BARRON'S
REAL
ESTATE
HANDBOOK

Jack C. Harris, PhD
Associate Research Economist
Real Estate Center
Texas A&M University

Jack P. Friedman, PhD, CPA, SRPA
Laguarta Professor of Real Estate
Department of Finance/Real Estate Center
Texas A&M University

SECOND EDITION

BARRON'S

New York • London • Sydney • Toronto

ACKNOWLEDGMENTS

We wish to express appreciation to the people who were instrumental in bringing this handbook to fruition. In particular, we thank Richard L. Floyd, Director Real Estate Center, and Benton Cocanougher, Dean of the College of Business at Texas A&M University for their support, encouragement, and for creating an appropriate atmosphere. We thank Lucy Morgan and Kammy Senter for preparing the manuscript and correspondence. Original works by Don Stebbins, Eileen Snyder and Harold Jambers were adapted for portions of the manuscript. Finally, we thank Don Reis and the staff at Barron's Educational Series for their perceptiveness and diligence throughout the editorial process.

The book *Houses*, by Henry Harrison, was used as a source for some drawings and definitions used in this book. Drawings of dormer, gable roof, gambrelroof, mansard roof, mobile home, shed roof, termite, window, and hip roof, plus drawings and definitions of "A" frame, American mansard, brownstone, bungalow, California bungalow, California ranch, Cape Cod colonial, Dutch colonial, Eastlake house, Elizabethan, Federal, French provincial, functional modern, Georgian, high Victorian, international architecture, Italian villa, log cabin, mission house. Monterey architecture, New England colonial, New England farm house, prairie house, pueblo or adobe, Queen Anne house, regency, salt box colonial, southern colonial, Spanish villa, stick style or Swiss chalet, tudor, western row, and Williamsburg came from this source. © Copyright REALTORS NATIONAL MARKETING INSTITUTE® of the NATIONAL ASSOCIATION OF REALTORS® 1973 and 1976. All rights reserved. Reprinted from *Houses* with permission of the Copyright Proprietor.

All inquiries should be addressed to:
Barron's Educational Series, Inc.
250 Wireless Boulevard
Hauppauge, New York 11788

Library of Congress Catalog Card No. 88-3345

International Standard Book No. 0-8120-5758-9

Library of Congress Cataloging-in-Publication Data

Harris, Jack C. *Barron's Real Estate Handbook*.
1. Real estate business — Handbooks, manuals, etc.
2. Real estate business — Dictionaries.
3. Business mathematics — Real estate business — Tables.
I. Friedman, Jack P., 1945-. II. Title. III. Title: Real estate handbook.
HD1375.H349 1988 333.33 88-3345
ISBN 0-8120-5758-9
PRINTED IN THE UNITED STATES OF AMERICA
8901 8800 9 8 7 6 5 4 3 2

CONTENTS

PREFACE

Real estate, like most business fields, has its own unique jargon. You must speak the language in order to understand and be understood. Real estate is also a field of numbers and formulas. Closing a simple transaction may involve calculating future mortgage payments and depreciation allowances or prorating closing costs. Furthermore, new terminology, types of mortgage loans and depreciation methods emerge constantly, taxing the ability of the professional to keep up.

Whether you are a real estate professional or someone who occasionally gets involved, the *Real Estate Handbook* will be indispensable. Reading through the glossary with its numerous examples will provide a course in the essentials of real estate. You will find legal terms to help take the mystery out of contract documents, financial terms to aid in structuring deals, architectural terms for traditional and contemporary buildings, and other helpful real estate words.

This second edition of the *Handbook* includes sections explaining some of the techniques used in real estate, as well as guides to real estate careers and government regulations. New homebuyers and sellers sections are designed to help readers make more informed decisions when involved in these common transactions. A section on investment analysis shows the reader how to estimate income and returns from a real estate project. The careers section compares the many employment opportunities related to real estate. A comprehensive list of regulations involving the use and development of real property is intended to prepare readers to deal with government agencies.

The tables will allow you to solve real estate problems using only simple mathematics. Monthly mortgage payment and amortization schedules can be constructed for mortgage loans with a variety of interest rates and terms. The critical early years of a graduated payment mortgage can be analyzed. Depreciation schedules can be computed whether the old or new rules apply. The effects of discount points can be determined. Property sellers who provide financing will find special tables for estimating the premium they should receive for the financing and be able to estimate how much their loan is worth in the seconday market. Each table has been specially prepared to make its use as simple as possible. Instructions precede each table stating the information needed to use the table and including example solutions to common real estate problems.

We hope that you, the reader, have an enjoyable experience whether you use this handbook as a reference guide or as a way to learn about real estate and its business environment.

Jack C. Harris
Jack P. Friedman

HOME BUYERS GUIDE

The Home Buying Process

Buying a home can be one of the most important decisions a person will make in his or her lifetime. A buyer is required to make several legal and financial commitments. For the first-time buyer, and even some veteran homeowners, this process can be confusing. Therefore, it is vital that the prospective buyer understand the process that must take place between the initial decision to move and the eventual possession of the new home. In this section, a typical home-buying process is followed, and the necessity for each step is explained.

Making the Decision

There are many reasons why people change homes. Frequently, people are forced to move because they change jobs and need to relocate to another town. For these people, buying a new home takes on some amount of urgency. They cannot afford to wait for the perfect house. For others, moving is a way to upgrade or modify their housing. They may desire more space or less space than they currently have. They may seek a more desirable neighborhood. There may be features of a home they do not presently have but want. They may just be renters who are ready to enjoy the benefits of homeownership. These groups can take a more leisurely approach to selecting a home.

A first step in making an intelligent choice is to decide exactly what you want in the new home. It might be helpful to detail the features of the "ideal" home, then decide what you would forego if you have to scale back. (Check the section on housing options, page 5.) Establishing your priorities will help you to evaluate homes and to describe to sales agents what you are looking for.

Setting a Price Range

Before going out and seriously looking at homes, you might call some lenders to get an idea of current mortgage rates. Loan terms will help determine how much you will be able to afford.

When you apply for a mortgage loan, the lender will apply certain criteria to determine how large a loan to make. The amount depends mainly on your income and how much debt you currently have. You can run through a similar analysis to provide an estimate of your loan limit. (See the section on prequalifying, page 9.)

1

Home Shopping

You will need to do some information gathering. First try to get an idea of the prices being asked for homes on the market. Read the classified ads and visit new home subdivisions. You may even pick up variations between certain locations. You should begin to select neighborhoods that appear desirable. A neighborhood can be favored because of the style of homes there, convenience to work or other points, or its reputation for retaining property values. If you know where you would like to live, you can save much time when you begin to look at houses.

Now you are ready to start the search process in earnest. There are several sources for available homes. Some owners try to sell their own homes without the aid of an agent. Check classified ads and *for sale* signs in front yards for these offers. Builders often advertise open house showings and may provide sales offices on the premises. Real estate brokerage firms represent many home sellers and also advertise with newspaper ads and yard signs. However, a visit to the brokerage office allows you to find out about a large number of homes on the market by looking through *exclusive* and *multiple* listings with an agent. (Exclusives are homes that are offered through a single broker; multiple listings are offered in cooperation with all brokers who are members of the service. (See Types of Listings, page 22.) The agent can also help you narrow down the list to the location, features, and price you desire. In addition, the agent can provide an inspection tour of available homes.

Negotiation

When you find the home you wish to buy, you can make an offer by submitting a *sales contract*. (This document may have another name in your state. For example, in Texas it is an *earnest money contract*.) The contract states what you are willing to pay (in most cases, it is not necessary to offer the full asking price), when you would like to take possession, and under what conditions the sale will be completed. These conditions generally include a provision that you are able to obtain financing at certain specified terms. This frees you of the obligation to go through with the purchase if you are turned down for a loan. Another common provision is that the house is free of defects over a specified amount of repairs that the seller agrees to make before closing. Other contingencies can be included, such as a provision that you must first sell your current home. (See the sales contract, page 665.)

Your offer will be accompanied by a check to signify serious intent. This earnest money is typically less than five percent of the price of the home and is forfeited if you back out of the contract. (If the deal falls through because of one of the conditions in the contract, your deposit is returned.) Of course, the contract is not binding until the seller signs it. The seller may accept your offer by signing the contract, reject the offer by sending it back, or propose a counteroffer by modifying the contract and signing it. Since a counteroffer is a substitute offer, it constitutes

2

rejection of the contract. If the counteroffer is acceptable, you may initial the contract to validate it. Alternatively, you may make another counteroffer; or you may reject the counteroffer, refuse to negotiate further, and take back your earnest money. This negotiation can go back and forth until an agreement (or an impasse) is reached. Of course, until a contract is signed by both parties, the seller may entertain offers from other buyers.

The sales contract designates the date at which property ownership will change. This is called a *closing*. In the meantime, you need to arrange financing. Since this typically takes from three to eight weeks, a loan application should be filed soon after signing the sales contract.

Getting Financing

Most home mortgage loans are made by lending institutions, such as savings and loan associations or banks, and mortgage bankers. Information on available terms can be obtained by calling a number of these lenders. There may be several types of loans available. Compare terms since they may vary significantly among lenders. (See the sections on loan sources and loan types, page 11 and page 12.)

When you have decided on a lender and type of loan, you can prepare to make a loan application. Take some time to gather information on your current income, major debts and available cash (or assets that can be converted to cash readily). If you are self-employed or work on commission, you may need income tax returns for the last three years to establish your income. (See page 664 for worksheets that can be used to calculate your qualifying income.)

When you visit the lender, you will need to take along a copy of the sales contract. You will fill out an application form stating your income, debts, and assets. You will also sign forms that allow the lender to verify some of the information you have provided (such as salary and bank account balances). Finally there will be a nonrefundable fee of at least $200 to cover the expense of an appraisal and credit review.

During the next several weeks, the lender analyzes your application to determine if a loan commitment can be issued. The home will be appraised to see if it is worth enough to cover the loan. Your credit history will be reviewed. Your income and debt will be evaluated to see if you can reasonably afford to make the payments on the loan. Finally, the lender will check to see if you have enough cash to make the required down payment on the house. If you require mortgage insurance, you will apply for it during this period.

The final decision to make the loan is generally made by a loan committee that meets periodically. If the decision is favorable, you will be given a commitment for the loan, sometimes with a locked-in interest rate. The commitment is good for a stated period from the time of the application, and the rate is good for a shorter period. For example, the commitment for the loan might be good for six months, with the rate valid for 45 days.

3

Preparing for Closing

In the time before the closing, there are several things that must be done. Practices vary from place to place. In many areas it is customary for the seller to arrange for a title search and, at closing, purchase a title insurance policy in the name of the lender and/or buyer. This policy assures good title and protects against claims of ownership or partial interests. The buyer must arrange for a hazard and liability insurance policy to be written for the new house. Such a policy is required for the mortgage loan. A new survey will be made of the property to make sure no building is encroaching on surrounding property. A termite inspection is typically required. The buyer may exercise the right under the contract to hire a housing inspector to report any non-functioning equipment or unsafe building condition. Recall that the sales contract may require the seller to repair any broken component up to a certain dollar limit. Such repairs should be completed before closing.

In some cases it may be necessary for the buyer to move into the house before the closing. Possibly a lease has expired or a previous house has closed before the buyer takes possession. If the new house is vacant, the buyer may arrange with the seller to rent the house in the interim. This is usually done at a nominal rental rate or may even be rent-free, particularly if the buyer is merely storing possessions but not actually living in the home.

In any event, the buyer must obtain the seller's agreement to the arrangement, preferably in writing. The buyer should also check with his or her insurance carrier to see if the policy covers the possessions while in the new house.

Closing

On closing day, all parties will meet and execute the necessary paperwork to pass title of the property. (For more details, see section on closing procedures, page 16.) Closing generally takes place at the offices of the title insurance company. The buyer and seller are present or represented, along with legal counsel, if desired. Also present will be the real estate broker, if one has been involved, and a representative of the mortgage lender. Closing day is considered the first day of ownership for the buyer, and all benefits and responsibilities are conferred at this time.

At the closing, the seller delivers a deed to the home, signifying passage of legal title to the buyer. The deed is a document that describes the title conveyed and acknowledges the identity of the new owner. The buyer provides any down payment required and signs the mortgage documents releasing the borrowed funds to the seller. These documents include a note acknowledging the debt and promising to repay the loan in a specific manner and a mortgage pledging the home to back up the borrower's promise. The seller then uses a portion of the money to retire any existing loans on the property (except for those that are

assumed by the buyer), pays the expenses of sale, and receives a check for the balance.

Most of the costs associated with the sale are paid at closing. The agents receive their commissions and the attorneys their fees. There also may be costs involved in inspections, surveys and various legal requirements. The one-time premiums for title insurance are paid. The lender may require payments toward setting up an *escrow* for the payment of future property taxes, insurance premiums and interest to cover the time from closing until the end of the month. From that point on, mortgage interest is paid at the end of the month as part of the regular monthly payment. In most cases, property taxes are due toward the end of the year. To adjust for this, the seller pays the buyer a prorated share of the tax.

After the closing, the buyer can begin to enjoy the full benefits of the new home. The purchase process can be time-consuming and expensive but, if done right, results in security and satisfaction for the new homeowner.

Housing Options

The housing market has developed a number of options that have more to do with the legal rights you possess as a homeowner than with the physical style of the building. Since your ownership interest can be important in determining your satisfaction with the home and the investment rewards of the purchase, try to settle on the type you prefer before you start your housing search.

Single-family Detached

The *single-family detached* unit, which is the most common type of housing structure, is what most people have in mind when they think of buying a home. It is simply a house designed for use by one household that sits on its own plot of land without being connected to a neighboring structure. When you buy a single-family detached home, you own the house and land and are solely responsible for their upkeep. You are free to modify the structure and landscape or build outbuildings as long as you comply with local ordinances and codes and any deed restrictions.

Attached or Cluster Housing

In large cities and areas where space is limited, several housing units may be combined into one structure. Such *attached* or *cluster housing* units are separated by party walls and have individual entrance ways. They may also have small lawns or courtyards in front and/or in back. In some areas, these units are called *row houses* or *brownstones*, but more generally are referred to as *townhouses*. Some townhouse complexes are set up as *condominiums*, which are described in the next sec-

tion. However, many townhouses, particularly older units, are individually owned. In these cases, the homeowner shares ownership of the party wall with each neighbor having an easement legally protecting the integrity of the wall.

In some newer subdivisions, housing units are clustered together to provide additional open space. These may be called *patio homes* or *zero lot line homes*. The arrangement often involves some type of shared wall, driveway or common grounds which are protected by easements as in townhouse units. The practical meaning of any of these types of housing arrangements is that the owner may be restricted in how he or she uses the component covered by the easement. The prospective buyer should become familiar with the specific restrictions that may apply.

Condominiums

The term *condominium*, which describes joint sovereignty, refers to the way individual property rights are exercised among the participating homeowners. Condominiums are made up of a number of dwelling units combined in a single building, complex, or subdivision. In a strict sense, the individual homeowner has ownership of only the interior of the dwelling unit. The structure of the buildings, the grounds, and any facilities on the grounds are common areas controlled by the homeowners' association. Every owner is a member of the association, paying periodic fees and having a vote in deciding its actions. The association generally maintains the common areas and sets rules for their use. In practical terms this means that the homeowner can enjoy common facilities, such as a swimming pool, at a fraction of the cost of providing one for individual use. It also means that the homeowner may be much more restricted in what can be done with his or her home than the owner of a single-family detached home. If you are considering a condominium, you should examine the association by-laws prior to making an offer. Some associations prohibit pets or even children.

Condominiums can be large or small, can be part of complexes with hundreds of units or a few units, and can be in the form of high-rise buildings, garden apartments, townhouses, or detached homes. Some units will be among the lowest priced housing available, while others are among the highest priced. The more inexpensive units are usually designed to take advantage of the lower land costs associated with high density development. The high priced units are usually located in highly desirable areas and include many luxury features. Condominiums appeal to people who don't care to do home maintenance chores.

Cooperatives

Like condominiums, *cooperatives* involve sharing ownership of property with other homeowners. The cooperative buyer purchases shares in a corporation holding title to the building. The shares give the owner the right to occupy an apartment in the building. Each share-

holder pays a portion of all financing, tax, and operating expenses associated with the building. The important differences between a cooperative and a condominium are related to mortgage financing and resales. In a cooperative a single mortgage loan is taken out by the corporation; in a condominium individual loans are obtained by each tenant. The cooperative arrangement may prove advantageous during periods of high interest rates as the new purchaser does not have to obtain new financing. However, failure of some cooperative shareholders to pay their share of expenses places a burden on all other owners to avoid foreclosure of the loan. Regarding resales, cooperative owners are free to offer their shares on the market, but transferring their right to occupy a unit must be approved by the other shareholders. In most cases, this procedure causes no problem, but does present one potential snag to reselling the unit.

Duplexes

Homes designed to accommodate two households are called *duplexes*. There are also *triplexes* and *quadraplexes* for three and four households. The building is divided into separate living areas, each with its own bath and kitchen facilities, as well as outside entrance. A duplex can often be purchased for little more than a single-family home and offers the opportunity to generate rental income. The owner may live in one half and rent the other to help defray housing expenses. If you like the idea of being a homeowner and landlord at the same time, a duplex may be for you.

Manufactured Housing

Once referred to as mobile homes, *manufactured homes* are usually sold without a lot and can be moved to a site that is owned or leased by the buyer. These homes can be as large and luxurious as many site-built homes but cost substantially less. However, the market for used manufactured homes is not as broad as that for site-built homes. This means that a manufactured home will probably have no real appreciation in value. Many communities severely restrict where manufactured homes may be placed, so before you consider this alternative, check on where such homes are permitted.

Lease Options

Sometimes it is possible to try out a home before committing to a purchase. A *lease option* is a lease with an option to buy within some time period. The tenant may be asked to pay a fee for the option. This fee will be applied toward the purchase price if the option is exercised, but forfeited if it is not. In markets where homes are hard to sell, however, option fees are usually not charged. In addition, the seller may be willing to apply some of the rent toward the purchase price. Lease

options are good ways to find out about a home before buying, and may provide a way to save a down payment for a home.

Equity Sharing

One way to buy a home when cash for a down payment is short is to arrange to co-purchase the home with an investor. The investor contributes a large portion of the down payment and you get to live in the home. Generally you must pay some form of rent on the investor's interest in the home. When the home is sold, you and the investor share in the proceeds. Before entering into an equity-sharing arrangement, it is essential to have in writing exactly what your rights and responsibilities are and the conditions under which the home can be sold.

Finding a new home can be a long and trying process. Fortunately, there are experienced professionals who can help in the search. Licensed real estate brokers can show you homes that are on the market, suggest sources of financing and help you in other aspects of the home purchase. Even with this assistance, however, you will find the process less confusing if you know a few basics. You will find it helpful if you know how to estimate the highest price you can afford to pay, how to size up the market, and how to make an offer.

Financing Options and Procedures

By far the biggest hurdle in buying a home is getting a loan. To qualify for a loan, you must have enough cash for the down payment and other closing costs and enough income to handle the loan payments. By comparing these requirements to your income and cash on hand, you may figure out how much you can afford.

Determining your Financial Status

The first step is to put together an accounting of current income and debts. The lender will want to see these items when you apply for the loan. It is a good idea to do this before you look at homes, so you don't waste your time with homes you can't afford.

Salaries Include what you make from your regular job. You may also include a spouse's salary if the job is steady and you can show that the income is dependable. The same goes for second jobs, bonuses and overtime pay. Are they a dependable source of income or just a temporary arrangement? If you are self-employed or work on commission, you should average the income received over the last several years. The object is to total the income you expect to make on a continuing basis.

Investments The money you get from your investments may be included if it is large enough to be meaningful (in most cases, $100 per month). This income includes interest from bank accounts, bonds and mutual funds, and dividends from stocks and bonds. You should not include assets you intend to sell to raise cash to purchase the home.

Once again, the idea is to include sources of income to be used for making the loan payments. If real estate is included, use net income after taking out routine expenses.

Alimony and child support Include these sources of income if they are not subject to termination in the near future. For example, child support is generally terminated when the child reaches a certain age. If you expect to receive this income for only the next few years, it should not be included.

Liabilities Now, make a list of your debts that require periodic payments. Include long term installment debt with a remaining term of more than ten months. Typically, this will include car loans, furniture loans, and other loans for major purchases. If you carry a balance on your credit cards, you should include the average monthly payment. Also include any other real estate mortgages you have, for example, the one on the rental property you listed in the income section. Finally, if you pay alimony or child support, you should include that payment.

Prequalifying: How Much House Can You Afford?

Lenders have different *ratios* they apply to your income alone and to your income minus debt obligations. You can use these ratios to get an idea of the largest loan you can obtain. You should apply both ratios because you must qualify under both criteria.

The most common loan is the conventional mortgage loan. This is one with no government insurance or guarantee to cover the lender's risk that you may fail to keep up the payments. Most lenders require the ratios that are required to sell the loan in the secondary market. Currently, the Federal National Mortgage Association, a major investor in home mortgages, requires that total mortgage payments plus insurance and taxes be no more than 28 percent of gross monthly income. Also, these expenses plus other debt payments can be no more than 36 percent of gross monthly income.

An example will show how these ratios can be used to estimate the maximum affordable loan. Mr. and Mrs. Brown receive $3,500 per month salary plus an average of $500 per month from investments. Their total monthly income is $4,000. Their mortgage payment may be no more than 28 percent of this income, or $1,120. An approximation of monthly escrow payments is one-fifth of the total payment. In the example, that would be $224, leaving $896 for principal and interest. They find that a mortgage loan can be obtained at 10 percent interest for 30 years. They look at a mortgage payment table and find that the largest loan they could afford is for $102,100.

The Browns also pay an average of $400 per month on their credit cards and car loan payments. Using the 36 percent ratio, they have $1,440 to use for all debt payments. Taking out the $400 they spend on current debts leaves them with $1,040 a month for mortgage expenses. After deducting one-fifth for taxes and insurance, the remainder for principal and interest is $832. This payment would support a loan of

$94,800 at 10 percent interest. Since this is less than the amount indicated by the simple income ratio, it represents the effective maximum loan obtainable. With a 20 percent down payment, they could afford a home priced at $118,500. Such a purchase would require a down payment of $23,700 plus closing costs of approximately $3,000, depending on how much the seller is willing to pay toward closing costs.

HOW MUCH CAN YOU AFFORD?
(CONVENTIONAL LOAN EXAMPLE)

1. Using the income to payment ratio
Monthly income

Salary	$3,500
Investment income	500
Total	$4,000
	× .28

Maximum mortgage payment	$1,120	
Tax and insurance	− 224	(payment divided by 5)
Maximum principal and interest payment	$ 896	

Maximum loan @ 10% (30 years)
Locate page of mortgage payment tables for 10%.
Find column for 30 years.
Find highest payment amount less than 896.
Note amount of loan in far left hand column.
Subtract payment in table from maximum payment.
Repeat previous three steps with the difference.

Maximum Payment	Amount in table	Difference	Loan Amount
$896.00	$877.58	$18.42	$100,000
18.42	17.56	.86	2,000
.86	.88	−.02	100
Total loan amount			$102,100

2. Using the total debt to income ratio

Monthly income	$4,000
	× .36
Income to pay all debt payments	$1,440
Average credit card payment	− 100
Installment loan payments	− 300
Existing mortgage payments	0
Maximum mortgage payment	$1,040
Tax and insurance	− 208
Maximum principal and interest payment	$832

(payment divided by 5)

(Note: if larger than amount in income part, stop)

Maximum loan amount:

Maximum payment	Amount in table	Difference	Loan Amount
$832.00	$789.82	$42.18	$90,000
42.18	35.11	7.07	4,000
7.07	7.03	.04	800
Total loan amount			$94,800

Sources

The first step in getting a loan is to find out what is available in the market. It is a good idea to check on several sources before committing, since the variation in interest rates, discount points and types of loans offered can be great.

Mutual savings banks and *Savings and loan associations.* Thrifts are institutions that specialize in home mortgage loans. Like commercial banks, they take in and pay interest on deposits from individual savers; then they lend these funds out to borrowers. Thrifts should be one of the first places you check for a loan.

Commercial banks do most of their lending on a short-term basis, such as auto loans and business loans. At times, however, they also make long-term mortgage loans.

Mortgage companies are prime sources for mortgage loans. Unlike savings and loans, mortgage companies do not collect deposits from savers. They obtain their funds by selling the loans they originate to investors, other lenders and the major secondary market agencies. Incidentally, it makes little difference to the borrower whether the loan is

11

retained by the lender or sold in the market. In most cases, the originator will continue to collect payments and manage the escrow account. *Credit unions* have been known to make home mortgage loans. This source could be worth checking if you are a member of a credit union. *Home finance companies* rarely make first mortgage loans for purchasing a home, but may be a source for second mortgages to help finance the down payment on a home.

Individuals also make home loans. Most often, these individuals are sellers who are willing to help finance the sale. When interest rates are high, or loans from established lenders hard to find, sellers may offer to take back a note as a way to clinch the sale. Seller financing differs in several important ways from a loan from a third-party lender. The financing is tied to a particular home offered at a particular price (which may be higher than the price you would pay without the financing). The loan is usually short term with a balloon payment. That means you must refinance the loan after a few years. These loans are meant for special situations, but can be worthwhile when those situations occur.

Government agencies sometimes make loans. In general, these loans are highly restricted to certain income groups or other target groups. Some state and local governments have money available from the sale of bonds to make home loans to first-time buyers. The loans are originated by established lenders, so inquire about these when you check out rates.

Federal Housing Administration (FHA) and Veterans Administration (VA) loans are made by private lenders using their own funds. The government backs up these loans if the borrower fails to make payments and the home is foreclosed. For FHA loans, the government provides insurance against default. The borrower pays a premium for this insurance. Similar insurance is provided by private companies for conventional loans. VA loans are guaranteed by the government and are available as a benefit to qualified military veterans. If you qualify, bring your DD214 form to the lender. The main advantage of these types of loans is the lower down payment required. In addition, FHA and VA loans may be assumed without an increase in the interest rate.

Loan Types

In many cases, getting the right loan can determine whether or not you can afford to buy the house you desire. Some loans require large cash down payments, while others call for relatively modest investments. Some have larger monthly payments than others. With some loans, the monthly payments vary over time. You will want to find the least expensive financing that fits your financial situation with adequate security.

Over the last several years, a great number of financial variations have developed for home buyers. At one time, the fixed-rate, fixed-payment loan was used exclusively by home buyers. Now there are loans whose payments vary as interest rates change, and those whose pay-

ments start out low and rise over the years. Loans with relatively short terms (such as 15 years instead of 30) are growing in popularity. This expanded list of options makes the loan selection decision a complicated one.

Fixed rate mortgage The standard loan covers 80 percent of the cost of the home, or the appraised value, whichever is lower. (Some lenders may offer loans in excess of 80 percent, but these higher *loan-to-value ratio* loans usually carry higher interest rates and costs.) The remainder of the cost is the cash down payment that you must provide at closing. Lenders also charge *discount points* as a condition of making the loan. Each point charged requires the buyer to pay an amount equal to one percent of the loan amount in cash at closing. An estimate of all these expenses will be given to you when you apply for the loan.

Each monthly payment on the fixed-rate loan includes interest on the outstanding principal plus repayment of a part of the principal borrowed. In this way the loan will be completely paid off at the end of the mortgage term. If you pay the loan back before the end of the term, the amount of principal you owe will be less than the amount you borrowed. The gradual reduction in principal is called *amortization*. Each payment of principal and interest is equal over the life of the loan. Since you are gradually paying back the principal with each payment, the amount of payment devoted to interest decreases over time. This means the amount of principal paid back increases with each payment. Therefore, the older the loan the faster you are paying the loan off. Each monthly payment may include a payment to an escrow account used for paying hazard insurance premiums and property taxes. While the interest and principal remain unchanged, the total payment may change over time because of increases or decreases in the escrow payment required.

It is possible to get mortgage loans for more than 80 percent of cost if the loan is insured. (This should not be confused with mortgage life insurance, which pays off the loan in the event of death or disability of the borrower.) The FHA insures home loans for up to 97.5 percent of value. Limits on the dollar amount of the loan make FHA insurance appropriate for low to moderate priced houses. Loans not insured by the FHA (or guaranteed by the VA) are called *conventional loans*. These loans can be insured by Private Mortgage Insurance (PMI) companies. PMI loans are not as restrictive in amount as FHA loans. Insurance, either PMI or FHA, requires additional premium payments at closing and may require an annual fee of one-quarter to one-half of one percent of the principal.

Adjustable rate mortgages Since 1980, *adjustable rate mortgages (ARMs)* have become an important part of the mortgage market. One reason is that lenders like the protection that ARMs give them from the effects of rising interest rates. Another reason is that ARMs usually start out with lower interest rates than comparable fixed-rate mortgages. Some home buyers find they can afford to borrow more with an ARM than they could with a higher interest rate fixed-rate mortgage. The main difference between ARMs and fixed-rate loans is that the

interest rate on the ARM may vary periodically. At pre-established intervals ranging from three months to five years the lender may change the interest rate. This is done by monitoring an *index of interest rates* and maintaining a set relationship between the interest rate and the index. The index may be the market yield on some government security, the average mortgage interest rate in the nation, or the cost of the money used by lenders to make loans. When the interest rate on the loan is changed, the monthly payment will change accordingly. This means the amount you pay on your loan for principal and interest may vary significantly over time. One way borrowers are protected from large changes in payments is through pre-set limits, or *caps*, placed on the interest rate adjustment. Some loans have caps that apply to the periodic adjustment and a cap on the overall change in the interest rate over the life of the loan. Some loans also have limits on the amount of change in the payment, but not on the interest rate. This type of cap can create *negative amortization*, a situation in which the amount of principal owed may increase over time. (For more information on these loans and helpful tables for analysis, see *Adjustable Rate Mortgages*, in Barron's Financial Guide series.)

Graduated payment mortgages The FHA also insures loans in which the interest rate is fixed, but the payment rises according to a pre-set schedule. These are called *Graduated Payment Mortgages (GPM)* because the payments are increased each year during the early life of the loan. The effect is to reduce the payment level in the first few years and to increase it somewhat in the middle and later years. The GPM is intended for young home buyers whose relatively low income is expected to grow over the years. The predetermined amount of change in the payment is not dependent on the movements of an index, although there are loans which combine the features of the GPM and the ARM. The common type of GPM involves negative amortization for the first several years.

Interest saving loans Some home buyers become dismayed when they learn the amount of money they must spend in interest over the life of a long-term mortgage loan. The total costs may be several times the price of the home. This concern has drawn attention to loans designed to cut down on the interest expense. In all cases, these types of loans require larger or more frequent payments.

One type of interest-saving loan is a fixed-rate loan with a 15-year term. Total interest expense can be reduced significantly, although the monthly payments are somewhat higher. For example, a loan of $50,000 at 10 percent interest requires a principal and interest payment of $438.79 when paid over 30 years. The total interest paid is $107,963. If the same loan is paid over 15 years, the monthly payment increases to $537.30, or about $100 more per month. Total interest paid, however, is only $46,714, a savings of over $60,000.

Other types of loans have been developed to save interest by paying

off the loan faster. One type is the Growing Equity Mortgage (GEM) which has a payment that increases periodically. Unlike the ARM or GPM, the increase in the payment is devoted to reducing the loan principal, so that the loan is retired in about half the original term. Another type, the *biweekly*, requires payments at two-week intervals (coinciding with payday for many workers) of half the normal monthly payment. Since there are 26 two-week intervals in the year, the borrower pays the equivalent of 13 months of payments, and the principal is paid down much faster.

Loan assumptions In some cases, it may not be necessary to obtain a new loan. Some sellers have existing mortgage loans that can be assumed by the buyer. When interest rates have risen, existing loans may have interest rates, and payments, much lower than those required with new loans. The buyer may be able to avoid many of the closing costs associated with new loans as well. Assumable conventional loans are becoming rare because in recent years lenders have included "due on sale clauses" in the loans. These provisions entitle the lender to call the loan due or raise the interest rate if the house is sold. Loans insured by the FHA or guaranteed by the VA are generally assumable at the original interest rate.

There are several drawbacks with assumable loans. The seller may want a higher price because of the loan; and the loan may cover a relatively small proportion of the cost of the home. In some cases, the latter problem has been overcome by the seller taking a second mortgage as part of the purchase price.

QUICK GUIDE TO CHOOSING A MORTGAGE LOAN

Borrower Concern	Possible Solution
Need low down payment	Conventional loan with private insurance FHA insured mortgage
Need low monthly payments in early years to help qualify	Adjustable Rate Mortgage with low initial interest rate Graduated Payment Mortgage Assumption with or without seller financing
Desire to reduce interest paid over loan term	Loan with 15-year term Growing Equity Mortgage Biweekly mortgage

The Closing

Closing day marks the time when all accounts are settled and title to the house passes to the buyer. In one simultaneous procedure:

- The seller receives the price of the house and retires the old loan (unless the buyer is assuming the loan).
- The sales agent receives a commission. (The commission may be split between a listing broker and a selling broker.)
- All fees are paid. These include title insurance premiums, survey costs, and fees for filing documents. They may also include attorneys' fees and inspectors' charges if these have not been paid previously.
- The lender supplies the proceeds from the loan and collects origination fees and discount points. This is the first day of the new loan which from then on begins to accrue interest. The lender usually requires interest be paid at the closing to cover the period from closing day to the end of the month. All other interest payments are made at the end of each month.
- The buyer receives documents which signify the passage of ownership of the property from the seller to the buyer.

For all practical purposes, the closing ends all negotiations and contingencies associated with the transaction. For that reason, it is important that all parties clear all these matters before the closing day. If not, the closing may be delayed, which can be very inconvenient for both seller and buyer.

The most common reasons that closings do not proceed as scheduled are connected with failures to make the necessary preparations. Sometimes the seller has a problem clearing a title. There may be existing liens, claims filed by those with partial interests in the property, or an ex-spouse with community property rights that complicate the process. If the property becomes involved in a lawsuit, the title may be impossible to clear for several years. Problems also occur when the buyer has trouble arranging a mortgage loan. The appraisal may be too low to justify the loan amount requested, or the buyer may not qualify. When loan activity is heavy, approval times can be delayed because the lender's staff is inadequate.

The seller can entertain contingent contracts from other buyers after the first contract is signed. These contracts have no effect on the original contract as long as the deadlines on contingencies are not exceeded. However, if the buyer is turned down for a mortgage, the house may be sold to another buyer before the first buyer can reapply.

Here is a good way that you, as the buyer, can prepare for a closing. Assume you have a mortgage commitment already approved. The following steps should be followed:

- Get a good estimate of the cash required at closing. The title company handling the closing can provide a reasonably accurate accounting. Make sure you can provide a certified check for your share of expenses on closing day.
- Have all inspections made and make sure all required repairs are com-

pleted. Unless agreed to in writing, the seller has no responsibility for repairs after closing. If any condition of the property is misrepresented, however, you still have remedies against the seller. Basically, the property is yours *as is* after closing.

- You may want to get an attorney to review all documents and represent you at the closing. Arrange for this beforehand.
- Arrange for a hazard insurance policy to be written on the property. The lender will require the house to be insured for at least the amount of the loan. At closing you will have to pay the first year's premium plus an amount to start the escrow account (usually two or three months prorated premium).
- Make sure the survey is completed as required by the lender.

If it looks as if the closing will be delayed due to some problem in getting everything done, it may be possible to move the closing date. The date stated in the sales contract is understood to be an approximation. Unless the market is unusually active, with many buyers vying for each home, the seller should be willing to comply. If the closing is delayed, you may be caught without a place to move into after vacating your previous residence. You may arrange with the seller to lease the new house on a temporary basis prior to closing if the home will be vacant during that time.

At closing, you will sign several documents. The following are most common:

- *Settlement statement* This shows the closing costs charged to each party in an itemized list. Of special note are the various prorated expenses. Property taxes, insurance premiums and other recurring expenses are generally paid once a year. If already paid by the seller, you are charged a proportional amount based on the remaining number of days in the year. If due after the closing, you will be given a credit for the days in which the seller owned the home.
- *Loan disclosure* This gives you certain information about the mortgage loan. The Annual Percentage Rate (APR) of interest is calculated. This amount takes into account the discount points paid at closing assuming their costs are spread out over the term of the loan. Also shown is the total amount of interest paid over the loan term, the monthly payment of interest and principal, the number of payments over the term and the date at which the first payment is due.
- *Mortgage note* This signifies your responsibility to pay back the amount borrowed on the mortgage.
- *Deed of trust* (*security deed*, *bond*, etc.) This pledges the house as security for the mortgage loan.
- *Deed* This transfers the title of the property to your name. In most cases you will receive a *general warranty deed*, meaning that the seller guarantees that the title is clear and will be clear in the future (not clouded by prior claims). In some cases, the seller may give a *special warranty deed*, which guarantees that any claims arising during the seller's ownership have been settled. Any additional liability stemming from a warranty deed are assumed by the title company.
- *Title policy* This provides protection should legitimate claims to the title of the property arise.
- *Additional documents* You may request copies of other documents asso-

ciated with the transaction. These include the survey map, the appraisal, and any inspection certificates prepared. These are desirable to have for future reference.

Tax Benefits of Homeownership

Many of the costs of owning a home are deductible from individual federal income taxes. Therefore, tax savings from these deductions may reduce homeownership costs. In addition, there are tax benefits when a home is sold.

Mortgage Interest Payments

The interest portion of mortgage monthly payments is deductible. Each year, the borrower receives a statement from the lender indicating how much interest was paid for the tax year. This amount should be included on schedule A of the 1040 tax form. In addition, for the year of purchase, discount points paid to the lender may qualify as interest payments. When they are a customary charge in the area, paid with a separate check, and not considered an origination fee, points should be deductible. When an origination fee is charged, it normally is only a portion of the discount point payment. Check with the lender to see how much is considered a fee. Remember that each point is one percent of the amount borrowed. For example, if three points were paid on a $100,000 loan, the total charge would be $3,000. Suppose one point was considered a fee and the rest discount points. An amount of $2,000 could be deducted as interest in the year of purchase.

Interest Expense Limits on Home Mortgages

Interest on up to $1,000,000 of mortgage debt to buy a home or a second home is fully deductible. Interest on up to $100,000 of home equity debt is generally fully deductible regardless of how the money is used. Interest is deductible on additional home equity debt if the loan is used to buy or improve a home. Interest on home equity loans used for educational or medical expenses is also deductible.

Property Taxes Paid to Local Governments

In most cases, these taxes are paid by the lender from an escrow account kept current by part of your monthly payments. The annual statement from the lender will indicate how much was paid in taxes for the year. If you pay taxes directly, you will have a statement from the

local taxing authority to indicate the amount of taxes paid. When you sell the home, do not forget to include any prorated taxes you may have paid to the buyer.

These benefits also apply to a second home, but not to any additional homes you may own. If you own houses as rental property, a different set of rules apply.

Capital Gains

When you buy your first home, the purchase price becomes the property's basis for calculating capital gains. At resale, taxes may be required on any profits realized. A profit is indicated if the sales price exceeds the basis. However, the cost of selling (commissions, advertising, etc.) may be deducted from the sales price. Major improvements, not just repairs, to the home while you own it may be added to the original basis. All of these things help to reduce the taxable capital gain.

As an example, suppose a home was purchased for $50,000 in 1960. In 1969, a second bath was added at a cost of $5,000. The house is sold in 1988 for $80,000. The seller paid a commission of $4,000 and $1,000 of the buyer's closing costs.

Original cost	$50,000
Improvements	5,000
Basis	$55,000
Sales price	$80,000
Sales expense	5,000
Net sales price	$75,000
Capital gain	$20,000

Capital gains taxes may be deferred if a replacement home is purchased within 24 months of the sale. The 24-month period may extend before or after the sale. The cost of the new home must be at least as much as the net sales price of the home sold. No tax is due in the year of sale but the basis of the new home is reduced by the amount of gain deferred. Suppose the seller of the home above buys a new home for $85,000. The new basis is $85,000 minus the $20,000 of gain deferred, or $65,000. As long as the procedures are followed, deferral of capital gains taxes can go on indefinitely, each time reducing the basis by the taxes deferred. After the age of 55, a homeowner may sell and receive an exemption of $125,000 in deferred gain. This can be elected only once in a lifetime.

HOME SELLERS GUIDE*

The typical American spends less than 12 years in any given house. This is the average. You may be the person transferred by an employer every year, or the one who lives in the same house for your entire life. Sooner or later, however, most of us need to sell a home. It may be because an altered family situation makes a larger or smaller house more desirable. Changing tastes, a job change, or the desire to be closer to schools or shopping facilities are other reasons commonly cited for moving. Hopefully, real estate market conditions will be favorable when you need to sell but this is not always the case. For example, a job or business location change often requires a move from an economically depressed to a booming area; consequently a house must be sold in a sluggish market, and another bought in a vibrant one. Still, the transaction process need not be fraught with hazards. Some considerations are discussed below.

Selling Yourself or Using a Broker

Many homeowners sell their own homes successfully. Those who do so save the sales commission, usually six percent of the home's price, or they may choose to speed up the sale by passing part of the savings on to the buyer. However, most home owners turn the job over to a real estate broker who has the experience, expertise and business connections to locate buyers and offer other services to a seller. After weighing the factors involved, a seller may first proceed without professional assistance, resorting to a broker only if these efforts prove unsuccessful.

If a broker is engaged, a *listing* is the contract of employment between the owner of the property and the broker hired to sell it. Under the terms of the listing contract, the owner agrees to pay the broker a commission when the broker locates a party who is ready, willing, and able to buy the property at its list price. Should an offer be tendered for less than the list price, the broker is entitled to a commission when the transaction is consummated.

Normally, the seller pays the commission at closing. However, it is possible for a buyer to agree to pay a commission in lieu of the seller or in addition to the seller, so long as all parties are aware of the circumstances.

*The authors gratefully acknowledge the contributions of Eileen Snyder and Don Stebbins who wrote, *Preparing Your Home for Sale*, and *Some Important Tax Considerations*, respectively, and the Real Estate Center at Texas A&M for allowing use of some of their materials.

Types of Listings

Listings can be categorized as *Open*, *Exclusive agency*, or *Exclusive right to sell*. In turn, any of these three basic types can be categorized as being, *Net* and/or *Multiple*.

Open listings Using an open listing, the seller or *principal* offers the broker a commission provided that the broker secures a purchaser. The listing is considered "open" because the owner reserves the right to list the property with other brokers or to sell it independently. All open listings are automatically canceled upon a sale of the property, so that the seller pays no more than one commission.

Exclusive agency listings Under an exclusive agency listing, one broker is employed to the exclusion of all others. The owner retains the right to sell the property independently without paying a commission. However, if the property is sold by a broker other than the listing broker, the listing broker is entitled to a full commission.

Exclusive right to sell listings An exclusive right to sell provides the employed broker a commission upon the sale, no matter who sells the property. Such a contract may appear to be to a seller's disadvantage. Even if the seller or another broker finds a buyer, the listing broker earns a commission. But this rigid arrangement, which gives the listing broker complete protection, can work to the seller's advantage. Under an exclusive right to sell, the employed broker has more incentive to spend time and money to promote the sale of the listed property. Brokers employed through other types of listings may not make as much effort precisely because the property can be sold by the owner or another broker. In recognition of this, most real estate boards emphasize the exclusive right to sell listing, particularly for single-family dwellings.

Net listings Any one of the above listings may also be a net listing if the property owner fixes the minimum acceptable net amount from a sale. For example, the seller informs the broker that he or she wants $100,000 from the sale. The broker may keep any amount as a commission so long as the seller "nets" $100,000. Thus, if the sale price is $100,001, the commission is $1; a sale at $104,000 yields a $4,000 commission.

In some states, net listings are illegal. In states where they are permitted, many real estate brokerage organizations suggest that, when offered a net listing, the broker add the customary charge to the net amount and then inform the seller of the resulting list price. For example, a six percent commission rate added to a $100,000 net figure results in a $106,383 offering price. As a check on the math, six percent of $106,383 is $6,383 leaving $100,000 for the seller. The arithmetic is as follows:

$$\frac{\text{Net amount to seller}}{\substack{\text{Fraction of sales price to seller} \\ \text{(100\% less commission)}}} = \text{List price with commission}$$

Using the $100,000 net figure and the 6 percent rate of commission, the list price becomes:

$$\frac{\$100,000}{.94} = \$106,383$$

Multiple listings Some brokers in a given geographical area may agree to pool all of their listings. They form a *multiple listing service* (MLS) to coordinate activities. Through this association, brokers agree to share their listings. Then, any cooperating broker may sell property that another has listed. Upon the sale of multiple-listed property, the commission is split between the listing and the selling broker in accordance with the agreement established by the multiple listing association. A small fraction of the commission is paid to the association to cover its expenses of operation. The MLS maximizes exposure of the property to prospective purchasers. Even in areas where there isn't a formal MLS organization, cooperation between brokers is quite common.

Rate of Commission

As a matter of law, commission rates for the sale of real estate are negotiable between the principal and the broker. The rate or amount should be specified in the listing contract to avoid misunderstandings. In most cases the rate is a percentage of the sales price (often four to seven percent), which is paid at closing.

Listing Period

Listing contracts should have a fixed expiration date. Most provide 60 to 120 days for the sale of single-family homes and up to six months for commercial property and apartment complexes. The law does not establish limits, so the actual period is a matter of negotiation.

If a house is unsold at the expiration of the stipulated period, the owner and broker can renew the listing. However, the broker is paid nothing as brokers are typically compensated only upon a sale. An owner may decide to try a different broker if the first one failed to produce satisfactory results or activity.

Occasionally, after having been shown a particular piece of property through a broker, a prospect and the property owner may arrange a sale "behind the broker's back." Together they wait for the listing to expire, then contract for the sale without advising the broker, in an attempt to elude the payment of a commission. Despite the fact that the listing has expired, courts are likely to require payment to a licensed broker, if it can be shown that the broker was the procuring cause of the sale.

Expectations of Broker Services

Upon listing your house, you can expect a broker to help you decide on an offering price, advertise the property, and show the house to prospective buyers. Typically, the broker places a *For Sale* sign on the front

lawn, advertises in newspapers or local magazines, and may hold an open house. The listing will be included in the book or computer of the multiple listing service if your broker belongs to the MLS.

How To Choose a Broker

Try to determine the broker's level of activity in your neighborhood. A broker with numerous for sale signs would be a likely one to select, especially if there is also a liberal sprinkling of "sold" signs. Check for the integrity and professional reputation of the firm by asking people you know to recommend a broker. Ask friends who recently sold a house in your area to describe the transaction. Did they feel they received the best possible personal treatment and financial result? Specifically, ask about pricing, time on the market, selling efforts, courtesy, and procedure for showing the home.

Call brokers and ask them to visit. Usually they will be prepared to discuss how best to market your home, including a suggested selling price or range. Ask the broker for information about transactions in your neighborhood: What has sold? At what price? What hasn't sold and why? Ask what advertising the broker would use: Which media? What frequency? Would he or she hold an "open house." Discuss the type of listing, especially if you have names of prospects who are considering buying from you. A firm that participates in a multiple listing service may increase market exposure, while national franchises or local firms that belong to national referral services are more likely to reach home-buyers who are relocating to your area. Bear in mind, however, that a local firm may give more attention to each listing.

The Real Estate Market

The real estate market is peculiar. Though you need only one buyer for your home, you never know when that buyer will appear. A buyer could come the day your ad first appears or not until a year or so later. When there are plenty of houses for sale and they don't seem to be selling — at least not quickly — there is a *buyer's market*. In this situation, buyers have many houses to choose from and can negotiate a tough bargain.

In a *seller's market*, the opposite is true. There are few houses for sale, and when one does become available, it is snapped up immediately — often at a higher price than was paid earlier for similar houses. Sometimes even a higher price is paid than was originally asked. Obviously, this is the type of market that sellers prefer.

A market is called *balanced* when most houses priced for sale at *market value* sell within a normal period of time. A "normal" or "reasonable" period is 30 to 180 days.

Nearly all home buyers have two concerns. First, they must like the house. Next, the price or payments must be affordable. These two elements must be present before a buyer will make an offer. Buyers can

usually be categorized as either *taste-conscious* or *price-conscious*. *Taste* buyers find the home of their choice and buy it if the price is within reason. *Price* buyers want a bargain. They could easily afford a higher-priced house in which they might actually prefer to live. Instead, they opt for the bargain — something that is not exactly what they want, but they grab it nevertheless because of its low price and resale potential.

Few buyers are guided exclusively by either taste or price considerations; most fall somewhere in between the two extremes and are willing to sacrifice some of the features they want for a good price, or vice versa.

Pricing

It is obvious that sellers want the highest possible price for their home. Buyers want the lowest. Most transactions take place at or near *market value*, which may be briefly defined as the highest price a buyer, willing but not compelled to buy, will pay a seller, willing but not compelled to sell, both acting with reasonable knowledge of the market.

Buyers become acquainted with the market by shopping. After visiting several homes, buyers will get a feel for what homes are worth. They don't know exactly what a house will cost until they try to buy one, but they are told the asking price for each one they visit. They understand they can buy any house for its asking (listed) price, and that most homes will actually sell for less.

As a seller you can sample the market the same way. Read ads in the newspapers. Find out how much neighbors are asking and visit their homes. You'll get a rough idea of what you should ask for your home.

It is also a good idea to phone some real estate brokerage agencies. Good agents will volunteer to visit your home just to meet you and offer their services in the hope that you'll list with them. You won't obligate yourself just by asking how much they would advise listing your home for. Good agents will let you know. They want your business. As a matter of professionalism and thoroughness, agents may offer an analysis of comparable sales ("comps"). Comps that have sold (as opposed to those that are for sale) provide actual prices, which are better indicators than offering prices. Agents will frequently leave a copy of their analyses with you.

Another way of estimating a price is to call a professional independent fee appraiser. Look in the Yellow Pages of your phone book under "Appraisers." Those with professional designations of SRA, RA, MAI, SRPA, or SREA have met high professional standards. Ask one or two for an appraisal. Fees typically range from $150 to $300. (Some appraisers will charge more, especially if your house is particularly unusual.) In any case, an appraiser's fee may be money well spent, especially since an appraiser may be able to suggest ways to increase the market value of your home.

Consider asking an appraiser these questions:

1. Which local mortgage lenders accept his or her valuations. If the appraiser is accepted by most local savings and loan associations, that appraisal can be used for a new loan application without paying another fee. You've saved your buyer some money, perhaps some time, and you can point that out when negotiating on other items.
2. Ask the appraiser what forms will be used. Ideally, the appraiser will use the most recent FHLMC/FNMA standard form. Most lenders want this form so that the loans they produce can be more readily sold.
3. Tell the appraiser you want a market value estimate, and, further, that you would like to know a probable sales price range. *Don't attempt to maneuver an appraisal into a specific amount.* Professional ethics will require the appraiser's resignation from any assignment where a client pushes for a high value. Ask for the price range in which your home is most likely to sell. A good appraiser will understand and oblige. He or she recognizes that the formal estimate is of market value, but that homes sell for more (and less). Generally, an appraiser will provide this range verbally.
4. Ask about market conditions. Is it a seller's market? A buyer's market? A balanced market? How long do houses like yours stay on the market. Is this a good time to sell?
5. Ask the appraiser to give you a list of items that should be repaired or "cured" in your home. The appraiser may be able to point out important things that you have overlooked, such as carpet that should be cleaned, faded paint, or broken fixtures. You should then take care of these things before buyers turn you down.
6. Ask whether you can later ask brief questions about the appraisal. A good appraiser will go over the report with you and later answer questions about how it was prepared.

An appraiser and the appraisal report can really be useful. The $150 to $300 appraisal cost can provide plenty of information. Once you have that appraisal report, study it carefully.

Forget about what you paid for your home. Whether you bought it for $10,000 or $500,000 makes no difference. When you want to sell it, the question is its *current value* — not your cost. The question of value is answered by that appraisal report. An appraisal should not refer to your original cost. That is a historic fact which has nothing to do with its present market value.

After estimating the market value, a seller should consider other matters. First, buyers typically want to negotiate price or other concessions. So the offering price should be raised above market value to leave room for flexibility. (Again, keep in mind whether you are in a buyer's or seller's market.) Next, the seller must consider how quickly a sale is needed. Pricing will be structured differently depending on whether the seller can wait for a good offer or is anxious or even desperate to sell. A lower price normally results in a quicker sale; a higher price could, but doesn't always, materialize only after the home is on the market for some time. Finally, a seller should consider whether the market is rising or falling. In a rising

market time is on the seller's side — there is a tendency to hold out for a high price. However, when prices are falling a seller will want a fast sale.

Some sellers adopt a policy of starting at a high price, then lowering it over time. This approach avoids selling for too low a price. However, a home with several price drops may give the impression that something is wrong with it. Sales agents are more reluctant to encourage the purchase of an overpriced house than one that is priced at the market.

Fixing Up

It is obvious that a house in a good state of repair and maintenance will sell faster and/or for a higher price than one that needs work. Before putting your house on the market, check its appearance and condition of its components.

Exterior Appearance

A prospective buyer will see the exterior first. Since first impressions count heavily, the exterior may well determine whether the prospect will want to look further. A good-looking, well-cared-for exterior is important in setting the value of a home. Consider the following factors:

- Does the house need a fresh coat of paint? Do pulled-away shingles need to be replaced? Do mortar joints need to be repointed?
- Has the roof been checked to ensure there is no cracking or drying out?
- Are the gutters and downspouts free of debris?
- Are there any cracks that need repair?
- Do the window screens need to be repaired?
- Do windows need recaulking and reglazing?
- Is the property well-landscaped, with the lawn trimmed and edged and the yard free of trash?
- Are there any cracks in the patio or driveway?
- Is the fence in good repair?
- Is the swimming pool clean and in good repair?
- Has an exterminator examined the house lately?

Interior Appearance

Particular care must be given to the interior. It is important to keep your home as neat and clean as possible to best display its assets. For example, excessive furniture needs to be removed so rooms do not appear crowded. In addition, the following suggestions should be considered:

- Are the walls faded, wallpaper smudged and woodwork worn? (If the interior needs painting, use neutral colors.)
- Does the carpet or floor need to be cleaned or repaired?
- Loose knobs, sticking doors and windows, warped cabinet drawers, and other minor flaws detract from home value and can be fixed easily.

- Kitchen and bathrooms are of particular interest to buyers and need to be kept clean and orderly. Repair caulking in bathtubs and showers.
- Keep stairways clear to avoid a cluttered appearance and possible injuries.
- Spacious closets are important to most buyers, so take the time to clean them.
- Display the full value of your attic, basement and other utility space by removing all unnecessary articles.

Mechanical Systems

After the exterior and interior of the home have been checked, the mechanical systems should be inspected to ensure their proper working order. Plumbing is a prime concern of buyers and can be observed readily. In these days of energy awareness, the heating and cooling plant will also be of great interest to prospective buyers.

Check the pipes and fix any leaky faucets. Old or corroded sections of the pipes should be replaced, loose joints tightened, and broken fixtures replaced.

The heating and cooling units also should be checked. A dirty heating plant tends to break down more frequently and does an inefficient job of heating. Before a home goes on the market, the owner should check the air-conditioner condenser and recharge the freon if necessary. It is unlikely every part of the home checked will require maintenance.

When improvements or repairs are indicated, decide whether the cost will be justified in the selling price.

Showing Your House

When your home is listed with a real estate broker, expect him or her and other brokers to *preview* it. The broker will show the home to prospects while you are away. Unless there is a compelling reason for you to stay, it is best to leave the showing to your broker.

Most active brokers in metropolitan areas are members of an MLS. Weekly or monthly a group of brokers will travel as a *caravan* to see the new listings. Allow them to do so as this enhances market exposure: possibly an agent has been looking for a house exactly like yours on behalf of a client. Your broker may also suggest putting a *lock box* on your door. That is a small metal box, opened by a key, in which your house key is put. All MLS members have a key to the box and, thus, have access to your home. If you have a compelling reason to avoid the lock box — such as fear of burglary — do not allow it. This could cause logistical problems because you, or someone else with a key, must be present to allow entry. However, your peace of mind is worth this inconvenience. (Should you have moved away from the house, a lock box may be the only practical solution.)

Buyers or their brokers should make an appointment to view your home. This will give you time to prepare. Whether you show your own home or leave the showing to a broker, plan your approach, determining

in advance the features to be called to the attention of the potential buyer. Often it is these unique or special features that prove to be persuasive. It could be the oak mantle or the view from the kitchen window that makes the potential buyer want to purchase your home.

It is important to be truthful about both good and negative points of the home. The potential buyer then will be more confident you are being completely honest. Point out the advantages an older home offers over a newly built home: it is in an established neighborhood whose character is apparent; the yard is already landscaped with more mature trees and shrubs; most minor problems with the home already should have been solved.

Before appointment time, pretend that you are the prospect and go on a tour. Start outside. Be sure that there's a place for the visitor to park — either on the street or in the driveway. From the logical parking spots, be certain that there's a clear path to the front door. If there is snow or ice on the ground, clear it or sprinkle sand. Stand just outside the front door. Look up, down and to all sides. Any cobwebs to be removed? Screws to be tightened? Does the doorbell work? Are there any visible cosmetic problems that your prospect will readily observe? Quickly repair them. Do your best to give the front door area an attractive appearance. People want to be proud of their front door area, even if it is seldom used.

Walk through your home with the intent of doing any last minute dusting, vacuuming, replacing electric bulbs, and so on. Your prospective buyers will arrive any minute so there's not time for major repairs. Just do the last minute cleaning and cosmetics.

When showing the home, consider these tips:

• A home that is well lighted is inviting. Open draperies during the day and turn on all lights in the evening.
• Turn off the radio and television so there will be no distractions.
• Keep pets out of the house during inspections.

Helpful Information

Any information that may facilitate the sale should be available to prospective buyers. Try to have the following information readily written and accessible to answer any questions that might arise:

• The date you are planning to move
• Why you are selling
• How old the home is, and who built it
• Records of utility expenses, maintenance costs and annual taxes
• Insulation material
• Draperies, appliances and other items included in the sale
• Recent improvements or additions, such as new appliances or a ceiling fan

Sales Contract

Due to the complexities of a real estate transaction, the most certain way to be sure a sale is properly closed is to use the services of an attorney. Care must be taken to see that both the buyer's and seller's legal rights are fully protected. This involves a knowledge of what these rights are and what must be done to keep them from being violated. State law contains many pitfalls in the sale and purchase of real property. Consequently, counsel by an attorney with experience in residential real estate transactions is advisable.

To consummate any sales agreement, the buyer and seller should sign a sales contract. The contract should contain the following elements:

- Signatures of competent parties
- An offer and an acceptance
- An adequate legal description of the property
- The sales price and the terms of financing
- An escrow deposit to bind the parties to the contract
- A description of the type of *deed* to be used in conveying *title*
- Any other provisions pertinent to the agreement.

A sample contract of sale is shown on page 665. However, a certain form may be preferred or mandated for use in your state.

Parts of a Real Estate Contract of Sale

A contract of sale for real estate will normally contain certain parts. These and their purpose are as follows:

Part	Purpose
Parties	States the names of the seller (*vendor*) and buyer (*vendee*).
Property description	Provides an adequate legal description of the subject property and fixtures included.
Sales price	States the amount to be paid in cash at closing and from the proceeds of financing.
Financing conditions	Purchaser stipulates acceptable conditions of financing, including the type of loan, loan-to-value ratio, interest rate, monthly payments.
Earnest money	The amount of the good faith deposit presented to the seller or agent. Also called *hand money* or *escrow money*.
Type of deed	Describes the type of deed to be given at closing.
Title evidence	Describes the type of evidence to be considered satisfactory assurance that the seller can give title.
Title approval	Describes rights of purchaser and seller in the event that purchaser objects to a flaw in the title.

Property condition	States whatever changes (if any) are required to the property, and required inspections such as for structural integrity, electrical, mechanical, and plumbing systems, and for wood destroying insects.
Prorations	Calls for the proration of prepaid or unpaid taxes, insurance, rents, etc., between buyer and seller.
Loss	Affixes responsibility for casualty losses until closing.
Possession	Establishes a date for possession.
Closing	Establishes a date for closing.
Broker	Acknowledges the existence of a real estate broker, the commission rate, and which principal is to pay the commission.
Default	Describes the obligations of parties in the event one fails to perform.
Miscellaneous provisions	States whatever other provisions buyer and seller agree upon.
Signatures	Principals, brokers, escrow agents.

A worksheet, shown on page 673, can be used to estimate the amount a seller receives upon the sale.

There may be considerable negotiations before prices and terms are agreed to. Usually, a prospective buyer makes an offer on a *sales contract* and tenders *earnest money*. If the seller accepts, the money should be placed in escrow by the broker, or with an attorney or title insurance company. However, if the seller changes any of the terms, it is a rejection of the offer and the substitution of a new offer to sell to the buyer. Negotiations may then proceed until the contract is consummated or may be broken off.

Tax Considerations on The Sale of Your Home

Two major tax provisions pertain to the sale of a taxpayer's principal residence after July 20, 1981.

For Homeowners 55 and Older

The first provision of the act pertains to taxpayers who are 55 or older at the time of the sale (only one spouse needs to be 55). Qualifying taxpayers can elect to exclude from gross taxable income up to $125,000 of any gain realized from the sale of a principal residence ($62,500 for married individuals filing separate returns). However, this election can be exercised only once in a lifetime and is binding on both spouses. Additionally, the taxpayer must have owned and occupied the property

as a principal residence for three or more years during the five-year period before the sale.

Since the exclusion may be elected only once, this provision has important implications for married taxpayers who elect it during a marriage which may later be dissolved by divorce or by the death of a spouse. Remarriage will not reinstate the election.

For Homeowners of Any Age

A second provision of the act applies to homeowners of any age. It requires taxpayers to defer taxes on a gain realized from the sale of a principal residence if a replacement residence that costs at least as much as the sale price of the residence sold is purchased or built within 24 months of the sale. Normally, only one tax-deferred sale is allowed during each 24-month period; an exception in the act permits more than one such transaction (usually called a *roll-over*) within 24 months if the taxpayer relocates for employment purposes. The same standards currently in effect concerning deductibility of moving expenses are used to determine if the sale was caused by a change of employment location.

The act permits taxpayers who are 55 or older to use both provisions to minimize taxes on the sale of their home. For example, suppose a 55 or older taxpayer realizes a $200,000 gain on the sale of a principal residence for $400,000. If that taxpayer purchases or builds a replacement for $275,000 within 24 months, taxes on the entire gain are minimized. This homeowner could postpone $75,000 through the roll-over provision and exclude $125,000 by the election available to older taxpayers. This permits those 55 or over to "step down" in the housing market and minimize their tax burden.

IRS Form 2119

The Internal Revenue Service has provided Form 2119, entitled "Sale or Exchange of Principal Residence," to help taxpayers calculate: (1) the gain on the sale of the old residence, (2) the adjusted sales price of the old residence, (3) the amount of taxable gain and (4) the adjusted basis of the replacement residence (if any). Form 2119 is reproduced on page 676.

Moving Expenses: Tax Implications

If you move to a residence 35 miles closer to where you work than you now live, most of your moving expenses may be tax deductible.

For example, if you lived 50 miles from your office and moved to within 15 miles, you moved 35 plus miles closer and qualify. However, if you moved from 50 miles from work to a new residence that is 20 miles from work, the 30 mile difference is not enough to qualify. Generally, one must work in the new area for 39 weeks during the first year after the move.

You cannot deduct the same expense twice. For example, expenses of selling your old home may be used either as moving expenses or subtracted from the old home selling price, but not both.

If you qualify as having moved to a new job location, direct and indirect moving costs are deductible. Direct costs are for moving personal and household goods from the old to the new home, and traveling, including lodging, from old to new. If one's auto is used, the allowance is nine cents per mile, or actual operating expenses but not depreciation. Generally, only 80 percent of the amount spent for meals is deductible. There is no other limit on the amount of deduction for direct expenses.

House hunting expenses are deductible, including meals at 80 percent. The cost of lodging while in temporary quarters at the general area of the new job site is also deductible for up to 30 days.The deduction for house hunting plus temporary living expenses cannot exceed $1,500.

Qualified real estate sale expenses include the real estate broker's commission, escrow fees, advertising expenses, deed preparation, state transfer taxes, points on a buyer's FHA mortgage, and any loss on the sale. On the home purchase, one may deduct legal, title, appraisal, and loan costs (but not interest). The costs of breaking a lease (but not rent) are deductible. Real estate expenses are also indirect expenses, and total indirect expenses may not exceed $3,000. Limits are higher for moves to and from a foreign country.

A sample IRS Form 3903 is provided on page 677.

Closing

Closing, in a real estate transaction, is when money and property change hands. In most states a title company, abstract company, or lawyer is responsible for preparing and recording the necessary documents and accounting for money. A sample form, *Seller's Estimated Receipts,* appears in the Appendix, page 673.

An abbreviated closing statement is shown below.

SAMPLE CLOSING STATEMENT

	Seller		Buyer	
	Debit	Credit	Debit	Credit
Real property		$80,000	$80,000	
Prepaid taxes		670	670	
Sales commission	$2,400			
Survey fee			75	
Cash paid by buyer to close ..				$80,745
Cash received by seller	78,270			
Totals	$80,670	$80,670	$80,745	$80,745

Items that affect only one party will be shown as a debit or a credit only on the statement of the party affected. For example, if the sales commission is paid by the seller, the amount will appear only on the seller's closing statement. If the buyer pays for a survey, it will appear on the buyer's statement only.

Items of value that are sold, exchanged, or transferred between buyer and seller will be shown in *opposite* columns of *both* parties. For example, the transferred property is shown as a credit to the seller *and* as a debit to the buyer. Never should an item transferred, exchanged, or taken over be shown as a credit to both parties or as a debit to both. If an item is transferred, sold, or exchanged, it will be a debit to one party and a credit to the other.

Items usually *debited* (charged) to the buyer include the following:

1. Purchase price of the real property
2. Purchase price of personal property
3. Deed recording fees
4. Title examination
5. Title insurance
6. Hazard insurance
7. Survey
8. Appraisal fee (sometimes charged to seller)
9. Prepaid taxes
10. Loan assumption fees

Items that are likely to be *credited* to the buyer are:

1. Earnest money deposits
2. Proceeds of a loan the buyer borrows
3. Assumption of a loan
4. Mortgage to the seller (purchase money)
5. Current taxes unpaid to closing
6. Tenant rents paid in advance (the seller collected these)
7. Balance due from purchaser to close (paid by buyer to close)

Items likely to be *debited* to a seller are:

1. Sales commission
2. Current but unpaid taxes
3. Existing debt—whether assumed or to be paid off
4. Loan prepayment penalties
5. Discount points for buyer's VA or FHA loan. Discount points on *conventional* loans may be charged to buyer or to seller depending on contractual arrangements, custom in the area, local law, etc.
6. Rent received in advance
7. Deed preparation

Items usually *credited* to a seller are:

1. Sales price of real property
2. Sales price of personal property

3. Prepaid taxes
4. Prepaid insurance (only if policy is assumed by buyer)
5. Escrow balance held by lender

When selling your home you may ask the person responsible for closing to allow you to review the figures a day or two prior to closing. If any amount does not appear correct or you have questions concerning charges, get the problem resolved then. It is awkward to resolve matters at the last minute.

Many people are frightened by real estate transactions. There is no need to be apprehensive when one's homework has been properly done.

ANALYZING REAL ESTATE INVESTMENT OPPORTUNITIES

Real estate investment analysis is the process of determining the suitability of a proposed real estate investment to a specific investor. The process involves weighing the expected benefits of property ownership against the possible risks and matching them with a potential investor. The validity of this analysis rests on the assumptions that are used. When overly optimistic assumptions are input, the investment will appear deceptively attractive. Further, returns from real estate take several forms and are more complex than other investments. For these reasons, real estate investment analysis requires a great deal of knowledge, sound judgment, and careful consideration.

Financial Benefits of Investing in Real Estate

Financial benefits of investing in real estate are classified into four major categories:

1. Cash flow
2. Income tax advantages
3. Capital appreciation (including inflation hedge)
4. Equity build-up via mortgage reduction

These four benefits, plus additional financial and non-financial reasons for investing in real estate, are described below. Because of inherent conflicts in the benefits it is very difficult for an investor to maximize all four from the same property. An investor should seek the one or two that are the most important in satisfying his or her goals.

Cash Flow

Cash flow is the excess of rentals over combined operating expenses and debt service. Cash flow alone may provide a rate of return on equity that is competitive with other investment alternatives.

Income Tax Advantages

Improved real estate can generate income tax losses that may offset income from other sources. Ordinary and necessary operating expenses, depreciation, and interest on indebtedness in a trade or business are allowable tax deductions. If total allowable deductions exceed rental income, a tax loss is generated. Since depreciation is a noncash

37

accounting deduction, rental property can generate a tax loss while providing cash flow and value appreciation. However, the use of such passive losses to offset active or portfolio income was severely restricted by the Tax Reform Act of 1986.

Capital Appreciation

There are good prospects for *capital appreciation* of land and improved properties in addition to inflation gains. Speculators and other landowners in the path of growth can enjoy windfall gains as rural areas become urbanized. Residential owners gain price increases because stricter environmental regulations and building codes, and higher interest rates increase replacement costs. In areas of growth, prices of existing units tend to rise with replacement costs. Higher interest rates require rents to rise before new construction becomes feasible. Furthermore, the number of residential units needed has been increasing due to the trend toward smaller household size.

Hedge against inflation Many investors acquire real estate as a *store of value*. In the long run, land prices tend to rise with inflation, keeping pace with the price level of other commodities. Improvements to and on land are considered to be long-lasting. As the price of bricks, lumber, concrete and other building materials rise along with higher wages, replacement costs for improved real estate increase. Prices paid for existing real estate rise with higher replacement costs.

Equity Build-Up

Equity build-up is a method of forced saving while owning real estate. Most real estate mortgages require at least some *amortization* (principal payments) to reduce the debt over time. The benefit of this payment is returned to the investor upon a sale or perhaps a refinancing of the property.

Additional Financial and Nonfinancial Benefits

Pride of Ownership and Control

The tangible nature of real estate provides advantages. Prestigious location, size, impressive architecture, or even a modest but well maintained property can add much to the psychological satisfaction of the owner. Control and use of property are also important aspects of ownership.

Leverage

Leverage provides the traditional key to building wealth with real

estate. By using borrowed money to purchase real estate, an investor can magnify the benefits of value appreciation. Advisors do point out the risk-return effect of leverage and counsel some middle ground for security. To the investor recognizing the trade-off between risk and reward in investments, there is a prudent amount of leverage.

Estate Building

All investors desire to accumulate wealth, and real estate is recognized as an excellent vehicle for this purpose. Traditional investors recognize the power of appreciation combined with leverage to build wealth. By controlling an appreciating asset using borrowed funds, owner's equity can grow quickly. Experience has shown that appreciation is not universal nor constant over time. Thus, investors spend much effort searching for properties with the best prospects for appreciation and plan to hold each property for five or more years.

Security of Capital

There is a certain security in real estate because it is highly unlikely that the asset will ever become worthless (in contrast to stocks and bonds). If an investor is interested in security, then judicious use of leverage, long-term leasing to high quality tenants, and diversification are advised.

Balancing Investment Portfolios

Spreading the risk among various investments — *diversification* — can serve to preserve principal and income. Diversification relates to the type of investment and to the geographical distribution of holdings. Large pension plans and life insurance companies acquire — in addition to securities — real estate and mortgages in many different locations. Additional diversification can be achieved through investments in different types of real property, e.g., shopping centers, office buildings, or apartments.

Opportunity for Abnormal Returns

Because each parcel of real property includes a unique location in geographic space, its owners enjoy some monopoly power. Investors who can obtain the more desired locations can derive above average returns. Such returns are achieved either by luck or through use of entrepreneurial skill. Consistent winners must be able to find those locations that will be in demand in the near future, create competitive advantages for their development, select the proper time for acquiring and disposing of property through knowledge of business cycles, or know how to overcome government-imposed constraints on the use of land.

Disadvantages of Investing in Real Estate

Among the reasons investors expect to receive relatively high returns from real estate investment are the extensive risks involved. To the careful investor, these risks represent challenges calling for expert knowledge. To the risk-taker, they are minor hurdles that discourage the uninitiated and timid.

Illiquidity

Real property is very costly; it is also time-consuming to buy and sell. Transaction costs are high compared to those associated with other assets. The market is more difficult to evaluate. Selection of a property requires analysis of the local economy and the location, as well as the specific attributes of the property under consideration. Locating a buyer generally requires the services of a professional agent. Furthermore, advantageous purchases and sales depend on proper market timing. Money invested in real estate, therefore, is apt to be tied up for a considerable period of time.

Management Burden

Real property ownership entails the responsibility for maintaining the property and collecting rents. This calls for continuous personal involvement on the part of the investor. Many have found that ownership of property outside their home area is impractical.

Economic Depreciation

Not only do properties require upkeep to offset physical deterioration, but periodic remodeling is needed to keep the property competitive in the market. Keeping a reserve account to handle these tasks is prudent.

Government Controls

The property owner may be restricted in several ways in the use of the property. Zoning and subdivision controls affect changes in the use of the site. Housing codes may require a specified level of maintenance (not necessarily in line with what the market demands). Rent controls can prevent recouping investments spent to upgrade property.

Legal Complexity

The buying and selling of real estate involves a succession of legal commitments with potentially serious consequences. It is not uncommon for both buyer and seller to be represented by legal counsel even in a simple transaction.

Lack of Information

Buyers and sellers of real estate are handicapped by limited information about current market conditions and the properties they are considering. It is important to negotiate the best deal, and up-to-date information is essential to that end. Such information is costly to obtain. (This is not so important for those who intend to use property for personal purposes; the greater part of their evaluation rests on the suitability of the property for their own use.)

Benchmark Example

At this juncture, a benchmark example of a proposed real estate investment will be used to introduce investment analysis. Variations on the basic case will highlight certain points. The benchmark is simplified into basic components from these standpoints:

1. Physical composition
2. Financial composition
3. Rights to use
4. Income and expenses

Physical Composition

Our hypothetical benchmark property is a 50-unit apartment complex which cost $2 million — $200,000 in land value, plus $1,800,000 of depreciable improvements. To simplify the illustration, all of the improvements are depreciated using a 27½ year life. Depreciation was calculated at 3.64 percent of the asset cost annually on a straight-line basis, except for the first year which is $23/24$ of that rate because of the midmonth convention introduced by the 1986 tax act. Land is not depreciated; only improvements are depreciable.

The property was expected to increase in value by three percent annually, compounded. Transaction costs to sell the property at the end of the projection period were three percent of the resale price.

Financial Composition

The mortgage-equity components of our benchmark property included a $1,600,000 loan at 11 percent interest, with monthly payments, self-amortizing over a 25-year period. The $400,000 balance of the purchase price was considered to be paid in cash at closing.

Rights to Use

It was assumed that the landlord held all of the rights and privileges of ownership, subject to tenant leases that were arranged on a short-

ANALYZING INVESTMENT OPPORTUNITIES

term (typically one-year) basis. Thus, periodic rent increases were
likely.

Income and Expenses

Each apartment rents for $550 per month. A 10 percent vacancy and
collection allowance was assumed in the example. Miscellaneous
income (such as from laundry and vending machines) was $5,000 for
the first year. Operating expenses, (such as utilities, maintenance, real
estate taxes, and insurance) were $100,000 for the first year.

These figures were incremented annually at three percent for reve-
nues, and five percent for operating expenses. A higher rate of increase
was used for operating expenses than revenues because as rental prop-
erty ages its market appeal diminishes, yet it requires more
maintenance.

Computer Simulation

A computer program can be used to project future income expected
from the investment, or results can be projected by hand, preferably
with a calculator. The computer program used for this illustration
allows the user to input separately, the potential gross income, miscel-
laneous income, vacancy and collection allowance, and operating
expenses. A compounded growth rate is allowed for the relevant
variables.

A 20-year projection of cash flow and taxable income or loss for the
subject property was performed, based on the assumptions stated.
Results are shown on the following pages. (Contact the authors at Texas
A&M University, College Station, Texas 77843, concerning availabil-
ity of the computer program which generated this output.)

Column 1 shows the *potential gross income* each year. This is the
amount of rental income that would be received if all units were occu-
pied and paid for each month.
Column 2 shows the *vacancy allowance* each year. Some allowance is
needed for vacant apartment units, and for the failure to collect some
rent.
Column 3 shows *miscellaneous income* each year. Typically, this
derives from laundry or vending machine concessions.
Column 4 shows *operating expenses* each year. These expenditures are
necessary to operate the property, even if it were bought free of debt.
Expenses include insurance, real estate taxes, repairs and maintenance,
replacement of worn carpets and appliances, property management,
and the like.
Column 5 shows *net operating income (NOI)* each year for 20 years.
(Column 1 plus column 3 minus columns 2 and 4.)

Year	1. Potential Gross Income	2. Vacancy Allowance	3. Misc. Income	4. Operating Expenses
1	330,000	33,000	5,000	100,000
2	339,900	33,990	5,150	105,000
3	350,097	35,010	5,305	110,250
4	360,600	36,060	5,464	115,762
5	371,418	37,142	5,628	121,551
6	382,560	38,256	5,796	127,628
7	394,037	39,404	5,970	134,010
8	405,858	40,586	6,149	140,710
9	418,034	41,803	6,334	147,745
10	430,575	43,058	6,524	155,133
11	443,492	44,349	6,720	162,889
12	456,797	45,680	6,921	171,034
13	470,501	47,050	7,129	179,586
14	484,616	48,462	7,343	188,565
15	499,155	49,915	7,563	197,993
16	514,129	51,413	7,790	207,893
17	529,553	52,955	8,024	218,287
18	545,440	54,544	8,264	229,202
19	561,803	56,180	8,512	240,662
20	578,657	57,866	8,768	252,695

Year	5. Net Operating Income	6. Interest Expense	7. Principal Amortization	8. Before-Tax Cash Flow
1	202,000	175,367	12,815	13,818
2	206,060	173,884	14,298	17,878
3	210,142	172,229	15,953	21,960
4	214,241	170,383	17,798	26,060
5	218,353	168,324	19,858	30,172
6	222,473	166,026	22,156	34,291
7	226,594	163,462	24,720	38,413
8	230,712	160,601	27,580	42,530
9	234,819	157,409	30,772	46,637
10	238,909	153,849	34,333	50,727
11	242,973	149,875	38,306	54,792
12	247,005	145,443	42,739	58,823
13	250,994	140,497	47,684	62,813
14	254,932	134,979	53,203	66,751
15	258,809	128,823	59,359	70,627
16	262,613	121,954	66,228	74,432
17	266,334	114,290	73,892	78,152
18	269,958	105,739	82,442	81,777
19	273,473	96,199	91,983	85,291
20	276,864	85,555	102,627	88,682

ANALYZING INVESTMENT OPPORTUNITIES

Year	9. Depreciation Expense	10. Taxable Income	11. Passive Loss Used	12. Passive Loss Carryover	13. Tax Paid (− Savings)	14. After-Tax Cash Flow
1	62,640	− 36,007	0	36,007	0	13,818
2	65,520	− 33,344	0	69,350	0	17,878
3	65,520	− 27,607	0	96,958	0	21,960
4	65,520	− 21,662	0	118,620	0	26,060
5	65,520	− 15,490	0	134,110	0	30,172
6	65,520	− 9,073	0	143,183	0	34,291
7	65,520	− 2,387	0	145,571	0	38,413
8	65,520	4,591	− 4,591	140,980	0	42,530
9	65,520	11,890	− 11,890	129,090	0	46,637
10	65,520	19,540	− 19,540	109,550	0	50,727
11	65,520	27,578	− 27,578	81,972	0	54,792
12	65,520	36,042	− 36,042	45,931	0	58,823
13	65,520	44,977	− 44,977	954	0	62,813
14	65,520	54,433	− 954	0	14,974	51,776
15	65,520	64,466	0	0	18,051	52,577
16	65,520	75,140	0	0	21,039	53,393
17	65,520	86,524	0	0	24,227	53,926
18	65,520	98,699	0	0	27,636	54,141
19	65,520	111,754	0	0	31,291	54,000
20	65,520	125,789	0	0	35,221	53,461

Sale Year	15. Selling Price Before Expenses	16. Selling Expenses	17. Selling Price After Expenses	18. Mortgage Balance	19. Adjusted Tax Basis
1	2,060,000	61,800	1,998,200	1,587,185	1,937,360
2	2,121,800	63,654	2,058,146	1,572,887	1,871,840
3	2,185,454	65,564	2,119,891	1,556,935	1,806,320
4	2,251,018	67,531	2,183,487	1,539,137	1,740,800
5	2,318,548	69,556	2,248,992	1,519,279	1,675,280
6	2,388,105	71,643	2,316,461	1,497,123	1,609,760
7	2,459,748	73,792	2,385,955	1,472,403	1,544,240
8	2,533,540	76,006	2,457,534	1,444,822	1,478,720
9	2,609,546	78,286	2,531,260	1,414,050	1,413,200
10	2,687,833	80,635	2,607,198	1,379,717	1,347,680
11	2,768,468	83,054	2,685,414	1,341,411	1,282,160
12	2,851,522	85,546	2,765,976	1,298,673	1,216,640
13	2,937,067	88,112	2,848,955	1,250,988	1,151,120
14	3,025,179	90,755	2,934,424	1,197,786	1,085,600
15	3,115,934	93,478	3,022,456	1,138,427	1,020,080
16	3,209,413	96,282	3,113,130	1,072,199	954,560
17	3,305,695	99,171	3,206,524	998,307	889,040
18	3,404,866	102,146	3,302,720	915,865	823,520
19	3,507,012	105,210	3,401,802	823,882	758,000
20	3,612,222	108,367	3,503,855	721,256	692,480

Sale Year	20. Passive Loss Released	21. Taxable Gain On Sale	22. Tax On Gain (− Savings)	23. After-Tax Resale Proceeds	24. Internal Rate Of Return On Init Equity
1	36,007	24,833	6,953	404,062	4.47%
2	69,350	116,956	32,748	452,511	10.18%
3	96,958	216,613	60,652	502,304	11.98%
4	118,620	324,067	90,739	553,612	12.77%
5	134,110	439,601	123,088	606,625	13.19%
6	143,183	563,518	157,785	661,554	13.41%
7	145,571	696,144	194,920	718,632	13.54%
8	140,980	837,834	234,539	778,118	13.61%
9	129,090	988,969	276,911	840,298	13.64%
10	109,550	1,149,967	321,991	905,490	13.65%
11	81,972	1,321,281	369,959	974,044	13.65%
12	45,931	1,503,405	420,953	1,046,350	13.64%
13	954	1,696,881	475,127	1,122,840	13.62%
14	0	1,848,824	517,671	1,218,968	13.60%
15	0	2,002,376	560,665	1,323,364	13.57%
16	0	2,158,570	604,400	1,436,532	13.52%
17	0	2,317,484	648,896	1,559,321	13.48%
18	0	2,479,200	694,176	1,692,679	13.42%
19	0	2,643,802	740,264	1,837,655	13.37%
20	0	2,811,375	787,185	1,995,415	13.31%

Sale Year	25. Overall Rate Of Return	26. Debt Service Coverage Ratio	27. Before-Tax Cash Flow To Inital Equity	28. After-Tax Cash Flow To Inital Equity
1	10.100%	107.343%	3.455%	3.455%
2	10.003%	109.501%	4.470%	4.470%
3	9.904%	111.670%	5.490%	5.490%
4	9.803%	113.848%	6.515%	6.515%
5	9.700%	116.033%	7.543%	7.543%
6	9.595%	118.222%	8.573%	8.573%
7	9.488%	120.413%	9.603%	9.603%
8	9.379%	122.601%	10.633%	10.633%
9	9.268%	124.783%	11.659%	11.659%
10	9.155%	126.956%	12.682%	12.682%
11	9.040%	129.116%	13.698%	13.698%
12	8.922%	131.259%	14.706%	14.706%
13	8.802%	133.379%	15.703%	15.703%
14	8.680%	135.471%	16.688%	12.944%
15	8.555%	137.532%	17.657%	13.144%
16	8.428%	139.553%	18.608%	13.348%
17	8.299%	141.530%	19.538%	13.481%
18	8.166%	143.456%	20.444%	13.535%
19	8.032%	145.324%	21.323%	13.500%
20	7.895%	147.126%	22.171%	13.365%

Year	29. Gross Rent Multiplier	30. Break-Even Ratio
1	6.061	87.328%
2	6.061	86.255%
3	6.061	85.243%
4	6.061	84.288%
5	6.061	83.392%
6	6.061	82.522%
7	6.061	81.767%
8	6.061	81.036%
9	6.061	80.359%
10	6.061	79.734%
11	6.061	79.161%
12	6.061	78.638%
13	6.061	78.165%
14	6.061	77.741%
15	6.061	77.366%
16	6.061	77.038%
17	6.061	76.757%
18	6.061	76.522%
19	6.061	76.333%
20	6.061	76.190%

Column 6 shows *interest expense* for each of 20 years based on the $1,600,000, 25-year monthly payment mortgage at 11 percent interest. Note how the interest portion of the constant payment diminishes over time as the principal is retired.

Column 7 shows the *principal payment* on the mortgage: this is the annual equity build-up. Note that principal payments (called *mortgage amortization*) require cash and are not tax-deductible.

Column 8 Before-tax cash flow is the difference between NOI in column 5 and the debt service requirement (principal and interest, the sum of columns 6 and 7).

Column 9 Depreciation was based on 3.64 percent per year, the straight-line rate that approximates a 27½year life. Depreciation provides a tax deduction without a cash outflow. Note: the first year is slightly less than other years because of the midmonth convention under the 1986 tax act.

Column 10 Taxable income (or *loss*) is the result of subtracting interest and depreciation from net operating income, specifically column 5 minus columns 6 and 9. Note that losses occur during the first seven years of ownership; these losses diminish with reduced mortgage payments and increased NOI. In later years taxable income increases sharply; however, projected taxable income is less than before-tax cash flow for the first 15 years. This occurs because depreciation exceeds the mortgage principal payment each year until the sixteenth year.

46

Column 11 In this projection it was assumed that tax losses generated in early years could not be applied against other income. Instead, the losses are suspended until this property generates positive taxable income; then they are released to offset such income or gain from the sale. *Passive losses* may be used earlier depending on the investor's other income and personal circumstances. An "active" property owner who meets certain requirements may deduct up to $25,000 of passive losses against non-passive income.

Column 12 The *passive loss carry-over* column accumulates the property's passive losses, net of annual application.

Column 13 The owner was assumed to be in the 28 percent marginal and average tax bracket. The *tax paid* column offers the amount of tax attributable to the property. For the first seven years the property offers tax losses but they are suspended because of passive loss limitations. Taxable income generated during the next six years is offset by releasing the suspended losses. Consequently, no income taxes are due for the first 13 years. In the fourteenth year, some taxes are due, continuing through the end of the projection.

Column 14 *After-tax cash flow* is before-tax cash flow (column 8) modified by taxes paid or saved (column 13). The investor keeps these dollars.

Resale Simulation

The eventual resale of our benchmark property will create a taxable gain (or loss) and cash proceeds (or cash deficits). We know that real estate is not a liquid asset, and it may take months or years just to realize market value in a sale. Furthermore, values are subject to fluctuation in an unpredictable manner. In an effort to simplify this analysis, our benchmark property was assumed to grow in value at a three percent rate, compounded annually. Transaction costs, estimated at a one-time charge of three percent, were subtracted. The mortgage balance and adjusted tax basis could be projected mathematically. Other details are shown in the projections.

Please note that columns 15 through 24 may be used for any year of sale and are valid only for that year because the property can be sold only once. All years are shown in the table to offer complete information for decision making purposes. For example, for a presumed sale in year 10, read across the line for year 10 of columns 15 — 24. That is the only relevant line across these columns for a 10 year projection. Results of operations would be applicable for years 1 through 10; but operations in years 11 through 20 should be ignored as they would be extraneous.

Column 15 The *selling price before expenses* is the initial cost increased by three percent compounded annually. The projection offers the price for any year, based on the assumed increase.

Column 16 *Selling expenses*, or *transaction costs*, are three percent of the resale price. This would include a brokerage commission and legal expenses.

Column 17 The *selling price after expenses* is the difference between column 15 and 16.

Column 18 Future *mortgage balances* were based on scheduled amortization. Neither accelerated payments nor delinquencies were considered for this projection. Refinancing was not attempted.

Column 19 The *adjusted tax basis* for each year is the initial cost less annual depreciation.

Column 20 Unused *passive losses* are assumed to be released upon a sale, and reduce the taxable gain.

Column 21 The *selling price* (column 15) minus the sum of selling expenses (column 16), adjusted tax basis (column 19), and passive loss released (column 20) result in a taxable gain or loss on a sale.

Column 22 A 28 percent tax rate was applied to the amount in column 21 to indicate the *tax on the gain*.

Column 23 The *after-tax resale proceeds* are the selling price after expenses (column 17) less the sum of the mortgage balance (column 18) and tax on the gain (column 22). This is the net cash amount the sale will provide.

Column 24 The *internal rate of return* is a complicated mathematical calculation that compares the equity paid with the after-tax cash flows forecast, including the cash proceeds from resale. Suppose the investor had instead put the cash down payment in a bank savings account and withdrew the same annual cash flows as the property is expected to generate. Then, the interest rate that the bank must pay to sustain the withdrawals would be equal to the internal rate of return.

Column 25 The *overall rate of return* is the net operating income (column 5) divided by the selling price before expenses for the previous year (column15 for 1 year earlier). This percentage may provide an indication of whether the estimated resale price is in line with the income at the time of resale.

Column 26 The *debt service coverage ratio* is net operating income (column 5) divided by the combined principal and interest payment (column 6 plus 7). It indicates to a lender whether the property can support the debt service payment.

Column 27 Before-tax cash flow (column 8) divided by initial equity is a percentage rate that compares the equity investor's rate of cash flow to the equity contributed; it is commonly known as the equity dividend rate.

Column 28 After-tax cash flow (column 14) compared to initial equity is an after-tax equity dividend rate.

Column 29 *Gross rent multiplier* is the selling price divided by the potential gross income expected for the next year (column 15 divided by Column 1 for the next year).

Column 30 The *break-even ratio* is the percentage occupancy rate that is needed to pay for operating expenses, interest and principal (sum of columns 4, 6, 7). Divide that sum by column 1 to derive the percentage.

Conflicts Among Financial Benefits

Property may be carved into several pieces to offer different investors the one or two types of financial benefits they desire. However, one investor will not be able to maximize simultaneously all potential financial benefits from the same property because of inherent conflicts. Some of these conflicts are discussed below.

Cash Flow versus Taxable Income

It is difficult to maximize cash flow and tax savings at the same time. Depreciation, a noncash tax deduction, makes possible the simultaneous receipt of cash flow and tax losses. However, further tax losses must be accompanied by a cash flow reduction — such as would result from receiving less rent, incurring higher operating expenses, or a higher interest cost.

Increases in cash flow will be accompanied by increases in taxable income. It is always preferable to receive cash and pay a tax on the income than it is to pay cash and possibly receive tax losses.

Cash Flow versus Mortgage Reduction

An investor can increase the equity build-up benefit by accelerating mortgage principal payments. Most lenders will allow that; however, loans on commercial property often have prepayment penalties of one to five percent and some have closed periods, meaning they cannot be prepaid for the first five to ten years.

Since cash is required to reduce the principal balance, there is an inherent trade-off of cash flow versus equity buildup. Most investors prefer to receive spendable cash flow unless the mortgage interest rate is higher than their earnings rate. Then, it may be preferable to reduce the mortgage debt. Fast mortgage amortization also reduces the future interest payment, so it inherently conflicts with tax savings.

Cash Flow versus Appreciation

An owner can attempt to enhance property value by plowing back cash flow into property maintenance, repairs, and capital expenditures. Conversely, an owner can attempt to maximize cash flow by skimping on maintenance. An owner must make this choice, keeping in mind present needs for cash contrasted with future value enhancement. When choosing, an owner should remember there are many properties that suffer from deferred maintenance or neglect and consequently lose value. The longer this process continues, the more difficult it is to reverse by rehabilitation or modernization.

49

Tax Shelter versus Appreciation in Value

There is an inherent conflict between tax savings and appreciation. When the effect of general economic inflation is removed, land tends to rise in value with population pressures, while improved real estate tends to wear out. An investor who seeks income tax savings would prefer to purchase depreciable improvements, whereas one who seeks appreciation would prefer land. Consequently, though it is possible to gain some of both benefits, it is very difficult for one investor to maximize both appreciation and tax shelter simultaneously. Furthermore, if appreciation does materialize, the property must be sold to recognize the gain and income taxes paid.

Judging Income Stream Quality

The value of real estate is based on its expected future income. To estimate future income, the following must be considered:

1. The amount of net operating income.
2. When the income will be received.
3. The expected net proceeds from the sale of the property.

Many real estate investors, especially those who are just beginning, may rely on professional appraisers to assist them with these projections. An appraiser should possess knowledge of market rental rates, operating expenses and values for the property being considered.

The Amount of Net Operating Income

Market data on competitive properties will provide benchmarks against which to judge the property being analyzed. This information might include market rental rates, vacancy rates, and typical expense ratios. Appraisal reports on income-producing properties should include these items.

Potential gross income In estimating the potential gross income, there is a difference between *market rent* and *contract rent*. Market rent is the prevailing market rate for similar properties. Contract rent is the sum agreed to between a landlord and a tenant. If the existing leases are for a long term, the contract rent serves as an important ingredient in calculating the investment value of the project. It is possible, for example, that the amount the property owner actually receives for the term of a lease may be considerably less than market rent. In the case of short-term agreements, a potential buyer should determine whether it is reasonable for contract rent to equal the market rent at the time leases are renegotiated. With several leases encumbering a property, it is good to prepare a schedule with the expiration date of each lease. This will assist in estimating the quality and duration of the known portion of the income stream.

Special problems can occur in analyzing projects occupied by a single tenant. One may evaluate the credit worthiness of the tenant and the length of the lease to judge the probability of a vacancy in the future and when this vacancy would be likely to occur.

Vacancy and collection allowance The potential gross income is the amount received if every unit were rented at full rates all of the time. From this must be subtracted the loss from expected vacancies and an allowance for unpaid rents. The vacancy allowance depends on real estate market conditions (overbuilding is often problematical), regulatory requirements, and marketing.

Miscellaneous income Miscellaneous income includes revenues from laundry rooms, concession income, and the rental of parking spaces and storage bins.

Operating expenses Operating expenses are either fixed or variable. *Fixed expenses* do not change as the rate of occupancy changes. *Variable expenses* are directly related to the occupancy rate. As more people occupy and use a building, variable expenses increase.

Fixed expenses include property taxes, license and permit fees, and property insurance. Variable expenses include cost of utilities, management fees, payroll and payroll taxes, security costs, annual landscaping costs, advertising fees, and the cost of supplies and fees for various services provided by local government or private contractors. Operating rental property differs from most other businesses in that, whether a property is fully occupied or mostly vacant, the cost of real estate operations hardly changes.

A prospective purchaser should review utility bills, property tax assessments, insurance policies, receipts and reports from property management companies, title insurance policies, W-2 forms and other wage information for employees, copies of the actual leases in force, and income tax forms pertaining to the operation of the project.

When The Income Will Be Received

Cash flows are negative during *new construction*. The expected duration of construction is estimated by examining schedules and expected times of completion. During this period, interest is to be paid to the construction lender or added to the loan balance. A forecast must be made assessing the expected interest costs during construction, and whether it is to be funded by the construction loan, or paid in cash.

During the *leasing phase*, cash flows will rise as the project is leased to tenants. Upon attainment of break-even occupancy, often 80 to 85 percent, the project generates adequate income to provide cash flow. Hopefully, full occupancy occurs and continues until the project approaches the end of its economic useful life.

The Expected Net Proceeds From The Sale of Property

One of the most difficult tasks is to estimate the net proceeds expected from the resale of the subject property at the end of its holding

period. The following factors should be considered:

Possible appreciation of the land Depending on what happens to the surrounding area, the land could increase or decrease in value. For example, if the local government plans to build a highway interchange at the site, the highest and best use of the land and its value will change accordingly. Conditions of future scarcity of buildable sites with similar location qualities might also be viewed as upward value indications. On the other hand, if future land uses are adverse, the land value may decline.

Depreciation of the improvements In real economic terms, that is, after correcting for price level inflation, the value of improvements is expected to decline over time. The rate of this depreciation can be estimated by the experience of similar properties.

Income taxes Because income tax laws are subject to the political process, over the long run there is no certainty as to how much tax must be paid at the time of disposition. Over the short run, income taxes can be determined with reasonable accuracy.

Inflation Consideration must be given to expected inflationary pressures on real estate values. In times of high inflation, measurements are more difficult especially as investor expectations drive up prices.

Leverage

Leverage is the use of "other peoples' money" in an effort to enhance the equity investor's rate of return. In real estate, leverage can be extensive: while most properties are acquired with some equity, it is possible to borrow the entire property cost in many situations. Leverage is positive when the property provides income at a rate greater than the interest rate; the rate of return to equity is then enhanced.

However, if the property fails to provide income or appreciate faster than the interest rate, leverage is negative. The owner not only loses money, but loses at a rapid rate because the losses apply to the total cost, both debt and equity. The ability to employ leverage successfully can greatly enhance an owner's wealth, while failure results in huge losses.

Techniques to Measure Rate of Return from Real Estate

There are two major techniques to measure rate of return from a real estate investment: *ratio* and *yield*. Ratio involves a simple arithmetic computation that relates some level of periodic income to a corresponding asset value. Yield computation is based on *discounting* future income to account for the *time value of money*. The time (or *present*) value of money is today's value of a future payment, or series of payments, discounted at some appropriate rate. Yield analysis is more

sophisticated than ratio analysis but more difficult to perform. A discussion of both ratio and yield techniques follows for our benchmark example.

Ratio Models

The periodic real estate income can be divided by an asset or investment amount to result in a percentage. Alternatively, the income can be divided into an asset value, which results in a *multiplier*. For example, suppose monthly rent for a house is $800 and its estimated value is $80,000. The ratio, $800/$80,000 tells us that rent is one percent of value. Alternatively, $80,000/$800 provides a rent multiplier of 100, which tells us that value is 100 times monthly rent. The result, whether a percentage or multiplier, provides a unit of comparison to judge proposed investments.

Ratio techniques are numerous and include the *gross rent multiplier, overall rate of return, equity dividend*, and *net spendable income*. Whichever method is used, one must take care to assure that the proper amount of income is compared to the corresponding asset or capital amount. For example, cash flow to equity should be compared to the amount of equity, and not to the total cost of mortgaged property. When preparing computations, avoid a mismatch of cash returns to one investor with money invested by two investors.

Gross rent multiplier The gross rent multiplier (GRM) is the relationship of the purchase price to the gross rental income. As it is defined, either potential gross income (before vacancies and collection allowances have been subtracted) or effective gross income (net of a vacancy and collection allowance) may be used. In the benchmark example, the GRM is 6.061 as shown in column 29, computed as follows:

$$\frac{\text{Purchase Price}}{\text{Annual Rental Income}} \quad \frac{\$2,000,000}{\$330,000} = 6.061$$

This method is one of the most widely used techniques because it is easy to compute and involves readily available figures. However, its widespread use stems from the ease of computation and comparison to other projects—not from its reliability as a measuring device.

The GRM fails to account for operating expense variations among projects, financing, resale prices, and income taxes. It disregards the amounts and timing of after-tax cash flows to the equity investor.

Overall rate of return (OAR) The overall rate of return is computed by dividing the net operating income (NOI) by the purchase price. The result is the rate of return on the entire purchase capital, without regard to the contributor (i.e., equity investor or mortgage lender).

Applied to the benchmark example, the OAR fluctuates as shown in column 25:

$$\frac{\$202,000}{\$2,000,000} = \frac{\text{NOI}}{\text{Price}} = 10.1\%$$

The OAR improves on the GRM in that operating expenses are taken into account. The OAR is a good ranking device for comparable, unmortgaged properties since it evaluates properties free and clear of any financing. However, when property is subject to an existing mortgage, a market-derived OAR fails to acknowledge the particulars of existing debt.

An OAR also fails to reflect an individual's income tax situation. With modifications it can include provisions for specific before-tax equity rates, mortgage loans, loan-to-value ratios, and forecast property appreciation. The OAR is frequently used by appraisers to estimate the market value of property, but it does not necessarily indicate the value to a specific investor.

Equity dividend rate The equity dividend rate is also called the *cash-on-cash return* method, the *cash return on cash invested* method, and the *percentage cash flow technique*. Computation involves dividing the before-tax cash flow (column 8) by the initial equity investment and converting the decimal result to a percentage. Results for each year are shown in column 27.

The equity dividend rate fails to acknowledge income tax implications, resale implications including property value changes, and reductions of mortgage principal. It also fails to describe a yield rate to maturity. Therefore it does not consider the investment life cycle. This technique, however, is commonly used by real estate investors.

As it applies to the benchmark property, the rate is as follows:

Year	Fraction		Equity Dividend Rate
1	$\dfrac{\$13,818}{\$400,000}$	$=$	3.455%
2	$\dfrac{\$17,878}{\$400,000}$	$=$	4.470%
3	$\dfrac{\$21,960}{\$400,000}$	$=$	5.490%

Net spendable income technique. When this technique is used, the rate is computed by dividing the sum of before-tax cash flow and the tax savings or payment (after-tax cash flow) by the initial equity investment. The resulting after-tax cash flow is compared to initial equity, as shown in column 28. The method is deficient for the same reasons as those advanced for the equity dividend rate; further, the rate fails to reflect taxes upon a sale.

As applied to the benchmark property, the net spendable income rate is the same as the equity dividend rate for the first 13 years. Although the equity dividend rate and net spendable income techniques do not account for all income sources from a property, they may be appropriate for certain types of investors. Tax-exempt or low tax bracket investors and those who do not anticipate selling the property (elderly or retired

individuals) might consider these indicators adequate for decision purposes. Also, these techniques may be used to compare a group of properties with similar tax implications and appreciation potential.

Other Ratios

Other ratios are useful in describing characteristics of the property although they are not valuation techniques. These may come from the balance sheet or cash flow statement. Balance sheet ratios include the *improvement*, *loan-to-value*, and *equity* ratios. Cash flow ratios include *vacancy*, *break-even*, *operating expense*, *debt service coverage*, and *operating expense* ratios.

Improvement ratio The ratio of buildings and site improvements to the total price of the property is the improvement ratio. It is 90% for our benchmark example. The improvement ratio generally indicates the fraction of total cost that can be depreciated for income tax purposes. The higher the fraction, the greater the noncash tax deductions.

A low improvement ratio generally indicates that land is a large component of value. While such property offers less to depreciate for tax purposes, it is likely to retain high values as land is not subject to genuine economic depreciation in value.

The improvement ratio generally ranges from 60 to 95 percent. Shopping centers need expensive land for access and driving convenience, as well as lots of land for parking and because buildings are only one or two stories. Consequently, shopping centers tend to have a relatively low improvement ratio. High-rise buildings will have a higher ratio because of the ability to spread the land cost over more improvements.

Loan-to-value ratio The loan-to-value ratio is the ratio of the mortgage debt to the property value — 80 percent in the benchmark example. The ratio indicates the degree of leverage. Higher ratios mean more leverage; lower ratios mean more equity.

From a lender's standpoint, higher ratios imply a greater risk of default and foreclosure. Institutional lenders have certain limits for loan-to-value ratios. (Life insurance companies in many states cannot lend more than 75 percent of the value of property that they finance.)

Equity ratio. This is the reciprocal of the loan-to-value ratio, indicating the percentage of equity included. When additional value is created in real estate it is possible to refinance and extract all of the equity that was paid in. A question then arises as to how much equity is in the project, that is whether equity is based on actual contributions or on current values. For decision-making purposes, use of current market values, although sometimes difficult to obtain, is more useful than historic accounting information.

Vacancy ratio. Collection allowances are usually lumped together with vacancies. Maintaining a low vacancy ratio for real estate is important because most cash outflows are fixed. Real estate taxes, insurance, and debt service show little variation for most properties regardless of occupancy. The variable cost of renting to a tenant is small, so nearly all of

the space should be rented to maximize income. Generally, it is preferable to have a 90 to 100 percent occupied building at slightly below market rates than an 80 percent or lower occupancy rate at above market rental rates.

Vacancy rates range widely with the type of property. Hotels and resorts expect a lower occupancy rate than do stores or apartment buildings. For resorts, this is due to the seasonal nature of their business. Hotel occupancy may vary for this reason or because of weekend traffic and conventions. Managers of apartments and office buildings generally try to maintain 93 to 97 percent occupancy. When leased property is fully occupied, there is an obvious opportunity for a rental rate increase. This may increase total rental income despite an accompanying occupancy rate decline. Conversely, management may offer rental concessions to gain more tenants when occupancy is less than 80 percent.

Break-even ratio Also called *default point*, this is the occupancy ratio needed to cover cash expenses. Shown in column 30, it is the sum of operating expenses and debt service, divided by the potential gross income. For the benchmark, the break-even ratio for the first year is about 87 percent, computed as follows:

$$\frac{\$100,000 \text{ operating expense} + \$188,182 \text{ debt service}}{\$330,000 \text{ potential gross income}} = 87.328\%$$

The break-even ratio allows investors to determine the minimum occupancy rate at which there will be some cash throw-off. The term *default point* implies that the owner will default on the mortgage payment when the occupancy rate falls below that point. That suggestion is misleading. Nearly all investors will remain even when the ratio drops below the default point in the hope of income increases and/or capital gain upon resale.

Debt service coverage ratio This is found by dividing the annual debt service into the net operating income. In column 26 of the sample, the debt service coverage ratio is only 1.073 for the first year. Like the break-even ratio, it offers information comparing the net operating income to debt service.

The debt service coverage ratio offers important information that is of concern to both lenders and investors. Many lenders impose minimum coverage ratios which vary according to each property, economic conditions, and the geographic area. For example, a 1.05 ratio may be an acceptable ratio for a free-standing store that is net-leased over a long term (as long as the mortgage term) to an AAA credit-rated tenant. For a shopping center with 50 percent "credit" tenants, a 1.2 — 1.25 ratio would be appropriate. Apartments and some office buildings, will require a 1.25 — 1.50 ratio. The variability of hotel and resort income creates the need for a higher ratio.

Operating expense ratio This is the ratio of operating expenses to potential gross income — 100,000/330,000 = 30% in the benchmark

example. Operating expenses are those necessary to maintain and run the property. Operating expenses include utilities, repairs, replacement reserves, real estate taxes, management, insurance, payroll, payroll taxes, advertising, postage, and other items. Debt service, depreciation, and income taxes are excluded. When property is subject to a net lease, the tenant pays all operating expenses, and the real estate owner incurs none. The ratio then is zero. The ratio may be below 15 percent on semi-net leased property where the owner is responsible for items such as insurance or real estate taxes. For most apartments, the typical ratio is 33 to 45 percent, unless the rental rate includes all utilities; then it may go above 50 percent. Office buildings that include cleaning services and elevators, lobbies, and restrooms, will have a high (45 to 60 percent) operating expense ratio.

Yield Models

Yield models consider an annual compound interest factor that reflect the time value of money. Most models derive the value of equity in this manner, and add that to the mortgage balance. All of the income the equity investor expects to receive during the holding period should be included—specifically, annual after-tax cash flow and the after-tax proceeds from resale.

Small-to-medium sized investors or those who invest in real estate as a part-time activity typically do not use a yield model. More time and effort might be required for appropriate use than benefit received from an occasional application.

There are two major varieties of yield models: those that solve for project value (*net present value*), and those that solve for rate (*internal rate of return*). Both types have strengths and weaknesses. The choice often depends on the income configuration and analyst's approach.

Net present value The net present value (NPV) technique involves discounting and summing investment inflows to a present value at a specified discount rate. The resulting present value is then compared to the investment outflow(s); if the present value of outflow(s) exceeds the present value of inflow(s), the proposed investment is rejected because the investment fails to return the minimum acceptable rate of return. Otherwise, the proposed investment is considered.

In theory, the specified discount rate used for net present value computations is the entity's cost of capital. In practice, however, measurement of the cost of capital is subjective which adds to the difficulty of implementation.

As the NPV relates to the sample property, if a 15 percent or greater rate were used as the minimum acceptable (so called *hurdle*) rate, the subject property would not be acquired because the net present values are negative at 15 percent. Acceptance would be allowed if 10 percent or less were the cutoff point and a projection period in excess of one year was considered.

Internal rate of return The internal rate of return (IRR) is usually defined as the rate at which the present value of investment outflows and investment inflows are equal. The formula, shown below, requires a trial-and-error method for solution.

$$\sum_{t=1}^{n} \frac{\text{periodic } cash\ flow}{(1\ +\ i)^t} = \text{investment amount}$$

where i = internal rate of return
 t = each time interval
 n = total time intervals
 \sum = summation

As it relates to the subject property, the periodic cash flow is the annual after-tax cash flow and any after-tax proceeds from resale, while the investment amount is the cash down payment plus subsequent cash payments.

The IRR, in column 24, shows the annual rate of return on capital generated by an investment. It is a compounded rate of earnings per investment dollar per time period and often is a useful device for ranking alternative investments. One drawback lies in its *reinvestment assumption* — after-tax cash flows from the investment must be reinvested at the internal rate of return for the rate to be a valid indicator of investment profitability.

Conclusion

When an individual considers acquiring real estate, he or she should analyze the potential costs and benefits of that property. Real estate investments can be lucrative by providing cash flow, appreciation, and a hedge against inflation. However, drawbacks include complex transactions, a need for business and management skills, and a potentially high risk of loss especially with financial leverage, and illiquidity. Careful analysis can increase the likelihood of a successful investment.

REAL ESTATE REGULATIONS*

The following offers a brief description of some of the prominent federal regulations that affect real estate. At the end of each entry appears the agency (or agencies) assigned to enforce the described regulation. State and local regulations should also be checked by homebuyers, investors, developers, and mortgage lenders.

Agricultural Foreign Investment Disclosure Act (1978)

Requires foreign persons who acquire, transfer, or hold interests in agricultural land to report transactions and holdings to the Secretary of Agriculture (U.S. Department of Agriculture, ERS, 500 12th St. S.W., Rm. 240, Washington, D.C. 20250) and directs the Secretary to analyze reports for effects these transactions and holdings may have on family farms and rural communities. Department of Agriculture.

Black Lung Revenues Act (1981)

Contains language that pertains to rentals to family members and shared-equity mortgages; provides two tax advantages to lessors who rent to family members: (1) larger depreciation deductions because of accelerated cost recovery and (2) more allowable tax losses; provides for participation of parents and other relatives in a shared-equity mortgage with the same tax deductions as an unrelated party. (Circumstances greatly affect the applicability of this tax law; seek tax counseling or legal advice prior to making decisions on provisions.) Internal Revenue Service.

Clean Air Amendments Act (1970) [Amendments (1977)]

Gives the Environmental Protection Agency (EPA) the power to establish standards and gives citizens and public interest groups the right to bring suit against alleged polluters, federal agencies, and the EPA administrator. Amendments establish new standards to protect areas with clean air from deterioration of air quality and extend some deadlines for city and industry compliance with air-quality standards. Federal Energy Regulatory Commission, Environmental Protection Agency.

*Much of this material is also described in the *Sourcebook*, Real Estate Center, Texas A&M University, compiled by Harold Jambers.

Clean Water Act (1972 and 1977)

Provides primary authority for water-pollution control, including effluent limitations, wastewater discharge permits, water-quality standards, municipal pollution control, and waste treatment. Environmental Protection Agency.

Coastal Zone Management Act (1972) [Amendment (1976)]

Declares a national policy to preserve, protect, develop, and, where possible, to restore or enhance coastal resources for all generations. Encourages and assists states in effectively exercising coastal zone responsibilities through development and implementation of management programs to achieve wise use of coastal land and water resources, giving full consideration to ecological, cultural, historic, and esthetic values, as well as to the need for economic development. Amendment of 1976 creates an energy-impact fund to assist states in providing public facilities and managing growth in coastal areas. Department of Commerce.

Community Reinvestment Act (1977)

Requires financial institution regulators to (1) encourage banks under their supervision to meet credit needs of their communities, including low- and middle-income neighborhoods and (2) scrutinize a lender's inner-city credit activities when the lenders seek to undertake certain prescribed activities. Federal Reserve System, Federal Deposit Insurance Corporation, Comptroller of Currency, Federal Home Loan Bank Board, Department of Housing and Urban Development.

Condominium and Cooperative Abuse Relief Act (1980)

Seeks to (1) minimize adverse impacts of condominium and cooperative conversions on the housing opportunities of low-income, moderate-income, elderly, and handicapped persons, (2) ensure that fair and equitable principles are followed in the establishment of condominiums and cooperatives, and (3) provide appropriate relief where long-term leases of recreation and other cooperative- and condominium-related facilities are determined to be unconscionable. Department of Housing and Urban Development.

Consumer Credit Protection Act (1960)

Requires accurate credit reports; allows consumers to correct inaccurate information in their reports; requires that credit reports be kept confidential, allowing access by properly authorized parties only; assures a meaningful disclosure of credit terms, allowing the consumer to compare other available credit terms to avoid uninformed use of credit; and to protect against inaccurate and unfair credit billing and credit card practices. Titles of this act that affect mortgage lending are

found in the Truth in Lending Act (I) and the Fair Credit Reporting Act (VI). Federal Deposit Insurance Corporation.

Consumer Home Mortgage Assistance Act (1974)

Authorizes federal savings-and-loan associations to invest an amount not greater than (1) the sum of its surplus and undivided profits and reserves or (2) five percent of its residential real estate loans within 100 miles of its home office or within the state in which such office is located. Federal Home Loan Bank Board.

Depository Institutions Deregulation and Monetary Control Act (1980)

Extends reserve requirements to all financial institutions; provides for orderly phaseout of limitations on the maximum rates of interest and dividends paid on deposits and accounts; allows thrift institutions to offer an expanded range of financial services and increases federal deposit insurance to $100,000 per depositor; preempts state usury ceilings for federally related, conventional, residential first mortgage loans unless a state enacts overriding legislation by April 1, 1983; requires depository institutions to report their liabilities and assets to the Federal Reserve Board at intervals the board determines so that the board can monitor and control finances and credit. Federal Deposit Insurance Corporation, Federal Home Loan Bank Board, Comptroller of Currency.

Economic Recovery Tax Act (1981)

Makes numerous adjustments in the Internal Revenue Code affecting real estate; affects replacement periods on sales of personal residences; contains income-producing property provisions that deal with cost recovery (depreciation) methods, depreciation recapture, rehabilitation expenditures, construction period interest and taxes for low-income housing, investment credit for certain building rehabilitation, investment tax credit for Section 38 property, additional first-year depreciation and imputed interest; addresses tax rate changes regarding individual income tax rates, corporate taxes, maximum tax, and alternative minimum tax. Internal Revenue Service.

Emergency Home Finance Act (1970) (Title III)

Creates the Federal Home Loan Mortgage Corporation (Freddie Mac) to operate a secondary market in conventional home mortgages. Federal Home Loan Bank Board.

Energy Conservation Standards for New Buildings Act (1976)

Requires Department of Housing and Urban Development to implement building energy standards for new residential and commercial

construction. Department of Housing and Urban Development.

Equal Credit Opportunity Act (1974) [Amendment (1976)]

Requires financial institutions and other firms engaged in the extension of credit to make all credit equally available to all credit-worthy customers without regard to sex or marital status. Compliance standards to prohibit discrimination are regulated by credit standards and loan application procedures prescribed by the board of governors of the Federal Reserve System.

The amendment of 1976 prohibits discrimination in lending on the basis of age, color, race, religion, national origin, or receipt by applicant of public assistance. A lender must notify the prospective buyer of action taken on the loan within 30 days of application, and if requested by applicant, a reason for denial of loan must be given. Steady part-time earning must be considered by the lender in evaluating a loan application. Federal Home Loan Bank Board, Comptroller of Currency, Federal Deposit Insurance Corporation, Federal Reserve System.

Fair Housing Laws

Prohibits discrimination on the basis of minority status in the sale or rental of any house, apartment (or other residential structure), and vacant land; requires that each client be treated as an individual and be served according to individual needs and desires.

The major laws that comprise the regulations prohibiting discrimination are:

Civil Rights Act of 1866
Civil Rights Act of 1964 (Title VI, Nondiscrimination in Federally Assisted Programs)
Civil Rights Act of 1968 (Title VIII—Fair Housing)
Department of Housing and Urban Development.

Farm Credit Act (1971)

Provides for the farmer-owned cooperatives system of credit for farmers and ranchers and their cooperatives, rural residences, associations, and other entities on which farming depends, to provide an adequate and flexible flow of money into rural areas and to modernize and consolidate existing farm credit laws to meet current and future rural credit needs. Farm Credit Administration.

Farmers Home Administration (FmHA) Act (1946)

Replaces the Farm Security Administration; continues government loan programs established under the Resettlement Administration; gives FmHA authority to insure loans made by banks, other agencies, and individuals. Farmers Home Administration.

Federal Flood Insurance Program (1968) and National Flood Insurance Act (1968)

Makes flood insurance available at reasonable rates to property owners in flood-prone areas; protects property owners against loss from flood damage not generally covered by commercial insurers at feasible rates. (Bank regulators require flood insurance when a mortgage is made in a flood-hazard area of a community participating in the national flood insurance program.) Department of Housing and Urban Development.

Federal Trade Commission Improvement Act

See Magnuson-Moss Warranty (1975).

Federal Home Loan Bank Act (1932)

Creates the Federal Home Loan Bank Board and the Federal Home Loan Bank System; establishes a reserve system for home financing to provide a permanent credit source for home mortgage lending institutions. Federal Home Loan Bank Board.

Federal Water Pollution Control Act and Amendments (1972)

Establishes regulatory and grant programs to "reach and maintain the chemical, physical, and biological integrity of the nation's waters;" sets up a program of state grants for construction of sewage treatment plants; establishes stiff industrial and municipal pollutant discharge permit programs. Federal Energy Regulatory Commission, Environmental Protection Agency.

Flood Disaster Protection Act (1973) [Amendments (1975 and 1976)]

Expands the national flood insurance program by substantially increasing limits of coverage and total amount of insurance authorized to be outstanding and by requiring known flood-prone communities to participate in the program; provides for the expeditious identification and dissemination of information concerning flood-prone areas; requires states or local communities — as a condition of future federal financial assistance — to participate in the flood insurance program and to adopt adequate flood plain ordinances and effective enforcement provisions; requires the purchase of flood insurance by property owners acquiring or improving property in flood-hazard areas and assisted by federal programs or institutions. Amendment of 1975 prohibits federally regulated lending institutions from making loans for mobile home purchases or for commercial or personal construction occurring in flood-hazard areas unless flood insurance is available for loan protection. Amendment of 1976 allows certain property exemptions from

sanctions in communities not participating in the flood insurance program. Department of Housing and Urban Development.

Foreign Investment in Real Property Tax Act (1980) [Amendment (1984)]

Eliminates techniques by which a nonresident alien (a foreign national temporarily present in the United States) or a foreign corporation could sell U.S. real estate without being subject to U.S. tax laws. Internal Revenue Service.

Garn-St. Germain Depository Institutions Act (1982)

Liberalizes procedures for rescuing insured saving and loan associations in distress, gives associations greater freedom to convert to stock form of ownership, expands the type of assets an association may hold, and reduces the differentiation between thrift institutions and banks. Federal Deposit Insurance Corporation, Federal Savings and Loan Insurance Corporation, Federal Home Loan Bank Board.

Home Mortgage Disclosure Act (1975)

Provides information to assist in determining whether depository institutions are serving the housing needs of their communities and neighborhoods; helps public officials determine the distribution of public sector investments in a manner designed to improve the private investment environment, contains a detailed reporting system. Federal Home Loan Bank Board, Comptroller of Currency, Federal Deposit Insurance Corporation, Federal Reserve System.

Interstate Land Sales Full Disclosure Act (1968) [Amendments (1979)]

Requires developers of subdivisions with 25 lots or more to file a property report and a statement of record with the Office of Interstate Land Sales and with the secretary of the Department of Housing and Urban Development prior to promoting or offering subdivision land for sale or lease; applies to land sold or leased in interstate commerce; recent revisions involve property reports and regulations for filing financial reports and advertising. Department of Housing and Urban Development.

Land and Water Conservation Act

Establishes financial assistance and grants to states and their political subdivisions for comprehensive planning, land acquisition, and facility development. Bureau of Resources.

Magnuson-Moss Warranty (Federal Trade Commission Improvement Act) (1975)

Establishes mandatory standards for warranties on consumer products to improve consumer information, prevent deception, and improve competition in the marketing of consumer products; requires written warranty, as required by the rules of the Federal Trade Commission, to fully and conspicuously disclose in simple language the terms and conditions of the warranty; includes new home appliances and other equipment that are an integral part of plumbing, electrical, and heating systems. (Wiring, piping, and other similar items are not covered; however, home builders are responsible for satisfying warranty claims with respect to any warranties they provide on these items.) Federal Trade Commission.

National Historic Preservation Act (1966)

Authorizes the Secretary of the Interior to (1) expand and maintain a national register of districts, sites, buildings, structures, and objects significant in American history, architecture, archaeology, and culture to be referred to as the National Register and to grant funds to states for preparing comprehensive statewide historic surveys and plans, in accordance with criteria established by the Secretary, for the preservation, acquisition, and development of such properties; (2) establish a program of matching grants-in-aid to states for public benefit, designed to preserve properties that are significant in American history, architecture, archaeology, and culture; (3) establish a program of matching grants-in-aid to the National Trust for Historic Preservation in the United States. Department of the Interior.

National Mobile Home and Construction Safety Standards Act (1974)

Establishes federal standards for the construction, design, performance, and safety of mobile homes. Department of Housing and Urban Development.

Neighborhood Self-Help Development Act (1978)

Authorizes the Secretary of the Department of Housing and Urban Development to make grants and provide other forms of assistance to neighborhood organizations to prepare and implement specific housing, economic and community development projects, other appropriate neighborhood conservation and revitalization projects, and to assist these organizations in implementing such projects in partnership with local government and other public and private entities; designed to involve low- and moderate-income neighborhood residents through their contribution of time and resources. Department of Housing and Urban Development.

Occupational Safety and Health Act (OSHA) (1970)

Establishes OSHA and sets up the Occupational Safety and Health Review Commission and the National Institute for Occupational Safety and Health; gives OSHA the power to promulgate and enforce worker safety and health standards, conduct inspections and investigations, and require employers to keep detailed records on worker injuries and illnesses; gives OSHA power to conduct research. Occupational Safety and Health Administration, Department of Labor.

Real Estate Settlement Procedures Act (RESPA) (1974) [Amendment (1975)]

Encourages homeownership by regulating certain lending practices, and closing and settlement procedures in federally related mortgage transactions to minimize unnecessary costs and difficulties of home purchase; provides the prospective borrower an information booklet on the nature and costs of real estate settlement services when application for a mortgage loan is made. (Booklets may be printed and distributed by lenders if form and content are approved by the HUD Secretary.) A 1975 amendment permits the HUD secretary to exempt certain localities, where settlement statements are not customarily provided, from the required uniform settlement statement and permits the statement to be modified for different parts of the United States. Federal Home Loan Bank Board, Department of Housing and Urban Development, Federal Deposit Insurance Corporation, Comptroller of Currency.

Regulation B (Title VII, Consumer Credit Protection Act) (Amendments)

Requires lenders to notify potential borrowers of action taken on their loan applications and to provide a written report on adverse action or a written statement of the prospective borrower's right to receive this information; addresses the terms under which a creditor can and cannot deny credit. Federal Reserve System.

Regulation BB

Implements the Community Reinvestment Act (CRA) requiring financial institution regulators to encourage state-chartered banks and savings-and-loan associations under their supervision to meet the credit needs of their community; requires financial institution regulators or supervisory agencies to scrutinize lenders' credit activities and compliance with these regulations when considering any application requiring federal approval. (A notice describing the act and written comments on the lender's performance must be posted in the bank or savings-and-loan association and made available to the public.) Federal Reserve System.

Regulation D

Governs certain offers and sales of securities that do not require registration under the Securities Act of 1933; revokes three exemptions under Rules 146, 240, and 242 including the related filing forms; simplifies and clarifies existing exemptions, to expand their availability and achieve uniformity between federal and state exemptions to facilitate capital formation consistent with the protection of investors; allows increased use of private offering investment vehicles to raise equity for real estate investment. (Regulation D is part of the Securities Act. See Securities Act.) Securities and Exchange Commission.

Regulation Z

Includes regulations pertaining to consumer-credit disclosure issued by the board of governors of the federal reserve system pursuant to Title I (Truth in Lending Act) and Title V (General Provisions) of the Consumer Credit Protection Act. (See Truth-in-Lending.) Federal Trade Commission.

Resource Conservation and Recovery Act (1976)

Sets safety standards for handling and storage of hazardous wastes; requires permits for the operation of hazardous waste treatment, storage, and disposal operations; gives the Environmental Protection Agency authority to make state grants for hazardous waste-treatment programs. Environmental Protection Agency.

Section 8 Program

Assists low- and moderate-income families in obtaining decent, newly constructed, and substantially rehabilitated housing, in accordance with provisions; promotes economically mixed housing; includes a federal rent-subsidy program for low- and moderate-income tenants and permits developers of new or substantially rehabilitated multifamily housing to contract for housing assistance payments on any or all units and be eligible for financing with mortgages insured under the National Housing Act; was created by the Housing and Community Development Act of 1974. Department of Housing and Urban Development.

Securities Act 1933

Requires any firm or individual issuing securities for sale in interstate commerce or through the mail to file financial and other data about the issuer and its securities with the Securities Exchanges Commission before the securities can be placed on the market.

Detailed information on this act, its amendments, and specific sections can be obtained from the Office of Chief Counsel, Securities and

Exchange Commission, 500 N. Capitol Street, N.W., Washington, D.C. 20549. A brief description of selected sections follows:

SEC Regulation A Offering Set forth Rules 252 – 263 and affects the registration exemption of qualified small offerings.

SEC Rule 144 Permits holders of restricted securities, and affiliates of an issuer of the securities, to sell their securities publicly without registration.

SEC Rule 147 Removes some of the uncertainties arising under the intrastate offering exemption.

Senior Citizens Housing Act (1962)

Establishes loan programs for low-rent apartments for individuals age 62 and over and authorizes loans to establish recreational facilities. Farmers Home Administration.

Sherman Antitrust Act (1890)

Protects trade and commerce against unlawful restraints and monopolies and establishes a policy in favor of competition; a recent supreme court ruling includes real estate agents under the purview of this pioneer antitrust statute; this ruling establishes that real estate agents who charge identical commissions in the same area may be sued for price fixing. Federal Trade Commission.

Tax Equity and Fiscal Responsibility Act (1982)

Affects real estate investment and development through modification of rules concerning accelerated cost recovery, investment tax credits, corporate construction-period interest and taxes, industrial development bonds, and the completed-contract method of accounting. Internal Revenue Service.

Tax Reform Act (1984)

Increases real estate asset recovery periods under the Accelerated Capital Recovery System to 18 years, places time limits on delayed 1031 exchanges, and establishes Original Issue Discount rules for seller-financed real estate transactions. Internal Revenue Service.

Tax Reform Act (1986)

Greatly reduces the ability to derive tax shelters from real estate investments, lengthens depreciable lives of assets, eliminates favorable treatment of capital gains, restricts use of installment sales, creates Real Estate Mortgage Investment Conduits (REMICs) to assist in issuing of mortgage-backed securities, substantially reduces the number of tax brackets for individual taxpayers, and eliminates or phases out certain itemized deductions. Internal Revenue Service.

Truth-in-Lending Act (1968)

Assures a meaningful disclosure of credit terms so consumers know of the cost of credit and can more readily compare terms and avoid uninformed use of credit; promotes economic stabilization and strengthens competition among financial institutions and other firms that extend consumer credit. Federal Trade Commission, Federal Home Loan Bank Board, Comptroller of Currency, Federal Deposit Insurance Corporation, Federal Reserve System.

Truth-in-Lending Simplification and Reform Act (1980)

Amends the Truth-in-Lending Act of 1968, making significant changes in credit disclosures that creditors must make to borrowers. (Information required by this act must be disclosed conspicuously, and the terms "annual percentage rate" and "finance charge" must be disclosed more conspicuously than any other terms, data, or information provided in connection with a transaction, except information relating to the identity of the creditor.) Federal Trade Commission, Federal Home Loan Bank Board, Comptroller of Currency, Federal Deposit Insurance Corporation, Federal Reserve System.

Uniform Relocation Assistance and Real Property Acquisition Policies Act (1970)

Establishes a uniform policy for the fair and equitable treatment of persons displaced by federal and federally assisted programs so such people will not suffer disproportionate injuries as a result of programs designed for the benefit of the public as a whole. Department of Housing and Urban Development.

Veterans' Housing Benefits Act (1978)

Amends title 38 of the United States Code to improve the housing benefits programs of the Veterans' Administration: provided for increased loan-guarantee and direct-loan amounts, authorized the Veteran's Administration to approve loans for home improvements involving installation of energy-conserving devices such as solar heating and cooling systems, reduced the amount of time of service required for Vietnam veterans to be eligible for loans. Veterans' Administration.

CAREERS IN REAL ESTATE

Opportunities in the real estate business are as varied and versatile as the properties themselves. Whether a person is entrepreneurial and wishes to start a business, or prefers to earn a fixed salary or an income based on productivity, opportunities abound. One of the drawbacks is the cyclical nature of the real estate business, which generally has higher peaks and lower troughs than the economy as a whole.

Real estate businesses and developments are among the few enterprises that one can still enter with little capital. A real estate broker, appraiser, or developer can start "on a shoestring"; a desk and telephone are the essential tools. Overhead can be kept low until enough income and work are generated to justify office space, advertising, and clerical help. Some of the largest real estate businesses in America were started only a few years ago by a single enterprising individual with little or no capital! Energy, a basic knowledge of real estate, and the ability to work with people is all that is needed.

Most jobs in real estate are compensated by commissions. Payment is made according to financial performance, whether it be sales, leasing, or mortgage arrangement. Some property managers are given incentive pay and the same holds for employees of some developers. Working on straight commissions can be extremely lucrative during good times, especially for experienced commercial real estate salesmen. However, those who start in the business must be prepared in every way — emotionally and financially — for the inevitable frustrations and setbacks that will occur during the early years.

Salaried jobs do exist in real estate, but they generally pay less than commissioned jobs. Clerical personnel are needed in every office, and there are some highly compensated opportunities in the production function for those with special skills. These jobs will be competitive in salary with comparable positions in other businesses and may offer more opportunities. Still, salaried workers tend to make less in real estate than those on commission.

As has been stated, the real estate business is rather cyclical. When interest rates are low and local business conditions good, real estate activity booms. However, high interest rates, tight money, or poor business conditions can play havoc with incomes generated from real estate, even for salaried employees. Since these economic factors are beyond the individual's control, people who earn their living from real estate must prepare for slow periods, if they are to remain in the business.

This section offers introductory career information concerning some of the better-defined occupations in real estate. These include appraisers, brokers, salespersons, counselors, developers, subdividers, educa-

71

tors, mortgage lenders, planners, and property managers. For each occupation, an overview is provided of the nature of the work, responsibilities, opportunities, hours, travel, educational requirements, and professional associations. The list of occupations covered is not intended to be exhaustive. Millions of others are engaged full time in real estate activities. These include lawyers, architects, engineers, accountants, surveyors, building inspectors, and construction workers. Most of these occupations have educational and career paths that are separate from the traditional real estate program.

Real Estate Appraiser

Nature of Work

The *real estate appraiser* answers questions about the value, quality, and use of real property. The appraiser is a problem solver who collects, studies, and interprets relevant facts and information.

A real estate appraiser is likely to evaluate these types of property:

- Single-family dwellings, including condominiums, cooperatives, and townhomes
- Apartment buildings
- Office buildings and complexes
- Shopping centers
- Industrial properties
- Hotels and motels
- Farms and ranches
- Undeveloped land

Appraisers are also sought to comment on the value and use of partial interests in real estate, such as:

- Air rights
- Easements
- Leaseholds
- Life estates
- Mortgage participation
- Partnership shares
- Syndication units

They may be called to testify in zoning hearings or in litigation of various property matters or to give advice on the viability of proposed developments, including subdivisions and income-producing properties. They may also testify in condemnation hearings, which occur frequently and can be quite lucrative.

Responsibilities

Appraisers are responsible for estimating the value of real estate. They are relied upon by individuals, businesses, and financial institutions for various purposes. For example, appraisals are desired by:

- Buyers and sellers, to establish a purchase (or sales) price
- Mortgage lenders who are lending a percentage of appraised value
- Insurance underwriters who want a value estimate of property they will insure
- Governments and public utilities, when condemning land for a public use
- Businesses planning mergers or dissolutions
- Individuals, for such personal reasons as estate planning and divorce settlements
- Publicly held entities including limited partnerships and real estate investment trusts.

The soundness of our nation's financial institutions depends, in part, upon the validity of appraisal reports. Thus, appraisers are responsible for providing decision-making information to individuals, corporations, and governments, and they contribute to the nation's financial soundness.

Advancement Opportunities

Many appraisers aspire to be self-employed independent fee appraisers (those who are paid fees by customers for appraisals) while others strive to be officers and directors of banks, savings and loan associations, or insurance companies. Still others enter the occupation merely to gain experience leading to positions in development, mortgage banking, asset management, and counseling.

Government agencies that employ appraisers include the Federal Deposit Insurance Corporation, Federal Savings & Loan Insurance Corporation, Department of Housing and Urban Development, General Services Administration, Federal Asset Disposal Agency, Justice Department, Federal Home Loan Bank Board, and Federal Reserve Board.

Entry-level positions are typically available as assistants to experienced appraisers. At first, assignments may be limited to field work such as obtaining measurements of homes and land. Getting sales and telephone verification of sales prices and terms are the next step. Once the apprentice gains sufficient experience to learn the appraisal process and sources of market information, he or she would be in a position to draft form reports for residential appraisals.

Depending upon education and experience, a beginner can expect to acquire more responsibility within one to two years. Tasks include field work and report preparation with moderate supervision and assisting in the appraisal of more complex properties. During this time, the professionally motivated appraiser will begin work leading to a professional designation. Most designations require experience, coursework, and examinations. Within five years from entry, the appraiser will be ready to supervise others and to accept more challenging and rewarding experiences.

A professional designation is conferred by appraisal organizations as a sign of a candidate's attainment of professional status. Eight major appraisal organizations and their designations are shown below.

Hours and Travel

Like other professionals, an appraiser can expect to put in far more than 40 hours per week. Providing prompt service to clients, maintaining professional skills, and contributing to one's community and professional associations requires time and commitment. Although some appraisers may regularly shut their office doors behind them at 5 P.M. (particularly those who work for a government or bank), most are constantly concerned with their clients' problems and find that they must work some evenings and weekends.

Local travel to the real estate being appraised and to comparable property that has recently been sold is essential. As an appraiser grows in reputation and status, or develops a unique specialty, he or she will be in demand for out-of-town assignments. Travel may also be needed to support professional associations and to maintain educational skills. It is difficult for the best appraisers to avoid travel, even when there is ample work available in their home town.

Educational Requirements

Education is required for prestigious professional designations; usually a bachelor's degree from a four-year accredited college or equivalent is necessary for the most coveted designations. In addition, the candidate must take certain courses and pass examinations. Some colleges and universities offer a real estate curriculum within the business college that includes appraisal courses, allowing the student to undertake professional association examinations without taking association-sponsored courses.

Professional and Trade Associations

American Institute of Real Estate Appraisers
430 N. Michigan Ave.
Chicago, IL 60611
312/329-8538
Professional Designations: RM, MAI
Publications: *Appraisal Journal*
The Appraiser

American Society of Appraisers
Dulles International Airport
P.O. Box 17265
Washington, D.C. 20041
703-478-2228
Professional Designation: ASA
Publication: *Newsline*

American Society of Farm Managers and Rural Appraisers
950 S. Cherry St., Suite 106

Denver, Colorado 80222
303-758-3513
Professional Designations: AFM, ARA
Publications: *Property Tax Journal*
 Assessment Digest
International Association of Assessing Officers
1313 East 60th Street
Chicago, IL 60637
312-947-2069
Professional Designations: CAE, CRE
Publications: *Property Tax Journal*
 Assessment Digest

International Right of Way Association
9920 La Cienega
Englewood, CA 90301
213-649-5323
Professional Designations: SR/WA

National Association of Independent Fee Appraisers
7501 Murdoch Ave.
St. Louis, MO
314-781-6688
Professional Designations: IFA, IFAS, IFAC

National Society of Real Estate Appraisers
1265 E. 105th Street
Cleveland, Ohio 44108
216-795-3445
Professional Designations: RA, CRA, MREA
Publications: *National Report*
 Income Property Appraisal and Analysis

Society of Real Estate Appraisers
225 N. Michigan Ave.
Chicago, IL 60601
312/346-7422
Professional Designations: SRA, SRPA, SREA
Publications: *The Real Estate Appraiser and Analyst SREA Briefs*

Real Estate Broker and Salesperson

Nature of Work

The principal function of a *real estate broker* is to bring together buyers and sellers or owners and tenants. Most brokers secure a *listing* which offers property for sale or lease, from a seller. A fee is earned

when the broker finds a ready, willing, and able purchaser at terms the seller will accept. By law, a licensed real estate broker can also perform other activities such as managing property, appraising, and auctioning.

Most real estate brokers specialize, especially those in metropolitan areas. Residential sales is considered a specialty, although some brokers further limit their activity to a certain price range and/or a certain geographical area. Commercial property brokerage is another specialty, with some brokers working only in the office building market, others in shopping centers, warehouses or industrial properties. Some brokers concentrate on farms and ranches or undeveloped land.

Real estate salespersons in all states must be licensed and associated with a licensed broker. All of their activities must be approved by their broker. (Activities that must be approved include acquiring listings, acquiring sales contracts, and performing appraisal work.) Real estate brokers and salespersons must complete an educational program and pass an exam.

Responsibilities

Real estate brokers are governed by the law of agency. They act in a fiduciary capacity and must place the interests of their clients above their own and be fair to all parties. Brokers must exercise integrity in the discharge of their responsibilities and must be prudent and cautious to avoid misrepresentation by omission or commission. They must be knowledgeable in the real estate business, stay informed on state and local issues that affect the real estate industry, and exercise skill and judgment in performing their work.

Advancement Opportunities

Opportunities in real estate brokerage are very broad and exciting. Many people are content to earn a sales or broker license and maintain it with no further work effort. Some wish to build an empire. Real estate brokerage is one of the few businesses where this is possible because capital requirements for entry are minimal.

With a broker's license a person may operate a business independently, and should feel like an independent entrepreneur. A broker can sell or lease the property of his or her choice, manage others' property or personnel, or open an independent brokerage office. Most states require applicants for broker's licenses to have held a salesperson's license for a certain minimum time, and to meet additional educational requirements.

The promotion ladder, for some brokers, means graduating from one type of property (single-family houses) to more complicated types such as office buildings. Others find property development or syndication a more challenging and/or more lucrative occupation.

Hours and Travel

Some licensees are content to stay home and wait for the phone to ring. However, brokerage is a 24-hour job for those who are truly active. They must sow seeds in the market area they define and develop market expertise and a reputation. Brokers and salespersons must be prepared to meet clients, whether residential or commercial, at a moment's notice. Their family activities are often subordinated to the needs of clients whom the broker may have to meet at an airport or subdivision with no advance notice, any time of day, any day of the week. Commercial real estate brokers may find themselves chasing people and deals all over the city, state, and country. Their lives can be hectic. Salespersons or brokers who find themselves or their families unable to cope with an unpredictable schedule often return to jobs with regularly scheduled hours.

Whether commercial or residential, brokers and salespersons are typically responsible for all of their own business expense. They must pay for the automobile that is used in business, air travel, professional association dues, and educational materials. Most brokerage firms provide a desk and telephone to sales personnel, but some firms charge salespersons for that, too. Commission splits between salesperson and broker firm are negotiable.

Educational Requirements

Typically, to be licensed as a salesperson or broker, one must:

- Be a U.S. Citizen or lawful alien
- Be 18 years or older
- Have been a state resident for 60 days
- Be honest and competent (competency is demonstrated by examination)
- If a corporation, be represented by a designated officer who meets broker qualifications
- Meet educational requirements
- Serve a specified time as salesperson before becoming broker

Professional and Trade Associations

National Association of Real Estate Brokers (NAREB)
1104 14th Street, N.W.
Washington, D.C. 20005
202/966-5100

National Association of Realtors (NAR)
430 N. Michigan Ave.
Chicago, IL 60611
312/329-8200
Publications: *Real Estate Today* and others

Society of Industrial Realtors
925 Fifteenth St., N.W.
Washington, D.C. 20005

Real Estate Counselor*

Nature of Work

A *real estate counselor* provides competent, disinterested, and unbiased advice, professional guidance, and sound judgment on diversified problems in the broad field of real estate. Any and all segments of the business, such as merchandising, leasing, management, planning, and financing, may be involved.

A counselor performs a separate and distinct function from that of the real estate broker. The professional service offered is advice born of experience, blended with wisdom, tempered by judgment, and supported by facts. The relationship between counselor and client is similar to the professional bond existing between lawyer and client.

The counselor translates knowledge of the past into projections for the future. Broad experience equips the counselor to comprehend the most sophisticated situations in the real estate field, which may include conservation of property as well as analysis of its diversified uses and potentials. In studies of the many complicated and challenging problems encountered in the broad spectrum of real estate, the counselor's perspective, professional objectivity, and detachment permit recognition and selection of the alternative courses of action most beneficial to the client. Skills in communicating findings and recommendations to clientele render the counselor's services valuable in the most practical way.

Advancement Opportunities

Few real estate counselors began their careers in that capacity. Most started in a related field such as appraising, property management, or brokerage. After demonstrating an exceptional ability to analyze and solve difficult problems associated with real estate, they find themselves being sought after for advice and counsel. Most counselors are independent professionals who perform their work for a fee, often being employed on a retainer. Some counselors are employees of corporations, developers, or consulting firms.

Hours and Travel

Complex real estate problems that require professional counselors arise infrequently in any one location. Further, owners cannot wait long

*Adapted with permission from "Real Estate Counseling" published by the American Society of Real Estate Counselors.

for solutions. Consequently, counselors must travel to out-of-town engagements and expend intensive efforts until appropriate solutions can be presented. Relatively few counselors have every evening and weekend free for personal pleasure; if they did, it would indicate a lack of demand for their skills.

Educational Requirements

Membership in the American Society of Real Estate Counselors requires, among other things, practical experience in the real estate field for at least ten years. This requirement may be modified on the basis of postgraduate academic achievements and/or degree achievements.

While it is possible to become a counselor with a degree in any field, an education in finance and real estate will be helpful. Real estate courses include investment analysis, appraisal, finance, law, and land use. Also helpful would be building construction, urban planning, and zoning. A broad academic base, such as that offered by a degree in business administration (BBA or MBA), would prove helpful. Courses offered by professional associations should be taken; continuing professional education is an essential part of a counselor's career.

Professional and Trade Association

American Society of Real Estate Counselors
430 North Michigan Ave.
Chicago, IL 60611
312/329-8427
Publications: *Real Estate Issues*

Real Estate Developer and Subdivider

Nature of Work

A *real estate subdivider* acquires a piece of land and makes it usable by rezoning, bringing utilities to the site, creating streets or roads, and/or providing other amenities such as parks and school sites. The final product is marketed to builders or other consumers.

A *developer* goes one step further. He or she builds a structure on the land. A successful developer or subdivider is like an artist: land is the canvas and the final product is worth more than the cost of raw materials.

Responsibilities

A developer is an entrepreneur — the focal point of a real estate project. He or she must envision a product that has market feasibility. The developer must be concerned with physical, financial, legal, and social

aspects of the property and its infrastructure (streets, utilities, police, and fire protection).

Development is a high-risk business with potentially high rewards. The developer is responsible for acquiring and financing land, then processing it to a buildable state. There are numerous pitfalls for the unwary: financing requirements, legal considerations, the local political situation, environmental concerns, design, and construction. Of course, the project must be sold or leased to yield a profit.

Advancement Opportunities

Most developers are individual entrepreneurs. They see or create their own opportunities, then acquire land using money they borrow from financial institutions. Progress is often measured by the size of their projects. Large developers create high-rise office buildings and regional malls. Small ones develop mini-warehouses, freestanding buildings, and small subdivisions. Few developers remain in a certain niche for very long.

Some individuals gain their first experience by working for another developer. Most developers begin their careers as appraisers, mortgage lenders, or real estate brokers. They envision development activity as offering more lucrative opportunities.

Hours and Travel

A developer's work load may be erratic. One may work around the clock for several weeks, then do virtually nothing for several months. A crash effort may be needed to solve a crisis — and many legal and financial matters have the potential for causing a crisis. When a project is progressing smoothly, there may be time to search for the next project. However, it is sometimes difficult to locate a feasible endeavor, as the local real estate or mortgage markets are not always ripe for continued development.

A developer must be prepared to build in another city when opportunities are greater there than at home. Developers who have exhibited great skill by regularly completing projects on time and within budget are in demand everywhere.

Educational Requirements

There are no special requirements for developers. Those who seem to be most successful have business, architecture, or law degrees. However, many successful developers have little advanced education.

Professional and Trade Associations

American Land Development Association
1220 L Street, 5th Floor
Washington, D.C.
202/371-6700

International Conference of Building Officials
5360 South Workman Mill Road
Whittier, CA 90601
213/699-0541

National Association of Home Builders
15th & M Streets, N.W.
Washington, D.C. 20005
202/822-0200

Urban Land Institute
1090 Vermont Ave, Suite 300
Washington, D.C. 20005

Real Estate Educator

Nature of Work

Real estate educators teach and provide educational and research materials in real estate matters. Core real estate courses include real estate principles, appraisal, law, finance, marketing, mathematics, brokerage, investments, and property management.

Real estate is taught at different types of educational institutions and instructors at each have different commitments and obligations. The institutions include colleges and universities, junior or community colleges (which provide credit and noncredit courses), and proprietary schools.

Educators at some institutions are only required to appear in class; at others they have a student advisement or counseling role as well. Some educators help students locate jobs and/or work with their local real estate associations to help solve business problems. At colleges and universities, full-time real estate instructors serve on various university committees, perform scholarly research, write books and articles, and are committed to community service (in addition to teaching and counseling requirements).

Responsibilities

Educators are responsible for assuring a minimum level of proficiency for their students. When the primary goal is education for licensing, educators are responsible for efforts that enable their students to pass the sales and broker's exams, as well as for efforts leading to protection of the public (which is the purpose of licensing). Thus, educators impart information and are role models for their students in ethical and legal behavior.

Those teaching real estate courses to the general public are responsible for supplying unbiased information on home buying or selling and

81

investing in real estate. Those teaching at the college or junior college level are responsible for career preparation of real estate majors.

Advancement Opportunities

Real estate teachers in licensed preparation schools and junior colleges, advance with their teaching skills experience, and reputation. Faculty in senior colleges must hold advanced degrees and publish scholarly works.

Hours and Travel

Schedules will vary with the institution that employs the educators. While most proprietary schools offer courses locally, some cross state boundaries and may require an hour or two of highway travel. Beyond that range, it is generally more efficient to find a local instructor. Most college and junior college courses are offered locally, but professors often travel to present research reports to colleagues or attend meetings of professional associations.

Many real estate courses are offered evenings and weekends. Instructors must be prepared to meet these demands.

Educational Requirements

Proprietary school teachers and those at junior colleges are generally required to be licensed as real estate brokers or salespersons and have three years of business experience. A master's degree is helpful but may not be required.

College and university faculty at fully accredited institutions are generally required to have a master's degree plus professional designation (JD or CPA). Many colleges require a PhD of their permanent full-time faculty, but may offer part-time or full-time non-tenure-track faculty appointments to qualified persons without the PhD.

Professional Associations

American Real Estate Society
c/o J.R. Webb
Dept. of Finance
University of Akron
Akron, Ohio 44325
Publications: *Journal of Real Estate Research*

American Real Estate and Urban Economics Association
c/o Jeffrey Fisher
School of Business
Indiana University
Bloomington, Ind. 47405
Publications: *AREUEA Journal*

Real Estate Chairholders and Director's Association
c/o Dr. J. Boykin
Virginia Real Estate Center
Virginia Commonwealth University
Richmond, VA 23284

Real Estate Educators Association
230 N. Michigan Ave., Ste. 1200
Chicago, IL 60601

Mortgage Loan Officer

Nature of Work

Mortgage loan officers typically work for a mortgage banking firm, savings and loan association, commercial bank, or insurance company. There are four separate functions that a loan officer can fulfill: loan origination, underwriting, servicing, and marketing — all of which may be performed for residential housing or for commercial property. Most individuals specialize in either residential or commercial property; few do both.

Loan originators (loan solicitors) seek out property buyers in an attempt to get their business. Before the loan is approved, however, *underwriters* investigate the likelihood of a default by considering the property and borrower. If the loan is extended, *servicers* make sure the monthly payments are received, property taxes are paid, and the property is adequately insured. *Marketing* refers to selling loans. Mortgage bankers sell nearly all the loans they originate, and savings and loan associations are doing the same in increasing numbers.

In sum, mortgage officers lend and collect mortgage money, which is the lifeblood of real estate activity.

Responsibilities

Mortgage officers are responsible for the safety and security of funds for their institutions and investors. They must exercise skill and judgment in lending money, and consider the property, borrower, and terms of the loan. Although individual home loan amounts may be only in the tens of thousands, a few days' work can run well into millions of dollars — as do most loans on commercial real estate. An interest rate error as small as half of one percent can be very costly. A default is also extremely costly.

Advancement Opportunities

Many successful loan officers started as loan originators or processors, or in supporting functions at a branch office. They progressed to branch manager, then to corporate executive.

Hours and Travel

Loan originators generally enjoy flexible hours. However, most will put in more than the minimum required. When business is good, extra effort pays off handsomely; when business is slow, as it often is when interest rates are high, extra effort is needed to maintain adequate income.

Travel is generally local for residential mortgage bankers. Those in the commercial business may travel all over the country to garner business from lenders or investors.

Educational Requirements

While there are no specific degree requirements for being a mortgage officer, the Mortgage Bankers Association of America suggests that education is a prime factor in recruitment for the income property field. A candidate should have a solid background in finance and banking. Moreover, the candidate should possess a basic knowledge of many aspects of real estate, including appraising, underwriting, negotiating, financial statement, lease analysis, and legal matters, in addition to having established contacts throughout the real estate community. A good mortgage banker will gain the trust and confidence of investors through knowing and even anticipating their investment tastes. A person with good fiduciary judgment, coupled with the ability to develop a bond of mutual respect with an investor, should find a career in income property mortgage banking personally challenging and financially rewarding.

Professional and Trade Associations

The Mortgage Bankers Association of America
1125 Fifteenth St., N.W.
Washington, D.C. 20005
202/861-6500
Publications: *Mortgage Banking*
Real Estate Finance Today
Professional Designation: Certified Mortgage Banker

U.S. League of Savings Associations
111 East Wacker Drive
Chicago, IL 60601
312/644-3100

Real Estate Planner*

Nature of Work

There are several areas of specialization for *real estate planners*, each entailing diversified challenges. Some planners are employed by cities, others by real estate developers. Specialties include:

Land Use Planning This is probably the oldest area of specialization within planning. It is concerned with the orderly, efficient, and equitable development of land. Important issues include environmental conservation, regulation of the use of land, recreation, ecological balance, and land management.

Housing and Community Development Specialists in this area analyze the housing stock and residential neighborhoods to identify shelter needs and deficiencies. They work to develop strategies to improve environments where housing is substandard or overcrowded, the rental rates are excessive, or the neighborhood is undesirable. These may involve work in developing countries in Africa, Asia, and Latin America.

Planning degrees can lead to opportunities across disciplines and fields such as transportation, economics, program management, environment, government, social policy, international development, research, education, and consulting, in either the public or the private sector.

Responsibilities

Planners formulate plans and policies to meet social, economic, and physical needs, and they develop the strategies to make these plans work. Planning is both science and art. It demands technical competence as well as creativity, hardheaded pragmatism as well as an ability to envision alternatives to the physical and social environments in which we live. It is an excellent career choice for those who desire a role in shaping the future.

The planning process typically involves the performance of a number of roles. Some planners function primarily as technical analysts or researchers, others as designers or program developers, and still others as managers or educators. Some planners will focus on only one of these roles; most, however, will perform several of them at different stages of their lives. In all phases of their careers, planners will find that planning is an interdisciplinary profession, and they will draw upon the resources and expertise of a wide variety of fields. Planners develop comprehensive approaches that attempt to show how best to use a community's land: where residential, commercial, industrial, recreational, and other human activities should take place. More and more, comprehensive plans emphasize the process of change and outline the social, economic, and environmental consequences.

*Adapted from *Had You Planned to Be a Planner?* published by the American Planning Association.

Opportunities

Employment prospects for planning graduates during the 1980s will be very good according to the U.S. Bureau of Labor Statistics. Though there have been cutbacks in planning in some areas of government, the slack has been compensated for by the private sector. Communities in rapidly growing areas of the country will be seeking additional professional planning help in dealing with urbanization and population growth. The energy-rich states will offer opportunities for planners to help guide the development of growing towns and to protect the environment. Older cities will continue to need planners to deal with housing, transportation, and redevelopment issues. The many types of private firms mentioned earlier will also be seeking planners. Policy planning and other new fields will provide fresh opportunities for which urban planning is excellent preparation. For a formal forecast of jobs in planning, see the U.S. Department of Labor, Bureau of Labor Statistics, *Exploring Careers: Office Occupations* (Bulletin 2001-3).

Hours and Travel

Most salaried planners keep regular office hours during business days; however, there are times when late hours are required to complete urgently needed plans. Those in private practice do not have such regular hours and may travel frequently to seek and perform out-of-town assignments.

Educational Requirements

Most professionals enter the field by earning a degree from a recognized school of planning. Several schools offer an undergraduate degree in planning, but most planners hold a master's degree with a solid base in a related undergraduate field. The typical graduate program involves two years of study. In many schools the students take part in practical field work during both the summer and in conjunction with courses offered during the academic year.

Students enter graduate planning programs from virtually all undergraduate fields. Most come directly from their undergraduate studies, but more and more have had previous experience in urban and regional planning or allied fields.

Professional Association

American Planning Association
1313 East 60th St.
Chicago, IL 60637
1776 Massachusetts Avenue, N.W.
Washington, D.C. 20036
Publication: *Planning Magazine*
Professional Designation: AICP

Property Manager

Nature of Work

Property managers handle the daily business activities for owners of income-producing real estate, such as apartments, shopping centers, and office buildings. Many developments have an on-site manager responsible for the project in addition to a centralized headquarters that issues instructions for managing all properties.

Property managers handle tenant-related activities of building use, and assure the sound mechanical state of the property and the efficient running of all systems. They may show and lease space to prospective users, determine tenant eligibility, and conduct credit checks. They set up accounting systems for the collection of rent and payment of operating expenses, with appropriate descriptions of accounts to determine income or loss of each profit center.

Property management varies greatly with the type of property — an apartment complex, office building, or shopping center — particularly in the areas of leasing and tenant mix. Since expertise learned in one type of property is not always transferable to another, specialization is important.

Responsibilities

Property managers are responsible for assuring the smooth operation of their property so as to assure the long-run profitability of the project and its value. They must comply with all laws including general commercial business practices, building codes, and affirmative action. Managers must work with tenants and tenant organizations, assure compliance with lease agreements, and report to the owner on the financial situation each month and on legal and marketing aspects when needed.

Advancement Opportunities

Property managers frequently begin as on-site managers of small properties (under 100 apartment units, for example) then move up to larger ones. Experienced personnel have many opportunities to move up in a large property management firm.

In most states a real estate broker's license is needed for most property management situations. Many real estate brokers enter the property management field because it provides a regular source of income regardless of business conditions. Other brokers begin to manage property as a service for owners of property they brokered.

Hours and Travel

On-site property managers may conduct most of their business during normal business hours. However, they may be called upon at any

time to show or lease space or respond to a security problem.

Those at higher management levels also conduct their business during normal hours but may be called on at any time for urgent security problems. In addition, they may travel to visit properties they manage out of town and to report to owners who live at a distance from the property.

Educational Requirements

There are no mandatory educational requirements, although courses are offered by several trade associations. Courses deal with on-site management; apartment, office building, and retail space management; and managing investment real estate.

Professional and Trade Associations

Building Owners and Managers Association
1221 Massachusetts Ave., N.W.
Washington, D.C. 20005
202/638-2929
Publication: *Annual Office Building Experience Exchange Report*

Community Association Institute
1423 Powhattan St., Suite 7
Alexandria, VA 22314
703/548-8600

Institute for Real Estate Management
430 N. Michigan Ave.
Chicago, IL 60611
312/661-1930
Publication: *Journal of Property Management*
Professional Designation: Certified Property Manager (CPM)

National Apartment Association
1101 14th St., N.W., Suite 804
Washington, D.C.
202/842-4050
Publication: *Units*
Professional Designation: Certified Apartment Manager (CAM)

Alphabetization: All words are alphabetized by letter rather than by word. Thus, for the purpose of arrangement, all multiple word terms are treated as if they were one word. For example, the word "ad valorem" follows "adult," rather than preceding as would be the case if "ad" were treated as a separate word. Abbreviations, in the rare instance that they appear as entries, are treated as if they were a word. The term "MAI," which stands for "Member, Appraisal Institute," appears before "maintenance fee." A separate list of abbreviations is included, so as a general rule, abbreviations and acronyms do not appear as entries. In the case of "MAI," the initials are understood by many who are not familiar with the formal name. Thus, MAI becomes the entry.

Parentheses: Parentheses are used in two instances. The first application is to indicate an abbreviation commonly applied to the term. For example, "ADJUSTABLE RATE MORTGAGE (ARM)" indicates that the abbreviation "ARM" commonly refers to adjustable rate mortgages. The second application is to indicate the context of the term as defined. For example, "TO RETIRE (A DEBT)" indicates the context under which the word "retire" is defined is when it is applied to retiring a debt. The definition is not appropriate to other legitimate uses of the word retire, such as in the expression "retirement benefits."

Cross References: When an entry is used in the definition or example for another entry, the term is printed in **boldface type.** This provides a cross reference in case the term is used in the definition is unclear to the reader. In general, the term is printed in boldface only the first time it appears in the definition. Occasionally, when a term is a closely related concept or provides contrast, it is cross-referenced, even though not used in the definition. In the former case, the term is referenced as follows: "See **cash flow.**" In the latter case, the reference appears as: "Contrast with **net lease.**" When an entry is merely another expression for a term defined elsewhere in the book, a reference rather than a definition is provided; for example, "NOMINAL RATE same as **face rate.**"

Examples and Addresses: At least one example is given for each definition in the book. In the case of organizations listed as entries, a current address is supplied in lieu of an example. The examples are intended to illustrate how the term is used in a sentence or to provide a sample of specific things which fall under the purview of the term. For example, under the entry for "closing costs" a list of specific closing cost items is provided. When an entry has more than one definition, an example is provided for each definition. Where applicable, an illustration is provided as an example. e.g., under "cluster housing," an illustration of a sample cluster housing plan is included.

A

ABANDONMENT the voluntary surrender of property, owned or leased, without naming a successor as owner or tenant. The property will generally revert to one holding a prior interest or, in cases where no owner is apparent, to the state. Abandonment does not relieve obligations associated with lease or ownership unless the abandonment is accepted by the entity to which the obligation is owed.
Example: Abel owns a dilapidated apartment house with 2 years delinquent property taxes. Rather than pay the back taxes, Abel *abandons* the building by disclaiming ownership.

ABATEMENT a reduction in amount or intensity.
Example: A manufacturing plant may install equipment for pollution *abatement*.
Example: Tenants may ask for an *abatement* in rent over a period when their use of the property has been interrupted or inhibited by actions of the landlord, such as renovation of the structure.

ABSENTEE OWNER an owner who does not personally manage or reside at property owned.
Example: Abel, living in New York, purchases an apartment building in Houston. Abel is an *absentee owner*.

ABSORPTION RATE an estimate of the expected annual sales or new occupancy of a particular type of land use.
Example: The demand for new homes in a market area is estimated to be 500 per year. Developer Abel's new subdivision, when completed, is expected to capture 10% of the market. Therefore Abel's subdivision has an expected *absorption rate* of 50 homes per year (10% of 500 = 50).

ABSTRACT OF TITLE a historical summary of all of the recorded instruments and proceedings that affect the title to property.
Example: A title insurance company will have an attorney prepare an *abstract of title* prior to granting a title insurance policy.
Example: An abstract company will compile an *abstract of title* with copies of all recorded instruments affecting title to a specific tract.

ABUT adjoining or meeting. See also **adjacent**.
Example: The 2 properties shown in Figure 1 *abut* one another. The property on the right also *abuts* the road.

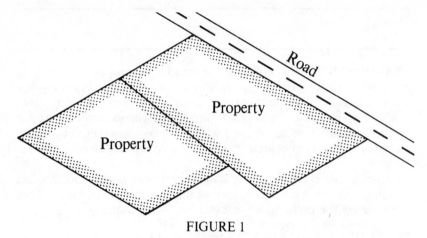

FIGURE 1

ACCELERATED COST RECOVERY SYSTEM (ACRS) a method of depreciation introduced by the Economic Recovery Tax Act of 1981 and modified by the Tax Reform Acts of 1984 and 1986. As *ACRS* applies to real estate, depreciable lives for buildings depend on when they are placed in service. See Table 1 for depreciable lives and rates.

Example: If an apartment building were purchased in January 1988 for $1,000,000 exclusive of land, $34,800 (3.48%) could be claimed as depreciation in 1988, and $36,400 each year for the following 26 years.

ACCELERATED DEPRECIATION depreciation methods, chosen for income tax or accounting purposes, that offer greater deductions in early years. See **accelerated cost recovery system, double declining balance, sum-of-years-digits depreciation.**

Example: One method of *accelerated depreciation* is the double declining balance method (DDB). If straight-line deductions equal 5% of depreciable basis, DDB allows a deduction of 10% (200% of 5%), but applied to the undepreciated basis. Thus the deductions decline each year (Figure 2).

ACCELERATION CLAUSE a loan provision giving the lender the right to declare the entire amount immediately due and payable upon the violation of a specific loan provision, such as failure to make payments on time.

Example: Collins sells her house to Baker, who assumes the existing 8% interest rate mortgage. They do not notify the lender of the sale. Clause 17 in the mortgage states that the full principal *accelerates* unless the lender approves of the sale. Collins must now pay the balance of the principal.

TABLE 1

Post-1986 Recovery Percentages for Residential Rental Depreciable Property

Recovery Year	Month Placed in Service											
	1	2	3	4	5	6	7	8	9	10	11	12
1	3.48	3.18	2.88	2.58	2.27	1.97	1.67	1.36	1.06	.76	.45	.15
2–27	3.64	3.64	3.64	3.64	3.64	3.64	3.64	3.64	3.64	3.64	3.64	3.64
28	1.88	2.18	2.48	2.78	3.09	3.39	3.64	3.64	3.64	3.64	3.64	3.64
29	0	0	0	0	0	0	.05	.36	.66	.96	1.27	1.57

Post-1986 Recovery Percentages for Non-residential Depreciable Property

Recovery Year	Month Placed in Service											
	1	2	3	4	5	6	7	8	9	10	11	12
1	3.04	2.78	2.51	2.25	1.98	1.72	1.46	1.19	.93	.66	.40	.13
2–31	3.17	3.17	3.17	3.17	3.17	3.17	3.17	3.17	3.17	3.17	3.17	3.17
32	1.86	2.12	2.39	2.65	2.92	3.17	3.17	3.17	3.17	3.17	3.17	3.17
33	0	0	0	0	0	0	.27	.54	.80	1.07	1.33	1.60

ACCEPTANCE

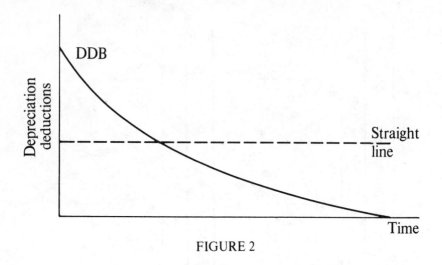

FIGURE 2

ACCEPTANCE the act of agreeing to accept an offer.
Example: Abel offers property for sale, Baker makes an offer to buy the property for a specified price. Upon Abel's *acceptance* a sales contract is complete.

ACCESSION additions to property as a result of annexing fixtures or alluvial deposits.
Example: The lease on a restaurant expires. The proprietor of the restaurant leaves some counters and bar stools. They become a part of the property by *accession*.
Example: Property bordering on a river is legally enlarged by soil deposited by the river (**alluvium**).

ACCESS RIGHT the right of owners to get to and from their property.
Example: If Baker is granted an *access right* to the property in Figure 3, a curb cut may be made onto the highway.

ACCOMMODATION PARTY one who has signed an agreement without receiving value for it, for the purpose of lending his or her name so that another person can secure a necessary loan or other arrangement.
Example: The young developer asked an experienced friend to act as an *accommodation party*. The experienced developer signed the loan agreement even though there was no monetary benefit to him.

94

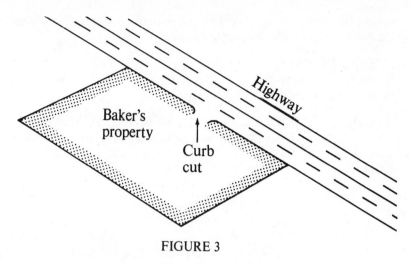

FIGURE 3

ACCRETION the addition to land through processes of nature, such as deposits of soil carried by streams. See **alluvium.**
Example: Figure 4.

Original island

River flow

Land added by *accretion*

FIGURE 4

ACCRUAL METHOD a method of accounting that requires income or expense to be entered when the amount is earned or the obligation is payable. Distinguished from **cash method** in which amounts are posted when paid or received.
Example: The home buyer bought and paid for a 3-year hazard insurance policy at closing. On the *accrual method,* only the current year's expense is indicated.
Example: Interest on a loan is 3 months delinquent. The expense, though unpaid, appears in the current year's financial statement

under the *accrual method*. Under the cash method it would appear on the financial statements when paid.

ACCRUED INTEREST interest that has been earned but not paid.
Example: If 6% interest is earned on a $100 deposit, then $6 of interest has *accrued* to the depositer.

ACKNOWLEDGMENT a declaration by a person who has signed a document that such signature is a voluntary act, made before a duly authorized person.
Example:

```
    I, Albert Abel, hereby deed to Robert Baker,
the land that I own in Fair County, further
described below.

                              Albert Abel
                              _____
                              Albert Abel

                              Jack Jones
                              _____
          Sigz R. Real        Witness
    _____
    Notary Public            George Smith
    Acknowledgment           _____
                              Witness
```

FIGURE 5

ACCUMULATED DEPRECIATION in accounting, the amount of **depreciation** expense that has been claimed to date. Same as accrued depreciation. See **adjusted tax basis.**
Example: A building was bought for $100,000. The annual **straight-line depreciation** expense is $2,500. The *accumulated depreciation* in 3 years is $7,500.

ACQUISITION COST the price and all fees required to obtain a property.
Example: Abel purchases a property for $90,000 plus $5,000 in **closing costs** (attorney's fees, loan fees, **appraisal** costs, **title insurance**, and loan **discount points**). Abel's *acquisition cost* is $95,000.

ACQUISITION LOAN money borrowed for the purpose of purchasing a property.

Example: The developer negotiated an *acquisition loan* for the purchase of land and a construction loan to improve the land for home sites.

ACRE a 2-dimensional measure of land equaling 160 square rods, 10 square chains, 4,840 square yards, or 43,560 square feet.

Example: A land survey shows that Abel owns 1.3774 *acres* of land (Figure 6).

Abel's land

200 ft 300 ft

60,000 sq ft = 1.3774 acres

FIGURE 6

ACTIVE PARTICIPATION type of investor position which determines how rental income is taxed. Requirements for *active participation* are less stringent than for **material participation.** An investor may have a manager for rental real estate and still be considered an active participant. Indicators of *active participation* in real estate are:
• Approving new tenants
• Deciding on rental terms
• Approving capital or repair expenditures
Active participation excludes:
• Owners of a 10% interest or less
• Limited partners
An active participant with adjusted gross income under $100,000 without regard to passive losses, may deduct up to $25,000 of passive losses against other income. This allowance is phased out on a 50% ratio as adjusted gross income increases from $100,000 to $150,000.

Example: Anna earns $40,000 from her job as an attorney, and is an active investor in an apartment complex. If the apartments generate a tax loss, she may offset up to $25,000 of her salary with the loss.

ACTIVE SOLAR HEATING a system that uses energy from sunlight to heat a structure and/or provide hot water. Contrasted with **passive solar heating** by the use of pumps or fans to move the energy-transporting medium through the system. Installation of active solar heating equipment is eligible for certain income tax credits.

Example: A schematic of a typical *active solar heating* system is shown in Figure 7.

FIGURE 7

ACT OF GOD an unpreventable destructive occurrence of the natural world.
Example A **contract** has a provision that allows the buyer to **default** if the property is damaged by an *act of God*.
Examples of an *act of God* are:
• earthquake
• flood
• hurricane
• lightning
• tornado

ADDENDUM (plural: ADDENDA) something added, as an attachment to a **contract**.
Example: An *addendum* to the **contract of sale** described the type of **financing** that the buyer must secure to be required to purchase the property.
Commonly added *addenda* in real estate purchase agreements are for financing terms and property **inspection** requirements.

ADDITIONAL FIRST-YEAR DEPRECIATION (TAX) under the 1986 tax act, up to $10,000 of depreciable personal property purchased each year may be expensed, rather than depreciated, provided not more than $200,000 is purchased in a year. The $10,000 is phased out, dollar for dollar, when purchases exceed $200,000 in a year.
Example: Barbara is a real estate broker. She bought a $4,000 computer to assist with her business; she may expense the cost in the year purchased, rather than depreciate the equipment.

ADD-ON INTEREST interest that is added to the principal of a loan. The amount of interest for all years is computed on the original amount borrowed.
Example: Abel borrows $1,000 at 8% *add-on interest* for 4 years. Total interest is $320 (8% of $1,000 for 4 years). Abel will repay the $1,320 total in equal monthly installments.

ADJACENT nearby but not necessarily **adjoining.**
Example: Lot B is *adjacent* to lot A (Figure 8).

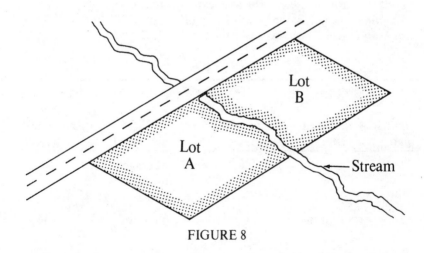

FIGURE 8

ADJOINING **contiguous;** attaching; sharing a common border.
Example: A warehouse with *adjoining* office space (Figure 9).

ADJUSTABLE MORTGAGE LOAN (AML) a mortgage instrument authorized by the Federal Home Loan Bank Board in 1981 for use by all federally chartered savings and loan associations. The *AML* provides to local associations maximum flexibility in selecting the terms under which interest rates and payments may be adjusted

FIGURE 9

over the maturity of the loan. See **adjustable rate mortgage, rene-gotiated rate mortgage, variable rate mortgage.**

Example: Major Savings and Loan offers several types of *adjustable mortgage loans* as described in Table 2.

TABLE 2

Loan plan	Interest rate adjusted every:	Payments adjusted every:	Index used	Maximum rate change each year
1	year	year	average mortgage rate	2%
2	6 months	3 years	6-month treasury bill rate	none
3	year	year	average cost of funds	none
4	3 years	3 years	3-year treasury bond yield	1%

ADJUSTABLE RATE MORTGAGE (ARM) a mortgage loan that allows the interest rate to be changed at specific intervals over the maturity of the loan.

Example: A person obtains an *adjustable rate mortgage* to finance the purchase of a home. After a 2-year period, the lender may adjust the rate of interest on the loan in accordance with an established index.

ADJUSTED SALES PRICE 1. In appraisal, the indicated price of a comparable property after adjustments have been made to account for differences between the comparable and the subject property. 2. In income taxation, the selling price of a home less expenses of sale, less fixing-up expenses. When the purchase price of a new principal residence equals or exceeds the *adjusted sales price* of a former residence, any gain on the sale of the former residence will be deferred. See **Section 1034.**

Example: The comparable is identical to the subject property except that the comparable has an additional half bath. The sales price of $70,000 is adjusted by subtracting $3,000 for the extra bath. The *adjusted sales price* is $67,000.

Example: A principal residence sold for $90,000. Just prior to the sale the seller had a contractor paint at a cost of $3,000; sales commissions and other seller-paid closing costs were $7,000. If the seller acquires another residence for $80,000 or more, there will be no income tax due on the sale of the former home.

ADJUSTED TAX BASIS the original cost or other basis of property, reduced by **depreciation** deductions and increased by **capital expenditures.**

Example: Collins buys a lot for $10,000. She erects a retail facility for $60,000, then depreciates the improvements for tax purposes at the rate of $4,000 per year. After 3 years her *adjusted tax basis* is $58,000. ($10,000 + $60,000 − 3 × $4,000)

ADJUSTMENTS (IN APPRAISAL) dollar value or percentage amounts that, when added to or subtracted from the sales price of a **comparable,** provide an indication of the value of a subject property. *Adjustments* are necessary to compensate for variation in the features of the comparable relative to the subject.

Example: An appraisal is to be made of a three-bedroom house. One **comparable** is a similar house with two bedrooms which sold for $50,000. The appraiser makes an adjustment of $1,000 to the comparable to account for the difference of bedrooms. The adjusted sales price of the **comparable** is $51,000.

ADMINISTRATOR a person appointed by a court to administer the estate of a deceased person who left no will.

Example: The *administrator* of the estate called a meeting of the deceased's relatives for the purpose of dividing the property.

ADMINISTRATOR'S DEED a **deed** conveying the property of one who died without a will **(intestate).**
Example: At the hearing called by the administrator, the heir received an *administrator's deed* to her father's home.

ADULT one who has attained the age of **majority.**
Example: Abel enters into a contract to purchase land. Because he is 17 years of age he. is a **minor** (not an *adult*) and may **void** the contract.

AD VALOREM according to value. See **ad valorem tax.**

AD VALOREM TAX a tax based on the value of the thing being taxed.
Example: If the *ad valorem tax* rate is 1%, the tax would be $1 per $100 of assessed value.

ADVERSE POSSESSION a means of acquiring title to real estate where an occupant has been in actual, open, **notorious,** exclusive, and continuous occupancy of property for the period required by state law.
Example: Although the elderly Ms. Davis held no official **deed** to the land, she was awarded title by *adverse possession,* since she had lived on the property all her life and the legal owner was unknown.

AFFIDAVIT a written statement, sworn to or **affirmed** before an officer who is authorized to administer an oath or affirmation.
Example: The *affidavit* affirmed that the landlord was solely entitled to lease out the property.

AFFIRM to confirm; to ratify; to verify.
Example: At a meeting between the buyer, seller, and broker, the voidable sales contract was *affirmed* by the party who could have voided it. All parties are now bound by the stipulations of the contract.

"A" FRAME a post World War II style house with a frame in the shape of one or more "A's."
Example: Figure 10.

AFTER-TAX CASH FLOW **cash flow** from income-producing property, less income taxes, if any, attributable to the property's income. If there is a tax loss which can provide a tax saving from the shelter of income earned outside the property, that savings is added to the **cash flow** that is earned by the property.
Example: A property generates $1,000 per year of cash flow. In the first year of ownership, depreciation and interest deductions pro-

"A" shape frame

Steep gable roof

Large windows

Shingles

FIGURE 10

vide a tax loss of $3,000. The loss saves $900 of income taxes that the investor would otherwise pay on salary earned as a teacher. The *after-tax cash flow* is $1,900.

AGENCY the legal relationship between a principal and his **agent** arising from a contract in which the principal engages the agent to perform certain acts on the principal's behalf.
Example: Under the law of *agency*, agents must be loyal to their employers. Therefore broker Roberts submits to employer Davis all offers on property.

AGENT one who undertakes to transact some business or to manage some affair for another, with the authority of the latter.
Example: An owner engages a **broker** to act as *agent* in selling real property; the broker in turn engages salespersons to act as *agents* to sell the same property.

AGREEMENT OF SALE a written agreement between seller and purchaser in which the purchaser agrees to buy certain real estate and the seller agrees to sell upon terms of the agreement. Also called **offer and acceptance, contract of sale, earnest money** contract.
Example: Abel's **broker** prepared an *agreement of sale* to sell a home to Baker. Both principals signed it. It states that the price of $50,000 is to be paid in cash at closing, subject to Baker's ability to arrange a $40,000 loan at a 12% interest rate.

AIR RIGHTS the right to use, control, or occupy the space above a designated property. Air rights can be leased, sold, or donated to another party.
Example: The Pan Am building in New York City is situated in the *air rights* of Grand Central Station (Figure 11).

Air rights

Pan Am building

Grand Central Station

FIGURE 11

ALIENATION to convey or transfer **title** and **possession** of property. May be voluntary (by the owner) or involuntary (without the owner's consent) such as in **condemnation.**
Example: By signing a **deed,** there is an *alienation* of property.

ALLODIAL SYSTEM a legal system that allocates full property ownership rights to individuals. The allodial system is the basis for property rights in the United States.
Example: Under the *allodial system,* an individual may obtain **fee simple** ownership of a parcel of real estate. This allows the individual to enjoy the full set of rights entailed in property ownership, subject to restriction only by governmental powers of taxation, **police power,** and **eminent domain.**

ALLUVIUM (or ALLUVION) soil deposited by **accretion.** Usually considered to belong to the owner of the land to which it is added.
Example: Figure 12.

FIGURE 12

ALTERNATIVE MINIMUM TAX a type of flat-rate tax that applies to individual taxpayers who have certain types of income. A 21% rate applies to broadly based income. If this tax exceeds the regular income tax, then the *alternative minimum tax* is to be paid instead of the regular income tax. See **tax preference items.**

ALTERNATIVE MORTGAGE INSTRUMENT (AMI) any mortgage other than a fixed interest rate, level payment **amortizing** loan.
Examples:
Various types of *AMI's:*
• **variable rate mortgages**
• **rollover loans**
• **graduated payment mortgages**
• **shared appreciation mortgages**
• **adjustable rate mortgages**
• **growing equity mortgages**

AMENITIES in **appraisal,** the nonmonetary benefits derived from property ownership, such as pride of home ownership.
Example: Graham bought a **condominium** overlooking Lake Michigan with a prestige address, thus enhancing the *amenities* of ownership.

AMERICAN INSTITUTE OF REAL ESTATE APPRAISERS (AIREA) a professional organization of real estate appraisers affiliated with the **National Association of Realtors®.** AIREA publishes the *Appraisal Journal* and several reference works on appraisal, provides educational services, and confers the professional designations of **MAI** (Member, Appraisal Institute) and RM (**Residential Member).**
Address:
American Institute of Real Estate Appraisers
430 North Michigan Avenue
Chicago, Illinois 60611

AMERICAN LAND TITLE ASSOCIATION (ALTA) a national association of title companies, abstractors, and attorneys established to promote uniformity and quality in **title abstract** and insurance policies.

Example: The title company employed in the purchase of the property is a member of the *American Land Title Association* and, therefore, used standard ALTA forms when underwriting the title policy.

AMERICAN MANSARD OR SECOND EMPIRE STYLE a nineteenth century style house whose main and distinguishing characteristic is the roof design. The mansard roof slopes gently back from the wall line and then is topped with an invisible (from the street) section resembling a conventional hip roof. Multiple dormers protrude through the roof.

Example: Figure 13.

Mansard roof

Massive cornice and supporting brackets

Decorative iron work

Many dormers

Colored glass windows

French doors

FIGURE 13

AMERICAN PLANNING ASSOCIATION (APA) a professional organization of regional and urban planners for the purpose of promoting professional standards, research, and education. APA was formed by the merger of the American Institute of Planners (AIP) and the American Society of Planning Officials (ASPO). APA publishes a monthly magazine, *Planning,* and a quarterly journal, *Journal of the APA.*

Address:
American Planning Association
1313 East 60th Street
Chicago, Illinois 60637

**AMERICAN REAL ESTATE AND URBAN ECONOMICS ASSOCI-
ATION (AREUEA)** an organization of scholars, researchers, and
practitioners concerned with economic analysis of real estate
related problems. Publishes the *AREUEA Journal* quarterly.
Address:
Jeffrey Fisher
Secretary-Treasurer
College of Business Administration
Indiana University
Bloomington, Indiana 47401

AMERICAN REAL ESTATE SOCIETY (ARES) an organization of
scholars, researchers and practitioners who are mainly concerned
with solving business problems related to real estate.
Address:
James L. Kuhle
Secretary/Treasurer
College of Business
California State University
Sacramento, CA 95819

AMERICAN SOCIETY OF APPRAISERS (ASA) a professional
organization of appraisers (not restricted to real estate). ASA pub-
lishes the biannual journal, *Valuation*.
Address:
American Society of Appraisers
International Headquarters
Dulles International Airport
P.O. Box 17265
Washington, D.C. 20041

**AMERICAN SOCIETY OF REAL ESTATE COUNSELORS
(ASREC)** a professional organization of real estate investment
counselors and consultants. Affiliated with the **National Associa-
tion of Realtors®**. Awards the designation of Counselor of Real
Estate (CRE). Publishes the biannual journal, *Real Estate
Issues*.
Address:
American Society of Real Estate Counselors
430 North Michigan Avenue
Chicago, Illinois 60611

AMORTIZATION a gradual paying off of a debt by periodic install-
ments.

Example: A $100,000 loan is arranged at a 12% interest rate. The borrower pays $13,500 in the first year. Of the payment, $12,000 is for interest, $1,500 for *amortization*. After the payment, the loan balance is amortized to $98,500.

AMORTIZATION SCHEDULE a table that shows the periodic payment, interest and principal requirements, and unpaid loan balance for each period of the life of a loan.

Example: An *amortization schedule* for a $1,000 principal, 5-year self-amortizing loan at 10% interest with annual payments is shown in Table 3.

TABLE 3

End of year	Payment required	Interest at 10% of unpaid balance	Principal retirement	Unpaid balance at end of year
1	$263.80	$100.00	$163.80	$836.20
2	263.80	83.62	180.18	656.02
3	263.80	65.60	198.20	457.82
4	263.80	45.78	218.02	239.80
5	263.78	23.98	239.80	0
Total retired			$1000.00	

ANCHOR TENANT the main tenant in a shopping center.
Example: Big Buy Foods is the *anchor tenant* in Figure 14. (Note: Large scale centers may have more than one anchor tenant).

FIGURE 14

ANNEXATION the process by which an incorporated city expands

its boundaries to include a specified area. The rules of annexation are established by state law and generally require a public ballot within the city and the area to be annexed. Other incorporated areas are generally protected from annexation by an adjacent city.

Example: *Annexation* is generally sought by a city to expand its boundaries by taking in an area to which it may already be providing services. Many unincorporated suburban areas, however, resist efforts to annex them into the city because of possibly higher tax rates and loss of local control over schools and other services.

ANNUAL CAP a limit on the amount of adjustment in the interest rate on an **adjustable rate mortgage** over a twelve month period. See **cap.**

Example: An adjustable rate mortgage has a current interest rate of 8% and an *annual cap* of 2 percentage points. After one year, the highest the interest rate can be is 10% and the lowest it can be is 6%, due to the cap.

ANNUAL DEBT SERVICE required annual principal and interest payments for a loan.

Example: A loan of $100,000 calls for 300 equal monthly payments to fully **amortize** the principal. Interest is 15% annually. Monthly payments are $1280.83. *Annual debt service* is the sum of 12 monthly payments, or $15,369.96.

ANNUAL MORTGAGE CONSTANT the amount of **annual debt service** compared to the principal; also expressed as a dollar amount. The formula is:

$$\text{Annual mortgage constant} = \frac{\text{annual debt service}}{\text{mortgage principal}}$$

Example: A loan, at a 15% interest rate, is amortizing over 30 years with monthly payments. The *annual mortgage constant* is 15.1733%. Total principal and interest payments in a year are 15.18 per $100 borrowed. Note: the annual mortgage constant must exceed the interest rate for **amortization** to occur.

ANNUAL PERCENTAGE RATE the effective rate of interest for a loan per year, disclosure of which is required by the **Truth-In-Lending** Law. See **yield to maturity.**

Example: Abel gets a loan for $50,000 at 10% interest plus 2 **discount points,** payable over 30 years. Because of the discount points $49,000 has been effectively borrowed but $50,000 must be repaid with 10% interest on $50,000. Considering the effective amount borrowed, the *annual percentage rate* is 10.25%.

ANNUITY a series of equal or nearly equal periodic payments or receipts.

Example: The receipt of $100 per year for the next 5 years constitutes a $100 five-year *annuity*.

109

ANNUITY DUE

ANNUITY DUE same as **ordinary annuity.**

ANNUITY IN ADVANCE a series of equal or nearly equal payments, each payable at the beginning of the period.
Example: A landlord leases property for 5 years. The rent, payable at the beginning of each period, constitutes an *annuity in advance* (Figure 15).

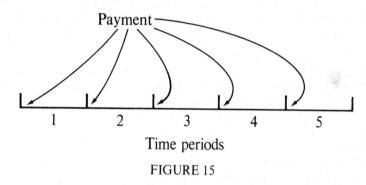

Payment

Time periods

FIGURE 15

ANNUITY IN ARREARS same as **ordinary annuity.**

ANNUITY FACTOR a mathematical figure that shows the present value of an income stream that generates one dollar of income each period for a specified number of periods.
Example: Collins is to receive $1,000 each year for 10 years for rental of her land. To value this income, she used an *annuity factor* at a 10% rate that is 6.144. The estimated rent has a present value of $6,144 (6.144 × $1,000).

$$\text{Annuity factor} = \frac{1 - \dfrac{1}{(1 + i)^n}}{i}$$

where *i* is the periodic interest rate in decimal form and *n* is the number of periods that the income stream will last.

ANTITRUST LAWS federal and state acts to protect trade and commerce from monopolies and restrictions.
Example: In the early 1960's several real estate boards required all members to charge the same rate of commission. Some boards were found to be in violation of *antitrust laws.* Now there are no boards that require specific commission rates.

APARTMENT (BUILDING) a dwelling unit within a multifamily structure, generally provided as rental housing. An apartment building is a structure with individual apartment units but a common entrance and hallway. See **multifamily housing.**
Example: *Apartments* may vary in size from small, 1-room effi-

ciencies to large, multibedroom units. *Apartment buildings* may be as small as a 1-story, 4-unit building to a high-rise building with hundreds of units and retail and office space included.

APPORTIONMENT 1. the **prorating** of property expenses, such as taxes and insurance, between buyer and seller.
Example: A house is sold on July 1. Property taxes, paid in **arrears,** are due on January 1 of the following year. At closing taxes are *apportioned,* so the seller pays the buyer one half of the estimated taxes as his share of the estimated tax payment due in January.
2. the partitioning of property into individual parcels by tenants in common.
Example: A sister and a brother inherit a property and hold it as tenants in common. The brother wishes to sell. The property is *apportioned* into 2 separate parcels to allow for the sale.

APPRAISAL an opinion or estimate of the value of a property.
Examples: A property owner may have an *appraisal* made of a specific property to:

• determine a reasonable offering price in a sale
• determine the value at death for estate tax purposes
• allocate the purchase price to the land and improvements
• determine the amount of **hazard insurance** to carry

APPRAISAL APPROACH one of 3 methods to estimate the value of property: **cost approach, income approach,** and **market comparison approach.**
Example: An independent fee appraiser generally uses each of the 3 *appraisal approaches* when preparing an appraisal report.

APPRAISAL BY SUMMATION same as **cost approach.**

APPRAISER one qualified to estimate the value of real property.
Example: One may hire an *appraiser* to render an opinion of a property's market value. In a court of law, an *appraiser* may be called upon for expert testimony.

APPRECIATION an increase in the value of property.
Example: Abel sold for $100,000 land that he purchased 10 years ago for $60,000. During that time the amount of *appreciation* was $40,000.
Appreciation gains from investment property are generally subject to favorable **capital gains** tax rates.

APPROPRIATION setting aside land for a public use.
Example: Abel plans to develop a subdivision in Pleasantville. In order to obtain permission from the city council, Abel is required

to *appropriate* 2 acres to the city for construction of an elementary school.

APPURTENANCE something that is outside the property itself but is considered a part of the property and adds to its greater enjoyment, such as the right to cross another's land (i.e., **easement** or **right-of-way**).
Example: *Appurtenances* (Figure 16).

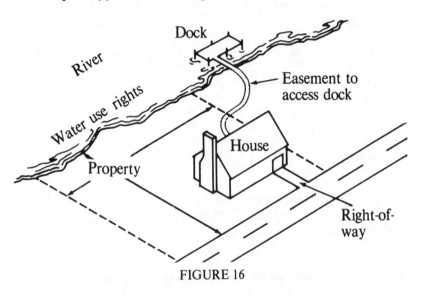

FIGURE 16

ARBITRAGE 1. buying in one market, selling simultaneously in another to make a profit.
Example: Graham bought gold in London for $500 per ounce; simultaneously she sold it in New York for $502. The *arbitrage* allowed $2 profit per ounce, less transaction costs.
2. buying one type of security and selling an equivalent to make a profit.
Example: Baker bought bonds for $5000 that could be converted into 500 shares of stock. Simultaneously, he sold 500 shares of stock at $11 per share. He earned $500 for this *arbitrage,* minus transaction costs.

ARCHITECTURE the manner in which a building is constructed, including the layout, **floor plan,** style and appearance, materials used, and the building technology used.
Example: The *architecture* of the houses in the neighborhood is characteristic of the design common to the 1930's: small rooms, much attention to detail, an elaborate **facade,** high ceilings, and thick walls.

AREA a 2-dimensional space defined by boundaries; such as floor area, area of a lot, and market area.

Example: A rectangular lot is 50 × 100 feet in dimension. Its *area* is 5,000 square feet or 0.11 acre.

ARM'S LENGTH TRANSACTION a transaction among parties, each of whom acts in his or her own best interest.

Examples: Transactions between the following parties would, in most cases, *not* be considered arm's length:
• a husband and wife
• a father and son
• a corporation and one of its subsidiaries

ARREARS 1. at the end of a term.

Example: Interest on mortgage loans is normally paid in *arrears*. This means that interest is paid at the end of a month or other period. Generally, rent and insurance are paid in advance.

2. sometimes used to signify default; overdue in payment.

ARTESIAN WELL a deep-drilled shaft that reaches water that rises because of natural underground pressure.

Example: Schematic drawing of an *artesian well* (Figure 17).

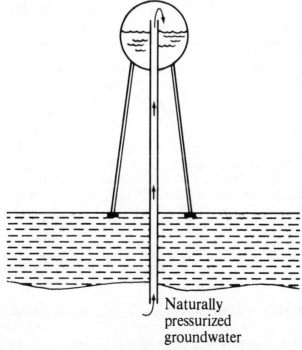

Naturally
pressurized
groundwater

FIGURE 17

AS IS without guarantees as to condition, as in a sale.
 Example: Baker purchases a building from Abel with the understanding that the building is to be conveyed *as is*. When Baker discovers that the roof leaks, Abel is not legally responsible for repairs.

ASKED the amount a property owner sets as a selling price for his property.
 Example: Abel has *asked* $75,000 for 20 acres of land, even though its **appraised** value is only $60,000.

ASKING PRICE the list price that an owner would like to receive.
 Example: Abel advertises a property for sale at a price of $100,000. The advertised price is Abel's *asking price*.

ASSEMBLAGE combining of 2 or more parcels of land. See **plottage value.**
 Example: Abel buys 2 **adjoining** properties of land for $10,000 each. The large unified tract is worth $25,000. The process is *assemblage*.

ASSESSED VALUATION the value established for property tax purposes.
 Example: Abel receives a statement indicating that, in the judgment of the local tax **assessor,** Abel's property is worth $40,000. By law, properties in this jurisdiction are assessed at 75% of **market value.** Thus Abel's *assessed valuation* is $30,000 (75% of $40,000) and property taxes will be based on this assessed amount.

ASSESSMENT 1. the amount of tax or special payment due to a municipality or association.
 Example: Abel owns a parcel of land assessed on the tax roll for $40,000. The tax rate is $1.00 per $100 of value. The tax *assessment* for Abel's land is $400.
 2. an owner's or lessee's proportionate share of a common expense.
 Example: Abel rents office space under a **net lease.** Abel pays an *assessment* each month for maintenance of the building lobby and elevators.

ASSESSMENT RATIO the ratio of assessed value to **market value.**
 Example: A county requires a 40% *assessment ratio* on all property to be taxed. Property with a $10,000 market value is therefore

assessed at $4000 (40% of $10,000), and the **tax rate** is applied to $4000.

ASSESSMENT ROLL a public record of the assessed value of property in a taxing jurisdiction.
Example: The *assessment roll* of Anytown, USA lists each individual tract of land within its taxing jurisdiction and shows the assessed value of each. The total assessed value of property is $10 million.

ASSESSOR an official who determines property tax assessments.
Example: Jones inspects Abel's property and estimates its value at $50,000 for property tax purposes. Jones is an *assessor*.

ASSET something of value.
Example: Land, houses, cars, furniture, cash, bank deposits, and securities owned are *assets*.

ASSET DEPRECIATION RANGE generally applies to property purchased before 1981. Limitations on the period over which assets may be depreciated. Generally allows depreciable lives 20% longer or shorter than the guidelines provided by the Internal Revenue Service. Also provides maximum amounts that can be spen annually on assets and still be a deductible repair.
Example: Farm buildings purchased before 1981 may be depreciated over 25 years or within a range of 20 to 30 years, according to the *asset depreciation range*. Up to 5% of the cost can be spent annually and be treated as repair, not as a capital improvement.

ASSIGNEE the person to whom an agreement or contract is sold or transferred.
Example: See **assignor.**

ASSIGNMENT the method by which a right or contract is transferred from one person to another.
Example: A tenant signs an *assignment* giving another the rights to use the leased space.

ASSIGNMENT OF LEASE the transfer of rights to use leased property. The **assignee** acquires the same rights and privileges as the **assignor.** The assignor remains liable unless released by the landlord.
Example: Abel signs a 20-year lease for a warehouse. After 5 years, Abel no longer needs the warehouse and *assigns the lease* to Baker.

ASSIGNOR a party who assigns or transfers an agreement or contract to another.
Example: Davis has an option to buy certain land. She assigns her

rights to Baker, so that Baker now has the same rights. Davis is the *assignor*. Baker is the **assignee**.

ASSUMABLE LOAN a mortgage loan which allows a new home purchaser to undertake the obligation of the loan with no change in loan terms. This is generally true of loans without **due-on-sale clauses**. Most FHA and VA mortgages are assumable.
Example: Abel sells a home with an *assumable loan* to Baker. Baker takes over the payments of the loan and accepts liability under the mortgage note.

ASSUMPTION OF MORTGAGE the purchase of mortgaged property whereby the buyer accepts liability for the debt that continues to exist. The seller remains liable to the lender unless the lender agrees to release him.
Example: Abel owes a 30-year mortgage loan of $50,000 against his house. Baker wants to buy the house and keep the same mortgage. Baker pays $20,000 cash for the **equity** and *assumes* the mortgage. Baker becomes liable for the debt, but Abel remains liable also.

AT-RISK RULES tax laws that limit the amount of tax losses an investor (particularly a **limited partner**) can claim. *At-risk rules* were extended to real estate by the 1986 tax act, and apply to property placed in service after 1986. This means that losses on real estate investments will be deductible only to the extent of money the equity investor stands to lose.
Example: If an investor has $10,000 at risk in a real estate investment that generates $3,333 per year in tax losses, the losses may be used for only three years. Thereafter, the losses may be used only if the investor contributes more money or property (net of withdrawals) or becomes liable to repay borrowed money. Amounts at-risk include:
• Cash contributed to the activity.
• Borrowed money for which the investor is personally liable.
• Property pledged as security for the real estate activity, provided the property is not used in the activity.
An exception is made for qualified third party non-recourse financing. These loans may be treated as amounts at-risk provided:
• A third-party, unrelated to the investor, provides the loan.
• The third-party lender is neither the seller of the property nor related to the seller.
• The lender is not paid a fee with respect to the equity investor's investment in the property.
Related Parties: Non-recourse loans from related parties qualify as amounts at-risk only if the terms are "commercially reasonable" and on substantially the same terms as loans involving unrelated persons.

Partnerships. A partnership's non-recourse financing may increase a general or limited partner's amount at risk provided the financing is qualified non-recourse for both the partner and the partnership. However, the amount treated at risk cannot be more than the total qualified non-recourse financing at the partnership level.

ATTACHMENT legal seizure of property to force payment of a debt.
Example: The landlord obtained an *attachment* that created a **lien** on the tenant's property to enforce payment of back rent.

ATTEST to witness by observation and signature.
Example: Many contracts require a third party to *attest* to the signing by the principals.

ATTORNEY-IN-FACT one who is authorized to act for another under a **power of attorney,** which may be general or limited in scope.
Example: Collins wishes to sell her home but is planning a 6-month vacation in the Middle East. She gives authorization to her friend Baker to sign the **deed** over to a buyer. Baker becomes her *attorney-in-fact* for this situation.

ATTORNMENT a tenant's formal agreement to be a tenant of a new landlord.
Example: Abel defaulted on the mortgage against his shopping center, so the Happy Life Insurance Company **foreclosed** and became the landlord. Happy Life asked all tenants to sign an *attornment* recognizing the new landlord.

AUCTION a way of marketing property to the highest bidder. **Bids** are taken verbally or simultaneously through mail or telegrams, and the property is sold to the highest bidder. Auctioning real estate may require both an auctioneer's license and a real estate license.
Example: Land in Iowa, since it is relatively homogeneous, lends itself to *auction* sales where it is sold to the highest verbal bidder.
Example: **Fannie Mae** agrees to buy mortgages once a week via an *auction*. Mortgage sellers state the price or yield they want, and Fannie Mae accepts the highest yields offered.

AVULSION the sudden removal of land from one parcel to another, when a body of water, such as a river, abruptly changes its channel. Contrast to **accretion.**
Example: Because of the change in the river's channel, in Figure 18 parcel A gains use of a portion of the land in the original river

117

bed through *avulsion*. Similarly, parcel B loses land which is now covered by the river.

FIGURE 18

B

BACKFILL the replacement of excavated earth into a hole or against a structure.

Example: Figure 19.

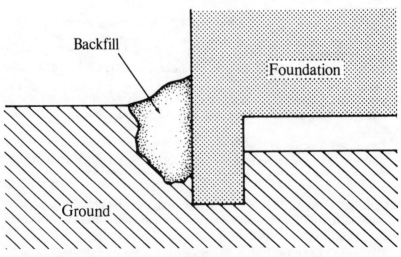

FIGURE 19

BACKUP CONTRACT a contract to buy real estate that becomes effective if a prior contract fails to be consummated.
Example: Abel contracts with Baker to sell a property contingent on Baker's ability to obtain financing within 30 days. In the meantime, Abel arranges a *backup contract* to sell to Collins, should Baker fail to obtain financing.

BALANCE SHEET a financial statement in table form showing **assets**, liabilities, and **equity**, in which assets equal the sum of **liabilities** plus **equity**.
Example: Table 4:

TABLE 4

BALANCE SHEET

Assets		Liabilities & Equity	
Cash	$1,000	Charge account debts	$500
Cars	5,000	Auto loan balance	2,000
Furniture	5,000	Home mortgage	28,500
House	50,000	Equity	40,000
Stocks	10,000		
Total assets	$71,000	Total liabilities & equity	$71,000

BALLOON MORTGAGE a mortgage with a **balloon payment**.
Example: The *balloon mortgage* called for payments of $500 per month for 5 years, followed by a **balloon payment** of $50,000.

BALLOON PAYMENT the final payment on a loan, when that payment is greater than the preceding installment payments and pays the loan in full.
Example: A debt requires interest-only payments annually for 5 years, at the end of which time the principal balance (a *balloon payment*) is due, as seen in Figure 20.

BAND OF INVESTMENT an income property **appraisal** technique where the overall interest rate is derived from weighting **mortgage** and **equity** rates.
Example: Table 5.

BANKRUPTCY the financial inability to pay one's debts when due. The debtor seeks relief through court action that may work out or erase debts.
Example: Carter lost his job but continued to live extravagantly on **credit.** When accounts were overdue, Carter filed a *bankruptcy* petition. The court allowed him to pay creditors 10 cents per dollar of debt, payable over 3 years.

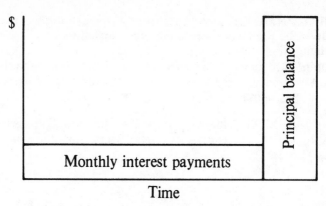

FIGURE 20

TABLE 5

Source of purchase capital	Percentage contributed	×	Rate of interest	=	Weighted rate
Mortgage	60%		15%		9%
Equity	40%		20%		8%
Band of investment rate					17%

BARGAIN AND SALE DEED in which the **grantor** implies to have or have had an interest in the property but offers no warranties of title to the **grantee.** This type of deed is typically used in many states to transfer title. Contrast **general warranty deed, quitclaim deed, special warranty deed.**
Example: Abel gives Baker a *bargain and sale deed* which includes no warranty of title but states, "for $10 and other valuable consideration, the grantor does hereby grant and release to the grantee, the following property."

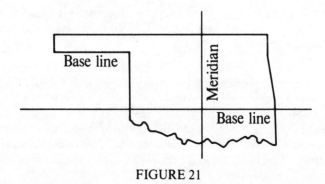

FIGURE 21

120

BASE AND MERIDIAN imaginary lines used by **surveyors** to find and describe the location of land. The base line is east-west; the meridian line is north-south.
Example: Principal *base and meridian* lines for Oklahoma (Figure 21).

BASE LINE part of the **Rectangular Survey** or **Government Rectangular Survey** method of land description. The *base line* is the major east-west line to which all north-south measurements refer.
Example: See **base and meridian.**

BASE RENT the minimum rent due under a lease that has a percentage or participation requirement.
Example: Spinning Records leases retail space in Majestic Mall. Under the lease Spinning Records must pay a *base rent* of $2,000 per month plus 5% of all sales revenue over $50,000 per month.

BASIC INDUSTRY MULTIPLIER in economic base analysis, the ratio of total population in a local area to employment in basic industry. Basic industry is considered to be any concern which attracts income from outside the local area. The job added in basic industry may also contribute to the need for local service jobs (telephone operator, nurse, waitress, etc.); and, if the workers have families, additional new people may be brought to the area.
Example: The Maintown economic base has a *basic industry multiplier* of 6. It is estimated that each new job added at Maintown's basic industries will increase the town's population by 6.

BASIS (TAX) the point from which gains, losses, and **depreciation** deductions are computed. Generally the cost or purchase price of an asset.
Example: Collins purchases land for $10,000 and erects a store for $80,000. Her *tax basis* is $90,000. If she then sells the property for $95,000 she has a $5,000 gain. If she instead depreciates the property, the $80,000 cost basis of improvements are depreciable; the $10,000 *basis* of the land remains because land is not depreciable.

BASIS POINT one 100th of 1%.
Example: Mortgage loan interest rates are 12.75% this week. They were 12.25% last week. The increase was 50 *basis points* (1275 minus 1225 equals 50).

BEARER INSTRUMENT a **security** that does not indicate the owner; payable to whoever presents it.
Example: A *bearer instrument* is open to theft because it can be redeemed without proof of legitimate ownership.

BEDROOM COMMUNITY a residential community in the **suburbs,** often near an employment center, but itself providing few employment opportunities.
Example: *Bedroom communities* frequently offer uncrowded schools, uncongested streets, and less noise and air pollution than the nearby industrial city. However, property tax rates are generally higher than in the city.

BEFORE-TAX CASH FLOW cash flow prior to deducting income tax payments or adding income tax benefits. See **cash throw-off.**
Example: After deducting **debt service** of $500 from a **net operating income** of $1000, Abel has a *before-tax cash flow* of $500.

BENCHMARK a permanently affixed mark that establishes the exact elevation of a place; used by **surveyors** in measuring site elevations, or as a starting point for **surveys.**
Example: The U.S. Coast and Geodetic Survey implants brass markers in the sidewalks of downtown areas to serve as *benchmarks*. The benchmark indicates the official elevation above sea level for the spot at which the marker is placed.

BENEFICIARY the person who receives or is to receive the benefits resulting from certain acts.
Example: Whitman takes out a $10,000 life insurance policy with her husband as the *beneficiary*. Should Whitman die, her husband will receive the benefits from the policy.

BEQUEATH to specify by **will** the recipient of personal property. Compare **devise.**
Example: In Abel's will he *bequeaths* his automobile and wrist watch to his son.

BEQUEST that personal property given by the terms of a **will.**
Example: Collins received a set of sterling silverware as a *bequest* from her deceased aunt.

BETTERMENT an improvement to real estate.
Example: Abel purchases a **site** and constructs a building. The building is considered a *betterment* to the site.

BIANNUAL occurring twice a year. Same as **semiannual.** Contrast **biennial.**
Example: Under a lease, Abel is required to make *biannual* rent payments, one in January and one in July (Figure 22).

BID the amount someone offers to pay.
Example: Abel places a property for sale at an **asking price** of $90,000. Baker makes a *bid* of $65,000 for the property, indicating he is willing to pay that amount for the property.

FIGURE 22

BIENNIAL occurring every 2 years.
 Example: Abel arranges to pay premiums on a property insurance policy on a *biennial* basis. If the current premium is paid in 1984, the next premium is due in 1986 (Figure 23).

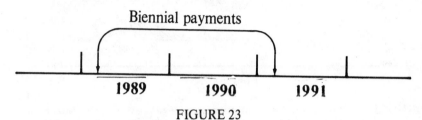

FIGURE 23

BILATERAL CONTRACT a contract under which each party promises performance. See **unilateral contract.**
 Example: A sales contract is a *bilateral contract,* since the seller promises to convey a property and the buyer agrees to pay a specified sum, given certain conditions.

BI-LEVEL a house built on 2 levels in which the main entrance is situated above the lower level but below the upper level.
 Example: Drawing of a *bi-level* house (Figure 24):

FIGURE 24

BILL OF SALE a written **instrument** given to pass **title** of personal property from a seller to a buyer. Used when furniture and portable appliances are sold.
Example: Figure 25.

Bill of Sale

I, Ernest Abel, do hereby sell my dining room suite, which I represent to be free and clear, to Bill Baker.

Signed,

Ernest Abel

FIGURE 25

BINDER an agreement, accompanied by a **deposit,** for the purchase of real estate, to evidence **good faith** on the part of the purchaser.
Example: Abel gave Baker a *binder* on the house; Abel then contacted his attorney to prepare the papers for a contract.

BIWEEKLY LOAN a mortgage which requires principal and interest payments at two-week intervals. The payment is exactly half of what a monthly payment would be. Over a year's time, the 26 payments are equivalent to 13 monthly payments on a comparable mortgage loan. As a result, the loan will amortize much faster than loans with monthly payments.
Example: A 30-year mortgage for $70,000 at 12 percent interest requires monthly payments of $720. A *biweekly loan* for the same amount and interest rate requires a payment of $360 every two weeks. The biweekly mortgage will be fully amortized (paid off) after 19 years.

BLANKET MORTGAGE a single **mortgage** that covers more than one parcel of real estate.
Example: A developer subdivides a tract of land into lots and obtains a *blanket mortgage* on the whole tract. A **release** provision in the mortgage allows the developer to sell individual lots over time without **retiring** the entire mortgage.

BLENDED RATE an **interest rate,** applied to a **refinanced** loan, that is higher than the rate on the old loan but lower than the rate offered on new loans. Generally offered by the lender to induce home buyers to refinance existing, low-interest rate loans as an

alternative to assuming the existing loan. Compare **assumption of mortgage.**
Example: Jones wishes to sell a home to Brown. Brown can assume the existing loan of $20,000 at an interest rate of 8%. Jones' lender offers the alternative of refinancing the loan for $40,000 at a *blended rate* of 10%. Brown could get a new loan at a rate of 12%.

BLIGHTED AREA a section of a city in which a majority of the structures are dilapidated.
Example: Urban renewal is planned for several *blighted areas* of the city. Within these areas, houses that do not meet **housing codes** are to be rehabilitated or demolished and new buildings constructed.

BLIND POOL an investment program in which monies are invested into an association without investors knowing which properties will be purchased.
Example: Each of 100 investors contributes $5,000 into a joint venture. The **syndicator** has not located the property to be purchased, so the investment money is said to be a *blind pool.*

BLOCKBUSTING a racially discriminatory and illegal practice of coercing a party to sell a home to someone of a minority race or ethnic background, then using scare tactics to cause others in the neighborhood to sell at depressed prices.
Examples: A sales agent arranges a sale in which a minority family enters a previously all-white neighborhood. The agent then engages in *blockbusting* by contacting other owners in the neighborhood and informing them that their property's value will fall if they don't sell right away at a depressed offered price.

BLUE-SKY LAWS state laws requiring the offeror of securities to give full disclosure, and register the offering as required by federal and state law.
Example: A **syndicator** wishes to sell 10,000 units of a partnership to investors throughout the U.S. He registers the offering with the **Securities and Exchange Commission** and complies with *blue-sky laws* in 50 states. The term comes from fraudulent practices of exaggerated offerings to investors, including part of the blue sky.

BOARD OF EQUALIZATION a government entity whose purpose is to assure uniform property tax assessments.
Example: A *board of equalization* at the local level may review **assessments** to be certain that the assessment for each parcel is fair; at the state level, the board will assure that each county is assessing property at the mandated proportion of market value.

BOARD OF REALTORS® a local group of real estate licensees who are members of the State and **National Association of Realtors®.**
Example: The Springfield *Board of Realtors®* has 200 members. They meet monthly to discuss business matters, and form the **multiple listing** service in Springfield.

BOILER PLATE standard language found in contracts. Preprinted material.
Example: Collins decided to lease her property. At a stationery store she finds a preprinted *boiler plate* form. She fills in rental rates and dates in the blank places, than asks her tenant, Baker, to sign the lease.

BONA FIDE in **good faith,** without fraud.
Example: To be certain that the signatures to the deed were *bona fide,* the county clerk insisted they be **notarized.**

BOND a certificate that serves as evidence of a debt and of the terms under which it is undertaken. See **promissory note.**
Example: Abel loans $10,000 to Baker, who gives a **note** or *bond* to evidence the debt (Figure 26).

Bill Baker owes Ernest Abel $10,000, payable at maturity in 10 years with interest payable semiannually at 10%.

Signed

Bill Baker

Bill Baker
August 15, 1989

FIGURE 26

BOOK VALUE the carrying amount of an **asset,** as shown on the books of a company. Generally the amount paid for an asset, less depreciation.
Example: X Corporation purchases a building for $100,000, then **depreciates** it by $10,000 on its financial statements. The *book value* was $100,000 and is now $90,000.

BOOT unlike property included to balance the value of like properties exchanged.
Example: In an exchange of property under **Section 1031** of the

Internal Revenue Code, Collins exchanges her warehouse worth $100,000 and receives Baker's land worth $125,000. Collins pays $15,000 cash and a car worth $10,000 to *boot* in order to equalize the values of properties exchanged. The car and cash are *boot* (Figure 27).

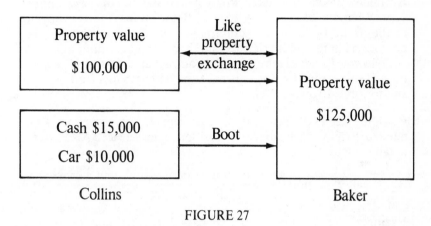

FIGURE 27

BOTTOMLAND 1. low land near a river, lake, stream, which is often flooded, see **flood plain.**
Example: Figure 28.

FIGURE 28

2. land in a valley or dale.
Example: Figure 29.

FIGURE 29

BOUNDARY same as **property line.**

BREACH OF CONTRACT a violation of the terms of a legal agreement; **default.** Breach of contract allows the nonbreaching party to rescind the contract, sue for damages, or sue for performance of the contract.
Example: Baker contracts with owner Brown to purchase a property. When the closing date arrives, Brown refuses to **convey** title to the property. Brown's action is not supported by any special conditions in the sales contract and therefore constitutes a *breach of contract.* Baker may rescind the contract and recover his **deposit,** may sue Brown for any expenses and damages incurred, or may sue to force Brown to sell.

BREAK-EVEN POINT the amount of **rent** or the **occupancy level** needed to pay **operating expenses** and **debt service.** Also called **default** point.

$$\text{Break-even point} = \frac{\text{operating expenses and debt service}}{\text{potential gross income}}$$

Example: Annual operating expenses for a 100-unit apartment complex are estimated at $200,000 per year. Debt service requirements are $250,000 per year. Therefore, total cash requirements are $450,000. If all apartments are rented all year, the **gross income** would be $600,000. The *break-even point* is at 75% occupancy. At that level, gross income would exactly equal cash requirements.

BRIDGE LOAN mortgage financing between the termination of one loan and the beginning of another loan.
Example: Collins, who is a developer, has a construction loan outstanding. She is in the process of negotiating better terms for permanent financing than the commitment previously arranged. She has arranged a *bridge loan* to pay off the construction loan when it is due. When new permanent financing is arranged, that loan will pay off the bridge loan.

BROKER a state-licensed **agent** who, for a fee, acts for property owners in real estate transactions, within the scope of state law.
Example: A person wishing to sell or lease property often engages a *broker* to arrange the sale or locate tenants. A broker may also be engaged by a prospective buyer or tenant to locate acceptable property.

BROKERAGE 1. the business of being a **broker.**
Example: One may open a *brokerage* office, upon receiving a broker's license, for the purpose of engaging in brokerage.
2. the **commission** received by a broker for his services.
Example: The *brokerage* was $6,000 on the sale of a $100,000 house.

128

BROWNSTONE, BRICK ROW HOUSE, OR EASTERN TOWN-HOUSE a nineteenth century style house, usually having 4 or 5 stories with a stoop leading up to the first floor. They have common side walls with the house on either side.
Example: Figure 30.

Brownstone trim

4 or 5 stories

Simple double-hung windows

Stoop up to first floor

Common walls Brick Flat roof

FIGURE 30

BUDGET MORTGAGE a **mortgage** that requires monthly payments for taxes and insurance in addition to interest and principal.
Example: Abel borrows $50,000 on a *budget mortgage* at 12% interest. His monthly mortgage payment is $700, which consists of $514 principal and interest, $150 taxes, and $36 insurance.

BUFFER ZONE a transitional area between 2 areas of different predominant land uses.
Example: In Figure 31 a *buffer zone* of **apartments** separates an area of **single-family** houses from a **commercial property** area:

FIGURE 31

BUILDER WARRANTY a guarantee on the quality of construction offered by the developer or building contractor. See **homeowner warranty program.**

Example: Abel buys a newly built home. The home carries a *builder warranty* which guarantees that the home is free of structural defects for a period of time.

BUILDING AND LOAN ASSOCIATIONS see **savings and loan associations.**

BUILDING CODES regulations established by local governments describing the minimum structural requirements for buildings; includes foundation, roofing, plumbing, electrical, and other specifications for safety and sanitation.

Example: Abel is developer who wishes to construct houses. He must comply with the standards of the local *building codes* and submit to inspections by a building inspector.

BUILDING LINE a line fixed at a certain distance from the front and/or sides of a lot, beyond which the building may not project.

Example: Figure 32.

FIGURE 32

130

BUILDING LOAN AGREEMENT an agreement whereby the lender advances money to an owner at specified stages of construction, i.e., upon completion of the foundation, framing, etc. Same as **construction loan** agreement.

BUILDING OWNERS AND MANAGERS ASSOCIATION (BOMA) an organization of practitioners who own and manage buildings, notably office space.
Address:
1221 Massachusetts Ave., N.W.
Washington, D.C. 20005

BUILDING PERMIT permission granted by a local government to build a specific structure at a particular site.
Example: Abel desires to construct a small office building at the corner of First and Main. A *building permit* must be obtained from the city to allow the construction to proceed legally.

BUILDING RESIDUAL TECHNIQUE an **appraisal** technique whereby income to land is subtracted from **net operating income** to result in the building income. Building income is capitalized into building value.
Example: Table 6:

TABLE 6

Net operating income	$13,000
Less: Land income	− 5,000
(Land value $50,000×10% rate of return)	
Building income	$8,000
Divided by building rate of return	÷ .12
(10%+2% **depreciation**)	
Building value	$66,666

BUNDLE OF RIGHTS THEORY the theory that ownership of realty implies a group of rights such as occupancy, use and enjoyment, and the right to sell, **bequeath**, give, or **lease** all or part of these rights.

Example: Under the *bundle of rights* concept, Abel may sell mineral rights, hunting rights, **easements**, and other partial interest, then give a **life estate** to his wife with the **remainder** to their daughter.

BUNGALOW a small, early twentieth century style, 1-story house that usually has an open or enclosed front porch.
Example: Figure 33.

Open or enclosed front porch

1 story

Shingle roof

FIGURE 33

BUSINESS DAY a standard day for conducting business. Excludes weekends and holidays.
Example: On Monday, July 1, Abel agrees to buy real estate. Closing will be 5 *business days* later, which is July 9 (Table 7):

TABLE 7

		Business days
Tuesday	July 2	1
Wednesday	July 3	2
Thursday	July 4	holiday
Friday	July 5	3
Saturday	July 6	weekend
Sunday	July 7	weekend
Monday	July 8	4
Tuesday	July 9	5

BUY-BACK AGREEMENT a provision in a contract under which the seller agrees to repurchase the property at a stated price upon the occurrence of a specified event within a certain period of time.
Example: The *buy-back agreement* in the sales contract requires the builder-seller to buy the property back if Collins, the buyer-occupant, is transferred by her company within 6 months.

BUY DOWN 1. the action to pay additional **discount points** to a lender in exchange for a reduced rate of interest on a loan. The reduced rate may apply for all or a portion of the loan term. 2. a loan that has been bought down by the seller of the property for the benefit of the buyer.
Example: In order to achieve a sale of a property, Jones arranged for a *buy down* loan. If a seller agreed to Jones' price, Jones would *buy down* the interest rate for the first 3 years by paying the lender 5% of the loan amount at closing.

BUYER'S BROKER an agent hired by a prospective purchaser to find an acceptable property for purchase. The broker then represents the buyer and negotiates with the seller in the purchaser's best interest.
Example: Abel wishes to purchase a small apartment complex. Abel hires Baker, a licensed real estate broker, to find such a property. Baker is acting as a *buyer's broker* and earns a commission from Abel when an acceptable property is found and the owner is willing to sell.

BUYER'S MARKET a situation where buyers have a wide choice of properties and may negotiate lower prices. Often caused by over-building, local population decreases, or economic slump.
Example: Abel can purchase properties below their appraised values because of the existence of a *buyer's market*.

BUY-SELL AGREEMENT a pact among partners or stockholders under which some agree to buy the interests of others upon some event.
Example: Collins and Baker are partners. In the event Baker dies, Collins has agreed to buy Baker's interest for $25,000. If Collins dies first, Baker will buy her interest for $25,000.

BYLAWS a set of regulations by which an organization conducts its activities.
Example: An association of **condominium** owners prepares *bylaws* that state the minimum number of owners to conduct a meeting, to decide on policies, to elect officers, and other matters.

C

CALIFORNIA BUNGALOW a 1-story, small, compact, early twentieth century house.
Example: Figure 34

Small, compact shape 1 story

FIGURE 34

CALIFORNIA RANCH a post-World War II style, 1-story, ground-hugging house with a low, pitched roof.
Example: Figure 35.

CALL PROVISIONS clauses in a loan that give the lender the right to accelerate the debt upon the occurrence of a specific event or date. See **acceleration clause.**
Example: Abel, the **mortgage** lender, notices that Baker, the homeowner, has begun to demolish the property. *Call provisions* in the loan allow Abel to claim that the full debt is now due.

CANCELLATION CLAUSE a contract provision that gives the right to terminate obligations upon the occurrence of specified conditions or events.
Example: a *cancellation clause* in a **lease** may allow the landlord to break the lease upon the sale of the building.

CAP in adjustable rate mortgages, a limit placed on adjustments to protect the borrower from large increases in the interest rate or the payment level. See **annual cap, life-of-loan cap, payment cap.**

CAPACITY OF PARTIES one of the requirements for a valid contract. Parties with less than full capacity include **minors,** the mentally insane, and those who are intoxicated.
Example: Collins, at age 17, entered into a contract to buy a tract of land. Collins can void that contract because it was entered into without full legal capacity.

Low-
1 story pitched Picture Ground- Sliding
 roof windows hugging windows

FIGURE 35

CAPE COD COLONIAL an early American style 1½ story compact house that is small and symmetrical with a central entrance. The roof is the steep gable type covered with shingles. The authentic types have low central chimneys, but end chimneys are very common in the new versions. Bedrooms are on the first floor. The attic may be finished into additional bedrooms and a bath. A vine covered picket fence is traditional.
Example: Figure 36.

Shingles Gable roof 1½ stories

Central
entrance

FIGURE 36

CAPITAL ASSET an asset defined in **Section 1221** of the **Internal Revenue Code** that once received favorable tax treatment upon sale. Excludes **inventory,** property held for resale, property used in a trade or business, copyrights in certain instances, and certain U.S. government obligations. There is no favorable tax treatment for *capital assets* sold after 1987.
Example: The dwelling that one owns and lives in, investment land, a limited partnership interest, or securities held for investment are *capital assets.*

CAPITAL EXPENDITURE an improvement (as distinguished from a **repair**) that will have a life of more than one year.
Example: Collins adds a new 25-room wing to her motel, at a cost of $250,000. The new wing is a *capital expenditure.*
Example: Baker, a rancher, has a fence that is in such poor condition it cannot be repaired. He makes a $50,000 *capital expenditure* to replace the fence.

CAPITAL GAIN gain on the sale of a **capital asset.** The 1986 tax act provides a maximum tax rate of 28% for *capital gains* in 1987; in 1988 and thereafter, there is no distinction in rates for *capital gains* as compared with **ordinary income.** There are limits on the deduction of **capital losses** against ordinary income.
Example: Collins purchases land, for investment purposes, for $10,000. Thirteen months later she sells it for $14,000. She reports the $4,000 profit as a long-term *capital gain* on her income tax return.

CAPITAL IMPROVEMENT same as **capital expenditure.**

CAPITAL RECOVERY see **recapture rate.**

CAPITALIZATION 1. in finance, a process whereby anticipated future income is converted to one lump sum capital value. A **capitalization rate** is divided into the expected periodic income to derive a capital value for the expected income. Sum of **interest rate** and **recapture rate.** See **capitalization rate.**
Example: A property is expected to produce an annual income of $10,000. It is judged to have a value of $80,000, which represents *capitalization* of the $10,000 per year income stream. Also, when taxes on the property increased by $500 per year, the property's value was reduced by $6,000 due to the *capitalization* process.
2. in accounting, setting up an **asset** on the financial records, rather than deducting it currently.
Example: *Capitalization* is required for an asset that has a 15-year **depreciable life;** the cost will be deducted over that time period, not deducted currently.

CAPITALIZATION RATE a rate of return used to derive the capital value of an **income stream.** The formula is

$$\text{Value} = \frac{\text{annual income}}{\text{capitalization rate}}$$

Example: The estimated net operating income of an office building is $12,000 per year. An appraiser decides the appropriate *capitalization rate* is 12%, comprised of a 10% return on investment and 2% for **depreciation.** The estimated value of the building is $100,000.

CAPITALIZE 1. to estimate the present lump sum value of an **income stream..** See **capitalization rate.**
Example: An **income stream** of $1,000 per year expected for 20 years is *capitalized* to result in a value of $8,513, based on a 10% interest rate.
2. to set up the cost of an asset on financial records.
Example: Abel acquires a building at a cost of $100,000. Since the cost cannot be deducted in the year paid, the $100,000 is *capitalized* as an asset and **depreciates** over its estimated useful life.

CAPITAL LOSS loss from the sale of a **capital asset.**
Example: Collins, an investor, purchases land for $10,000. Two years later she sells it for $8,000. The $2,000 difference is a *capital loss,* since the land is a capital asset. Note: There are limitations on the amount of loss that can be used to offset **ordinary income.**

CAP RATE same as **capitalization rate.**

CAPTURE RATE the sales or leasing rate of a real estate development compared to the sales or leasing rate of all developments in the market area.
Example: Two thousand condominium units are built in a rapidly growing metropolitan area, including one project of 500 units built by the Gibraltar Development Company. Sales in the area during July are 200 units, of which half are sold by Gibraltar. Gibraltar's *capture rate* is 50%.

CARRYING CHARGES expenses necessary for holding property, such as taxes and interest on idle property or property under construction.
Example: The annual *carrying charges* on a $100,000 tract of land are: $2,000 for taxes and $12,000 for interest.

CARRYOVER BASIS in a tax-deferred exchange, the **adjusted tax basis** of the property surrendered that is used to determine the tax basis of the property acquired. See **basis (tax)..**
Example: Abel exchanges land with Baker in a tax-deferred

exchange. Abel's **adjusted tax basis** in the **land** given up was $10,000. The *carryover basis* will therefore be $10,000 and (in the absence of **boot**) that will be Abel's tax basis in the land acquired from Baker.

CASH METHOD a method of accounting based on cash receipts and disbursements. Contrast **accrual method.**
Example: Abel, a *cash method* taxpayer, has the carpets in his office building shampooed on December 20 and immediately gets a bill for the service. He pays the bill on January 1 so the tax deduction is taken in the next year.

CASH FLOW periodic amounts available to an **equity** investor after deducting all periodic cash payments from rental income. See **before-tax cash flow, cash throw-off, after-tax cash flow.**
Example: Table 8.

TABLE 8

potential gross income	$10,000
less: vacancy and collection allowance	− 1,000
add: miscellaneous income	+ 500
effective gross income	9,500
less: operating expenses	− 3,000
less: replacement reserve	− 500
net operating income	6,000
less: interest	− 4,000
less: principal payment	− 500
cash flow	$1,500

CASH THROW-OFF same as **cash flow.**

CAVEAT EMPTOR "let the buyer beware." The buyer must examine the goods or property and buy at his own risk, except for **latent defects.**
Example: Often a property is offered "as is," with no expressed or implied guarantee of quality or condition. When entering such transactions, *caveat emptor* is a worthy admonishment.

CENTRAL BUSINESS DISTRICT (CBD) the downtown section of a city, generally consisting of retail, office, hotel, entertainment, and governmental land uses with some high **density** housing.
Example: Elaine chose to live in the suburb of Great Neck because it is only 30 minutes from the Manhattan CBD.

CERTIFICATE OF DEPOSIT (CD) a type of savings account that carries a specified minimum deposit and **term** and generally pro-

vides a higher **yield** than passbook-type savings accounts.
Example: Carny purchases a 3-year *certificate of deposit* from
Local Savings and Loan. Carny must deposit at least $1000 and
may not withdraw the money for 3 years without forfeiting a por-
tion of the interest earned. Carny receives a yield of 8% annual-
ly.

CERTIFICATE OF ELIGIBILITY issued by the Veterans Adminis-
tration to those who qualify for a **VA loan.**
Example: A person honorably discharged after serving a certain
number of days on active duty in the armed forces is entitled to a
certificate of eligibility. It indicates eligibility for a VA mortgage
loan.

CERTIFICATE OF INSURANCE a document issued by an insur-
ance company to verify the coverage.
Example: Under the **net lease,** the tenant had to keep adequate
insurance and provide the landlord with a *certificate of insurance*
as evidence.

CERTIFICATE OF NO DEFENSE same as **estoppel certificate.**

CERTIFICATE OF OCCUPANCY a document issued by a local
government to a **developer** permitting the structure to be occupied
by members of the public. Issuance of the certificate generally
indicates that the building is in compliance with public health and
building codes.
Example: Upon obtaining **zoning** and **subdivision** approvals and
passing inspection by code enforcement officials, the developer is
issued a *certificate of occupancy.*

CERTIFICATE OF REASONABLE VALUE a document issued by
the Veteran's Administration, based on an approved **appraisal.**
Establishes a ceiling on the maximum **VA mortgage loan** princi-
pal.
Example: A *certificate of reasonable value* (CRV) was received
for a home that was under a **contract of sale.** Since the CRV was
$1,000 more than the contracted price, the VA lent the full pur-
chase price.

CERTIFICATE OF TITLE an opinion rendered by an attorney as to
the status of **title** to a property, according to the public records.
See **title search.**
Example: Abel's attorney issues a *certificate of title* that indicates
no public record of claims against Abel's ownership of the prop-
erty.

CERTIFIED COMMERCIAL INVESTMENT MEMBER (CCIM) a
designation awarded by the **Realtors National Marketing Institute,**
which is affiliated with the **National Association of Realtors®.**

Address:
Realtors National Marketing Institute
430 N. Michigan Ave.
Chicago, Illinois 60611

CERTIFIED HISTORIC STRUCTURE see **historic structure.**

CERTIFIED PROPERTY MANAGER (CPM) a professional designation awarded to real estate managers by the **Institute of Real Estate Management,** an affiliate of the **National Association of Realtors®.**
Address:
Institute of Real Estate Management
430 N. Michigan Ave.
Chicago, Illinois 60611.

CERTIFIED RESIDENTIAL BROKER (CRB) a designation awarded by the **Realtors National Marketing Institute,** which is affiliated with the **National Association of Realtors®.**
Example: Upon completing the necessary requirements, Abel was awarded the title of *Certified Residential Broker.*

CERTIFIED RESIDENTIAL SPECIALIST (CRS) a professional designation awarded by the **Realtors National Marketing Institute,** based on education and experience in residential sales. Candidates must hold the **GRI** designation.

CHAIN a linear unit of land measurement used in surveying: 66 feet in length. Each chain consists of 100 links.
Example: A plot 66 ft square measures 1 chain by 1 chain.

CHAIN OF TITLE a history of **conveyances** and **encumbrances** affecting a **title** from the time that the original **patent** was granted, or as far back as records are available. See **abstract of title, certificate of title.**
Example: An abstractor can research title to property going back to the date that the property was granted to the United States. This *chain of title* is helpful in preparing an attorney's **opinion of title,** as to whether the owner has a marketable or **insurable interest.** See **marketable title.**

CHATTEL personal property. Anything owned and tangible, other than real estate. See **personalty.**
Example: Furniture, automobiles, and jewelry are all *chattels.*

CHATTEL MORTGAGE a pledge of personal property as **security** for a **debt.**
Example: Abel borrows money against his automobile; the lender grants a *chattel mortgage.*

CLEAR TITLE a **marketable title;** one free of **clouds** and disputed interests.
Example: It is necessary to obtain *clear title* in order to convey a general **warranty deed** in a transaction.

CLIENT the one who engages a **broker,** lawyer, accountant, **appraiser,** etc.
Example: Unless otherwise specified in the sales contract, the *client* of the broker, most often the seller, pays the **brokerage** commission.

CLOSING 1. the act of transferring ownership of a property from seller to buyer in accordance with a sales contract. 2. the time when a closing takes place.
Example: Abel agrees to purchase a property from Baker. A *closing* is set up for June 15, at which time Abel and Baker will sign all documents and pay all expenses necessary to transfer ownership and secure financing.

CLOSING COSTS various fees and expenses payable by the seller and buyer at the time of a real estate **closing** (also termed transaction costs).
Examples: The following are some *closing costs:*
• **brokerage** commissions
• lender **discount points**/other fees
• **title insurance** premium
• deed **recording** fees
• loan **prepayment penalty**
• **inspection** and **appraisal** fees
• attorney's fees

CLOSING DATE the date on which the seller delivers the **deed** and the buyer pays for the property.
Example: The sales contract generally establishes a *closing date,* at which time the parties will meet and settle all accounts necessary to transfer **title** to the property.

CLOSING STATEMENT an accounting of funds from a real estate sale, made to both the seller and the buyer separately. Most states require the **broker** to furnish accurate closing statements to all parties to the transaction.
Example: Table 9

CLOUD ON THE TITLE an outstanding claim or **encumbrance** that, if valid, would affect or impair the owner's **title.** Compare **clear title.**
Example: Abel dies and in his will leaves land to Baker. Abel's widow is contesting the validity of Abel's will. During this period there is a *cloud on* Baker's *title* to the land.

TABLE 9

	Seller		Buyer	
	Debit	Credit	Debit	Credit
Real property		$40,000	$40,000	
Prepaid taxes		670	670	
Sales commission	$ 2,400			
Survey fee			75	
Cash paid by buyer to close				$40,745
Cash received by seller	38,270			
Totals	$40,670	$40,670	$40,745	$40,745

CLUSTER HOUSING a **subdivision** technique in which detached dwelling units are grouped relatively close together, leaving open spaces as **common areas.**.

Example: A *cluster housing* development (Figure 37).

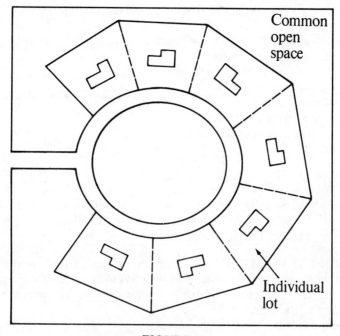

FIGURE 37

CODE see **building code, code of ethics, housing code.**

CODE OF ETHICS a statement of principles concerning the behavior of those who subscribe to the code.

Example: All Realtors® are required to subscribe to a *code of ethics* that defines proper professional behavior and practices that are considered unbecoming a professional real estate **agent.**

COINSURANCE a clause in an insurance policy stating the minimum percentage of value to be insured in order to collect the full amount of loss.

Example: Abel has a building worth $100,000. He figures that the maximum loss in the event of a disastrous fire will be $60,000, and insures it to $60,000. The policy has an 80% *coinsurance* clause. Since he did not insure it to 80% of its value, he will not receive the full amount of loss. The ratio he will receive is:

$$\frac{\text{amount carried}}{\substack{\text{amount should carry} \\ \text{(property value} \times \text{coinsurance rate)}}} = \frac{\$60,000}{\$80,000} \times \text{loss}$$

= maximum recovery, subject to maximum carried

COLD CANVASS the process of contacting homeowners in an area in order to solicit **listings.**
Example: Abel discovers a growing demand for older homes that are close to the central business district. To increase the number of listings of such homes, Abel *cold canvasses* several older neighborhoods to determine owners' interest in selling.

COLLAPSIBLE CORPORATION a term that applies to some corporations that are dissolved within 3 years. The IRS treats gain on the sale or **liquidation** of the corporation as **ordinary income** to the stockholder.
Example: Abel forms a corporation and is the sole stockholder. The corporation builds 50 houses and estimates that each is worth $10,000 more than it costs. Abel liquidates the corporation and claims a $500,000 **capital gain** on the corporate stock. The **Internal Revenue Service** claims the gain is ordinary income because of the existence of a *collapsible corporation.*

COLLATERAL property pledged as **security** for a **debt.**
Example: A borrower who arranges a **mortgage** loan pledges the property as *collateral.*

COLLATERALIZED MORTGAGE OBLIGATION (CMO) a security backed by a pool of mortgage loans that may be separated into various classes with varying maturities. Note that **REMICs,** intro-

duced by the Tax Reform Act of 1986, are expected to become the standard vehicle for investing in mortgage instruments.

Example: Fidelity Savings and Loan pools $2 million worth of home mortgages to create a *collateralized mortgage obligation.* Investors in the *CMO* receive periodic interest and principal payments as well as return of principal as the loans are repaid.

COLOR OF TITLE that which appears to be good title but is not.
Example: Abel gives Baker a **deed** to land that he has never actually owned; Baker farms the land under a *color of title.*

COMMERCIAL BANK a financial institution authorized to provide a variety of financial services, including consumer and business loans (generally short-term), checking services, credit cards and savings accounts. Certain deposits at most commercial banks are insured by the **Federal Deposit Insurance Corporation.** Commercial banks may be members of the **Federal Reserve System.**
Example: Although *commercial banks* do make long-term mortgage loans, they have traditionally concentrated on short-term loans and are good sources for home-improvement loans and second loans secured by home equity.

COMMERCIAL BROKER one who **lists** and sells **commercial property,** which may include shopping, office, industrial and apartment projects. Contrast **residential broker.**
Example: Collins sells apartment complexes to earn a brokerage fee. She is considered a *commercial broker* despite the fact that apartments are residences.

COMMERCIAL PROPERTY property designed for use by retail, wholesale, office, hotel, or service users.
Example: An investor is interested in purchasing *commercial property* for investment. A **broker** might show the investor shopping centers, office buildings, hotels and motels, resorts or restaurants.

COMMINGLE to mingle or mix, such as the deposit of another's money in a broker's personal account.
Example: State law prohibits the *commingling* of **earnest money** deposits with a broker's own money. Most states require a separate account for earnest money held by a **broker.**

COMMISSION 1. an amount earned by a real estate broker for his services.
Example: Broker Roberts sells a $50,000 home for a client. At a 6% commission rate the client owes the broker a $3,000 *commission.*
2. the official body that enforces real estate license laws. See Figure 38.

Example: The State Real Estate *Commission* administers the real estate licensing examination, collects license fees, hears testimony from those who claim misconduct on the part of a licensee, and may punish offenders.

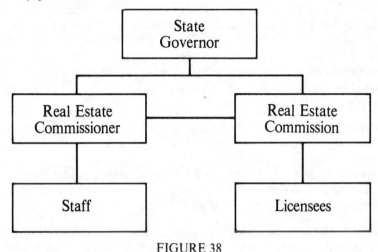

FIGURE 38

COMMISSIONER the head administrator of the State **Real Estate Commission.**
Example: As *commissioner,* Jones is responsible for maintaining records of licensees and administering examinations (Figure 38).

COMMISSION SPLIT the arrangement of sharing commissions earned between a sales agent and sponsoring broker, or between the selling broker and listing broker. See **cooperating broker.**
Example: The seller of a $100,000 house paid a $6,000 commission at closing. The *commission split* was 50–50 between the listing and selling broker. Each broker then split the fee received with the sales agent responsible for the sale, in accordance with each firm's *commission split* schedule.

COMMITMENT a pledge or promise; a firm agreement.
Example: Collins obtains a *commitment* from a **savings and loan association** for a $50,000 loan on a house she wants to buy. She is then assured of the loan so business will proceed to **closing.**

COMMON AREAS areas of a property that are used by all owners or tenants.

Example: The following are examples of *common areas.*
• the clubhouse and pool of a condominium development
• the hallways and stairs of an apartment building
• the elevators in an office building
• the mall area of a shopping center

COMMON ELEMENTS in a **condominium,** those portions of the property not owned individually by unit owners but in which an indivisible interest is held by all unit owners. Generally includes the grounds, parking areas, recreational facilities, and external structure of the building. See **community association.**
Example: In a condominium building, each resident unit owner owns the interior space within that unit. The remainder of the building and **site** are *common elements* enjoyed by each resident according to the condominium bylaws. The common elements are maintained by the owners' association, to which each owner pays a fee.

COMMON LAW the body of law that has grown out of legal customs and practices that developed in England. Common law prevails unless superseded by other law.
Example: In many disputes between neighboring landowners over damages from the activities of one or the other, the courts apply *common law* to reach a settlement.

COMMUNITY ASSOCIATION general name for any organization of property owners to oversee some common interest. In a **condominium** or planned unit development, the association has the responsibility of managing the **common elements** in the project. A **homeowners' association** may be established in a **subdivision** to enforce deed **covenants.**
Example: The **Community Associations Institute (CAI)** is a not-for-profit organization to assist in the establishment and operation of *community associations*. Their materials are helpful in setting up the association, maintenance of common elements, enforcing bylaws, and collecting monthly fees.

COMMUNITY ASSOCIATIONS INSTITUTE (CAI) a nonprofit educational and research organization concerned with the problems of managing homeowners' associations and other community associations (such as **condominium** owners associations). CAI sponsors educational seminars and publishes various handbooks and brochures.
Address:
Community Associations Institute
3000 South Eads St.
Arlington, Va. 22202

COMMUNITY PROPERTY property accumulated through joint efforts of husband and wife and owned by them in equal shares. This doctrine of ownership now exists in Arizona, California, Idaho, Louisiana, Nevada, New Mexico, Texas, and Washington State.
Example: Mary and Jim are getting divorced. During their mar-

146

riage she inherited $100,000, which is kept in a separate bank account. All other property was acquired during their marriage. Although she never worked outside the home, half of all property acquired by joint effort during the marriage is hers under the *community property* laws of the state. Her $100,000 is entirely her separate property.

CO-MORTGAGOR one who signs a **mortgage** contract with another party or parties and is thereby jointly obligated to repay the loan. Generally a co-mortgagor provides some assistance in meeting the requirements of the loan and receives a share of ownership in the encumbered property.
Example: Brown and Jones agree to purchase and share residence in a home. They jointly apply for and receive a mortgage loan to make the purchase and, thereby, become *co-mortgagors*.
Example: Sims wishes to assist her son to purchase a home. Sims provides a portion of the **down payment** money and signs the loan contract as a *co-mortgagor*.

COMPARABLES properties that are similar to the one being sold or appraised. See **market approach.**
Example: A subject property is a detached, 3-bedroom house that is 30 years old and will be bought with an **FHA loan.** *Comparables* would be recently sold houses with similar styling, age, location, and financing. Slight variations in characteristics may be taken into account when making the analysis.

COMPETENT PARTIES persons legally capable of entering a **contract.** Must be of legal age, not be insane or a drunkard.
Example: If Abel is a **minor** he may generally **void** contracts he entered to buy or sell real estate because the law does not consider him to be a *competent party*.

COMPLETION BOND a legal instrument used to guarantee the completion of a development according to specifications. More encompassing than a **performance bond,** which assures that one party will perform under a contract on condition that the other party performs. The completion bond assures production of the development without reference to any contract and without the requirement of payment to the **contractor.**
Example: A developer proposes to build a **subdivision** that necessitates a rezoning. The **zoning** commission requires the developer to post a *completion bond* prior to granting a permit for the development.

COMPONENT DEPRECIATION dividing real estate improvements into various parts such as the roof, plumbing, electrical system, and shell, then depreciating each component separately for tax purposes. Eliminated by the 1981 Tax Act, for acquisitions after

1980.

Example: Abel builds a shopping center. The $1 million total cost was spent on the components with useful lives indicated in Table 10. Abel claims *component depreciation* on each part based on its estimated useful life.

TABLE 10

roof	$100,000	15-year life
plumbing	$100,000	20-year life
electrical	$100,000	15-year life
heating & A/C	$100,000	10-year life
paving	$100,000	15-year life
building foundation and structure	$500,000	50-year life

COMPOUND INTEREST interest paid on the original principal and also on the unpaid interest that has accumulated. Contrast with **simple interest.**

Example: $100 deposited in a 5% savings account earns $5 interest the first year. Its second-year earnings are 5% of $105, or $5.25. Each year, interest is received on previously earned but undistributed interest, so interest compounds.

CONCESSIONS benefits granted by a seller/**lessor** to induce a sale/ **lease.**

Example: Abel is leasing out space in an office building. In order to get the Granite Insurance Co. to sign a lease, Abel offers a *concession* in the form of a $2000 remodeling allowance.

Example: Baker is converting apartments to **condominium** units. In order to induce tenants to purchase their units, Baker offers a *concession* of a 20% discount on the sales price, available only to tenants.

CONDEMNATION 1. taking private property for public use with compensation to the owner under **eminent domain.** Used by governments to acquire land for streets, parks, schools, etc., and by utilities to acquire necessary property. Compare **appropriation.**

Example: Abel's home is in the **right-of-way** of the new highway. When Abel refused to sell, the highway department acquired the property through *condemnation,* paying Abel an amount based on a **fair market value** appraisal.

2. declaring a structure unfit for use.

Example: The state health department, acting through its *condemnation* powers, prevented use of an old, dilapidated shack because of violations of the **housing code.**

CONDITION(S) provision(s) in a contract that some or all terms of the contract will be altered or cease to exist upon a certain event.

See **cancellation clause.**

Example: If a house is destroyed by fire before closing, the buyer is not obligated to complete the purchase.

Example: If a loan that is described as a *condition* cannot be arranged, the buyer is not required to complete the transaction and may receive a refund of any **earnest money.**

CONDITIONAL COMMITMENT an agreement by a lender to provide a loan to a qualified borrower, within a specified time period, but without stating who the borrower will be.

Example: The Solid Rock Development Company is completing a project with 200 condominiums. They arrange financing with the Trusty Mortgage Company to provide 90% loan-to-value financing at a 10% interest rate to qualified buyers. Trusty Mortgage issues a *conditional commitment* and will make such loans to qualified buyers.

CONDITIONAL OFFER purchase contract tendered to the seller that stipulates one or more requirements to be satisfied before the purchaser is obligated to buy.

Example: Baker offers to buy Collins' farm, conditioned on its rezoning for use as a shopping center prior to purchase. If it is not rezoned, Baker can get the earnest money, tendered with the *conditional offer,* refunded.

CONDITIONAL SALES CONTRACT a contract for the sale of property stating that the seller retains **title** until the conditions of the contract have been fulfilled.

Example: A **contract for deed** or a **land contract** is a *conditional sales contract.* Until the buyer makes full payment, the seller retains title to the property.

CONDOMINIUM a system of ownership of individual units in a multiunit structure, combined with joint ownership of commonly used property (sidewalks, hallways, stairs, etc.). See **common elements.**

Example: A midrise *condominium* (Figure 39).

CONDOMINIUM OWNERS ASSOCIATION an organization of all unit owners in a **condominium** to oversee the **common elements** and enforce the bylaws. See **community association.**

Example: When Vivian and Paul Carter purchase a unit in the condominium, they are automatically members of the *owners association.* As such, they are entitled to vote on decisions before the association regarding changes in bylaws, development and repair of common elements, and other matters. They are also required to pay a monthly fee to cover expenses of the association.

149

Individual units

Common elements

Parking

FIGURE 39

CONFORMITY PRINCIPLE an **appraisal** principle that holds that property tends to reach maximum value when the neighborhood is reasonably homogeneous in social and economic activity.
Example: Under the *conformity principle*, a house that cost $300,000 in a neighborhood of $50,000 homes is not worth as much as if it were in a neighborhood of $300,000 homes.

CONSIDERATION anything of value given to induce entering into a **contract;** it may be money, personal services, love and affection, etc.
Example: Abel ran out of gasoline while driving down the highway. Baker, a passing motorist, gave him a ride to the nearest filling station. Abel promised Baker a $50,000 tract of land for his help, but Baker cannot enforce the promise because of the absence of *consideration.*

CONSTANT PAYMENT LOAN a loan on which equal payments are made periodically so as to pay off the debt when the last payment is made. See **level payment mortgage, variable payment plan.**
Example: Baker obtains a *constant payment loan* to purchase a home. The loan requires a payment of $450.00 per month (principal and interest) for 30 years. At the end of 30 years, the principal balance will be zero.

CONSTRUCTION LOAN one that finances **subdivision** costs and/or improvements to real estate. See **building loan agreements.**
Example: Collins plans to develop an office building. She receives a **commitment** for permanent financing and approaches a **commercial bank** for a *construction loan.* The bank agrees to advance money as construction progresses (Figure 40).

FIGURE 40

CONSTRUCTIVE NOTICE the law presumes that everyone has knowledge of a fact when the fact is a matter of public record.
Example: Abel buys land from Baker, believing that Baker is the owner. Since Carter's **deed** had been properly recorded, Abel had *constructive notice* of Carter's ownership and cannot claim ownership against Carter.

CONTIGUOUS actually touching; contiguous properties have a common boundary.
Example: Lots A and B in Figure 41 are *contiguous*. Lot C is **adjacent** to A and B but not *contiguous*.

CONTINGENCY CLAUSE see **condition.**

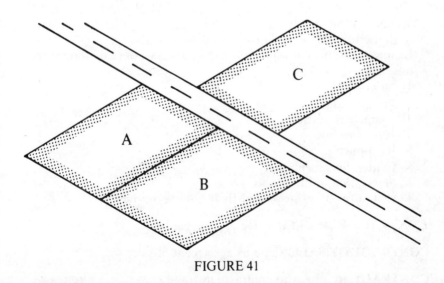

FIGURE 41

CONTOUR MAP a map that displays the **topography** of the **site.** A map with contour lines that indicate various elevations.

151

Example: A *contour map* of a building **site** (Figure 42).

FIGURE 42

CONTRACT an agreement between competent parties to do or not to do certain things for a **consideration.**
Example: To have a valid *contract* for the sale of real estate there must be:
1. an **offer**
2. an **acceptance**
3. **competent parties**
4. **consideration**
5. **legal purpose**
6. **written documentation**
7. **description of the property**
8. **signatures by principals** or their **attorney-in-fact**

CONTRACT FOR DEED same as **land contract.**

CONTRACT OF SALE same as **agreement of sale.**

CONTRACTOR one who contracts to supply specific goods or services, generally in connection with development of a property.
Example: Abel is developing a residential **subdivision.** In the

152

course of the project, Abel secures the services of various *contractors,* such as landscapers, carpenters, plumbers, and architects.

CONTRACT PRICE (TAX) in an **installment sale,** for tax purposes, generally the selling price less existing mortgages assumed by the buyer. See also **installment sale.**
Example: Abel sells land for $100,000 subject to an existing $60,000 first mortgage. Abel receives $5,000 cash in the year of sale and a $35,000 second mortgage from the buyer. The *contract price* is $40,000. Note, if Abel's **adjusted tax basis** in the land exceeds the first mortgage, such excess is a payment in the year and reduces the contract price.

CONTRACT RATE same as **face interest rate.**

CONTRACT RENT the amount of rent that has been set forth in a contract. Contrast with **economic rent.**
Example: Abel signs a lease requiring rent payments of $400 per month. The *contract rent* is $400 per month.

CONTRIBUTION a principle of valuation that states that the value of any portion of a property is determined by how it affects the performance of the total property. Therefore, a property is considered a combination of features, each of which adds something to the total value based on its *contribution* to the property's usefulness.
Example: The value of an improvement can be appraised based on the principle of *contribution.* If a swimming pool adds $25,000 to the value of a house in a prestigious San Diego neighborhood, then its *contribution* is $25,000 regardless of what it costs to build.

CONVENTIONAL LOAN 1. a mortgage loan other than one guaranteed by the Veterans Administration or insured by the **Federal Housing Administration.** See **VA loan, FHA loan.**
Example: Abel applies for a *conventional loan* from his **savings and loan association.** If Abel wants to borrow more than 80% of the value of the mortgaged property, he must buy private **mortgage insurance.**
2. A fixed-rate, fixed-term mortgage loan.
Example: Alternative mortgage instruments, by commonly used definition, are not *conventional loans.*
Example: A *conventional mortage loan* requires a fixed principal and interest payment over its term.

CONVERSION 1. changing property to a different use or form of ownership, such as when **apartments** are transformed to **condominiums.**
Example: A **condominium** *conversion* allows existing tenants to remain until the expiration of their **lease** and often allows them to

purchase the unit at terms more favorable than those offered to general public.

2. the taking away of property that belongs to another person. See also **involuntary conversion.**

Example: An illegal *conversion* of the landlord's property occurred when the tenant removed the landlord's light fixture from the apartment.

3. a change in the ownership form of a **savings and loan association.**

Example: Friendly Savings applies to the **Federal Home Loan Bank** Board for *conversion* from a **mutual savings bank** to a stockholder-owned company.

CONVEY to **deed** or transfer **title** to another.

Example: At the **closing,** Abel will *convey* the property to Baker.

CONVEYANCE the transfer of the **title** of real estate from one to another; the means or medium by which title of real estate is transferred.

Example: A **warranty deed** is most often used as a *conveyance* at the **closing.**

CO-OP 1. an arrangement between 2 real estate **agents** that generally results in splitting the **commission** between them.

Example: Abel obtains a **listing** contract on a piece of property. Baker agrees to find a buyer in exchange for a portion of the commission. Abel and Baker have arranged a *co-op* agreement.

2. a type of housing in which each tenant is a shareholder in a **corporation** that owns the building. Also termed **cooperative.**

Example: Upon moving to New York, Abel obtains an apartment in a *co-op.* This requires purchase of shares in the apartment corporation.

COOPERATING BROKER one who agrees to share the **commission** with another broker. See **commission split.**

Example: The broker who secured the listing is a *cooperating broker* with the one who brought the purchaser. The brokers agree to a **commission split.**

COOPERATIVE a type of corporate ownership of real property whereby stockholders of the corporation are entitled to use a certain dwelling unit or other units of space. Special income tax laws allow the tenant stockholders to deduct interest and property taxes paid by the corporation. See **co-op.**

Example: Apartment buildings in New York City are occasionally converted to *cooperatives.* In simple terms, this requires forming a

corporation to own the building and selling shares to those who wish to live in the building.

CORPORATION a legal entity properly registered with the secretary of state. Can have **limited liability,** perpetual life, freely transferable shares, and centralized management.
Example: Abel wants to start a real estate **brokerage** business with $10,000 of his own money. He asks his attorney to form a *corporation* with Abel as the sole stockholder. The corporation may **bankrupt** but Abel's other assets are not affected.

CORPOREAL visible or tangible real or personal property.
Example: Buildings, pavement, fences, and the like are *corpo᠃᠃al.* **Easements** are incorporeal.

COSIGNER same as **accommodation party.**

COST APPROACH a method of **appraising** property based on the **depreciated** reproduction or replacement cost (new) of improvements, plus the market value of the **site.**
Example: Table 11:

TABLE 11

Reproduction cost (new)		$100,000
Minus: Physical deterioration	$25,000	
Functional obsolescence	$10,000	
Economic obsolescence	$5,000	
Total accrued depreciation	$40,000	−$40,000
Depreciated value of improvements		$60,000
Add: Site value		$20,000
Value indicated by *cost approach*		$80,000

COST OF LIVING INDEX an indicator of the current price level for goods and services related to some base year.
Example: The Consumer Price Index (CPI), published by the Bureau of Labor Statistics, indicates that the price level for goods and services in 1986 was 330.1 This means that, on average, prices were 230% higher in 1986 than in 1967 (when the CPI was 100). A **lease** made in 1967 with initial annual payments of $1000 and indexed to the CPI, would call for payments of $3,330 in 1986. See **index lease.**

COTENANCY any of a number of forms of multiple ownership such as **tenancy in common** and **joint tenancy.**

Example: Abel and Baker decide to invest in a parcel of land. Both names are to be on the **deed.** Abel and Baker join together as *cotenants;* each owns one half of the property.

COUNSELING the act of advising clients on a variety of real estate investment or development matters.
Example: Abel wishes to invest in an office building. Baker offers *counseling* by advising Abel on how to select a property, how to legally structure the investment and how to maximize after-tax returns from the investment.

COUNSELOR OF REAL ESTATE (CRE) a member of the **American Society of Real Estate Counselors (ASREC).** Membership is based on experience and professional conduct as a real estate counselor.

COUNTEROFFER rejection of an **offer** to buy or sell, with a simultaneous substitute offer.
Example: A property is put on the market. An investor offers $75,000 in cash. The owner rejects the offer but submits a *counteroffer* to sell for $80,000. Offers and counteroffers may be negotiated on factors other than price, e.g., **financing** arrangements, **apportionment** of **closing costs,** inclusion of personal property.

COVENANT NOT TO COMPETE a clause in an agreement where one party promises not to offer to sell or produce the same goods and services in proximity to the other party.
Example: Abel sells his realty firm to Baker. In the sales contract, Abel gives Baker a *covenant not to compete.* This bars Abel from opening a competing realty firm in the same immediate area as Baker.

COVENANTS promises written into **deeds** and other instruments agreeing to performance or nonperformance of certain acts, or requiring or preventing certain uses of the property.
Examples: Deed *covenants* are often used to:
• maintain a land parcel in a specified use, such as residential
• enforce architectural and design standards
• control the **density** of future development
• prohibit certain practices, such as the sale of liquor

CREATIVE FINANCING any **financing** arrangement other than a traditional **mortgage** from a third-party lending institution.
Example: *Creative financing* devices include:
• loans from the seller
• **balloon payment** loans
• **wraparound mortgages**
• **assumption of mortgage**

- **sale-leasebacks**
- **land contracts**
- alternative mortgage instruments

CREDIT 1. in finance, the availability of money.
Example: When money and *credit* are readily available, it is easier to buy real estate. Credit policy is determined to a large extent by the **Federal Reserve System.**
2. in accounting, a **liability** or **equity** entered on the right side of the ledger.
Example: In **closing statements,** the *credit* column shows what is due and payable. The buyer is *credited* with amounts paid, the seller is *credited* with the price of the real property and prepaid items.

CREDITOR one who is owed money.
Examples: *Creditors* include:
- bond holders
- loan companies
- mortgage lenders

CREDIT RATING (REPORT) an evaluation of a person's capacity (or history) of debt repayment. Generally available for individuals from a local retail credit association; for businesses by companies such as Dunn & Bradstreet; and for publicly held bonds by Moody's, Standard & Poors, and Fitch's. Individuals have access to their own files.
Example: Goodmoney Savings Association received and studied the *credit report* on Collins before they issued her a mortgage loan. The report stated credit limits at various stores, current balances, and repayment terms in days. It would have noted **defaults** and slow repayments.

CUL-DE-SAC a street with an intersection on one end and a closed turning area on the other. Often valued in the design of residential **subdivisions** for the privacy provided to homes on the street.
Example: A **subdivision** plan showing a *cul-de-sac* (Figure 43).

CURABLE DEPRECIATION **depreciation** or deterioration that can be corrected at a cost less than the value that will be added.
Example: An apartment owner estimates that remodeling the dwelling units would allow an increase in rent of $20 per month. The cost of remodeling is $1,500 per unit. The prevailing **gross rent multiplier** in the neighborhood is 100. Thus the value added by remodeling is 100×$20 = $2,000 per unit. Thus, the outmoded appearance of the units is a form of *curable depreciation.*

Lots

Cul
de
sac

Street

FIGURE 43

CURRENT YIELD a measurement of investment returns based on the percentage relationship of annual cash income to the investment cost. The formula is

$$\text{Current yield} = \frac{\text{current income}}{\text{investment cost}}$$

Example: Abel purchases a parking lot for $10,000. It provides $5,000 of parking revenues each year. Property taxes and insurance total $3,500, leaving $1,500 of annual before-income-tax **cash flow.** The *current yield* is 15%:

$$\frac{\$1,500}{\$10,000} = 15\%$$

CURTESY the right of a husband to all or part of his deceased wife's realty regardless of the provisions of her will. Exists in only a few states.
Example: Under the *curtesy* law of some states, a widower may claim a **life estate** to part of the property left by his deceased wife, provided they had a child in their marriage.

CUSTOM BUILDER one who builds unique houses; contrast with **tract house.**

Example: Abel, a *custom builder,* erects unique homes from plans provided by architects and buyers. Each home is unique, whether built for a specific customer or speculatively.

D

DAMAGES the amount recoverable by a person who has been injured in any manner, including physical harm, property damage, or violated rights, through the act or default of another.
Example: Abel forfeited his **earnest money** to the owner of property as *damages* for failing to purchase as agreed.

DEALER (TAX) one who buys and sells for his or her own account. The merchandise is **inventory,** consequently any gain on the sale is **ordinary income.**
Example: Davis purchases mobile homes from several manufacturers, and sells them to her customers. Davis is a *dealer* and all gains from sales are ordinary income.

DEBENTURE an unsecured **note** or **bond.**
Example: Abel invests in *debentures* of the XYZ Corporation; Baker invests in a **first mortgage** on a building owned by XYZ Corporation. The XYZ Corporation **bankrupts.** Ultimately Baker receives full payment for the mortgage upon the **foreclosure sale.** Abel is a general creditor and receives only 18 cents per dollar owed to him.

DEBIT 1. in a **closing statement** (settlement), an item that is charged to a party. Contrast with **credit.**
Examples: The buyer is charged with these typical *debits:*
• purchase price
• taxes prepaid by seller
• deed recording fees
The seller is charged with these typical *debits:*
• cost to **retire** existing mortgage principal.
• **accrued interest** on mortgage being relieved
• **termite inspection** fee
2. in accounting, entries on the left side of the general ledger. Contrast with **credit.**
Examples: Debits include:
• acquisition cost of **assets**
• amounts of deductible expenses

DEBT an obligation to pay.
Example: Abel borrows $1,000 from Baker and thereby incurs a *debt.*

DEBT COVERAGE RATIO the relationship between **net operating income** (NOI) and **annual debt service** (ADS). Often used as an **underwriting** criterion for **income property** mortgage loans.
Example: Annual debt service for a mortgage loan on a certain office building is $10,000. The property generates $25,000 in annual gross rent, and requires $7,000 for expenses of operation, leaving $18,000 net operating income. The *debt coverage ratio* is 1.80, calculated by the following formula:

$$\frac{NOI}{ADS} = \frac{\$18,000}{\$10,000} = 1.8$$

DEBT SERVICE see **annual debt service.**

DECLARATION 1. formal pleadings by a plaintiff as to the facts and circumstances that gave rise to his cause of action. Also, a statement made out of court.
Example: The unhappy land buyer offered a *declaration* explaining the claim that the property was misrepresented.
2. a legal document used to create a **condominium.** Includes a description of the property and the uses to which it is restricted, a description of individual ownership units, **common elements,** and procedures for amending the declaration.
Example: A developer constructs apartments and wishes to market them as a condominium. He prepares and records a *declaration,* which describes the division of individual and common ownership, a set of bylaws and a master **deed** for the project.

DECLARATION OF TRUST a written statement by a **trustee** to acknowledge that the property is held for the benefit of another.
Example: A *declaration of trust* was signed by a **trustee** to state that certain valuable land was being held in **trust** for certain orphaned children.

DECLINING BALANCE DEPRECIATION a method of **depreciation,** often used for income tax purposes, whereby a rate is applied to the remaining balance to derive the depreciation deduction. Compare **accelerated depreciation.**
Example: Table 12 shows the depreciation schedule for a property with a **tax basis** of $10,000 and **depreciable** life of 5 years, using the 125% *declining balance* method:

DECREE an order issued by one in authority; a court order or decision.
Example: The court issued a *decree* stating that Abel owed $10,000 to Baker for failing to perform under a **contract.**

DEDICATION the gift of land by its owner for a public use and the acceptance of it by a unit of government. See also **appropriation.**

160

TABLE 12

Year	Remaining balance	Rate*	Annual deduction
1	$10,000	0.25	$2,500
2	7,500	0.25	1,875
3	5,625	0.25	1,406
4	4,219	0.25	1,055
5	3,164	0.25	791

*A 5-year life results in 20% per year depreciation using the straight-line method. The 125% declining balance method results in an annual percentage of 25 for an asset with this life (125% of 20% = 25%).

Example: A **developer** of a large **subdivision** makes to the local government a *dedication* of the streets, the flood-prone areas and one **acre** of land for a public school. This obligates the government to **maintenance** of these areas and relieves the developer of a property tax liability on the dedicated lands.

DEED a written document, properly signed and delivered, that conveys **title** to real property. See **general warranty deed, quitclaim deed, special warranty deed.**
Example: In exchange for the agreed upon terms of a **contract,** including the purchase price, at **closing** the seller delivers a *deed* to the buyer.

DEED IN LIEU OF FORECLOSURE the act of giving property back to a lender without **foreclosure.**
Example: Abel, a builder, has a **construction loan** with a $100,000 balance against the house he is building. He offers the house for sale at $100,000 but no one buys it. He does not have the cash to continue to pay interest on the construction loan, and is in **default.** The lender asks for a *deed in lieu of foreclosure.*

DEED OF TRUST an instrument used in many states in lieu of a **mortgage.** Legal title to the property is **vested** in one or more **trustees** to secure the repayment of the loan.
Example: Abel borrows $50,000 on his property in Texas from the Good Money Savings Association. He gives a *deed of trust* that is held in the name of I.M. Honest, a trustee. If Abel **defaults** it will not be difficult for Good Money to gain possession.

DEED RESTRICTION a clause in a deed that limits the use of land. See **covenants.**
Example: A deed might stipulate that alcoholic beverages are not to be sold on the land for 20 years. This is a *deed restriction.*

DEFAULT failure to fulfill an obligation or promise, or to perform specified acts.
Example: The **contract** required the buyer to close within 3 business days. His failure to appear at **closing** constituted a *default* under the contract.

DEFEASANCE a clause in a **mortgage** that gives the borrower the right to redeem the property after **default,** usually by paying the full indebtedness and fees incurred.
Example: Graham defaults on the **balloon payment** of the mortgage. Three days later she pays the balance in cash. The *defeasance* clause allows her to redeem the property. It overrides the provision that grants the property to the lender upon default.

DEFECT IN TITLE any recorded **instrument** that would prevent a **grantor** from giving a **clear title.**
Example: A **mechanic's lien** that was recorded against the property when it was remodeled was a *defect in title*. The grantor had to clear the **lien** by paying the amount due the electrician who filed the lien.

DEFENDANT the party sued in an action at law.
Example: Abel brings suit against a former landlord, Baker, for refusing to return a **security deposit.** In the suit, Baker is the *defendant*.

DEFERRED MAINTENANCE in appraisal, a type of physical **depreciation** owing to lack of normal upkeep.
Example: The appraiser found the following examples of *deferred maintenance* on the subject property:
• broken window glass
• missing roof shingles
• peeling paint
• broken guttering

DEFERRED PAYMENTS payments to be made at some future date.
Example: On a **graduated payment mortgage** the **principal** payments and some interest payments are *deferred* for the first 3 to 5 years.

DEFICIENCY JUDGMENT a court order stating that the borrower stills owes money when the **security** for a loan does not entirely satisfy a defaulted debt.
Example: Upon **default** by the **mortgagor,** a lender **forecloses** on the mortgage. The unpaid balance of the loan is $60,000. The property is sold at public **auction** and brings $50,000. The lender then seeks a *deficiency judgment* against the mortgagor to recover the $10,000 shortage.

DELAYED (TAX-FREE) EXCHANGE a transaction in which a property is traded for the promise to provide a replacement **like-kind property** in the near future. The Tax Reform Act of 1984 allows investment real estate or real property used in a trade or business to be sold with the tax on the gain deferred, provided replacement property is identified within 45 days and closed within 180 days. Other strict requirements must be observed. See also **tax-free exchange.**

DELIVERY transfer of the **possession** of a thing from one person to another.
Example: A man dies leaving no will. A search of his possessions uncovers a **deed** giving valuable land to his nephew. Since the deed has not been *delivered,* the court ruled that the land does not belong to the nephew.

DEMAND LOAN a loan that may be called by the lender at any time.
Example: Abel borrows $10,000 from a bank on a *demand loan* and uses the cash for the downpayment on a parcel of land. The bank may call in the loan and Abel may be forced to sell the property at a distressed price to meet the *demand loan.*

DEMISED PREMISES property subject to lease.
Example: An apartment is rented under a written lease. In the lease, the apartment is referred to as the *demised premises.*

DEMOGRAPHIC pertaining to characteristics of the population, such as race, sex, age, household size, and to population growth and **density.**
Example: As a first step in estimating the demand for new housing units, a **developer** commissions a *demographic* study. The study describes the current population density and rate of growth, the age distribution of the population, and average size of households in the local **market area.**

DEMOLITION destruction and removal of an existing structure from a **site;** necessary to prepare a site for new construction.
Example: A block of old houses in the city is to be converted into a new shopping mall. This conversion will require *demolition* of the houses, site preparation and construction of the mall.

DENSITY the intensity of a land use. See also **land use intensity.**
Example: A 10-acre **subdivision** contains 30 single-family houses. The *density* is 3 dwelling units per **acre.**

DENSITY ZONING laws that restrict **land use intensity.**
Example: A **zoning ordinance** states that all zones designated "R-2" may contain no more than 4 **detached housing** units per **acre.** This is an example of *density zoning.*

DEPLETION a **tax deduction** to account for reduced **land** value due to removing minerals.
Example: The $10,000 tax deduction for *depletion* was allowed because coal was being removed and the land would become virtually worthless when all of the coal was gone.

DEPOSIT money paid in **good faith** to assure performance of a contract. Deposits are commonly used with **sales contracts** and **leases.** If the person who put up the deposit fails to perform, the deposit is forfeited, unless conditions in the contract allow a refund. **Brokers** are to put deposits in a separate checking account pending completion of the contract. See **earnest money.**
Example: Whitman presented a $1,000 check as an earnest money *deposit* on a home she would buy provided she could get a 10% rate, 30-year loan for 80% of the price. The broker deposited the check in an **escrow account,** and refunded it when Whitman could not arrange said loan.

DEPOSIT ACCOUNT an arrangement whereby an individual or organization may place cash under the safekeeping of a financial institution. It is understood that the institution may invest the cash and pay the depositor a specified amount of interest and that the depositor can reclaim the full value of the account according to the agreed upon procedures governing the account.
Example: Town Savings maintains several types of *deposit accounts* for the benefit of its depositors. The accounts provide funds which are used to make mortgage loans.

DEPOSITORY INSTITUTIONS DEREGULATION AND MONETARY CONTROL ACT federal law that represents significant decontrol of federally regulated banks and savings institutions, including gradual phase out of limits on interest rates paid on passbook accounts. **(Regulation Q).**
Example: The *Depository Institutions Deregulation and Monetary Control Act* is a major effort to reform the nation's banking regulations. Among its effects are:
• standardized reserve requirements for banks and **savings and loan associations**
• phase out of deposit interest rate limitations
• authorization for interest-bearing checking accounts
· increased ability for savings and loan associations to make consumer loans
• reduced applicability of state **usury** laws

DEPRECIABLE BASIS see basis (tax); see adjusted tax basis.

DEPRECIABLE LIFE 1. for tax purposes, the number of years over which the cost of an **asset** may be spread. See **accelerated cost recovery.**

Example: Abel buys an apartment complex. For tax purposes the building has a 27½-year *depreciable life.*
2. for **appraisal** purposes, the estimated useful life of an asset.
Example: Baker buys an apartment complex. An appraiser estimates that the roof will last for 15 years, so it has a 15-year *depreciable life.*

DEPRECIABLE REAL ESTATE (TAX) realty that is subject to deductions for **depreciation.** It generally includes property used in a trade or business, or an investment, subject to an allowance for depreciation under **Section 167** of the **Internal Revenue Code.**
Example: Abel buys an apartment complex for $1 million. Of the purchase price, $100,000 is the value of the land, the remaining $900,000 is the value of *depreciable real estate.* Abel uses the **straight-line depreciation** method and a 27½-year remaining depreciable life.

DEPRECIATION (ACCOUNTING) allocating the cost of an **asset** over its estimated **useful life.**
Example: Collins buys a warehouse for $550,000. Of the price, $50,000 is for land, which is not subject to depreciation. Of the remaining $500,000, she claims accounting *depreciation* of $10,000 per year over a 50-year **depreciable life,** despite the fact that the property is expected to increase in value because of the location of the land.

DEPRECIATION (APPRAISAL) a charge against the **reproduction cost** (new) of an **asset** for the estimated wear and **obsolescence.** Depreciation may be physical, functional, or economic.
Example: The estimated reproduction cost (new) of a theater being appraised is $500,000. **Wear and tear** sustained during its life is estimated at $100,000. Functional obsolescence caused by lack of air-conditioning and high ceilings causes an estimated loss of $100,000. It is in a decaying area of the city estimated at causing $100,000 of economic obsolescence. Total *depreciation* is estimated at $300,000.

DEPRECIATION RECAPTURE when real property is sold at a gain and **accelerated depreciation** had been claimed, the owner may be required to pay a tax at ordinary rates to the extent of the excess accelerated depreciation. Excess depreciation on residential real estate after 1980 is recaptured; all depreciation on commercial property after 1980 is recaptured when an accelerated method had been used, under **Section 1250** of the **Internal Revenue Code.** See Figure 44.
Note: The importance of *depreciation recapture* for real estate was minimized by the Tax Reform Act of 1986 which mandated straight-line depreciation for buildings bought after 1986, and eliminated favorable tax rates on long-term capital gains after 1987.

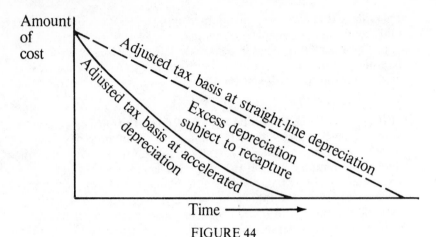

FIGURE 44

DEPTH TABLES a set of percentages indicating the proportion of
site value attributable to each additional amount of depth in the lot.
Example: A commonly used *depth table* (Figure 45).

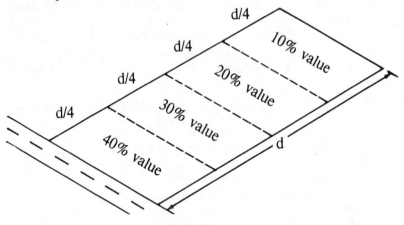

FIGURE 45

DESCRIPTION formal depiction of the dimensions and location of a
property; generally included in **deeds, leases, sales contracts,** and
mortgage contracts for **real property.** See **government rectangular
survey, lot and block, metes and bounds,** for specific methods of
legal description. See also **plat.**
Example: A **sales contract** is executed. A portion of the contract
contains a *description* of the property that simply states the street
address of the house. In the deed conveyed at **closing** a more pre-
cise metes and bounds *description* is included based upon a **survey**
of the property.

DESCRIPTIVE MEMORANDUM a term used to describe an offer-
ing circular of property or securities when a **prospectus** is not
required.

Example: A **syndicator** prepared a *descriptive memorandum* about the property after receiving an exemption from registering the offering by the **Securities and Exchange Commission (SEC).**

DESCENT the acquisition of property by an heir when the deceased leaves no will.
Example: Abel dies without having prepared a will. His wife and son are awarded **title** to Abel's estate by the courts. They are said to acquire title by *descent.*

DETACHED HOUSING **residential** buildings in which each **dwelling** unit is surrounded by freestanding walls and is generally sited on a separate lot. Contrast with **duplex, row house, town house.**
Example: Figure 46.

Detached housing Townhouses

FIGURE 46

DEVELOPER one who transforms **raw land** to **improved** property by use of labor, capital, and **entrepreneur** efforts.
Example: Abel buys 25 acres of land for $10,000 per **acre.** After putting in streets and utilities, dividing it into 100 lots, and building homes on each lot, Abel sells the homes. Abel is a *developer.*

DEVELOPMENT the process of placing improvements on or to a parcel of land. Such improvements may include drainage, utilities, subdividing, access, buildings and any combination of these elements. Also the project where such improvements are being made.
Example: Baker, a developer, acquired a large parcel of land and began the preparation of detailed plans and securing of government permits. Later, the site will be prepared and construction will commence. The *development* will be the first phase of a large multi-use subdivision.

DEVELOPMENT LOAN same as **construction loan.**

DEVISE a gift of real estate by **will** or last testament. Compare **bequeath.**
Example: In his will, Abel *devises* his home to his daughter. He **bequeaths** his automobile to his son.

DEVISEE one who inherits real estate through a will.
Example: Abel dies. The *devisee* in his will receives his land.

DIRECTIONAL GROWTH the location or direction toward which a city is growing.
Example: the *directional growth* of Boom Town is toward the northeast (Figure 47).

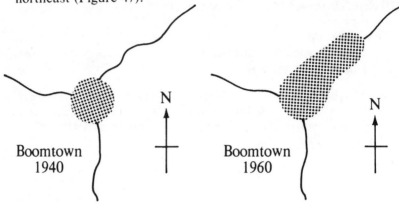

Boomtown 1940 N

Boomtown 1960 N

FIGURE 47

DIRECT REDUCTION MORTGAGE a loan that requires both **interest** and **principal** with each payment such that the level payment will be adequate for **amortization** over the loan's term. See **level payment mortgage.**
Example: Collins borrows $50,000 at 10% interest over a 30-year term, using a *direct reduction mortgage.* Her monthly principal and interest payment of $438.79 will fully amortize (pay off) the loan over 30 years.

DISCHARGE IN BANKRUPTCY the release of a bankrupt party from the obligation to repay **debts** that were, or might have been, proved in a **bankruptcy** proceeding.
Example: A real estate resort **developer** filed for bankruptcy. He owned 2,000 unsold vacation lots, and owed $2 million on land acquisition loans. The court granted a *discharge in bankruptcy* for these loans and allowed the creditor to dispose of the lots.

DISCLAIMER 1. a statement whereby responsibility is rejected.
Example: Abel, a certified public accountant, is asked to write up the **financial statements** of Baker without testing (auditing) the validity of the statements. Abel's report provides a *disclaimer* in which he states that he did not examine the financial statements and does not accept responsibility for their accuracy.
2. Renunciation of ownership of **property.**
Example: Because it was no longer profitable, Baker *disclaimed* apartments that had become dilapidated.

DISCOUNT the difference between the **face amount** of an obligation and the amount advanced or received.
Example: Abel sells land for $100,000 and receives a $60,000

mortgage at 7% interest as part of the payment. Abel then sells the mortgage (the right to collect payments on the mortgage) at a $15,000 *discount*, thereby receiving $45,000.

DISCOUNT BROKER a licensed broker who provides brokerage services for a lower commission than that typical in the market. Generally, the services provided are less extensive than those of a full service broker. Many discount brokers charge a flat fee rather than a percentage of the selling price. See **flat fee broker.**
Example: Henson, a *discount broker*, offers to list a property for a 3% commission. Henson will refer prospective buyers to the seller and prepare a sales contract. The seller is expected to show the property and negotiate directly with the buyer.

DISCOUNTED CASH FLOW a method of investment analysis in which anticipated future cash income from the investment is estimated and converted into a rate of return on initial investment based on the time value of money. In addition, when a required rate of return is specified, a net present value of the investment can be estimated.
Example: An asset may be purchased for $1,000. It is expected to generate $100 in income per year for 10 years, after which time it is expected to sell for $1,200. *Discounted cash flow* analysis shows that the internal rate of return on the investment is expected to be 11.2% per year.

DISCOUNTED LOAN one that is offered or traded for less than its face value. See **discount, discount points.**
Example: When the Deavers sold their house, they accepted a second mortgage as part of the purchase price. The Deavers then sold the loan to an investor for 75% of its face value. The purchaser of this *discounted loan* is entitled to all interest and principal payments stipulated in the mortgage contract.

DISCOUNT POINTS amounts paid to the lender (usually by the seller) at the time of origination of a loan, to account for the difference between the market interest rate and the lower face rate of the note (often required when **VA loans** are used).
Example: At the time of loan application, conventional mortgages are being made at 15%. The maximum rate on an FHA loan is 14½% with 4 *discount points* added to compensate for the lower face rate of interest. If the loan is for $50,000, the points will require an additional payment of $2,000 at closing. (The 4 points equals 4% of $50,000, which is $2,000.)

DISCOUNT RATE 1. a **compound interest** rate used to convert expected future income into a present value. See **capitalization rate, present value of annuity, present value of one.**
Example: A *discount rate* of 10% applied to a $100 sum expected to be received in one year results in a present value of $90.90. (The **present value of one** for one year is 0.909.)

2. the rate charged member banks who borrow from the **Federal Reserve System.** Same as **rediscount rate.**
Example: See **rediscount rate.**

DISCRIMINATION applying special treatment (generally unfavorable) to an individual solely on the basis of the person's race, religion, or sex.
Example: Abel is accused of *discrimination* under the Fair Housing Laws because he refused to rent apartments to nonwhite families.

DISINTERMEDIATION situation when deposits are removed from a financial intermediary, such as a **savings and loan association,** and invested in other **assets,** generally for the purpose of obtaining higher yields.
Example: Figure 48.

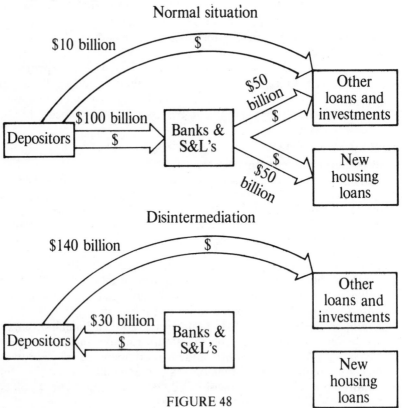

Normal situation

$10 billion — $
$100 billion $
Depositors → Banks & S&L's
$50 billion $ → Other loans and investments
$50 billion $ → New housing loans

Disintermediation

$140 billion — $
$30 billion $
Depositors ← Banks & S&L's
Other loans and investments
New housing loans

FIGURE 48

DISPOSSESS PROCEEDINGS the legal process by a **landlord** to remove a **tenant** and regain possession of property. See **eviction.**
Example: After not having received rent for 3 months, the landlord began *dispossess proceedings* to eject the tenant.

DISTRAINT the legal right of a **landlord** to seize a tenant's personal property to satisfy payment of back rent.

Example: Abel is 6 months in **arrears** on rent. Landlord Baker obtains a court order to seize Abel's furniture to satisfy the rent due. Baker is exercising his right of *distraint*.

See **workout.**

Example: An **apartment building** is financed with **mortgages** that require $25,000 in **annual debt service.** Because of high vacancies and rising expenses, **net operating income** drops to $20,000. The owners have ceased making loan payments because their resources are insufficient to pay the **negative cash flow.** The property is considered *distressed property.*

DISTRESSED PROPERTY real estate that is under **foreclosure** or impending foreclosure because of insufficient income production.

DOCUMENTARY EVIDENCE evidence in the form of written or printed papers.

Example: During court proceedings, a **sales contract** was entered in the record as *documentary evidence* of the agreement made between the **plaintiff** and the **defendant.**

DOMICILE the state in which one makes his or her principal residence.

Example: Mason's job requires her to travel throughout the United States. Although she owns property in several states, Mason's *domicile* is New York, where she has her principal residence. Mason is subject to the laws of New York concerning automobile registration, voting rights, payment of taxes, and other matters.

DOMINANT TENEMENT land that benefits from an **easement** on another property. The other property, which usually is **adjacent,** is the **servient tenant.**

Example: In Figure 49 the owner of Parcel A has a right-of-way easement to the road by going across Parcel B.

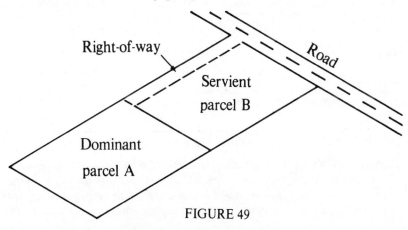

Right-of-way

Road

Servient parcel B

Dominant parcel A

FIGURE 49

DONEE a recipient; as of a gift.
 Example: Collins was the *donee* of an **estate;** she takes the **property** as a gift.

DONOR one who gives.
 Example: Whitman was the *donor* of land that she gave to charity; she had owned the land in **fee simple.**

DORMER 1. a window projecting through a sloping roof (single dormer); 2. the roofed structure containing such a window (shed dormer).
 Example: Figure 50.

Shed dormer
Single dormer

FIGURE 50

DOUBLE DECLINING BALANCE a method of **depreciation** for tax purposes whereby twice the **straight-line** rate is applied to the remaining depreciable balance of an asset. See **declining balance depreciation.**
 Example: Table 14 is a depreciation schedule for a property with depreciable basis of $10,000 and **depreciable life** of 5 years, using the **double declining balance** method.

TABLE 14

Year	Remaining balance	Rate*	Annual deduction
1	$10,000	.40	$4,000
2	6,000	.40	2,400
3	3,600	.40	1,440
4	2,160	.40	864
5	1,296	.40	518

*.40 = twice the straight-line rate of 20% per year for a 5-year life asset.

DOUBLE TAXATION taxation of the same income at 2 levels.
 Example: A corporation earns $25,000 of **net income.** The corporation pays a $5,000 corporate income tax, then distributes $20,000 in dividends to its shareholders, who pay an $8,000 tax on this

dividend income. The corporation's earnings are subject to *double taxation*.

DOWER under **common law,** the legal right of a wife or child to part of a deceased husband's or father's property. See **curtesy.**
Example: In some states a widow can enforce *dower* rights to claim part of her deceased husband's **estate,** regardless of provisions in his will.

DOWN PAYMENT the amount one pays for property in addition to the **debt** incurred.
Example: Abel buys a house for $50,000. He arranges a $30,000 **first mortgage** and a $5,000 **second mortgage.** The *down payment* he needs is $15,000, which he pays in cash at **closing.**

DOWNZONING the act of **rezoning** a tract of land for a less intensive use than the existing use or permitted use.
Example: Arlington had a booming single-family residential market, but was not attracting industry. The owner of a large tract of land zoned for industrial use asked for a *downzoning* to **single-family housing** use to develop the land immediately.

DRAGNET CLAUSE a provision in a **mortgage** that pledges several properties as **collateral.** A **default** on one mortgage constitutes a default on the one with the *dragnet*.
Example: A real estate investor was in financial straits. She failed to pay a certain **mortgage.** The holder of the mortgage on a different property, which was not in **default,** enforced the *dragnet* clause in its mortgage by **foreclosing.**

DRAW a periodic advance of funds from a construction lender to a **developer. Construction loans** generally provide for a schedule of draws, either at regular intervals during construction or pending construction of specific segments of the structures.
Example: A developer arranges a construction loan of $500,000. The funds are to be advanced in a series of *draws* as follows:
• $50,000 upon completion of final plans and **specifications**
• $200,000 upon completion of the foundation
• $150,000 upon completion of the frame, external surfaces, and roof
• $100,000 upon internal finishing

DRY MORTGAGE same as **nonrecourse** mortgage.

DUE-ON-SALE CLAUSE a provision in a **mortgage** that states the loan is due upon the sale of the property.
Example: Collins owes on a $30,000 mortgage loan against her house at an 8% interest rate. She wants to sell the house to a buyer who will assume the mortgage. The lender says that the $30,000

loan is *due upon the sale* of the house so it cannot be assumed by the buyer. The lender adds that he will **waive** the due-on-sale provision if the interest rate is escalated to 16%.

DUAL CONTRACT the illegal or unethical practice of providing 2 different **contracts** for the same transaction.
Example: Abel wants to purchase a home from a builder for $50,000 but has no cash for the **down payment.** The builder suggests that they prepare a fictitious contract for $60,000 and try to borrow 90% of $60,000. The bank's attorney discusses the *dual contract* and explains that they could be guilty of attempted **fraud.**

DUMMY an individual or **entity** that stands in the place of the **principal** to a transaction.
Example: Abel wants to borrow from a bank $100,000 to build houses to sell. Abel requests his attorney to establish a *dummy* **corporation** with $500 of **equity.** The dummy borrows the $100,000 from the bank and, in turn, lends it to Abel as a **nonrecourse** loan.

DUPLEX 1. two dwelling units under one roof.
Example: General floor plan for a *duplex* (Figure 51).
2. an apartment having rooms on two floors.
Example: An artist in a Manhattan *duplex* apartment enjoyed the sunlight that came in from the upper floor to his studio below.

FIGURE 51

DURESS compulsion to do something because of a threat.
Example: Abel tells Baker that unless Baker will sell his property to Abel for $1,000, Abel will physically harm Baker. Baker signs

the **contract** under *duress*, but can later **void** it by showing he acted under duress.

DUTCH COLONIAL an early American style, moderate sized, 2 to 2½ story house with a gambrel roof and eaves that flare outward.
Example: Figure 52.

Eaves flare outward
Off-center chimney
Central entrance
Dutch door
Gambrel roof
2 or 2½ stories
Small pane windows

FIGURE 52

DWELLING a place of residence.
 Examples: The following are *dwellings:*
 • apartment
 • hotel
 • mobile home
 • nursing home
 • single-family house

E

EARNEST MONEY a **deposit** made by a purchaser of real estate to evidence **good faith.**
 Example: It is customary for the buyer to give the seller *earnest money* at the time a **sales contract** is signed. The earnest money generally is credited to the **down payment** at **closing.** Until closing a

broker must hold earnest money in a separate account. See also **commingle.**

EASEMENT the right, privilege, or interest that one party has in the land of another.
Example: The right of public utility companies to lay their lines across others' property is a utility *easement.*

EASEMENT BY NECESSITY the right of an owner to cross over another's property for a special necessary purpose.
Example: Figure 53.

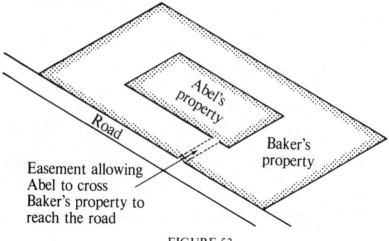

FIGURE 53

EASEMENT BY PRESCRIPTION continued use of another's property for a special purpose can ripen into a permanent use if conditions are met.
Example: Although Abel can reach the highway by another path, for the last 10 years, Abel has been traveling across Baker's property to reach the highway. Since Abel has been doing this for the length of time required by state law, Abel can continue to do so despite Baker's protests, because Abel has achieved an *easement by prescription* (Figure 54).

EASTLAKE HOUSE a nineteenth century style house with three-dimensional ornamentation made with a chisel, gouge, and lathe rather than the scroll saw. Many of the parts of the ornamentation resemble furniture legs and knobs. This distinctive type of ornamentation is the major characteristic of this style and separates the Eastlake style house from the Queen Anne or Carpenter Gothic style.
Example: Figure 55.

Abel's property

Abel's easement by prescription

Baker's property

Road

Highway

FIGURE 54

Shingle covered gable roof

Parts resemble furniture legs

Tower or turret

Open front porch

Rows of spindles

FIGURE 55

ECONOMIC BASE industry within a geographic **market area** that provides employment opportunities that are essential to support the community.

177

Example: Steel is the *economic base* for Pittsburgh. For each steelworker added to the economic base there is another job added in service employment (physician, lawyer, switchboard operator, barber). Each new job brings 2 people to the community (spouse, children, nonworking parents, etc.).

ECONOMIC DEPRECIATION loss of value from all causes outside the property itself. See **depreciation (appraisal).**
Example: An expensive private home may drop in value when an industrial plant is built nearby. This is a form of *economic depreciation* that must be considered in the appraisal of the property.

ECONOMIC LIFE that remaining period for which real estate **improvements** are expected to generate more income than **operating expenses** cost. See **useful life.**
Example: Figure 56.

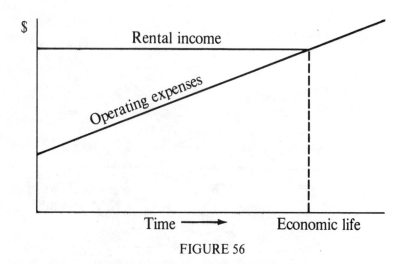

FIGURE 56

ECONOMIC OBSOLESCENCE Same as **economic depreciation.**

ECONOMIC RENT 1. in economics, the cost commanded by a factor that is unique or inelastic in supply.
Example: The portion of rental income attributable to the land is often considered *economic rent,* since the land will exist no matter what the rental rate. In this context, *economic rent* carries a connotation of being "unearned" by its owner.
2. in appraisal, the **market rent.** Contrast with **contract rent.**
Example: Big Buy Foods is using a store for $1,000 per month rent. If the landlord could rent the store on a new **lease** now, it would command $4,000 per month. The $1,000 is the **contract rent** and the $4,000 is the *economic rent.*

EFFECTIVE AGE the age of a property based on the amount of **wear and tear** it has sustained.
Example: Collins' house was built twelve years ago. Because she keeps it in excellent condition it shows only as much wear as a typical 5-year-old house. Collins' house therefore has an *effective age* of 5 years.

EFFECTIVE RATE the true rate of return considering all relevant **financing** expenses. See **annual percentage rate.**
Example: Abel borrows $10,000 on a one-year bank loan. He pays **2 discount points** and a 10% **face interest rate.** He repays the loan at the end of the year, with interest. Since he really received only $9,800 at the start of the loan and repaid $11,000, the *effective rate* was greater than 10%. It was approximately 12.25%.

EGRESS access from a land parcel to a public road or other means of exit.
Example: Figure 57.

A lot with *egress* A lot without *egress*

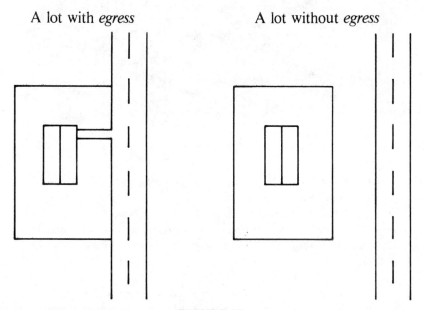

FIGURE 57

EJECTMENT action to regain possession of **real property,** when there is no **lease.**
Example: The holder of a **conditional sales contract,** through an action in *ejectment,* regains possession when the buyer **defaults.**

ELIZABETHAN OR HALF TIMBER STYLE an English style, 2- or 2½-story house, often with part of the second story overhanging

the first. It has less stone work and is less fortlike than the Tudor. Stone and stucco walls with half timbers are most common. **Example:** Figure 58.

Second
floor
overhangs 2 or 2½ stories Small
first floor leaded
 Complicated high- casement
Massive peaked roof windows
sculptured
chimney Half timbers

 Nogging

FIGURE 58

EMBLEMENT a growing crop. Annual crops are generally considered **personal property.**
Example: Abel, a **tenant,** planted corn on Baker's, land. Three days prior to harvesting, Baker informs Abel that the **land lease** has expired. Abel has the right to *emblements* and so can harvest the corn.

EMINENT DOMAIN the right of the government or a public utility to acquire property for necessary public use by **condemnation**; the owner must be fairly compensated.
Example: Ready Watts Electric Company is granted the power of *eminent domain* by the state government. This allows the company to acquire private property for specified purposes through the process of condemnation.

EMPTY NESTERS a couple whose children have established separate households; important segment of the housing market, since empty nesters often seek to reduce the amount of housing space

they occupy. Thus empty nesters are one source of demand for smaller housing units.

Example: The Etons have raised 2 children who are now grown and have families of their own. As *empty nesters,* the Etons no longer have need for the big 4-bedroom home they occupy. They purchase a 2-bedroom **town house,** which provides all the space they require.

ENCROACHMENT a building, a part of a building, or an obstruction that physically intrudes upon, overlaps, or **trespasses** upon the property of another.

Example: A part of the building on lot A is an *encroachment* on lot B. This situation probably occurred because of a faulty **survey** of lot A (Figure 59).

FIGURE 59

ENCUMBRANCE any right to or interest in land that affects its value. Includes outstanding **mortgage** loans, unpaid taxes, **easements, deed restrictions.**

Example: *Encumbrances* on Blackacres include 3 mortgages, 4 **leases,** a **mechanic's lien,** and a deed restriction preventing the sale of alcoholic beverages on the land.

END LOAN same as **permanent mortgage.**

ENDORSEMENT 1. the act of signing one's name, as the payee, on the back of a check or **note,** with or without further qualification; the signature itself.

Example: Figure 60.

2. offering support or credibility to a statement.

Example: The American Association of Homebuilders *endorses* the use of brick as a construction material.

181

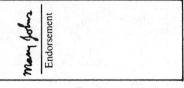

Pay $1000 to Mary Johns on August 20, 1989 *John Jones*	
Front	Back

FIGURE 60

ENERGY EFFICIENT as applied to buildings, generally indicating the existence of extra insulation, weatherproofing, and/or special features and equipment designed to reduce the cost of energy for heating, cooling and hot water.

Example: An *energy efficient* home might have an extra layer of insulation in the attic and walls, relatively air tight exterior, a heat pump and a solar hot water heater. An *energy efficient* furnace might be designed to burn fuel more completely and capture more of the heat generated.

ENERGY TAX CREDITS a reduction in income tax, generally based on the cost of installing insulation and other energy-saving devices.
Note: At the federal level, *energy tax credits* generally expired before 1987 and were not renewed by the 1986 tax act.

ENTITY the legal form under which property is owned. See also **corporation, limited partnership, partnership.**
Examples: The benefits and risks of owning real property may vary depending on the *entity* that is formed. Among the options are:
• corporation
• individual ownership (see **tenancy** entries)
• **joint venture**
• **limited partnership**
• **partnership**
• **real estate investment trust**

ENTREPRENEUR an individual who generates business activity. A businessman or businesswoman. Often associated with one who takes business risks.
Example: Business owned by *entrepreneurs* include:
• auto dealerships
• restaurants
• retail stores
• wholesale distributing companies

ENVIRONMENTAL IMPACT STATEMENT (EIS) an analysis of the expected effects of a development or action on the surrounding natural and fabricated environment. Such statements are required

for many federally supported developments under the National Environmental Policy Act of 1969.

Example: Abel seeks to develop a large **subdivision** and obtain **FHA-** insured financing for lot purchasers. Abel must prepare an *environmental impact statement* detailing the effects the development will have on the natural and fabricated environment.

ENVIRONMENTAL PROTECTION AGENCY (EPA) an agency of the U.S. government established to enforce federal pollution abatement laws and to implement various pollution prevention programs.

Example: The *Environmental Protection Agency* requires **permits** for the siting of manufacturing facilities that may introduce pollution into the air or public waters. The *EPA* also provides grants to local governments to assist in construction of sewage treatment plants.

EQUAL CREDIT OPPORTUNITY ACT a federal law, enacted in 1974, to discourage discrimination by lenders on the basis of sex or marital status. Amended in 1976 to prohibit discrimination on the basis of age, race, color, religion, national origin, or receipt of public assistance.

Example: Collins, a divorced woman, is denied a **mortgage** loan by a local **savings and loan association.** She feels she would have obtained the loan if she were a man. She sues the savings and loan under the *Equal Credit Opportunity Act.* Her steady, permanent part-time earnings are to be considered in granting the loan.

EQUALIZATION BOARD a government agency that determines the fairness of taxes levied against properties.

Example: Abel feels the **market value** estimate of his property made by the tax **assessor** is too high. Appeals to the assessor do not result in satisfying Abel's complaint. Abel may take his case to the *Equalization Board* in the hope of reducing the amount of his **assessment.**

EQUITABLE CONVERSION a legal doctrine in some states in which, under a **contract of sale,** buyers and sellers are treated as though the **closing** had taken place in that the seller in possession has an obligation to take care of the property. See **equitable title.** Note: A contract of sale may specify which party incurs risk of loss until closing.

Example: Though the legal **title** has not passed, the law holds that there has been an *equitable conversion* that effectively **vests** the property in the buyer.

EQUITABLE TITLE the interest held by one who has agreed to purchase but has not yet closed the transaction.

Example: Collins has agreed in writing to buy Baker's house, with **closing** to be arranged in 2 weeks. In the interim valuable minerals are found on the property. Since Collins has *equitable title,* the minerals belong to her. Similarly, if the property were **condemned** for public use, the value gain or loss would be hers.

EQUITY the interest or value that the owner has in real estate over and above the **liens** against it.

Example: A property has a **market value** of $100,000. The owner currently owes $60,000 in **mortgage** loans that are against the property. The owner's *equity* is $40,000. See Table 15

TABLE 15

Market value	$100,000
Liens	−60,000
Equity	$ 40,000

EQUITY KICKER see **kicker.**

EQUITY OF REDEMPTION the right of an owner to recover property that has been **foreclosed.**

Example: Abel's property has been foreclosed because he has not met his **mortgage** obligation. If he raises enough money within the period of time set by state laws, he may reclaim the property by paying the **principal, interest,** and legal expenses, under *equity of redemption* laws.

EROSION the gradual wearing away of land through processes of nature, as by streams and winds.

Examples:
- Deep gullies cut into unvegetated earth, caused by rainwater *erosion*
- The Grand Canyon formed by *erosion* from the Colorado River
- The Sphinx in Egypt, disfigured by wind *erosion*

ESCALATOR CLAUSE a provision in a **lease** that requires the **tenant** to pay more rent based on an increase in costs. Same as **stop clause.**

Example: A lease requires the tenant to pay increases in real estate taxes over the amount in the base year. Taxes were $1000 for the base year; and were $1,250 the following year. The tenant's rent is *escalated* by $250.

ESCHEAT the **reversion** of property to the state in the event that the owner dies without leaving a will and has no legal heirs.

Example: Abel dies without a will. No heirs are found. His property *escheats* to the state.

ESCROW an agreement between 2 or more parties providing that certain instruments or property be placed with a third party for safekeeping, pending the fulfillment or performance of a specified act or condition.

Example: The **deed** to the property and the **earnest money** were both placed in *escrow* pending fulfillment of other conditions to the **contract.**

ESCROW ACCOUNT same as **trust account.**

ESCROW AGENT any person engaged in the business of receiving **escrows** for deposit or delivery.

Example: The **title** company is serving as the *escrow agent.* It holds the **earnest money** and **deed,** pending fulfillment of other conditions to the **contract** (Figure 61).

FIGURE 61

ESTATE the degree, nature, and extent of interest that a person has in **real property.**

Example: The highest form of an *estate* is **fee simple,** under which the owner can use the property at will and dispose of it without restriction.

ESTATE AT SUFFERANCE the wrongful occupancy of property by a tenant after the **lease** has expired. See **dispossess proceedings.**

Example: Abel's lease expired and he remained on the property. He has an *estate at sufferance* and may be ejected at the landlord's whim.

ESTATE AT WILL the occupation of real estate by a tenant for an indefinite period, terminable by one or both parties at will.

Example: Under an *estate at will,* the landlord may evict the tenant at any time, and the tenant may vacate at any time. The tenant may have certain rights, however, such as ownership of **emblements** (crops as a result of annual cultivation).

ESTATE FOR LIFE an interest in property that terminates upon the death of a specified person. See **life estate.**

Example: Abel deeded his wife an *estate for her life.* When she dies the property will go to Abel's son. She may use the property and may not commit **waste,** but normal **wear and tear** is acceptable.

ESTATE FOR YEARS an interest in land allowing possession for a specified and limited time.
Example: The **tenant** under a 5-year **lease** holds an *estate for years*.

ESTATE IN REVERSION an **estate** left by the **grantor** for himself or herself, to begin after the termination of some particular estate granted by him or her.
Example: All landlords have an *estate in reversion* which becomes theirs to possess when the **lease** expires.

ESTATE IN SEVERALTY see **tenancy in severalty.**

ESTATE TAX a tax based on the value of property left by the deceased. Since 1987, the estate and gift tax laws exempt approximately $600,000 of property.
Example: Abel dies, leaving $800,000 worth of **assets.** The estate of Abel will pay an *estate tax.* Abel's heirs may also be liable for an **inheritance tax** under their state law.

ESTOPPEL a doctrine of law that stops one from later denying facts which that person once acknowledged were true and others accepted on **good faith.**
Example: Abel signs a certificate acknowledging that he owes $10,000 on a **mortgage** as of a certain date. Later he contends that he owed only $5,000. Abel is prevented from asserting this new contention under *estoppel.*

ESTOPPEL CERTIFICATE a document by which the **mortgagor** (borrower) certifies that the mortgage debt is a **lien** for the amount stated. The debtor is thereafter prevented from claiming that the balance due differs from the amount stated.
Example: The Good Money Savings Association asks Abel to sign an *estoppel certificate,* which he does. Good Money Savings then sells the mortgage to Baker, who buys with confidence. Abel is later estopped (prevented) from denying that he owed the money.

ESTOVERS the legally supported right to take necessities from property. Contrast with **waste.**
Example: Mason has a **life estate** on property. She needs to cut timber for firewood to heat the residence. The **remainderman,** Baker, complains that Mason is damaging the property. The law supports Mason's use of the *estovers* as she has been doing.

ET AL. abbreviation of the Latin *et alii,* "and others."
Example: Property owned by John Jones and several others may be referenced as "John Jones, *et al.*"

ET CON legal term signifying "and husband." See **et ux.**

Example: Hereby signed and delivered by Ellen Smith *et con.*

ET UX abbreviation of the Latin *et uxor,* which means "and wife."
Example: A house is sold by Bill Baker *et ux.* Baker and his wife both must sign the **deed.**

EVICTION a legal proceeding by a **lessor** (landlord) to recover possession of property.
Example: When the **tenant** fails to comply with the **lease** agreement (skipping rent payments, unauthorized use of the property, etc.), the landlord may seek *eviction* of the tenant. If successful, this action will terminate the rights of the tenant to use the property.

EVICTION, ACTUAL exists where one is removed from the property, either by force or by process of law.
Example: An apartment tenant may be subject to *actual eviction,* in which case, a notice will be served requiring the tenant to vacate the apartment within a specified time interval.

EVICTION, CONSTRUCTIVE exists when, through the fault of the landlord, physical conditions of the property render it unfit for the purpose for which it was leased.
Example: A landlord may allow the physical condition of an apartment building to deteriorate to the point that the premises are no longer safe for occupancy. A tenant may be able to terminate the **lease,** order *constructive eviction,* and end **liability** for future rent payments.

EVICTION, PARTIAL exists where the possessor of the property, such as a tenant, is deprived of a portion thereof.
Example: A law firm leases a floor of an office building. The **landlord** wishes to make substantial modifications to one side of the building. Because of the disruption caused by the work, the tenant and landlord agree to a *partial eviction* from the property affected by construction. The tenant's rent is reduced accordingly.

EVIDENCE OF TITLE documents, such as **deeds,** that demonstrate ownership.
Example: The property owner kept the **deed** in a bank vault because it is important *evidence of title.*

EXCHANGE under **Section 1031** of the **Internal Revenue Code, like-kind property** used in a trade or business or held as an investment can be exchanged tax-free. See also **boot, realized gain, recognized gain, delayed (tax-free) exchange.**
Example: Collins *exchanges* her farm worth $100,000, but subject to a $20,000 **mortgage,** for Baker's apartments worth $80,000.

187

EXCLUSIVE AGENCY LISTING employment **contract** giving only one **broker,** for a specified time, the right to sell the property and also allowing the owner alone to sell the property without paying a **commission.**
Example: Graham gives Quick Sale Realty an *exclusive agency listing* on her house. If an agent of Quick Sale or any other **brokerage** firm sells the house during the time of the listing, Quick Sale is entitled to a commission. If Graham sells the house herself, no commission is earned.

EXCLUSIVE RIGHT TO SELL LISTING employment **contract** giving the **broker** the right to collect **commission** if the property is sold by anyone, including the owner, during the term of the agreement. See also **multiple listing service.**
Example: Abel give Quick Sale Realty an *exclusive right to sell listing* on his house. If the house is sold during the time of the listing, Quick Sale is entitled to a commission.

EXCULPATORY CLAUSE a provision in a **mortgage** allowing the borrower to surrender the property to the lender without personal **liability** for the loan.
Example: Abel buys land for $100,000, paying $40,000 cash and gives a $60,000 mortgage to the seller with an *exculpatory clause.* The **market value** of the land drops suddenly to $55,000. Abel abandons the mortgaged property, losing the $40,000 investment but keeping everything else he owns.

EXECUTE to sign a **contract;** sometimes, to perform a contract fully.
Example: Generally when a buyer and seller sign a **sales contract,** they *execute* the contract.

EXECUTED CONTRACT a **contract** whose terms have been completely fulfilled.
Example: At the **closing,** all parties signed the contract, which made it an *executed contract.*

EXECUTOR a person named in a **will** to carry out its provisions for the disposition of the estate.
Example: Abel specifies in his will that his attorney shall serve as its *executor.* The attorney, at the appropriate time, assures that Abel's property is distributed according to the will.

EXECUTORY CONTRACT a **contract** under which one or more parties has not yet performed.
Example: Abel orally has agreed to buy Baker's land, and Baker's attorney has drafted a contract. At this stage it is *executory* because neither Abel nor Baker has signed it.

EXECUTRIX a woman who performs the duties of an **executor.**

Example: Abel appoints his wife as *executrix* for his estate. She will not need a real estate **license** to sell the property he leaves.

EXEMPTION an amount provided by law that reduces taxable income or taxable value.
Example: Personal exemptions, generally based on the number of people in a household, reduce taxable income.
Example: Homestead exemptions, offered in many jurisdictions, reduce the value of real estate that would otherwise be subject to **ad valorem tax.**

EXPOSURE (MARKET) the advertising, whether free or paid, of property that is for sale.
Example: Real estate agents provide market *exposure* through such devices as:
• classified ads in local papers
• for sale signs on the premises
• inclusion in **multiple listing service**
• displays in their office

EXTENDED COVERAGE insurance that covers specific incidences normally excluded from standard insurance policies.
Example: A homeowner who lives **adjacent** to a golf course discovers that the standard homeowners' insurance policy does not cover damage due to errant golf balls. An *extended coverage* policy may be obtained, however, to cover such damage.

EXTENSION an agreement between 2 parties to extend the time period specified in a **contract.**
Example: When a tenant is unable to **vacate** the property at the termination of the **lease,** an *extension* may be granted by the **landlord.**
Example: When a seller fails to clear the **title** in time for a **closing,** an *extension* of the closing date may be granted.

F

FACADE the outside front wall of a building.
Example: *Facade* materials for a building include:
• aluminum
• brick
• glass
• masonry
• wood

FACE AMOUNT same as **face value.**

FACE INTEREST RATE the percentage interest that is shown on the loan document. Compare with **annual percentage rate, effective rate.**
Example: A mortgage has an 8% *face interest rate,* $10,000 **face value,** and 30-year **amortization** term. If market interest rates are 12%, the **market value** of the loan is $7,200.

FACE VALUE the dollar amount, shown by words and/or numbers, on a document. Compare with **market value; see amortization.**
Example: A **mortgage** has a *face value* of $10,000, **amortization** term of 30 years, and 8% **face interest rate.** It will be amortized in 13 years to $8,000 by annual payments.

FAIR CREDIT REPORTING ACT a federal law that allows individuals to examine and correct information used by **credit** reporting services.
Example: Abel wishes to purchase property from Baker under an **installment land contract.** Baker refuses to make the contract because of Abel's poor **credit rating.** Under the *Fair Credit Reporting Act,* Abel may demand disclosure of Baker's source of information and then take steps to correct any misinformation in the report.

FAIR MARKET RENT the amount that a property would command if it were now available for **lease.** Contrast with **contract rent.** See **economic rent, rent control, Section 8 housing.**
Example: The *fair market rent* for an apartment is estimated at $400 per month. Under **Section 8,** the **tenant** is required to pay 20% of income toward rent; the **landlord** would receive a payment from the government to make up the difference.

FAIR MARKET VALUE a term, generally used in **property tax** and **condemnation** legislation, meaning the **market value** of a property.
Example: Property taxes generally are assessed at some ratio of *fair market value.*
Example: When property is condemned for public use, the owner is entitled to be compensated at *fair market value.*

FALSE ADVERTISING describing property in a misleading fashion.
Example: Examples of false advertising might include:
• representing a property as not being in a **floodplain** when, in fact, it is
• stating, without **caveat,** that a property will appreciate in value
• denying structural flaws that are known to exist

FANNIE MAE nickname for **Federal National Mortgage Association.**

FARMER'S HOME ADMINISTRATION (FmHA) an agency, within the U.S. Department of Agriculture, that administers assistance programs for purchasers of homes and farms in small towns and rural areas.
Example: Abel wishes to develop housing for the elderly in a rural area. He may apply to the *Farmer's Home Administration* for a special 40-year **mortgage** loan.

FEASIBILITY STUDY a determination of the likelihood that a proposed development will fulfill the objectives of a particular investor.
Example: A *feasibility study* of a proposed **subdivision** should:
• estimate the demand for housing units in the area
• estimate the **absorption rate** for the project
• discuss legal and other considerations
• forecast **cash flows**
• approximate investment returns likely to be produced

FEDERAL an early American style of house that is box-shaped and has a flat roof.
Example: Figure 62.

FIGURE 62

FEDERAL DEPOSIT INSURANCE CORPORATION (FDIC) a public corporation, established in 1933; insures up to $100,000 for each depositor in most **commercial banks**. Has own reserves and can borrow from the U.S. Treasury.
Example: The First National Bank has a **liquidity** difficulty and cannot pay depositors who want to withdraw their money. The *FDIC* pays each depositor the full **prinicpal** amount, up to $100,000.

FEDERAL FAIR HOUSING LAW a federal law that forbids **discrimination** on the basis of race, color, sex, religion, or national origin in the selling or renting of homes and apartments. See **steering**.
Example: Broker Abel is contacted by a black couple wishing to purchase a home. Although homes are currently for sale in several all-white neighborhoods, Abel maintains there are no houses available in these areas. Abel may be prosecuted under the *Federal Fair Housing Law*.

FEDERAL HOME LOAN BANK SYSTEM a federally created banking system primarily intended to assure **liquidity** to member **savings and loan associations**.
Example: *Federal Home Loan Bank System* (Figure 63).

FIGURE 63

FEDERAL HOME LOAN MORTGAGE CORPORATION (FHLMC) an organization that purchases **mortgage** loans, mostly from **savings and loan associations**.
Example: ABC Savings and Loan Association sells mortgage loans to the *Federal Home Loan Mortgage Corporation* to gain funds for originating new mortgage loans.

FEDERAL HOUSING ADMINISTRATION (FHA) an agency, within the U.S. Department of Housing and Urban Development, that

administers many loan programs, loan **guarantee** programs, and **loan insurance** programs designed to make more housing available.
Example: Abel wishes to purchase a home but lacks funds for a large **down payment.** Through a program provided by the *Federal Housing Administration,* Abel may obtain a loan for up to 97% of the purchase price.

FEDERAL NATIONAL MORTGAGE ASSOCIATION (FNMA) a corporation that specializes in buying mortgage loans, mostly from **mortgage bankers.** It adds **liquidity** to the mortgage market. Nicknamed **Fannie Mae,** FNMA is owned by its stockholders, who elect 10 to its Board of Directors. The U.S. president appoints the other 5 directors.
Example: A mortgage banker originates conventional and **FHA loans** and periodically sells them to the *Federal National Mortgage Association.*

FEDERAL RESERVE SYSTEM the central federal banking system that regulates and provides services to member **commercial banks.** Also has the responsibility for conducting federal monetary policy.
Example: The system consists of the Federal Reserve Board and a series of regional Federal Reserve Banks.

FEDERAL SAVINGS & LOAN ASSOCIATION a member of the **Federal Home Loan Bank System** and the **Federal Savings and Loan Insurance Corporation.**
Example: City Federal Savings and Loan is a *federal savings and loan association.* Its activities are regulated by the Federal Home Loan Bank Board. Home Savings is a state chartered savings and loan association regulated by state government.

FEDERAL SAVINGS AND LOAN INSURANCE CORPORATION (FSLIC) an agency of the federal government that insures depositors in **savings and loan associations** against loss of **principal.** Most deposits, including passbooks and saving certificates, are insured up to a maximum amount per account.
Address: Federal Savings and Loan Insurance Corporation
1700 G Street, N.W.
Washington, D.C. 20552
Example: Graham may deposit savings in a **savings and loan association** without fear of losing her money, since her deposit, up to $100,000, is insured by the *Federal Savings and Loan Insurance Corporation.*

FEDERAL TRADE COMMISSION (FTC) a federal agency, headquarters in Washington, D.C., that regulates advertising and other promotion and sales practices of firms engaged in interstate com-

merce. The FTC does *not* regulate interstate land sales (HUD), anticompetitive activities (JUSTICE), or sale of securities (SEC).

Example: Abel, a builder, was found guilty of false television advertising by the *FTC*.

FEE SIMPLE or FEE ABSOLUTE or FEE SIMPLE ABSOLUTE absolute ownership of **real property;** owner is entitled to the entire property with unconditional power of disposition during the owner's life, and upon his death the property descends to the owner's designated heirs.

Example: The only power that can require Abel to sell his land is **eminent domain;** he owns the property in *fee simple,* so there is no other interest.

FEE SIMPLE DEFEASIBLE a type of property ownership in which the grant of **title** or duration of ownership is dependent on a specified condition.

Example: A *fee simple defeasible* may be granted on the condition that the property be used for an orphanage home (termed "fee simple subject to a condition subsequent").

Example: A *fee simple defeasible* may be granted as long as the property is held as a wildlife refuge (termed "fee simple determinable").

FHA MORTGAGE LOAN a **mortgage** loan insured by the FHA. See **Federal Housing Administration.**

Example: Abel wishes to purchase a home but has insufficient cash to make a large down payment. By obtaining an *FHA mortgage loan,* Abel may borrow more than the customary 80% of value, with the FHA insuring the loan amount.

FHLB Federal Home Loan Bank; a federally chartered bank that supplies **credit** to member banks. See **Federal Home Loan Bank System.**

FIDELITY BOND an assurance, generally purchased by an employer, to cover employees who are entrusted with valuable property or funds.

Example: A landlord employs a resident manager who, among other duties, collects the **rent.** To safeguard these funds during the collection process, the landlord purchases a *fidelity bond* on the resident manager.

FIDUCIARY one who acts, in a financial role, in the best interests of others.

Example:
• a **broker** is a *fiduciary* for the seller
• a banker is a *fiduciary* for the bank's depositors

- an attorney may be a *fiduciary* for the client
- a **trustee** is a *fiduciary* for the **beneficiaries**

FILTERING DOWN the process whereby, over time, a housing unit or neighborhood is occupied by progressively lower-income residents.
Example: Many older residences near the downtown of big cities were once occupied by the upper classes, but have *filtered down* to the relatively poor. At some point in the filtering process, many large houses may be converted into rented **multifamily housing.**

FINANCE CHARGE interest or certain other fees charged to a **credit** customer.
Example: A customer makes purchases of $400 on credit. Payment is made one month later. Based on an annual percentage rate of interest of 18%, a *finance charge* of $6.00 ($.\frac{18}{12} \times \400) is added to the bill.

FINANCIAL INTERMEDIARY a firm, such as a bank or savings and loan association, which performs the function of collecting deposits from individuals and investing them in loans and other securities. Also includes credit unions and mutual savings banks. See **disintermediation.**
Example: First National Bank serves as a *financial intermediary* by taking in deposits and placing them in mortgage loans and various securities. In doing so, the bank links individual investors with demanders of credit and the financial markets.

FINANCIAL LEVERAGE the use of borrowed money to complete an investment purchase.
Example: The effects of *financial leverage* on return on **equity** are shown in Table 16.

(Note: If **debt service** required is high compared to income, effect of leverage may be to *reduce* return to equity.)

TABLE 16

No Leverage		Leverage with 50% Debt	
Cost	$100,000	Cost	$100,000
Debt	0	Debt	$50,000
Equity	$100,000	Equity	$50,000
Income	$20,000	Income	$20,000
Debt service	0	Debt service	−7,500
Cash to equity	$20,000	Cash to equity	$12,500
Return on equity	$\frac{20,000}{100,000} = 0.20$	Return on equity	$\frac{12,500}{50,000} = 0.25$

FINANCIAL MANAGEMENT RATE OF RETURN (FMRR) a method of measuring investment performance that is a variation on the **internal rate of return** method. The user specifies 2 after-tax reinvestment rates:

i_L: a safe, liquid rate, obtainable for liquid deposits.

i_R: a run-of-the-mill rate, which can be earned from typical investments over a long term.

Negative cash flows are generally **discounted** to a present value at the i_L rate, inflows are compounded to the investment resale date at i_R. The FMRR is the rate that equates the present value of negative cash flows to the future value of inflows.

Example: An investment requires a $10,000 negative cash flow for the first 3 years, then offers $8,500 of cash inflows for years 4-10. If i_L is 5%, the negative cash flows have a present value of $27,232. If i_R is 10%, the cash inflows will become $80,641. The *FMRR* is 11.47% because that is the rate at which $27,232 would grow to $80,641 in 10 years with **compound interest.**

FINANCIAL STATEMENT one that shows income and expense for an accounting period, or **assets, liabilities** and **equity** as of a point in time.
Example: Table 17.

Table 17

Income statement		Balance sheet		
Rental income	$5,000	Assets	Liabilities & equity	
Interest expense	−2,000			
Depreciation	−1,000	Buildings $40,000	Mortgage $30,000	
Real estate taxes	− 500	Land 10,000	Equity 20,000	
Net income	$1,500	Total $50,000	Total $50,000	

FINANCING borrowing money to buy property. See **creative financing.**
Example: The following are examples of *financing:*
• obtaining a **mortgage** loan on a purchase
• **assumptions of a mortgage** from a seller
• arranging for the seller to take a loan as part of the purchase price
• arranging an **installment sale**

FINDER'S FEE money paid to someone other than a **broker** who locates suitable property or a purchaser. Prohibited or limited in most states.
Example: Broker Abel has a **listing** on a particular property. Baker knows several people interested in such property. Abel arranges with Baker to provide a *finder's fee* should one of the **prospects** identified by Baker purchase the property.

FINISH OUT ALLOWANCE a provision in a lease for an office or retail space that provides a certain sum or amount per square foot to the **tenant** to customize the space provided.

Example: A retail tenant leases space for 5 years at a $10 per square foot annual rental rate. The **lessor** provides four concrete walls and a concrete floor, and will pay the tenant a *finish out allowance* of up to $4 per square foot for costs to customize the space.

FIREPROOF having all exposed surfaces constructed of noncombustible materials or protected by such materials.

Example: The exterior surface of the building was composed of brick, aluminum siding, and asbestos shingles, thereby making the exterior *fireproof*.

FIRE-RESISTIVE able to withstand exposure to flame of a specified intensity or for a specified time. Compare **fireproof**.

Example: The interior walls in the house were made of *fire-resistive* material. The walls were designed to resist igniting at temperatures below 1,000 degrees if not exposed for more than one hour.

FIRST MORTGAGE a **mortgage** that has priority as a **lien** over all other mortgages. In cases of **foreclosure** the first mortgage will be satisfied before other mortgages. See **junior mortgage, second mortgage.**

Example: A property costing $100,000 is financed with a *first mortgage* of $75,000, a second mortgage of $15,000, and $10,000 in cash. If the borrower **defaults** and the property is sold upon foreclosure for $80,000, the holder of the *first mortgage* will receive the full amount of the unpaid **principal** plus legal expenses. The second mortgage holder will receive any excess after the first mortgage has been satisfied.

FIRST REFUSAL RIGHT same as **right of first refusal.**

FIRST-YEAR DEPRECIATION same as **additional first-year depreciation.**

FISCAL YEAR a continuous 12-month time interval used for financial reporting; the period starts on any date after January 1 and ends one year later.

Example: For agencies of the federal government, *fiscal year* 1988 refers to the time between October 1, 1987 and September 30, 1988.

FIXED PAYMENT MORTGAGE a loan secured by real property which features a periodic payment of interest and principal which is constant over the term of the loan. All *fixed payment mortgages* are **fixed rate mortgages,** but some fixed rate mortgages may have variable payments, such as a **graduated payment mortgage.**

Example: A *fixed payment mortgage* calls for 360 monthly payments of interest and principal of $1,000. Added to that amount is a payment to an escrow account for taxes and insurance which may change from year to year.

FIXED RATE MORTGAGE a loan secured by real property featuring an interest rate that is constant for the term of the loan. Contrast **adjustable rate mortgage.**

Example: A *fixed rate mortgage* is originated with an interest rate of 10% for a term of 30 years. The rate will remain at 10% until the loan is retired or the **due-on-sale clause** is exercised at resale of the property.

FIXING-UP EXPENSES (TAX) expenses incurred for the purpose of physically preparing a personal residence for sale. Qualified fixing-up expenses may be deducted from the sales price to determine the price that must be spent in the purchase of another residence to defer **capital gains** taxes on the sale of the old one.

Example: Abel spends $500 for painting and repairs on a home prior to sale. The house sells for $75,500 and costs $7,000 in transaction costs. The adjusted sales price is calculated in Table 18.

TABLE 18

Sale price	$75,500
Fixing-up expenses	− 500
Selling expenses	− 7,000
Adjusted sales price	$68,000

Abel must spend at least $68,000 on a new residence to avoid **capital gains** on the sale.

FIXTURES **improvements** or **personal property** attached to the land so as to become part of the real estate. Tests to determine whether an item is a fixture include:
- intent of the parties (was it intended to remain?)
- method of annexation (how is it affixed?)
- relation of the parties (was it expected to be part of a tenant's business?)
- adaptation of the article (is it essential to the building?)

Example: Abel sells his house. The contract of sale includes all of the real estate. Baker, the buyer, believes that the ceiling fan in the dining room is a *fixture*, but Abel claims it as **personal property.**

FLAT 1. an apartment, generally on one level.

Example: A 2-room *flat* is an apartment having 2 rooms.

2. a **level payment mortgage** or **lease** requirement.

Example: A **flat lease** is one that requires level payments each month or other specified period.

FLAT FEE BROKER a licensed broker who charges a fixed fee for the provision of brokerage services instead of a commission based on a percentage of the sales price of the property. See **discount broker.**
Example: Kramden, a *flat fee broker,* charges $5,000 to arrange the sale of a home, no matter what price is agreed upon by the buyer and seller. If a sale is not consummated within the term of the listing contract, no fee is paid.

FLAT LEASE a rental agreement that requires periodic level rent payments.
Example: Pattern of payments for a one-year *flat lease* with monthly payments (Figure 64).

Flat lease payments

FIGURE 64

FLEXIBLE PAYMENT MORTGAGE (FPM) a home-purchase loan plan that allows the borrower to pay interest-only for the first several years of the term. FPM's were authorized by the **Federal Home Loan Bank** Board in 1974 with 2 restrictions:
1. monthly payments must be sufficient to cover **interest** on the **principal**
2. after 5 years, payments must be sufficient to amortize the principal over the remaining term
Example: A young couple purchases a home with a *flexible payment mortgage.* The principal is $50,000, interest rate at 14%, and term of 30 years. For the first 5 years, the monthly payments are $583.33. For years 6 through 30, payments will be $601.88. If they had obtained a **level payment mortgage,** monthly payments would have been $592.44 over the entire loan. See the mortgage tables in the Appendix.

FLOAT 1. the interval of time after a deposit or withdrawal is made and before the transaction is credited or deducted.
Example: Abel writes a check to pay a **debt** to Baker. Baker deposits the check in a bank other than the one used by Abel. Abel's bank may have a *float* of 2 or 3 days before Baker's bank collects the money.
2. the difference between a **variable interest rate** and the **index** to which it is pegged.

Example: A bank makes construction loans at 3% over the **prime rate.** The 3% is the *float.*
3. to incur a debt.
Example: To fund a project, Atlas Company may *float* a loan or *float* a **bond** issue.

FLOOD INSURANCE an insurance policy that covers property damage due to natural flooding. Flood insurance is offered by private insurers but is subsidized by the federal government.
Example: Abel owns a home within an area defined as a 100-year **floodplain.** If the local community is participating in a special federal program, Abel may purchase *flood insurance* to cover damage from periodic flooding.

FLOODPLAIN a level land area subject to periodic flooding from a **contiguous** body of water. Floodplains are delineated by the expected frequency of flooding. For example, an annual floodplain is expected to flood once each year.
Example: Figure 65.

FIGURE 65

FLOOR-AREA RATIO the arithmetic relationship of the total square feet of a building to the square footage of the land area.

FLOOR LOAN the minimum that a lender is willing to advance. See also **gap loan.**
Example: Abel, a lender, agrees to a $700,000 floor on a $1,000,000 permanent loan. When construction is complete, the borrower will receive a $700,000 *floor loan;* when the property is 80% occupied the full $1,000,000 will be loaned.

FLOOR PLAN the arrangement of rooms in a building, or a one-plane diagram of that arrangement.
Example: The home is difficult to sell due to its awkward *floor plan.* One must pass through a bedroom to enter the master bed-

Formula: floor-area ratio $= \dfrac{\text{building area}}{\text{land area}}$

The floor-area ratio is $0.25 \left(\dfrac{50' \times 50'}{100' \times 100'} \right)$

Example: Figure 66.

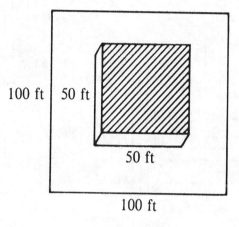

100 ft

50 ft

50 ft

100 ft

FIGURE 66

room. There is no direct access from the garage to the kitchen and the living room is too small.

FNMA Federal National Mortgage Association, which buys and sells existing residential mortgages; nicknamed **Fannie Mae.**

FORCE MAJEURE an unavoidable cause of delay or of failure to perform a **contract** obligation in time.
Example: A *force majeure* clause is often inserted in a construction contract to protect the **contractor** from delays due to weather, labor disputes, and other unavoidable incidents.

FORECLOSURE a termination of all rights of a **mortgagor** or the **grantee** in the property covered by the **mortgage.** Statutory foreclosure is effected without recourse to courts, but must conform to laws (statutes). Strict foreclosure forever bars **equity of redemption. See default.**
Example: The lender *forecloses* to gain possession of mortgaged land after the borrower missed 3 payments.

FORFEITURE loss of money or anything else of value because of failure to perform under **contract.**
Example: Because Baker, the prospective purchaser, failed to keep up payments under the **land contract,** he *forfeited* all his rights to the property.

FRAME HOUSE a house constructed with a wooden frame over which is placed some form of siding or **veneer**.
Example: A *frame house* (Figure 67).

Wood siding Wooden frame Brick veneer

FIGURE 67

FRANCHISE an arrangement between a franchisor and franchisee through which the franchisee uses the company name of the franchisor and is provided specified business services in exchange for a franchise fee. The fee is usually an initial purchase requirement plus an ongoing percentage of gross sales of the business.
Example: In real estate brokerage, locally owned firms may operate as *franchises* of such national companies as Century 21, Gallery of Homes and Red Carpet. The franchisor advertises the name and logo of the company, offers training for salespersons, and offers or provides other services to the franchisee.

FRAUD the intentional use of deception to cause another person to suffer loss.
Example: Abel purchases property from Baker. Abel later discovers that Baker did not hold **title** to the property and had no right to sell. Baker was guilty of *fraud* and is liable for damages suffered by Abel in the purchase of the property.

FREDDIE MAC nickname for **Federal Home Loan Mortgage Corporation.**

FREE AND CLEAR TITLE title to a property without **encumbrances.** Generally used to refer to a property free of **mortgage**

debt. See **clear title, marketable title.**

Example: *Free and clear title* is generally desired by the purchaser of a property. This requires clearing any **clouds on the title** and satisfying any **liens** that may exist.

FREEHOLD an interest in **real estate** without a predetermined time span.

Example: A **fee simple** or a **life estate** is considered a *freehold* estate because there is not a specified time limit. A **lease** is less than freehold because it has a specified termination date.

FRENCH PROVINCIAL a French style formal, 1½- to 2½-story house that is perfectly balanced with a high steep hip roof and curved-headed upper windows that break through the cornice.

Example: Figure 68.

1½ to 2½ stories Perfectly balanced
Curve-headed upper windows that break through cornice
Brick
Formal looking high steep hip roof
Some have 2 symmetrical 1-story wings
French windows and shutters

FIGURE 68

FRONTAGE the linear distance of a piece of land along a lake, river, street, or highway.
Example: Road *frontage* (Figure 69).

FIGURE 69

Example: Lake *frontage* (Figure 70).

FIGURE 70

FRONT FOOT a standard measurement of land, applied at the **front-age** of its street line. Used for lots of generally uniform depth in downtown arces.
Example: The lot in Figure 71 sold for $30,000, or $300 per *front foot.*

FRONT MONEY cash necessary to start a development project.
Example: *Front money* is generally required for purchasing a **site**, preparing plans and studies, obtaining **permits**, and obtaining loan **commitments.**

FIGURE 71

FSBO for sale by owner. A term referring to properties on the market that are not listed with a real estate broker. Pronounced "fizz-bo."
Example: The Mathers are attempting to find a buyer for their home by placing an ad in the paper and putting up a sign in the yard. Such activities indicate the existence of a *FSBO*.

FULL DISCLOSURE a requirement to reveal all information pertinent to a transaction.
Example: Under *full disclosure,* a **broker** is required to give the buyer all known facts about the physical, financial, and economic condition of the subject property.

FULLY INDEXED RATE in conjunction with **adjustable rate mortgages,** the interest rate indicated by the sum of the current value of the **index** and **margin** applied to the loan. This rate is the interest rate which is used to calculate monthly payments in the absence of constraints imposed by the **initial rate** or **caps.** See **teaser rate, adjustable rate mortgage.**
Example: An adjustable rate mortgage is indexed to the one-year treasury bill rate. The current value of the index is 6%. A margin of 2.5 percentage points is applied to the loan. The *fully indexed rate* is 8.5%. However, the loan has an initial rate of 7.5% which determines the interest rate for the first year. When the rate is adjusted, the *fully indexed rate* rises to 10%. A cap of 2 percentage points limits the adjustment in the rate to only 9.5%. If there had been no cap, the interest rate would have risen to 10%.

FUNCTIONAL DEPRECIATION loss of value from all causes within the property, except those due to physical deterioration. See **obsolescence.**
Example: A poor **floor plan** or outdated plumbing fixtures are types of *functional depreciation.*

FUNCTIONAL MODERN OR CONTEMPORARY HOUSE a post World War II style house with an exterior style that is an integral part of the overall design. Its function is to enclose some living areas with modern materials while integrating the indoor and outdoor space into one unit.
Example: Figure 72.

Extensive use of glass

No ornamentation

Modern building materials

FIGURE 72

FUNCTIONAL OBSOLESCENCE same as **functional depreciation.**

FUTURE INTEREST a property right or estate that may not be enjoyed until some time in the future.
Example: When a **life estate** is created, the **remainder** is a *future interest.*
Example: The lender's right to a portion of net **appreciation,** under a **shared appreciation mortgage**, is a *future interest.*

G

GABLE ROOF one with a triangle, with the ridge forming an angle at the top and each eave forming an angle at the bottom.
Example: Figure 73.

GAIN an increase in money or **property** value. See **capital gain, realized gain, recognized gain.**
Example: Abel sells for $10,000 land that he bought for $4,000. He recognizes a $6,000 gain excluding property and income taxes.

Gable

FIGURE 73

GAMBREL ROOF one having two slopes on two sides with a steeper lower slope than the upper, flatter sections.
Example: Figure 74.

Gambrel

FIGURE 74

GAP LOAN one that fills the difference between the **floor loan** and the full amount of the **permanent loan.**
Example: A **developer** arranges a permanent **mortgage** that will fund $1,000,000 when the apartments she is building are 80% occupied. From completion of construction until 80% occupancy is reached, the mortgage is only $700,000. The developer arranges a *gap loan* of $300,000 for the **rent-up period.**

GARDEN APARTMENTS a housing complex whereby some or all **tenants** have access to a lawn area.
Example: Abel is now enjoying a steak that he grilled outside his *garden apartment* (Figure 75).

GENERAL CONTRACTOR one who constructs a building or other **improvement** for the owner or **developer.** May retain a construction labor force or use **subcontractors.** See **contractor.**
Example: Collins, a landowner, has architectural plans and **specifications** for an office building. She enters into a **contract** with Baker, a *general contractor,* to build the structure. Baker hires

subcontractors who put up the foundation, walls, roof, electrical and plumbing systems, etc.

GENERAL LIEN a **lien** that includes all of the property owned by the debtor, rather than a specific property.
Example: Abel failed to pay 3 months of rent and moved out. Baker, the **landlord,** obtained a *general lien* against Abel by going to secure a **judgment** against Abel. If Abel doesn't pay the back rent, Baker will apply for a specific lien against Abel's furniture and then have it sold.

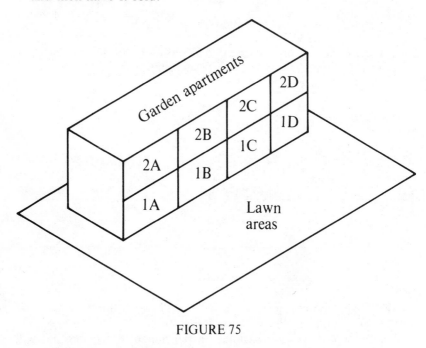

FIGURE 75

GENERAL PARTNER in a **partnership**, a partner whose **liability** is not limited. All partners in an ordinary partnership are general partners. A **limited partnership** must have at least one general partner.
Example: The *general partner* in a limited partnership is the **syndicator** who arranges the purchase, seeks investors, and assumes all liabilities of the partnership.

GENERAL WARRANTY DEED a **deed** in which the **grantor** agrees to protect the **grantee** against any other claim to **title** of the property and provides other promises. See **warranty deed.**
Example: Abel received a *general warranty deed* for land he bought from Baker. Five years later a defect is found. Mrs. Cabel, whose deceased husband sold the land to Baker, actually owns

one half of the property. Abel can claim restitution from Baker for the half because the deed warranties against all defects.

GENTRIFICATION the displacement of lower-income residents by higher-income residents in a neighborhood. Generally occurs when an older neighborhood is rehabilitated or revitalized.
Example: In the past, many large older homes in Inman Park, Atlanta, had been converted to boarding houses. Recently, middle-income families have been buying these houses and converting them back into **single-family homes.** The lower-income residents are often forced to move to surrounding areas and are replaced by the middle-income renovators. As this process is repeated, *gentrification* of the neighborhood occurs.

GEORGIAN a large, English style, formal 2- or 3-story rectangular house that is characterized by its classic lines and ornamentation.
Example: Figure 76.

Cornice with dentils

Gable or hip roof

2 or 3 stories

Balustrade

2 large chimneys high above each end

Palladian style window

Slate or copper roof

Double-hung windows

Glass lights

Quoins

Brick

FIGURE 76

GIFT DEED a **deed** for which **consideration** is love and affection, and no material consideration is involved.

Example: Abel, who is on the brink of **bankruptcy, executes** a *gift deed* to his wife. Since there is no consideration and the apparent reason for the transfer was to remove the property from the reach of Abel's creditors, the deed might not be valid. In other situations the gift deed would be upheld.

GIFT TAX federal tax upon a monetary gift to a relative or friend. Generally, each person may give up to $10,000 per year to each **donee** without imposition of a federal gift tax. On higher gifts, there may be a gift tax, or the gift may affect the **donor's estate tax.**
Example: Mr. and Mrs. Abel together give $20,000 this year to each of 3 sons ($60,000 total). There will be no *gift tax* imposed.

GI LOAN same as **VA loan.**

GINNIE MAE nickname for **Government National Mortgage Association.**

GINNIE MAE PASS THROUGH a **pass-through certificate** secured by a pool of mortgage loans insured by the Government National Mortgage Association, an arm of the federal government.
Ginnie Mae pass throughs often provide high yields with security to investors, although the returns may be affected by the pattern of loan repayments on the mortgages in the pool.

GOOD FAITH an act done honestly.
Example: Abel pays $1,000 to Baker as a *good faith* **deposit** on land Baker offers for sale. Baker doesn't own the land and doesn't plan to buy it, so his acceptance of the deposit was not in *good faith.*

GOODWILL a business **asset** of **intangible value** created by customer and supplier relations.
Example: Diversified Enterprises, Inc. bought Acme Hardware Co. They paid a total of $200,000, which included $100,000 for the **property**, $50,000 for **inventory**, and $50,000 for *goodwill.*

GOVERNMENT NATIONAL MORTGAGE ASSOCIATION (GNMA) a government organization to assist in housing finance. There are 2 main programs:
1. to **guarantee** payments to investors in mortgage-backed securities
2. to absorb the **write-down** of low-interest rate loans that are used to finance **low-income housing**
 See **secondary mortgage market.**
Example: Good Money Mortgage Bankers, who have originated $3,000,000 of **FHA** and **VA mortgages**, have issued **participation**

mortgage certificates, backed by the mortgages, to investors. *GNMA* guarantees the participation certificates (Figure 77).

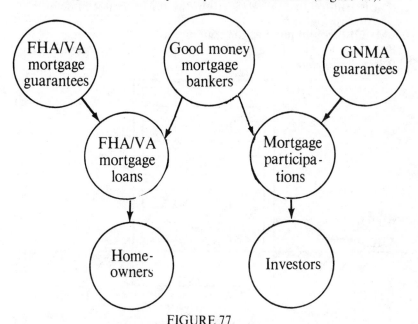

FIGURE 77

GOVERNMENT RECTANGULAR SURVEY a rectangular system of land **survey** that divides a district into 24-square mile **quadrangles** from the **meridian** (north-south line) and the **base line** (east-west line); the tracts are divided into 6-mile-square parts called *townships,* which are in turn divided into 36 tracts, each 1 mile square, called **sections**.

Example: *Government Rectangular Survey* System (Figure 78).

FIGURE 78

GRACE PERIOD the period during which one party may fail to perform without being considered in **default**.

Example: Rent is due on the first of each month, but the tenant requested and received a 10-day *grace period* from the landlord. If rent is paid on or before the 10th, the tenant is not in default.

GRADE 1. ground level at the foundation.
Example: Part A of the building in Figure 79 is above *grade;* Part B is below *grade*.

FIGURE 79

2. to prepare a smooth surface on a site.

Example: Machinery was brought to the **site** to *grade* the **land** in preparation for the foundation.

GRADED LEASE same as **graduated lease.**

GRADIENT the slope, or rate of increase or decrease in the elevation of a surface; usually expressed as a percentage:

$$\text{Gradient} = \frac{\text{vertical rise or fall}}{\text{horizontal distance}}$$

Example: The lot in Figure 80 has a 10% *gradient:*

$$\frac{10'}{100'} = 0.10$$

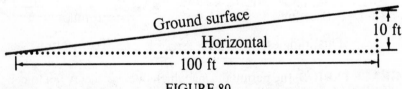

FIGURE 80

GRADUATED LEASE a lease that provides for graduated changes, at stated intervals, in the amount of rent.

Example: A 5-year *graduated lease* calls for annual rent increases of 5%. The yearly payments are shown in Figure 81.

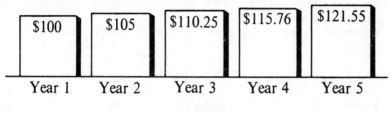

| $100 | $105 | $110.25 | $115.76 | $121.55 |
| Year 1 | Year 2 | Year 3 | Year 4 | Year 5 |

FIGURE 81

GRADUATED PAYMENT MORTGAGE (GPM) a mortgage requiring lower payments in early years than in later years. Payments increase in steps each year until the installments are sufficient to amortize the loan.

Example: A *GPM* may be made in which monthly payments rise by a set percentage after each year for the first 4 years. The payments would look like Figure 82.

FIGURE 82

GRADUATE REALTORS® INSTITUTE (GRI) an educational program sponsored by the **National Association of Realtors®** or State Boards.

Example: Broker Abel attends 3 approved courses offered by the California Association of Realtors®, and he passes the examinations. His new business cards read: Broker Albert Abel, *GRI*.

GRANDFATHER CLAUSE when a law is changed or a new law is passed, those whose specific activity was legal under the previous

law are often allowed to continue, by virtue of this provision.

Example: All real estate **brokers** are allowed to continue to practice as brokers after licensure requirements increase. The new law affects only new **licensees**; old licensees are *grandfathered*.

GRANT a technical term used in deeds of **conveyance** of property to indicate a transfer.

Example: In a **deed**, Abel *grants* his land to his daughter in **fee simple**.

GRANTEE the party to whom the **title** to **real property** is conveyed; the buyer.

Example: Edith Andrew Abel is the *grantee* under a **deed** from her father, Albert Abel.

GRANTOR anyone who gives a **deed**.

Examples: *Grantors* include:
• an individual (former) owner
• a bankruptcy **trustee**
• a **guardian** for an **incompetent**

G.R.I. graduate of the Realtors® Institute, which is affiliated with the **National Association of Realtors®. See Graduate Realtors Institute.**

GROSS AREA the total floor area of a building, usually measured from its outside walls.

Example: The *gross area* of a 2-story office building (Figure 83) that completely covers a 100′ X 100′ tract of land is 20,000 square feet (10,000 square feet for each story). Exterior walls, interior hallways, stairwells, and utility rooms absorb 4,000 square feet, so the **net leasable area** is 16,000 square feet.

GROSS INCOME total income from property before any expenses are deducted.

Example: A building with 10,000 net rentable square feet of floor space rents for an average of $10 per square foot. **Concessions** in the lobby produce an additional $20,000 in annual income. An average 5% **vacancy rate** is maintained. Two measures of *gross income* are shown in Table 19.

Table 19

Total **rent** income	$100,000	(10,000 × $10)
Concession income	20,000	
Potential gross income	$120,000	
Vacancy loss	− 5,000	(.05 × $100,000)
Effective gross income	$115,000	

FIGURE 83

GROSS INCOME MULTIPLIER (GIM) same as **gross rent multiplier.**

GROSS LEASE a lease of property whereby the landlord **(lessor)** is responsible for paying all property expenses, such as taxes, insurance, utilities, and repairs.
Example: In a certain apartment complex the **landlord** pays for all utilities and taxes. The lease is a *gross lease*, since the landlord receives rent as a gross figure and must pay **operating expenses.**

GROSS PROFIT RATIO in an **installment sale,** the relationship between the gross profit (gain) and the **contract price.** The resulting fraction is applied to periodic receipts from the buyer to determine the taxable gain from each receipt.
Example: Land, held as a **capital asset** by Collins, is sold for $10,000. Collins tax basis was $4,000, so the resulting gain was $6,000. The *gross profit ratio* is 60% ($6,000 divided by $10,000 equals 60%). Collins accepted a $1,000 cash **downpayment** with the $9,000 balance of the price to be paid over 3 years. Of each amount paid toward the principal, 60% is gain to be taxed and the balance is a nontaxable return of capital. See **contract price.**

GROSS RENT MULTIPLIER (GRM) the sales price divided by the **contract** rental rate.
Example: The sales price is $40,000; the gross monthly **contract rent** is $400; the *GRM* = $40,000 ÷ $400 = 100. GRM may also be expressed as the number of years of rent equaling the purchase price ($40,000 ÷ $4,800 annual rent = a *GRM* of 8.333).

215

GROUND LEASE one that rents the land only.
Example: The landowner, Abel, gives a 50-year *ground lease* to Baker. Baker must pay $5,000 per year rent. At the end of the 50-year period, Abel owns the land **free and clear** and whatever **improvements** that Baker left on the property.

GROUND RENT the rent earned by leased land.
Example: The Good Title Company owns an office building situated on a **site** owned by the Widget Makers Retirement Fund. The site is leased to Good Title on a long-term basis and requires the payment of *ground rent* to the Widget Makers Retirement Fund on a semiannual basis.

GROWING EQUITY MORTGAGE (GEM) a **mortgage** loan in which the payment is increased by a specific amount each year, with the additional payment amount applied to **principal** retirement. As a result of the added principal retirement, the **maturity** of the loan is significantly shorter than a comparable **level payment mortgage.**
Example: Long purchased her home with a *growing equity mortgage.* Long's monthly payments will increase by 5% each year, with the increased amount applied to principal. Long will **retire** the loan in about half the time required to retire a comparable loan with fixed payments.

(TO) GUARANTEE (A LOAN) to agree to **indemnify** the holder of a loan all or a portion of the unpaid **principal** balance in case of **default** by the borrower. See also **VA mortgage loan.**
Example: Abel takes out a **VA mortgage loan** to purchase a home. The Veterans Administration *guarantees* the loan. In case foreclosure is threatened because Abel fails to make the payments, the VA will reimburse the lender for losses up to the amount guaranteed.

GUARANTY an assurance provided by one party that another party will perform under a contract.
Example: Fred Garrison is an experienced developer. His daughter, Ruth, decides to branch out and start her own company. The construction lender requires a *guaranty* from Fred Garrison before granting Ruth Garrison a loan for her first project.

GUARDIAN one appointed by a court to administer the personal affairs or property of an individual who is not capable of such duties.
Example: The *guardian* of an orphan **minor** signs a **deed** to sell property inherited by the minor, to pay the minor's educational expenses.

GUIDELINE LIVES depreciable lives, for buildings and equipment,

that are used in trade or business. Generally applied to **assets** bought before 1981; the **accelerated cost recovery system** applies to depreciable assets bought since then.

Example: *Guideline lives* for certain assets:
- apartments—40 years
- dwellings—45 years
- hotels—40 years
- warehouses—60 years

H

HABENDUM CLAUSE the "to have and to hold" clause that defines or limits the quantity of the **estate** granted in the **deed**.
Example: The *habendum clause* "to have and to hold for one's lifetime" creates a **life estate**.

HALF BATH a room in a residence which contains a toilet and wash basin but no bathing facilities, such as a bathtub or shower stall. A three-quarter bath contains a shower but no bathtub.
Example: The two story home has two full baths upstairs and a *half bath* downstairs.

HANDYMAN'S SPECIAL in real estate classified advertising, generally refers to a house that requires extensive repair and remodeling, selling at a relatively low price.
Example: The Williams' looked at a *handyman's special* that needed new carpeting and repainting. They bought it for $50,000, spent $12,000 (not counting the value of their own labor) to repair it, then resold it for $75,000, providing them with a $13,000 profit.

HANGOUT the remaining balance of a loan when the **term** of the loan is beyond the term of a **lease**.
Example: A lender offers a 30-year loan on property that is leased to Big Buy Foods for the next 25 years. In 25 years the loan balance will be $100,000, which is the *hangout*. The lender estimates that the land value in 25 years will greatly exceed $100,000, so concern for the hangout is minimized.

HAZARD INSURANCE a form of insurance that protects against certain risks, such as from fires or storms.
Example: **Mortgage** lenders frequently require that owners maintain *hazard insurance*, at least to the extent of the mortgage debt.

HEARING a formal procedure, with issues of fact or law to be tried, in which parties have a right to be heard. Similar to a trial and may

result in a final order.
Example: State **real estate commissions** hold *hearings* to investigate complaints filed against licensed salespersons.

HECTARE a metric land measurement equal to about 2.471 **acres** or about 107,637 square feet.
Example: Abel sold 6 *hectares* of land in Puerto Rico for $20,000.

HEIR one who inherits **property**.
Example: A person can decide on *heirs* by leaving a **valid** will. If one dies **intestate**, state laws determine who the heirs are.

HEIRS AND ASSIGNS a term often found in **deeds** and **wills** to grant a **fee simple** estate.
Example: Abel wills property to "Baker, *heirs and assigns*." Upon inheriting the property, Baker can sell it or will it to **heirs**.

HEREDITAMENTS any property, whether real or personal, tangible or intangible, that may be inherited.
Example: Buildings, lands, and **leaseholds** are examples of *hereditaments*.

HIGHEST AND BEST USE an **appraisal** term meaning the legally and physically possible use that, at the time of appraisal, is most likely to produce the greatest net return to the land and/or buildings over a given period.
Example: A vacant lot in the city is valued at $10,000 if developed for a **single-family house**, $20,000 as an **apartment building**, $25,000 as a retail store, and $30,000 as a small chemical processing plant. Because of **restrictions** on water supply and disposal, the chemical plant is not physically or legally possible. **Zoning** laws prohibit commercial development. Therefore, the *highest and best use* of the lot is for an apartment building.

HIGH RISE generally a building that exceeds 6 stories in height and is equipped with elevators.
Example: A *high-rise* building is constructed to include retail space on the first floor, 8 floors of office space, 10 floors of **condominium** units, and a club/restaurant on the 20th floor.

HIGH VICTORIAN ITALIANATE a nineteenth century style house with three different kinds of window arches, the primary distinguishing characteristic of this style. The arches are straight-sided, flat-topped and rectangular.
Example: Figure 84.

Flat-topped arch Large brackets

Straight-
sided arch Entrance way with Hip roof
columns supporting
Rectangular entablature Three
arch different
Symmetrical types
bays of arches

FIGURE 84

HIP ROOF one formed by four walls sloped in different directions
with the two longer sides forming a ridge at the top.
Example: Figure 85.

Hip

FIGURE 85

HISTORIC DISTRICT a designated area where the buildings are
considered to have some significant historic character. Such des-
ignation makes the area eligible for certain federal assistance pro-
grams and protects the area from clearance in conjunction with
federally sponsored programs.

Example: Older areas, such as the French Quarter in New Orleans, enjoy protection by being designated as *historic districts.*

HISTORIC STRUCTURE a building that is officially recognized for its historic significance has special status under the 1976 Tax Reform Act, which encourages **rehabilitation** and discourages **demolition** or substantial alteration of the structure. In 1981 a special tax law allowed a 25% **tax credit** for rehabilitation of **certified historic structures**, reduce to 20% in 1986.
Example: Because the old office building was designated a certified *historic structure*, its owner decided to restore the building to take advantage of allowable tax deductions.

HOLDBACK money not paid until certain events have occurred, such as a **floor loan** of a **loan commitment** or **retainage** on a construction contract.

Example: On a $1,000,000 loan the lender has a $300,000 *holdback* until the property is 80% rented.
Example: The developer has a 10% *holdback* from subcontractors until the building **inspection** is complete.

HOLDER IN DUE COURSE one who acquires a **bearer instrument** in **good faith** and is eligible to keep it even though it may have been stolen.
EXAMPLE: Abel receives from Baker a $100 bill in payment of rent on his apartment. Police inform Abel that the bill was stolen by Baker from Cobb. Since the bill is bearer paper and Abel accepted it without knowing about the theft, he became a *holder in due course* and is allowed to keep it.

HOLD HARMLESS CLAUSE in a **contract**, a clause whereby one party agrees to protect another party from claims.
Example: Big Buy Foods is leasing property from its landlord, Lucky Lessors. A customer is injured by a falling light fixture, and she sues both Big Buy Foods and Lucky Lessors. In the **lease**, Big Buy Foods agreed to a *hold harmless clause* whereby they **indemnified** Lucky Lessors against such events.

HOLDING COMPANY one that owns or controls another company(ies).
Example: Banks and public utilities are often owned or controlled by a *holding company*. Sometimes this arrangement allows more latitude for business practices than the operating company can achieve alone.

HOLDING COSTS same as **carrying costs**.

HOLDING PERIOD the time span of ownership, often for investment real estate.

Example: Some investors prefer short *holding periods* (under 5 years) in an attempt to retain high levels of financial **leverage**. Others hold property longer to reduce frequent **transaction costs** and avoid **depreciation recapture**.

HOLDOVER TENANT a **tenant** who remains in possession of leased property after the expiration of the lease **term**. See **tenancy at sufferance**.
Example: Abel leases an apartment for one year. At the end of the year, Abel is still in the process of finding a new home. As a *holdover tenant*, Abel may be evicted or allowed to remain on a month-to-month basis by continuing to pay rent, at the landlord's discretion.

HOME INSPECTOR a professional who evaluates the structural and mechanical condition of a home prior to its being sold. Some states require home inspectors to be bonded or licensed.
Example: Before closing on their new home, the Felixes hired a *home inspector* to check the condition of the structure. The inspector discovered an unsafe furnace burner and a leaking faucet. The seller agreed to have the problems repaired before the closing.

HOME LOAN see **mortgage**.

HOMEOWNER'S ASSOCIATION an organization of the homeowners in a particular **subdivision**, planned unit development, or **condominium**; generally for the purpose of enforcing **deed** restrictions or managing the **common elements** of the development. See **community association**.
Example: All unit owners of the Lakefront Condominiums are members of the Lakefront *Homeowners' Association*. The Association maintains the pool, grounds, and building structure, and regulates use of common elements. They assess each owner a $75 monthly fee.

HOMEOWNERSHIP the state of living in a structure that one owns. Contrasted with being a renter or **tenant** in one's home.
Example: *Homeownership* is a goal of many families. It provides security from the decisions of landlords, pride of ownership, and investment advantages in exchange for undertaking the responsibilities of a property owner.

HOMEOWNER'S POLICY an insurance policy designed especially for homeowners. Usually protects the owner from losses caused by most common disasters, theft, and **liability**. Coverage and costs vary widely.
Example: Whitman acquired a *homeowner's policy* for an annual premium of $500. It insures her home from fire losses (up to $100,000), theft (of household goods, excluding jewelry, paintings,

stamp collections, silverware), and gives up to $300,000 of **liability** protection.

HOMEOWNERS' WARRANTY PROGRAM (HOW) a private insurance program that protects purchasers of newly constructed homes, when the builder participates in the program, against structural and mechanical faults.
Example: Abel purchases a new home. The builder participates in the HOW program and provides Abel with a *homeowner's warranty* to cover any faults or oversights in the construction.

HOMEOWNER WARRANTY INSURANCE same as **homeowner warranty program.**

HOMESTEAD status provided to a homeowner's principal residence by some state statutes; protects home against **judgments** up to specified amounts.
Example: *Homestead* laws in Texas prevent a lender, other than the **mortgage** lender, from forcing the sale of one's principal residence to satisfy a **debt.**

HOMESTEAD EXEMPTION in some jurisdictions, a reduction in the **assessed value** allowed for one's principal residence.
Example: The *homestead exemption* in Georgia enables a homeowner, upon application, to get $5,000 subtracted from the assesor's **appraisal** of the home. This reduces the property tax burden.

HOMOGENEOUS uniform, of like characteristics or quality. Opposite of heterogeneous. The values of an area tend to be maximized when properties are *homogeneous,* because low valued or unusual properties are likely to reduce the value of other nearby properties of higher cost.
Example: The houses in the neighborhood were *homogeneous,* all single-family, one-story buildings with brick exteriors. They were readily marketable with asking and selling prices in a tight range.

HORIZONTAL PROPERTY LAWS state statutes that enable **condominium** ownership of property. Whereas property laws generally recognize **ownership rights** to all space from the center of the earth to some distance in the air, condominium laws allow individual ownership to be split on a horizontal plane that generally limits the unit owner's interest to the inside dimensions of the unit. See **common elements.**
Example: Before passage of *horizontal property laws,* all owners in a condominium were obligated under each individual mortgage loan in the complex. If one owner **defaulted,** the lender could **foreclose** on the entire condominium. Now, to secure a loan, each owner pledges only his or her limited interest in the condominium.

HOUSING AND URBAN DEVELOPMENT (HUD) DEPARTMENT
a U.S. government agency established to implement certain federal housing and community development programs.
Example: Mason desires to develop a housing project for low-income families. She applies to the *Department of Housing and Urban Development* for a special low-interest loan for the development.

HOUSING CODE a local government **ordinance** that sets minimum standards of safety and sanitation for existing residential buildings. Contrast to **building codes**, which pertain to new construction.
Example: Because of violations of the *housing code*, including a badly leaking roof and rat infestation, the old apartment building was condemned.

HOUSING STARTS an estimate of the number of dwelling units on which construction has begun during a stated period.
Example: During the last month, *housing starts* were 20% lower than the same month a year ago, reflecting a lower demand for new houses caused by high **mortgage** rates.

HUNDRED PERCENT LOCATION see **one-hundred percent location.**

HYPOTHECATE to pledge a thing as **security** without having to give up possession of it.
Example: Through use of a **mortgage** or **deed of trust**, the buyer *hypothecates* a newly acquired home to the lender or **trustee**. The buyer uses and controls the property.

I

IMPLIED CONTRACT created by actions but not necessarily written or spoken. See also **Statute of frauds.**
Example: Abel posts a for-sale sign on his property that says, "See Your Broker." Davis submits an offer through her **broker** and buys the property. Abel refuses to pay the broker, who then goes to court contending that the sign created an *implied contract*.

IMPLIED EASEMENT See **easement by prescription.**

IMPLIED WARRANTY one that is not written but exists under the law. Contrasted with "expressed."
Example: Under the law in several states there is an *implied warranty* **of habitability** for apartments leased to tenants. This means

that the tenant has the right to a dwelling that is fit for living, i.e., there are no **building code** violations.

IMPROVED LAND land that has some improvements. Land that has been partially or fully developed for use.
Examples: Any of the following activities on a piece of **raw land** will result in *improved land*:
• landscaping and grading
• installation of utilities
• construction of roads, curbs, and/or gutters
• contruction of buildings

IMPROVEMENTS those additions to **raw land**, such as buildings, streets, sewers, etc., tending to increase value.
Example: A hypothetical example of how *improvement* costs may affect property and land values is shown in Table 20.

TABLE 20

Improvement	Cost of improvement	Total property value	Value of land
None	$ 0	$ 500	$ 500
Curbs, drainage, & utilities	3,000	5,000	2,000
House	70,000	85,000	15,000
Apartment building	250,000	290,000	40,000

IMPOUND ACCOUNT a fund set aside for future needs. See **reserve fund**, **escrow account**.
Example: Each month a homeowner deposits $\frac{1}{12}$ of the estimated annual **property tax** and insurance premium requirements into an *impound account*, so that the balance will be sufficient to pay amounts when they come due.

IMPUTED INTEREST implied interest. In a **mortgage** that states an insufficient interest rate, the law will impute that the rate is higher, and the **principal** is less.
Example: Abel sells property to Baker. Baker gives Abel a portion of the price in cash and Abel takes a **note** for the remainder. Since the gain on the sale is taxable at **capital gains** rates and the interest paid on the note is taxed as **ordinary income**, it is in Abel's favor to set a higher price in exchange for charging a low rate of interest on

the note. If this is done, the **Internal Revenue Service** will consider a portion of the principal paid on the note as *imputed interest* and tax that portion as ordinary income.

INCHOATE unfinished, begun but not completed. In real estate, this can apply to **dower** or **curtesy** rights prior to the death of a spouse.
Example: Collins dies, leaving dower rights *inchoate.* Her children by a former marriage sue her widower to recover her share of property he sold.

INCOME the money or other benefit coming from the use of property, skill, or business.
Examples: In real estate, *income* may be produced by:
• rents
• fees
• royalties
• sales of crops, timber, or livestock
• revenues derived from business activities on the property

INCOME APPROACH a method appraising real estate based on the property's anticipated future income. The formula for appraisal by the income approach is

$$\frac{\text{Expected annual income}}{\text{Capitalization rate}} = \text{Market value}$$

See **capitalization** and **gross rent multiplier**.
Example: A property is expected to produce a **net operating income** of $100,000 yearly. Recent sales data indicate that the **capitalization rate** for **comparable** properties is 10%. By the *income approach,* the property has a market value of

$$\frac{\$100,000}{.10} = \$1,000,000$$

INCOME PROPERTY real estate that generates rental income.
Examples: The following are types of *income property:*
• apartment buildings
• shopping centers
• office buildings
• industrial properties and warehouses
• resort and recreational properties
• hotels, motels, and restaurants
The following are generally not considered *income property:*
• personal residences
• undeveloped land (rental income is minimal)
• schools, churches, parks

INCOME STREAM a regular flow of money generated by a business or investment.

Example: A **net lease** that pays $1,000 per month **rent** for 10 years provides an *income stream*.

INCOMPETENT one not legally capable of completing a **contract**. Includes the mentally ill, **minors**, and others considered incapable.
Example: Abel, a moron, inherited $100,000, and wants to buy a tract of land. He enters into a contract, but his legal guardian **voids** it because the land is worth under $5,000. It is voidable because Abel is *incompetent*.

INCORPORATE 1. to form a **corporation** under regulations provided by the Secretary of State.
Example: Abel intends to enter the real estate **brokerage** business and wishes to protect his personal **assets**. He retains a lawyer whom he pays a $1,000 fee to *incorporate* the business. Abel is the sole stockholder and chairman of the board of directors. Abel's personal assets are protected because **liability** is limited to the assets owned by the corporation.
2. to provide a geographic area the legal status of a political subdivision of the state.
Example: A large **subdivision** outside a large city petitions the state legislature to *incorporate* as an independent city. The residents of the incorporated area may elect representatives and tax themselves to provide services.

INCORPOREAL PROPERTY legal interests in real property that do not entail the right of possession. See **easement, license.**

INCURABLE DEPRECIATION a defect that cannot be cured or that is not financially practical to cure; a defect in the "bone structure" of a building. Compare **curable depreciation**.
Example: It is estimated that if a specific house had a more convenient **floor plan**, it would sell for an additional $5,000. The cost of rearranging the partitions to improve the plan is $10,000. The poor floor plan is *incurable depreciation*.

INDEMNIFY 1. to protect another person against loss or damage.
Example: **FHA mortgage loans** *indemnify* the lender against the risk of a buyer's **default**.
2. to compensate a party for loss or damage.
Example: Upon **foreclosure**, the FHA *indemnified* the lender for losses on the defaulted loan.

INDENTURE a written agreement made between 2 or more persons having different interests.
Example: The *indenture* **trustee** enforces the agreement made between the **bond** issuer (borrower) and the lender.

INDEPENDENT CONTRACTOR a **contractor** who is self-

employed.

Example: Collins, a real estate salesperson, is an *independent contractor* engaged by **broker** Baker. She has not received any income in the last 3 months but is unable to collect unemployment insurance because she is an *independent contractor*. Last year she paid a self-employment tax instead of social security.

INDEX 1. a statistic that indicates some current economic or financial condition. Indexes are often used to make adjustments in wage rates, rental rates, loan interest rates, and pension benefits set by long-term contracts.

Example: Office building rental rates are sometimes adjusted in relation to the consumer price *index*.

2. to adjust contract terms according to an index. See **indexed loan**.

Example: Mortgage interest rates on **adjustable rate mortgages** are often *indexed* to the average mortgage rate for all lenders or the average cost of funds for all lenders.

INDEXED LOAN a long-term loan in which the **term**, payment, **interest rate**, or **principal** amount may be adjusted periodically according to a specific **index**. The index and the manner of adjustment are generally stated in the loan contract.

Example: An **adjustable rate mortgage** is an *indexed loan*. At specific intervals the **face interest rate** on the loan may be changed according to variations in the specified **index**.

INDEX LEASE a rental agreement that requires changes in rent based on a published record of cost changes. See **cost of living index**.

Example: A landlord makes an *index lease* with initial rent at $10,000 per year, adjusted annually by the Consumer Price Index (CPI). If the CPI is 100 at the time of the lease and increases to 110 in the second year, the rent for the second year will be 10,000 × 1.10 = $11,000.

INDUSTRIAL PARK an area designed and **zoned** for manufacturing and associated activities.

Example: Figure 86.

INDUSTRIAL PROPERTY property used for industrial purposes, such as factories.

Examples: Types of *industrial property:*
• factory-office multiuse property
• factory-warehouse multiuse property
• heavy manufacturing buildings
• industrial parks
• light manufacturing buildings
• research and development parks

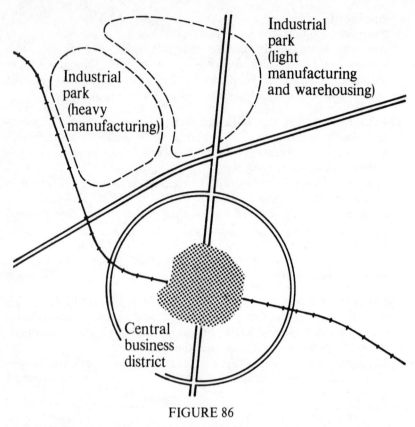

Industrial park (light manufacturing and warehousing)

Industrial park (heavy manufacturing)

Central business district

FIGURE 86

INFORMATION REPORTING reports provided to the Internal Revenue Service (IRS), such as commissions earned by real estate sales agents and real estate transactions of home sellers, reported by the broker.
Example: In January, Baker files a form 1099 with the IRS for real estate transactions she brokered during the past year. Such *information reporting* is required by the Tax Reform Act of 1986.

INHERITANCE TAX a tax, based on property **value**, imposed in some states on those who acquire property from a decedent. Compare **estate tax.**
Example: An estate tax is based on the value of all property left by the decedent, whereas an *inheritance tax* is based on the amount that an **heir** receives.

INJUNCTION an order issued under the seal of a court to restrain one or more parties to a legal proceeding, from performing an act deemed inequitable to another party or parties in the proceeding.
Example: Abel begins serving alcoholic drinks on property he bought from Baker. Baker claims that a **deed restriction** prevents

consumption of such beverages on the property, and sues Abel. Since the trial is set several months ahead, Baker requests an *iniunction* to prevent the sale of drinks until the trial.

INNER CITY generally the older and more urbanized area of a large city surrounding the **central business district.** The term often refers to densely populated blighted **areas** characterized by low-income residents and a high proportion of minority racial and ethnic groups.
Examples:
• Many *inner city* neighborhoods have been **rehabilitated** by **urban renewal** projects.
• Violence is a problem in some *inner city* schools.
• The mayor promises a construction program to rehabilitate the *inner city*.

IN REM Latin: "against the thing." A proceeding against the property directly, as distinguished from a proceeding against a person (used in taking land for nonpayment of taxes, etc.)
Example: Baker cannot collect on his past due loan from Abel. Baker, through court action, secures a **judgment** *in rem* against a building lot owned by Abel, which causes a lien against the lot.

INSIDE LOT in a **subdivision,** a lot surrounded on each side by other lots, as opposed to a corner lot, which has road **frontage** on at least 2 sides.
Example: An *inside lot* **adjoining** a corner lot (Figure 87).

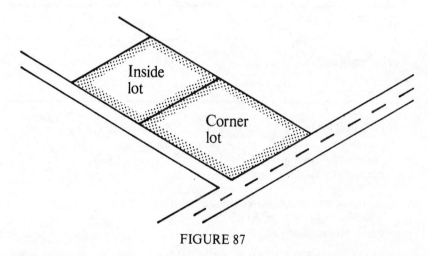

FIGURE 87

INSPECTION a physical scrutinizing review of property or of documents.
Example: *Inspections* may be required for the following purposes:

- compliance with **building codes**
- sale requirements as to property conditions, such as wood-destroying insects or structural soundness
- legal review of documents such as **leases** and **mortgages** to determine whether they are as purported

INSTALLMENTS parts of the same **debt**, payable at successive periods as agreed; payments made to reduce a **mortgage**.
Example: Abel purchases a property with a **land contract**. The contract calls for a payment of $30,000 at **closing**, with 10 annual *installments* of $15,000 each.

INSTALLMENT CONTRACT same as **land contract**.

INSTALLMENT SALE when a seller accepts a **mortgage** for part of the sale, the tax on the gain is paid as the mortgage **principal** is collected. See also **contract price, gross profit ratio, imputed interest**.
Example: Collins sells for $10,000 her land that she bought 3 years ago for $4,000. Her gain is $6,000. She received 10% ($1,000) as a cash **down payment** and a 90% ($9,000) **purchase money mortgage**. She will report 10% of the gain in the year of sale and the balance as she collects the principal of the purchase money mortgage. To do so, on her tax return she reports the sale as an installment sale. See Table 21.

TABLE 21

	Year of sale	Year 1	Year 2	Year 3
Principal paid	$1000	$3000	$3000	$3000
Taxable gain	600	1800	1800	1800
Interest income	0	900	600	300

INSTITUTE OF REAL ESTATE MANAGEMENT (IREM) a professional organization of property managers. Affiliated with the **National Association of Realtors®**. Publishes the *Journal of Property Management*.
Address:
Institute of Real Estate Management
430 North Michigan Avenue
Chicago, Illinois 60611

INSTITUTIONAL LENDER financial intermediaries who invest in loans and other securities on behalf of their depositors or customers; lending and investment activities are regulated by laws to limit risk.
Example: *Institutional lenders* are a prime source of real estate

loans. Many organizations, such as **savings and loan associations** and **commerical banks**, originate loans directly; others, such as insurance companies, lend through **mortgage brokers**.

INSTRUMENT a written legal document, created to establish the rights and liabilities of the parties to it.
Examples: The following are examples of instruments:
• **deed**
• mortgage
• land contract
• lease
• assignment

INSURABLE INTEREST an **interest** in a person or property that would cause one a loss if that person or property were injured. Must be present to collect from an insurance policy.
Example: The Good Money Savings Association lent $50,000 on Abel's house. Yesterday it was destroyed by fire. Good Money can collect on its insurance policy, because they were insured and had an *insurable interest*. Five Star Savings also had an insurance policy on the home but had no **lien**, so they couldn't collect.

INSURABLE TITLE a **title** that can be insured by a **title insurance** company.
Example: In some **contracts** for the sale of **real estate** the buyer must receive *insurable title* or he is not obligated to purchase the property.

INSURANCE COVERAGE total amount and type of insurance carried.
Example: The owner maintained $100,000 of hazard *insurance coverage* on the property, and $300,000 of **liability** *insurance coverage*. The **hazard insurance** coverage was adequate to meet the 80% **coinsurance** requirement in the policy.

INSURANCE (MORTGAGE) a service, generally purchased by a borrower, that will **indemnify** the lender in case of **foreclosure** of the loan. Indemnification is generally limited to losses suffered by the lender in the foreclosure process. See **FHA mortgage loan**, **private mortgage insurance**.
Example: Abel took out a **home loan** covered by *mortgage insurance*. After one year, Abel **defaulted** on the loan and the lender foreclosed. Abel owed $50,000, but the foreclosure sale produced only $40,000 in proceeds. The insurance company paid the lender the difference of $10,000.

INTANGIBLE VALUE value that cannot be seen or touched.
Example: The **goodwill** of an established business is an *intangible value*.

INTEREST 1. cost of the use of money.

Example: Lenders require payment of *interest* at a specified rate, to compensate for risk, deferment of benefits, inflation, and administrative burdens.

2. the type and extent of ownership.

Example: One may hold either a partial or **fee simple** *interest* in a property. That *interest* entitles one to specific ownership rights.

INTEREST DEDUCTIONS (UNDER THE 1986 TAX ACT)

Investment Interest. Investment interest deductions are limited to net investment income, which includes interest, dividends, long-term capital gains and income or loss from working interests in oil and gas interests. However, net investment income includes neither rental or other passive activity income or loss, nor interest paid to buy an ownership in a passive activity. The $10,000 allowance for investment interest expense above investment income allowed before the 1986 tax act is subject to a 4-year phase out, allowing 65% in 1987, then 40%, 20%, and 10%, for each subsequent year.

Construction Interest. Interest incurred during the construction and development of most real estate (but not a personal residence) must be capitalized, and deducted over its depreciable life beginning when the property is ready to be placed in service or sold.

Business Interest. Interest incurred in an active trade or business in which the investor materially participates is not investment interest, and is fully deductible.

Housing Interest. Interest on up to 2 personal residences is allowed as an itemized deduction, provided the mortgages did not exceed the value of the residences and were borrowed before August 17, 1986. However, deductible interest on mortgages borrowed after that is limited to the sum of the home cost, improvements, medical and educational expenses; provided the total debt does not exceed the market value of the residence.

Points paid on a mortgage to acquire a principal residence may be deductible if they are customary in the geographic area; points paid for other purposes such as refinancing are amortized rather than deducted currently.

Consumer Interest. Interest on credit cards and auto loans will not be deductible by 1990. The deduction is being phased out over 4 years, allowing 65% in 1987, then 40%, 2% and 10%.

INTEREST-ONLY LOAN a loan in which interest is payable at regular intervals until loan **maturity**, when the full loan balance is due. Does not require **amortization**. Contrast **self-amortizing mortgage**.

Example: Land was bought with a 5-year *interest-only loan* of $100,000 at 12%. The **interest** of $12,000 was paid annually for 4 years. The $100,000 **principal**, together with the last $12,000 interest payment, was due at the end of the fifth year.

INTEREST RATE 1. the percentage of a sum of money charged for its use.
2. the **rate of return** on an investment.
Example: A $50,000 mortgage loan is made at 12% interest and 4 **discount points**. The contract *interest rate* is 12% and determines the monthly payment amount. The **effective rate** of interest, which incorporates the effects of the discount points, is 12.55% and is the rate of return to the lender if the loan runs to maturity.

INTERIM FINANCING a loan, including a **construction loan**, used when the property owner is unable or unwilling to arrange permanent financing. Generally arranged for less than 3 years, used to gain time for financial or market conditions to improve.
Example: Monroe developed an office building but, in the expectation of falling **interest rates**, does not wish to use permanent financing at this time. He arranges a 2-year *interim* loan, during which time he seeks favorable permanent financing.

INTERNAL RATE OF RETURN (IRR) the true annual rate of earnings on an investment. Equates the value of cash returns with cash invested. Considers the application of **compound interest** factors. Requires a trial-and-error method for solution. The formula is

$$\sum_{t=1}^{n} \frac{\text{periodic } cash\ flow}{(1+i)^t} = \text{investment amount}$$

where i = internal rate of return
t = each time interval
n = total time intervals
Σ = summation

Example: Abel sells for $20,000 land that he bought 4 years earlier for $10,000. There were no **carrying charges** or **transaction costs**. The *internal rate of return* was about 19%. That is the annual rate at which compound interest must be paid for $10,000 to become $20,000 in 4 years.
Example: Baker received $3,000 per year for 5 years on a $10,000 investment. The *internal rate of return* was about 15%.

INTERNAL REVENUE CODE the law, passed by Congress, that specifies how and what income is to be taxed, and what may be deducted from taxable income.
Example: Court cases, regulations, revenue rules, and revenue procedures attempt to properly interpret the *Internal Revenue Code*.

INTERNAL REVENUE SERVICE (IRS) an agency of the federal government that is responsible for the administration and collection of federal income taxes. The IRS prints and distributes tax forms and audits tax returns.

Addresses:
Regional Offices

- Andover, MA 05501
- Atlanta, GA 31101
- Austin, TX 73301
- Cincinnati, OH 45999
- Fresno, CA 93888
- Holtsville, NY 00501
- Kansas City, MO 64999
- Memphis, TN 37501
- Ogden, UT 84201
- Philadelphia, PA 19255

INTERNATIONAL ARCHITECTURE an early twentieth century style house whose design is very simple with no ornamentation. The windows appear to be continuous rather than appearing to be holes in the walls.
Example: Figure 88.

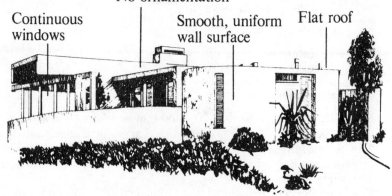

FIGURE 88

INTERNATIONAL ASSOCIATION OF ASSESSING OFFICERS (IAAO) a professional organization of property tax **assessors**. Awards the designation of Certified Assessment Evaluator (CAE). Publishes the quarterly *Assessors Journal*.
Address:
International Association of Assessing Officers
1313 East 60th Street
Chicago, Illinois 60637

INTERNATIONAL RIGHT OF WAY ASSOCIATION (IR/WA) an

234

individual membership association (no corporate membership) that offers courses covering various phases of **right-of-way** work. Educational curriculum includes law, engineering, **appraisal.** Offers a designation, SR/WA, and a bimonthly magazine.
Address:
International Right of Way Association
6133 Bristol Parkway, Suite 270
Culver City, California 90230

INTERSTATE LAND SALES ACT a federal law, administered by the Department of **Housing and Urban Development** (HUD), which requires certain disclosures and advertising procedures when selling land to purchasers in other states.
Example: Rollins, a developer, has a 200-acre **subdivision** in Florida and wishes to market lots nationally. Under the *Interstate Land Sales Act,* she must register with the Office of Interstate Land Sales Registration (OILSR, a division of HUD), and make certain disclosures in the **prospectus** sent to prospective purchasers.

INTER VIVOS during one's life.
Example: Abel makes an *inter vivos* gift of $10,000 to each of 3 children. The children spend the $10,000 and may inherit more money if Abel names them in the **will** he is preparing.

INTESTATE 1. (adj.) having made no valid will 2. (noun) a person who dies leaving no will or leaving one that is defective. Property goes to the legal **heirs** of the intestate.
Example: If Doris dies *intestate,* her heirs under state law will inherit her property. If she leaves no heirs her property will **escheat.**

INVENTORY property held for sale or to be used in the manufacture of goods held for sale. Does not qualify for **capital gains** tax treatment.
Examples: Examples of *inventory* are:
• raw materials
• work-in-progress
• finished goods
To a builder, property under construction and property completed are *inventory.* To a **subdivider,** vacant lots are *inventory.*

INVERSE CONDEMNATION a legal procedure to obtain compensation when a property **interest** has been taken or diminished in value by a government activity.
Example: Abel owns a home near a public airport. The city constructs a new runway that sends air traffic directly over Abel's house, seriously diminishing Abel's enjoyment of his property. Abel may sue for *inverse condemnation* and, if successful, may

INVESTMENT ANALYSIS a study of the likely return from a proposed real estate investment with the objective of evaluating the amount an investor may pay for it, the investment's suitability to that investor, or the feasibility of a proposed real estate development. Appraised value is based on a synthesis of people in the market whereas *investment analysis* is based on the value to a specific investor.

There are various methods of *investment analysis,* including:
• Cash on cash return
• Payback period
• Internal rate of return
• Net present value

Each provides some measure of the estimated return on an investment, based on various assumptions and investment horizons.

INVESTMENT LIFE CYCLE the time span from acquisition of an investment to final disposition.

Example: The best way to measure the **rate of return** from an *investment* is over its *life cycle.* All relevant investment contributions, **cash flows,** and resale proceeds are known (Figure 89).

FIGURE 89

INVESTMENT TAX CREDIT a reduction in income tax generally based on the cost and life of certain assets purchased.

Note: This was abolished by the Tax Reform Act of 1986; but see **rehabilitation tax credit** and **low-income housing (qualified).**

INVOLUNTARY CONVERSION condemnation or sudden destruction by nature.

Example: A property is taken by **eminent domain** for the purpose of constructing a public highway. This *involuntary conversion* of the property is contrasted with a sale that the owner enters into voluntarily.

INVOLUNTARY LIEN a **lien** imposed against property without consent of the owner (unpaid taxes, special assessments, etc.). Compare **mortgage lien**.
Example: The **absentee** land **owner** was not notified of the past-due tax bill. The tax **assessor** placed a lien on the property that was an *involuntary lien,* since the owner did not take action to cause the lien.

INWOOD ANNUITY FACTOR a number that, when multiplied by the periodic payment from a **level payment income stream**, indicates the present value of the income stream, based on a specific interest rate. Same formula as that for **annuity factor**.
Example: An investment is expected to provide income of $100 per month for 10 years. At the end of 10 years the investment has no value. At an interest rate of 10%, the present value (PV) of the investment is
$$PV = \$100 \times 75.67 = \$7,567$$
where 75.67 is the *Inwood annuity factor.*

INWOOD TABLES a set of **annuity factors** for various **interest rates** and **maturities**. See **Inwood annuity factor**.
Example: The *Inwood tables* show that the right to receive $1.00 at the end of each year for 10 years at 15% interest is worth $5.02 as of the beginning of the first year.

IRREVOCABLE incapable of being recalled or revoked; unchangeable.
Example: The bank issued an *irrevocable* **letter of credit** stating that if the terms of the **contract** were met the bank would lend the money requested.

ITALIAN VILLA a Latin style, massive 2- or 3-story house of masonry with large overhanging eaves.
Example: Figure 90.

J

JEOPARDY danger, **risk**.
Example: Property pledged as **security** for a delinquent loan is in *jeopardy* of **foreclosure**.

JOINT AND SEVERAL LIABILITY a **creditor** can demand full repayment from any and all of those who have borrowed. Each borrower is **liable** for the full debt, not just the **prorated** share.
Example: Abel and Baker are **general partners**. Together they borrow (or the **partnership** borrows) $10,000 from a bank, agreeing to

joint and several liability. Upon **default**, the bank can collect the remaining balance of the $10,000 from either party.

JOINT TENANCY ownership of **realty** by 2 or more persons, each of whom has an **undivided interest** with the **right of survivorship**. Typically used by related persons.
Example: Abel and Baker own land in *joint tenancy*. Each owns half of the entire (undivided) property. Upon Abel's death, Baker will own the entire property, and vice versa.

2 or 3 story

Massive

Some have quoins

Large overhanging eaves

Heavy cornice line

Decorative iron work

Brackets

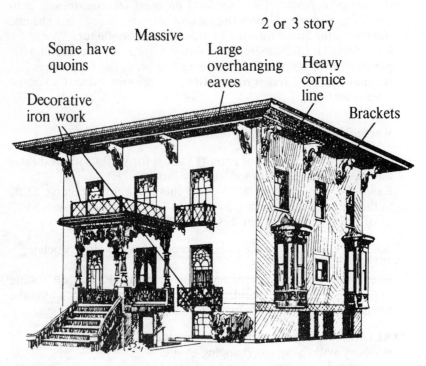

FIGURE 90

JOINT VENTURE an agreement between 2 or more parties who invest in a single business or property. See also **limited partnership**, **tenancy in common**.
Example: Abel and Baker form a *joint venture* to explore for minerals on Cobb's land. Abel and Baker use a **tenancy in common** arrangement for ownership of the mineral rights.

JUDGMENT a decree of a court stating that one individual is indebted to another and fixing the amount of the indebtedness.
Example: As a result of Abel's failure to pay disputed rent, the landlord obtained a court decision, or *judgment*, against Abel.

JUDGMENT CREDITOR one who has received a court decree or **judgment** for money due from the **judgment debtor**.

238

Example: To enforce the judgment awarded by court, the *judgment creditor* filed a **lien** against the **judgment debtor** Abel.

JUDGMENT DEBTOR one against whom a **judgment** has been issued by a court for money owed, and that remains unsatisfied.
Example: A judgment was entered into against Abel for nonpayment of rent. Abel is the *judgment debtor.*

JUDGMENT LIEN the claim upon the property of a debtor resulting from a **judgment**.
Example: Abel won't pay his debt to Baker. After establishing the debt in court, Baker may be allowed by the court to put a *judgment lien* on Abel's **real estate**.

JUDICIAL FORECLOSURE having a defaulted debtor's property sold where the court ratifies the price paid.
Example: Happy Mortgage Company is owed $50,000 on a first mortgage by Mr. Baker. At *judicial foreclosure,* Happy Mortgage Company **bids** $30,000 for the property, which is more than anyone else bids. They then claim the property and are awarded a $20,000 **deficiency judgment** against Mr. Baker.

JUNIOR MORTGAGE a **mortgage** whose claim against the property will be satisfied only after prior mortgages have been repaid. See **first mortgage, second mortgage**.
Example: Property is purchased for $100,000. A first mortgage is obtained covering $75,000 of the price. To reduce the cash requirements, a *junior mortgage* is arranged to cover $15,000 of the price. The remaining $10,000 is cash **equity**.

JURISDICTION geographic or topical area of authority for a specific government entity.
Example: The *jurisdiction* of the Lower Valley Consolidated Appraisal District is a 3 county area surrounding the city of Valleyview. The federal district court has *jurisdiction* in all cases involving violation of federal law.

JUST COMPENSATION the amount paid to the owner of a property when it is acquired under **eminent domain**. See **condemnation**.
Example: Property is condemned to construct a sewage treatment plant. The owner is entitled to *just compensation* equal to the **fair market value** of the property taken.

K

KICKER a payment required by a **mortgage** in addition to normal **principal** and **interest**. See **participation loan**.

Example: Abel obtains a loan to purchase a retail store building. The lender requires a *kicker* equal to 10% of gross sales in excess of $100,000 per month, in addition to principal and interest.

L

LACHES undue delay or negligence in asserting one's legal rights, possibly leading to **estoppel** of the negligent party's suit.
Example: Abel was estopped by *laches* after he knowingly delayed telling an **adjacent** property owner of an **encroachment**.

LAND the surface of the earth; any part of the surface of the earth. (Note: Legal definitions often distinguish land from water.)
Example: Extent of *land* as **real property** (Figure 91). **Air rights** may be limited to some defined altitude. Added **improvements** are distinguished from *land*.

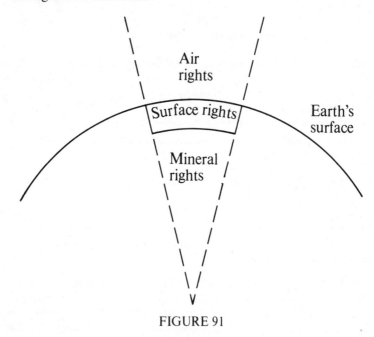

FIGURE 91

LAND BANKING the activity of purchasing land that is not presently needed for use.
Example: The Burger Company buys 8 **sites** that they plan to use 10 years from now. Wendy Ronald is in charge of *land banking* for The Burger Company.

LAND CONTRACT a real estate **installment** selling arrangement whereby the buyer may use, occupy, and enjoy land, but no **deed**

is given by the seller (so no **title** passes) until all or a specified part of the sale price has been paid. Same as **contract for deed** and **installment land contract**.

Example: Collins buys a recreational lot. Under the *land contract* she signed, she must pay $500 down and $100 per month for 7 years; then she is to receive a **general warranty deed**.

LAND LEASE only the ground is covered by the lease. See **ground lease**.

Example: Abel arranges a *land lease* from Baker for 50 years at a net annual rent of $5,000. Abel builds a shopping center on the land. At the end of 50 years the entire property will revert to Baker (Figure 92).

Building owner pays $5,000 per year rent on land

FIGURE 92

LANDLOCKED the condition of a lot that has no access to a public thoroughfare except through an **adjacent** lot. See **egress**. Compare **easement**, **right-of-way**.

Example: Figure 93.

LANDLORD one who rents property to another; a **lessor**. A property owner who surrenders the right to use property for a specific time in exchange for the receipt of rent.

Example: *Landlord*-tenant relationship (Figure 94).

LANDMARK a fixed object serving as a **boundary** mark for a tract of land. Same as **monument**.

Example: The tree and rail line may serve as *landmarks* in a land **description** (Figure 95).

LAND RESIDUAL TECHNIQUE in **appraisal**, a method of estimat-

ing the value of land when given **the net operating income (NOI)** and value of **improvements**. Used for **feasibility** analysis and **highest and best use**. See **income approach**.

Example: A property generates $10,000 net operating income ($15,000 rent less $5,000 operating expenses). The improvements cost $70,000 to construct and claim a 12% rate of return (10% interest plus 2% depreciation), which is $8,400. The remaining $1,600 income is capitalized at a 10% rate (divided by .10) to result in a $16,000 land value, using the *land residual technique*. See Table 22.

Table 22

Property NOI	$10,000
Income to improvement	− $8,400
Income to land	$1,600
Divided by required rate (10%)	$16,000 Land value

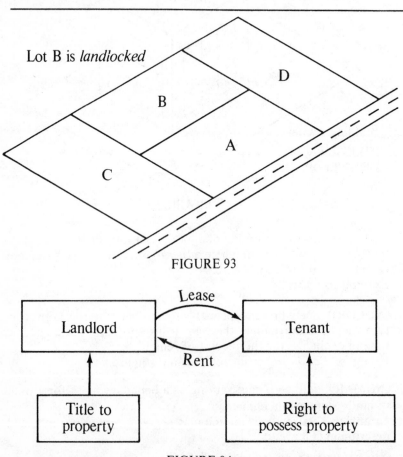

Lot B is *landlocked*

FIGURE 93

Lease

Rent

| Landlord | Tenant |

| Title to property | Right to possess property |

FIGURE 94

Tree

Railroad

FIGURE 95

LAND SALE-LEASEBACK the sale of land and simultaneous leasing of it by the seller, who becomes the **tenant**.
Example: Collins owns land and wants to raise cash to build a shopping center on it. She sells the land for $100,000 to Baker and leases it back for 50 years at a $5,000 annual rent. Collins can use the land for the lease **term** provided she pays the annual rent, so she builds the shopping center after the *land sale-leaseback* (Figure 96).

Cash price

sale

First owner becomes tenant

Land

Second owner becomes landlord

Lease

Annual rent

FIGURE 96

LANDSCAPE ARCHITECT a professional who designs building sites, subdivisions, and other projects which require work on drainage, grading, vegetation, installation of utilities and site improvements.
Example: On the office park project, a *landscape architect* advised the developer on the placement of drainage sewers, parking lots, plantings and other landscaping requirements.

243

LAND, TENEMENTS, AND HEREDITAMENTS a phrase used in early English law to express all sorts of **real estate**.
Example: The **bundle of rights** in real estate is expressed by the phrase *land, tenements and hereditaments*. It includes all **interests** in real estate.

LAND USE INTENSITY a measure of the extent to which a land parcel is developed in conformity with **zoning** ordinances.
Example: Under a local zoning ordinance, **developers** might be allowed a maximum *land use intensity* of 4,000 square feet of **improvements** per **acre** of land.

LAND USE PLANNING an activity, generally conducted by a local government, that provides public and private land use recommendations consistent with community policies. Generally used to guide decisions on **zoning**.
Example: As part of its *land use planning* efforts, the city planning department prepared maps of existing land uses, forecasts of future development, a list of planned new roads, **utility** extensions, and waste disposal facilities, a map of environmentally sensitive areas, and a map showing recommended future land uses.

LAND USE REGULATION government **ordinances**, codes, and permit requirements intended to make the private use of land and natural resources conform to policy standards. See also **zoning**.
Example: Local governments have several types of *land use regulation*. Commonly used types are:
• building codes
• curb-cut permit systems
• historic preservation laws
• housing codes
• subdivision regulations
• tree-cutting laws
• zoning

LAND USE SUCCESSION a change in the predominant use of a **neighborhood** or area over time. See also **neighborhood life cycle**.
Example: As the neighborhood aged, it began to make a transition from large **single-family housing** to **apartment buildings** through the process of *land use succession*.

LATENT DEFECTS flaws that are hidden but are apt to surface later.
Example: A building was found to have *latent defects* in the form of poor construction of subfloors and improper foundation support.

LATE PAYMENTS a fee added to a bill after the expiration of a specific grace period. Such payments are intended to encourage

timely payment of the bill.
Example: Largetown Federal Savings requires an additional 5% in *late payments* when a mortgage payment is made after the fifteenth of the month.

LEASE a **contract** in which, for a payment called **rent,** the one entitled to the **possession** of real property **(lessor)** transfers those rights to another **(lessee)** for a specified period of time.
Example: Abel leases office space from Baker. Under the *lease* signed by the parties, Abel is allowed to conduct business activities within the office space, subject to specified **restrictions,** for a specified period of time. Baker is entitled to receive a specified amount of rent payments according to a specified schedule of payments.

LEASEHOLD the **interest** or **estate** on which a **lessee (tenant)** of **real estate** has a **lease.**
Example: Mason possesses a long-term lease on a property. She may obtain a loan with the *leasehold* pledged as **collateral.** If the **contract rent** required by the lease is lower than **market rents,** Mason's *leasehold* will have a positive value.

LEASEHOLD MORTGAGE a **lien** on the tenant's **interest** in **real estate.**
Example: Abel is leasing land from Baker under a 50-year lease. Abel builds a shopping center and borrows money from the Big Money Assurance Company to do so. Big Money Assurance Company secures the loan with a leasehold mortgage. The mortgage will be lower in priority (subordinate) to land lease because the lease was contracted first. Had the mortgage been arranged before the lease, the mortgage would have priority. The holder of a prior **lien** has first claim to the income and assets if in default.

LEASE WITH OPTION TO PURCHASE a lease that gives the **lessee (tenant)** the right to purchase the property at an agreed-upon price under certain conditions.
Example: Abel *leases* property with an *option to purchase.* He must pay $500 per month rent for 5 years; after that he may buy the property (but is not forced to buy) for $100,000.

LEGAL AGE the official standard of maturity upon which one is held legally responsible for one's acts. Contracts for the sale or lease of real estate by a minor are voidable by the minor. See **minor.**
Example: Young, aged 17, signed a contract to purchase a home. Because Young was not of *legal age,* the seller could not enforce the contract when Young later decided not to go through with the purchase.

LEGAL DESCRIPTION legally acceptable identification of **real estate** by one of the following:
• the **government rectangular survey**
• metes and bounds
• recorded **plat** (**lot and block** number)
Example: The seller was required to include a *legal description* in the **deed**.

LEGAL NAME the name one has for official purposes.
Example: Though friends call him Fast Buck Jones, his *legal name* is Ferdinand Buchanan Jones. He may sign **contracts** with the name Ferdinand B. Jones.
Example: The *legal name* of GM is General Motors, Incorporated.

LEGAL NOTICE notification of others using the method required by law. See **constructive notice, notice**.
Example: Abel wishes to **rescind** an **offer** to buy real estate that has not been accepted by Baker. Abel sends a telegram and registered letter to Baker as *legal notice*.
Example: Collins bought land. She recorded the **deed** in the county courthouse as *legal notice* of ownership.

LEGATEE one who receives property by **will**. See **devisee**.
Example: Garrison wills all her property to Baker. Upon Garrison's death, Baker is the *legatee*.

LESSEE a person to whom property is rented under a **lease**. A **tenant**. Compare **lessor**.
Example: In the arrangement shown in Figure 97, Baker is the *lessee*.

FIGURE 97

LESSOR one who rents property to another under a **lease**. A **landlord**. Compare **lessee**.
Example: In the arrangement shown in Figure 98, Abel is the *lessor*.

LET to rent a property to a tenant.
Example: Larry *lets* an apartment to Simon for $300 per month.

LETTER OF CREDIT an arrangement, with specified conditions,

whereby a bank agrees to substitute its credit for a customer's.
Example: Abel, from Atlanta, wishes to buy property from Baker,
in Boston. Abel arranges a *letter of credit* with the Atlanta Trust
Company Bank to pay Baker upon **closing** in Boston.

LETTER OF INTENT the expression of a desire to enter into a con-
tract without actually doing so.
Example: After a preliminary meeting, the Five Stars Develop-
ment Company writes to a landowner, "We wish to enter into a
contract to buy your land and will further pursue this matter in
coming days. This *letter of intent* does not commit either party to
purchase, sell, or lease."

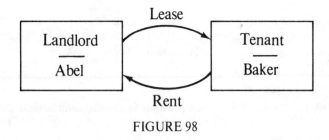

FIGURE 98

LEVEL PAYMENT INCOME STREAM see **annuity**.

LEVEL PAYMENT MORTGAGE requires the same payment each
month (or other period) for full **amortization**. See **mortgage con-
stant, flat**.
Example: Abel borrows $50,000 to buy a house. The *level pay-
ment mortgage* at 15% interest, payable over 30 years, requires a
$632.50 monthly payment for **principal** and **interest**. That payment
will be constant over the life of the loan.

LEVERAGE use of borrowed funds to increase purchasing power
and, ideally, to increase the profitability of an investment. See
positive leverage, reverse leverage.
Example: Collins wishes to invest in real estate. The property
costs $100,000 and produces **net operating income** of $10,000 per
year. If purchased with all cash, Collin's annual **rate of return** is
10% ($10,000÷$100,000). If she *leverages* the investment by bor-
rowing $75,000, her return may be higher. If the debt cost is 8%
($6,000) annually, the *leverage* results in a return of 16%
($4,000÷$25,000). However, if the debt cost is 12% ($9,000), the
leverage produces a return of 4% ($1,000÷$25,000).

LEVY to legally impose or collect that which is due.
Example: A tax assessor *levies* a tax.
Example: A judge *levies* a fine.

LIABILITY 1. a **debt** or financial obligation. Contrast with **asset**.
Example: One who borrows $75,000 for a **mortgage** loan incurs a *liability* to repay that loan.
Example: A **general partner** in a **partnership** has a personal *liability* for debts of the partnership in the event the partnership cannot repay its debt.
2. a potential loss.
Example: One should purchase sufficient *liability* insurance to protect against possible legal claims of someone who gets injured on one's property.

LIABILITY INSURANCE protection for a property owner from claims arising from injuries or damage to other people or property.
Example: Abel slipped on a broken step on the walkway in an apartment complex owned by Baker. Baker's *liability insurance* pays Abel for the doctor and hospital fees.

LIABLE responsible or obligated. Contrast with **exculpatory clause** and **nonrecourse**.
Example: One who borrows a **mortgage** loan generally becomes personally *liable* for its repayment. The lender can look to the **property** or the borrower personally for repayment.

LICENSE 1. permission
Example: If Abel did not secure *license* to cross Baker's property, it would be a **trespass**.
2. a right granted by a state to an individual to operate as a real estate **broker** or salesperson.
Example: The **real estate commission** issued a salesperson *license* to Rollins (Figure 99). Working under the supervision of her broker, Rollins can sell and lease real estate owned by others.

LICENSEE one who holds a real estate **license**; a licensed salesperson or **broker**. See **licensing examination**.
Example: A pocket card is held by *licensees*. The employing broker displays licenses in the office.

LICENSE LAWS laws that govern the activities of real estate salespersons.
Example: Abel, an unlicensed individual, sold a farm for Baker and a house owned by Collins. Under state *license laws* each violation subjects Abel to a $10,000 fine and a year imprisonment, or both.

LICENSING EXAMINATION a written test given to a prospective real estate **broker** or salesperson to determine ability to represent the public in a real estate transaction. Most states offer examinations on at least 5 dates each year.

Example: Educational Testing Services (ETS) in Princeton, New Jersey, and American College Testing (ACT) in Iowa City, Iowa, prepare *licensing examinations* for most states. Some states prepare their own *licensing examination.*

𝔖tate 𝔯eal 𝔈state Commission
═══ 1988 ═══

```
┌─────────────────────────────────────────────────┐
│                                                 │
└─────────────────────────────────────────────────┘
```

The Real Estate Commission hereby certifies that this License is issued in accordance with all legal requirements and shall remain in force and effect during the year shown above as long as the broker conforms with all obligations of the law.

	FILE	LICENSE
Charlie Baker	025	360245
101 Maple Road		
Springfield, MA 90001	October 15, 1990	

Application for annual certification of this license must be made between Sept 1st and Nov. 30th.

Andy Jensen

ADMINISTRATOR, THE REAL ESTATE COMMISSION
P.O. BOX 12188 CAPITOL STATION

THIS LICENSE MUST BE PROMINENTLY DISPLAYED IN THE OFFICE OF THE BROKER NAMED HEREON.

FIGURE 99

LIEN a charge against property making it **security** for the payment of a **debt, judgment, mortgage,** or taxes; it is a type of **encumbrance.** A specific lien is against certain property only. A **general lien** is against all of the property owned by the debtor.
Example: Abel failed to pay the **contractor** for work performed on his home. The contractor files a **mechanic's lien** against the property for the amount due.

LIEN, JUNIOR a **lien** that will be paid after earlier liens have been paid. See **junior mortgage, subordination.**
Example: Abel obtains a **mortgage** loan from Solid Savings to finance the acquisition of a property. To reduce the **down payment,** he takes out a **second mortgage** with Baker, an investor. Solid Savings has a first lien and has first **priority** to **foreclosure** sale proceeeds in case of a **default.** Baker has a *junior lien* and is entitled to whatever remains, up to the debt and costs, after Solid Savings is **indemnified.**

LIEN-THEORY STATES states whose laws give a **lien** on property to secure debt. Contrasted with **title theory states** in which the

lender becomes the **title** owner. In either case the borrower has the right to use and enjoy the property in the absence of **default**; in the event of default, lenders may **foreclose**.

Example: After **closing** the sale of a home in a *lien-theory state*, the lender acquires a **first mortgage** and may foreclose upon certain default.

LIFE ESTATE a **freehold** interest (in **real property**) that expires upon the death of the owner or some other specified person (**pur autre vie**).

Example: A retired couple purchase a *life estate* in a retirement village apartment unit. Upon death of both husband and wife, ownership of the unit will revert to the owner's association, who may then resell to another couple.

LIFE OF LOAN CAP a contractual limitation on the maximum interest rate that can be applied to an adjustable rate mortgage during the term of the loan. See **adjustable rate mortgage;** contrast **annual cap.**

Example: An adjustable rate mortgage is offered at the initial interest rate of 7.5% and has a *life of loan cap* of 5 percentage points. At no time during the term of the loan can the interest rate rise above 12.5%, regardless of how much the index rises.

LIFE TENANT one who is allowed to use property for life or the lifetime of another designated person. See **life estate.**

Example: Graham owns a life estate in a home. As a *life tenant,* Graham may enjoy full ownership rights to the home during her lifetime.

LIKE-KIND PROPERTY property having the same nature. See also **Section 1031** and **tax-free exchange.**

Example: Under the **Internal Revenue Code**, apartments and land are considered *like-kind property,* but animals of different sexes are not.

LIMITED LIABILITY the restriction of one's potential losses to the amount invested. The absence of personal liability. See **at-risk rules.**

Example: *Limited liability* is provided to stockholders in a **corporation** and limited partners of a **limited partnership**. Those parties cannot lose more than they contribute to the corporation, unless they agree to become personally liable. For example, if Collins buys stock in a corporation for $1,000, she cannot lose more than that amount. However, many lenders require personal guarantees of major stockholders before lending to corporations.

LIMITED PARTNERSHIP one in which there is at least one partner who is passive and limits **liability** to the amount invested, and at least one partner whose liability extends beyond monetary invest-

ment. See **general partner**, **partnership**.
Example: Abel, a **syndicator**, forms a *limited partnership* with Price, Stone, and Wise. Abel invests his time and talent, is the general partner, and owns 10% of the partnership. Price, Stone, and Wise each invested $30,000 cash and were limited partners. They buy property with a $90,000 **down payment** and a $500,000 mortgage. The property drops in value by $250,000. Price, Stone, and Wise lose their **equity**, and Abel, the general partner, is responsible for additional losses (Figure 100).

Limited partnership

Abel	Price	Stone	Wise
General partner	Limited partner	Limited partner	Limited partner
Entrepreneur and manager	Passive investor	Passive investor	Passive investor

FIGURE 100

LINE OF CREDIT an agreement whereby a financial institution promises to lend up to a certain amount without the need to file another application.
Example: Happy Homes Brokers, Inc., has a *line of credit* under which they can borrow up to $50,000 at 3% above the **prime rate** through The Goodmoney National Bank.

LIQUIDATE 1. to dissolve a business.
Example: A **corporation's** only asset is **real estate** which is encumbered by a **mortgage**. The stockholders decide to *liquidate* the corporation. They may have the corporation sell the real estate, **retire** the mortgage, and distribute the **resale proceeds** to stockholders. The corporation is said to be *liquidated*.
2. to **retire debts**.
Example: Abel *liquidates* a $1,000 **debt** by paying it off in full with cash.

LIQUIDATED DAMAGES an amount agreed upon in a contract that one party will pay the other in the event of a **breach of the contract**.
Example: Abel engages a builder to erect a house. The **contract** says that if the builder fails to complete it by March 1, 1985, the builder will pay $50 per day thereafter until completion, as *liquidated damages*.

LIQUIDITY ease of converting **assets** to cash.
Example: Common stocks and U.S. savings bonds have good *liquidity*. **Real estate** and many types of collectibles generally have poor *liquidity*.

LIS PENDENS Latin: "suit pending." Recorded **notice** of the filing of a suit, the outcome of which may affect **title** to a certain land.
Example: The unpaid **mortgage** holder filed a **foreclosure** suit. She gave notice of *lis pendens* to make others aware of the suit pending.

LIST to obtain a **listing**.
Example: Baker wanted to *list* as many properties as possible under an **exclusive right to sell** so he would earn a commission no matter who sold the property.

LISTING 1. a written engagement **contract** between a principal and an **agent**, authorizing the agent to perform services for the principal involving the latter's property. 2. a record of property for sale by a **broker** who has been authorized by the owner to sell. 3. the property so listed.
Example: Abel employs Baker to find a buyer for his home by giving Baker a *listing* contract. When prospective buyers visit Baker, they will examine the *listings* in Baker's office. If interested, a prospective buyer may wish to visit the *listing*.

LISTING BROKER (AGENT) the licensed real estate **broker** (agent) who secures a **listing** of the property. Contrast with **selling broker (agent)**.
Example: For most sales, the *listing broker* and the **selling broker** share **commissions** equally. In some locales, notably for new homes, the *listing broker* earns only 1%, whereas the **selling broker** earns 3% of the selling price.

LITIGATION the act of carrying on a lawsuit.
Example: *Litigation* is a contest in court to enforce a right.

LITTORAL part of the shore zone of a large body of water. Compare **riparian rights**.
Example: Lot A has *littoral* land. Lot B has **riparian** land (Figure 101).

LOAN APPLICATION document required by a lender prior to issuing a **loan commitment**. The application generally includes the following information:
1. name of the borrower
2. amount and terms of the loan
3. description of the subject property to be mortgaged

4. borrower's financial and employment data
Example: Lowry wishes to borrow money to purchase a home. At Friendly Savings, she completes a *loan application* and pays an application fee. Friendly Savings will **appraise** the house, examine Lowry's **credit rating**, and verify certain information on the application prior to approving or disapproving the application.
commitment from the local **savings and loan association** for permanent financing.

FIGURE 101

LOAN APPLICATION FEE a charge required by a loan originator to be paid by the borrower to cover the credit report, property appraisal and other incidental expenses associated with underwriting the loan. The fee is generally not refundable.
Example: Home Mortgage Company charges a *loan application fee* of $250 to process a mortgage application. The prospective property buyer/mortgage borrower brings the purchase contract to a loan officer at Home Mortgage Company.

LOAN CLOSING see **closing.**

LOAN COMMITMENT an agreement to lend money, generally of a specified amount, at specified terms at some time in the future.
Example: Before commencing development, Abel obtained a *loan*

LOAN CORRESPONDENT see **mortgage correspondent.**

LOAN ORIGINATION FEE see **origination fees.**

LOAN POINTS see **discount points.**

LOAN SERVICING see **servicing.**

LOAN-TO-VALUE RATIO (LTV) the portion of the amount borrowed compared to the cost or value of the property purchased.
Example: Abel bought a $100,000 house and arranged a $90,000

mortgage loan, resulting in a 90% *loan-to-value ratio*. Home mortgages at more than an 80% *LTV* ratio generally require **mortgage insurance**.

LOG CABIN an early American style house of unfinished logs. **Example:** Figure 102.

Chimneys at ends Shingle covered gable roof

Unfinished logs

FIGURE 102

LONG-TERM CAPITAL GAIN for income tax purposes, the gain on a **capital asset** held long enough to qualify for special tax considerations.
Note: The Tax Reform Act of 1986 eliminated the favorable treatment for *long-term capital gains*. The highest rate in 1987 for *long-term capital gains* is 28%; thereafter there is no distinction in tax rates as compared with ordinary income.

LOT AND BLOCK a method of locating a parcel of land. See **legal description.**
Example: The shaded property in Figure 103 is lot 4, block B of Rolling Acres **subdivision,** in Lincoln County, New Mexico.

LOT LINE a line bounding a lot as described in a property **survey.**
Example: Figure 104

LOW-INCOME HOUSING (QUALIFIED) housing that is eligible for special tax credits of up to 9% of their cost (4% in certain situations) under the 1986 tax act. Strict rules must be followed concerning tenant qualification, certification, and project financing.

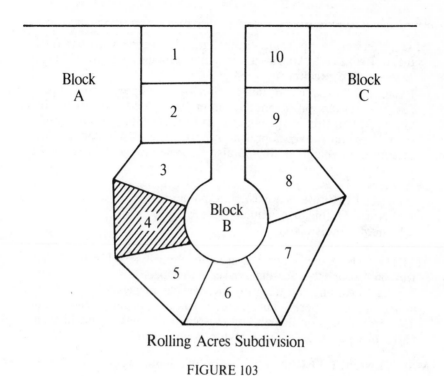

Rolling Acres Subdivision

FIGURE 103

Lot line

Lot line

FIGURE 104

M

MAI (Member, Appraisal Institute) a member of the **American Institute of Real Estate Appraisers,** which is affiliated with the **National Association of Realtors®.**

Example: To acquire the designation *MAI*, an **appraiser** must pass several written proficiency examinations, perform acceptable appraisal work for a specific period of time, and prepare a demonstration narrative appraisal report. The *MAI* signifies the appraiser is qualified to appraise a broad range of **real estate** types.

Address:
American Institute of Real Estate Appraisers
430 North Michigan Avenue
Chicago, Illinois 60611

MAINTENANCE activities required to compensate for **wear and tear** on a property. See **deferred maintenance.**

Example: Among the duties of **property management** is *maintenance* of the property. This includes routine upkeep of the building, repair and periodic painting as needed, keeping all mechanical parts in working order, and lawn maintenance.

MAINTENANCE FEE an assessment by a **homeowners' association** or a **condominium owners' association,** to pay costs of operating the **common elements.**

Example: A condominium association assesses each owner a *maintenance fee* of $100 per month for lawn maintenance and insurance costs.

MAJORITY 1. the age at which one is no longer a **minor** and is fully able to conduct one's own affairs; majority (full legal age) is 18 to 21 years, depending on the state.

Example: Abel, under 18 years of age, enters into a **contract** to buy land. Because he has not attained *majority*, he may **void** the contract if he chooses. Baker, the seller, is bound to the contract unless Abel voids it.

2. more than half.

Example: The bylaws of the **condominium owners' association** require a *majority* of the owners who vote to change to another management firm.

MALL a public area connecting individual stores in a **shopping center;** generally enclosed. Also, an enclosed shopping center.

Example: A large shopping *mall* was being developed south of town. It was designed to include over 40 stores connected by an

enclosed and air-conditioned *mall.*

MANAGEMENT AGREEMENT a **contract** between the owner of property and someone who agrees to manage it. Fees are generally 4-10% of the rental income. See **property management.**
Example: Abel has a *management agreement* with Baker for a 200-unit apartment complex. The contract provides that Baker will receive 5% of the rental income, and he will perform all duties concerning leasing, operating, and managing the property. He will maintain a separate bank checking account for receipts and disbursements, provide monthly accounting statements, and manage the property with competence.

MANSARD ROOF one having two slopes on all four sides, with the lower slope steeper than the upper, flatter sections.
Example: Figure 105

Mansard

FIGURE 105

MANUFACTURED HOME see **mobile home, mobile home park.**

MARGIN a constant amount added to the value of the **index** for the purpose of adjusting the interest rate on an **adjustable rate mortgage.**
Example: An adjustable rate mortgage is indexed to the 1 year Treasury yield and has a *margin* of 3 percentage points. If the index is currently 6%, the fully indexed rate on the loan is 9% (6% index plus 3% *margin*).

MARGINAL PROPERTY property that is barely profitable to use.
Example: The sale of cotton that has been efficiently raised **yields** $100; yet the cotton cost $99.99 to raise. The land on which the cotton was raised is therefore considered *marginal property.*
Example: A tract of undeveloped land is deemed *marginal property* because of lack of access to a roadway.

MARITAL DEDUCTION the tax-free amount one transfers by **will**

to one's spouse. The 1981 tax act allows an unlimited amount to be transferred without federal estate tax.

Example: The concept of a *marital deduction* is to treat husband and wife as one economic unit. Since 1981, a federal **estate tax** will be due only on taxable property that passes to another generation.

MARKETABLE TITLE a **title** so free from defect that a court will enforce the title's acceptance by a purchaser. Compare **cloud on the title.**

Example: Through a divorce settlement, Collins obtained certain ownership rights to a property. She now wished to sell the property. To obtain a *marketable title,* she must obtain a **quitclaim deed** from her former husband, thereby curing a defect in her title.

MARKET ANALYSIS a study of the supply and demand conditions in a specific area for a specific type of property or service. A *market analysis* report is generally prepared by someone with experience in real estate, economics, or marketing. It serves to help decide what type of project to develop and is also helpful in arranging permanent and construction financing for a proposed development.

Example: The developer commissioned a *market analysis* to evaluate the need for luxury apartments in the St. Louis suburban market. Copies of the report were supplied to prospective lenders for this type of development.

MARKET APPROACH same as **market comparison approach.**

MARKET AREA a geographic region from which one can expect the primary demand for a specific product or service provided at a fixed location.

Example: A regional shopping center has a larger *market area* than a neighborhood shopping center.

Example: A developer estimates that the *market area* for a **subdivision** covers the northeast section of the metropolitan area.

MARKET COMPARISON APPROACH one of 3 **appraisal approaches.** Value is estimated by analyzing sales prices of similar properties (**comparables**) recently sold.

Example: The subject property is a 3-bedroom, 2-bath house. Two recently sold comparables are found. The appraiser, using the *market comparison approach,* sets up Table 23.

MARKET DATA APPROACH same as **market comparison approach.**

MARKET DELINEATION the process of defining the geographic extent of the demand for a specific property.

Example: The *market delineation* for a new regional shopping center showed that shoppers are likely to be drawn from a 2 county area.

TABLE 23

Subject	Comparable #1	Comparable #2
Sale price	$70,500	$69,000
Date of sale	last week	3 months ago (+$1000)
3 bedrooms	3 bedrooms	3 bedrooms
2 baths	2½ baths (−$500)	2 baths
Adjusted price	$70,000	$70,000

The subject property is appraised for $70,000.

MARKET PRICE the actual price paid in a market transaction. Contrast with **market value.**
Example: A home was offered for sale at $100,000. It was appraised for $93,000, and actually sold for $95,000 in an **arm's length transaction.** The *market price* is $95,000.

MARKET RENT the **rent** that a comparable unit would command if offered in the competitive market. Contrast with **contract rent.**
Example: Long rents an apartment to Towns for $400 per month. Similar units are renting for $450 per month. The apartment's *market rent* is $450 per month.

MARKET SEGMENTATION the process of defining the socio-economic characteristics of the demand for a specific property or properties.
Example: *Market segmentation* shows that the tenants for a new garden apartment complex are likely to be young married couples with incomes between $15,000 and $30,000.

MARKET STUDY see **market analysis.**

MARKET VALUE the theoretical highest price a buyer, willing but not compelled to buy, would pay, and the lowest price a seller, willing but not compelled to sell, would accept.
Example: An **appraisal** of a home indicates its *market value* is $75,000. In a normally active market, the home should sell for this amount if allowed to stay on the market for a reasonable time. The owner may, however, **deed** the home to a relative for $250. The owner may also grow impatient and sell for $70,000. Conversely, an anxious buyer may be found who pays $80,000. Finally, the owner may provide favorable financing and sell for $85,000.

MASONRY construction made from brick, cement block, or stone.
Example: The ground floor of the house shown in Figure 106 is made of *masonry*. The upper floor is wooden frame with wooden siding.

FIGURE 106

MASTER DEED used by a condominium developer or converter for recording a **condominium** development. It divides a single property into individually owned units, includes restrictions on their use and provides for ownership of common areas.
Example: When a New York apartment building was converted into a condominium, the converter filed a *master deed* with the city to reflect separate ownership of individual units.

MASTER LEASE a controlling **lease.** Contrast with **sublease.** Note that one cannot grant a greater interest in real estate than one has; so if a *master lease* is for a 5-year term, a sublease cannot legally exceed 5 years.
Example: Abel leases 10,000 square feet of retail space to Baker. Baker then subleases the space to 5 different **tenants.** The lease between Abel and Baker is the *master lease.*

MASTER LIMITED PARTNERSHIP an ownership vehicle, espe-' cially used for real estate or oil and gas ventures. It is generally formed by a "roll up" of existing **limited partnerships** that own property, and typically has the advantage of ownership interests that are more marketable than individual limited partnerships.
Example: A real estate entrepreneur has syndicated 30 properties over the past 5 years, with each as a separate limited partnership. All were brought together as one large entity, a *master limited partnership,* with interests that were readily marketable.

MASTER PLAN a document that describes, in narrative and with maps, an overall development concept. The master plan is used to coordinate the preparation of more detailed plans or may be a collection of detailed plans. The plan may be prepared by a local government to guide private and public development or by a **developer** on a specific project.
Example: The city planners checked to see if the **zoning** request complied with the city's *master plan*.
Example: The *master plan* for further development of the resort **condominium** is displayed in the sales office.

MATERIAL FACT a fact that is germane to a particular situation; one that participants in the situation such as a trial, may reasonably be expected to consider.
Example: If *material facts* about the investment property lying in a **floodplain** had been communicated to the buyer, he would not have bought. He is now charging **misrepresentation** against the seller and the **broker.**

MATERIALMAN a person who supplies materials used in the construction or repair of a building or other property.
Example: Since the *materialman* was not paid for lumber, he filed a **mechanic's lien** against the property.

MATERIAL PARTICIPATION a tax term introduced by the 1986 tax act, defined as year-round active involvement in the operations of a business activity on a regular, continuous and substantial basis. Three main factors to consider in determining the presence of *material participation* are:
• Is the activity the taxpayer's principal trade or business?
• How close is the taxpayer to the business?
• Does the taxpayer have knowledge and experience in the enterprise?
Retired Farmers A special exception is provided for retired farmers who are considered to continue to participate materially in that activity after retirement, as does the spouse of deceased farmers.
Limited Partners Limited partnership interests are considered inherently passive. However, the IRS may draft regulations to prevent persons from using the limited partnership vehicle for any business enterprise simply to generate passive income to offset passive losses.

MATURITY the due date of a loan.
Example: A **mortgage** loan may have a *maturity* of 30 years. Periodic payments are established so that the loan **principal** will **amortize** by the *maturity* date.
Example: A bond may have a *maturity* of 20 years. Generally, **interest** only will be paid, with the full principal repaid at *maturity*.

MECHANIC'S LIEN a **lien** given by law upon a building or other **improvement** upon land, and upon the land itself, as **security** for

the payment for labor done and materials furnished for improvement.
Example: The unpaid plumber filed a *mechanic's lien* against the property while it was under construction. The builder had to satisfy the lien in order to give **clear title** to the buyer.

MEETING OF THE MINDS agreement, by all parties to a **contract,** to the exact terms thereof.
Example: To have a *meeting of the minds* there must be:
1. an **offer** and **acceptance**
2. considering the subject property
3. **consideration**
4. **terms**

MERCHANTABLE TITLE see **marketable title.**

MERGER the fusion of 2 or more interests, such as businesses or investments.
Examples: Examples of *mergers* are:
• conglomerates—corporations that are not customers or suppliers to each other or competitors
• corporations—union of 2 or more by transferring property to one that survives, and issuing its shares to stockholders of the corporation that ceases to exist

MERIDIAN a longitudinal reference line that traverses the earth in a north-south direction; all meridians circle the earth through the equator and converge at the north and south poles; used by **surveyors** in describing property under the **government rectangular**

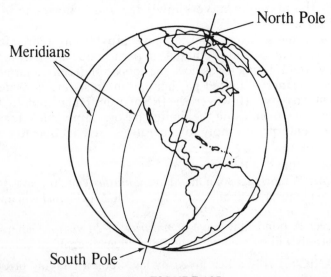

FIGURE 107

survey method.
Example: Figure 107

METES AND BOUNDS a land **description** method that details all the **boundary** lines of land, together with their terminal points and angles.
Example: *Metes and bounds* description: Beginning at a point on the northeasterly corner of the intersection of South St. and West Rd.; running thence northerly along West Rd. 200 feet; thence easterly parallel to South St. 150 feet; thence southerly parallel to West Rd. 200 feet; thence westerly along South St. 150 feet to the point of beginning (Figure 108).

FIGURE 108

METROPOLITAN AREA generally the developed region economically attached to a large central city; same as **standard metropolitan statistical area.**
Example: The *metropolitan area* of Atlanta, Georgia covers 15 counties and contains over 2 million people.

MILL one tenth of a cent. Used in expressing tax rates on a per-dollar basis.
Example: A tax rate of 60 *mills* means that taxes are 6 cents per dollar of **assessed valuation.**

MILLAGE RATE a tax rate applied to property. Each **mill** represents $1 of tax **assessment** per $1,000 of assessed property value.
Example: The *millage rate* for property taxes in the Bumpton school district is 20 mills. A home with assessed value of $100,000 pays $2,000 a year in property taxes to the district.

MINERAL RIGHTS the privilege of gaining **income** from the sale of oil, gas, and other valuable resources found on land.
Example: Abel purchases a property that contains underground oil deposits. Abel may:
• develop these *mineral rights* by drilling a well
• sell the rights for a price to an oil company
• **lease** the rights to an oil company in exchange for a **royalty**

MINIMUM LOT AREA the smallest building lot area allowed in a **subdivision,** generally specified by a **zoning ordinance.**
Example: Baker owns land that is zoned "R-4." If Baker develops the land, it must be used for residential purposes and lots must have a *minimum lot area* of ¼ acre.

MINOR a person under the age of **majority** specified by law (18 to 21 years, depending on the state).
Example: Contracts for the sale or use of real estate, entered into by a *minor,* are voidable by the minor. Note that the other party is bound; only the minor may void them.

MISREPRESENTATION an untrue statement, whether unintentional or deliberate. It may be a form of nondisclosure where there is a duty to disclose or the planned creation of a false appearance. Where there is misrepresentation of **material fact,** the person injured may sue for **damages** or **rescind** the **contract.** See **false advertising.**
Example: The **broker** represented the home as being structurally sound. The broker did not know that **termites** were destroying the wood. The buyer sued the broker for *misrepresentation.*

MISSION HOUSE a nineteenth century style house that looks like the old mission churches and houses of Southern California. The doors and windows are arch-shaped.
Example: Figure 109

MISTAKE an unintentional error made in preparing a **contract;** may be corrected by mutual consent of all parties without voiding contract.
Example: Abel and Baker agree to a sales contract for a property located at 100 Main Street. In preparing the contract the address is listed as 100 Main Blvd. The *mistake* is discovered at the **closing,** and correction is made with the consent of both parties.

MOBILE HOME a dwelling unit (Figure 110) manufactured in a factory and designed to be transported to a **site** and semipermanently attached.
Example: One option for low-cost housing is purchase of a *mobile home,* which generally costs much less than site-built housing. *Mobile homes* may be placed on the purchaser's lot or in a **mobile home park** for a monthly rental.

Looks like old mission church

Arch-shaped doors and windows

Pyramid-shaped roof

Parapet

Tile roof

Stucco walls

FIGURE 109

Up to 72 ft long

Metal roofing and siding

About 12 ft wide

Removable wheels

Relocatable

Factory made

FIGURE 110

MOBILE HOME PARK a **subdivision** of plots designed for siting of mobile homes. Plots are generally leased to mobile home owners and include **utilities,** parking space, and access to utility roads. Many parks also include such **amenities** as swimming pools and clubhouses.
Example: A typical *mobile home park* design (Figure 111).

MODEL UNIT a representative home, apartment, or office space used as part of a sales campaign to demonstrate the design, structure, and appearance of units in a development.

265

MODERNIZE

Example: A **developer** constructs a *model unit* in an effort to **pre-lease** units in a development. Prospective tenants are invited to tour the *model unit* to gain an appreciation for the design and appearance of the development.

MODERNIZE to alter a property by installing up-to-date equipment, making contemporary cosmetic improvements, and deleting obsolete facilities.
Example: The redeveloper *modernized* the apartment building by installing dishwashers, wall-to-wall carpeting, a new gas furnace and by removing the coal storage bin.

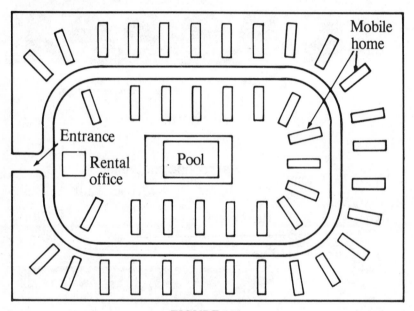

Mobile home

Entrance

Rental office

Pool

FIGURE 111

MODULAR HOUSING dwelling units constructed from components **prefabricated** in a factory and erected on the **site**.
Example: In a *modular housing* project, site preparation may be performed while structural panels are being fabricated by mass production techniques in a factory. The panels are then shipped to the site and erected in place.

MOISTURE BARRIER a layer of foil, plastic, or paper used in the construction of exterior walls, ceilings, and foundations to prevent moisture penetration into wooden members or insulation.
Example: The *moisture barrier* in an exterior wall (Figure 112).

MONETARY INSTITUTION DEREGULATION ACT same as **Depository Institutions Deregulation and Monetary Control Act.**

266

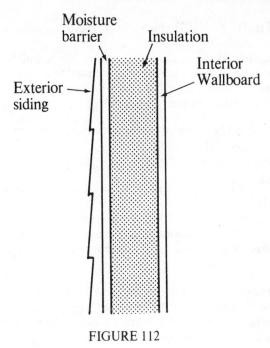

Moisture barrier

Insulation

Interior Wallboard

Exterior siding

FIGURE 112

MONTEREY ARCHITECTURE a nineteenth century style, 2-story house with a balcony across the front at the second floor level. **Example:** Figure 113

Balcony across front at second floor

Shingle roof

2 stories

Rail simple iron or wood

FIGURE 113

MONTH-TO-MONTH TENANCY lease agreement extendable or cancelable each month.
Example: Abel rents an apartment from Baker on a *month-to-month tenancy* basis. Abel may remain as long as he pays rent and Baker does not give notice to cancel the lease. Abel may also cancel the lease upon giving notice.

MONUMENT a fixed object and point established by surveyors to determine land locations.
Example: See **landmark.**

MORATORIUM a time period during which a certain activity is not allowed.
Example: Fair City passes an **ordinance** that establishes a 6-month *moratorium* on condominium **conversions.** During the period, no one may legally convert an apartment complex into **condominium** units.

MORTGAGE a written **instrument** that creates a **lien** upon **real estate** as **security** for the payment of a specified debt.
Example: Lowry wants to buy a home. She needs a loan to complete the purchase. As **collateral,** Lowry offers a *mortgage* on the property to the lender.
Note that the borrower gives the mortgage, which pledges the property as collateral. The lender gives the loan.

MORTGAGE ASSUMPTION same as **assumption of mortgage.**

MORTGAGE BACKED SECURITY a bond or other financial obligation secured by a pool of mortgage loans. See **collateralized mortgage obligations, REMICs.**
Example: The Sachs Mortgage Broker Company purchased $100 million worth of mortgage loans on private homes. To fund the purchase, Sachs created a *mortgage backed security* secured by the pool of mortgages and sold the security to investors.

MORTGAGE BANKER one who originates, sells, and services **mortgage** loans. Most loans are insured or guaranteed by a government agency or private mortgage insurer. See **mortgage insurance.**
Example: The Mortgage Store, a *mortgage banker,* originates 100 loans totaling $5,000,000. They sell this package of loans to an out-of-state investor for $5,010,000. They continue to collect monthly payments from homeowners and assure that property taxes are paid and insurance is maintained. They charge the investor an annual fee of ⅜ of 1% of the loan **principal,** each month remitting to the investor the rest of the monthly payments from homeowners.

MORTGAGE BANKERS ASSOCIATION (MBA) an organization that provides educational programs and other services for **mortgage bankers.** Offers the Certified Mortgage Banker (CMB) designation. Publishes *Mortgage Banker* magazine.
Address: Mortgage Bankers Association of America
1125 Fifteenth Street, N.W.
Washington, D.C. 20005

MORTGAGE BONDS tax-exempt securities sold by municipal and state authorities for the purpose of providing low-interest rate **mortgage** loans to qualified individuals. For most programs, mortgage borrowers must be first-time home buyers with moderate income.
Example: Local Housing Finance Agency, a creation of the city of Local, sold $50 million of *mortgage bonds.* The proceeds from the sale were used to originate loans through local mortgage lenders for first-time home buyers within the city. Interest on the bonds was tax-exempt to the bond-holders, thereby allowing the agency to borrow money at an **interest rate** below 8%. The mortgage loans could be originated at rates below 9% at a time when market mortgage interest rates were above 10%.

MORTGAGE BROKER one who, for a fee, places loans with investors, but does not service such loans.
Example: The Ace Development Company wants to build a shopping center. A *mortgage broker* charges a 1% fee for each construction loan (placed with a commercial bank) and the permanent loan (placed with an insurance company).

MORTGAGE COMMITMENT an agreement between a lender and a borrower to lend money at a future date, subject to the conditions described in the agreement.
Example: Baker wishes to build a home. Construction will require 6 months. Baker obtains a *mortgage commitment* from Home Town Savings and Loan for permanent financing of the home at the time of its completion.

MORTGAGE CONSTANT the percentage ratio between the annual **debt service** and the loan **principal.** The formula is

$$\frac{\text{Ann. debt serv.}}{\text{Loan prin.}} = \text{mort. const.}$$

Example: A loan of $10,000 at 12% interest for 5 years requires annual payments of $2774. The *mortgage constant* is

$$\frac{2,774}{10,000} = .2774 \text{ or } 27.74\%$$

Annual debt service for the loan is

$$0.2774 \times \$10,000 = \$2,774$$

MORTGAGE CORRESPONDENT one who services loans for a fee. Compare **mortgage broker.**
Example: The Good Money Savings Association bought a package of 1,000 loans in another state. They arrange with a *mortgage correspondent* to collect monthly payments, pay real estate taxes, and assure that the property is insured. The *mortgage correspondent* keeps as a fee ⅜ of 1% of the mortgage balance each year.

MORTGAGE DISCOUNT amount of **principal** that lenders deduct at the beginning of the loan. See **discount points.**
Example: Abel obtains a mortgage loan in the amount of $50,000. The loan is discounted by 2 **points,** each point equaling 1% of the **principal.** At **closing** Abel will receive $49,000, yet will owe $50,000. The $1,000 difference is the *mortgage discount.*

MORTGAGEE one who holds a **lien** on property or **title** to property, as **security** for a debt.
Example: Abel obtains a **mortgage** loan from Homebuyers Savings. Homebuyers Savings serves as the *mortgagee.*

MORTGAGE GUARANTEE INSURANCE CO. (MGIC) a private company that insures, to lenders, loan repayment in the event of **default** and/or **foreclosure.** See **mortgage insurance.**
Example: Collins wants to arrange a loan for 90% of the cost of the home she is buying. The lender applies to *MGIC* for **private mortgage insurance.** MGIC accepts and, for a **premium,** stands willing to accept any losses on the mortgages up to 25% of the **principal.**

MORTGAGE INSURANCE 1. a policy that guarantees repayment of a mortgage loan in the event of death or, possibly, disability of the **mortgagor.** 2. protection for the lender in the event of **default,** usually covering the top 25% of the amount borrowed. See **private mortgage insurance.**
Example: Manning obtains a mortgage loan and, for an additional monthly **premium,** purchases *mortgage insurance.* Should Manning die before loan **maturity,** the policy will pay the remaining balance of the loan. This protects Manning's survivors from losing the property because of inability to continue the loan payments, and also protects the **mortgagee.**

MORTGAGE LIEN an **encumbrance** on property used to secure a loan. The holder of the **lien** has a claim to the property in case of loan **default.** The **priority** of the claim depends on the order of **recording** and any **subordination** agreements. Thus a **first mortgage** generally has prior claim to all other mortgage lien holders. See also **second mortgage.**
Example: Minton obtains a mortgage loan to purchase a house. Minton signs a **note** and mortgage contract. The lender obtains a

mortgage lien on the house. Should Minton default on the loan, the lender may **foreclose** and exercise the lien to force a sale, the proceeds of which are used to satisfy Minton's debt.

MORTGAGE OUT to obtain financing in excess of the cost to construct a project. In the early 1970's **developers** could mortgage out by obtaining a permanent **loan commitment** based on a high percentage of the completed project's value. This enabled the developer to borrow more than the cost of developing the project. Since then opportunities to mortgage out have been virtually eliminated by lower **loan-to-value ratios,** higher **capitalization rates** and higher construction costs.
Example: A proposed office building is projected to produce annual **net operating income** of $100,000. At a capitalization rate of 10%, the building is worth $1,000,000. A **takeout** loan commitment is obtained for 80% of value, or $800,000. The developer requires only $750,000 to purchase the land and construct the building. The $50,000 excess represents the results of the developer *mortgaging out.*

MORTGAGE POOL a collection of loans of similar nature which are sold as a unit in the secondary market or used to back a security which is then sold in the capital markets.
Example: Lenders Mortgage Company packaged a *mortgage pool* consisting of $50 million worth of VA guaranteed loans. The package was sold to a group of investors who each put up a minimum of $25,000.

MORTGAGE RELIEF acquired freedom from mortgage debt, generally through **assumption of mortgage** by another party or **debt** retirement. In a tax-free exchange, mortgage relief is considered **boot** received.
Example: Collins exchanged her mortgaged office building, receiving land worth $25,000 and *mortgage relief* of $75,000. The total value received was $100,000.

MORTGAGOR one who pledges property as **security** for a loan.
Example: Abel obtains a mortgage loan from Homebuyers Savings. Abel serves as a *mortgagor.*

MULTIFAMILY HOUSING a type of residential structure with more than one **dwelling** unit in the same building.
Example: *Multifamily housing* is divided into 2 categories:
2-4 dwelling units: **duplexes,** triplexes, and quadraplexes
5 or more units: apartment buildings
Multifamily housing may be tenant-occupied, owner-occupied (as in a **condominium** or cooperative project), or mixed (as many duplexes with the owner occupying one side).

MULTIPLE LISTING an arrangement among a group of real estate **brokers;** they agree in advance to provide information about some

or all of their **listings** to the others and also agree that **commissions** on sales of such listings will be split between listing and selling brokers.

Example: A broker lists a home under an **exclusive right to sell.** The broker belongs to a *multiple listing* association. After 5 days the broker turns in a description of the home to the association. Any cooperating broker can sell the home and will receive half of the commission. The broker who obtained the **exclusive right to sell** is assured of earning half the commission upon the sale.

MULTIPLE LISTING SERVICE (MLS) an association of real estate **brokers** that agrees to share **listings** with one another. The listing broker and the selling broker share the **commission.** The MLS usually distributes a book with all listings to its members, updating the book frequently. Prospective buyers benefit from the ability to select from among many homes from any member broker.

Example: Abel and Baker, both brokers, are members of the *multiple listing service.* A home that was listed by Abel under an **exclusive right to sell** is sold by Baker. The two brokers share the commission.

MUNIMENTS OF TITLE documents, such as **deeds** or **contracts,** one uses to indicate ownership.

Example: In order to register **title** under the **Torrens system,** the owner offered *muniments of title.*

MUTUAL SAVINGS BANKS mostly in the northeastern U.S., these state-chartered banks are owned by the depositors and operated for their benefit. Most of these banks hold a large portion of their **assets** in home mortgage loans.

Example: Abel deposits his savings in a *mutual savings bank* in New York. As a depositor-shareholder, Abel receives a proportionate distribution of the bank's earnings.

N

NATIONAL APARTMENT ASSOCIATION (NAA) an organization of apartment owners, with local chapters in metropolitan areas, that provides information and services for members concerning apartment rentals, **lease** forms, occupancy rates, and other matters.

Address:
National Apartment Association
1825 K Street, N.W.
Washington, D.C. 20006

NATIONAL ASSOCIATION OF CORPORATE REAL ESTATE EXECUTIVES (NACORE) membership includes those active with purchasing, selling, and managing **real estate** held by **corporations.**
Address:
National Association of Corporate Real Estate Executives
7799 Southwest 62nd Avenue
South Miami, Florida 33143, N.W.

NATIONAL ASSOCIATION OF HOME BUILDERS (NAHB) an organization of home builders, providing educational, political information and research services. Publishes a monthly magazine, *Builder.*
Address:
National Association of Home Builders
15th and M Street, N.W.
Washington, D.C. 20005

NATIONAL ASSOCIATION OF REAL ESTATE BROKERS (NAREB) an organization mostly of minority real estate salespersons and **brokers** who are called **Realtists.**
Address:
National Association of Real Estate Brokers
9th floor, Suite 900
1101 14th Street, N.W.
Washington, D.C. 20005

NATIONAL ASSOCIATION OF REAL ESTATE LICENSE LAW OFFICIALS (NARELLO) membership is composed of commissioners from state real estate licensing agencies.
Address:
National Association of Real Estate License Law Officials
2580 South 90th Street
Omaha, Nebraska 68124

NATIONAL ASSOCIATION OF REALTORS® (NAR) an organization of **Realtors®**, devoted to encouraging professionalism in **real estate** activities. There are over 600,000 members of NAR, 50 state associations, and several affiliates. Members are required to abide by the **Code of Ethics** of the NAR.
Address:
National Association of Realtors®
430 N. Michigan Avenue
Chicago, Illinois 60611

NATIONAL SOCIETY OF REAL ESTATE APPRAISERS an affiliate of the National Association of Real Estate Brokers that offers the professional designations RA, CRA, MREA.

NEGATIVE AMORTIZATION

Address:
National Society of Real Estate Appraisers
1265 East 105th Street
Cleveland, Ohio 44108

NEGATIVE AMORTIZATION an increase in the **outstanding balance** of a loan resulting from the failure of periodic **debt service** payments to cover required interest charged on the loan. Generally occurs under **indexed loans** for which the applicable **interest rate** may be changed without affecting the monthly payments. *Negative amortization* will occur if the indexed interest rate is increased.

Example: A loan is originated at 15% interest with a **maturity** of 30 years. The interest rate may be adjusted each 6 months, but monthly payments remain a constant $632. After 6 months, the interest rate is raised to 16.5%, which would require a monthly payment of $692 to fully amortize the loan. At the new interest rate, $687 is required to pay interest. The $55 difference between the payment and interest due is added to the principal in month 7 as *negative amortization* (Figure 114).

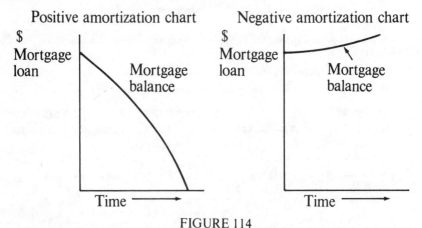

Positive amortization chart Negative amortization chart

FIGURE 114

NEGATIVE CASH FLOW situation in which a property owner must make an outlay of funds to operate a property.
Example: Baker acquires an apartment building with the first year income statement shown in Table 24.

Baker must spend $5,000 to operate the building for the first year, because of a *negative cash flow*.

NEGATIVE LEVERAGE same as **reverse leverage.**

NEGOTIABLE INSTRUMENT a promise to pay money, transferable from one person to another.
Example: Abel gave Baker a *negotiable instrument* that contained

274

a promise to pay $1000 on July 22 of this year. Baker sold the note for $900 cash to Collins by endorsing and delivering it. Collins became a **holder in due course.**

TABLE 24

Potential **gross income:**	$50,000
Vacancy loss	− 5,000
Effective gross income	45,000
Operating expenses	−30,000
Net operating income	15,000
Debt service	−20,000
Negative cash flow before tax	$5,000

NEGOTIATION the process of bargaining that precedes an agreement. Successful negotiation generally results in a **contract** between the parties.
Example: Nelson wishes to purchase a property from Newman. Nelson is willing to pay up to a certain price and desires certain **conditions** placed on the sale. Newman will accept anything over a certain price and may be willing to help finance the purchase for a higher price. In *negotiation* Nelson and Newman attempt to come to an agreement over the price and conditions. When they agree, a sales contract is **executed.**

NEIGHBORHOOD a district or locality characterized by similar or compatible land uses. Neighborhoods are often identified by a place name and have boundaries composed of major streets, barriers, or abrupt changes in land use.
Example: Residential *neighborhoods* are often identified with a **subdivision,** an elementary school attendance zone, a major public facility, such as a college, or a small town within a larger urban area. Homes in the neighborhood are of similar style, age, and value.
Example: Commercial *neighborhoods* are generally associated with a major road, shopping center, or **central business district.**
Example: Industrial *neighborhoods* are generally identified by common use of a transportation linkage.

NEIGHBORHOOD LIFE CYCLE a generalized pattern that describes the physical and social changes that residential areas experience over time. See also **abandonment, filtering down, urban renewal, land use succession.**
Example: Richard Andrews' *neighborhood life cycle* (Figure 115).

275

NET INCOME

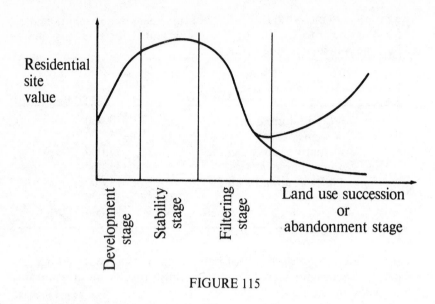

FIGURE 115

NET INCOME 1. in accounting, the amount remaining after all expenses have been met.
Example: Table 25
2. in **appraisal,** same as **net operating income.**

TABLE 25

Rental income		$10,000
Less:		
Utilities	$1,500	
Property taxes	1,000	
Management fee	500	
Maintenance expenses	2,000	
Interest	2,000	
Depreciation	1,000	
Income taxes	1,000	
Subtotal		− 9,000
Net income		$1,000

NET LEASABLE AREA in a building or project, floor space that may be rented to tenants. The area upon which rental payments are based. Generally excludes common areas and space devoted to the heating, cooling, and other equipment of a building.
Example: A building with 10 floors, each containing 3,000 square feet of space, may have a *net leasable area* of 25,000 square feet. Elevators, hallways etc. absorb the remaining 5,000 square feet.

NET LEASE a **lease** whereby, in addition to the rent stipulated, the **lessee** (tenant) pays such expenses as taxes, insurance, and **maintenance.** The landlord's rent receipt is thereby "net" of those expenses.

Example: Baker leases retail space from Abel on a *net lease*. Abel can expect to receive the full rent without deducting for **operating expenses,** which are paid by Baker. In practice, various levels of net leases are often used to designate arrangements where the tenant pays only some types of expenses and the landlord pays other types.

NET LISTING a listing in which the brokers's **commission** is the excess of the sale price over an agreed-upon (net) price to the seller; illegal in some states.

Example: Abel agrees to sell Baker's house on a *net listing*. They set the net price at $70,000. Abel finds a buyer willing to pay $75,000. Abel's commission is $5,000. Note that should Abel find a buyer offering $70,000, Abel would earn no commission.

NET OPERATING INCOME (NOI) income from property or business after **operating expenses** have been deducted, but before deducting income taxes and financing expenses (**interest** and **principal** payments). The formula is:

NOI = gross income − operating expenses

Example: A property produces rental income of $100,000 during the year. The expenses incurred are shown in Table 26.

TABLE 26

Operating expenses:	
Maintenance	$20,000
Insurance	5,000
Property taxes	10,000
Management	10,000
Utilities	15,000
	$60,000
Debt service:*	
Interest	$18,000
Principal	2,000
	$20,000
Income taxes*	($5,000)

*Excluded from the computation.

NOI = $100,000 − $60,000 = $40,000 (*net operating income*)

NET PRESENT VALUE a method of determining whether expected

performance of a proposed investment promises to be adequate. See also **internal rate of return, present value of one.**
Example: A proposed land investment requires $10,000 of cash now, and is expected to be resold for $25,000 in 4 years. For the **risks** involved, the investor seeks a 20% **discount rate** (same as **compounded rate of return**). The $25,000 amount to be received in 4 years, when discounted by 20% annually, is worth $12,056 now. Since the investment costs $10,000, the *net present value* is $2,056.

$$\frac{\$25,000}{(1 + 0.20)^4} - \$10,000 = \$2,056$$

NET WORTH the excess of **assets** over **liabilities.** The amount of **equity.**
Example: Table 27:

TABLE 27

Balance Sheet

Assets		Liabilities	
Land	$10,000	Mortgage	$75,000
Buildings	90,000	Net worth	25,000
Total	$100,000	Total	$100,000

NET YIELD the return on an investment after subtracting all expenses. See also **current yield, yield to maturity.**
Example: Equity paid for an investment is $10,000. **Net income** is $1,000. Therefore, the investment generates a $1,000 *net yield.*

NEW ENGLAND COLONIAL an early American style, 2½ story boxlike house that is generally symmetrical, square, or rectangular with side or rear wings. The traditional material is narrow clapboard siding. The roof is usually the gable type covered with shingles.
Example: Figure 116.

NEW ENGLAND FARM HOUSE an early American style of house that is simple and box-shaped. The traditional material for the exterior siding is white clapboard. A steep pitched roof is used to shed heavy snow.
Example: Figure 117.

NEW TOWN a large mixed-use development designed to provide residences, general shopping, services, and employment. The basic concept of a new town is to construct a community in a previously undeveloped area under a central plan, to avoid

Cornice with dentils

Chimney at each end

Small pane double-hung windows

Side lights

Gable roof

2½ stories

Wing

Working wood shutters

FIGURE 116

White clapboard

Steep, pitched roof simple box shape

FIGURE 117

unplanned development. Some European and South American countries use new towns to attract population into less developed regions.

Example: The popularity of *new towns* reached a peak in the early 1970's under financial assistance from the federal government.

Possibly the most famous modern *new towns* in the U.S. are Columbia, Maryland and Reston, Virginia. *New towns* have been developed to serve as national capitals, such as Washington, D.C., Brasilia, Brazil, and Canberra, Australia.

NOMINAL LOAN RATE same as **face interest rate.**

NOMINEE one who, in a limited sense, acts for or represents another.
Example: Davis with consent, used her secretary's name as the **grantee** to property she buys. Her secretary was considered her *nominee.* Simultaneously, her secretary **deeded** the property to Davis. There was a **mortgage** on the property. Davis acquired the property from the *nominee* **subject to** the mortgage. By doing so, Davis is not personally liable for the mortgage loan.

NO MONEY DOWN general term referring to real estate acquisition strategies based on seller provided financing and/or existing loan assumption and minimal use of cash down payments. It is a method of achieving maximum profits from real estate investments.
Example: Allen purchased three houses using a *no money down* strategy. In one transaction, Allen assumed the existing mortgage of $55,000, gave the seller a note for an additional $30,000 and transferred ownership of an automobile worth $5,000 to finance the $90,000 house with no cash down payment.

NONCONFORMING USE a use that violates **zoning** regulations or codes but is allowed to continue because it began before the zoning **restriction** was enacted.
Example: Carter owns a commercial building constructed in 1920. In 1935, the city enacted a **zoning ordinance** that prescribes residential use for the area in which the building is located. Under *noncomforming use,* the building may remain, but Carter is restricted in the extent to which he may improve or restore the building.

NONDISTURBANCE CLAUSE 1. an agreement in mortgage contracts on income-producing property that provides for the continuation of **leases** in the event of loan **foreclosure.**
Example: The tenant was concerned that he would be **evicted** if the landlord went **bankrupt.** He insisted on a *nondisturbance clause* so the lease would continue in the event of foreclosure.
2. an agreement in a sales contract, when the seller retains **mineral rights,** that provides that exploration of minerals will not interfere with surface development.
Example: When the seller negotiated the **oil and gas lease,** she was assured by the oil company that the property could be **conveyed** with a *nondisturbance clause.*

NONEXCLUSIVE LISTING same as **open listing.**

NONRECOURSE no personal **liability.** Lenders may take the property pledged as **collateral** to satisfy a **debt,** but have no **recourse** to other **assets** of the borrower.
Example: Downing purchases a property with a *nonrecourse* loan. Should Downing **default,** the lender may **foreclose** and acquire the property but is barred from seeking a **judgment** against other properties held by Downing.

NORMAL WEAR AND TEAR physical **depreciation** arising from age and ordinary use of the property.
Example: An **appraiser** estimates that a certain type of carpeting, subject to *normal wear and tear,* should have a physical life of 5 years.

NOTARIZE to attest, in one's capacity as a **notary public,** to the genuineness of a signature.
Example: Before a county clerk will record certain types of documents, they must be *notarized* to assure the signature is not forged.

NOTARY PUBLIC an officer who is authorized to take **acknowledgments** to certain types of documents, such as **deeds, contracts,** and **mortgages,** and before whom **affidavits** may be sworn.
Example: Eakins and Finwick agree to transfer a piece of property. At the **closing,** a *notary public* serves to witness the signing of all documents.

NOTE a written **instrument** that acknowledges a **debt** and promises to pay.
Example: Greer borrows money from Thrifty Savings to purchase a home. Greer signs a *note* to acknowledge the debt, to promise to pay under specified terms, and to prescribe a procedure for curing **default.** A **mortgage** will also be signed that pledges the home to the lender as **security** for the note.

NOTICE official communication of a legal action or one's intent to take an action. See also **public offering, public sale.**
Example: A landlord may be required to give a tenant 30 days *notice* before terminating the **lease.**
Example: A lender may be required to give a debtor *notice* that a **default** has occurred before initiating **foreclosure** proceedings. See **notice of default.**
Example: **Recording** a deed serves to give **constructive notice** to the public of one's ownership of a property.

NOTICE OF DEFAULT a letter sent to a defaulting party as a reminder of the **default.** May state a **grace period** and the **penalties**

for failing to cure the default.
Example: Vacation Lot Sales Corp. sent a *notice of default* to Abel. It offered a 7-day grace period, after which they would consider his **interest** as forfeited unless he paid the delinquent **installment.**

NOTICE TO QUIT 1. a notice to a tenant to **vacate** rented property.
Example: After the lease expired the tenant remained in **possession.** The landlord sent a *notice to quit* by January 31.
2. sometimes used by a tenant who intends to vacate on a certain date.

NOTORIOUS POSSESSION generally acknowledged **possession** of **real estate.** One of the requirements to gain ownership of real estate through **adverse possession.**
Example: A squatter, who was in *notorious possession* of land, was thought by neighbors to be the owner of record.

NOVATION a 3-party agreement whereby one party is released from a **contract** and another party is substituted.
Example: Baker wants to buy Abel's home and assume the mortgage. Abel wants to be released from all mortgage **liability.** Good Money Savings Association cooperates. The 3 sign a *novation* whereby Baker is substituted for Abel on the mortgage.

NUISANCE a land use whose associated activities are incompatible with surrounding land uses.
Example: Zoning laws and private **deed restrictions** are used to prevent the development of *nuisances,* such as:
• activities that produce noxious fumes or air pollution in residential areas
• commercial uses that generate large volumes of automobile traffic in residential areas
• junkyards in highly visible areas
• activities considered socially offensive, such as sale of pornographic materials, in residential areas

NULL AND VOID that which cannot be legally enforced, as with a **contract** provision that is not in conformance with the law.
Example: Ivenson sells a property and places in the **deed** a **covenant** that the property may never be sold to someone of a minority race. Since this provision is in defiance of the U.S. Constitution, it could never be enforced and is thereby *null and void.*

O

OBLIGEE the person in whose favor an obligation is entered into.
Example: Jackson promises to manage the property of Kindall, an out-of-town investor. In this arrangement, Kindall is the *obligee;* Jackson is the **obligor.**

OBLIGOR the person who binds himself or herself to another; one who has engaged to perform some obligation; one who makes a **bond.**
Example: See **obligee.**

OBSOLESCENCE a loss in value due to reduced desirability and usefulness of a structure because its design and construction has become obsolete; loss due to a structure's becoming old-fashioned, not in keeping with modern needs, with consequent loss of income. See **economic depreciation, functional depreciation, functional obsolescence.**
Example: An old house may suffer from the following examples of *obsolescence:*
• rooms of improper size
• features no longer useful, such as a coal chute with a gas-fired furnace
• out-of-date plumbing, heating, and electrical fixtures and systems
• inadequate insulation
• unsuitable architectural style
• construction materials that require excessive **maintenance**
• undesirable location

OCCUPANCY AGREEMENT, LIMITED one that allows a prospective buyer to obtain **possession** under a temporary arrangement, usually prior to **closing.**
Example: Abel, the seller, signs a *limited occupancy agreement* with Baker that allows Baker possession of the property at rent of $25 per day for up to 30 days or the day of closing, whichever occurs first.

OCCUPANCY LEVEL percentage of currently rented units in a building, city, neighborhood, or complex. Contrast with **vacancy rate.**
Example: Today the Holiday Hotel has 90 of its 100 rooms booked and filled. Its *occupancy level* is 90%. Conversely, its vacancy rate is 10%.

OFFER an expression of willingness to purchase a property at a specified price.
Example: Lincoln places a property on the market. Murray makes an *offer* to buy the property for $150,000. Lincoln may accept the offer, reject the offer, or propose a **counteroffer.**

OFFER AND ACCEPTANCE see **agreement of sale.**

OFFEREE one who receives an offer. Generally a buyer offers a purchase contract to an owner, which makes the owner the *offeree*. When the seller offers a contract to a buyer, the buyer is the *offeree*.
Example: Brewster offers Smithton a contract in which Brewster offers to pay $120,000 for a property. Smithton is the *offeree*.

OFFEROR one who extends an offer to another.
Example: Brewster offers Smithton $120,000 for a property. Brewster is the *offeror*.

OFFICE OF INTERSTATE LAND SALES REGISTRATION (OILSR) a division of the U.S. Department of **Housing and Urban Development** that regulates offerings of land for sale across state lines. See **Interstate Land Sales Act.**
Example: Norwood **subdivides** a large land parcel in Arizona and wishes to market the lots to investors across the nation. Norwood is required to register the offering with *OILSR* and follow certain procedures intended to inform buyers of the characteristics of their investment.

OFF-SITE COSTS expenditures related to construction that are spent away from the place of construction.
Example: Owens is developing a **subdivision.** Certain *offsite costs* are incurred, such as the costs of extending roads, sewers, and water lines to the **site.** Site costs include landscaping and other site **improvements.**

OFF-SITE IMPROVEMENTS the portions of a **subdivision** or development that are not directly on the lots to be sold.
Example: Access streets, curbs, sewers, and utility connections are common examples of *off-site improvements*.

OIL AND GAS LEASE an agreement that gives the right to explore for oil, gas, and sometimes other minerals and to extract them from the ground. Provisions include the granting of subsurface and surface rights, **lease** duration, **extension** terms, **royalties,** surface damages, **assignments,** and **warranties.** See **mineral rights.**
Example: In an *oil and gas lease,* the owner is to receive $100 per acre as a bonus payment, and one eighth of the value of minerals found on the property.

ONE-HUNDRED-PERCENT LOCATION a point in space where a

retail establishment would achieve maximum sales volume compared to other locations in the local market area.
Example: The corner of First and Main is the busiest intersection downtown. It represents the *hundred-percent location* for a department store.

OPEN-END MORTGAGE a **mortgage** under which the **mortgagor** (borrower) may secure additional funds from the **mortgagee** (lender), usually stipulating a ceiling amount that can be borrowed.
Example: Poole obtains an *open-end mortgage* to purchase a home. Under the mortgage agreement, Poole may borrow additional funds over the **maturity** of the loan as long as the unpaid **principal** does not exceed 80% of the home's **appraised** value.

OPEN HOUSE a method of showing a home for sale whereby the home is left open for inspection by interested parties.
Example: A **broker** advertises an *open house* to promote the sale of a **listing.** On the specified date, prospective buyers may inspect the house during the hours of the *open house*.

OPEN HOUSING a condition under which housing units may be purchased or **leased** without regard for racial, ethnic, color, or religious characteristics of the buyers or tenants.
Example: The intent of government antidiscrimination laws applied to housing is to provide *open housing* under which anyone with sufficient funds may purchase or rent available housing units.

OPEN LISTING a **listing** given to any number of **brokers** without **liability** to compensate any except the one who first secures a buyer who is ready, willing, and able to meet the terms of the listing or secures the seller's **acceptance** of another **offer.** The sale of the property automatically terminates all open listings.
Example: Quarry offers an *open listing* to 2 brokers, Ridley and Sims. Ridley presents a buyer who eventually purchases the property. Ridley is entitled to a **commission;** Sims is not.

OPEN MORTGAGE a **mortgage** that has **matured** or is overdue and is therefore open to **foreclosure** at any time.
Example: Towns sells a property to Udall. Towns provides financing for the sale in the form of a 5-year, **interest-only** loan. At the end of 5 years, Udall does not pay the **principal** and Towns allows the loan to become an *open mortgage*. This arrangement allows Udall to pay off the loan at any time or Towns to call the loan at any time.

OPEN SPACE land, within a developed area, that is left undeveloped and serves as an **amenity** to surrounding occupants.
Example: A 20-acre **planned unit development** contains 12 acres

that are covered by structures and pavement. The remaining 8 acres are left in *open space*.

OPERATING EXPENSES amounts paid to maintain property, such as **property taxes, utilities, hazard insurance.** Excludes **financing** expenses and **depreciation.**
Example: The following are expenses incurred in operating a property:
Operating expenses
 • maintenance
 • management
 • real estate taxes
 • hazard and liability insurance
 • utilities
 • supplies
The following are not categorized as operating expenses:
debt service
 • principal payments
 • interest
 • loan fees
 • participation payments
depreciation
income taxes

OPERATING LEASE a **lease** between the **lessee** and the **sublessee** who actually occupies and uses the property. See **sublease.**
Example: Figure 118.

FIGURE 118

OPINION OF TITLE a certificate, generally from an attorney, as to the validity of **title** to property being sold. See **title abstract.**
Example: Based upon the attorney's *opinion of title,* the **title insurance** company insured title to the property.

OPTION the right to purchase or **lease** a property upon specified terms within a specified period.

Example: Moore purchases an *option* on a piece of land. The option runs 90 days and costs $500 per acre. If Moore wishes to purchase the land, she has 90 days to exercise her right and may buy the land for $5,000 per acre. If she decides not to purchase, she **forfeits** the $500 per acre.

OPTIONEE one who receives or purchases an option.
Example: Brewster pays Smithton $5,000 for the right to purchase a property for $120,000 within the next year. Brewster is the *optionee*.

OPTIONOR one who gives or sells an option.
Example: Brewster pays Smithton $5,000 for the right to purchase a property for $120,000 within the next year. Smithton is the *optionor*.

ORAL CONTRACT a verbal agreement. With few exceptions, verbal agreements for the sale or use of **real estate** are unenforceable. In most states, contracts for the sale or rental of real estate are, unless they are in writing, unenforceable under the **Statute of Frauds.** Verbal leases for a year or less are often acceptable.
Example: Abel agrees to sell property to Baker. Their contract is oral. Abel changes his mind. He faces no **penalty** because *oral contracts* for the sale of real estate are unenforceable.

ORDINANCES municipal rules governing the use of land.
Examples: Local governments may pass *ordinances* to:
• specify certain land uses in certain areas
• regulate **nuisances**
• specify the manner in which structures are constructed or maintained
• specify the manner in which **subdivisions** are designed
• regulate rental practices
• regulate condominium **conversion** practices

ORDINARY AND NECESSARY BUSINESS EXPENSES a tax term that allows a current deduction for business expenses. Contrasted with **capital expenditures** and unreasonable expenses.
Example: Each day the apartment manager enjoyed a 3-martini lunch with his friend. He claimed a tax deduction for the lunch expense. The **Internal Revenue Service** contests the deductions because they were not *ordinary and necessary business expenses.*

ORDINARY ANNUITY a series of equal payments, each payment occurring at the end of each equally spaced period.
Example: For a lender the **income stream** from a standard, fixed rate mortgage loan provides an *ordinary annuity* (Figure 119).

ORDINARY INCOME defined by the **Internal Revenue Code** to include salaries, fees, **commissions,** interests, dividends, and many

287

other items. Taxed at regular tax rates. Contrasted with long-term **capital gains,** which receive more favorable tax treatment.
Example: Abel would prefer to convert *ordinary income* into long-term capital gains. He wants to change the nature of property he has from **inventory** to investment.

Loan
origination

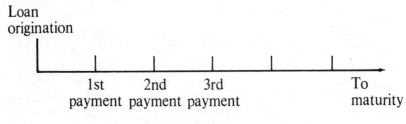

1st 2nd 3rd To
payment payment payment maturity

FIGURE 119

ORDINARY LOSS for income tax purposes a loss that is deductible against **ordinary income.** Usually more beneficial to a taxpayer than a **capital loss,** which has limitations on deductibility.
Example: The sale of **inventory** at a loss results in an *ordinary loss,* whereas the sale of an investment at a loss results in a capital loss.

ORIENTATION the position of a structure on a **site** relative to sunlight angles and prevailing winds.
Example: A house in Figure 120 has a north-south *orientation* designed to maximize the natural heating effect of the sun in the winter:

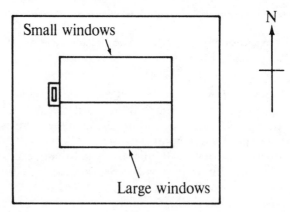

FIGURE 120

ORIGINATION FEES charges to a borrower to cover the costs of issuing the loan, such as **credit** checks, **appraisal,** and **title** expenses.
Example: The lender issued a $50,000 **mortgage** loan and charged a 1% *origination fee* ($500).

OUTSTANDING BALANCE the amount currently owed on a
debt.
Example: Whitman borrowed $10,000. She then paid $1,200 of
interest and $500 toward **principal.** Her *outstanding balance* is
$9,500 ($10,000 minus $500).

OVERAGE in leases for retail stores, amounts to be paid, based on
gross sales, over the **base rent.** See **percentage lease.**
Example: Winfield leases retail space in a shopping center. The
lease calls for a base rent of $2,500 per month plus 5% of gross
sales over $10,000. The first month, Winfield has sales of $20,000.
In addition to the $2,500 base rent, Winfield pays an *overage* of
$500 [.05 × ($20,000 − $10,000)].

OVER AGE 55 HOME SALE EXEMPTION in taxation, an individ-
ual over age 55 can sell principal residence at a gain and exclude up
to $125,000 of the gain from taxation. Allowed regardless of the
purchase of another home. Must have used the property as a **prin-
cipal residence** for 3 of the last 5 years.
Example: Abel, *over age 55*, sells his principal residence, which
he has lived in for the last 3 years, at a $150,000 gain. He may
exclude $125,000 of the gain from taxation. The rest of the gain is
taxable as a **capital gain.**

OVERALL RATE OF RETURN (OAR) the percentage relationship
of **net operating income** divided by the purchase price of property.
See **capitalization rate.**
Example: Property that sells for $1,000,000 is anticipated to
produce a net operating income of $100,000 per year. The indi-

cated *overall rate of return* is 0.10 or 10% $\left(\dfrac{\$100,000}{\$1,000,000}\right)$.

OVERIMPROVEMENT a land use considered too intense for the
land.
Example: A proposed house costs $100,000 to construct on a **site**
valued at $20,000. It is estimated that the completed house would
have a market value of only $110,000. The proposed house is an
overimprovement of the site.

OVERRIDE 1. a fee paid to someone higher in the organization, or
above a certain amount.
Example: In the agreement the salesman was required to pay an
override of 10% of his gross **commissions** to the managing **bro-
ker.**
2. an **estate** carved out of a working interest in an **oil or gas**

lease.
Example: The *overriding* **royalty** required 2% of the production of the well be paid to the attorney who negotiated the oil lease.

OWNER OCCUPANT a tenant of a residence who also owns the property.
Example: Homer lives in a home that he also owns. Landon owns a home but rents it to Renton. Homer is an *owner occupant*, Landon is an **absentee owner**, and Renton is a rental tenant.

OWNERSHIP FORM methods of owning **real estate**, which affect **income** tax, **estate tax**, continuity, **liability, survivorship**, transferability, disposition at death and at **bankruptcy.**
Example: *Ownership* forms include:
• **corporation**
• joint tenancy
• **limited partnership**
• **partnership**
• **Subchapter S corporation**
• **tenancy by the entireties**
• **tenancy in common**
• **tenancy in severalty**

OWNERSHIP RIGHTS TO REALTY possession, enjoyment, control, and disposition. See also **fee tail, interest, tenancy.**
Example: By virtue of **title** to the property, Overton enjoys full *ownership rights to realty*. This enables Overton to use the property, **lease** out the property, pledge it as **security** on loans, and sell the property within the restrictions of the law.

P

PACKAGE MORTGAGE a **mortgage** arrangement whereby the **principal** amount loaned is increased because **personalty** (e.g., appliances), as well as **realty** serve as **collateral.**
Example: Simmons applied for a *package mortgage* in order to spread the cost of appliances over 25 years and to pay for them with her home mortgage payment.

PAPER credit given, evidenced by a written obligation that is backed by **property.**
Example: Dunn sells his property for $100,000. He receives $20,000 cash and $80,000 of *paper* that is payable over 20 years at 10% interest.

PARCEL a piece of property under one ownership; a lot in a **subdivision.**

Example: In order to construct the highway, the state must acquire parts of *parcels* A and C in Figure 121. *Parcels* B and D are unaffected.

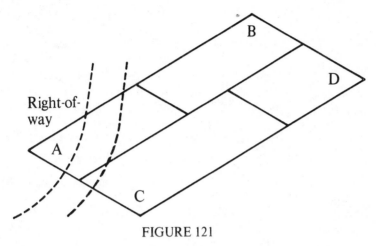

FIGURE 121

PAROL EVIDENCE oral evidence, rather than that contained in documents. The parol evidence rule states that when parties put their agreement in writing, all previous oral agreements merge into the written agreement. The written agreement cannot be contradicted by oral testimony, unless there was a **mistake** or **fraud.**
Example: Carter agrees to buy a house from Dooley, and both sign a written agreement. Carter later argues that Dooley said he'd pay all the loan **discount points.** Under the *parol evidence* rule, courts will interpret the **contract** as it is written.

PARTIAL RELEASE a provision in a **mortgage** that allows some of the property pledged to be freed from serving as **collateral.**
Example: Baker sold 3 acres of land (Figure 122), and accepted a $30,000 purchase money mortgage. *Partial releases* in the mortgage require that, upon each $10,000 **principal** payment, one acre be freed from serving as collateral. The sequence of release was **platted,** and described in the mortgage.

PARTIAL TAKING acquisition by **condemnation** of only part of the property or some property rights.
Examples: Situations calling for *partial takings* (Figure 123).

PARTICIPATION MORTGAGE one that allows the lender to share in part of the income or resale proceeds.
Example: A loan is given on an office building. In addition to a fixed payment of **principal** and **interest,** the lender is entitled to 2% of gross rental income. This is a *participation loan* in which the lender participates in the **income stream** provided by the property.

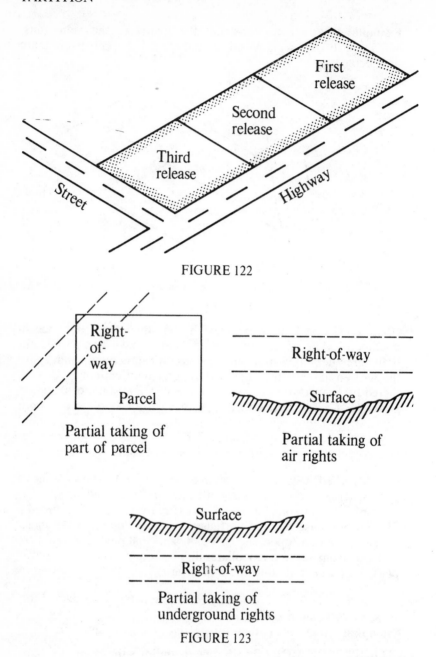

FIGURE 122

Partial taking of
part of parcel

Partial taking of
air rights

Partial taking of
underground rights

FIGURE 123

PARTITION the division of **real property** between those who own it
with **undivided interest.**

Example: Abel and Baker own land by **tenancy in common** until
they *partition* it. Thereafter, each owns a particular tract of land
(Figure 124).

Before partition	After partition

Abel and Baker, as tenants in common, are owners of one parcel.

Abel owns this half.	Baker owns this half.

FIGURE 124

PARTNERSHIP an agreement between 2 or more entities to go into business or invest. Either partner may bind the other, within the scope of the partnership. Each partner is liable for all the partnership's debts. A partnership normally pays no taxes, but merely files an information return. The individual partners pay personal income tax on their share of **income**. See also **general partner, limited partnership**. Compare **corporation**.
Example: Abel and Baker form a *partnership* to buy land. The partnership owns the property, rather than Abel and Baker.

PARTY WALL a wall built along the line separating 2 properties, partly on each **parcel**. Either owner has the right to use the wall and has an **easement** over that part of the **adjoining** owner's land covered by the wall.
Example: The structures built on lots A and B in Figure 125 are separated by a *party wall*.

FIGURE 125

PASSIVE ACTIVITY INCOME under the 1986 tax act, is generated by: 1. Any trade or business conducted for profit in which the taxpayer does not materially participate. 2. Any rental activity, whether or not the taxpayer materially participates.

Rental activities are presumed to be passive. These include all activities that generate income from payments for the use of property rather than for the performance of services. Rental activities include long-term rentals of apartments, net leased property, office equipment, and automobiles. In contrast, the rental of hotel rooms

293

or transient apartments and short-term car rentals are not passive because of the extent of services provided.

Because rental real estate is a passive activity, owners may not use losses to shelter other types of income. These are exceptions:

1. Phase-out for property acquired before October 22, 1986, the enactment date of the 1986 tax act. Losses on property acquired before then are allowed as follows:

1987 65%
1988 40%
1989 20%
1990 10%

Property acquired after the October 22, 1986 date is not eligible for the phase-out.

2. Real estate dealers .

3. **"Active" participants** in rental real estate are allowed to shelter up to $25,000 per year of losses against nonpassive income. A less stringent definition of active participation is provided as compared to **material participation**.

4. Mortgage interest on a principal or second residence is not subject to these rules even when the residence is rented out.

5. A closely held *C* corporation (other than a personal services corporation) may use passive losses and credits to offset its net active income, but not portfolio income. An *S* corporation may not apply passive losses and credits against other income.

Example: Paul bought an apartment complex in 1988, which generated a $30,000 tax loss. If Paul meets the test of an active investor, up to $25,000 of the loss may be used to offset active or portfolio income. If not, the entire loss remains suspended until Paul earns passive income.

PASSIVE INCOME 1. generally, income from **rents, royalties**, dividends, interest, and gains from the sale of securities. 2. A new meaning created by the Tax Reform Act of 1986, distinguishes *passive income* or loss from **active income** and **portfolio income**. See **passive activity income**.

PASSIVE INCOME GENERATOR a business or investment that produces **passive income** which can be used to offset passive losses.

Example: Perry owns rental real estate which provides a tax loss. Under the 1986 tax act, the loss may be offset by passive income, but not by **portfolio income** or **active income**. Without a *passive income generator* to offset the loss, the loss will be carried forward in a suspense account.

PASSIVE INVESTOR 1. one who invests money but does not manage the business or property. 2. See **passive income, portfolio income**.

Example: Dooley has neither time nor skills to manage the prop-

erty that he wants to invest in. He forms a **partnership** with a real estate syndicator who will devote time and expertise to manage the property for profit. Dooley contributes money but not effort, so he is a *passive investor*.

PASSIVE SOLAR HEATING a system of features incorporated into a building's design to use and maximize the effects of the sun's natural heating capability. See **active solar heating.**
Example: *Passive solar heating* systems use some type of collection and storage element, such as a water-filled partition, which is exposed to the sun during the day and radiates heat to the structure at night. Other features, such as south-facing windows, site **orientation,** roof overhangs, are included to enhance the effects of the sun's heat.

PASS-THROUGH CERTIFICATES interests in a pool of mortgages sold by **mortgage bankers** to investors. Money collected as monthly mortgage payments is distributed to those who own certificates. Often **guaranteed** by **Ginnie Mae.**
Example: A mortgage banker sells $5,000,000 of *pass-through certificates* in $10,000 denominations, supported by an equal amount of **VA** and **FHA mortgages.** Monthly collections of **interest** and **principal** are remitted to certificate holders, except for $^{44}/_{100}$ of 1% of the annual principal, kept by the mortgage banker as a **servicing** fee (Figure 126).

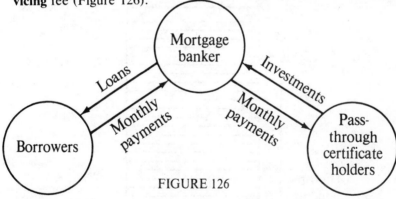

FIGURE 126

PATENT conveyance of **title** to government land.
Example: The federal government grants a *patent* on land they sell to a mining company.

PAYBACK PERIOD the amount of time required for cumulative estimated future income from an investment to equal the amount initially invested. It is used to compare alternative investment opportunities.
Example: Purchase of an apartment building requires an equity investment of $20,000. Annual cash flow is expected to be $2,000. The *payback period* for the investment is 10 years.

295

PAYMENT CAP a contractual limit on the percentage amount of adjustment allowed in the monthly payment for an adjustable rate mortgage at any one adjustment period. Generally it does not affect the interest rate charged. If the allowable payment does not cover interest due on the principal at the adjusted rate of interest, **negative amortization** will occur.

Example: An adjustable rate mortgage has a *payment cap* of 7% a year. The monthly payment in year 1 is $500.00. When the interest rate is adjusted in year 2, the new payment would be $550.00 to pay interest and amortize the principal. However, due to the *payment cap*, the maximum payment for year 2 is $535.00.

PENALTY money one will pay for breaking a law or violating part or all of the **terms** of a **contract.**

Example: *Penalties* are often imposed for:
• prepaying a loan
• failing to complete a contract of sale
• breaking a lease

PENTHOUSE a luxury housing unit located on the top floor of a high-rise building.

Example: A *penthouse* (Figure 127).

Penthouse

High rise building

FIGURE 127

PERCENTAGE LEASE a **lease** of property in which the rental is based on a percentage of the volume of sales made upon the leased premises. It usually stipulates a minimum rental and is regularly used for retailers who are **tenants**. See **overage**.
Example: The *percentage lease* required the jewelry store to pay as additional rent 6% of annual sales in excess of $100,000. The **base rent** is $6,000 per year.

PERCOLATION TEST a procedure to measure the drainage characteristics of the soil on a lot. Required in the proper design of septic tank drainfields.
Example: Carter is developing a **subdivision** in the county. As part of site preparation, Carter runs *percolation tests* on the soil. From this information, the engineer can determine the proper size of the lots and placement of septic tanks.

PERFORMANCE BOND issued by an insurance company; posted by a party who is to perform certain work. If the work is not performed, the insurer promises to complete the work or pay damages up to the amount of the bond. Contrast with **completion bond.**
Example: The contract requires the **contractor** to put up a $10,000 *performance bond*. If the contractor fails to do the job, the property owner has assurances of compensatory payment from the insurance company.

PERMANENT MORTGAGE a mortgage for a long period of time (over 10 years).
Example: The **savings and loan association** promises to originate a 25-year **self-amortizing** *permanent mortgage* when construction is completed. A permanent **mortgage commitment** is often needed before a **construction** loan can be arranged.

PERMIT a document, issued by a government regulatory authority, that allows the bearer to take some specific action.
Example: An occupancy *permit* allows the owner of a building to occupy or rent the building.
Example: A building *permit* allows a builder to construct or modify a structure.

PERPETUITY the condition of being never ending. Most states attempt to outlaw perpetuities because of potential problems. A perpetual income stream may cause bankruptcy. A **deed** that keeps property in a family in *perpetuity* can cause financial hardship.
Example: A bank offers to pay a 10% interest rate in *perpetuity*. A $10,000 deposit should receive $1,000 annual income for as long as the deposit remains in the account.

PERSON in law, an **entity** having legal responsibility. Legally, a natural person is a human being who has reached **majority.** (Compare **minor.**) An artificial person may be a **corporation;** in some instances **partnerships,** governments, and certain other bodies are considered persons.
Example: When negotiating a contract it is important to deal with a **person;** otherwise the contract may be unenforceable.

PERSONAL PROPERTY same as **personalty.**

PERSONALTY personal property, i.e., all **property** that is not **realty.** Property that is movable, not fixed to land. See **chattel**
Example: The following are *personalty:*
• appliances not permanently attached to **real property**
• cash and securities
• furniture and household items
• **mobile homes** not permanently affixed to a **site**
• vehicles

PER STIRPES a legal method of distributing an **estate** to include the descendants of a deceased legatee, whose share is apportioned among linear descendants.
Example: A person dies intestate. State law requires a *per stirpes* distribution of assets. The decedent had 4 children. Three are surviving; the fourth child died as an adult and left 5 children. The estate is divided into 4 equal parts. Each surviving child of the decedent gets one fourth, and the 5 orphaned grandchildren, as a group, share one fourth.

PHOTOVOLTAIC the process of converting light directly into electricity using specially designed silicon cells.
Example: The house has a *photovoltaic* system which supplies power to the filter pumps of the swimming pool.

PHYSICAL DEPRECIATION OR DETERIORATION the loss of value from all causes of age and action of the elements.
Example: Sources of *physical depreciation:*
• breakage
• deferred maintenance
• effects of age on construction material
• normal wear and tear

PIGGYBACK LOAN 1. a combination of the **construction loan** with the permanent **loan commitment.**
Example: The permanent lender would issue a commitment at a 15% rate, effective upon completion of construction. As assurance that the loan will be borrowed even if rates are lower later, the commitment is *piggybacked* to the construction loan, and must be drawn down upon **retiring** the construction loan.

2. one mortgage held by more than one lender, with one lender holding the rights of the others in **subordination.**
Example: A loan is made for 90% of the home price; 80% of the price is supplied by a **savings and loan association,** 10% by an individual, who then has a *piggyback loan.* The piggyback agreement allows the S&L to have priority in **foreclosure.**

PITI principal, interest, taxes and insurance. Refers to the monthly payment required for most home mortgage loans. The tax and insurance portion of the payment is the monthly deposit to the escrow account used to pay property taxes and hazard insurance premiums.
Example: A mortgage loan requires monthly payments of principal and interest of $600. In addition, monthly deposits to maintain the escrow account are $150. *PITI* is $750.

PLAINTIFF the person who brings a lawsuit. Contrast with **defendant.**
Example: A *plaintiff* sued for **specific performance** to force the owner of land to sell at the agreed upon terms.

PLANNED UNIT DEVELOPMENT (PUD) a **zoning** classification that allows flexibility in the design of a **subdivision.** Planned Unit Development zones generally set an overall **density** limit for the entire subdivision, allowing the dwelling units to be clustered to provide for common open space. See also **cluster housing, common areas.**
Example: A typical *planned unit development* (Figure 128).

Common areas

FIGURE 128

PLANNING COMMISSION a group of citizens appointed by local government officials to conduct hearings and recommend amend-

ments to the **zoning ordinance.** The planning commission generally oversees the work of a professional planning department, which prepares a comprehensive plan. May also be called a planning board, zoning commission, or zoning board, depending on locality.

Example: Moore wishes to have her land **rezoned** from low **density** to high density **residential.** She submits her request to the *planning commission.* The commission holds a public hearing and asks the planning department to evaluate the change. Following the review, the commission makes a recommendation to the city council on whether or not to grant the request.

PLAT a plan or map of a specific land area. See also **description, government rectangular survey.**
Example: *Plat* of a **subdivision** (Figure 129).

PLAT BOOK a public record containing maps of land, showing the division of the land into streets, blocks, and lots and indicating the measurements of the individual **parcels.**
Example: Sample entry in a *plat book* for property number 001 in district 07-510-AZ (Figure 130).

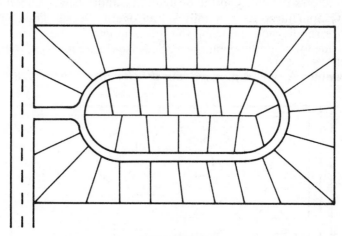

FIGURE 129

PLEDGED ACCOUNT MORTGAGE (PAM) a type of home purchase loan under which a sum of cash contributed by the owner is set aside in an account pledged to the lender. The account is drawn down during the initial years of the loan to supplement periodic mortgage payments. The effect is to reduce the payment amounts in early years. See **graduated payment mortgage.** Compare **collateral.**
Example: Abel obtains a *pledged account mortgage.* The loan

07-510-AZ

FIGURE 130

principal is $40,000 and Abel makes a down payment of $10,000. $5,000 of this amount is put in a pledged account. Abel makes payments based on a mortgage principal of $45,000 but the payments are reduced in the first 3 years by drawing upon the $5,000 pledged account.

PLOT PLAN a diagram showing the proposed or existing use of a specific **parcel** of land.
Example: A *plot plan* submitted to a **zoning** review board (Figure 131).

PLOTTAGE VALUE increment in the value of land comprised by **assemblage** of smaller plots into one ownership.
Example: A and B are **adjacent** lots, each worth $10,000 (Figure 132). By combining them under one owner the entire **tract** becomes large enough for use as a restaurant **site,** worth $50,000. The *plottage value* is $30,000.

POCKET CARD required for salespersons and **brokers** in most states. Issued by the state licensing agency, it identifies its holder as a **licensee** and must be carried at all times.
Example: Figure 133

POINTS fees paid to induce lenders to make a **mortgage** loan. Each point equals 1% of the loan **principal.** Points have the effect of reducing the amount of money advanced by the lender. Same as *discount points.*

Example: Mortgage lenders commonly charge one *point* as a loan **origination fee.** Additional points may be charged to raise the loan **yield** to current **market interest rates.** If only one point is required, a borrower requesting a loan of $50,000 would actually receive only $49,500. The $500 cost of the point is a **closing** cost.

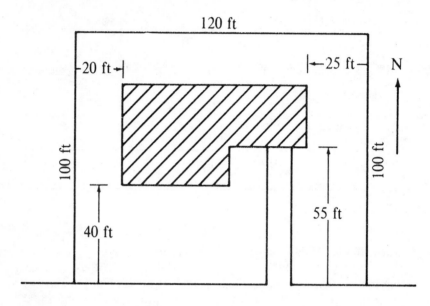

FIGURE 131

POLICE POWER the right of any governmental body to enact and enforce regulations for the order, safety, health, morals, and general welfare of the public.
Example: Types of *police power* mechanisms applied to **real property:**
• **condemnation** proceedings
• **housing codes**
• public **nuisance** ordinances
• **rent controls**
• special operating **licenses**
• **subdivision** regulations
• **zoning**

PORTFOLIO INCOME interest, dividends, royalties (unless earned in the ordinary course of business) and gains from the sale of property that generates this type of income. Under the Tax Reform Act of 1986 this type of income cannot be used to offset passive activity losses. See **passive income.**

POSITIVE LEVERAGE the use of borrowed funds that increases the return on an investment.
Example: See **leverage.**

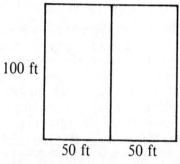

50 ft 50 ft
Two lots valued at $10,000 each

100 ft
Lots combined with value of $50,000

FIGURE 132

Real Estate Broker Identification Card

Expires 3-1-92

Charlie Baker
101 Maple Road
Springfield, MA 90001

FILE 025 LICENSE 360245
(NOT A LICENSE — FOR IDENTIFICATION ONLY)

FIGURE 133

POSSESSION the holding, control, or custody of property for one's use, either as owner or person with another right. See also **ownership rights to realty, title.**
Example: Actual *possession:* within immediate occupancy
Adverse *possession:* see definition
Constructive *possession:* as stated in the public record

POTENTIAL GROSS INCOME the amount of income that could be produced by a real property assuming no vacancies or collection losses. Does not include miscellaneous income. Contrast **cash flow, net operating income.**
Example: An office building has 10,000 square feet of rentable space and rents for an average of $12 per square foot. *Potential gross income* for the building is $120,000 per year. Concessions on the ground floor that contribute $1,000 of annual revenue, and a 5% vacancy and collection allowance are not included in *potential gross income.*

POWER OF ATTORNEY an **instrument** authorizing a person to act as the **agent** of the person granting it. See **attorney-in-fact.**
Example: Abel is going on a 6-month vacation to China. He wants to sell his house in Colorado for $75,000 but will not be present to sign the **deed.** He gives his trusted friend Baker the *power of attorney* so Baker may deed the property to a **grantee** while Abel is in China.

POWER OF SALE a clause sometimes inserted in **mortgages** or **deeds of trust;** grants the lender (or **trustee**) the right to sell the property upon certain **default.** The property is to be sold at **auction** but court authority is unnecessary.
Example: The **savings and loan association** exercises the *power of sale* clause in the mortgage by selling the defaulted property at public auction for $100,000. Since the debt was $60,000 and expenses of sale $5,000, the $35,000 surplus belongs to the borrower.

PRAIRIE HOUSE an early twentieth century style house with a long, low roof line, continuous row of windows and an unornamented exterior. Designed to satisfy the physical and psychological needs of the inhabitants, it is unlike the traditional concept of a house that is a box subdivided into smaller boxes (rooms), each with some doors and windows.
Example: Figure 134.

PRECLOSING a rehearsal of the **closing** whereby **instruments** are prepared and signed by some or all parties to the **contract.** Used when closings are expected to be complicated.
Example: *Preclosings* are used when there are many parties to an agreement. This sometimes occurs when there are multiple loans

Continuous
row of
windows

Long, low roof line
Unornamented
exterior

FIGURE 134

to be arranged and/or multiple buyers or sellers, as when **syndicating** property or converting an apartment complex to a **condominium.**

PREEXISTING USE See **nonconforming use.**

PREFABRICATED 1. constructed, as building components, in a factory prior to being erected or installed on the construction site. 2. constructed, as a house, of prefabricated components. See **modular housing.**
Example: The **subdivision** is developed with *prefabricated* housing. The roof, exterior walls, and interior partitions are *prefabricated* in a factory in Dallas.

PRELEASE to obtain **lease** commitments in a building or complex prior to its being available for occupancy.
Example: As a requirement for obtaining a **permanent mortgage,** a developer must *prelease* 50% of the space in the office building.

PREMISES land and **tenements;** an **estate;** the subject matter of a **conveyance.**
Example: In selling the property, Carter **deeds** the *premises* to Dawson. Dawson later **leases** the *premises* to Enwright.

PREMIUM 1. the cost of an insurance policy.
Example: Annual or monthly *premiums* are generally required for **hazard insurance, liability insurance,** and life insurance. **Title insurance** *premiums* are paid only once.
2. the value of a **mortgage** or **bond** in excess of its **face amount.**
Example: When the face rate of a mortgage exceeds the prevailing **market interest rate,** the mortgage may be worth a *premium* over its **face value.**

305

PREPAID EXPENSES amounts that are paid prior to the period they cover.
Example: Simmons pays the full **premium** on a 3-year insurance policy. When her accountant prepares Abel's financial statement, the proportionate value of the unused premium is presented as a *prepaid expense*.

PREPAID INTEREST interest paid in advance of the time it is earned.
Example: Prior to 1968, up to 5 years of prepaid interest could be deducted from taxable income; until 1976 up to one year could be deducted. Since then *prepaid interest* has not been deductible. An exception is for **points** paid to purchase one's residence, provided that the practice and amount is customary in the local area.

PREPAYMENT CLAUSE a clause in a **mortgage** that gives a **mortgagor** (borrower) the privilege of paying the mortgage indebtedness before it becomes due. Sometimes there is a **penalty** for prepayment, with **waiver** of the interest that is not yet due.
Example: The *prepayment clause* in the mortgage allows the unpaid **principal** to be **retired** by the owner with a 1% penalty.

PREPAYMENT PENALTY fees paid by borrowers for the privilege of **retiring** a loan early.
Example: Abel borrowed $50,000 last year at 15% interest on a 30-year mortgage. If he pays the remaining **principal** now, in one lump sum, there will be a 5% *prepayment penalty* that amounts to $2,500.

PREPAYMENT PRIVILEGE the right of a borrower to **retire** a loan before **maturity**.
Example: A loan on **commercial property** is closed (no *prepayment privilege*) for the first 5 years. Afterwards it can be prepaid without **penalty**.

PREPAYMENTS advance payments of expenses such as insurance and taxes, often into an escrow account.
Example: At the closing of a residence they bought, the Pollards made *prepayments* equal to 14 months of hazard insurance and 6 months of property taxes.

PRESALE sale of proposed properties, such as **condominiums**, before construction begins.
Example: The developer *presold* 40% of the condominium units at a $5,000 **discount** for each unit before construction began. Based on the *presales*, the developer was able to get a favorable **construction loan**.

PRESCRIPTION acquiring rights through **adverse possession**.

Example: For years, Fulson, owner of a **landlocked** parcel, has continually and openly crossed the property of Grissom to reach the highway. Fulson eventually acquires an **easement** by *prescription* to the access route, thus preventing Grissom from blocking his way.

PRESENT VALUE OF ANNUITY the value now of a level stream of income to be received each period for a finite number of periods. See **ordinary annuity.**

$$\text{Present value of annuity} = \frac{1 - \dfrac{1}{(1 + i)^n}}{i}$$

where i = interest rate
n = number of periods
Example: The *present value of an annuity* of $1.00 per year for 10 years, discounted at 12%, is $5.65. Selected present values of annuity factors for annual income of 1 are shown in Table 28.

Table 28

Life of the Annuity (years)	Discount Rates			
	5%	10%	15%	20%
1	.952	.909	.870	.833
2	1.859	1.736	1.626	1.528
3	2.723	2.487	2.283	2.016
4	3.546	3.170	2.855	2.589
5	4.329	3.791	3.352	2.991
10	7.722	6.144	5.019	4.192
15	10.380	7.606	5.847	4.675
20	12.462	8.514	6.259	4.870
25	14.094	9.077	6.464	4.948
30	15.372	9.427	6.566	4.979

PRESENT VALUE OF ONE the value today of an amount to be received in the future, based on a **compound interest** rate.
Example: At a 12% interest rate, the receipt of one dollar one year from now has a *present value* of $.89286 (slightly more than 89 cents). One dollar to be received in 2 years has a *present value* of $.79719 (under 80 cents). Factors are based on the following formula:

$$\text{Present worth (1 factor)} = \frac{1}{(1 + i)^n}$$

where i = interest rate
n = number of periods
See Table 29.

TABLE 29

Number of Years until $1 Is Received

Rates

	5%	10%	15%	20%
1	.952381	.909091	.869565	.833333
2	.907029	.826446	.756144	.694444
3	.863838	.751315	.657516	.578704
4	.822702	.683014	.571753	.482253
5	.783526	.620921	.497177	.401878
10	.613913	.385543	.247185	.161506
15	.481017	.239392	.122894	.0649055
20	.376889	.148644	.0611003	.0260841
25	.295302	.092296	.0303776	.0104826
30	.231377	.057308	.015103	.004212

PRICE LEVEL ADJUSTED MORTGAGE a loan whose payment is adjusted according to the rate of inflation. The payments are generally quite low, typically 3 to 5% annually of the debt. This type of mortgage is not commonly used in the U.S.

Example: A *price level adjusted mortgage* is made for $100,000. Monthly payments in the first year are $400. After the first year, the principal balance is reduced to $98,000. The inflation rate for the year was 10%. The principal balance is adjusted to $107,800 and the payments for the second year are increased to $440 per month.

PRIMARY LEASE a **lease** between the owner and a tenant whose **interest,** all or in part, has been sublet.

Example: Figure 135.

PRIMARY MORTGAGE MARKET that portion of the credit market that originates mortgage loans, including institutional lenders, such as savings and loan associations and banks, and mortgage bankers and brokers. Contrast with **secondary mortgage market.**

The *primary mortgage market* originates and services mortgage loans. Many of these loans are packaged and sold in the secondary mortgage market.

PRIME CONTRACTOR see **general contractor.**

PRIME RATE the lowest commercial **interest rate** charged by banks on short-term loans to their most credit-worthy customers. The prime rate is not the same as the long-term mortgage rate, though it may influence long-term rates. Also, it is not the same as the consumer loan rate that is charged on personal property loans and credit cards. Mortgage rates and consumer loan rates are generally

higher than the prime rate, but exceptions occur at times.
Example: The Chemical Bank and the Chase Manhattan Bank offer a *prime rate* of 12%. Gulf Oil is a prime customer and at that rate may borrow loans up to 270 days. Chemical Bank offers construction loans at 4 **points** over the *prime rate*.

PRIME TENANT in a shopping center or office building, the tenant who occupies the most space. Prime tenants are considered credit worthy and attract customers or traffic to the center. See also **anchor tenant.**
Example: Huntley is developing an office building with 40,000 square feet of leasable space. Of this, 20,000 square feet are **preleased** to a *prime tenant*, Diesoil. The **credit rating** and prestige of the prime tenant allow Huntley to obtain **financing** and prelease the remaining space to other tenants.

PRINCIPAL 1. the one who owns or will use property.
Example: The *principals* to the **lease** are the **landlord** and **tenant;** *principals* to a sale are the buyer and seller.
2. One who contracts for the services of an **agent** or **broker,** the broker's or agent's **client.**
Example: Grey wishes to purchase a shopping center. Grey engages Jamison, a mortgage broker, to arrange **financing.** Jamison arranges a loan in the name of the *principal*, Grey. The loan is payable as **interest** only for 5 years, with the *principal* payable as a **balloon payment** at the end of year 5.
3. the amount of money raised by a mortgage or other loan, as distinct from the **interest** paid on it.

FIGURE 135

PRINCIPAL AND INTEREST PAYMENT

Example: Abel arranged a loan with $100,000 principal on his home. The first monthly payment is $1,200 including $1,000 interest and $200 that **amortized** the *principal*.

PRINCIPAL AND INTEREST PAYMENT (P&I) a periodic payment, usually paid monthly, that includes the **interest** charges for the period plus an amount applied to **amortization** of the **principal** balance. Commonly used with amortizing loans. See **mortgage constant, amortization.**
Example: A $1,200 annual *principal and interest payment* is required by a $10,000 **face value** amortizing mortgage at a 10% **interest rate.** $1,000 of the first year payment is required for interest; $200 reduces the outstanding balance to $9,800.

PRINCIPAL BROKER the licensed broker responsible for the operations conducted by the **brokerage** firm.
Example: As *principal broker*, Collins receives a 10% **override** on all sales **commissions** earned by the other **agents.**

PRINCIPAL, INTEREST, TAXES and INSURANCE PAYMENT (PITI) the periodic (typically monthly) payment required by an amortizing loan that includes **escrow** deposits. Each periodic payment includes a **principal and interest payment** plus a contribution to the escrow account set up by the lender to pay insurance premiums and property taxes on the mortgaged property.
Example: Abel's monthly *PITI payment* is $950. This includes $750 for **principal and interest,** $150 for **ad valorem taxes** and $50 for insurance.

PRINCIPAL MERIDIAN one of the prime **meridians** used in the **government rectangular survey** method of land **description** to locate **range lines.**
Example: *Principal meridians* within the state of California are shown in Figure 136.

PRINCIPAL RESIDENCE the place one lives in most of the time. May be a single-family house, **condominium,** trailer, or houseboat. To defer **capital gain** taxes on the profit from a home, the home must be used as the taxpayer's *principal residence*.
Example: Collins spends 10 months each year living in a rented apartment in downtown Seattle. She spends 2 months in a home she owns in San Diego. The rented apartment is her *principal residence*.

PRIORITY legal precedence; having preferred status. Generally, upon **foreclosure,** lenders are repaid according to priority.
Example: Abel's home was foreclosed and sold for $25,000. Unpaid taxes and attorney's fees were accorded *priority*, and paid in full. The rest of the sales proceeds was applied against the **first**

mortgage. There was nothing for the **second mortgage,** because it was lower in *priority*.

PRIVATE MORTGAGE INSURANCE **default** insurance on conventional loans, provided by private insurance companies. See **mortgage insurance.**
Example: Lawton wishes to obtain a home purchase loan covering 90% of value. The lender requires Lawton to acquire *private mortgage insurance* as a condition for granting any loan for more than 80% of value.

Humboldt meridian

Mt. Diablo meridian

San Bernardino meridian

FIGURE 136

PRIVATE OFFERING an investment or business offered for sale to a small group of investors, generally under exemptions to registration allowed by the **Securities and Exchange Commission** and state securities registration laws.
Example: The **syndicator** prepared a *private offering* of the **equity** in the apartments. Up to 35 persons are allowed to participate in the purchase. If more persons are allowed, the **syndicator** must register a **public offering** with the state securities commissioner or the U.S. Securities and Exchange Commission (SEC).

PROBATE OR PROVE to establish the validity of the **will** of a deceased person.

Example: Hughes died. The **executor** appealed to the *probate* court that a certain document was the **valid** will that Hughes left.

PROCEEDS FROM RESALE same as **resale proceeds.**

PROCURING CAUSE a legal term that means the cause resulting in accomplishing a goal. Used in **real estate** to determine whether a **broker** is entitled to a **commission.**

Example: A real estate broker introduced parties and they agreed to enter into a transaction to sell a home. The broker claimed she was entitled to a commission but had to show in court that she was the *procuring cause.*

PRO-FORMA STATEMENT according to form. Financial statements showing what is expected to occur.

Example: The **broker** prepared a *pro-forma* statement for the prospective purchaser (Table 30). It showed expected cash flows for the property:

TABLE 30

Pro-forma Cash Flow Statement
Next Year, Projected

Rental income		$10,000
Taxes	−$2,000	
Utilities	−1,000	
Miscellaneous	− 500	
Subtotal expenses		−3,500
Cash flow		$6,500

PROGRESS PAYMENTS in construction, loan payments issued to the builder as building is completed. See **draw.**

Example: For the $100,000 **construction loan,** the *progress payments* were $20,000 upon buying the lot and a like amount upon pouring the foundation, roofing, wiring, and completion of all work.

PROMISSORY NOTE a promise to pay a specified sum to a specified **person** under specified **terms.** See also **note.**

Example: Figure 137.

PROPERTY 1. the rights that one individual has in lands or goods to the exclusion of all others; rights gained from the ownership of

```
                    Promissory Note

      I, June Monroe, do promise to pay City
   Finance Co. the sum of $50,000. Repayment is
   to be made in the form of 300 equal payments
   at 12% interest, or $526.61 payable on the
   1st of each month, beginning 8/1/88 until the
   total debt is satisfied.

                    Signed,

                      June Monroe
                         7/15/88
```

FIGURE 137

wealth. See **real property, personalty; possession, title.**
Example: An individual may own *property* with the associated rights to enjoyment, control over others' use of the property, and disposition, subject to government-imposed **restrictions.** Groups of individuals may own *property,* with ownership rights shared collectively. Governments may also own *property,* held for public use.
2. real estate
Example: The appraiser needed to inspect the *property* prior to establishing its value.

PROPERTY LINE the recorded **boundary** of a plot of land.
 Example: Figure 138.

FIGURE 138

PROPERTY MANAGEMENT the operation of property as a business, including rental, rent collection, **maintenance,** etc.

Example: The following tasks are often required in the ownership of property:
Property management
• accounting and reporting
• leasing
• maintenance and repair
• paying taxes
• provision of utilities and insurance
• remodeling
• rent rate setting and collection
Investment management
• acquisition and disposition
• development and rehabilitation feasibility
• financing
• income tax accounting

PROPERTY REPORT required by the **Interstate Land Sale Act** for the sale of **subdivisions** of 50 lots or more, if the subdivisions are not otherwise exempt. Filed with HUD's **Office of Interstate Land Sales Registration (OILSR).**
Example: A **subdivider** wishes to sell lots in a 55-lot development, through an interstate commerce promotional plan. She is required to file a *property report* with OILSR.

PROPERTY RESIDUAL TECHNIQUE in **appraisal,** a method for estimating the value of property based on estimated future income and the **reversionary value** of the building and land. See **income approach.**
Example: Table 31.

TABLE 31

Level annual **net operating income**		$10,000
Multiplied by: **annuity factor** of appropriate rate for number of years (say 12%, 30 years)		× 8.0552
Value of income		$80,552
Estimated *property residual* in 30 years	$50,000	
Multiply by: Present worth of one factor at 12%	× .03338	
Present worth of reversion		$1,669
Estimated property value		$82,221

PROPERTY TAX a government **levy** based on the **market value** of privately owned property. Sometimes referred to as **ad valorem tax** or real estate tax.

Example: Homeville assesses a *property tax* at the rate of $.50 per $100 of market value. Kilmer pays a tax of $500 on a property valued at $100,000.

PROPRIETARY LEASE in a cooperative apartment building, the lease a corporation provides to the stockholders which allows them to use a certain apartment unit under the conditions specified.
Example: The Coopers purchase a unit in a cooperative on Fifth Avenue. Their ownership provides 450 shares of stock in the cooperative and a *proprietary lease* to a unit in the apartment building.

PRORATE to allocate between seller and buyer their proportionate share of an obligation paid or due; for example, to prorate real **property taxes** or insurance.
Example: Property taxes were $730, assessed for the calendar year and paid by the seller on April 30. The property was sold on September 15 (Figure 139). It is necessary to *prorate* property taxes so that the buyer and seller each pay a proportionate share for his or her ownership period. There are 107 days from September 15 to December 31. Therefore the buyer must pay $214 at **closing,** based on a daily rate of $2.00.

FIGURE 139

PROSPECT a **person** considered likely to buy. A prospective purchaser.
Example: All of the persons who request further information about the advertised property are considered *prospects.*

PROSPECTUS a printed descriptive statement about a business or investment that is for sale, to invite the interest of prospective investors.
Example: A **syndicator** prepared a *prospectus* that disclosed all **material facts** about the property being offered. Before it is approved by the SEC or state securities commissioner, it is called a **red herring.** If it need not be approved, it is called a **descriptive memorandum.**

PROXY a person who represents another, particularly in some meeting. Also, the document giving to another the authority to represent.
Example: Abel could not be at the **cooperative** apartment association's annual meeting, so he cast his vote by *proxy.*

PUBLIC HOUSING government-owned housing units made available to low-income individuals and families at no cost or for nominal rental rates. Contrast to **low-income housing.**
Example: The Metropolitan Housing Authority operates several *public housing* projects for those who cannot afford decent housing on the rental market.

PUBLIC LANDS acreage held by the government for conservation purposes. Public lands are generally undeveloped, with limited activities such as grazing, wildlife management, recreation, timbering, mineral development, water development, and hunting.
Example: Many western states, such as Alaska and Nevada, have large amounts of *public lands.* A part of this area is held by the federal government and is dedicated to national parks, wilderness, and wildlife refuges. Some oil and mineral exploration is allowed under **lease** to private firms.

PUBLIC OFFERING soliciting the general public for the sale of investment units. Generally requires approval by the SEC and/or state securities agencies. Contrast with **private offering.**
Example: The **syndicator** who wishes to sell **limited partnership** interests to over 35 investors should register this *public offering* with the SEC or state securities commissioner.

PUBLIC RECORD usually refers to land transaction records kept at the county courthouse.
Example: Documents that are evidence of real estate transactions should be taken to the county courthouse to be officially entered in the *public record.* Recording gives **constructive notice** of a document's existence.

PUBLIC SALE an **auction** sale of property with **notice** to the general public.
Example: After **foreclosure,** a *public sale* was effected. It was advertised in the local newspaper in advance. The property was auctioned off on the courthouse steps to the highest bidder.

PUEBLO OR ADOBE an early twentieth century house that is made of adobe brick or some other material made to look like adobe brick. The characteristic projecting roof beams are called viga.
Example: Figure 140.

PUFFING overstating the qualities of a property.
Example: "This house has the most efficient floor plan of any home in the world" is an example of a salesperson's *puffing.*

PUNCH LIST an enumeration of items that need to be corrected prior to a sale.

Example: The buyer refuses to close the purchase until the builder fixes the leaky roof and replaces the defective carpeting—the 2 items on the buyer's *punch list.*

PUR AUTRE VIE for the life of another. An **estate** one person grants to another, only for the duration of the life of a third person. **Example:** Abel grants a **life estate** to Baker to use Abel's ranch until Baker's wife dies. Baker has a life estate *pur autre vie.*

PURCHASE AGREEMENT same as **contract of sale.**

Projecting roof beams (viga)

Real or simulated adobe brick

Flat roof

Massive looking

FIGURE 140

PURCHASE MONEY MORTGAGE a **mortgage** given by a **grantee** (buyer) to a **grantor** (seller) in part payment of the purchase price of **real estate.**
Example: Lamar wishes to purchase a house from Murphy. The sale price is $75,000. Lamar will assume Murphy's existing mortgage in the amount of $50,000. In addition, Lamar gives Murphy a *purchase money mortgage* of $15,000, plus $10,000 in cash to close the sale.
(note: a purchase money mortgage can be a **first mortgage** or junior **lien,** depending on its **priority**).

Q

QUADRANGLE a square-shaped land area, 24 miles on each side, used in the **government rectangular survey** method of land **description**. Each quadrangle contains 16 **townships**.
Example: See example for **government rectangular survey**.

QUANTITY SURVEY a method used by **appraisers** to estimate **reproduction cost** (new) of an **improvement**; detailed cost estimate of all materials, labor, and overhead required to reproduce a structure. See **cost approach**.
Example: A simplified *quantity survey* estimate of reproduction cost (new) is shown in Table 32.

TABLE 32

Item	Cost
site preparation	$5,000
cement	10,000
masonry	15,000
lumber	25,000
fasteners	5,000
siding	15,000
roof cover	10,000
labor	30,000
fees	5,000
financing	10,000
Total cost	$130,000

QUEEN ANNE HOUSE a nineteenth century style house that is unique-looking, multi-story, and irregular in shape with a variety of surface textures, materials, and colors. The term Queen Anne has come to be applied to any Victorian house that cannot be otherwise classified.
Example: Figure 141.

QUIET ENJOYMENT the right of an owner or any other **person** legally entitled to **possession** to the use of property without interference.
Example: The landlord, unhappy with a low rental rate, continually blocks the driveway of the tenant. The tenant sues for *quiet enjoyment*.

QUIET TITLE (ACTION) court action to settle a title dispute.
Example: People may use quiet **title** action to:
• substantiate the **title** of a squatter

- extinguish **easements**
- release a **dower** interest
- remove any **cloud on title**

QUIET TITLE SUIT (OR ACTION) a suit in court to remove a defect, **cloud on the title,** or suspicion regarding legal rights of an owner to a certain **parcel** of **real property.**
Example: In an *action to quiet title,* the landowner of record brought the **adverse possessor** to court that required him to establish his claim or be forever barred from claiming the property.

QUITCLAIM DEED a **deed** that conveys only the **grantor's** rights or interest in real estate, without stating the nature of the rights and with no **warranties** of ownership. Often used to remove a possible **cloud on the title.** Contrast with **general warranty deed.**
Example: It is discovered during a **title** search that a certain property was at one time held by a **partnership** that later **abandoned** the property. To obtain a **marketable title,** the current owner obtains *quitclaim deeds* from all partners in the old partnership.

Projecting upper stories

Unique looking

Multi-story

Turrets

Bay windows

Big chimneys

Variety of surface textures

Various forms of windows

Many small details

FIGURE 141

319

R

RANGE LINES lines parallel to a **principal meridian,** marking off the land into 6-mile strips known as ranges; they are numbered east or west of a principal meridian in the **Government Rectangular Survey.** See **base line.**
Example: Figure 142.

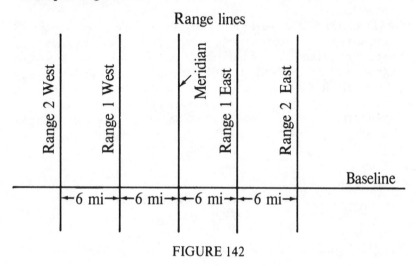

FIGURE 142

RATE OF RETURN the percentage relationship between the earnings and the cost of an investment. See **internal rate of return, overall rate of return.**
Example: Nickson deposits $100 in a savings account. At the end of the year Nickson receives a payment of $10. Nickson's *rate of return* is 10%.

RATE OF RETURN OF INVESTMENT same as **recapture rate.**

RAW LAND acreage with no added **improvements,** such as landscaping, drainage, streets, **utilities,** and structures.
Example: The developer bought 50 acres of *raw land* upon which to develop a **subdivision.**

READY, WILLING, AND ABLE capable of an action and disposed to act.
Example: A home is listed with a **broker** who finds a *ready, willing and able* person who agrees to buy under the terms of the **listing.** The seller refuses to sell. The broker has earned a **commission** because she fulfilled the requirements of the listing.

320

REAL ESTATE 1. in law, land and everything more or less attached to it. Ownership below to the center of the earth and above to the heavens. Distinguished from **personal property**. Same as **realty**. **Example:** Figure 143.

2. in business, the activities concerned with ownership and use transfers of the physical property.
Example: The following are engaged in *real estate* business activities:
* **accountants**
* **appraisers**
* attorneys
* **brokers**
* counselors
* government regulators
* **mortgage brokers**
* mortgage lenders
* salespersons
* **surveyors**
* **title** companies

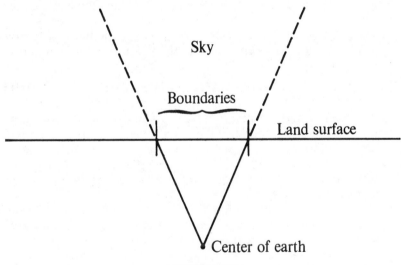

FIGURE 143

REAL ESTATE COMMISSION state agency that enforces real estate **license** laws.
Example: The *Real Estate Commission* is usually comprised of between 5 and 15 members who are appointed for a term (2 to 6 years) by the governor, generally confirmed by the state senate. They enforce the real estate laws and regulations, subject to judicial authority. The real estate **commissioner,** a full time employee of the Real Estate Commission, conducts the routine activities of licensing, collecting fees, and other matters.

REAL ESTATE INVESTMENT TRUST (REIT) a real estate mutual fund, allowed by income tax laws to avoid the corporate income tax. It sells shares of ownership and must invest in real estate or **mortgages.** It must meet certain other requirements, including minimum number of shareholders, widely dispersed ownership, **asset** and income tests. If it distributes 95% of its income to shareholders, it is not taxed on that income, but shareholders must include their share of the *REIT's* income in their personal tax returns.
Example: During the early 1970's, many *real estate investment trusts were created.* They raised money from investors for investment in mortgages and real estate **equities.** An individual could buy shares on the stock market in such a **trust.** Its unique feature is to allow small investors to participate, without **double taxation,** in large real estate ventures. The trust is not subject to corporate income tax as long as it complies with the tax requirements for a *REIT.*

REAL ESTATE MARKET the potential buyers and sellers of real property at the current time, and the current transaction activity for real property. It includes markets for various property types, such as housing market, office market, condominium market, land market.
Example: The local *real estate market* is very active. There have been a record number of sales and there still are many properties on the market.

REAL ESTATE MORTGAGE INVESTMENT CONDUIT (REMIC) The Tax Reform Act of 1986 created a new entity, the *REMIC.* The purpose of a *REMIC* is to hold a fixed pool of mortgages and issue interests in itself to mortgage investors. A *REMIC* may be a partnership, corporation, trust, or separate pool of assets. *REMICs* are intended to become the exclusive means for issuing multiple-class mortgage backed securities in a form that avoids the corporate double tax.

Substantially all of a *REMIC's* assets must be qualified mortgages (mortgages secured by real estate) but it may also hold some short-term liquid assets that produce interest income, and assets held in a special reserve fund, and foreclosed properties.

All interests in a *REMIC* must be classified as regular or residual. Regular interests entitle the holder to interest and principal income, through debt, stock or some other ownership form. Residual interests provide income that is more contingent in nature.

A *REMIC* will not, in general, be a taxable entity, although it must comply with tax requirements and is subject to a 100% tax on prohibited transactions. Regular interest holders will be taxed as if their interests were debt obligations subject to their share of the *REMIC's* income on an accrual basis. Gain or loss on the sale of a regular interest will be ordinary to the extent of their share of original issue discount. Residual interest holders generally receive their share of *REMIC* income as ordinary. (Although the Tax

Reform Act of 1986 makes no distinction in rates for capital gains after 1987, the character of capital gains remains in the tax code, perhaps paving the way for a rate distinction in the future.)

REAL ESTATE OWNED (REO) property acquired by a lender through foreclosure and held in inventory. Commonly referred to as REO.

Example: Because of a large number of recent mortgage foreclosures, the bank's *real estate owned* has grown to 5% of all assets, or $25 million.

REAL ESTATE SECURITIES AND SYNDICATIONS INSTITUTE (RESSI) an organization of **syndicators** affiliated with the **National Association of Realtors®.** Offers a newsletter, *RESSI Review,* on current developments affecting **syndications,** and educational courses.

Address: Real Estate Securities and Syndications Institute
430 N. Michigan Avenue
Chicago, Illinois 60611

REAL ESTATE SETTLEMENT PROCEDURES ACT (RESPA) a law that states how **mortgage** lenders must treat those who apply for federally related real estate loans on property with 1-4 dwelling units. Intended to provide borrowers with more knowledge when they comparison shop for mortgage money.

Example: Within 3 days after Abel applies for a loan on a house he wants to buy, the lender is to provide a **good faith** estimate of settlement **(closing)** costs, and a booklet about *RESPA.* In addition, one day before closing, the borrower is entitled to review the closing papers, including all amounts that are known at that time.

REALIZED GAIN in a tax-free exchange, a gain that has occurred financially, but is not necessarily taxed. See **boot, recognized gain, Section 1031.**

Example: Abel's land has a tax **basis** of $10,000. Its **market value** is $75,000. He exchanges the land, tax-free under Section 1031, for Baker's warehouse, which was appraised at $75,000. Abel's *realized gain* is $65,000. None of Abel's *realized gain* is recognized, because he did not receive boot.

REAL PROPERTY the rights to use real estate. Sometimes also defined as **real estate.**

Example: *Real property* includes, but is not limited to:
• personal residence owned in **fee simple**
• a **life estate** to a farm
• rights to use land under a **lease**
• **easements** and other partial interests

REALTIST a member of the **National Association of Real Estate Brokers,** a group comprised of mainly minority brokers.

Example: Abel, a black real estate broker, paid dues to the National Association of Real Estate Brokers and subscribed to its code of ethics. Abel is a *Realtist.*

REALTOR® a professional in real estate who subscribes to a strict **Code of Ethics** as a member of the local and state boards and of the **National Association of Realtors®**.
Example: Much of the general public are surprised to discover that only about 40% of licensed real estate **brokers** are eligible to use the designation *Realtor®*.

REALTOR®-ASSOCIATE a licensed salesperson (not **broker**) who is a member of the **National Association of Realtors®**.
Example: Downing passed the salesman's **licensing exam** and is sponsored by a **Realtor®-broker**. Upon being sworn in to the national and state association, Downing is appropriately described as a *Realtor®-Associate*.

REALTORS® NATIONAL MARKETING INSTITUTE (RMNI) an affiliate of the **National Association of Realtors®**; mainly concerned with educational programs and literature for members. Publishes *Real Estate Today* (monthly) and *Real Estate Perspectives* (bimonthly).
Address:
Realtors® National Marketing Institute
430 N. Michigan Avenue
Chicago, Illinois 60611

REALTY same as **real estate**.

REAPPRAISAL LEASE a **lease** where the rental level is periodically reviewed by independent **appraisers**. Often, the **lessor** and **lessee** will each select an appraiser; if they do not agree on a value, they will choose a third appraiser.
Example: In the 20-year *reappraisal lease*, Big Buy Foods agrees to pay the landlord an annual rent of 12% of the property value. Every 5 years the property will be reappraised to determine the rent.

REASSESSMENT the process of revising or updating the value estimate of property for **ad valorem tax** purposes.
Example: Local **property tax** assessors are required to periodically conduct a *reassessment* of all property. Value estimates are revised based on recent sales and other data, and tax **assessments** are based on the new estimates.

REBATE 1. a refund resulting from a purchase or tax.
Example: To encourage sales of the **condominium** project, the developer offered a $2,500 *rebate* to each purchaser.
2. a kickback of a charge, often illegal if done without knowledge of all parties.
Example: the broker accepted a $50 *rebate* from the insurer each time he sold a home carrying a homeowner's **warranty**.

RECAPTURE CLAUSE in a contract, a clause permitting the party who grants an **interest** or right to take it back under certain conditions.
Example: Carter grants a **lease** to Frank's Furniture, with rent set at 6% of retail sales. The lease contains a *recapture clause* whereby Carter can regain the property unless sales are over $1 million per year.

RECAPTURE OF DEPRECIATION same as **depreciation recapture.**

RECAPTURE RATE in **appraisal,** a term used to describe the rate of recovery of an investment in a **wasting asset.** This rate is added to the **discount rate** to derive a **capitalization rate** in appraisal terminology. May be based on the straight line, **sinking fund,** or annuity method.
Example: A building with a 50-year estimated **useful life** has a 2% straight-line *recapture rate.* At a discount rate of 10%, the capitalization rate is 12%.

RECASTING the process of adjusting a loan arrangement, especially under the threat of **default.** See **workout.**
Example: Pope owns an apartment building with a **mortgage** loan requiring **debt service** of $25,000 per year. Because of a period of high vacancies, Pope's **net operating income** falls to $20,000 per year. To eliminate the **negative cash flow,** Pope appeals to the lender to *recast* the loan by extending the **maturity** and reducing the **interest rate** for the next 2 years.

RECIPROCITY mutual agreement to accept, such as a state's acceptance, as **valid** the real estate **license** one has earned in another state.
Example: In the absence of *reciprocity,* Moore must take a new examination to obtain a real estate license in the state which she moves. With *reciprocity* she needs only to present her previously earned license.

RECOGNIZED GAIN in a **tax-free exchange,** the portion of gain that is taxable. A **realized gain** will generally be recognized to the extent of **boot** received. See **Section 1031.**
Example: Abel's land has a tax **basis** of $10,000. It is worth $75,000. He exchanges the land under Section 1031 for Baker's warehouse worth $70,000 and $5,000 of cash. Of Abel's $65,000 realized gain, $5,000 will be *recognized.*

RECONCILIATION in **appraisal,** the process of adjusting **comparables** to estimate the value of the subject being appraised.
Example: An **appraiser** arrives at the market value estimates shown in Table 33 following application of the 3 traditional approaches.

TABLE 33

market comparison:	$85,000
cost approach:	$89,000
income approach:	$84,000

In *reconciliation*, the appraiser considers the appropriateness of each approach to the subject, the quality of available data, and the amount of judgmental **adjustment** required to reach each estimate. Following this review, the appraiser settles on an estimate of $85,000 as her opinion of **market value.**

RECONVEYANCE occurs when a **mortgage** debt is **retired.** The lender **conveys** the property back to the **equity** owner, free of the debt.
Example: The *reconveyance* took place after Abel paid off the loan; Abel promptly **recorded** the *reconveyance* **instrument.**

RECORDING the act of entering in a book of public records **instruments** affecting the **title** to **real property.** Recording in this manner gives **notice** to the world of facts recorded. See **constructive notice, ownership rights to realty.**
Example: By *recording* the **deed** from a sale of property, the purchaser assumes that all subsequent interested parties are given notice of the purchaser's ownership **interests** in the property. **Leases** and **liens** may also be recorded.

RECOURSE the ability of a lender to claim money from a borrower in **default,** in addition to the property pledged as **collateral.**
Example: Ross obtains a **mortgage** loan from Local Savings. Should Ross default on the loan, Local Savings may **foreclose** and force the sale of the mortgaged property. Should the sale fail to satisfy the unpaid loan **principal,** Local Savings has *recourse* to other assets of Ross.

RECOVERY FUND generally administered by the **Real Estate Commission.** Requires **licensees** to contribute, then reimburses aggrieved persons who are unable to collect from **brokers** for wrongdoings.
Example: A typical state's *recovery fund* law requires all new licensees to contribute $10 to the fund. Anytime the fund account balance drops below $500,000, all licensees will be assessed. Payments from the fund to an aggrieved person may not exceed $10,000; total payments on behalf of any licensee may not exceed $25,000. The recovery fund pays only when the broker does not.

RECTANGULAR SURVEY same as **government rectangular survey method.**

REDEMPTION, EQUITY OF same as **equity of redemption.**

REDEMPTION PERIOD the period during which a former owner can reclaim **foreclosed** property. See **equity of redemption.**
Example: Collins' property was foreclosed. If she acts within her state's *redemption period,* she can reclaim her property by paying the **debt** and legal fees.

REDEVELOP the process of demolition of the existing improvements and construction of new improvements on a site. The new improvements are often of a different type from the old.
Example: Since the old building has outgrown its usefulness, the owner plans to *redevelop* the site as the location of a new office tower.

RED HERRING a proposed **prospectus** that has not been approved by the **Securities and Exchange Commission** (SEC) or state securities commission. See **public offering.**
Example: A *red herring* is shown in Table 34.

TABLE 34

Proposed Prospectus

A registration statement has been filed with the Securities and Exchange Commission but is subject to change. The securities described herein may not be sold until approval becomes effective.

REDISCOUNT RATE the rate of interest charged to member banks when they borrow from the **Federal Reserve System.** Also called **discount rate.**
Example: The First and Citizens Banks borrows funds from the Federal Reserve for one day and is charged interest at the *rediscount rate.*

REDLINING the illegal practice of refusing to originate **mortgage** loans in certain **neighborhoods** on the basis of race or ethnic composition.
Example: A **savings and loan association** may be accused of practicing *redlining* if it is found that no loans have been originated in predominantly nonwhite neighborhoods. The term derives from the alleged practice of drawing a red line on a map around certain neighborhoods to designate them as off limits for loan approvals.

REDUCTION CERTIFICATE

REDUCTION CERTIFICATE a document in which the **mortgagee** (lender) acknowledges the sum due on the **mortgage** loan. Used when mortgaged property is sold and the buyer assumes the debt.
Example: Abel buys Baker's home and agrees to assume the existing mortgage. They obtain a *reduction certificate* from the mortgage lender stating that the remaining balance is $34,567.89.

REFERRAL the act of suggesting the use of a certain **broker.**
Example: Smith receives several **listings** based on *referrals* from former customers.
Example: A broker agrees to pay a 1% *referral* fee to out-of-state brokers who suggest families that are moving into the area.

REFINANCE the substitution of an old loan(s) with a new loan(s).
Example: Garner has a $30,000 loan against her house. She desires cash to pay for a college education. By *refinancing* the home with a new $40,000 loan, she will realize $9,000 in cash after paying $1,000 in **transaction costs.** See Table 35.

TABLE 35

New loan	$40,000
Old debt	-30,000
Cost of loan	- 1,000
Refinancing: cash proceeds	$9,000

REGENCY an English style 2- or 3-story, symmetrical house with a hip roof. A small octagonal window over the front door is traditional.
Example: Figure 144

REGISTRAR the person who is to maintain accurate official records, such as for **deeds, mortgages,** and other recorded **documents.**
Example: After **closing,** the buyer brought the deed to the *registrar* of deeds for **recording** in the county records.

REGRESSION a statistical technique used to estimate mathematical models of economic and other processes. It is used to find a mathematical expression which best fits the relationship between a group of random variables as indicated by a sample of data.
Example: An appraiser wants to find the relationship between sales prices for homes and their physical characteristics. Data are collected on the prices of a group of homes and their size, number of rooms, location and age. Linear *regression* is used to analyze

328

the relationship expressed by the data. The *regression* model can then be used to estimate prices for other similar houses on the market.

REGULATION D a regulation of the **Securities and Exchange Commission** that sets forth conditions necessary for a **private offering** exemption.

Example: Syndicator Stuart wants to sell 35 **limited partnership** interests in an office building. He applies for an exemption under *Rule 146* to avoid the need of registering a **public offering;** he thereby saves over $100,000 and avoids a 4-month delay.

Simple informal style
Small
octagonal Brick
window 1 chimney
Double- Hip roof at side
hung
windows

FIGURE 144

REGULATION Q a federal law that specified the maximum interest rates that banks and **savings and loan associations** could pay on various types of deposits. It was phased out by the **Depository Institutions Deregulations and Monetary Control Act of 1980.**

Example: Under *Regulation Q*, Hometown Savings could offer no more than a 5% yield on its passbook accounts. Today, it can offer any rate required to attract deposits.

REGULATION Z a federal regulation requiring **creditors** to provide full disclosure of the terms of a loan. Compliance is compulsory for anyone who arranges **credit** for more than 5 sales of **residential** real estate in a year. **Terms** of the loan must be disclosed. The **interest rate** must be stated as an **annual percentage rate** (APR).

329

REHABILITATE

See also **rescind, rescission.**
Example: Figure 145.

Convenient Savings and Loan

Michael Jones
500 Walnut Court, Little Creek, U.S.A.

Account number: 4862-38

Annual Percentage Rate The cost of your credit as a yearly rate	Finance Charge The dollar amount the credit will cost you	Amount Financed The amount of credit provided to you or on your behalf	Total of Payments The amount you will have paid after you have made all payments as scheduled
15.37%	$177,970.44	$43,777	$221,548.44

Your payment schedule will be:

Number of Payments	Amount of Payments	When Payments Are Due	
12	$446.62	Monthly beginning	6/1/88
12	$479.67	" "	6/1/89
12	$515.11	" "	6/1/90
12	$553.13	" "	6/1/91
12	$593.91	" "	6/1/92
300	varying from $637.68 to $627.37	" "	6/1/93

Security: You are giving a security interest in the property being purchased.

Late Charge: If a payment is late, you will be charged 5% of the payment.

Prepayment: If you pay off early, you
☒ may ☐ will not ☐ have to pay a penalty.
☒ may ☐ will not ☐ be entitled to a refund of part of the finance charge.

Assumption: Someone buying your home cannot assume the remainder of the mortgage on the original terms.

See your contract documents for any additional information about nonpayment, default, any required repayment in full before the scheduled date, and prepayment refunds and panalties.

e means an estimate

FIGURE 145

REHABILITATE to restore a structure to a condition of good repair.
Example: An old building has deteriorated to the point of prohibiting profitable operation. The owner faces the choice of **demolition** of the structure and rebuilding or *rehabilitation* to restore the building to a competitive position.

REHABILITATION TAX CREDIT the Tax Reform Act of 1986 provides a 20% tax credit for rehabilitating certified historic structures, and a 10% credit for other buildings that were placed in service after 1936. However, there are certain conditions or requirements that are imposed.
• The credit may be used to offset a maximum of $25,000 of nonpassive income, but is phased out on a 50% basis between $200,000 and $250,000 of adjusted gross income. Thus, the credit is not of use to high income investors.
• The tax basis of the property is reduced by the full amount of the credit.
• Transition rules are provided for those with binding contracts for rehabilitations between March 1, 1986 and October 22, 1986; these rules require such property be placed in service before 1994.

RELEASE to free real estate from a **mortgage**. See **partial release**.
Example: Reynolds owns 100 **acres** of land that is mortgaged for $10,000. If she pays the $10,000, the land will be *released* from the lender's **lien** on the property.

RELEASE CLAUSE in a **mortgage,** a clause that gives the owner the privilege of paying off a portion of the mortgage indebtedness, thus freeing a portion of the property from the mortgage.
See **partial release**.
Example: Smith, a **developer,** is **subdividing** land that is **financed** under a mortgage. A *release clause* in the mortgage allows Smith to sell individual lots from the **tract** by retiring portions of the loan. Without the clause, Smith would have to **retire** the entire loan before selling any lots.

RELICTION gradual subsidence of waters, leaving dry land.
Example: As the Great Salt Lake in Utah becomes smaller by evaporation, *reliction* occurs. Generally the new land belongs to the party who owned the rights to the water area (Figure 146).

FIGURE 146

331

RELOCATION CLAUSE a **lease** stipulation that allows the landlord to move the tenant within the building.
Example: The landlord of an office building requires *relocation clauses* in all leases for space that does not include an entire floor. When a new client wishes to lease an entire floor, the landlord may relocate tenants in such a way as to provide the desired space.

RELOCATION NETWORK a geographically diversified group of independent real estate brokerage companies, generally not members of a franchise, that share information with one another concerning potential customers.
Example: A broker in Atlanta, Georgia lists a home for sale which is owned by a family who is moving to Dallas, Texas. The broker, who is a member of a certain *relocation network,* finds a counterpart member/broker in Dallas and refers the family to the Dallas broker. If they buy a home through the Dallas broker, the Atlanta broker will receive a referral fee.

RELOCATION SERVICE a company which contracts with other firms to arrange the relocation of employees from one city to another. The service generally handles the sale of the employee's home and purchase of a new home. Furniture moving services may be included also.
Example: The Beeker Company wishes to open a new office in Denver. Most of the staff for the new office will be relocated from Miami. Beeker hires a *relocation service* to sell the employees' homes and to help them find new homes in the Denver area.

REMAINDER an **estate** that takes effect after the termination of a prior estate, such as a **life estate.**
Example: At the death of her husband, Polly Rowen inherits a **life estate** in their home. The *remainder* is **devised** to their son, Paul Rowen. When Polly dies, Paul will gain **title** to the house. Paul is the **remainderman.**

REMAINDERMAN the person who is to receive **possession** of the property after the death of a **life tenant.**
Example: See example under **remainder.**

REMODEL to change the appearance and functional utility of a building. This may include painting, repairing and replacing of fixtures and equipment.
Example: The Moodys wish to *remodel* the kitchen in their home. They plan to refinish the cabinets, repaint the walls, install a new floor covering and replace the range and sink.

RENEGOTIATE to legally revise the **terms** of a **contract.**
Example: Abel owes $10,000 to Baker at 7% interest. Abel and Baker *renegotiate* so that Baker agrees to lend $15,000 at 13% interest instead of the original loan.

RENEWAL OPTION the right, but not the obligation, of a **tenant** to continue a **lease** at specified **term** and **rent**.
Example: Abel leases property from Baker for 20 years at $500 monthly rent. A *renewal option* in the lease gives Abel the right to continue leasing for 5 years beyond the original term (Figure 147).

FIGURE 147

RENOVATE general term applied to the process of upgrading an existing improvement. Usually there is an attempt to keep the same general appearance of the building with new materials or to return the building to its original appearance.
Example: The city bought several dilapidated homes in the neighborhood. They plan to *renovate* the homes by bringing them up to the current housing code standards. The renovated homes will be sold to city residents.

RENT a charge for the use of space. See **contract rent, economic rent.**
Example: Abel allows Baker to use property, provided that Baker pays $500 per month (Figure 148). The charge is *rent*.

RENTABLE AREA same as **net leasable area.**

RENTAL RATE the periodic charge per unit for the use of a property. The period may be a month, quarter or year. The unit may be a dwelling unit, square foot or other unit of measurement.
Example: The *rental rate* for the 2-bedroom apartments is $400 per month. The *rental rate* for office space is $12 per square foot per year.

RENT BID MODELS a conceptual tool used to explain how land is allocated in competitive markets. The model is based on the assumption that space is controlled by the activity which offers the highest bid for the site.
Example: A simple *rent bid model* of urban land is formulated. The model predicts that commercial uses will occupy land near the city's center, while residential land will spread around the core .

333

RENT CONTROL laws that govern the rate that may be charged for space.
Example: Since the 1940's, apartment owners in New York City have been restricted by law in the rent that they may charge. *Rent control* laws have been adopted by Boston, Washington, D.C., Los Angeles, and many cities in New Jersey, among others.

RENT-FREE PERIOD a portion of the term of a lease when no rent is required. It is offered by a landlord as a rental concession to attract tenants.
Example: In order to attract tenants to the new office building, the landlord is offering a 3-month *rent-free period* to all tenants who sign a 2-year lease.

RENT-UP PERIOD the time it takes for newly constructed properties to be fully occupied.
Example: Figure 149.

Rent-up period

Occupancy rate

Preleasing Construction Full occupancy
 completion

Time ⟶

FIGURE 149

REO see **real estate owned.**

REPAIRS work performed to return property to a former condition without extending its **useful life,** as distinguished from **capital improvements.** In **income property,** repairs are an **operating expense** for accounting and tax purposes.
Examples: Patching a hole in the roof (but not replacing the roof) and mending (but not rebuilding) a fence are *repairs.*

REPLACEMENT COST the cost of erecting a building to replace or

serve the functions of a previous structure. See **reproduction cost.**

Example: Abel wishes to insure a building against accidental destruction. The policy should be written so that in the event of destruction of the building, Abel may replace it with a structure that serves an identical function. Therefore, Abel should insure the building in an amount equal to its *replacement cost,* which is likely to be greater than its **market value.**

REPLACEMENT RESERVE an amount set aside from **net operating income** to pay for the eventual wearing out of short-lived **assets.** See **reserve fund.**

Example: Singer buys new apartments, each containing $1,000 worth of carpeting and appliances that have a 10-year **useful life.** Each year she deposits $100 in a *replacement reserve* account to pay for recarpeting in 10 years.

REPRODUCTION COST the cost of exact duplication of a property as of a certain date. Reproduction differs from replacement in that replacement requires the same functional utility for a property, whereas reproduction is an exact duplication. See **replacement cost.**

Example: In the **cost approach** to property valuation, the **appraiser** estimates the *reproduction cost* of the subject structure. Various deductions are then made to account for **depreciation** in value from the time the building was constructed. These deductions reflect the fact that the building is not new, may not be of modern design, and may have suffered adverse effects due to its location.

RESALE PROCEEDS the amount a former owner receives upon a sale after paying **transaction costs,** remaining debt, and, sometimes, income taxes. Same as **proceeds from resale.**

Example: Table 36.

TABLE 36

Selling price		$100,000
Less: Commissions	$5,000	
Closing costs	1,000	
Unpaid mortgage	60,000	
Capital gains tax	$14,000	− $80,000
Resale proceeds		$20,000

RESCIND to withdraw an **offer** or contract. **Regulation Z** allows a 3-day period in which to *rescind* certain credit transactions.

Example: Abel offers to buy a certain house from Baker. Before Baker accepts, Abel *rescinds* the offer and, therefore, is not obligated to follow through on the purchase.

RESCISSION the act of cancelling or terminating a **contract**. Rescission is allowed when the contract was induced by **fraud, duress, misrepresentation,** or **mistake**. **Regulation Z** allows one to **rescind** certain credit transactions within 3 business days (not applicable to **first mortgages** on a home); purchasers of certain land that must be registered by **Department of Housing and Urban Development** **(HUD)** may rescind within 3 business days. See **rescind**.
Example: *Rescission* was allowed by the court for a contract that Abel was induced to enter on the threat of death.

RESERVE FUND an account maintained to provide funds for anticipated expenditures required to maintain a building. A reserve may be required by a lender in the form of an **escrow** to pay upcoming taxes and insurance costs. A **replacement reserve** may be maintained to provide for **replacement cost** of short-lived components, such as carpets, heating equipment, or roofing. Deposit of money into such a fund does not achieve a tax deduction.
Example: A **property management** firm anticipates that property taxes will be due in 6 months, insurance must be renewed in 2½ years, and carpeting must be replaced in 6 years. Accordingly, she establishes a *reserve fund* by depositing a portion of monthly revenues in an account. Monies from the fund will be used at the appropriate time to meet the future expenditures.

RESIDENCE the place where one lives, particularly the **dwelling** in which one lives. See **domicile**.
Example: Baker owns several houses, one of which is Baker's *residence,* another is a vacation home, and the others are **income properties** rented to tenants.

RESIDENTIAL pertaining to housing. See **residential property**.

RESIDENTIAL BROKER one who **lists** and sells houses or **condominiums**. Contrast **commercial broker**.
Example: Baker earned a livelihood as a *residential broker* selling **single-family housing**.

RESIDENTIAL MEMBER (RM) a professional designation offered by the **American Institute of Real Estate Appraisers**.
Example: Collins passed several examinations, prepared demonstration **appraisal** reports, and acquired several years of experience in the appraisal of **residential property**. She has been awarded the *RM* designation, which acknowledges her skills as a residential appraiser.

RESIDENTIAL PROPERTY 1. in real estate **brokerage** terminology, owner-occupied housing.
Example: Rollins is in *residential* real estate. She secures **listings** for **single-family housing** and sells homes.

2. in income taxation terminology, rental units used for **dwelling** purposes, not of a transient (hotel, motel) nature. To qualify as residential, at least 80% of a building's income should be derived from dwelling units.

Example: *Residential* rental *property* owners may be subject to different methods of **depreciation (accelerated cost recovery)** and/or **depreciation recapture** than **commercial property** owners.

RESIDENTIAL SERVICE CONTRACT an insurance **contract** or home **warranty**, generally for one year, covering the plumbing, mechanical, and electrical systems of a home. It is available in most areas upon the purchase of an existing home. Either the buyer or seller can pay for the contract.

Example: Ricky and Rebecca Miller purchase a home. The sellers paid $300 for a *residential service contract*. Three months later, the air-conditioner compressor breaks and costs $800 to repair. The Millers must pay the $100 deductible, and the contract covers the balance of the cost of repair.

RESIDENT MANAGER one who supervises the care of an apartment complex while living in one of the units in the complex.

Example: Carter employs Downs as a *resident manager*. Downs' duties include showing vacant units to prospective tenants, making sure the building is kept clean, and providing entry to repair persons. In return, Downs receives an apartment rent-free.

RESIDUAL value or income remaining after deducting an amount necessary to meet fixed obligations.

Example: After deducting **operating expenses, debt service,** and income taxes from **gross income,** the **equity** investor is entitled to the *residual*. Note, there is no assurance that a residual will exist.

In **appraisal,** a portion of stabilized **net operating income** is deducted to support the value of the **improvements.** The *residual* net operating income is then left to support the value of the **site.**

RESPONDEAT SUPERIOR in **agency** law, the doctrine that a **principal** is liable for the acts of an **agent.**

Example: A real estate **agent** misrepresented the facts about property that was offered for sale. The injured party sued the **agent** and the **broker.** The **broker** was held liable under the doctrine of *respondeat superior.*

RESTORE to return a building to its original quality and appearance. While modern materials are used, the emphasis is on faithful reproduction of the original style.

Example: The Hollys bought an old Victorian style home which had been converted into a duplex. They plan to *restore* the home by removing partitions, refinishing the hardwood floors, repairing the fireplaces and other improvements to return the building to its original style.

RESTRAINT ON ALIENATION a limiting condition on the right to transfer property. If the condition is against public policy or is unreasonable, courts will **void** the condition.
Example: The **deed** that Lowell received when she bought property specifies that she may not resell the property to certain ethnic minorities. Since the clause is illegal, she went to court to remove this *restraint on alienation*.

RESTRICTION a limitation placed upon the use of property, contained in the **deed** or other written **instrument** in the **chain of title** or in local **ordinances** pertaining to land use. See **encumbrance.**
Example: The ownership of property is subject to several *restrictions*. A deed **covenant** may restrict development alternatives, as may a local **zoning ordinance. Easements** may restrict use of parts of the property. **Liens** may restrict sales. **Building** codes may restrict construction practices.

RESTRICTIVE COVENANT see **restriction.**

RETAIL GRAVITATION the drawing power of a shopping center; generally, the larger the center, the greater its ability to draw from distant areas.

RETAINAGE in a construction **contract,** money earned by a **contractor** but not paid to the contractor until the completion of construction or some other agreed-upon date.
Example: The **general contractor** earns $5,000 upon pouring the foundation, plus $15,000 upon completion of the frame, plus $10,000 upon completion of the roof. Of each payment, 10% is held back as *retainage*. It is paid after a **certificate of occupancy** is issued.

RETALIATORY EVICTION the requirement that a tenant vacate a unit in response to a complaint from the tenant concerning the condition of the building. Landlord-tenant laws in many states forbid such **evictions** if proper channels are taken to lodge the complaint.
Example: Six months after Romney moved into an apartment, the heating system stopped operating. The landlord failed to repair the system, and Romney filed a formal complaint with the city **housing code** enforcement office. When the landlord received notice from the city to repair the system, he evicted Romney in a *retaliatory eviction*. The eviction was stopped in court.

RETIRE (A DEBT) to pay off the **principal** on a loan, thereby fulfilling the obligation under the loan contract. See also **amortization.**
Example: When Smith made the last monthly payment on his mortgage loan, he *retired* the debt.

Example: Jones arranged to *retire* her home improvement loan by paying an amount equal to the remaining principal balance.

REVALUATION CLAUSE see **reappraisal lease.**

REVERSE ANNUITY MORTGAGE a type of **mortgage,** designed for elderly homeowners with substantial **equity,** by which a lender periodically (monthly, for example) pays an amount to the borrower. The loan balance increases with interest and periodic payments, causing **negative amortization.**
Example: Roper, age 70, who retired from his job, owns his home **free and clear** of any **liens.** His pension is inadequate to pay expenses. He seeks a *reverse annuity mortgage* that will pay him $200 per month. At a 15% interest rate, he will owe $55,043 in 10 years.

REVERSE LEVERAGE a situation in which financial benefits from ownership accrue at a lower rate than the mortgage interest rate. See **leverage.**
Example: Net-leased property is purchased for $100,000 with a $75,000 mortgage at 12% interest and $25,000 of **equity.** The net rent is $10,000 per year; interest expense is $9,000 per year. The $1,000 difference (**cash flow**) provides a 4% return to the equity owner. In the absence of debt, the owner would receive a 10% return. *Reverse leverage* works against the property owner.

REVERSION the right of a **lessor** to **possess** leased property upon the termination of a **lease.**
Example: Evans purchases the home of Felker, a senior citizen, and leases the home back to Felker for life. Evans has the right to receive rental payments from Felker plus a *reversion* in the property at Felker's death.

REVERSIONARY FACTOR the mathematical factor that indicates the present worth of one dollar to be received in the future. Same as **present value of one.** The formula is

$$\text{Reversionary factor} = \frac{1}{(1 + i)^n}$$

where i = interest rate
n = number of years (or periods)

Example: The *reversionary factor* for 30 years at 12% is .03338. The present value of the receipt of land that will be worth $50,000 in 30 years is $1,690 (.03338 x $50,000).

REVERSIONARY VALUE the value of property at the expiration of a certain time period.

Example: A **lease** will expire in 30 years. The landlord estimates that the *reversionary value* of the property will be $50,000; that is, the property can be sold in 30 years for $50,000.

REVERSIONARY INTEREST the **interest** a person has in property upon the termination of the preceding **estate.**
Example: Abel is the **remainderman** in property that was granted to Baker for life. Abel has a *reversionary interest* in the property.

REVOCATION an act of recalling a power of authority conferred, as a revocation of a **power of attorney**, a **license**, an **agency**, etc.
Example: The *revocation* of Abel's broker's license, caused by his fraudulent acts, prevented him from earning a living in **real estate.**

REZONING an action to change the designation of a subject **parcel** or group of parcels on the **zoning** map. The effect of a rezoning is to change the permitted uses for the affected parcels. See **downzoning.**
Example: Brown, whose property was zoned for low-**density** residential, petitioned the city for a *rezoning* to allow construction of an **apartment building.**

RIDER an amendment or **attachment** to a **contract.**
Example: A *rider* to Owen's **homeowner's policy** insured the valuable paintings against fire and theft losses.

RIGHT OF FIRST REFUSAL the opportunity of a party to match the **terms** of a proposed contract before the contract is **executed.**
Example: In some states, tenants whose apartments are converted to **condominium** are given a *right of first refusal* for the unit when it is sold. This means the tenant may purchase the unit at the same price and terms of any outside purchaser.

RIGHT OF SURVIVORSHIP the right of a surviving joint tenant to acquire the **interest** of a deceased joint owner; the distinguishing feature of both **joint tenancy** and **tenancy by the entirety.**
Example: Frank Adams and Anna Adams own property as joint tenants with the *right of survivorship*. When either dies, the entire property will pass to the other without **probate.**

RIGHT-OF-WAY 1. the right to use a particular path for **access** or passage; a type of **easement.**
Example: Lot A has acquired a *right-of-way* across lot B (Figure 150).
2. the areas of subdivisions **dedicated** to government for use for streets, roads, and other public access to lots.
Example: A section of a subdivision with a *right-of-way* for a public road (Figure 151).

FIGURE 150

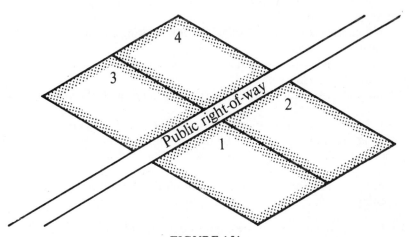

FIGURE 151

RIPARIAN OWNER one who owns land bounding upon a lake, river, or other body of water. See also **littoral.**
Example: The owner of lot A in Figure 152 is a *riparian owner,* whose ownership rights include access to the river and use of its waters, or **riparian rights.** The owner of lot B has no riparian rights.

RIPARIAN RIGHTS rights pertaining to the use of water on, under, or **adjacent** to one's land. May be qualified to avoid **nuisance** and pollution. Riparian rights are recognized in most eastern states but rarely in western states, where they recognize **usufructory rights.**
Example: See **riparian owner.**

341

FIGURE 152

RISK 1. uncertainty or variability. The possibility that returns from an investment will be greater or less than forecast. Diversification of investments provides some protection against risk.
Example: Types of *risk* in real estate:
• business risk—rents, vacancies, or **operating expenses** vary from projected amounts
• interest risk—property may be subject to a higher rate **mortgage** than the **market rate**
• market rental rate—a long-term lease may lock the owner into low rents
• principal risk—resale proceeds may be less than anticipated
2. the possibility of a loss. Insurance can offer protection against certain risks.
Example: Owners insure buildings against *risk* of loss caused by fires, storms, and other hazards by taking out a **hazard insurance** policy.

ROD a linear unit of measurement equal to 16½ feet.
Example: A certain lot has 165 feet, or 10 *rods,* of road **frontage.**

ROLLOVER LOAN a type of **mortgage** loan, commonly used in Canada, in which the **amortization** of **principal** is based on a long **term** but the **interest rate** is established for a much shorter term. The loan may be extended, or rolled over, at the end of the shorter term at the current market interest rate.
Example: Abel obtains a *rollover loan.* The amortization term is 30 years. The interest rate is 14% for 2 years. After 2 years, Abel must renew the loan at the going interest rate or **refinance** with a new loan.

ROW HOUSE **single-family** dwelling units attached to one another by common walls, generally with a common **facade.** See **town-**

house.
Example: A group of *row houses* (Figure 153).

A group of *row houses*

FIGURE 153

ROYALTY money paid to a property owner for extraction of some valuable resource from the land.
Example: Richman owns a 500-**acre** ranch in west Texas. An oil company negotiates a **lease** with Richman to explore for oil on the ranch. Under the agreement, Richman will receive a *royalty* in proportion to the number of barrels of oil pumped from the ranch.

RULE OF 72's an approximation of the time it takes for money to double when earning **compound interest.** Divide the percentage rate into 72 to derive the number of years to double the **principal.**
Example: A $1,000 **certificate of deposit** pays a 9% interest rate with annual compounding. In about 8 years the balance will be $2,000. (72 ÷ 9% = 8 years)

RULE OF 78's a method for computing unearned interest used on installment loans with **add-on interest.** The number 78 is based on the sum of the digits from 1 to 12.
Example: A 12-month loan is made for $1,000 with 8% add-on interest. The loan payments are based on a total of $1,080, payable at the rate of $90 per month for 12 months. If the borrower prepays the loan at the end of 1 month, $\frac{12}{78}$ of the $80 interest is charged; the balance of interest is refunded. If the borrower prepays at the end of the second month, $\frac{12+11}{78} = \frac{23}{78}$ is charged. Prepayment at the end of the eleventh month results in a $\frac{1}{78}$ refund.

RUN WITH THE LAND an expression indicating a right or **restriction** that affects all current and future owners of a property. Contrasted to an agreement, between a current owner and other parties, that is not passed on to future owners in a **deed.**
Example: A **covenant,** written into the **deed,** prohibits the property from being used as a liquor store. The restriction *runs with the land,* and all future owners are restrained from violating the covenant.

RURBAN areas, on the fringe of urban development, that are in the process of being developed for urban uses.
Example: Figure 154.

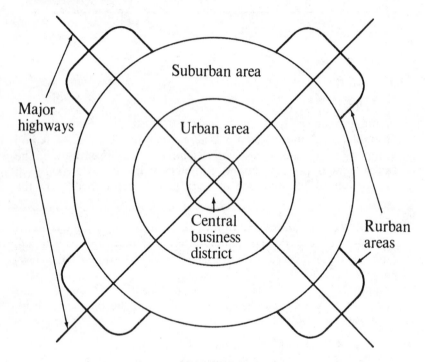

FIGURE 154

RURAL pertaining to the area outside the larger and moderate-sized cities and surrounding population concentrations. Generally characterized by farms, ranches, small towns and unpopulated regions. Compare **suburb.**
Example: Garrison grew up on a farm in a *rural* area of Indiana. She later moved to Chicago and lived in a suburban town nearby. Garrison invested in *rural* land, hoping to be able to return at retirement.

R VALUE a measure of the heat conductivity of material. The higher the *R value,* the better the material serves as insulation from heat

transfer. *R value* generally applies to insulating materials, roofs, exterior walls and windows and doors.

Example: The walls in a building have an estimated *R value* of 20. Fiberglass insulation with an *R value* of 34 was installed in the walls to make the building more energy efficient.

S

SALES CONTRACT a **contract** by which the buyer and seller agree to the **terms** of sale. Same as **agreement of sale, earnest money** contract.

Example: Carter and Dooley sign a *sales contract,* which specifies the property to be sold, type of **deed, closing date,** price, **financing** conditions, and other details.

SALE-LEASEBACK the simultaneous purchase of property and **lease** back to the seller. The lease portion of the transaction is generally long-term. The seller-lessee in the transaction is converted from an owner to a tenant.

Example: ABC Corporation owns an office building. It arranges a *sale-leaseback* for the building **site** with the Carpenters Pension Fund. ABC receives cash and a 25-year lease to the site. In addition, ABC might **depreciate** the value of the building for income taxes. The Fund receives an **income stream** for 25 years and a **reversion** to the property at the end of the lease.

SALESPERSON one who is licensed to deal in real estate or perform any other act enumerated by state real estate **license** laws, while under the supervision of a **broker** licensed by the state.

Example: A *salesperson* arranges a 90-day **listing** on a house, which is accepted by the broker. Another *salesperson* shows the home to a prospective buyer. The sale is closed, and **commissions** are collected by the broker and shared with the *salespersons.*

SALT BOX COLONIAL OR CATSLIDE (IN SOUTH) an early American style, 2 or 2½-story house that is square or rectangular with a steep gable roof that extends down to the first floor in the rear.

Example: Figure 155:

SALVAGE VALUE the estimated **value** that an **asset** will have at the end of its **useful life.**

Example: An appraiser estimates the useful life of a building at 40 years; she also estimates that the building's *salvage value* would be $10,000 in 40 years. Consequently, all but $10,000 of the building cost is to be **depreciated** over 40 years.

Steep gable roof extended to first floor in rear

No windows in rear

Large central chimney

2 or 2½ stories

Square or rectangular shape

Small glass panes in double-hung windows

FIGURE 155

SANDWICH LEASE lease held by a **lessee** who becomes a **lessor** by subletting. Typically, the sandwich leaseholder is neither the owner nor the user of the property. See **sublease.**
Example: Figure 156

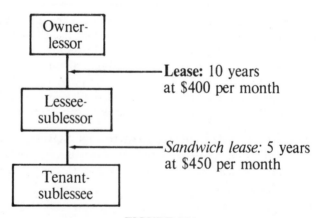

Owner-lessor

Lessee-sublessor

Tenant-sublessee

Lease: 10 years at $400 per month

Sandwich lease: 5 years at $450 per month

FIGURE 156

SATISFACTION PIECE an **instrument** for recording and acknowledging final payment of a **mortgage** loan.
Example: After the mortgage loan was paid off, the borrower received a *satisfaction piece,* which she promptly **recorded,** officially.

SAVINGS & LOAN ASSOCIATIONS (S&Ls) depository institutions that specialize in originating, servicing, and holding **mortgage** loans, primarily on owner-occupied, **residential property.** See **Federal Savings and Loan Association.**
Example: Most home buyers finance the purchase with a mortgage loan from a *savings and loan association.* Such associations receive most of their investment funds from the deposits of small individual savers. All savings and loan associations are subject to regulation from federal or state government.

SCALE the proportional relationship between the dimensions of a drawing, plan, or model to the dimensions of the physical object it represents.
Example: A **subdivision** plan is prepared at a *scale* in which one inch equals 1,000 feet. A distance of one inch on the drawing is intended to signify 1,000 feet on the **site.**
Example: A *scale* model of a building has a *scale* of one to 25. Each inch on the model represents 25 inches on the actual building.

SCENIC EASEMENT an **encumbrance** on the **title** to a property to preserve it in a more-or-less natural or undeveloped state. See **easement.**
Example: Smith owns a house with a view of the ocean (Figure 157). Snyder owns the property between the Smith house and the beach. To preserve the view of the ocean, Smith purchases a *scenic easement* to Snyder's property. Snyder is then prevented from developing the property in such a manner as to obstruct Smith's view.

FIGURE 157

SEASONED LOAN a loan on which several payments have been collected.
Example: The seller accepts a **second mortgage** on the property sold. After he collects 12 months of payments, the loan is considered *seasoned* and can more easily be sold to a second mortgage investor.

SECONDARY FINANCING see **junior mortgage, second mortgage.**

SECONDARY MORTGAGE MARKET the mechanisms available to buy and sell mortgages, mainly residential **first mortgages.** There is no set meeting place for the secondary mortgage market. **FNMA** and **Freddie Mac** hold **auctions** weekly to buy those mortgages offered at the highest **effective rate. Bids** are collected from all over the country.
Example: The Good Money Mortgage Bankers originated 100 residential first mortgages with a total **face value** of $5 million. They sell the mortgages in the *secondary mortgage market* for a $1,000 profit on each.

SECOND HOME a residence that is not one's **principal residence.** Under the Tax Reform Act of 1986, a taxpayer may deduct interest on 2 personal residences.
Example: Senator Goodwill maintains his principal residence in Hometown, Iowa and a *second home* in Washington, D.C. He is allowed to deduct interest paid on both as an itemized deduction.

SECOND MORTGAGE a **subordinated lien,** created by a mortgage loan, over the amount of a **first mortgage.** Second mortgages are used at purchase to reduce the amount of a cash **down payment** or in **refinancing** to raise cash for any purpose. See **subordination.**
Example: A house costs $100,000. Available **financing** is a mortgage loan covering 80% of value, or $80,000. The required cash **down payment** is $20,000. A *second mortgage* is available for an additional $10,000 of value, reducing the down payment to $10,000. The *second mortgage* will generally carry a higher **interest rate** than the first mortgage to reflect the inferior position and greater **risk** of the second mortgage.

SECTION (OF LAND) one square mile in the **government rectangular survey.** There are 36 sections in a 6-mile square **township.**
Example: A township, containing 36 *sections* (Figure 158).

SECTION 8 HOUSING privately owned rental **dwelling** units participating in the low-income rental assistance program created by 1974 amendments to Section 8 of the 1937 Housing Act. Under the program, landlords receive rent subsidies on behalf of qualified low-income tenants, allowing the tenants to pay a limited propor-

tion of their incomes toward the rent.

Example: A **landlord** elects to participate in the *Section 8 housing* program. A prospective tenant's income is $800 per month—low enough to qualify for the program. A **fair market rent** for the unit is established by the **Department of Housing and Urban Development** as $200 per month. The tenant pays 20% of income, or $160 per month, and HUD supplements $40 per month to the landlord.

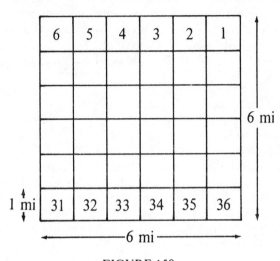

FIGURE 158

SECTION 167 the part of the **Internal Revenue Code** that deals with **depreciation**.
Example: Improvements to **real estate** are depreciable in accordance with *Section 167* of the Internal Revenue Code.

SECTION 1031 the section of the **Internal Revenue Code** that deals with **tax-free exchanges** of certain property. General rules for a **tax-free exchange** of real estate are:
The properties must be:
1. exchanged
2. **like-kind property** (real estate for real estate)
3. held for use in a trade or business or held as an investment
See also **tax-free exchange, boot, delayed exchange.**
Example: Under *Section 1031*, Lowell trades her **appreciated** land for Baker's shopping center. **Equities** are the same. Lowell's **adjusted tax basis** in the land becomes her **adjusted tax basis** in the shopping center.

SECTION 1034 the section of the **Internal Revenue Code** dealing with sales of personal residences. Generally, there is no **recognized gain** or loss on the sale of a personal residence, provided another

one is purchased within 2 years of the sale date of the old one. The new one must cost at least as much as the adjusted sales price of the old one (sales price, less expenses of sale, less fixing-up expenses).

Example: Under *Section 1034*, Abel can defer tax on the $10,000 gain on the home he sold for $65,000 by buying a new one that costs more.

SECTION 1221 the part of the **Internal Revenue Code** that defines a **capital asset.** It actually states what is not a capital asset.

Examples: Under *Section 1221* the following are not **capital assets:**
• inventory (such as lots of a subdivider)
• receivables collected in the course of business (such as **notes** received from the sale of lots by a **subdivider**)
• copyrights and the like held by the creator or certain other parties
• certain U.S. securities
The following are capital assets:
• the personal **residence** that one owns
• **raw land** held as an investment
• **mortgages** held as investments
Note: The importance of capital gains has been diminished by the Tax Reform Act of 1986 which applies the same tax rate to capital gains after 1987 as it does to ordinary income. However, there remain important distinctions as to capital loss limitations, so *Section 1221* remains relevant.

SECTION 1231 the section of the **Internal Revenue Code** that deals with **assets** used in a trade or business. Generally, gains on Section 1231 assets are taxed at **capital gains** rates (except for **depreciation recapture**) and losses are **tax deductible** as **ordinary income.** See also **Section 1245, Section 1250.**
Example: *Section 1231* assets include:
• vehicles used in business
• machinery used in business
• hotels, office buildings, warehouses, apartments

SECTION 1245 the section of the **Internal Revenue Code** dealing with **gains** from **personal property** on which **depreciation** had been claimed. Generally, gains are taxed at **capital gains** rate except to the extent of depreciation claimed.
Note: The Tax Reform Act of 1986 provides the same tax rate for ordinary income as for capital gains after 1987. Therefore the nature of the gain has diminished in importance, though *Section 1245* remains in the Internal Revenue Code.

SECTION 1250 the section of the **Internal Revenue Code** dealing with **gains** from **real estate** on which **accelerated depreciation** had been claimed. Under the Tax Reform Act of 1986, the tax rate for ordinary income is the same as for capital gains after 1987, and straight-

line depreciation is mandated for most buildings. Consequently, the importance of *Section 1250* has been minimized. Under prior law, gains on **residential property** were generally treated as **capital gains** except to the extent of accelerated depreciation claimed (Figure 159 and Table 37). Gains on nonresidential property on which accelerated depreciation was claimed were all **recaptured** to the extent of gain or depreciation, whichever is less.

TABLE 37

TREATMENT OF GAIN
AFTER USE OF DEPRECIATION METHOD

1. Accelerated Method

	Nonresidential	*Residential*
Capital gain	A — B	A — C
Ordinary income	B — D	C — D

2. Straight-line

	Nonresidential	*Residential*
Capital gain	A — B	A — C
Ordinary income	none	none

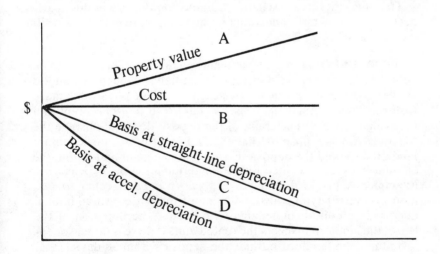

FIGURE 159

SECURITIES AND EXCHANGE COMMISSION (SEC) the federal agency created in 1934 to carry out the provisions of the Securities Exchange Act. Generally, the agency seeks to protect the investing public by preventing **misrepresentation, fraud,** manipulation, and other abuses in the securities markets.

Example: The **Securities and Exchange Commission** requires their review of proposed **public offerings** of securities, registration of listed securities, and other matters. They do not, however, guarantee the investor against loss.

SECURITIZATION the process of creating a security marketable in the capital markets and backed by a package of assets such as mortgage loans. See **real estate mortgage investment conduit, mortgage pools, collateralized mortgage obligation.**
Example: Mortgage loans insured by the Federal Housing Administration are good assets for *securitization*. A lender can organize a pool of such loans and create a collateralized mortgage obligation for sale to investors.

SECURITY 1. property that serves as **collateral** for a **debt.**
Example: **Real estate** serves as *security* for a **mortgage** loan. In the event of **default** on the loan, the lender may sell the property to satisfy the debt.
2. a document that serves as evidence of ownership.
Examples: The following are securities:
• common and preferred stocks
• **bonds**
• **mortgages**
 The **Securities and Exchange Commission** defines **limited partnership** interests and **condominiums** and **cooperatives** in certain situations as *securities*.

SECURITY DEPOSIT a cash payment required by a landlord, to be held during the **term** of a **lease** to offset damages incurred due to actions of the tenant. Such damages may include physical damage to the property, theft of property, failure to pay back rent and breaking the lease. **Forfeiture** of the deposit does not absolve the tenant of further financial **liability.** Laws in most states require landlords to hold the deposit in a separate account and refund the amount within a specified time after termination of the lease.
Example: A landlord requires a *security deposit* equal to one month's rent, payable at the signing of the lease. An additional deposit is required for tenants with pets. At termination of the lease, the landlord inspects the rented unit. If there is no reason for forfeiture, the landlord refunds the deposit within 30 days.

SECURITY INTEREST an interest in **real estate** in which the real estate serves as **collateral.**
Example: A **mortgage** lender holds a *security interest* in real estate. He doesn't own the real estate, but does have a **lien** against it.

SEED MONEY amounts needed to begin a real estate development, prior to being able to borrow under a **mortgage** loan. Required

costs include those for a **feasibility study, loan application** and **loan commitment** fees, attorney and accountant fees, land **option** costs, and others. See **front money.**
Example: To begin a $2,000,000 **condominium** development, about 2% of the total cost is needed as *seed money.*

SEISIN the **possession** of **realty** by one who claims to own a **fee simple** estate or a **life estate** or other salable **interest.** See also **ownership rights to realty, title.**
Example: *Seisin* is used to describe the **possession** of real estate by one who claims a **freehold** interest.

SELF-AMORTIZING MORTGAGE one that will **retire** itself through regular **principal and interest payments.** Contrast with **balloon mortgage, interest-only loan.**
Example: Collins borrowed $100,000 with a *self-amortizing mortgage* at 12% **interest** with a 30-year **term. Principal and interest payments** are $1,029 each month for the 30 years, at the end of which her loan will be amortized fully.

SELF-HELP the efforts of a landlord to cure a **default** on the **lease** without aid of legal proceedings. In most states, self-help remedies are not considered a legitimate substitute for a legal **eviction.**
Example: When Simmons' tenant fell 3 months behind in rent, Simmons changed the locks on the apartment and cut off the heat. The tenant took Simmons to court and forced him to follow eviction procedures in lieu of these *self-help* activities.

SELLER'S MARKET economic conditions that favor sellers, reflecting rising prices and market activity. Contrast with **buyer's market.**
Example: *Seller's markets* in real estate are often caused by:
• population influx
• lower interest rates
• lack of building activity

SELLING BROKER (AGENT) the licensed real estate **broker (agent)** that brings forth the buyer. Contrast with **listing broker (agent).**
Example: Abel was the *selling broker* under a **multiple listing** agreement. He showed the property to Collins, the buyer. Abel will share the **commission** with the listing broker.

SEMIANNUAL twice a year; same as **biannual.**

SENSITIVITY ANALYSIS a technique of investment analysis whereby different values of certain key variables are tested to see how sensitive investment results are to possible change in assumptions. It is a method of evaluating the riskiness of an investment.

Example: *Sensitivity analysis* was applied to a certain income property investment. It was found that forecasting a 15% vacancy rate produced a rate of return on investment of 16% versus an 18% rate of return for a 5% vacancy factor. On the other hand, varying the property's appreciation rate from 10% per year to 5% reduced the return from 20% to 4%.

SEPARATE PROPERTY property acquired by either spouse prior to marriage or by gift or **devise** after marriage, as distinct from **community property.**
Example: At a divorce trial, each party tries to show that property owned prior to marriage or acquired in his or her own right is *separate property.*

SERVICING the act of billing, collecting payment, and filing reports for a **mortgage** loan; may also include loan analysis, **default** follow-up, and management of tax and insurance **escrow** accounts. Often performed for a fee by **mortgage bankers** after loans are sold to investors.
Example: Gray, a mortgage banker, originates loans and markets them in groups to large investors. On each loan originated, Gray receives a monthly fee for *servicing,* thereby freeing the investors of loan management burdens. The fee is ⅜ of 1% of the loan balance.

SERVIENT TENANT contrast with **dominant tenant.**

SETBACK the distance from the curb or other established line within which no buildings may be erected. See also **building line.**
Example: A 50-ft setback is shown in Figure 160.

FIGURE 160

SETTLEMENT same as **closing.**

SETTLEMENT STATEMENT same as **closing statement.**

SEVERALTY the ownership of **real property** by an individual as an individual. See **tenancy in severalty.**
Example: The owner in *severalty* enjoys working the land without partners in its ownership.

SEVERANCE DAMAGES an element of **value** arising out of a **condemnation** to which a **tract** was a part.
Example: The state highway department needed a strip of land 100 feet wide from the middle of Dooley's farm. They awarded $1,000 per **acre** for the land taken, plus $15,000 *severance damages* for Dooley's inconvenience in getting from one side of the highway to the other.

SEWER a system of pipes, containments, and treatment facilities for the disposal of plumbing wastes.
Example: A sanitary *sewer* collects waste water from individual buildings and homes, for treatment and disposal at a public facility.
Example: To prevent flooding, a storm *sewer* collects water drainage from streets and other surfaces.

SHARED APPRECIATION MORTGAGE a residential loan with a fixed **interest rate** set below **market rates,** with the lender entitled to a specified share of **appreciation** in property **value** over a specified time interval. Loan payments are set to **amortize** the loan over a long-term **maturity,** but repayment is generally required after a much shorter term. The amount of appreciation is established by sale of the home or by **appraisal** if no sale is made.
Example: Hogan obtains a *shared appreciation mortgage.* The interest rate on the loan is 10%, with the lender receiving ⅓ of any appreciation after 10 years. At the end of 10 years, Hogan does not wish to sell the home. An appraisal is made to establish the appreciation amount. Hogan must **retire** the loan by **refinancing** with a new loan the amount of the unpaid balance plus the appreciation share.

SHARED EQUITY MORTGAGE a home **loan** in which the lender is granted a share of the **equity,** thereby allowing the lender to participate in the proceeds from resale. After satisfying the unpaid balance of the loan, the borrower splits the residue of the proceeds with the lender. Shared equity plans often require the lender to buy a portion of the equity by providing a portion of the **down payment.**
Example: Ingram obtains a *shared equity mortgage* from a **mortgage banker.** The lender provides one half of the necessary down

payment. Ingram makes loan payments on a fixed-rate, level payment basis. At resale, Ingram and the lender split the proceeds after repayment of the balance of the loan.

SHED ROOF one having a single, sloped side.
Example: Figure 161.

Shed

FIGURE 161

SHOPPING CENTER a collection of retail stores with a common parking area and generally one or more large department, discount, or food stores; sometimes including an enclosed **mall** or walkway. See also **anchor tenant.**
Example: *Shopping centers* developed after World War II as population shifted to the suburbs. Providing a variety of stores with easy access and ample parking, the centers became a strong alternative to downtown retail centers. Types of shopping centers are shown in Table 38.

SHORT-FORM an **instrument,** seldom more than 2 pages, that refers to another document. The short form is often recorded in lieu of a cumbersome longer document.
Example: The Giant Development Company leased part of a shopping center to Malee's Department Store. The **lease** required 150 printed pages. A *short-form* lease was recorded.

SHORT-TERM CAPITAL GAIN gain on the sale of a **capital asset** that was held, generally, for less than 6 months. A taxpayer's *short-term capital gains* and losses are merged, the net is then merged with net long-term capital gains.
Example :An investor sold land that was owned for 4 months at a $10,000 profit The sale was the investor's only capital transaction that year, so the $10,000 *short-term capital gain* is added to ordinary income.
 The difference in tax treatment of various kinds of income has been diminished by the Tax Reform Act of 1986 which generally taxes all income at the same rate. Consequently, short- and long-term capital gains are, in general, taxed at the same rate after 1987.

TABLE 38

	Building area, sq ft	Anchor tenant
Neighborhood	30,000–100,000	supermarket or drugstore
Community	100,000–500,000	junior department store and supermarket
Regional	500,000–1,000,000	at least one major department store
Superregional	over 1,000,000	several major department stores

SIMPLE INTEREST a method of calculating the future value of a sum assuming that interest paid is not compounded, i.e., that interest is paid only on the **principal.** See also **compound interest.**

Example: An account is established paying *simple interest* of 10% on a principal of $1,000. Table 39 shows the current value of the account for the next 5 years.

TABLE 39

Year	Value
1	$1100
2	1200
3	1300
4	1400
5	1500

SINGLE-FAMILY HOUSING a type of residential structure designed to include one **dwelling.** Adjacent units may share walls and other structural components but generally have separate access to the outside and do not share plumbing and heating equipment.

Example: *Single-family housing* includes:
• **detached housing** units
• **town houses**
• **zero lot line** homes

SINKING FUND an account that, when compounded, will equal a specified sum after a specified time period. See **compound interest.**

357

Example: The Johnsons wish to buy a home 3 years from now. They estimate the **down payment** will equal $5,000. To accumulate the necessary money, they set up a *sinking fund* at the local bank. At 5% interest, the fund requires monthly deposits of $129. After 36 payments, the account will contain $5,000.

SITE a plot of land prepared for or underlying a structure or development. The location of a property.
Example: The Smith Building is located on a half-**acre** *site* in downtown Smithville. Several new buildings are being constructed on *sites* nearby.

SITE PLAN a document which describes how a parcel of land is to be improved. It includes the outlines of all structures and site improvements, such as driveways, parking lots, landscaping and utility connections.
Example: The *site plan* indicates that the office tower will be set back 100 feet from the street and be surrounded by surface parking for 2,000 cars.

SITUS the economic attributes of location, including the relationship between the property and surrounding properties, as well as distant points of interest and the linkages to those points. *Situs* is considered to be the aspect of location that contributes to the market value of a real property.
Example: The *situs* of a commercial property includes surrounding commercial establishments, the location of suppliers' warehouses, competing establishments, and the homes of employees and customers.

SMALL BUSINESS ADMINISTRATION (SBA) a federal government agency in Washington, D.C. that encourages small business.
Example: The *SBA* offers low-interest rate loans to qualified businessmen and businesswomen.
Address:
Small Business Administration
1441 L Street, N.W.
Washington, D.C. 20416

SOCIETY OF INDUSTRIAL REALTORS® **(SIR)** an organization, affiliated with the **National Association of Realtors®**, whose members are mainly concerned with the sale of warehouses, factories, and other **industrial property.** Confers SIR designation. Publishes *SIR Market Letter* (bimonthly) and *SIR Newsletter* (monthly).
Address:
Society of Industrial Realtors®
925 Fifteenth Street, N.W.
Washington, D.C. 20005

SOCIETY OF REAL ESTATE APPRAISERS (SREA) an organization in Chicago, Illinois dedicated to professionalism in real estate **appraisal.** They award designations, **SRA, SRPA, SREA.**
Address:
Society of Real Estate Appraisers
645 N. Michigan Avenue
Chicago, Illinois 60611

SOFT MONEY 1. in a development or an investment, money contributed that is **tax-deductible.**
Example: **Equity** required for a development is $100,000, of which 50% is promised to be tax-deductible and therefore is *soft money.*
2. sometimes used to describe costs that do not physically go into construction, such as interest during construction, architect's fees, legal fees, etc.

SOIL BANK land held out of agricultural production in an effort to stabilize commodity prices and promote soil conservation. Subsidies to farmers participating in the soil bank program are provided by the U.S. Department of Agriculture.
Example: A farmer normally plants her land in corn. To avoid a surplus of corn production, the federal government pays the farmer to hold the land out of production for a year. The farmer is participating in the *soil bank* program.

SOLAR HEATING, HOT WATER see **active solar heating, passive solar heating.**

SOLE PROPRIETORSHIP ownership of a business, with no formal entity as a vehicle or structure. Contrast **corporation, limited partnership, partnership.**
Example: Jessica goes into the real estate appraising business with all business activities in her own name and no partners. She is a *sole proprietor.*

SOUTHERN COLONIAL a large, early American style, 2 or 3-story frame house with a characteristic colonnade extending across the front. The roof extends over the colonnade.
Example: Figure 162.

SPANISH VILLA a Latin style, asymmetrical, 1- to 3-story house with painted stucco exterior walls and red tile roof.
Example: Figure 163.

SPEC HOUSE a **single-family** dwelling constructed in anticipation of finding a buyer.
Example: Keene, a **developer,** is convinced there is local demand for 3-bedroom houses priced in the $80,000 range. Keene therefore

constructs a number of *spec houses* and mounts a marketing campaign.

Symmetrical

2 or 3 stories

Column-supported colonnade across front

FIGURE 162

1 to 3 stories

Red tile roof

Painted stucco exterior walls

Oval-top doors

FIGURE 163

SPECIAL AGENT one who is engaged to act for another, with limited authority.
Example: A real estate **broker,** engaged by an owner to find a buyer, is considered a *special agent* of the owner.

SPECIAL ASSESSMENT an **assessment** made against a property to pay for a public **improvement** by which the assessed property is supposed to be especially benefited.
Example: The Lawsons own a house in a developing section of the city. When the city constructs curbs and gutters along their street, the Lawsons are levied a *special assessment,* in the form of a one-time tax, to pay for the construction.

SPECIALIST IN REAL ESTATE SECURITIES (SRS) a professional designation awarded by the **Real Estate Securities and Syndication Institute (RESSI).** Qualification is based on experience, education, examination, and demonstration of expertise in preparing a **syndication** report.

SPECIAL USE PERMIT a right granted by a local **zoning** authority to conduct certain activities within a zoning district. Such activities are considered conditional uses, which are permitted within the zone only upon special approval of the zoning authority. Also termed a "conditional use permit."
Example: A local government allows, as a conditional use, the operation of parking lots within its high-**density** residential zoning districts. A landowner wishing to operate a parking lot must obtain a *special use permit* following review of the plans of the development.

SPECIAL WARRANTY DEED a **deed** in which the **grantor** limits the title **warranty** given to the **grantee** to anyone claiming by, from, through, or under him, the grantor. The grantor does not warrant against **title** defects arising from conditions that existed before he owned the property. See **warranty deed.**
Example: Because of **bankruptcy** of its owner, a property goes under trusteeship. When the property is sold to satisfy creditor claims, the **trustee** conveys a *special warranty deed* to the buyer. This provides the buyer with warranty against claims incurred only during the time the property was held by the trustee.

SPECIFICATIONS detailed instructions provided in conjunction with plans and blueprints for construction. Specifications may stipulate the type of materials to be used, special construction techniques, dimensions, and colors.
Example: The building *specifications* state that:
• number 3 lumber shall be used for all framing
• studs are to be on 16-inch centers
• all exterior surfaces shall be painted white

SPECIFIC PERFORMANCE a legal action in which the court requires a party to a **contract** to perform the **terms** of the contract when he has refused to fulfill his obligations. Used in real estate, since each **parcel** of land is unique.

Example: Baker agrees in writing to sell his house to Abel. Baker changes his mind when his adult daughter decides to buy the house. Baker offers to refund Abel's **earnest money** and pay living expenses for one month, but Abel insists on buying the house as agreed and sues for *specific performance*.

SPECULATOR one who invests with the anticipation that an event or series of events wil occur to increase the value of the investment.
Example: The value of **single-family houses** has been appreciating rapidly for several months. Munson, a *speculator*, purchases several houses in anticipation that this rapid rate of **appreciation** will continue.

SPENDABLE INCOME same as **after-tax cash flow.**

SPOT ZONING the act of rezoning a **parcel** of land where all surrounding parcels are zoned for a different use, in particular where the rezoning creates a use which is incompatible with surrounding land uses. Spot **zoning** is generally disallowed in the courts.
Example: Figure 164 may be construed as *spot zoning.*

Low density residential zone

Rezoned to commercial use

FIGURE 164

SPREAD 1. the difference between the **bid** price and **asking price.**
Example: The buyer offers to pay $1,000 per **acre,** but the seller asks $1,300. The *spread* is $300.
2. the difference between the cost of money and the earnings rate.
Example: Good Money Savings and Loan pays an average interest rate of 10% to its depositors. It earns an average of 12% on its investments. The 2 point *spread* is adequate to pay **operating expenses** and leave some profit.

SPREADING AGREEMENT an agreement that extends the **collateral** of a loan to include several properties.
Example: Abel owns 7 shopping centers; all have **first mortgages.** He wants to borrow $5 million from a lender. The lender insists he

sign a *spreading agreement* that gives a second **lien** on all 7 shopping centers.

SQUARE FOOTAGE the area, measured in square feet, of a piece of **real estate**. Generally measured from outside the exterior walls in the case of structures.
Example: The outside dimension of a rectangular home is 40 × 50 feet. Its *square footage* is 2,000.

SQUATTER'S RIGHTS the legal allowance to use the property of another in absence of an attempt by the owner to force **eviction;** this right may eventually be converted to **title** to the property over time by **adverse possession,** if recognized by state law.
Example: Various poor families take up residence in a vacant building, acquiring *squatter's rights.* Since ownership of the property is uncertain, no one attempts to evict the families.

SRA a person who is a Senior Residential Appraiser, a designation awarded by the **Society of Real Estate Appraisers** for residential **appraisers.**
Example: To assure that the appraiser was ethical and qualified, Good Money Savings Association engaged one with the *SRA* designation.

SREA Senior Real Estate Analyst, the highest designation awarded by the **Society of Real Estate Appraisers.**
Example: A complicated **condemnation** of multiuse properties required the services of an *SREA*.

SRPA Senior Real Property Appraiser. Awarded by the **Society of Real Estate Appraisers** to those qualified to appraise **residential** and income-producing **property.**
Example: The *SRPA* is careful in estimating the **market value** of the subject office building. She considers all **appraisal** approaches before arriving at a value estimate.

STANDARD METROPOLITAN STATISTICAL AREA (SMSA) a designation of the U.S. Census Bureau for **metropolitan areas** with a central city having a specified minimum population (50,000 in the 1970 census) and including all counties that are economically linked to the central city. Statistics compiled for the SMSA are considered more descriptive of the importance of a city than those for the political jurisdiction of the city only.
Example: In 1980, the city of Houston had a population of 1.5 million. The Houston *standard metropolitan statistical area,* which included 6 counties, had a population of almost 3 million.

STANDBY FEE the sum required by a lender to provide a standby **commitment.** See **standby loan.** The fee is **forfeited** should the loan

not be closed within a specified time.

Example: A **developer** obtains a **standby loan** on a project to be developed. The developer hopes **interest rates** will decline during the construction period so that permanent **financing** may be arranged with **terms** better than those on the standby loan. However, a permanent loan commitment is required to obtain a **construction loan.** The developer pays a *standby fee* to compensate the lender for making the standby loan commitment. At the completion of construction, the developer has the **option** of exercising the standby commitment or forfeiting the fee.

STANDBY LOAN a **commitment** by a lender to make available a sum of money at specified terms for a specified period. A **standby fee** is charged for this commitment. The borrower retains the **option** of closing the loan or allowing the commitment to lapse.
Example: See **standby fee.**

STATUTE a law established by an act of legislature.
Example: When a bill is passed by the legislature and signed by the governor, it becomes a state *statute.* Similarly, when a bill is passed by Congress and signed by the President, it becomes a federal *statute.*

STATUTE OF FRAUDS a state law that provides that certain **contracts** must be in writing in order to be enforceable. Applied to **deeds, mortgages,** and other **real estate** contracts, with the exception of **leases** for periods shorter than one year.
Example: An oral contract for the sale of land is considered unenforceable under the *statute of frauds.*

STATUTE OF LIMITATIONS a specified statutory period after which a claimant is barred from enforcing his claim by suit.
Example: Abel bought a **limited partnership** interest in a real estate transaction. The **syndicator** failed to mention in the **prospectus** that the land is in a flood-prone area. Abel discovers the fact and sues 4 years later but is barred from collecting under the *statute of limitations.*

STEERING an illegal practice of limiting the housing shown to a certain ethnic group.
Example: Though the minority couple wanted to be shown all available rental housing that they could afford, the unlicensed person *steered* them from certain neighborhoods.

STEPPED-UP BASIS an income tax term used to describe a change in the **adjusted tax basis** of property, allowed for certain transactions. The old basis is increased to **market value** upon inheritance, as opposed to a **carry-over basis** in the event of a

tax-free exchange.
Example: Dooley dies, leaving land worth $100,000. The land was purchased for $20,000, but the heirs receive a *stepped-up basis* to the **fair market value** at death. The $80,000 **unrealized gain** to Dooley escapes **capital gains** tax.

STEP-UP LEASE see **graduated lease.**

STICK STYLE OR CARPENTER GOTHIC a nineteenth century style house with exposed framing members, high steep roofs, complex silhouettes, diagonal braces, and a large amount of gingerbread trim.
Example: Figure 165.

Exposed framing members

High steep roof

Lots of "Gingerbread"

Ornate windows and doors

Complex silhouette

FIGURE 165

STIPULATIONS the **terms** within a written **contract.**
Example: A sales contract contains *stipulations* concerning the type of **financing** the buyer must be able to obtain, the price, proration of **closing** cost between buyer and seller, and the date and location of the closing.

STOP CLAUSE in a **lease,** stipulates an amount of **operating expense** above which the tenant must bear. Often the base amount is the amount of expense for the first full year of operation under the lease.
Example: The *stop clause* requires the tenant to pay all **utilities** in excess of $2,500 per year. If utilities are less than that amount, the landlord pays them.

STRAIGHT LEASE see **flat lease.**

STRAIGHT-LINE DEPRECIATION equal annual reductions in the **book value** of property. It is used in accounting for replacement and tax purposes. See **depreciation (accounting).**
Example: A property has a **depreciable basis** of $275,000. For tax purposes, a **useful life** of 27½ years is used with no **salvage value.** Using *straight-line depreciation,* the book value of the property is decreased by $10,000 ($275,000/27.5) per year. The tax deduction for depreciation is $10,000 per year.

STRAIGHT-LINE RECAPTURE RATE the part of a **capitalization rate** that accounts for the annual erosion of a **wasting asset** by assuming an equal amount of loss in value each year of the **useful life** of the asset.
Example: A retail building's **useful life** is estimated at 50 years. The *straight-line recapture rate* is 2% per year, which will recover the asset cost over its estimated useful life. The 2% should be added to the **discount rate** to derive the **capitalization rate.**

STRAW MAN one who purchases property that is, in turn, **conveyed** to another for the purpose of concealing the identity of the eventual purchaser.
Example: A **developer** is assembling land, for a **subdivision,** from a large number of individually owned plots. To avoid the possibility that a few landowners will hold out for high prices, the developer uses *straw men* to purchase the **parcels. Agents** of the developer purchase plots in their own names and later convey the land to the developer.

STRIP DEVELOPMENT a form of commercial land use in which each establishment is afforded direct access to a major thoroughfare; generally associated with intensive use of signs to attract passersby.
Example: Map of *strip development* (Figure 166).

STRUCTURE any constructed improvement to a **site.**
Examples: *Structures* include:
• buildings
• fencing and enclosures
• garages

366

• gazebos, greenhouses, and kiosks
• sheds and utility buildings

Auto parts store	Fast food	Tire store	Car wash	Service station

Fast food	Shoe store	Hardware store	Fast food

FIGURE 166

SUBCHAPTER S CORPORATION a **corporation** with a limited number of stockholders (35 or fewer) that elects not to be taxed as a regular corporation, and meets certain other requirements. Shareholders include, in their personal tax return, their pro-rata share of **capital gains, ordinary income, tax preference** items, and so on. See **passive income.**
Example: To avoid **double taxation,** the ABC Real Estate Corporation elects *Subchapter S* status. Its shareholders will include corporate income in their own tax return, whether or not they receive a dividend. The corporation itself will not pay an income tax, but will file a tax return.

SUBCONTRACTOR one who performs services under **contract** to a **general contractor.**
Example: A general contractor agrees to construct a building for a **developer.** The contractor arranges with individual *subcontractors* who are specifically responsible to the contractor for performance of carpentry, plumbing, electrical, and masonry work.

SUBDIVIDER one who partitions a **tract** of land for the purpose of selling the individual plots. If the land is improved in any way, the subdivider becomes a **developer.**
Example: Olsen, a *subdivider,* purchases a 100-acre tract of land. The tract is subdivided into 5-acre plots that are marketed to investors and developers.

SUBDIVIDING dividing a **tract** of land into smaller tracts.
Example: See **subdivider.**

SUBDIVISION a **tract** of land divided into lots suitable for home-building purposes. Some states and localities require that a subdivision **plat** be recorded.
Example: A residential *subdivision* (Figure 167).

FIGURE 167

SUBJECT PROPERTY in appraisal, the property being appraised.
Example: The *subject property* compares favorably with other homes in the neighborhood.

SUBJECT TO acquiring property with an existing mortgage, but not becoming **personally liable** for the debt. Contrast with **assumption of mortgage.**
Example: Abel bought **land** for $1,000 cash, *subject to* a $99,000 mortgage. If Abel defaults on the **mortgage** he will lose the cash **down payment** but is not responsible for the $99,000 **debt.**

SUBJECT TO MORTGAGE circumstance in which a buyer takes **title** to mortgaged **real property** but is not personally liable for the payment of the amount due. The buyer must make payments in order to keep the property; however, with default, only the buyer's **equity** in that property is lost. Contrast **assumption of mortgage.**
Example: Queen purchases a house from Parsons *subject to* the existing *mortgage.* Parson's mortgage has an outstanding balance of $40,000 and the sales price is $60,000. Queen pays Parsons $20,000 in cash and takes over the payments on the mortgage. Should Queen **default,** Parsons is liable under the **promissory note** given to the lender.

SUBLEASE a **lease** from a **lessee** to another lessee. The new lessee is a sublessee or subtenant. See **sandwich lease.**
Example: Acme, Inc., leases office space under a 10-year lease. Acme wishes to relocate but cannot break the lease. With the landlord's permission, Acme finds a subtenant, Medcorp, to sign a *sublease* for the space. Medcorp pays rent to Acme, which, in turn, continues to pay rent to the landlord.

SUBLET see **sublease.**

SUBORDINATION moving to a lower **priority,** as a **lien** would if it changes from a **first mortgage** to a **second mortgage.**
Example: The land seller who held a first mortgage allowed *subordination* so the **development loan** could be arranged. In return, the seller is promised mortgage **retirement** in 2 years.

SUBORDINATION CLAUSE a clause or document that permits a **mortgage** recorded at a later date to take **priority** over an existing mortgage.
Example: Even though the **first mortgage** was recently **retired,** the **second mortgage** remained a second mortgage. The *subordination clause* in the second mortgage provided that a mortgage that replaces the existing first mortgage will become a first mortgage; the second mortgage will not move up in priority.

SUBSTITUTION in appraisal, the principle that market value is indicated by the value of another property with similar utility. A typical buyer is assumed to be indifferent to substituting one property for the other.
Example: By the principle of *substitution,* the market value of a property can be estimated by analyzing sales prices of comparable properties.

SUBSURFACE RIGHTS same as **mineral rights.**

SUBURB a town or unincorporated developed area in close proximity to a city. Suburbs, largely residential, are often dependent on the city for employment and support services; generally characterized by low-**density** development relative to the city.
Example: Figure 168.

SUMMARY POSSESSION same as **eviction, actual.**

SUM-OF-YEARS-DIGITS DEPRECIATION in tax and accounting, a method of allocating the cost of an **asset** over its **useful life.** It requires a fraction to be computed each year, which is applied against the depreciable amount. The numerator is the number of years left to be depreciated. The denominator is the sum of the years digits of the depreciable life. The formula for the denominator is:

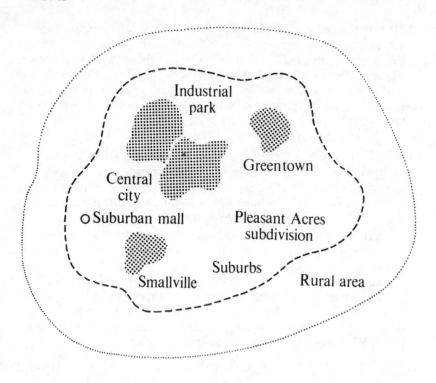

FIGURE 168

$$\frac{N(N + 1)}{2}$$

where N = the depreciable life. See **accelerated depreciation**.
Example: An automobile used in business cost $10,000 and has a
4-year depreciable life. *Sum-of-the-years-digits depreciation*
results in the deductions shown in Table 40.

TABLE 40

Year	Fraction	Asset	Depreciation deduction
1	⁴⁄₁₀	$10,000	$4,000
2	³⁄₁₀	10,000	3,000
3	²⁄₁₀	10,000	2,000
4	¹⁄₁₀	10,000	1,000

SUMP as part of a drainage system, a pit in the basement to collect
excess moisture and liquids. To avoid flooding, a *sump* pump may
be installed to remove accumulated water in the sump pit.
Example: Figure 169

FIGURE 169

SUNSPACE a room, generally with glass walls and roof, designed to collect solar heat.
Example: By adding a *sunspace* to the south side of their home, the Sols were able to save money on their winter heating bills.

SURETY one who guarantees the performance of another.
Example: Ridley employs a **contractor** to construct a house. Under the **contract,** the contractor is required to obtain a **performance bond** against failure to perform the work. Ace Bonding Co. provides the bond, thereby acting as a *surety.* Should the contractor fail to perform, Ace compensates Ridley for damages.

SURRENDER the cancellation of a **lease** by mutual consent of the **lessor** and the **lessee.**
Example: Simmons rents a house under a 2-year lease. Simmons is forced to move due to a job transfer. The landlord agrees to allow Simmons to *surrender* the **premises** if Simmons finds an acceptable new tenant.

SURVEY 1. the process by which a **parcel** of land is measured and its area ascertained. 2. the plan showing the measurements, boundaries, area, and contours.
Example: A simplified *survey* (Figure 170).

SURVEYOR one who prepares **surveys.**
Example: Prior to selling her property, Collins had to hire a *surveyor* to prepare a survey of the land.

SURVIVORSHIP the right of a joint tenant or tenants to maintain ownership rights following the death of another joint tenant. Survivorship prevents heirs of the deceased from making claims against the property. See **joint tenancy.**
Example: Travers and Vance Mead are brothers who own an

371

apartment building, with the right of survivorship. When Travers Mead dies, Vance Mead, through *survivorship*, becomes sole owner of the building.

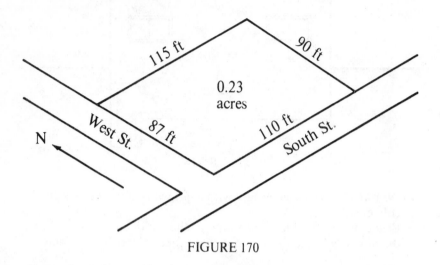

FIGURE 170

SWEAT EQUITY value added to a property due to **improvements** as a result of work performed personally by the owner.
Example: The Watsons purchase an old house for $20,000. Working in their spare time, the Watsons repair and repaint the structure to the point that the property is valued at $30,000. The $10,000 increment is *sweat equity*.

SWISS CHALET a Swiss style 1½- to 2½-story, gable roof house with extensive natural decorative woodwork on the exterior.
Example: Figure 171.

SYNDICATION a method of selling property whereby a sponsor (or **syndicator**) sells interests to investors. May take the form of a **partnership, limited partnership, tenancy in common, corporation,** or **subchapter S Corporation.**
Example: A *syndication* was formed whereby limited partnership interests were sold to investors. The partnership bought land with the **equity** raised.

SYNDICATOR a person in business who sells an investment in shares or units.
Example: Collins, licensed as both a real estate **broker** and a **securities** salesperson, is a *syndicator*. She contracts with investors to buy shopping centers, then sells **partnership** interests conveying ownership in the centers to 30 different investors.

1½ to 2½ stories Large glass windows

Gable roof

Decorative wood work

Natural wood look

Open porches

Curved cornice

FIGURE 171

T

TACKING adding on to a time period.
Example: A squatter was on property for 10 years, moved away for one year, then returned for 10 years. If he were allowed to *tack* both 10-year periods, his claim to **squatter's rights** to the land would be a strong one.

TAKEOUT FINANCING a **commitment** to provide permanent **financing** following construction of a planned project. The takeout commitment is generally predicated upon specific conditions, such as a certain percentage of unit sales or leases, for the permanent loan to "takeout" the **construction loan.** Most construction lenders require takeout financing.
Example: Young, a developer, applied for a construction loan on a small office building. The construction lender requires Young to obtain *takeout financing* in the form of a commitment from a permanent lender. The takeout loan will be granted following con-

373

struction and leasing of at least 65% of **net rentable area** to creditworthy tenants.

TAKING 1. acquisition of a **parcel** of land through **condemnation.**
Example: The Highway Department acquires much of its **right-of-way** for new roads through *takings*. These are usually parcels whose owners are unwilling to settle on a price through negotiation.
2. in land use law, application of **police power** restrictions to a parcel of land that are so restrictive as to preclude any reasonable use.
Example: A local community zones a parcel of land for agricultural use. The owner argues the land is unsuitable for growing crops but could be used for building homes. The owner's argument is the **zoning** is a *taking* of the property without just compensation, which is contrary to the Fourteenth Amendment to the U.S. Constitution.

TANDEM PLAN a program of the **Government National Mortgage Association (GNMA)** working together with the **Federal National Mortgage Association (FNMA)** to provide low interest rate home loans.
Example: Under the *tandem* plan, FNMA purchases qualified low-interest rate mortgages at a discount from GNMA. GNMA absorbs the loss as a subsidy to the qualified low-income home buyer.

TANGIBLE PROPERTY real estate and other valuables which can be seen and touched.
Example: A home, farm, furniture and fixtures are types of *tangible properties*. In contrast, a deed, mortgage, or stock certificate are intangibles in that they represent ownership in something but are not the thing itself.

TAX a charge levied upon persons or things by a government.
Example:
• ad valorem *tax*
• county *tax*
• excise *tax*
• income *tax*
• property *tax*
• sales *tax*
• school *tax*
• use *tax*

TAXABLE VALUE see **assessed value.**

TAX AND INSURANCE ESCROW an account required by a mortgage lender to fund annual property tax assessments and hazard

insurance premiums for the mortgaged property. Funded through monthly contributions by the mortgagor. See **PITI.**
Example: When the mortgage loan was originated, a *tax and insurance escrow* was set up by the lender to pay tax and insurance expenses. The borrower's monthly mortgage payment was increased by an amount necessary to accumulate a balance in the account sufficient to cover these expenses.

TAX ASSESSOR see **assessor.**

TAX BASE the collective value of property, income or other taxable activity or assets subject to a tax. Tax revenues are computed as the tax base times the tax rate. For property taxation, the tax base is the total assessed value of all taxable property less exemptions.
Example: American Widgetworks plans to build a new plant in Centerville. The plant will add $15 million to the property *tax base* of the city.

TAX BASIS same as **basis (tax); see adjusted tax basis.**

TAX BRACKET marginal rate for income taxes; the percentage of each additional dollar in income required to be paid as income taxes.
Example: Abel is considering an investment that will produce $1,000 in taxable income for the next year. Abel's taxable income is currently $20,000, which places Abel in the 28% *tax bracket.* Thus, should Abel make the investment, $280 of the $1,000 will be paid in taxes.

TAX CREDIT a reduction against income tax payments that would otherwise be due. Contrast with **tax deductions** that reduce taxable income.
Example: *Tax credits* that are available to real estate owners include:
• rehabilitation tax credits for older properties and **historic structures**
• low income housing .

TAX DEDUCTIBLE a type of expense that can be used to reduce taxable income. See **tax deduction.**
Example: Interest and **ad valorem** taxes are generally *tax deductible* for all types of property. **Depreciation,** repairs, **maintenance, utilities,** and other ordinary and necessary expenses are *tax deductible* for **income property.**

TAX DEDUCTION one that can be used to reduce taxable income. See **tax deductible.** Contrast with **tax credit.**
Example: Abel has a $75,000 annual salary and $25,000 worth of *tax deductions.* Taxes for the year are figured on taxable income of $50,000.

TAX DEED the type of instrument given to a **grantee** by a government that had claimed the **property** for unpaid taxes.

Example: The city acquired a **parcel** of land because the former owner failed to pay **ad valorem** taxes. The city then auctioned it. Baker, the highest bidder, received a *tax deed* as evidence of ownership.

TAX-EXEMPT PROPERTY real property that is not subject, in whole or in part, to **ad valorem** property taxes.
Examples: In many local communities, the following types of property are *tax-exempt property:*
• churches
• government land and buildings
• **homesteads** (in part)
• solar-powered heating systems

TAX FORECLOSURE the process of enforcing a lien against property for nonpayment of delinquent property taxes. Taxing authorities hold a superior lien against all taxable property to enforce the payment of their taxes. See **foreclosure.**
Example: The owner of the old apartment house had failed to pay property taxes on the building for the past 2 years. The county was forced to pursue a *tax foreclosure* against the property and have it sold at auction.

TAX-FREE EXCHANGE same as tax-deferred exchange.

TAX LIEN a **debt** attached against **property** for failing to pay taxes.
Example: A *tax lien* may be imposed for failing to pay the following taxes:
• city
• county
• estate
• income
• payroll
• sales
• school

TAX MAP a document showing the location, dimensions, and other information pertaining to a **parcel** of land subject to **property taxes.** Maps are generally bound into books and kept as public records at the local tax office.
Example: A *tax map* showing parcel 65 in district A5-300 (Figure 172).

TAX PREFERENCE ITEMS certain types of **income** or deductions that are added to adjusted **gross income** to calculate the **alternative minimum tax.**
Examples: *Tax preference items* in 1987 and thereafter include:
• **depreciation** on **real estate** to the extent it exceeds 40-year straight-line depreciation

- **accelerated depreciation** on leased **personal property** to the extent it exceeds **straight-line depreciation**
- bargain element of an incentive stock option
- certain rapid write-offs
- losses from passive activity investment
- certain itemized deductions (state and local income taxes, real estate taxes, medical expenses not greater than 10% of adjusted gross income)
- miscellaneous deductions in excess of 2% of adjusted gross income
- all interest expense, except home mortgage interest and investment interest, to the extent of net investment income
- interest on certain tax exempt bonds issued after August 7, 1986
- the excess of value deducted over the cost of property given to charitable organizations.

A5-300-65

FIGURE 172

TAX RATE the ratio of a tax **assessment** to the amount being taxed.
Example: In a certain community, the *tax rate* for **property taxes** is $0.35 per $100 of **assessed value**. A home is valued at $20,000. A **homestead exemption** of $2,000 is allowed for this type of property. The tax collected is

$$\$0.35 \times \frac{(\$20,000 - \$2,000)}{\$100} = \$63.00$$

TAX ROLL the list of all properties subject to a tax in a county or other property taxing jurisdiction. It identifies all properties and indicates their assessed values.

Example: A *tax roll* was prepared by the county tax assessor's office, showing $100 million worth of assessed value in the jurisdiction. The county commissioners needed to collect $1 million of taxes to run the government this year, so they applied a 10 mill tax rate to the tax roll.

TAX SALE the sale of property after a period of nonpayment of taxes. The **grantee** receives a **tax deed**. In most states the **defaulting** party has a **redemption period** during which he may pay the unpaid taxes, interest, court costs, and the purchase price to redeem the property.
Example: The failure to pay property **ad valorem** taxes resulted in a *tax sale* of Abel's land. Since the property was worth more than the back taxes, Abel erred by failing to pay.

TAX SHELTER an investment that produces after-tax income that is greater than before-tax income. The investment may produce **before-tax cash flow** while generating losses to shield, from taxation, income from sources outside the investment.
Example: Dunn purchases an income-producing property which provides *tax shelter*. In the first year, the property produces a **net operating income** of $100,000. **Debt service** is $80,000, of which $75,000 is **interest**. Dunn's **before-tax cash flow** is $20,000. First-year **depreciation** is $50,000, so that a tax loss is generated as shown in Table 41.

TABLE 41

$100,000	Net operating income
75,000	Interest deduction
50,000	Depreciation deduction
(25,000)	Taxable income (loss)

Dunn not only pays no tax on the $20,000 cash flow but might be allowed to shelter $25,000 of income from other sources. The Tax Reform Act of 1986 places limits and restrictions on the deductibility of passive losses. See **passive income, active participation, material participation.**

TAX STOP a clause in a **lease** that stops a **lessor** from paying **property taxes** above a certain amount. See **escalator clause, stop clause.**
Example: The *tax stop* in the lease required the tenant to pay all property taxes in excess of $1,200.

TEASER RATE a contract interest rate charged on an adjustable rate mortgage for the initial adjustment interval that is significantly lower than the fully indexed rate at the time. It is an incentive to encourage borrowers to accept adjustable rate mortgage loans. In

general, the interest rate reverts to the fully indexed rate at the first adjustment date. See **fully indexed rate.**
Example: An adjustable rate mortgage is indexed to the average contract rate for mortgage loans made by all lenders. Although the current average rate is 10%, the loan is offered at a *teaser rate* of 8%.

TENANCY the right of possession of real property. See **tenancy in common, joint tenancy.**

TENANCY AT SUFFERANCE tenancy established when a person who had been a lawful tenant wrongfully remains in **possession** of property after expiration of a **lease.**
Example: A *tenant at sufferance* may be ejected from the property anytime the landlord decides to do so.

TENANCY AT WILL a **license** to use or occupy lands and buildings at the will of the owner. The tenant may decide to leave the property at any time or must leave at the landlord's will. Agreement may be oral or written. See also **emblements.**
Example: Under an oral agreement, Abel is using Baker's property. Baker may ask Abel to leave at any time; Abel may leave at any time.

TENANCY BY THE ENTIRETY an **estate** that exists only between husband and wife with equal right of **possession** and enjoyment during their joint lives and with the **right of survivorship,** i.e., when one dies, the property goes to the surviving tenant. Recognized in some states.
Example: A married couple owns property as *tenants by the entirety.* Neither can convey his or her part of the property during their lives unless the other consents. Divorced spouses become tenants in common. See **tenancy in common.**

TENANCY FOR YEARS created by a **lease** for a fixed term, such as 2 months, 3 years, 10 years, and so on.
Example: Big Buy Groceries leased a building for 10 years, beginning April 1, 1984 and ending March 31, 1994, 10 years later. The company has a *tenancy for years.*

TENANCY IN COMMON an ownership of **realty** by 2 or more persons, each of whom has an **undivided interest,** without the right of **survivorship.** Upon the death of one of the owners, the ownership share of the decedent is inherited by the party or parties designated in the decedent's **will.** Compare **partition.** See **syndication.**
Example: A syndicate is formed using a *tenancy in common.* Under this arrangement all of the investors have to sign the **deed** for the entire property to be conveyed. Each tenant may convey his or her share independently.

TENANCY IN SEVERALTY ownership of property by one person or one legal entity (corporate ownership).
Example: Abel owns land as a *tenant in severalty*. He enjoys the absence of partners or cotenants.

TENANT one who is given **possession** of real estate for a fixed period or at will. See **lessee, tenancy at will.**
Example: Enwright signs a **lease** to rent office space. Enwright is a *tenant* of the office building.

TENDER 1. an **offer** to perform an obligation, together with actual performance or evidence of present ability to perform. 2. to perform under a contract 3. to pay or deliver.
Example: Abel thought Baker would **default** under the **sales contract** but did not know for certain until Baker *tendered* the **deed.**

TENEMENTS 1. possessions that are permanent and fixed; structures attached to land.
Example: Real property consists of *tenements* and hereditaments: tenements are the physical and legal property that may be enjoyed by the owner; hereditaments are property one can pass on to one's heirs.
2. older apartment units.
Example: In the inner city, many people live in *tenements*.

TENURE the nature of an occupant's ownership rights; an indication of whether one is an owner or a tenant.
Example: For economic analysis, one may differentiate the occupied housing stock by *tenure:* one portion may be owner-occupied; the other portion may be renter-occupied.

TENURE IN LAND the mode in which a person holds an **estate** in lands.
Example: If one purchases all rights to real estate, *tenure in land* is **fee simple** ownership. A tenant's *tenure in land* is a **leasehold.**

TERM the period of time during which something is in effect.
Example: Fowler leases an apartment for a *term* of one year. At the end of the year, Fowler moves from the apartment and buys a house. To finance the purchase, Fowler gets a mortgage loan with a *term* of 30 years. At the end of 30 years, the loan will be paid off.

TERM, AMORTIZATION for a loan, the period of time during which **principal and interest** payments must be made; generally the time needed to amortize the loan fully.
Example: *Amortization terms* of 25 and 30 years are commonly

used on real estate mortgage loans. Monthly principal and interest payments are set to fully liquidate loans over the **term.**

TERMITE INSPECTION an examination of a structure by qualified personnel to determine the existence of infestation by **termites.** Often required by the **terms** of a **sales contract.** See **wood-destroying insect.**
Example: Gross sells a house to Handy. As protection for Handy, the sales contract stipulates that a *termite inspection* will be performed at Gross' expense and the sale is contingent on a finding of no termite infestation.

TERMITE CLAUSE a provision in a sales contract that allows the buyer to have the property inspected for termite infestation. In general, if termites are discovered, the buyer may require the seller to treat the property or the buyer may cancel the contract. Most clauses now use the term **wood-destroying insects** to protect against other types of insects that harm structures, such as the powder post beetle and old house borer.
Example: Under the *termite clause* in the sales contract, the buyer may get the home inspected before the closing. The seller will pay to exterminate any termites found. The buyer pays for the inspection.

TERMITES insects that bore into wood and destroy it.
Example: *Termites* are a threat to any wooden structure or members of a structure. *Termites* generally act to weaken support members in proximity to the ground or in contact with it. *Termites* are often confused with winged adult ants. The differences are shown in Figure 173.

TERM LOAN one with a set maturity date, typically without **amortization.**
Example: Terry purchased a tract of land for $15,000, and borrowed $10,000 from a lender with a 5-year *term loan.* The interest rate is 10% annually; the entire principal is due at the end of the 5-year term.

TERMS conditions and arrangements specified in a **contract.**
Example: A **sales contract** will generally include *terms* relating to the price, **financing** available to the buyer, contingencies based on the condition of the property, **how to prorate closing costs,** and items of personal property included in the sale. See also **as is, cancellation clause, contingency clause.**

TESTAMENT a **will.** Generally to dispose of **personal property.** Common usage employs the words **will,** *testament,* and *last will and testament* as synonyms.
Example: Ewen wrote her *testament* that directed the disposition of her property upon her death.

TESTATE having made a valid **will.** Contrast **intestate.**

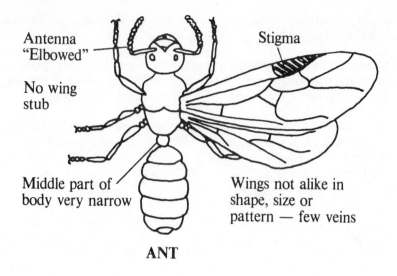

Antenna "Elbowed"

Stigma

No wing stub

Middle part of body very narrow

Wings not alike in shape, size or pattern — few veins

ANT

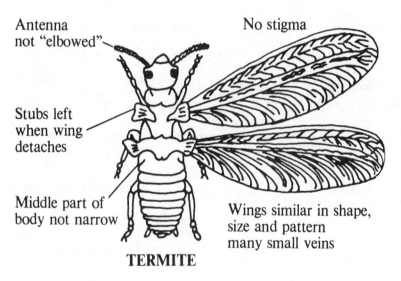

Antenna not "elbowed"

No stigma

Stubs left when wing detaches

Middle part of body not narrow

Wings similar in shape, size and pattern many small veins

TERMITE

FIGURE 173

Example: A person who dies *testate* has left a will disposing of property.

TESTATOR a person who makes a **will.**
Example: By will the *testator* left his property to his wife.

TESTATRIX a woman who makes a **will.**
Example: By will the *testatrix* left her property to her husband.

TESTIMONIUM a clause that cites the act and date in a **deed** or

382

other **conveyance.** Before signing a deed, the grantor should make sure that everything is in order, e.g., the spelling of names and legal descriptions. This is the *testimonium* clause.

Example: *Testimonium* clause: "In witness whereof, the parties to these presents have hereunto set their hands and seals this day and year written above."

THIRD PARTY one who is not directly involved in a transaction or **contract** but may be involved or affected by it.

Example: An apartment owner sells the property to a **condominium** converter. The **tenants,** as *third parties,* may be forced to move or buy their units at the expiration of their **lease.**

Example: A trusted *third party* was designated as **escrow** agent by the **principals.**

TIME IS OF THE ESSENCE a phrase that, when inserted in a **contract,** requires that all references to specific dates and times of day noted in the contract be interpreted exactly. In its absence extreme delays might be acceptable.

Example: A **sales contract** contains the clause: *time is of the essence.* This statement reinforces the content of other clauses, such as the time provided to the buyer to arrange **financing** and the date of **closing.**

TIME-SHARING a form of property ownership under which a **property** is held by a number of people, each with the right of **possession** for a specified time interval. Time-sharing is most commonly applied to resort and vacation properties.

Example: Ingram is an owner in a *time-sharing* arrangement for a lakefront cottage. Ingram is entitled to use the cottage each year from July 1 to July 15. Use of the property during the remainder of the year is divided among other owners. All property expenses are paid by an owner's association to which Ingram pays an annual fee.

TITLE evidence that the owner of land is in lawful **possession** thereof; evidence of ownership. See also **adverse possession,** certificate of title, **clear title, color of title, cloud on the title, marketable title.**

Example: *Title* to land does not merely imply that a person has the right of **possession,** because one may have the right to possession and have no title. Title does ordinarily signify rights to possession in addition to evidence of ownership.

Example: Abel sold land to Baker. *Title* to the **property** was transferred at closing by the deed Baker received.

TITLE ABSTRACT see **abstract of title.**

TITLE COMPANY one in the business of examining **title** to real

TITLE DEFECT

estate and/or issuing **title insurance.**
Example: The Chicago Lawyer Title Company searched courthouse records to be sure that Whitman would get **marketable title** on a house she planned to buy. They charged a $500 one-time **premium.** The bank wouldn't issue a loan without the policy.

TITLE DEFECT an unresolved claim against the ownership of property which prevents presentation of a marketable title. Such claims may arise from failure of the owner's spouse, or former part owner, to sign a deed, current liens against the property, or an interruption in the title records to a property. See **cloud on the title.**
Example: Prior to the closing, the attorney for the title insurance company discovered a *title defect* which delayed the transaction. It seems the property had once been owned by the seller's parents and a deed had never been signed over to the seller.

TITLE INSURANCE an insurance policy that protects the holder from loss sustained by **defects in the title.**
Example: When property is purchased, most **mortgage** lenders require the buyer to obtain *title insurance.* After a satisfactory **title search** and in exchange for a one-time **premium,** the title company insures the buyer against most claims to the title of the property.

TITLE REPORT a document indicating the current state of the **title,** such as **easements, covenants, liens** and any **defects.** The title report does not describe the **chain of title.** See **abstract of title.**
Example: A buyer wishes to assure receipt of **clear title** to a property. The buyer authorizes a *title search* by an experienced attorney. The attorney examines the public records for all recorded encumbrances and past claims. The attorney renders to the buyer an **abstract of the title.**

TITLE SEARCH an examination of the public records to determine the ownership and **encumbrances** affecting **real property.**
Example: A buyer wishes to assure receiving **clear title** to a property. The buyer authorizes a *title search* by an experienced attorney. The attorney examines the public records for all recorded encumbrances and past claims. The attorney renders to the buyer an **abstract of the title.**

TITLE THEORY STATES states in which the law splits the **title** of mortgaged property into legal title, held by the lender, and **equitable title,** held by the borrower. The borrower gains full title to the property upon **retiring** the mortgage debt. The lender is granted more immediate cure to a **default** than in **lien theory states.** Contrast **lien theory states.**
Example: In *title theory states,* mortgage lenders may possess the

property upon default of the borrower. In **lien theory states,** lenders must go through the process of **foreclosure.**

TOPOGRAPHY the state of the surface of the land; may be rolling, rough, flat, etc.
Example: The *topography* in Oklahoma is mostly flat; in West Virginia, mountainous; in Ohio, rolling.

TORRENS SYSTEM a **title** registration system used in some states; the condition of the **title** can easily be discovered without resorting to a **title search.**
Example: A property owner in Chicago wishes to register the property under the *Torrens System.* An application is made with the appropriate court. Following a title examination and **notice** to all who wish to make a claim, the court issues a **certificate of title** setting forth the nature of the applicant's title. When the owner sells the property, a new certificate is issued to the buyer. Anyone establishing a claim to the property following registration is compensated from a special fund for any losses suffered.

TORT a wrongful act that is neither a crime nor a **breach of contract,** but that renders the perpetrator **liable** to the victim for damages.
Examples:
• **nuisance**
• **trespass**
• negligence
An example of negligence is a landlord's failure to fix reported defective wiring. The law provides remedy for damages from resulting fire.

TOWN HOUSE a **dwelling** unit, generally having 2 or more floors and attached to other similar units via **party walls.** Town houses are often used in **planned unit developments** and **condominium** developments, which provide for clustered or attached housing and common open space. See **cluster housing, row house, brownstone.**
Example: Figure 174.

TOWNSHIP a 6-mile square **tract** delineated by **government rectangular survey.**
Example: 16 *townships* (Figure 175).

TRACT a **parcel** of land, generally held for **subdividing;** a **subdivision.**
Example: Reynolds, a **subdivider** purchases a *tract* of land. For marketing purposes, she subdivides the *tract* into lots (Figure 176).

385

FIGURE 174

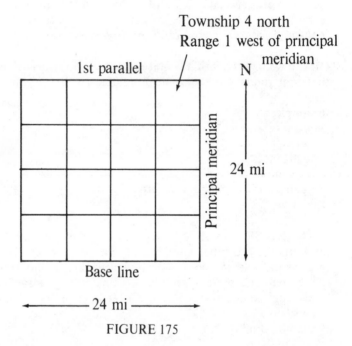

Township 4 north
Range 1 west of principal
meridian

1st parallel

N

Principal meridian

24 mi

Base line

◄──────── 24 mi ────────►

FIGURE 175

TRACT HOUSE a dwelling that has a similar style and **floor plan** to those of all other houses in a development. Contrast **custom builder.**
Example: Pleasant Acres is a **subdivision** of *tract houses.* Each home is a 3-bedroom ranch style house with the same basic floor plan.

TRADE FIXTURE articles placed in rented buildings by the tenant to help carry out trade or business. The tenant can remove the

386

fixtures before the expiration of the **lease,** but if the tenant fails to do so shortly after the lease expires, the fixtures become the landlord's property.
Examples: *Trade fixtures* include:
• bar stools
• neon signs
• decorative or functional light fixtures
• stoves and refrigerators

75 ft	75 ft	75 ft	70 ft	70 ft
1	2	3	4	5

200 ft

South St.

FIGURE 176

TRAILER PARK same as **mobile home park.**

TRANSACTION COSTS the costs associated with buying and selling **real estate.**
Examples: The following are *transaction costs:*
• **appraisal** fees
• **brokerage** commission
• legal fees
• mortgage **discount points**
• mortgage **origination fees**
• **recording** fees
• **survey** fees
• **title search**

TRANSFER DEVELOPMENT RIGHTS a type of **zoning ordinance** that allows owners of property zoned for low-density development or conservation use to sell development rights to other property owners. The development rights purchased permit the landowners to develop their **parcels** at higher **densities** than otherwise. The system is designed to provide for low-density uses, such as historic preservation, without unduly penalizing some landowners.
Example: Under a *transfer development rights* system, a land-

owner whose property is restricted to open space is assigned development rights in proportion to some overall desirable density for the jurisdiction. The landowner cannot utilize the rights but may sell them on the open market to landowners in other locations who are allowed to develop their properties. The rights may be used to develop additional structures on the unrestricted properties. In this way, restricted areas may be maintained as open space without completely destroying the development value of the properties.

TRANSFER TAX one paid upon the passing of **title** to property or to a valuable **interest.**
Example: In a state that imposes a high *transfer tax* on the sale of **real estate,** the seller formed a **corporation** as the owner of a valuable building and sold stock that was subject to a lower transfer tax. The state is claiming that it was a sale of real estate.

TRESPASS unlawful entry or **possession** of property.
Example: Thompson rents an apartment from Turner. When Thompson is away, Turner enters with a passkey and checks on the apartment's condition. Even though Turner owns the property, he is guilty of *trespass,* since the right to possession has been granted to Thompson exclusively. It is possible for Turner to reserve the right to enter the property periodically.
Example: Smith fenced in his farm and posted signs to prevent *trespass* by hunters.

TRIPLE-NET LEASE one in which the tenant is to pay all **operating expenses** of the property; the landlord receives a net rent.
Example: Big Buy Supermarkets enters into a *triple-net lease.* They are to pay for all the taxes, **utilities,** insurance, repairs, janitorial services, and license fees; any **debt service** and the landlord's income taxes are the responsibility of the landlord.

TRUST an arrangement whereby property is transferred to a trusted **third party** (trustee) by a **grantor** (trustor). The **trustee** holds the property for the benefit of another **(beneficiary).**
Example: An **inter vivos** *trust* was established by a living person who gave her warehouse to a trustee for the benefit of her children.
Example: A testamentary *trust* was established upon the death of a trustor, according to his **will.**

TRUST ACCOUNT a separate bank account segregated from a broker's own funds, in which the **broker** is required by state law to deposit all monies collected for clients. In some states called an **escrow** account.
Example: A broker who fails to deposit **earnest money** into a sep-

arate *trust account* may be held **liable** for penalties under the state's real estate **license** laws.

TRUST DEED a **conveyance** of real estate to a **third party** to be held for the benefit of another. Commonly used in some states in place of **mortgages** that conditionally convey **title** to the lender.
Example: Same as **deed of trust.**

TRUSTEE one who holds property in **trust** for another to secure performance of an obligation; the neutral party in a **trust deed** transaction.
Example: Johnson purchases property and finances it with a **deed of trust** from a lender. The **title company** is the *trustee,* holding legal title to the property pending Johnson's satisfaction of the debt. Should Johnson **default** on the loan, the trustee may sell the property to satisfy the debt.

TRUTH IN LENDING see **Regulation Z.**

TUDOR an English style imposing looking house with fortress-lines. Siding is chiefly stone and brick with some stucco and half timbers. Windows and doors have moulded cement or stone trim around them.
Example: Figure 177.

Fort-like appearance

2 to 3 stories High chimney

Semi-hexagonal Chimney pots Moulded
Brick or bays stone trim
stone walls

Stone
mullions

FIGURE 177

TURNKEY PROJECT a development in which a **developer** completes the entire project on behalf of a buyer; the developer turns over the keys to the buyer at completion.
Example: Many government-owned public housing projects are *turnkey projects*. A private developer undertakes all activities necessary to producing the project, including land purchases, **permits, plans,** and construction, and sells the project to the housing authority.

U

UNDERIMPROVEMENT a structure or development of lower cost than the **highest and best use** of the site. Compare **overimprovement.**
Example: Construction of a $40,000 bungalow on a vacant lot in a **neighborhood** of $100,000 homes would represent an *underimprovement* of the **site.**

UNDERLYING MORTGAGE refers to the first mortgage when there is a **wraparound mortgage.**
Example: A wraparound for $100,000 includes a $60,000 *underlying mortgage* in its balance, so the additional funds provided by the wrap are $40,000.

UNDERWRITER one who insures another or takes certain **risks.** In **mortgage** lending, the one who approves or denies a loan based on the property and the applicant. In securities, it is the **broker** that sells the issue and, unless sold on a "best efforts" basis, agrees to purchase the shares not bought by the public.
Example: The *underwriter* analyzed the loan submission package carefully, because she didn't want her firm to accept excessive risk.

UNDIVIDED INTEREST an ownership right to use and possession of a property that is shared among co-owners, with no one co-owner having exclusive rights to any portion of the property. Compare **partition.**
Example: Ten investors form a **tenancy in common** and purchase a 100-**acre** tract of land. Each cotenant obtains an *undivided interest* in the property. All decisions as to the use and disposition of the land are made collectively by all cotenants. No one cotenant may unilaterally mortgage, develop, or sell a portion of the **tract.**

UNEARNED INCREMENT an increase in the **value** of real estate unrelated to effort on the part of the owner; often due to an increase in population.
Example: Murphy buys a **tract** of land in the county for $2,000 per

acre. As the city grows, the surrounding county begins to develop, with paved highways eventually extended to Murphy's land. Murphy sells the land for $5,000 per acre, realizing an *unearned increment* in value of $3,000 per acre.

UNENCUMBERED PROPERTY real estate with **free and clear title.**
Example: Nash owns an *unencumbered property.* Nash's **interest** is **fee simple,** there are no **mortgage, vendor, mechanic's** or **tax liens** on the property, no **restrictive covenants** exist, and no **easements** have been granted.

UNIFORM COMMERCIAL CODE (UCC) a group of laws to standardize the state laws that are applicable to commercial transactions. Few of the laws have relevance to **real estate.**
Example: The *Uniform Commercial Code* applies to **chattel mortgages, promises, commercial paper, securities, etc.**

UNILATERAL CONTRACT an obligation given by one party contingent on the performance of another party, but without obligating the second party to perform. Compare **bilateral contract.**
Example: A **broker** makes a *unilateral contract* with her associates. She offers a trip to Hawaii to any salesman who sells one million dollars of property during the month. None of the salesmen is obligated to meet the goal, but the broker is obligated to provide the trip should any salesman perform the feat.

UNIMPROVED PROPERTY land that has received no development, construction, or **site** preparation. See **raw land.**
Example: O'Brien is **subdividing** a **tract** of land and selling lots to investors. In all marketing materials, O'Brien must disclose the fact that the land is *unimproved property* that must receive extensive development before being suitable for urban uses.

UNINCORPORATED ASSOCIATION an organization formed by a group of people. If the organization has too many characteristics of a **corporation** it may be treated like one for income tax purposes.
Example: Many **condominium** associations, **limited partnerships,** and real estate investment **trusts** are examples of *unincorporated associations.*

UNIT in multi-family residential property, a suite of rooms making up a residence for 1 tenant. It is generally characterized by a private entrance and some method of individuality from other units in the building or complex.
Example: The apartment building has 45 dwelling *units.* Each *unit* has a private bath and kitchen. Some are 2 bedroom *units* and others have 3 bedrooms.

UNIT-IN-PLACE METHOD a technique used by **appraisers** to estimate the **reproduction cost** (new) of a structure. The method involves estimating the cost of producing and installing individual components, such as the foundation, exterior walls, and plumbing. Similar methods include the trade-breakdown method and segregated-costs method. See **cost approach.**
Example: A simplified cost estimate using the *unit-in-place method* is shown in Table 42.

TABLE 42

Item	Cost per unit ($/ft^2)	Cost
Foundation 1500 ft^2	2	$3,000
Walls 1600 ft^2	4	6,400
Roof 1500 ft^2	3	4,500
Flooring 1500 ft^2	2	3,000
Plumbing		2,500
Heating		1,500
Electrical		2,000
Total		$22,900
Fees, interest and overhead (10%)		2,290
Reproduction cost (new)		$25,190

UNREALIZED GAIN the excess of current **market value** over cost for an asset that is unsold.
Example: Collins bought land for $10,000; she had an offer to sell it for $15,000, but decided to keep the land. Her *unrealized gain* is $5,000.

UNRECORDED DEED an **instrument** that transfers **title** from one party **(grantor)** to another party **(grantee)** without providing public **notice** of change in ownership. **Recording** is essential to protect one's **interest** in **real estate.**
Example: Uncas purchases a lakefront lot from Upson. At **closing,** Uncas receives a **deed** but fails to record it at the county courthouse. In the meantime, Upson fradulently sells the lot to Ustinov. Ustinov's attorney does a **title search** but, because of the *unrecorded deed*, does not turn up the sale to Uncas. When Uncas discovers what has occurred, he is forced to pursue legal proceedings against Upson for recovery. Ustinov, who purchased in **good faith,** owns the land.

UPSET PRICE the minimum acceptable price for property being auctioned. See also **asking price, bid.**
Example: If the bidding at **auction** fails to reach the *upset price,* the property will not be sold.

URBAN LAND INSTITUTE (ULI) a nonprofit organization providing research and information on land use and development. Among the many publications of the ULI are the periodicals, *Urban Land* and *Environmental Comment*, and several development guides for specific types of land use.
Address:
Urban Land Institute
1200 18th St. N.W.
Washington, D.C. 20036

URBAN PROPERTY real estate located in an urban area, generally characterized by relatively high-**density** development and extensive availability of city water and sewer services.
Example: Typical development of 3 types of property is shown in Table 43.

TABLE 43

Urban	Suburban	Rural
High-rise office	Office parks	Farms
High-rise apartment	Industrial parks	Low-density housing
Department stores	Shopping centers	Recreational lands
Public buildings	Garden apartments	Summer camps
Moderate density single-family housing	Low-density housing	

URBAN RENEWAL the process of redeveloping deteriorated sections of the city, often through **demolition** and new construction. Although urban renewal may be privately funded, it is most often associated with government renewal programs.
Example: Most large cities have experienced some *urban renewal* in the last 20 years. The typical program attempts to demolish concentrations of dilapidated housing and attract **developers** of middle-income or mixed housing. Often, however, urban renewal areas become **sites** for new public buildings, such as civic auditoriums, sports arenas, and universities.

USEFUL LIFE the period of time over which a building is expected to provide a competitive return. *Useful life* provides the basis for allowable **depreciation** deductions on properties acquired prior to 1981. For tax purposes, this was replaced in 1981 by the **accelerated cost recovery system.**

393

Example: A property acquired in 1980 has a **depreciable basis** of $100,000 and a *useful life* of 25 years. Using **straight-line depreciation,** the owner may deduct $4,000 per year for tax reporting.

USUFRUCTUARY RIGHTS interests that provide for the use of property that belongs to another. Compare **emblement.**
Example: The owner of land that bounds or contains a natural water channel has a *usufructory right* to use of the water. The water itself is considered to be held by the public with all **adjacent** property owners holding rights to its use. **Restrictions** on that use vary under state law.

USURY charging a rate of interest greater than that permitted by state law. In most states, usury limits vary according to the type of lender and type of loan. Federal laws have passed to preempt certain usury limits under certain conditions.
Example: The **interest rate** that must comply with *usury* limitation is defined differently in the various states. The stated maximum rate may apply to the **face interest rate, effective rate** to the borrower, or the actual **yield** to the lender. If a loan is found to be usurious, severe penalties may be imposed, including loss of the **principal,** interest, a multiple of the interest, and/or damages.

UTILITIES 1. services, such as water, sewer, gas, electricity, and telephones, that are generally required to operate a building.
2. the periodic charges for such services.
Example: The building will be ready for occupancy as soon as the *utilities* are connected. When available, the *utility* bill is expected to average $100 per month. All *utilities* are paid for by the **landlord.**

UTILITY EASEMENT use of another's property for the purpose of laying gas, electric, water, and sewer lines.
Example: A property owner grants a *utility easement* to the electric power company to extend power lines to the owner's home.

V

VACANCY RATE the percentage of all units or space that is unoccupied or not rented. On a **pro-forma** income **statement** a projected vacancy rate is used to estimate the vacancy allowance, which is deducted from potential **gross income** to derive effective gross income.
Example: The *vacancy rate* for apartment units in Boom City is currently 4.5%. For the Hightower Building, the *vacancy rate* is 9.5% (of 100,000 square feet of **net leasable area,** 9,500 square feet are not rented). If this 9.5% *vacancy rate* is expected to be the average through next year, a vacancy allowance of $95,000 (at $10

per square foot) should be deducted from potential rent when projecting income.

VACANT LAND land not currently being used. May have **utilities** and **off-site improvements.** Contrast with **raw land.**
Example: *Vacant land* was cleared and graded for future use as a **shopping center.**

VACATE to move out.
Example: A tenant *vacates* an apartment by terminating occupancy and removing all possessions. The tenant is responsible for **rent** to the end of the **lease** term.

VACATION HOME a dwelling used by the owner occasionally for recreational or resort purposes. It may be rented to others for a portion of the year. Income tax deductions pertaining to *vacation homes* depend on the frequency of use by the owner. Generally, a business loss cannot be claimed on a vacation home. See **second home.**
Example: The Travers have a *vacation home* in the mountains that they use on weekends during the summer. At other times it is rented to strangers on a weekly basis. If business deductions including depreciation exceed income, the loss cannot be deducted.

VALID having legally binding force; legally sufficient and authorized by law.
Examples: A *valid* **deed, will, lease, mortgage,** or other **contract.**

VA LOAN home loan **guaranteed** by the U.S. **Veterans Administration (VA)** under the Servicemen's Readjustment Act of 1944 and later. The VA **guarantees** restitution to the lender in the event of **default.** The **guaranty** is 60% of the loan, but not more than $27,500. Home must be a principal residence.
Example: Abel, a veteran of the U.S. Army, wishes to purchase a home. Abel may apply for a *VA loan* with the Veterans Administration and, if qualified, may obtain a **mortgage** loan from a lending institution with no **down payment.**

VALUABLE CONSIDERATION a type of promised payment upon which a promisee can enforce a claim against an unwilling promisor. Includes money, extension of time, and other equivalents for the grant. Distinguished from good **consideration,** which may be love and affection toward a relative, generosity, and the like.
Example: A man promised to give certain land to a suitor of his daughter, provided they marry. This was not considered *valuable consideration,* so the suitor could not enforce it and he did not marry the daughter.

VALUATION 1. estimated worth or price.

VALUE

Example: The *valuation* of the land is $100,000.
2. the act of estimating the worth of a thing. See **appraisal**.
Example: The *valuation* was prepared in accordance with instructions provided by the tax **assessor**.

VALUE the worth of all the rights arising from ownership; the quantity of one thing that will be given in exchange for another.
Example: A property may have a certain *value* to its owner (value in use) equal to the amount of other property (typically cash) that the owner would be willing to accept in exchange for the property without loss in wealth or well-being. The same property may have a different **market value** (value in exchange) equal to the amount of other property exchanged for the property when many typically motivated buyers and sellers are allowed to interact.

VARIABLE INTEREST RATE an amount of compensation to a lender that is allowed to vary over the **maturity** of a loan. The amount of variation is generally governed by an appropriate index. See **variable rate mortgage, renegotiated rate mortgage**.
Example: A 20-year loan is made with a *variable interest rate*. The initial rate is 14% but may be changed each year in relation to changes in a published index of average loan rates. If, at the end of the first year, the index has risen one percentage **point**, the rate on the loan may be raised to 15%. Similarly, a fall in the index at one point would allow a decrease in the loan rate to 13%.

VARIABLE MATURITY MORTGAGE a long-term **mortgage** loan, under which the **interest rate** may be adjusted periodically. Payment levels remain the same but the loan **maturity** is lengthened or shortened to achieve the adjustment.
Example: Abel obtains a *variable maturity mortgage* originated at 12% with a **term** of 25 years. At the end of one year, the interest rate is increased to 12¼%. Abel's monthly payment of $527 remains the same after the adjustment; however, the remaining term is no longer 24 years, but is increased to 27 years.

VARIABLE PAYMENT PLAN any **mortgage** repayment schedule that provides for periodic change in the amount of monthly payments. Changes may occur as a result of: the expiration of an interest-only period (**flexible payment mortgage**), a planned step-up in payments (**graduated payment mortgage**), or a change in the **interest rate** due to fluctuation in an index (**variable rate mortgage**).
Example: A loan is made with a *variable payment plan*. The interest rate on the loan may be adjusted once a year according to a published index. As the interest rate is changed, the monthly payment is adjusted to provide for full **amortization** of the outstanding **principal** over the remaining life of the loan.

VARIABLE RATE MORTGAGE (VRM) a long-term **mortgage** loan applied to residences, under which the **interest rate** may be adjusted on a 6-month basis over the **term** of the loan. Rate increases are restricted to no more than ½ **point** per year and 2½ points over the term.

Example: Abel obtains a *variable rate mortgage* originated at a 12% interest rate. In 6 months, the index upon which the rate is based increases by one percentage point. Abel's rate is adjusted to 12½% and cannot be further increased during the year because of the ½% annual cap.

VARIANCE permission granted by a **zoning** authority to a property owner to allow for a specified violation of the zoning requirements. Variances are generally granted when compliance is impossible without rendering the property virtually unusable.

Example: Sherman owns a lot that is zoned for low-**density** housing. Because of the peculiar shape and **topography** of the lot, Sherman cannot build a home with the required minimum floor area without violating the **setback** requirements for the area. Sherman may be granted a *variance* to either construct a smaller dwelling or encroach on the setback line.

VENDEE a buyer. Generally used for **real estate;** one who purchases **personal property** is usually called the buyer.

Example: The *vendee* is the party that pays for the real estate bought.

VENDEE'S LIEN a **lien** against property under a **contract of sale,** to secure the **deposit** paid by a purchaser.

Example: Moore, the vendee (buyer), gave a substantial deposit. Since Moore did not trust the seller, she secured a *vendee's lien* against the property. The lien provides the vendee with a claim against the property should the seller attempt to sell to another party prior to closing.

VENDOR a seller, usually of **real estate.** The term *seller* is commonly used for **personal property.**

Example: The *vendor* receives cash, **notes,** and **mortgage relief** from the **vendor.**

VENDOR'S LIEN see **purchase money mortgage.**

VENEER wood or brick exterior that covers a less attractive and less expensive surface.

Example: Beneath the sturdy-looking oak *veneer* was low-grade hollow board (Figure 178).

VENTURE CAPITAL money raised for high-risk investments.

Example: Money raised for oil exploration, theatrical produc-

tions, and the like is considered *venture capital.*

VERIFICATION sworn statements before a duly qualified officer that the contents of an **instrument** are correct.
Example: A tenant takes a landlord to court to recover a **security** deposit. The tenant files a claim describing the **conditions** under which the **deposit** is to be refunded and the manner in which the tenant complied with the conditions. The tenant then supplies *verification* of this description by a sworn statement.

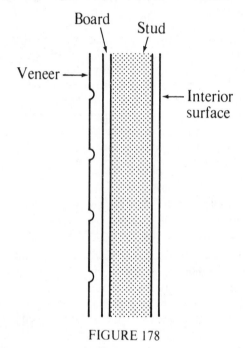

FIGURE 178

VEST to create an entitlement to a privilege or right.
Example: By crossing Baker's property regularly for 20 years, Abel's right to an easement became *vested.* Baker can no longer prevent Abel from crossing.
Example: If she stays employed by the same **brokerage** firm for 10 years, Collins' right to a pension will *vest.*

VETERANS ADMINISTRATION (VA) an agency of the federal government that provides services for eligible veterans. Generally, a veteran who has served (beyond basic training) more than 120 days active duty in the armed forces is eligible for a **home loan** with no **down payment.**
Address:
Veterans Administration
810 Vermont Avenue
Washington, D.C. 20420

VIOLATION an act or a condition contrary to law or to permissible use of **real property.**
Example: According to most **zoning ordinances,** operating a business from one's home is a *violation* of the restriction for a residential zone. In many cities, owning an occupied **apartment building** with nonfunctioning plumbing is a *violation* of the **housing code.**

VOID having no legal force or effect; unenforceable. See **null and void.**
Example: In a **listing** contract with a **broker,** Smith stipulates that the property be sold only to a person of a certain race. Since the stipulation is contrary to antidiscrimination laws, it is *void* and thereby unenforceable.

VOIDABLE capable of being voided, but not **void** unless action is taken to void it. A **contract** to **real estate** entered into by a **minor** is voidable only by the minor.
Example: A **landlord** leases an apartment to a minor. The minor may honor the **lease** and rent the apartment. However, should the minor decide not to rent the apartment, he may void the lease without **liability** for performance. The lease is a *voidable* contract.

VOLUNTARY LIEN a **debt** that the property owner agrees to have recorded. Typically a **mortgage.** Contrast **involuntary lien.**
Example: The **mortgage** was a *voluntary lien,* since the real estate owner agreed to pledge the property as **security.**

W

WAIVER the voluntary renunciation, **abandonment,** or surrender of some claim, right, or privilege.
Example: A **violation** of a contract causes the need for a *waiver* from the other party who does not feel injured.

WAREHOUSING (LOAN) the packaging of a number of **mortgage** loans for sale in the **secondary mortgage market** by a financial institution or **mortgage banker** who has originated the loans.
Example: Willard, a mortgage banker, is regularly engaged in loan *warehousing.* He would originate a number of FHA-insured mortgages and sell the package to **FNMA** at **auction.** After origination but before the sale to FNMA, the loans are considered to be in Willard's *warehouse.*

WARRANTY a promise contained in a **contract.**

Example: The **vendee** received a one-year *warranty* from the builder as to the structural soundness of the property.

WARRANTY DEED one that contains a **covenant** that the **grantor** will protect the **grantee** against any and all claims. Usually contains covenants assuring good **title**, freedom from **encumbrances,** and **quiet enjoyment.** See also **general warranty deed** and **special warranty deed.**
Example: The grantor was willing to give a *warranty deed* because she was confident that she had good title to the property.

WARRANTY OF HABITABILITY an implied assurance given by a **landlord** that an apartment offered for rent is free from safety and health hazards.
Example: Todd signed a one-year **lease** to rent an apartment from Landon. Todd later discovered that the apartment's heating system was not functioning. Todd sought to break the lease, claiming the apartment was deficient under Landon's implied *warranty of habitability.*

WASTE unauthorized use or neglect of property by a party with the right to **possession** when another party owns an **interest** in the property. The party may be a **tenant,** a **mortgagor,** or a **life tenant.**
Example: A tenant neglecting to heat an apartment in the winter with the result of damage to the plumbing.
Example: A mortgagor failing to pay property taxes, thereby risking a tax **foreclosure.**
Example: A life tenant converting a residential property into a production center for some specialized product.

WASTING ASSET something of value that deteriorates over time.
Example: Improvements to land will not last forever, so they are *wasting assets;* in contrast **land** is not wasting because it will last forever.

WATER RIGHTS see **riparian rights, usufructory** rights.

WATER TABLE the upper level at which underground water is normally encountered in a particular area.
Example: Cross section showing the *water table* (Figure 179).

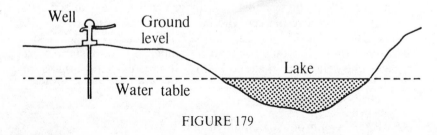

FIGURE 179

WEAR AND TEAR physical deterioration of property as the result of use, weathering, and age.
Example: A carpet is expected to last only 8 years because of *wear and tear*, or deterioration resulting from foot traffic and cleaning.

WESTERN ROW HOUSE OR WESTERN TOWNHOUSE a nineteenth century style house usually built to cover an entire street or block. It has common side walls with the house on either side.
Example: Figure 180.

Bay windows

Pitched roof

2 or 3 stories

Common side walls

Heavily decorated, painted

FIGURE 180

WETLANDS land, such as a marsh or swamp, normally saturated with water.
Example: A typical coastal *wetlands* (Figure 181).

WILL the disposition of one's property, to take effect after one's death. Same as **testament.**
Example: If one does not prepare a *will*, state law will govern the disposition of one's property after death.

WILLIAMSBURG GEORGIAN OR EARLY GEORGIAN an English style house built in Williamsburg and representative of the early Georgian houses built in America throughout the early 1700s. They had simple exterior lines and generally fewer of the

401

Dry
land

Coastal
marsh

Ocean

Island

FIGURE 181

decorative devices characteristic of the later Georgian houses. Most were 2- or 3-story rectangular houses with two large chimneys rising high above the roof at each end.
Example: Figure 182.

2 to 3 stories Simple exterior lines

Double-
hung
windows;
small
panes

Rectangular
shape

Large, high
chimneys

Simple
front

FIGURE 182

WINDOW an opening in the wall of a building to let in light and air. Most are made of transparent material and have the ability to be opened and closed.
Example: Figure 183.

Fixed

Sliding

Double or single-hung

Casement

Awning

Hopper

Center pivot

Jalousie

FIGURE 183

403

WITHOUT RECOURSE words used in endorsing a **note** or bill to denote that the holder is not to look to the debtor personally in the event of nonpayment: the creditor has **recourse** only to the property. A form of exculpation. Same as **nonrecourse**. See **endorsement, exculpatory clause.**
Example: Abel insisted that the **mortgage** to the seller be *without recourse*. In the event that the value of the property declines, Abel may lose the property but he loses nothing else.

WOMEN'S COUNCIL OF REALTORS® **(WCR)** an organization, affiliated with the **National Association of Realtors®**, devoted to preparing women in **real estate** for their emerging roles in society, to encouraging members to a productive career in real estate, and to developing leadership potential. Publishes *The Real Estate Scene* (monthly) and the *WCR Communiqué* (quarterly).
Address:
Women's Council of Realtors®
430 N. Michigan Avenue
Chicago, Illinois 60611

WOOD-DESTROYING INSECT a term used in certain home **inspection** forms; as a condition for purchase, the property must be free of these insects.
Examples:
• subterranean termites
• dry wood termites
• powder post beetles

WORKING CAPITAL the difference between current **assets** and current **liabilities.**
Example: The *working capital* is $2,500 ($4,000 minus $1,500) according to the balance sheet in Table 44.

WORKOUT a mutual effort by a property owner and lender to avoid **foreclosure** or **bankruptcy** following a **default;** generally involves substantial reduction in the **debt service** burden during an economic depression. See **distressed property.**
Example: Because of an economic slowdown, the hotel suffered high **vacancy rates** and failed to generate enough income to meet **mortgage** payments. The owner approached the lender about a *workout*. It was agreed to reduce the outstanding loan **principal** and extend the **maturity** date to reduce the debt service. In turn the lender would participate in the income when the economy recovered and hotel income exceeded a specified amount. See **participation mortgage.**

TABLE 44

Assets		Liabilities & equity	
Current		Current	
cash	$1,000		
acc'ts receivable	1,000	accounts payable	$ 500
inventory	2,000	3-month note	1,000
Current assets	$4,000	Current liabilities	$1,500
Fixed		Long-term	
Land	6,000	Mortgage	$10,000
Buildings	10,000	Equity	8,500
Total assets	$20,000	Total liabilities	$20,000
		and equity	

WRITE-DOWN to diminish in amount on the records, generally to reflect a **market value** loss.
Example: Bank auditors, upon discovering that a certain **mortgage** was worthless, insisted on a *write-down*. The bank recorded the value decline as a bad debt expense.

WRAPAROUND MORTGAGE a loan arrangement in which an existing loan is retained and an additional loan, larger than the existing loan, is made. The new lender accepts the obligation to make payments on the old loan. The existing loan generally carries an **interest rate** below the rate available on new loans. Consequently, the **yield** to the wraparound lender is higher than the rate charged on the new loan. Sellers are the most common wraparound lenders.
Example: Figure 184 and Table 45.

WRIT OF EJECTMENT see **ejectment.**

Y

YIELD 1. a measurement of the rate of earnings from an investment. See **current yield, yield to maturity.**
Example: A loan is arranged to *yield* 15% a year to the lender.
2. the productivity of agricultural land.
Example: A farm produces a *yield* of 5,000 bushels of corn per acre.

YIELD TO MATURITY the **internal rate of return** on an investment.

TABLE 45

Wraparound mortgage

Seller gets $10,000 from buyer
and $20,000 from wraparound
lender.
Wraparound lender makes
payments on existing
mortgage.
Buyer makes payments on
wraparound mortgage.
Lender gets payment of
$632
−336

$296 per month on $20,000
outlay for a yield over 25
years of 17.5%.

Home sale price: $70,000

Wraparound loan:
$60,000 12%
25 years $632 payments

Existing loan:
$40,000 principal
25 years left
9%
$336 payments

FIGURE 184

406

Considers all inflows and outflows of investment returns and their timing.
Example: An income-producing property requires a $10,000 investment. It promises a $1,000 annual return for 5 years, then resale proceeds of $15,000. The *yield to maturity* is 17.1%. See **internal rate of return** for formulas.

Z

ZERO LOT LINE a form of **cluster housing** development in which individual dwelling units are placed on separately platted lots but are attached to one another. See **planned unit development, plat, row house, town-house.**
Example: A representative *zero lot line* development (Figure 185).

FIGURE 185

ZONE an area set off by local **ordinance** for specific use, subject to certain **restrictions** or conditions. See **zoning.**
Example: A zoning map designates various *zones* with associated land use restrictions (Figure 186).
C-1: commercial (service station, convenience store, etc.)
R-2: low-**density** residential (**single-family** housing)
R-4: high-density residential (apartments)

ZONING a legal mechanism for local governments to regulate the use of privately owned **real property** by specific application of **police power** to prevent conflicting land uses and promote orderly development. All privately owned land within the jurisdiction is

FIGURE 186

placed within designated zones that limit the type and intensity of development permitted. See **zone.**

Example: Before a **tract** of land may be developed, the intended use must be permitted under the existing *zoning* classification. If the proposed use is not permitted, the developer must apply for an amendment to the **zoning ordinance,** or for rezoning. Such amendments are granted by the local governing body, generally following a public hearing and recommendation from the **planning commission.**

ZONING MAP a map of the local jurisdiction that indicates current **zoning** designations.
Example: A typical *zoning* map (Figure 187).

FIGURE 187

ZONING ORDINANCE act of city or county or other authorities specifying the type of use to which property may be put in specific areas. See **zone, zoning.**
Example: A typical *zoning ordinance* defines:
• the purpose for which the ordinance is adopted
• the various zoning classifications and permitted uses within each
• **restrictions,** such as height limitations
• the procedure for handling nonconforming uses
• the procedure for granting amendments, **variances,** and hearing appeals
• penalties for **violation** of the ordinance

TABLES

MONTHLY MORTGAGE PAYMENTS

The monthly payments table allows you to find out how much you would pay in interest and principal per month on an amortizing mortgage loan. To use the table you must know the following:

1. *The loan interest rate.* Each page is for a different interest rate as shown in the table's heading. Rates range from 7% to 21.75% by .25% intervals.

2. *The amount borrowed.* Amounts are shown in the column on the far left side of each table. To find the payment for an amount in between those shown, add up the payments as shown in the example below.

3. *The maturity or term of the loan.* This is the length of time over which the payments are set to run. Maturities of 10, 15, 20, 25, and 30 years are shown in the top row of each table.

The body of the table shows the monthly payment amount in dollars. This payment does not include escrow payments which may be required by the lender for insurance and property taxes. Such payments would be in addition to the amount shown in the table.

Example: Suppose you wish to borrow $47,850 to buy a home. The maturity of the loan is 25 years and the annual interest rate is 7%. To find the monthly payment, look at the first table where the annual interest rate is 7%. First look at where the row for "40,000" intersects the column for "25" years. The amount is 282.72. Next locate the row for "7,000" and column for "25" and see the amount of 49.48 at their intersection. Likewise, find the "800" row and "25" column (amount is 5.66) and the "50" row and "25" column (amount is .36). The total payment is the sum of these amounts:

40,000	282.72
7,000	49.48
800	5.66
50	.36
47,850	338.22

The total loan amount is $47,850 and the total monthly payment is $338.22.

Example: Suppose your monthly income is $2,000 and you can afford to pay up to 25% of that amount ($500) on mortgage payments. How big a loan can you get?

Assume the loan interest rate is 7% and 30 year loans are available. Look once again at the first table. Find the amount in the table under the "30" column which is closest but lower than 500. You should see the amount of 465.72 in the "70,000" row. The difference between 500 and 465.72 is 34.28. Find the closest lower amount in the "30" column. The answer is 33. 27 in the "5,000" row. You still have 34.28 minus 33.27, or 1.01 to

411

spend. In the "100" row you will find an amount of .67. You still have 1.01 −.67, or .34 to spend. In the "50" row you will find an amount of .34. Now add up all the amounts:

465.72	70,000
33.27	5,000
.67	100
.34	50
500.00	75,150

The highest payment you could afford is $500.00 which, at 7% over 30 years, will provide for a loan of $75,150.

MONTHLY PAYMENTS
ANNUAL INTEREST RATE: 7%

LOAN AMOUNT	LOAN MATURITY (YEARS)				
	10	15	20	25	30
50	0.59	0.45	0.39	0.36	0.34
100	1.17	0.90	0.78	0.71	0.67
200	2.33	1.80	1.56	1.42	1.34
300	3.49	2.70	2.33	2.13	2.00
400	4.65	3.60	3.11	2.83	2.67
500	5.81	4.50	3.88	3.54	3.33
600	6.97	5.40	4.66	4.25	4.00
700	8.13	6.30	5.43	4.95	4.66
800	9.29	7.20	6.21	5.66	5.33
900	10.45	8.09	6.98	6.37	5.99
1,000	11.62	8.99	7.76	7.07	6.66
2,000	23.23	17.98	15.51	14.14	13.31
3,000	34.84	26.97	23.26	21.21	19.96
4,000	46.45	35.96	31.02	28.28	26.62
5,000	58.06	44.95	38.77	35.34	33.27
6,000	69.67	53.93	46.52	42.41	39.92
7,000	81.28	62.92	54.28	49.48	46.58
8,000	92.89	71.91	62.03	56.55	53.23
9,000	104.50	80.90	69.78	63.62	59.88
10,000	116.11	89.89	77.53	70.68	66.54
20,000	232.22	179.77	155.06	141.36	133.07
30,000	348.33	269.65	232.59	212.04	199.60
40,000	464.44	359.54	310.12	282.72	266.13
50,000	580.55	449.42	387.65	353.39	332.66
60,000	696.65	539.30	465.18	424.07	399.19
70,000	812.76	629.18	542.71	494.75	465.72
80,000	928.87	719.07	620.24	565.43	532.25
90,000	1044.98	808.95	697.77	636.11	598.78
100,000	1161.09	898.83	775.30	706.78	665.31
110,000	1277.20	988.71	852.83	777.46	731.84
120,000	1393.30	1078.60	930.36	848.14	798.37
130,000	1509.41	1168.48	1007.89	918.82	864.90
140,000	1625.52	1258.36	1085.42	989.49	931.43
150,000	1741.63	1348.25	1162.95	1060.17	997.96
160,000	1857.74	1438.13	1240.48	1130.85	1064.49
170,000	1973.85	1528.01	1318.01	1201.53	1131.02
180,000	2089.95	1617.89	1395.54	1272.21	1197.55
190,000	2206.06	1707.78	1473.07	1342.88	1264.08
200,000	2322.17	1797.66	1550.60	1413.56	1330.61
250,000	2902.71	2247.07	1938.25	1766.95	1663.26
300,000	3483.25	2696.49	2325.90	2120.34	1995.91

413

MONTHLY PAYMENTS
ANNUAL INTEREST RATE: 7.25%

LOAN AMOUNT	LOAN MATURITY (YEARS)				
	10	15	20	25	30
50	0.59	0.46	0.40	0.37	0.35
100	1.18	0.92	0.80	0.73	0.69
200	2.35	1.83	1.59	1.45	1.37
300	3.53	2.74	2.38	2.17	2.05
400	4.70	3.66	3.17	2.90	2.73
500	5.88	4.57	3.96	3.62	3.42
600	7.05	5.48	4.75	4.34	4.10
700	8.22	6.40	5.54	5.06	4.78
800	9.40	7.31	6.33	5.79	5.46
900	10.57	8.22	7.12	6.51	6.14
1,000	11.75	9.13	7.91	7.23	6.83
2,000	23.49	18.26	15.81	14.46	13.65
3,000	35.23	27.39	23.72	21.69	20.47
4,000	46.97	36.52	31.62	28.92	27.29
5,000	58.71	45.65	39.52	36.15	34.11
6,000	70.45	54.78	47.43	43.37	40.94
7,000	82.19	63.91	55.33	50.60	47.76
8,000	93.93	73.03	63.24	57.83	54.58
9,000	105.67	82.16	71.14	65.06	61.40
10,000	117.41	91.29	79.04	72.29	68.22
20,000	234.81	182.58	158.08	144.57	136.44
30,000	352.21	273.86	237.12	216.85	204.66
40,000	469.61	365.15	316.16	289.13	272.88
50,000	587.01	456.44	395.19	361.41	341.09
60,000	704.41	547.72	474.23	433.69	409.31
70,000	821.82	639.01	553.27	505.97	477.53
80,000	939.22	730.30	632.31	578.25	545.75
90,000	1056.62	821.58	711.35	650.53	613.96
100,000	1174.02	912.87	790.38	722.81	682.18
110,000	1291.42	1004.16	869.42	795.09	750.40
120,000	1408.82	1095.44	948.46	867.38	818.62
130,000	1526.22	1186.73	1027.50	939.66	886.84
140,000	1643.63	1278.02	1106.53	1011.94	955.05
150,000	1761.03	1369.30	1185.57	1084.22	1023.27
160,000	1878.43	1460.59	1264.61	1156.50	1091.49
170,000	1995.83	1551.88	1343.65	1228.78	1159.71
180,000	2113.23	1643.16	1422.69	1301.06	1227.92
190,000	2230.63	1734.45	1501.72	1373.34	1296.14
200,000	2348.04	1825.74	1580.76	1445.62	1364.36
250,000	2935.04	2282.17	1975.95	1807.03	1705.45
300,000	3522.05	2738.60	2371.14	2168.43	2046.54

414

MONTHLY PAYMENTS
ANNUAL INTEREST RATE: 7.5%

LOAN AMOUNT	LOAN MATURITY (YEARS)				
	10	15	20	25	30
50	0.60	0.47	0.41	0.37	0.35
100	1.19	0.93	0.81	0.74	0.70
200	2.38	1.86	1.62	1.48	1.40
300	3.57	2.79	2.42	2.22	2.10
400	4.75	3.71	3.23	2.96	2.80
500	5.94	4.64	4.03	3.70	3.50
600	7.13	5.57	4.84	4.44	4.20
700	8.31	6.49	5.64	5.18	4.90
800	9.50	7.42	6.45	5.92	5.60
900	10.69	8.35	7.26	6.66	6.30
1,000	11.88	9.28	8.06	7.39	7.00
2,000	23.75	18.55	16.12	14.78	13.99
3,000	35.62	27.82	24.17	22.17	20.98
4,000	47.49	37.09	32.23	29.56	27.97
5,000	59.36	46.36	40.28	36.95	34.97
6,000	71.23	55.63	48.34	44.34	41.96
7,000	83.10	64.90	56.40	51.73	48.95
8,000	94.97	74.17	64.45	59.12	55.94
9,000	106.84	83.44	72.51	66.51	
10,000	118.71	92.71	80.56	73.90	69.93
20,000	237.41	185.41	161.12	147.80	139.85
30,000	356.11	278.11	241.68	221.70	209.77
40,000	474.81	370.81	322.24	295.60	279.69
50,000	593.51	463.51	402.80	369.50	349.61
60,000	712.21	556.21	483.36	443.40	419.53
70,000	830.91	648.91	563.92	517.30	489.45
80,000	949.62	741.61	644.48	591.20	559.38
90,000	1068.32	834.31	725.04	665.10	629.30
100,000	1187.02	927.01	805.60	738.99	699.22
110,000	1305.72	1019.72	886.16	812.89	769.14
120,000	1424.42	1112.42	966.71	886.79	839.06
130,000	1543.12	1205.12	1047.27	960.69	908.98
140,000	1661.82	1297.82	1127.83	1034.59	978.90
150,000	1780.52	1390.52	1208.39	1108.49	1048.83
160,000	1899.23	1483.22	1288.95	1182.39	1118.75
170,000	2017.93	1575.92	1369.51	1256.29	1188.67
180,000	2136.63	1668.62	1450.07	1330.19	1258.59
190,000	2255.33	1761.32	1530.63	1404.09	1328.51
200,000	2374.03	1854.02	1611.19	1477.98	1398.43
250,000	2967.54	2317.53	2013.98	1847.48	1748.04
300,000	3561.04	2781.03	2416.78	2216.97	2097.64

415

MONTHLY PAYMENTS
ANNUAL INTEREST RATE: 7.75%

LOAN AMOUNT	LOAN MATURITY (YEARS)				
	10	15	20	25	30
50	0.61	0.48	0.42	0.38	0.36
100	1.21	0.95	0.83	0.76	0.72
200	2.41	1.89	1.65	1.52	1.44
300	3.61	2.83	2.47	2.27	2.15
400	4.81	3.77	3.29	3.03	2.87
500	6.01	4.71	4.11	3.78	3.59
600	7.21	5.65	4.93	4.54	4.30
700	8.41	6.59	5.75	5.29	5.02
800	9.61	7.54	6.57	6.05	5.74
900	10.81	8.48	7.39	6.80	6.45
1,000	12.01	9.42	8.21	7.56	7.17
2,000	24.01	18.83	16.42	15.11	14.33
3,000	36.01	28.24	24.63	22.66	21.50
4,000	48.01	37.66	32.84	30.22	28.66
5,000	60.01	47.07	41.05	37.77	35.83
6,000	72.01	56.48	49.26	45.32	42.99
7,000	84.01	65.89	57.47	52.88	50.15
8,000	96.01	75.31	65.68	60.43	57.32
9,000	108.02	84.72	73.89	67.98	64.48
10,000	120.02	94.13	82.10	75.54	71.65
20,000	240.03	188.26	164.20	151.07	143.29
30,000	360.04	282.39	246.29	226.60	214.93
40,000	480.05	376.52	328.39	302.14	286.57
50,000	600.06	470.64	410.48	377.67	358.21
60,000	720.07	564.77	492.58	453.20	429.85
70,000	840.08	658.90	574.67	528.74	501.49
80,000	960.10	753.03	656.77	604.27	573.14
90,000	1080.11	847.16	738.86	679.80	644.78
100,000	1200.12	941.28	820.96	755.34	716.42
110,000	1320.13	1035.41	903.05	830.87	788.06
120,000	1440.14	1129.54	985.15	906.40	859.70
130,000	1560.15	1223.67	1067.24	981.93	931.34
140,000	1680.16	1317.80	1149.34	1057.47	1002.98
150,000	1800.17	1411.92	1231.43	1133.00	1074.63
160,000	1920.19	1506.05	1313.53	1208.53	1146.27
170,000	2040.20	1600.18	1395.62	1284.07	1217.91
180,000	2160.21	1694.31	1477.72	1359.60	1289.55
190,000	2280.22	1788.44	1559.81	1435.13	1361.19
200,000	2400.23	1882.56	1641.91	1510.67	1432.83
250,000	3000.29	2353.20	2052.38	1888.33	1791.04
300,000	3600.34	2823.84	2462.86	2266.00	2149.25

416

MONTHLY PAYMENTS
ANNUAL INTEREST RATE: 8%

LOAN AMOUNT	\multicolumn LOAN MATURITY (YEARS)				
	10	15	20	25	30
50	0.61	0.48	0.42	0.39	0.37
100	1.22	0.96	0.84	0.78	0.74
200	2.43	1.92	1.68	1.55	1.47
300	3.64	2.87	2.51	2.32	2.21
400	4.86	3.83	3.35	3.09	2.94
500	6.07	4.78	4.19	3.86	3.67
600	7.28	5.74	5.02	4.64	4.41
700	8.50	6.69	5.86	5.41	5.14
800	9.71	7.65	6.70	6.18	5.88
900	10.92	8.61	7.53	6.95	6.61
1,000	12.14	9.56	8.37	7.72	7.34
2,000	24.27	19.12	16.73	15.44	14.68
3,000	36.40	28.67	25.10	23.16	22.02
4,000	48.54	38.23	33.46	30.88	29.36
5,000	60.67	47.79	41.83	38.60	36.69
6,000	72.80	57.34	50.19	46.31	44.03
7,000	84.93	66.90	58.56	54.03	51.37
8,000	97.07	76.46	66.92	61.75	58.71
9,000	109.20	86.01	75.28	69.47	66.04
10,000	121.33	95.57	83.65	77.19	73.38
20,000	242.66	191.14	167.29	154.37	146.76
30,000	363.99	286.70	250.94	231.55	220.13
40,000	485.32	382.27	334.58	308.73	293.51
50,000	606.64	477.83	418.22	385.91	366.89
60,000	727.97	573.40	501.87	463.09	440.26
70,000	849.30	668.96	585.51	540.28	513.64
80,000	970.63	764.53	669.16	617.46	587.02
90,000	1091.95	860.09	752.80	694.64	660.39
100,000	1213.28	955.66	836.44	771.82	733.77
110,000	1334.61	1051.22	920.09	849.00	807.15
120,000	1455.94	1146.79	1003.73	926.18	880.52
130,000	1577.26	1242.35	1087.38	1003.37	953.90
140,000	1698.59	1337.92	1171.02	1080.55	1027.28
150,000	1819.92	1433.48	1254.66	1157.73	1100.65
160,000	1941.25	1529.05	1338.31	1234.91	1174.03
170,000	2062.57	1624.61	1421.95	1312.09	1247.40
180,000	2183.90	1720.18	1505.60	1389.27	1320.78
190,000	2305.23	1815.74	1589.24	1466.46	1394.16
200,000	2426.56	1911.31	1672.88	1543.64	1467.53
250,000	3033.19	2389.13	2091.10	1929.55	1834.42
300,000	3639.83	2866.96	2509.32	2315.45	2201.30

417

MONTHLY PAYMENTS
ANNUAL INTEREST RATE: 8.25 %

LOAN AMOUNT	LOAN MATURITY (YEARS)				
	10	15	20	25	30
50	0.62	0.49	0.43	0.40	0.38
100	1.23	0.98	0.86	0.79	0.76
200	2.46	1.95	1.71	1.58	1.51
300	3.68	2.92	2.56	2.37	2.26
400	4.91	3.89	3.41	3.16	3.01
500	6.14	4.86	4.27	3.95	3.76
600	7.36	5.83	5.12	4.74	4.51
700	8.59	6.80	5.97	5.52	5.26
800	9.82	7.77	6.82	6.31	6.02
900	11.04	8.74	7.67	7.10	6.77
1,000	12.27	9.71	8.53	7.89	7.52
2,000	24.54	19.41	17.05	15.77	15.03
3,000	36.80	29.11	25.57	23.66	22.54
4,000	49.07	38.81	34.09	31.54	30.06
5,000	61.33	48.51	42.61	39.43	37.57
6,000	73.60	58.21	51.13	47.31	45.08
7,000	85.86	67.91	59.65	55.20	52.59
8,000	98.13	77.62	68.17	63.08	60.11
9,000	110.39	87.32	76.69	70.97	67.62
10,000	122.66	97.02	85.21	78.85	75.13
20,000	245.31	194.03	170.42	157.69	150.26
30,000	367.96	291.05	255.62	236.54	225.38
40,000	490.61	388.06	340.83	315.38	300.51
50,000	613.27	485.07	426.04	394.23	375.64
60,000	735.92	582.09	511.24	473.07	450.76
70,000	858.57	679.10	596.45	551.92	525.89
80,000	981.22	776.12	681.66	630.76	601.02
90,000	1103.88	873.13	766.86	709.61	676.14
100,000	1226.53	970.14	852.07	788.45	751.27
110,000	1349.18	1067.16	937.28	867.30	826.40
120,000	1471.83	1164.17	1022.48	946.14	901.52
130,000	1594.49	1261.19	1107.69	1024.99	976.65
140,000	1717.14	1358.20	1192.90	1103.83	1051.78
150,000	1839.79	1455.21	1278.10	1182.68	1126.90
160,000	1962.44	1552.23	1363.31	1261.52	1202.03
170,000	2085.10	1649.24	1448.52	1340.37	1277.16
180,000	2207.75	1746.26	1533.72	1419.21	1352.28
190,000	2330.40	1843.27	1618.93	1498.06	1427.41
200,000	2453.05	1940.28	1704.14	1576.90	1502.54
250,000	3066.32	2425.35	2130.17	1971.13	1878.17
300,000	3679.58	2910.42	2556.20	2365.35	2253.80

MONTHLY PAYMENTS
ANNUAL INTEREST RATE: 8.5 %

LOAN AMOUNT	LOAN MATURITY (YEARS)				
	10	15	20	25	30
50	0.62	0.50	0.44	0.41	0.39
100	1.24	0.99	0.87	0.81	0.77
200	2.48	1.97	1.74	1.62	1.54
300	3.72	2.96	2.61	2.42	2.31
400	4.96	3.94	3.48	3.23	3.08
500	6.20	4.93	4.34	4.03	3.85
600	7.44	5.91	5.21	4.84	4.62
700	8.68	6.90	6.08	5.64	5.39
800	9.92	7.88	6.95	6.45	6.16
900	11.16	8.87	7.82	7.25	6.93
1,000	12.40	9.85	8.68	8.06	7.69
2,000	24.80	19.70	17.36	16.11	15.38
3,000	37.20	29.55	26.04	24.16	23.07
4,000	49.60	39.39	34.72	32.21	30.76
5,000	62.00	49.24	43.40	40.27	38.45
6,000	74.40	59.09	52.07	48.32	46.14
7,000	86.80	68.94	60.75	56.37	53.83
8,000	99.19	78.78	69.43	64.42	61.52
9,000	111.59	88.63	78.11	72.48	69.21
10,000	123.99	98.48	86.79	80.53	76.90
20,000	247.98	196.95	173.57	161.05	153.79
30,000	371.96	295.43	260.35	241.57	230.68
40,000	495.95	393.90	347.14	322.10	307.57
50,000	619.94	492.38	433.92	402.62	384.46
60,000	743.92	590.85	520.70	483.14	461.35
70,000	867.91	689.32	607.48	563.66	538.25
80,000	991.89	787.80	694.27	644.19	615.14
90,000	1115.88	886.27	781.05	724.71	692.03
100,000	1239.87	984.75	867.83	805.23	768.92
110,000	1363.85	1083.22	954.61	885.76	845.81
120,000	1487.84	1181.70	1041.40	966.28	922.70
130,000	1611.82	1280.17	1128.18	1046.80	999.59
140,000	1735.81	1378.64	1214.96	1127.32	1076.49
150,000	1859.80	1477.12	1301.74	1207.85	1153.38
160,000	1983.78	1575.59	1388.53	1288.37	1230.27
170,000	2107.77	1674.07	1475.31	1368.89	1307.16
180,000	2231.76	1772.54	1562.09	1449.42	1384.05
190,000	2355.74	1871.02	1648.87	1529.94	1460.94
200,000	2479.73	1969.49	1735.66	1610.46	1537.83
250,000	3099.66	2461.86	2169.57	2013.08	1922.29
300,000	3719.59	2954.23	2603.48	2415.69	2306.75

419

MONTHLY PAYMENTS
ANNUAL INTEREST RATE: 8.75 %

LOAN AMOUNT	LOAN MATURITY (YEARS)				
	10	15	20	25	30
50	0.63	0.50	0.45	0.42	0.40
100	1.26	1.00	0.89	0.83	0.79
200	2.51	2.00	1.77	1.65	1.58
300	3.76	3.00	2.66	2.47	2.37
400	5.02	4.00	3.54	3.29	3.15
500	6.27	5.00	4.42	4.12	3.94
600	7.52	6.00	5.31	4.94	4.73
700	8.78	7.00	6.19	5.76	5.51
800	10.03	8.00	7.07	6.58	6.30
900	11.28	9.00	7.96	7.40	7.09
1,000	12.54	10.00	8.84	8.23	7.87
2,000	25.07	19.99	17.68	16.45	15.74
3,000	37.60	29.99	26.52	24.67	23.61
4,000	50.14	39.98	35.35	32.89	31.47
5,000	62.67	49.98	44.19	41.11	39.34
6,000	75.20	59.97	53.03	49.33	47.21
7,000	87.73	69.97	61.86	57.56	55.07
8,000	100.27	79.96	70.70	65.78	62.94
9,000	112.80	89.96	79.54	74.00	70.81
10,000	125.33	99.95	88.38	82.22	78.68
20,000	250.66	199.89	176.75	164.43	157.35
30,000	375.99	299.84	265.12	246.65	236.02
40,000	501.31	399.78	353.49	328.86	314.69
50,000	626.64	499.73	441.86	411.08	393.36
60,000	751.97	599.67	530.23	493.29	472.03
70,000	877.29	699.62	618.60	575.51	550.70
80,000	1002.62	799.56	706.97	657.72	629.37
90,000	1127.95	899.51	795.34	739.93	708.04
100,000	1253.27	999.45	883.72	822.15	786.71
110,000	1378.60	1099.40	972.09	904.36	865.38
120,000	1503.93	1199.34	1060.46	986.58	944.05
130,000	1629.25	1299.29	1148.83	1068.79	1022.72
140,000	1754.58	1399.23	1237.20	1151.01	1101.39
150,000	1879.91	1499.18	1325.57	1233.22	1180.06
160,000	2005.23	1599.12	1413.94	1315.43	1258.73
170,000	2130.56	1699.07	1502.31	1397.65	1337.40
180,000	2255.89	1799.01	1590.68	1479.86	1416.07
190,000	2381.21	1898.96	1679.05	1562.08	1494.74
200,000	2506.54	1998.90	1767.43	1644.29	1573.41
250,000	3133.17	2498.63	2209.28	2055.36	1966.76
300,000	3759.81	2998.35	2651.14	2466.44	2360.11

420

MONTHLY PAYMENTS
ANNUAL INTEREST RATE: 9 %

LOAN AMOUNT	LOAN MATURITY (YEARS)				
	10	15	20	25	30
50	0.64	0.51	0.45	0.42	0.41
100	1.27	1.02	0.90	0.84	0.81
200	2.54	2.03	1.80	1.68	1.61
300	3.81	3.05	2.70	2.52	2.42
400	5.07	4.06	3.60	3.36	3.22
500	6.34	5.08	4.50	4.20	4.03
600	7.61	6.09	5.40	5.04	4.83
700	8.87	7.10	6.30	5.88	5.64
800	10.14	8.12	7.20	6.72	6.44
900	11.41	9.13	8.10	7.56	7.25
1,000	12.67	10.15	9.00	8.40	8.05
2,000	25.34	20.29	18.00	16.79	16.10
3,000	38.01	30.43	27.00	25.18	24.14
4,000	50.68	40.58	35.99	33.57	32.19
5,000	63.34	50.72	44.99	41.96	40.24
6,000	76.01	60.86	53.99	50.36	48.28
7,000	88.68	71.00	62.99	58.75	56.33
8,000	101.35	81.15	71.98	67.14	64.37
9,000	114.01	91.29	80.98	75.53	72.42
10,000	126.68	101.43	89.98	83.92	80.47
20,000	253.36	202.86	179.95	167.84	160.93
30,000	380.03	304.28	269.92	251.76	241.39
40,000	506.71	405.71	359.89	335.68	321.85
50,000	633.38	507.14	449.87	419.60	402.32
60,000	760.06	608.56	539.84	503.52	482.78
70,000	886.73	709.99	629.81	587.44	563.24
80,000	1013.41	811.41	719.78	671.36	643.70
90,000	1140.08	912.84	809.76	755.28	724.16
100,000	1266.76	1014.27	899.73	839.20	804.63
110,000	1393.43	1115.69	989.70	923.12	885.09
120,000	1520.11	1217.12	1079.67	1007.04	965.55
130,000	1646.78	1318.55	1169.64	1090.96	1046.01
140,000	1773.46	1419.97	1259.62	1174.88	1126.47
150,000	1900.13	1521.40	1349.59	1258.80	1206.94
160,000	2026.81	1622.82	1439.56	1342.72	1287.40
170,000	2153.48	1724.25	1529.53	1426.64	1367.86
180,000	2280.16	1825.68	1619.51	1510.55	1448.32
190,000	2406.83	1927.10	1709.48	1594.47	1528.79
200,000	2533.51	2028.53	1799.45	1678.39	1609.25
250,000	3166.88	2535.66	2249.31	2097.99	2011.56
300,000	3800.26	3042.79	2699.17	2517.59	2413.87

421

MONTHLY PAYMENTS
ANNUAL INTEREST RATE: 9.25%

LOAN AMOUNT	LOAN MATURITY (YEARS)				
	10	15	20	25	30
50	0.65	0.52	0.46	0.43	0.42
100	1.29	1.03	0.92	0.86	0.83
200	2.57	2.06	1.84	1.72	1.65
300	3.85	3.09	2.75	2.57	2.47
400	5.13	4.12	3.67	3.43	3.30
500	6.41	5.15	4.58	4.29	4.12
600	7.69	6.18	5.50	5.14	4.94
700	8.97	7.21	6.42	6.00	5.76
800	10.25	8.24	7.33	6.86	6.59
900	11.53	9.27	8.25	7.71	7.41
1,000	12.81	10.30	9.16	8.57	8.23
2,000	25.61	20.59	18.32	17.13	16.46
3,000	38.41	30.88	27.48	25.70	24.69
4,000	51.22	41.17	36.64	34.26	32.91
5,000	64.02	51.46	45.80	42.82	41.14
6,000	76.82	61.76	54.96	51.39	49.37
7,000	89.63	72.05	64.12	59.95	57.59
8,000	102.43	82.34	73.27	68.52	65.82
9,000	115.23	92.63	82.43	77.08	74.05
10,000	128.04	102.92	91.59	85.64	82.27
20,000	256.07	205.84	183.18	171.28	164.54
30,000	384.10	308.76	274.77	256.92	246.81
40,000	512.14	411.68	366.35	342.56	329.08
50,000	640.17	514.60	457.94	428.20	411.34
60,000	768.20	617.52	549.53	513.84	493.61
70,000	896.24	720.44	641.11	599.47	575.88
80,000	1024.27	823.36	732.70	685.11	658.15
90,000	1152.30	926.28	824.29	770.75	740.41
100,000	1280.34	1029.20	915.87	856.39	822.68
110,000	1408.37	1132.12	1007.46	942.03	904.95
120,000	1536.40	1235.04	1099.05	1027.67	987.22
130,000	1664.44	1337.96	1190.63	1113.30	1069.48
140,000	1792.47	1440.88	1282.22	1198.94	1151.75
150,000	1920.50	1543.80	1373.81	1284.58	1234.02
160,000	2048.54	1646.72	1465.40	1370.22	1316.29
170,000	2176.57	1749.64	1556.98	1455.86	1398.55
180,000	2304.60	1852.56	1648.57	1541.50	1480.82
190,000	2432.64	1955.48	1740.16	1627.13	1563.09
200,000	2560.67	2058.40	1831.74	1712.77	1645.36
250,000	3200.84	2572.99	2289.68	2140.96	2056.70
300,000	3841.00	3087.59	2747.61	2569.16	2468.03

422

MONTHLY PAYMENTS
ANNUAL INTEREST RATE: 9.5%

LOAN AMOUNT	LOAN MATURITY (YEARS)				
	10	15	20	25	30
50	0.65	0.53	0.47	0.44	0.43
100	1.30	1.05	0.94	0.88	0.85
200	2.59	2.09	1.87	1.75	1.69
300	3.89	3.14	2.80	2.63	2.53
400	5.18	4.18	3.73	3.50	3.37
500	6.47	5.23	4.67	4.37	4.21
600	7.77	6.27	5.60	5.25	5.05
700	9.06	7.31	6.53	6.12	5.89
800	10.36	8.36	7.46	6.99	6.73
900	11.65	9.40	8.39	7.87	7.57
1,000	12.94	10.45	9.33	8.74	8.41
2,000	25.88	20.89	18.65	17.48	16.82
3,000	38.82	31.33	27.97	26.22	25.23
4,000	51.76	41.77	37.29	34.95	33.64
5,000	64.70	52.22	46.61	43.69	42.05
6,000	77.64	62.66	55.93	52.43	50.46
7,000	90.58	73.10	65.25	61.16	58.86
8,000	103.52	83.54	74.58	69.90	67.27
9,000	116.46	93.98	83.90	78.64	75.68
10,000	129.40	104.43	93.22	87.37	84.09
20,000	258.80	208.85	186.43	174.74	168.18
30,000	388.20	313.27	279.64	262.11	252.26
40,000	517.59	417.69	372.86	349.48	336.35
50,000	646.99	522.12	466.07	436.85	420.43
60,000	776.39	626.54	559.28	524.22	504.52
70,000	905.78	730.96	652.50	611.59	588.60
80,000	1035.18	835.38	745.71	698.96	672.69
90,000	1164.58	939.80	838.92	786.33	756.77
100,000	1293.98	1044.23	932.13	873.70	840.86
110,000	1423.37	1148.65	1025.35	961.07	924.94
120,000	1552.77	1253.07	1118.56	1048.44	1009.03
130,000	1682.17	1357.49	1211.77	1135.81	1093.11
140,000	1811.56	1461.92	1304.99	1223.18	1177.20
150,000	1940.96	1566.34	1398.20	1310.55	1261.29
160,000	2070.36	1670.76	1491.41	1397.92	1345.37
170,000	2199.76	1775.18	1584.62	1485.29	1429.46
180,000	2329.15	1879.60	1677.84	1572.66	1513.54
190,000	2458.55	1984.03	1771.05	1660.03	1597.63
200,000	2587.95	2088.45	1864.26	1747.40	1681.71
250,000	3234.93	2610.56	2330.33	2184.24	2102.14
300,000	3881.92	3132.67	2796.39	2621.09	2522.57

MONTHLY PAYMENTS
ANNUAL INTEREST RATE: 9.75%

LOAN
AMOUNT

LOAN MATURITY (YEARS)

	10	15	20	25	30
50	0.66	0.53	0.48	0.45	0.43
100	1.31	1.06	0.95	0.90	0.86
200	2.62	2.12	1.90	1.79	1.72
300	3.93	3.18	2.85	2.68	2.58
400	5.24	4.24	3.80	3.57	3.44
500	6.54	5.30	4.75	4.46	4.30
600	7.85	6.36	5.70	5.35	5.16
700	9.16	7.42	6.64	6.24	6.02
800	10.47	8.48	7.59	7.13	6.88
900	11.77	9.54	8.54	8.03	7.74
1,000	13.08	10.60	9.49	8.92	8.60
2,000	26.16	21.19	18.98	17.83	17.19
3,000	39.24	31.79	28.46	26.74	25.78
4,000	52.31	42.38	37.95	35.65	34.37
5,000	65.39	52.97	47.43	44.56	42.96
6,000	78.47	63.57	56.92	53.47	51.55
7,000	91.54	74.16	66.40	62.38	60.15
8,000	104.62	84.75	75.89	71.30	68.74
9,000	117.70	95.35	85.37	80.21	77.33
10,000	130.78	105.94	94.86	89.12	85.92
20,000	261.55	211.88	189.71	178.23	171.84
30,000	392.32	317.81	284.56	267.35	257.75
40,000	523.09	423.75	379.41	356.46	343.67
50,000	653.86	529.69	474.26	445.57	429.58
60,000	784.63	635.62	569.12	534.69	515.50
70,000	915.40	741.56	663.97	623.80	601.41
80,000	1046.17	847.50	758.82	712.92	687.33
90,000	1176.94	953.43	853.67	802.03	773.24
100,000	1307.71	1059.37	948.52	891.14	859.16
110,000	1438.48	1165.31	1043.38	980.26	945.08
120,000	1569.25	1271.24	1138.23	1069.37	1030.99
130,000	1700.02	1377.18	1233.08	1158.49	1116.91
140,000	1830.79	1483.12	1327.93	1247.60	1202.82
150,000	1961.56	1589.05	1422.78	1336.71	1288.74
160,000	2092.34	1694.99	1517.63	1425.83	1374.65
170,000	2223.11	1800.93	1612.49	1514.94	1460.57
180,000	2353.88	1906.86	1707.34	1604.05	1546.48
190,000	2484.65	2012.80	1802.19	1693.17	1632.40
200,000	2615.42	2118.73	1897.04	1782.28	1718.32
250,000	3269.27	2648.42	2371.30	2227.85	2147.89
300,000	3923.12	3178.10	2845.56	2673.42	2577.47

MONTHLY PAYMENTS
ANNUAL INTEREST RATE: 10%

LOAN AMOUNT	LOAN MATURITY (YEARS)				
	10	15	20	25	30
50	0.67	0.54	0.49	0.46	0.44
100	1.33	1.08	0.97	0.91	0.88
200	2.65	2.15	1.94	1.82	1.76
300	3.97	3.23	2.90	2.73	2.64
400	5.29	4.30	3.87	3.64	3.52
500	6.61	5.38	4.83	4.55	4.39
600	7.93	6.45	5.80	5.46	5.27
700	9.26	7.53	6.76	6.37	6.15
800	10.58	8.60	7.73	7.27	7.03
900	11.90	9.68	8.69	8.18	7.90
1,000	13.22	10.75	9.66	9.09	8.78
2,000	26.44	21.50	19.31	18.18	17.56
3,000	39.65	32.24	28.96	27.27	26.33
4,000	52.87	42.99	38.61	36.35	35.11
5,000	66.08	53.74	48.26	45.44	43.88
6,000	79.30	64.48	57.91	54.53	52.66
7,000	92.51	75.23	67.56	63.61	61.44
8,000	105.73	85.97	77.21	72.70	70.21
9,000	118.94	96.72	86.86	81.79	78.99
10,000	132.16	107.47	96.51	90.88	87.76
20,000	264.31	214.93	193.01	181.75	175.52
30,000	396.46	322.39	289.51	272.62	263.28
40,000	528.61	429.85	386.01	363.49	351.03
50,000	660.76	537.31	482.52	454.36	438.79
60,000	792.91	644.77	579.02	545.23	526.55
70,000	925.06	752.23	675.52	636.10	614.31
80,000	1057.21	859.69	772.02	726.97	702.06
90,000	1189.36	967.15	868.53	817.84	789.82
100,000	1321.52	1074.61	965.03	908.71	877.58
110,000	1453.67	1182.07	1061.53	999.58	965.33
120,000	1585.82	1289.53	1158.03	1090.45	1053.09
130,000	1717.97	1396.99	1254.53	1181.32	1140.85
140,000	1850.12	1504.46	1351.04	1272.19	1228.61
150,000	1982.27	1611.92	1447.54	1363.06	1316.36
160,000	2114.42	1719.38	1544.04	1453.93	1404.12
170,000	2246.57	1826.84	1640.54	1544.80	1491.88
180,000	2378.72	1934.30	1737.05	1635.67	1579.63
190,000	2510.88	2041.76	1833.55	1726.54	1667.39
200,000	2643.03	2149.22	1930.05	1817.41	1755.15
250,000	3303.78	2686.52	2412.56	2271.76	2193.94
300,000	3964.54	3223.83	2895.07	2726.11	2632.72

425

MONTHLY PAYMENTS
ANNUAL INTEREST RATE: 10.25%

LOAN AMOUNT	LOAN MATURITY (YEARS)				
	10	15	20	25	30
50	0.67	0.55	0.50	0.47	0.45
100	1.34	1.09	0.99	0.93	0.90
200	2.68	2.18	1.97	1.86	1.80
300	4.01	3.27	2.95	2.78	2.69
400	5.35	4.36	3.93	3.71	3.59
500	6.68	5.45	4.91	4.64	4.49
600	8.02	6.54	5.89	5.56	5.38
700	9.35	7.63	6.88	6.49	6.28
800	10.69	8.72	7.86	7.42	7.17
900	12.02	9.81	8.84	8.34	8.07
1,000	13.36	10.90	9.82	9.27	8.97
2,000	26.71	21.80	19.64	18.53	17.93
3,000	40.07	32.70	29.45	27.80	26.89
4,000	53.42	43.60	39.27	37.06	35.85
5,000	66.77	54.50	49.09	46.32	44.81
6,000	80.13	65.40	58.90	55.59	53.77
7,000	93.48	76.30	68.72	64.85	62.73
8,000	106.84	87.20	78.54	74.12	.71.69
9,000	120.19	98.10	88.35	83.38	80.65
10,000	133.54	109.00	98.17	92.64	89.62
20,000	267.08	217.99	196.33	185.28	179.23
30,000	400.62	326.99	294.50	277.92	268.84
40,000	534.16	435.98	392.66	370.56	358.45
50,000	667.70	544.98	490.83	463.20	448.06
60,000	801.24	653.97	588.99	555.83	537.67
70,000	934.78	762.97	687.15	648.47	627.28
80,000	1068.32	871.96	785.32	741.11	716.89
90,000	1201.85	980.96	883.48	833.75	806.50
100,000	1335.39	1089.95	981.65	926.39	896.11
110,000	1468.93	1198.95	1079.81	1019.03	985.72
120,000	1602.47	1307.94	1177.98	1111.66	1075.33
130,000	1736.01	1416.94	1276.14	1204.30	1164.94
140,000	1869.55	1525.93	1374.30	1296.94	1254.55
150,000	2003.09	1634.93	1472.47	1389.58	1344.16
160,000	2136.63	1743.92	1570.63	1482.22	1433.77
170,000	2270.16	1852.92	1668.80	1574.86	1523.38
180,000	2403.70	1961.91	1766.96	1667.49	1612.99
190,000	2537.24	2070.91	1865.13	1760.13	1702.60
200,000	2670.78	2179.90	1963.29	1852.77	1792.21
250,000	3338.48	2724.88	2454.11	2315.96	2240.26
300,000	4006.17	3269.85	2944.93	2779.15	2688.31

426

MONTHLY PAYMENTS
ANNUAL INTEREST RATE: 10.5%

LOAN AMOUNT	LOAN MATURITY (YEARS)				
	10	15	20	25	30
50	0.68	0.56	0.50	0.48	0.46
100	1.35	1.11	1.00	0.95	0.92
200	2.70	2.22	2.00	1.89	1.83
300	4.05	3.32	3.00	2.84	2.75
400	5.40	4.43	4.00	3.78	3.66
500	6.75	5.53	5.00	4.73	4.58
600	8.10	6.64	6.00	5.67	5.49
700	9.45	7.74	6.99	6.61	6.41
800	10.80	8.85	7.99	7.56	7.32
900	12.15	9.95	8.99	8.50	8.24
1,000	13.50	11.06	9.99	9.45	9.15
2,000	26.99	22.11	19.97	18.89	18.30
3,000	40.49	33.17	29.96	28.33	27.45
4,000	53.98	44.22	39.94	37.77	36.59
5,000	67.47	55.28	49.92	47.21	45.74
6,000	80.97	66.33	59.91	56.66	54.89
7,000	94.46	77.38	69.89	66.10	64.04
8,000	107.95	88.44	79.88	75.54	73.18
9,000	121.45	99.49	89.86	84.98	82.33
10,000	134.94	110.55	99.84	94.42	91.48
20,000	269.88	221.09	199.68	188.84	182.95
30,000	404.81	331.63	299.52	283.26	274.43
40,000	539.75	442.17	399.36	377.68	365.90
50,000	674.68	552.71	499.20	472.10	457.37
60,000	809.62	663.25	599.03	566.51	548.85
70,000	944.55	773.79	698.87	660.93	640.32
80,000	1079.49	884.33	798.71	755.35	731.80
90,000	1214.42	994.87	898.55	849.77	823.27
100,000	1349.36	1105.41	998.39	944.19	914.74
110,000	1484.29	1215.95	1098.22	1038.61	1006.22
120,000	1619.23	1326.49	1198.06	1133.02	1097.69
130,000	1754.16	1437.03	1297.90	1227.44	1189.17
140,000	1889.10	1547.57	1397.74	1321.86	1280.64
150,000	2024.04	1658.11	1497.58	1416.28	1372.11
160,000	2158.97	1768.65	1597.41	1510.70	1463.59
170,000	2293.91	1879.19	1697.25	1605.12	1555.06
180,000	2428.84	1989.73	1797.09	1699.53	1646.54
190,000	2563.78	2100.27	1896.93	1793.95	1738.01
200,000	2698.71	2210.81	1996.77	1888.37	1829.48
250,000	3373.39	2763.51	2495.96	2360.46	2286.85
300,000	4048.07	3316.21	2995.15	2832.55	2744.22

427

MONTHLY PAYMENTS
ANNUAL INTEREST RATE: 10.75%

LOAN AMOUNT	LOAN MATURITY (YEARS)				
	10	15	20	25	30
50	0.69	0.57	0.51	0.49	0.47
100	1.37	1.13	1.02	0.97	0.94
200	2.73	2.25	2.04	1.93	1.87
300	4.10	3.37	3.05	2.89	2.81
400	5.46	4.49	4.07	3.85	3.74
500	6.82	5.61	5.08	4.82	4.67
600	8.19	6.73	6.10	5.78	5.61
700	9.55	7.85	7.11	6.74	6.54
800	10.91	8.97	8.13	7.70	7.47
900	12.28	10.09	9.14	8.66	8.41
1,000	13.64	11.21	10.16	9.63	9.34
2,000	27.27	22.42	20.31	19.25	18.67
3,000	40.91	33.63	30.46	28.87	28.01
4,000	54.54	44.84	40.61	38.49	37.34
5,000	68.17	56.05	50.77	48.11	46.68
6,000	81.81	67.26	60.92	57.73	56.01
7,000	95.44	78.47	71.07	67.35	65.35
8,000	109.08	89.68	81.22	76.97	74.68
9,000	122.71	100.89	91.38	86.59	84.02
10,000	136.34	112.10	101.53	96.21	93.35
20,000	272.68	224.19	203.05	192.42	186.70
30,000	409.02	336.29	304.57	288.63	280.05
40,000	545.36	448.38	406.10	384.84	373.40
50,000	681.70	560.48	507.62	481.05	466.75
60,000	818.04	672.57	609.14	577.26	560.09
70,000	954.38	784.67	710.67	673.47	653.44
80,000	1090.72	896.76	812.19	769.68	746.79
90,000	1227.05	1008.86	913.71	865.89	840.14
100,000	1363.39	1120.95	1015.23	962.10	933.49
110,000	1499.73	1233.05	1116.76	1058.31	1026.83
120,000	1636.07	1345.14	1218.28	1154.52	1120.18
130,000	1772.41	1457.24	1319.80	1250.73	1213.53
140,000	1908.75	1569.33	1421.33	1346.94	1306.88
150,000	2045.09	1681.43	1522.85	1443.14	1400.23
160,000	2181.43	1793.52	1624.37	1539.35	1493.58
170,000	2317.76	1905.62	1725.89	1635.56	1586.92
180,000	2454.10	2017.71	1827.42	1731.77	1680.27
190,000	2590.44	2129.81	1928.94	1827.98	1773.62
200,000	2726.78	2241.90	2030.46	1924.19	1866.97
250,000	3408.47	2802.38	2538.08	2405.24	2333.71
300,000	4090.17	3362.85	3045.69	2886.28	2800.45

MONTHLY PAYMENTS
ANNUAL INTEREST RATE: 11%

LOAN AMOUNT	LOAN MATURITY (YEARS)				
	10	15	20	25	30
50	0.69	0.57	0.52	0.50	0.48
100	1.38	1.14	1.04	0.99	0.96
200	2.76	2.28	2.07	1.97	1.91
300	4.14	3.41	3.10	2.95	2.86
400	5.51	4.55	4.13	3.93	3.81
500	6.89	5.69	5.17	4.91	4.77
600	8.27	6.82	6.20	5.89	5.72
700	9.65	7.96	7.23	6.87	6.67
800	11.02	9.10	8.26	7.85	7.62
900	12.40	10.23	9.29	8.83	8.58
1,000	13.78	11.37	10.33	9.81	9.53
2,000	27.55	22.74	20.65	19.61	19.05
3,000	41.33	34.10	30.97	29.41	28.57
4,000	55.10	45.47	41.29	39.21	38.10
5,000	68.88	56.83	51.61	49.01	47.62
6,000	82.65	68.20	61.94	58.81	57.14
7,000	96.43	79.57	72.26	68.61	66.67
8,000	110.20	90.93	82.58	78.41	76.19
9,000	123.98	102.30	92.90	88.22	85.71
10,000	137.75	113.66	103.22	98.02	95.24
20,000	275.50	227.32	206.44	196.03	190.47
30,000	413.25	340.98	309.66	294.04	285.70
40,000	551.00	454.64	412.88	392.05	380.93
50,000	688.75	568.30	516.10	490.06	476.17
60,000	826.50	681.96	619.32	588.07	571.40
70,000	964.25	795.62	722.54	686.08	666.63
80,000	1102.00	909.28	825.75	784.09	761.86
90,000	1239.75	1022.94	928.97	882.11	857.10
100,000	1377.50	1136.60	1032.19	980.12	952.33
110,000	1515.25	1250.26	1135.41	1078.13	1047.56
120,000	1653.00	1363.92	1238.63	1176.14	1142.79
130,000	1790.75	1477.58	1341.85	1274.15	1238.02
140,000	1928.50	1591.24	1445.07	1372.16	1333.26
150,000	2066.25	1704.90	1548.29	1470.17	1428.49
160,000	2204.00	1818.56	1651.50	1568.18	1523.72
170,000	2341.75	1932.22	1754.72	1666.20	1618.95
180,000	2479.50	2045.88	1857.94	1764.21	1714.19
190,000	2617.25	2159.54	1961.16	1862.22	1809.42
200,000	2755.00	2273.19	2064.38	1960.23	1904.65
250,000	3443.75	2841.49	2580.47	2450.29	2380.81
300,000	4132.50	3409.79	3096.57	2940.34	2856.97

429

MONTHLY PAYMENTS
ANNUAL INTEREST RATE: 11.25%

LOAN AMOUNT	LOAN MATURITY (YEARS)				
	10	15	20	25	30
50	0.70	0.58	0.53	0.50	0.49
100	1.40	1.16	1.05	1.00	0.98
200	2.79	2.31	2.10	2.00	1.95
300	4.18	3.46	3.15	3.00	2.92
400	5.57	4.61	4.20	4.00	3.89
500	6.96	5.77	5.25	5.00	4.86
600	8.36	6.92	6.30	5.99	5.83
700	9.75	8.07	7.35	6.99	6.80
800	11.14	9.22	8.40	7.99	7.78
900	12.53	10.38	9.45	8.99	8.75
1,000	13.92	11.53	10.50	9.99	9.72
2,000	27.84	23.05	20.99	19.97	19.43
3,000	41.76	34.58	31.48	29.95	29.14
4,000	55.67	46.10	41.98	39.93	38.86
5,000	69.59	57.62	52.47	49.92	48.57
6,000	83.51	69.15	62.96	59.90	58.28
7,000	97.42	80.67	73.45	69.88	67.99
8,000	111.34	92.19	83.95	79.86	77.71
9,000	125.26	103.72	94.44	89.85	87.42
10,000	139.17	115.24	104.93	99.83	97.13
20,000	278.34	230.47	209.86	199.65	194.26
30,000	417.51	345.71	314.78	299.48	291.38
40,000	556.68	460.94	419.71	399.30	388.51
50,000	695.85	576.18	524.63	499.13	485.64
60,000	835.02	691.41	629.56	598.95	582.76
70,000	974.19	806.65	734.49	698.77	679.89
80,000	1113.36	921.88	839.41	798.60	777.01
90,000	1252.53	1037.12	944.34	898.42	874.14
100,000	1391.70	1152.35	1049.26	998.25	971.27
110,000	1530.87	1267.59	1154.19	1098.07	1068.39
120,000	1670.04	1382.82	1259.11	1197.89	1165.52
130,000	1809.21	1498.06	1364.04	1297.72	1262.65
140,000	1948.37	1613.29	1468.97	1397.54	1359.77
150,000	2087.54	1728.52	1573.89	1497.37	1456.90
160,000	2226.71	1843.76	1678.82	1597.19	1554.02
170,000	2365.88	1958.99	1783.74	1697.01	1651.15
180,000	2505.05	2074.23	1888.67	1796.84	1748.28
190,000	2644.22	2189.46	1993.59	1896.66	1845.40
200,000	2783.39	2304.70	2098.52	1996.49	1942.53
250,000	3479.24	2880.87	2623.15	2495.61	2428.16
300,000	4175.08	3457.04	3147.78	2994.73	2913.79

MONTHLY PAYMENTS
ANNUAL INTEREST RATE: 11.5%

LOAN AMOUNT	LOAN MATURITY (YEARS)				
	10	15	20	25	30
50	0.71	0.59	0.54	0.51	0.50
100	1.41	1.17	1.07	1.02	1.00
200	2.82	2.34	2.14	2.04	1.99
300	4.22	3.51	3.20	3.05	2.98
400	5.63	4.68	4.27	4.07	3.97
500	7.03	5.85	5.34	5.09	4.96
600	8.44	7.01	6.40	6.10	5.95
700	9.85	8.18	7.47	7.12	6.94
800	11.25	9.35	8.54	8.14	7.93
900	12.66	10.52	9.60	9.15	8.92
1,000	14.06	11.69	10.67	10.17	9.91
2,000	28.12	23.37	21.33	20.33	19.81
3,000	42.18	35.05	32.00	30.50	29.71
4,000	56.24	46.73	42.66	40.66	39.62
5,000	70.30	58.41	53.33	50.83	49.52
6,000	84.36	70.10	63.99	60.99	59.42
7,000	98.42	81.78	74.66	71.16	69.33
8,000	112.48	93.46	85.32	81.32	79.23
9,000	126.54	105.14	95.98	91.49	89.13
10,000	140.60	116.82	106.65	101.65	99.03
20,000	281.20	233.64	213.29	203.30	198.06
30,000	421.79	350.46	319.93	304.95	297.09
40,000	562.39	467.28	426.58	406.59	396.12
50,000	702.98	584.10	533.22	508.24	495.15
60,000	843.58	700.92	639.86	609.89	594.18
70,000	984.17	817.74	746.51	711.53	693.21
80,000	1124.77	934.56	853.15	813.18	792.24
90,000	1265.36	1051.38	959.79	914.83	891.27
100,000	1405.96	1168.20	1066.43	1016.47	990.30
110,000	1546.56	1285.01	1173.08	1118.12	1089.33
120,000	1687.15	1401.83	1279.72	1219.77	1188.35
130,000	1827.75	1518.65	1386.36	1321.41	1287.38
140,000	1968.34	1635.47	1493.01	1423.06	1386.41
150,000	2108.94	1752.29	1599.65	1524.71	1485.44
160,000	2249.53	1869.11	1706.29	1626.36	1584.47
170,000	2390.13	1985.93	1812.94	1728.00	1683.50
180,000	2530.72	2102.75	1919.58	1829.65	1782.53
190,000	2671.32	2219.57	2026.22	1931.30	1881.56
200,000	2811.91	2336.39	2132.86	2032.94	1980.59
250,000	3514.89	2920.48	2666.08	2541.18	2475.73
300,000	4217.87	3504.58	3199.29	3049.41	2970.88

431

MONTHLY PAYMENTS
ANNUAL INTEREST RATE: 11.75%

LOAN AMOUNT	LOAN MATURITY (YEARS)				
	10	15	20	25	30
50	0.72	0.60	0.55	0.52	0.51
100	1.43	1.19	1.09	1.04	1.01
200	2.85	2.37	2.17	2.07	2.02
300	4.27	3.56	3.26	3.11	3.03
400	5.69	4.74	4.34	4.14	4.04
500	7.11	5.93	5.42	5.18	5.05
600	8.53	7.11	6.51	6.21	6.06
700	9.95	8.29	7.59	7.25	7.07
800	11.37	9.48	8.67	8.28	8.08
900	12.79	10.66	9.76	9.32	9.09
1,000	14.21	11.85	10.84	10.35	10.10
2,000	28.41	23.69	21.68	20.70	20.19
3,000	42.61	35.53	32.52	31.05	30.29
4,000	56.82	47.37	43.35	41.40	40.38
5,000	71.02	59.21	54.19	51.74	50.48
6,000	85.22	71.05	65.03	62.09	60.57
7,000	99.43	82.89	75.86	72.44	70.66
8,000	113.63	94.74	86.70	82.79	80.76
9,000	127.83	106.58	97.54	93.14	90.85
10,000	142.04	118.42	108.38	103.48	100.95
20,000	284.07	236.83	216.75	206.96	201.89
30,000	426.10	355.25	325.12	310.44	302.83
40,000	568.13	473.66	433.49	413.92	403.77
50,000	710.16	592.07	541.86	517.40	504.71
60,000	852.19	710.49	650.23	620.88	605.65
70,000	994.22	828.90	758.60	724.36	706.59
80,000	1136.25	947.31	866.97	827.84	807.53
90,000	1278.28	1065.73	975.34	931.32	908.47
100,000	1420.31	1184.14	1083.71	1034.80	1009.42
110,000	1562.34	1302.55	1192.09	1138.28	1110.36
120,000	1704.37	1420.97	1300.46	1241.76	1211.30
130,000	1846.40	1539.38	1408.83	1345.24	1312.24
140,000	1988.43	1657.79	1517.20	1448.72	1413.18
150,000	2130.46	1776.21	1625.57	1552.20	1514.12
160,000	2272.49	1894.62	1733.94	1655.68	1615.06
170,000	2414.52	2013.04	1842.31	1759.16	1716.00
180,000	2556.55	2131.45	1950.68	1862.64	1816.94
190,000	2698.58	2249.86	2059.05	1966.12	1917.89
200,000	2840.61	2368.28	2167.42	2069.60	2018.83
250,000	3550.76	2960.34	2709.28	2587.00	2523.53
300,000	4260.91	3552.41	3251.13	3104.40	3028.24

MONTHLY PAYMENTS
ANNUAL INTEREST RATE: 12%

LOAN AMOUNT	LOAN MATURITY (YEARS)				
	10	15	20	25	30
50	0.72	0.61	0.56	0.53	0.52
100	1.44	1.21	1.11	1.06	1.03
200	2.87	2.41	2.21	2.11	2.06
300	4.31	3.61	3.31	3.16	3.09
400	5.74	4.81	4.41	4.22	4.12
500	7.18	6.01	5.51	5.27	5.15
600	8.61	7.21	6.61	6.32	6.18
700	10.05	8.41	7.71	7.38	7.21
800	11.48	9.61	8.81	8.43	8.23
900	12.92	10.81	9.91	9.48	9.26
1,000	14.35	12.01	11.02	10.54	10.29
2,000	28.70	24.01	22.03	21.07	20.58
3,000	43.05	36.01	33.04	31.60	30.86
4,000	57.39	48.01	44.05	42.13	41.15
5,000	71.74	60.01	55.06	52.67	51.44
6,000	86.09	72.02	66.07	63.20	61.72
7,000	100.43	84.02	77.08	73.73	72.01
8,000	114.78	96.02	88.09	84.26	82.29
9,000	129.13	108.02	99.10	94.80	92.58
10,000	143.48	120.02	110.11	105.33	102.87
20,000	286.95	240.04	220.22	210.65	205.73
30,000	430.42	360.06	330.33	315.97	308.59
40,000	573.89	480.07	440.44	421.29	411.45
50,000	717.36	600.09	550.55	526.62	514.31
60,000	860.83	720.11	660.66	631.94	617.17
70,000	1004.30	840.12	770.77	737.26	720.03
80,000	1147.77	960.14	880.87	842.58	822.90
90,000	1291.24	1080.16	990.98	947.91	925.76
100,000	1434.71	1200.17	1101.09	1053.23	1028.62
110,000	1578.19	1320.19	1211.20	1158.55	1131.48
120,000	1721.66	1440.21	1321.31	1263.87	1234.34
130,000	1865.13	1560.22	1431.42	1369.20	1337.20
140,000	2008.60	1680.24	1541.53	1474.52	1440.06
150,000	2152.07	1800.26	1651.63	1579.84	1542.92
160,000	2295.54	1920.27	1761.74	1685.16	1645.79
170,000	2439.01	2040.29	1871.85	1790.49	1748.65
180,000	2582.48	2160.31	1981.96	1895.81	1851.51
190,000	2725.95	2280.32	2092.07	2001.13	1954.37
200,000	2869.42	2400.34	2202.18	2106.45	2057.23
250,000	3586.78	3000.43	2752.72	2633.07	2571.54
300,000	4304.13	3600.51	3303.26	3159.68	3085.84

MONTHLY PAYMENTS
ANNUAL INTEREST RATE: 12.25%

LOAN AMOUNT	LOAN MATURITY (YEARS)				
	10	15	20	25	30
50	0.73	0.61	0.56	0.54	0.53
100	1.45	1.22	1.12	1.08	1.05
200	2.90	2.44	2.24	2.15	2.10
300	4.35	3.65	3.36	3.22	3.15
400	5.80	4.87	4.48	4.29	4.20
500	7.25	6.09	5.60	5.36	5.24
600	8.70	7.30	6.72	6.44	6.29
700	10.15	8.52	7.83	7.51	7.34
800	11.60	9.74	8.95	8.58	8.39
900	13.05	10.95	10.07	9.65	9.44
1,000	14.50	12.17	11.19	10.72	10.48
2,000	28.99	24.33	22.38	21.44	20.96
3,000	43.48	36.49	33.56	32.16	31.44
4,000	57.97	48.66	44.75	42.87	41.92
5,000	72.46	60.82	55.93	53.59	52.40
6,000	86.96	72.98	67.12	64.31	62.88
7,000	101.45	85.15	78.30	75.03	73.36
8,000	115.94	97.31	89.49	85.74	83.84
9,000	130.43	109.47	100.68	96.46	94.32
10,000	144.92	121.63	111.86	107.18	104.79
20,000	289.84	243.26	223.72	214.35	209.58
30,000	434.76	364.89	335.57	321.53	314.37
40,000	579.68	486.52	447.43	428.70	419.16
50,000	724.60	608.15	559.29	535.88	523.95
60,000	869.52	729.78	671.14	643.05	628.74
70,000	1014.44	851.41	783.00	750.23	733.53
80,000	1159.36	973.04	894.86	857.40	838.32
90,000	1304.28	1094.67	1006.71	964.57	943.11
100,000	1449.20	1216.30	1118.57	1071.75	1047.90
110,000	1594.12	1337.93	1230.43	1178.92	1152.69
120,000	1739.04	1459.56	1342.28	1286.10	1257.48
130,000	1883.96	1581.19	1454.14	1393.27	1362.27
140,000	2028.88	1702.82	1566.00	1500.45	1467.06
150,000	2173.80	1824.45	1677.85	1607.62	1571.85
160,000	2318.72	1946.08	1789.71	1714.80	1676.64
170,000	2463.64	2067.71	1901.57	1821.97	1781.43
180,000	2608.56	2189.34	2013.42	1929.14	1886.22
190,000	2753.48	2310.97	2125.28	2036.32	1991.01
200,000	2898.40	2432.60	2237.13	2143.49	2095.80
250,000	3623.00	3040.75	2796.42	2679.36	2619.75
300,000	4347.60	3648.90	3355.70	3215.24	3143.69

434

MONTHLY PAYMENTS
ANNUAL INTEREST RATE: 12.5%

LOAN AMOUNT	\-	\-	LOAN MATURITY (YEARS)	\-	\-
	10	15	20	25	30
50	0.74	0.62	0.57	0.55	0.54
100	1.47	1.24	1.14	1.10	1.07
200	2.93	2.47	2.28	2.19	2.14
300	4.40	3.70	3.41	3.28	3.21
400	5.86	4.94	4.55	4.37	4.27
500	7.32	6.17	5.69	5.46	5.34
600	8.79	7.40	6.82	6.55	6.41
700	10.25	8.63	7.96	7.64	7.48
800	11.72	9.87	9.09	8.73	8.54
900	13.18	11.10	10.23	9.82	9.61
1,000	14.64	12.33	11.37	10.91	10.68
2,000	29.28	24.66	22.73	21.81	21.35
3,000	43.92	36.98	34.09	32.72	32.02
4,000	58.56	49.31	45.45	43.62	42.70
5,000	73.19	61.63	56.81	54.52	53.37
6,000	87.83	73.96	68.17	65.43	64.04
7,000	102.47	86.28	79.53	76.33	74.71
8,000	117.11	98.61	90.90	87.23	85.39
9,000	131.74	110.93	102.26	98.14	96.06
10,000	146.38	123.26	113.62	109.04	106.73
20,000	292.76	246.51	227.23	218.08	213.46
30,000	439.13	369.76	340.85	327.11	320.18
40,000	585.51	493.01	454.46	436.15	426.91
50,000	731.89	616.27	568.08	545.18	533.63
60,000	878.26	739.52	681.69	654.22	640.36
70,000	1024.64	862.77	795.30	763.25	747.09
80,000	1171.02	986.02	908.92	872.29	853.81
90,000	1317.39	1109.28	1022.53	981.32	960.54
100,000	1463.77	1232.53	1136.15	1090.36	1067.26
110,000	1610.15	1355.78	1249.76	1199.40	1173.99
120,000	1756.52	1479.03	1363.38	1308.43	1280.72
130,000	1902.90	1602.29	1476.99	1417.47	1387.44
140,000	2049.28	1725.54	1590.60	1526.50	1494.17
150,000	2195.65	1848.79	1704.22	1635.54	1600.89
160,000	2342.03	1972.04	1817.83	1744.57	1707.62
170,000	2488.41	2095.30	1931.45	1853.61	1814.34
180,000	2634.78	2218.55	2045.06	1962.64	1921.07
190,000	2781.16	2341.80	2158.67	2071.68	2027.80
200,000	2927.54	2465.05	2272.29	2180.71	2134.52
250,000	3659.42	3081.32	2840.36	2725.89	2668.15
300,000	4391.30	3697.58	3408.43	3271.07	3201.78

MONTHLY PAYMENTS
ANNUAL INTEREST RATE: 12.75%

LOAN AMOUNT	LOAN MATURITY (YEARS)				
	10	15	20	25	30
50	0.74	0.63	0.58	0.56	0.55
100	1.48	1.25	1.16	1.11	1.09
200	2.96	2.50	2.31	2.22	2.18
300	4.44	3.75	3.47	3.33	3.27
400	5.92	5.00	4.62	4.44	4.35
500	7.40	6.25	5.77	5.55	5.44
600	8.88	7.50	6.93	6.66	6.53
700	10.35	8.75	8.08	7.77	7.61
800	11.83	10.00	9.24	8.88	8.70
900	13.31	11.24	10.39	9.99	9.79
1,000	14.79	12.49	11.54	11.10	10.87
2,000	29.57	24.98	23.08	22.19	21.74
3,000	44.36	37.47	34.62	33.28	32.61
4,000	59.14	49.96	46.16	44.37	43.47
5,000	73.92	62.45	57.70	55.46	54.34
6,000	88.71	74.94	69.23	66.55	65.21
7,000	103.49	87.42	80.77	77.64	76.07
8,000	118.28	99.91	92.31	88.73	86.94
9,000	133.06	112.40	103.85	99.82	97.81
10,000	147.84	124.89	115.39	110.91	108.67
20,000	295.68	249.77	230.77	221.82	217.34
30,000	443.52	374.66	346.15	332.72	326.01
40,000	591.36	499.54	461.53	443.63	434.68
50,000	739.20	624.42	576.91	554.53	543.35
60,000	887.04	749.31	692.29	665.44	652.02
70,000	1034.88	874.19	807.67	776.34	760.69
80,000	1182.72	999.07	923.05	887.25	869.36
90,000	1330.56	1123.96	1038.44	998.15	978.03
100,000	1478.40	1248.84	1153.82	1109.06	1086.70
110,000	1626.24	1373.73	1269.20	1219.96	1195.37
120,000	1774.08	1498.61	1384.58	1330.87	1304.04
130,000	1921.92	1623.49	1499.96	1441.77	1412.71
140,000	2069.76	1748.38	1615.34	1552.68	1521.38
150,000	2217.60	1873.26	1730.72	1663.58	1630.04
160,000	2365.44	1998.14	1846.10	1774.49	1738.71
170,000	2513.28	2123.03	1961.49	1885.39	1847.38
180,000	2661.12	2247.91	2076.87	1996.30	1956.05
190,000	2808.96	2372.80	2192.25	2107.20	2064.72
200,000	2956.80	2497.68	2307.63	2218.11	2173.39
250,000	3696.00	3122.10	2884.53	2772.64	2716.74
300,000	4435.20	3746.52	3461.44	3327.16	3260.08

MONTHLY PAYMENTS
ANNUAL INTEREST RATE: 13%

LOAN AMOUNT	10	15	20	25	30
		LOAN MATURITY (YEARS)			
50	0.75	0.64	0.59	0.57	0.56
100	1.50	1.27	1.18	1.13	1.11
200	2.99	2.54	2.35	2.26	2.22
300	4.48	3.80	3.52	3.39	3.32
400	5.98	5.07	4.69	4.52	4.43
500	7.47	6.33	5.86	5.64	5.54
600	8.96	7.60	7.03	6.77	6.64
700	10.46	8.86	8.21	7.90	7.75
800	11.95	10.13	9.38	9.03	8.85
900	13.44	11.39	10.55	10.16	9.96
1,000	14.94	12.66	11.72	11.28	11.07
2,000	29.87	25.31	23.44	22.56	22.13
3,000	44.80	37.96	35.15	33.84	33.19
4,000	59.73	50.61	46.87	45.12	44.25
5,000	74.66	63.27	58.58	56.40	55.31
6,000	89.59	75.92	70.30	67.68	66.38
7,000	104.52	88.57	82.02	78.95	77.44
8,000	119.45	101.22	93.73	90.23	88.50
9,000	134.38	113.88	105.45	101.51	99.56
10,000	149.32	126.53	117.16	112.79	110.62
20,000	298.63	253.05	234.32	225.57	221.24
30,000	447.94	379.58	351.48	338.36	331.86
40,000	597.25	506.10	468.64	451.14	442.48
50,000	746.56	632.63	585.79	563.92	553.10
60,000	895.87	759.15	702.95	676.71	663.72
70,000	1045.18	885.67	820.11	789.49	774.34
80,000	1194.49	1012.20	937.27	902.27	884.96
90,000	1343.80	1138.72	1054.42	1015.06	995.58
100,000	1493.11	1265.25	1171.58	1127.84	1106.20
110,000	1642.42	1391.77	1288.74	1240.62	1216.82
120,000	1791.73	1518.29	1405.90	1353.41	1327.44
130,000	1941.04	1644.82	1523.05	1466.19	1438.06
140,000	2090.35	1771.34	1640.21	1578.97	1548.68
150,000	2239.66	1897.87	1757.37	1691.76	1659.30
160,000	2388.97	2024.39	1874.53	1804.54	1769.92
170,000	2538.28	2150.91	1991.68	1917.32	1880.54
180,000	2687.59	2277.44	2108.84	2030.11	1991.16
190,000	2836.91	2403.96	2226.00	2142.89	2101.78
200,000	2986.22	2530.49	2343.15	2255.67	2212.40
250,000	3732.77	3163.11	2928.94	2819.59	2765.50
300,000	4479.32	3795.73	3514.73	3383.51	3318.60

437

MONTHLY PAYMENTS
ANNUAL INTEREST RATE: 13.25%

LOAN	LOAN MATURITY (YEARS)				
AMOUNT	10	15	20	25	30
50	0.76	0.65	0.60	0.58	0.57
100	1.51	1.29	1.19	1.15	1.13
200	3.02	2.57	2.38	2.30	2.26
300	4.53	3.85	3.57	3.45	3.38
400	6.04	5.13	4.76	4.59	4.51
500	7.54	6.41	5.95	5.74	5.63
600	9.05	7.70	7.14	6.89	6.76
700	10.56	8.98	8.33	8.03	7.89
800	12.07	10.26	9.52	9.18	9.01
900	13.58	11.54	10.71	10.33	10.14
1,000	15.08	12.82	11.90	11.47	11.26
2,000	30.16	25.64	23.79	22.94	22.52
3,000	45.24	38.46	35.69	34.41	33.78
4,000	60.32	51.27	47.58	45.87	45.04
5,000	75.40	64.09	59.48	57.34	56.29
6,000	90.48	76.91	71.37	68.81	67.55
7,000	105.56	89.73	83.27	80.27	78.81
8,000	120.64	102.54	95.16	91.74	90.07
9,000	135.72	115.36	107.05	103.21	101.32
10,000	150.79	128.18	118.95	114.68	112.58
20,000	301.58	256.35	237.89	229.35	225.16
30,000	452.37	384.53	356.83	344.02	337.74
40,000	603.16	512.70	475.78	458.69	450.31
50,000	753.95	640.87	594.72	573.36	562.89
60,000	904.74	769.05	713.66	688.03	675.47
70,000	1055.53	897.22	832.61	802.70	788.05
80,000	1206.32	1025.39	951.55	917.37	900.62
90,000	1357.11	1153.57	1070.49	1032.04	1013.20
100,000	1507.90	1281.74	1189.44	1146.71	1125.78
110,000	1658.68	1409.92	1308.38	1261.38	1238.36
120,000	1809.47	1538.09	1427.32	1376.05	1350.93
130,000	1960.26	1666.26	1546.27	1490.72	1463.51
140,000	2111.05	1794.44	1665.21	1605.39	1576.09
150,000	2261.84	1922.61	1784.15	1720.06	1688.67
160,000	2412.63	2050.78	1903.09	1834.73	1801.24
170,000	2563.42	2178.96	2022.04	1949.40	1913.82
180,000	2714.21	2307.13	2140.98	2064.07	2026.40
190,000	2865.00	2435.31	2259.92	2178.74	2138.97
200,000	3015.79	2563.48	2378.87	2293.41	2251.55
250,000	3769.73	3204.35	2973.58	2866.76	2814.44
300,000	4523.68	3845.22	3568.30	3440.11	3377.33

MONTHLY PAYMENTS
ANNUAL INTEREST RATE: 13.5%

LOAN AMOUNT	LOAN MATURITY (YEARS)				
	10	15	20	25	30
50	0.77	0.65	0.61	0.59	0.58
100	1.53	1.30	1.21	1.17	1.15
200	3.05	2.60	2.42	2.34	2.30
300	4.57	3.90	3.63	3.50	3.44
400	6.10	5.20	4.83	4.67	4.59
500	7.62	6.50	6.04	5.83	5.73
600	9.14	7.79	7.25	7.00	6.88
700	10.66	9.09	8.46	8.16	8.02
800	12.19	10.39	9.66	9.33	9.17
900	13.71	11.69	10.87	10.50	10.31
1,000	15.23	12.99	12.08	11.66	11.46
2,000	30.46	25.97	24.15	23.32	22.91
3,000	45.69	38.95	36.23	34.97	34.37
4,000	60.91	51.94	48.30	46.63	45.82
5,000	76.14	64.92	60.37	58.29	57.28
6,000	91.37	77.90	72.45	69.94	68.73
7,000	106.60	90.89	84.52	81.60	80.18
8,000	121.82	103.87	96.59	93.26	91.64
9,000	137.05	116.85	108.67	104.91	103.09
10,000	152.28	129.84	120.74	116.57	114.55
20,000	304.55	259.67	241.48	233.13	229.09
30,000	456.83	389.50	362.22	349.70	343.63
40,000	609.10	519.33	482.95	466.26	458.17
50,000	761.37	649.16	603.69	582.83	572.71
60,000	913.65	778.99	724.43	699.39	687.25
70,000	1065.92	908.83	845.17	815.96	801.79
80,000	1218.20	1038.66	965.90	932.52	916.33
90,000	1370.47	1168.49	1086.64	1049.08	1030.88
100,000	1522.74	1298.32	1207.38	1165.65	1145.42
110,000	1675.02	1428.15	1328.12	1282.21	1259.96
120,000	1827.29	1557.98	1448.85	1398.78	1374.50
130,000	1979.57	1687.82	1569.59	1515.34	1489.04
140,000	2131.84	1817.65	1690.33	1631.91	1603.58
150,000	2284.11	1947.48	1811.07	1748.47	1718.12
160,000	2436.39	2077.31	1931.80	1865.04	1832.66
170,000	2588.66	2207.14	2052.54	1981.60	1947.21
180,000	2740.94	2336.97	2173.28	2098.16	2061.75
190,000	2893.21	2466.81	2294.01	2214.73	2176.29
200,000	3045.48	2596.64	2414.75	2331.29	2290.83
250,000	3806.85	3245.80	3018.44	2914.12	2863.53
300,000	4568.22	3894.95	3622.13	3496.94	3436.24

MONTHLY PAYMENTS
ANNUAL INTEREST RATE: 13.75%

LOAN AMOUNT	LOAN MATURITY (YEARS)				
	10	15	20	25	30
50	0.77	0.66	0.62	0.60	0.59
100	1.54	1.32	1.23	1.19	1.17
200	3.08	2.63	2.46	2.37	2.34
300	4.62	3.95	3.68	3.56	3.50
400	6.16	5.26	4.91	4.74	4.67
500	7.69	6.58	6.13	5.93	5.83
600	9.23	7.89	7.36	7.11	7.00
700	10.77	9.21	8.58	8.30	8.16
800	12.31	10.52	9.81	9.48	9.33
900	13.84	11.84	11.03	10.67	10.49
1,000	15.38	13.15	12.26	11.85	11.66
2,000	30.76	26.30	24.51	23.70	23.31
3,000	46.14	39.45	36.77	35.55	34.96
4,000	61.51	52.60	49.02	47.39	46.61
5,000	76.89	65.75	61.28	59.24	58.26
6,000	92.27	78.90	73.53	71.09	69.91
7,000	107.64	92.05	85.78	82.93	81.56
8,000	123.02	105.20	98.04	94.78	93.21
9,000	138.40	118.35	110.29	106.63	104.87
10,000	153.77	131.50	122.55	118.47	116.52
20,000	307.54	263.00	245.09	236.94	233.03
30,000	461.31	394.50	367.63	355.41	349.54
40,000	615.07	526.00	490.17	473.87	466.05
50,000	768.84	657.50	612.71	592.34	582.56
60,000	922.61	789.00	735.25	710.81	699.07
70,000	1076.38	920.50	857.79	829.27	815.58
80,000	1230.14	1052.00	980.33	947.74	932.10
90,000	1383.91	1183.50	1102.87	1066.21	1048.61
100,000	1537.68	1315.00	1225.41	1184.67	1165.12
110,000	1691.45	1446.49	1347.95	1303.14	1281.63
120,000	1845.21	1577.99	1470.49	1421.61	1398.14
130,000	1998.98	1709.49	1593.03	1540.07	1514.65
140,000	2152.75	1840.99	1715.58	1658.54	1631.16
150,000	2306.52	1972.49	1838.12	1777.01	1747.67
160,000	2460.28	2103.99	1960.66	1895.47	1864.19
170,000	2614.05	2235.49	2083.20	2013.94	1980.70
180,000	2767.82	2366.99	2205.74	2132.41	2097.21
190,000	2921.58	2498.49	2328.28	2250.87	2213.72
200,000	3075.35	2629.99	2450.82	2369.34	2330.23
250,000	3844.19	3287.48	3063.52	2961.67	2912.79
300,000	4613.03	3944.98	3676.23	3554.01	3495.34

440

MONTHLY PAYMENTS
ANNUAL INTEREST RATE: 14%

LOAN AMOUNT	LOAN MATURITY (YEARS)				
	10	15	20	25	30
50	0.78	0.67	0.63	0.61	0.60
100	1.56	1.34	1.25	1.21	1.19
200	3.11	2.67	2.49	2.41	2.37
300	4.66	4.00	3.74	3.62	3.56
400	6.22	5.33	4.98	4.82	4.74
500	7.77	6.66	6.22	6.02	5.93
600	9.32	8.00	7.47	7.23	7.11
700	10.87	9.33	8.71	8.43	8.30
800	12.43	10.66	9.95	9.64	9.48
900	13.98	11.99	11.20	10.84	10.67
1,000	15.53	13.32	12.44	12.04	11.85
2,000	31.06	26.64	24.88	24.08	23.70
3,000	46.58	39.96	37.31	36.12	35.55
4,000	62.11	53.27	49.75	48.16	47.40
5,000	77.64	66.59	62.18	60.19	59.25
6,000	93.16	79.91	74.62	72.23	71.10
7,000	108.69	93.23	87.05	84.27	82.95
8,000	124.22	106.54	99.49	96.31	94.79
9,000	139.74	119.86	111.92	108.34	106.64
10,000	155.27	133.18	124.36	120.38	118.49
20,000	310.54	266.35	248.71	240.76	236.98
30,000	465.80	399.53	373.06	361.13	355.47
40,000	621.07	532.70	497.41	481.51	473.95
50,000	776.34	665.88	621.77	601.89	592.44
60,000	931.60	799.05	746.12	722.26	710.93
70,000	1086.87	932.22	870.47	842.64	829.42
80,000	1242.14	1065.40	994.82	963.01	947.90
90,000	1397.40	1198.57	1119.17	1083.39	1066.39
100,000	1552.67	1331.75	1243.53	1203.77	1184.88
110,000	1707.94	1464.92	1367.88	1324.14	1303.36
120,000	1863.20	1598.10	1492.23	1444.52	1421.85
130,000	2018.47	1731.27	1616.58	1564.89	1540.34
140,000	2173.74	1864.44	1740.93	1685.27	1658.83
150,000	2329.00	1997.62	1865.29	1805.65	1777.31
160,000	2484.27	2130.79	1989.64	1926.02	1895.80
170,000	2639.54	2263.97	2113.99	2046.40	2014.29
180,000	2794.80	2397.14	2238.34	2166.78	2132.77
190,000	2950.07	2530.32	2362.70	2287.15	2251.26
200,000	3105.34	2663.49	2487.05	2407.53	2369.75
250,000	3881.67	3329.36	3108.81	3009.41	2962.18
300,000	4658.00	3995.23	3730.57	3611.29	3554.62

441

MONTHLY PAYMENTS
ANNUAL INTEREST RATE: 14.25%

LOAN AMOUNT	LOAN MATURITY (YEARS)				
	10	15	20	25	30
50	0.79	0.68	0.64	0.62	0.61
100	1.57	1.35	1.27	1.23	1.21
200	3.14	2.70	2.53	2.45	2.41
300	4.71	4.05	3.79	3.67	3.62
400	6.28	5.40	5.05	4.90	4.82
500	7.84	6.75	6.31	6.12	6.03
600	9.41	8.10	7.58	7.34	7.23
700	10.98	9.45	8.84	8.57	8.44
800	12.55	10.79	10.10	9.79	9.64
900	14.11	12.14	11.36	11.01	10.85
1,000	15.68	13.49	12.62	12.23	12.05
2,000	31.36	26.98	25.24	24.46	24.10
3,000	47.04	40.46	37.86	36.69	36.15
4,000	62.71	53.95	50.47	48.92	48.19
5,000	78.39	67.43	63.09	61.15	60.24
6,000	94.07	80.92	75.71	73.38	72.29
7,000	109.75	94.41	88.33	85.61	84.33
8,000	125.42	107.89	100.94	97.84	96.38
9,000	141.10	121.38	113.56	110.07	108.43
10,000	156.78	134.86	126.18	122.30	120.47
20,000	313.55	269.72	252.35	244.59	240.94
30,000	470.32	404.58	378.52	366.88	361.41
40,000	627.10	539.44	504.69	489.18	481.88
50,000	783.87	674.29	630.86	611.47	602.35
60,000	940.64	809.15	757.04	733.76	722.82
70,000	1097.42	944.01	883.21	856.05	843.29
80,000	1254.19	1078.87	1009.38	978.35	963.75
90,000	1410.96	1213.73	1135.55	1100.64	1084.22
100,000	1567.73	1348.58	1261.72	1222.93	1204.69
110,000	1724.51	1483.44	1387.90	1345.22	1325.16
120,000	1881.28	1618.30	1514.07	1467.52	1445.63
130,000	2038.05	1753.16	1640.24	1589.81	1566.10
140,000	2194.83	1888.01	1766.41	1712.10	1686.57
150,000	2351.60	2022.87	1892.58	1834.40	1807.04
160,000	2508.37	2157.73	2018.75	1956.69	1927.50
170,000	2665.14	2292.59	2144.93	2078.98	2047.97
180,000	2821.92	2427.45	2271.10	2201.27	2168.44
190,000	2978.69	2562.30	2397.27	2323.57	2288.91
200,000	3135.46	2697.16	2523.44	2445.86	2409.38
250,000	3919.33	3371.45	3154.30	3057.32	3011.72
300,000	4703.19	4045.74	3785.16	3668.79	3614.07

MONTHLY PAYMENTS
ANNUAL INTEREST RATE: 14.5%

LOAN AMOUNT	LOAN MATURITY (YEARS)				
	10	15	20	25	30
50	0.80	0.69	0.64	0.63	0.62
100	1.59	1.37	1.28	1.25	1.23
200	3.17	2.74	2.56	2.49	2.45
300	4.75	4.10	3.84	3.73	3.68
400	6.34	5.47	5.12	4.97	4.90
500	7.92	6.83	6.40	6.22	6.13
600	9.50	8.20	7.68	7.46	7.35
700	11.09	9.56	8.96	8.70	8.58
800	12.67	10.93	10.24	9.94	9.80
900	14.25	12.29	11.52	11.18	11.03
1,000	15.83	13.66	12.80	12.43	12.25
2,000	31.66	27.32	25.60	24.85	24.50
3,000	47.49	40.97	38.40	37.27	36.74
4,000	63.32	54.63	51.20	49.69	48.99
5,000	79.15	68.28	64.00	62.11	61.23
6,000	94.98	81.94	76.80	74.53	73.48
7,000	110.81	95.59	89.60	86.96	85.72
8,000	126.63	109.25	102.40	99.38	97.97
9,000	142.46	122.90	115.20	111.80	110.22
10,000	158.29	136.56	128.00	124.22	122.46
20,000	316.58	273.11	256.00	248.44	244.92
30,000	474.87	409.66	384.00	372.65	367.37
40,000	633.15	546.21	512.00	496.87	489.83
50,000	791.44	682.76	640.00	621.09	612.28
60,000	949.73	819.31	768.00	745.30	734.74
70,000	1108.01	955.86	896.00	869.52	857.19
80,000	1266.30	1092.41	1024.00	993.74	979.65
90,000	1424.59	1228.96	1152.00	1117.95	1102.11
100,000	1582.88	1365.51	1280.00	1242.17	1224.56
110,000	1741.16	1502.06	1408.00	1366.38	1347.02
120,000	1899.45	1638.61	1536.00	1490.60	1469.47
130,000	2057.74	1775.16	1664.00	1614.82	1591.93
140,000	2216.02	1911.71	1792.00	1739.03	1714.38
150,000	2374.31	2048.26	1920.00	1863.25	1836.84
160,000	2532.60	2184.81	2048.00	1987.47	1959.29
170,000	2690.88	2321.36	2176.00	2111.68	2081.75
180,000	2849.17	2457.91	2304.00	2235.90	2204.21
190,000	3007.46	2594.46	2432.00	2360.12	2326.66
200,000	3165.75	2731.01	2560.00	2484.33	2449.12
250,000	3957.18	3413.76	3200.00	3105.41	3061.40
300,000	4748.62	4096.51	3840.00	3726.50	3673.67

443

MONTHLY PAYMENTS
ANNUAL INTEREST RATE: 14.75%

LOAN AMOUNT	LOAN MATURITY (YEARS)				
	10	15	20	25	30
50	0.80	0.70	0.65	0.64	0.63
100	1.60	1.39	1.30	1.27	1.25
200	3.20	2.77	2.60	2.53	2.49
300	4.80	4.15	3.90	3.79	3.74
400	6.40	5.54	5.20	5.05	4.98
500	8.00	6.92	6.50	6.31	6.23
600	9.59	8.30	7.80	7.57	7.47
700	11.19	9.68	9.09	8.84	8.72
800	12.79	11.07	10.39	10.10	9.96
900	14.39	12.45	11.69	11.36	11.21
1,000	15.99	13.83	12.99	12.62	12.45
2,000	31.97	27.66	25.97	25.23	24.89
3,000	47.95	41.48	38.96	37.85	37.34
4,000	63.93	55.31	51.94	50.46	49.78
5,000	79.91	69.13	64.92	63.08	62.23
6,000	95.89	82.96	77.91	75.69	74.67
7,000	111.87	96.78	90.89	88.31	87.12
8,000	127.85	110.61	103.87	100.92	99.56
9,000	143.83	124.43	116.86	113.54	112.01
10,000	159.81	138.26	129.84	126.15	124.45
20,000	319.62	276.51	259.68	252.30	248.90
30,000	479.43	414.76	389.51	378.44	373.35
40,000	639.24	553.01	519.35	504.59	497.80
50,000	799.04	691.26	649.18	630.74	622.24
60,000	958.85	829.51	779.02	756.88	746.69
70,000	1118.66	967.76	908.85	883.03	871.14
80,000	1278.47	1106.01	1038.69	1009.18	995.59
90,000	1438.27	1244.26	1168.53	1135.32	1120.03
100,000	1598.08	1382.51	1298.36	1261.47	1244.48
110,000	1757.89	1520.76	1428.20	1387.62	1368.93
120,000	1917.70	1659.01	1558.03	1513.76	1493.38
130,000	2077.50	1797.26	1687.87	1639.91	1617.82
140,000	2237.31	1935.51	1817.70	1766.06	1742.27
150,000	2397.12	2073.76	1947.54	1892.20	1866.72
160,000	2556.93	2212.01	2077.37	2018.35	1991.17
170,000	2716.73	2350.26	2207.21	2144.50	2115.61
180,000	2876.54	2488.51	2337.05	2270.64	2240.06
190,000	3036.35	2626.76	2466.88	2396.79	2364.51
200,000	3196.16	2765.01	2596.72	2522.93	2488.96
250,000	3995.19	3456.27	3245.89	3153.67	3111.19
300,000	4794.23	4147.52	3895.07	3784.40	3733.43

MONTHLY PAYMENTS
ANNUAL INTEREST RATE: 15%

LOAN AMOUNT	LOAN MATURITY (YEARS)				
	10	15	20	25	30
50	0.81	0.70	0.66	0.65	0.64
100	1.62	1.40	1.32	1.29	1.27
200	3.23	2.80	2.64	2.57	2.53
300	4.85	4.20	3.96	3.85	3.80
400	6.46	5.60	5.27	5.13	5.06
500	8.07	7.00	6.59	6.41	6.33
600	9.69	8.40	7.91	7.69	7.59
700	11.30	9.80	9.22	8.97	8.86
800	12.91	11.20	10.54	10.25	10.12
900	14.53	12.60	11.86	11.53	11.38
1,000	16.14	14.00	13.17	12.81	12.65
2,000	32.27	28.00	26.34	25.62	25.29
3,000	48.41	41.99	39.51	38.43	37.94
4,000	64.54	55.99	52.68	51.24	50.58
5,000	80.67	69.98	65.84	64.05	63.23
6,000	96.81	83.98	79.01	76.85	75.87
7,000	112.94	97.98	92.18	89.66	88.52
8,000	129.07	111.97	105.35	102.47	101.16
9,000	145.21	125.97	118.52	115.28	113.80
10,000	161.34	139.96	131.68	128.09	126.45
20,000	322.67	279.92	263.36	256.17	252.89
30,000	484.01	419.88	395.04	384.25	379.34
40,000	645.34	559.84	526.72	512.34	505.78
50,000	806.68	699.80	658.40	640.42	632.23
60,000	968.01	839.76	790.08	768.50	758.67
70,000	1129.35	979.71	921.76	896.59	885.12
80,000	1290.68	1119.67	1053.44	1024.67	1011.56
90,000	1452.02	1259.63	1185.11	1152.75	1138.00
100,000	1613.35	1399.59	1316.79	1280.84	1264.45
110,000	1774.69	1539.55	1448.47	1408.92	1390.89
120,000	1936.02	1679.51	1580.15	1537.00	1517.34
130,000	2097.35	1819.47	1711.83	1665.08	1643.78
140,000	2258.69	1959.42	1843.51	1793.17	1770.23
150,000	2420.02	2099.38	1975.19	1921.25	1896.67
160,000	2581.36	2239.34	2106.87	2049.33	2023.12
170,000	2742.69	2379.30	2238.55	2177.42	2149.56
180,000	2904.03	2519.26	2370.22	2305.50	2276.00
190,000	3065.36	2659.22	2501.90	2433.58	2402.45
200,000	3226.70	2799.18	2633.58	2561.66	2528.89
250,000	4033.37	3498.97	3291.98	3202.08	3161.11
300,000	4840.04	4198.76	3950.37	3842.49	3793.34

445

MONTHLY PAYMENTS
ANNUAL INTEREST RATE: 15.25%

LOAN AMOUNT	LOAN MATURITY (YEARS)				
	10	15	20	25	30
50	0.82	0.71	0.67	0.66	0.65
100	1.63	1.42	1.34	1.31	1.29
200	3.26	2.84	2.68	2.61	2.57
300	4.89	4.26	4.01	3.91	3.86
400	6.52	5.67	5.35	5.21	5.14
500	8.15	7.09	6.68	6.51	6.43
600	9.78	8.51	8.02	7.81	7.71
700	11.41	9.92	9.35	9.11	9.00
800	13.03	11.34	10.69	10.41	10.28
900	14.66	12.76	12.02	11.71	11.57
1,000	16.29	14.17	13.36	13.01	12.85
2,000	32.58	28.34	26.71	26.01	25.69
3,000	48.87	42.51	40.06	39.01	38.54
4,000	65.15	56.68	53.42	52.02	51.38
5,000	81.44	70.84	66.77	65.02	64.23
6,000	97.73	85.01	80.12	78.02	77.07
7,000	114.01	99.18	93.48	91.02	89.92
8,000	130.30	113.35	106.83	104.03	102.76
9,000	146.59	127.51	120.18	117.03	115.61
10,000	162.87	141.68	133.53	130.03	128.45
20,000	325.74	283.36	267.06	260.06	256.90
30,000	488.61	425.03	400.59	390.08	385.34
40,000	651.48	566.71	534.12	520.11	513.79
50,000	814.35	708.38	667.65	650.13	642.23
60,000	977.22	850.06	801.18	780.16	770.68
70,000	1140.09	991.73	934.71	910.19	899.13
80,000	1302.96	1133.41	1068.24	1040.21	1027.57
90,000	1465.83	1275.08	1201.77	1170.24	1156.02
100,000	1628.70	1416.76	1335.30	1300.26	1284.46
110,000	1791.57	1558.43	1468.83	1430.29	1412.91
120,000	1954.44	1700.11	1602.36	1560.32	1541.36
130,000	2117.31	1841.78	1735.89	1690.34	1669.80
140,000	2280.18	1983.46	1869.42	1820.37	1798.25
150,000	2443.05	2125.13	2002.95	1950.39	1926.69
160,000	2605.92	2266.81	2136.48	2080.42	2055.14
170,000	2768.79	2408.48	2270.01	2210.44	2183.58
180,000	2931.65	2550.16	2403.54	2340.47	2312.03
190,000	3094.52	2691.83	2537.07	2470.50	2440.48
200,000	3257.39	2833.51	2670.60	2600.52	2568.92
250,000	4071.74	3541.88	3338.25	3250.65	3211.15
300,000	4886.09	4250.26	4005.90	3900.78	3853.38

MONTHLY PAYMENTS
ANNUAL INTEREST RATE: 15.5%

LOAN AMOUNT	LOAN MATURITY (YEARS)				
	10	15	20	25	30
50	0.83	0.72	0.68	0.66	0.66
100	1.65	1.44	1.36	1.32	1.31
200	3.29	2.87	2.71	2.64	2.61
300	4.94	4.31	4.07	3.96	3.92
400	6.58	5.74	5.42	5.28	5.22
500	8.23	7.17	6.77	6.60	6.53
600	9.87	8.61	8.13	7.92	7.83
700	11.51	10.04	9.48	9.24	9.14
800	13.16	11.48	10.84	10.56	10.44
900	14.80	12.91	12.19	11.88	11.75
1,000	16.45	14.34	13.54	13.20	13.05
2,000	32.89	28.68	27.08	26.40	26.10
3,000	49.33	43.02	40.62	39.60	39.14
4,000	65.77	57.36	54.16	52.79	52.19
5,000	82.21	71.70	67.70	65.99	65.23
6,000	98.65	86.04	81.24	79.19	78.28
7,000	115.09	100.38	94.78	92.39	91.32
8,000	131.53	114.72	108.32	105.58	104.37
9,000	147.97	129.06	121.85	118.78	117.41
10,000	164.42	143.40	135.39	131.98	130.46
20,000	328.83	286.80	270.78	263.95	260.91
30,000	493.24	430.20	406.17	395.93	391.36
40,000	657.65	573.60	541.56	527.90	521.81
50,000	822.06	717.00	676.94	659.88	652.26
60,000	986.47	860.40	812.33	791.85	782.71
70,000	1150.88	1003.80	947.72	923.83	913.17
80,000	1315.29	1147.20	1083.11	1055.80	1043.62
90,000	1479.70	1290.60	1218.50	1187.78	1174.07
100,000	1644.11	1433.99	1353.88	1319.75	1304.52
110,000	1808.52	1577.39	1489.27	1451.72	1434.97
120,000	1972.93	1720.79	1624.66	1583.70	1565.42
130,000	2137.34	1864.19	1760.05	1715.67	1695.88
140,000	2301.75	2007.59	1895.44	1847.65	1826.33
150,000	2466.16	2150.99	2030.82	1979.62	1956.78
160,000	2630.57	2294.39	2166.21	2111.60	2087.23
170,000	2794.98	2437.79	2301.60	2243.57	2217.68
180,000	2959.39	2581.18	2436.99	2375.55	2348.13
190,000	3123.80	2724.58	2572.38	2507.52	2478.59
200,000	3288.21	2867.98	2707.76	2639.49	2609.04
250,000	4110.26	3584.98	3384.70	3299.37	3261.30
300,000	4932.31	4301.97	4061.64	3959.24	3913.56

MONTHLY PAYMENTS
ANNUAL INTEREST RATE: 15.75%

LOAN AMOUNT	LOAN MATURITY (YEARS)				
	10	15	20	25	30
50	0.83	0.73	0.69	0.67	0.67
100	1.66	1.46	1.38	1.34	1.33
200	3.32	2.91	2.75	2.68	2.65
300	4.98	4.36	4.12	4.02	3.98
400	6.64	5.81	5.50	5.36	5.30
500	8.30	7.26	6.87	6.70	6.63
600	9.96	8.71	8.24	8.04	7.95
700	11.62	10.16	9.61	9.38	9.28
800	13.28	11.62	10.99	10.72	10.60
900	14.94	13.07	12.36	12.06	11.93
1,000	16.60	14.52	13.73	13.40	13.25
2,000	33.20	29.03	27.46	26.79	26.50
3,000	49.79	43.54	41.18	40.18	39.74
4,000	66.39	58.06	54.91	53.58	52.99
5,000	82.98	72.57	68.63	66.97	66.24
6,000	99.58	87.08	82.36	80.36	79.48
7,000	116.18	101.60	96.08	93.76	92.73
8,000	132.77	116.11	109.81	107.15	105.97
9,000	149.37	130.62	123.53	120.54	119.22
10,000	165.96	145.14	137.26	133.93	132.47
20,000	331.92	290.27	274.51	267.86	264.93
30,000	497.88	435.40	411.77	401.79	397.39
40,000	663.84	580.53	549.02	535.72	529.85
50,000	829.80	725.66	686.27	669.65	662.31
60,000	995.76	870.79	823.53	803.58	794.78
70,000	1161.72	1015.92	960.78	937.51	927.24
80,000	1327.68	1161.05	1098.03	1071.44	1059.70
90,000	1493.63	1306.18	1235.29	1205.37	1192.16
100,000	1659.59	1451.31	1372.54	1339.30	1324.62
110,000	1825.55	1596.45	1509.79	1473.22	1457.08
120,000	1991.51	1741.58	1647.05	1607.15	1589.55
130,000	2157.47	1886.71	1784.30	1741.08	1722.01
140,000	2323.43	2031.84	1921.55	1875.01	1854.47
150,000	2489.39	2176.97	2058.81	2008.94	1986.93
160,000	2655.35	2322.10	2196.06	2142.87	2119.39
170,000	2821.31	2467.23	2333.31	2276.80	2251.85
180,000	2987.26	2612.36	2470.57	2410.73	2384.32
190,000	3153.22	2757.49	2607.82	2544.66	2516.78
200,000	3319.18	2902.62	2745.07	2678.59	2649.24
250,000	4148.98	3628.28	3431.34	3348.23	3311.55
300,000	4978.77	4353.93	4117.61	4017.88	3973.86

MONTHLY PAYMENTS
ANNUAL INTEREST RATE: 16%

LOAN AMOUNT	\multicolumn LOAN MATURITY (YEARS)				
	10	15	20	25	30
50	0.84	0.74	0.70	0.68	0.68
100	1.68	1.47	1.40	1.36	1.35
200	3.36	2.94	2.79	2.72	2.69
300	5.03	4.41	4.18	4.08	4.04
400	6.71	5.88	5.57	5.44	5.38
500	8.38	7.35	6.96	6.80	6.73
600	10.06	8.82	8.35	8.16	8.07
700	11.73	10.29	9.74	9.52	9.42
800	13.41	11.75	11.14	10.88	10.76
900	15.08	13.22	12.53	12.24	12.11
1,000	16.76	14.69	13.92	13.59	13.45
2,000	33.51	29.38	27.83	27.18	26.90
3,000	50.26	44.07	41.74	40.77	40.35
4,000	67.01	58.75	55.66	54.36	53.80
5,000	83.76	73.44	69.57	67.95	67.24
6,000	100.51	88.13	83.48	81.54	80.69
7,000	117.26	102.81	97.39	95.13	94.14
8,000	134.02	117.50	111.31	108.72	107.59
9,000	150.77	132.19	125.22	122.31	121.03
10,000	167.52	146.88	139.13	135.89	134.48
20,000	335.03	293.75	278.26	271.78	268.96
30,000	502.54	440.62	417.38	407.67	403.43
40,000	670.06	587.49	556.51	543.56	537.91
50,000	837.57	734.36	695.63	679.45	672.38
60,000	1005.08	881.23	834.76	815.34	806.86
70,000	1172.60	1028.10	973.88	951.23	941.34
80,000	1340.11	1174.97	1113.01	1087.12	1075.81
90,000	1507.62	1321.84	1252.14	1223.01	1210.29
100,000	1675.14	1468.71	1391.26	1358.89	1344.76
110,000	1842.65	1615.58	1530.39	1494.78	1479.24
120,000	2010.16	1762.45	1669.51	1630.67	1613.71
130,000	2177.68	1909.32	1808.64	1766.56	1748.19
140,000	2345.19	2056.19	1947.76	1902.45	1882.67
150,000	2512.70	2203.06	2086.89	2038.34	2017.14
160,000	2680.22	2349.93	2226.02	2174.23	2151.62
170,000	2847.73	2496.80	2365.14	2310.12	2286.09
180,000	3015.24	2643.67	2504.27	2446.01	2420.57
190,000	3182.76	2790.54	2643.39	2581.89	2555.04
200,000	3350.27	2937.41	2782.52	2717.78	2689.52
250,000	4187.84	3671.76	3478.15	3397.23	3361.90
300,000	5025.40	4406.11	4173.77	4076.67	4034.28

449

MONTHLY PAYMENTS
ANNUAL INTEREST RATE: 16.25%

LOAN AMOUNT	LOAN MATURITY (YEARS)				
	10	15	20	25	30
50	0.85	0.75	0.71	0.69	0.69
100	1.70	1.49	1.42	1.38	1.37
200	3.39	2.98	2.83	2.76	2.73
300	5.08	4.46	4.24	4.14	4.10
400	6.77	5.95	5.65	5.52	5.46
500	8.46	7.44	7.06	6.90	6.83
600	10.15	8.92	8.47	8.28	8.19
700	11.84	10.41	9.88	9.65	9.56
800	13.53	11.89	11.29	11.03	10.92
900	15.22	13.38	12.70	12.41	12.29
1,000	16.91	14.87	14.11	13.79	13.65
2,000	33.82	29.73	28.21	27.58	27.30
3,000	50.73	44.59	42.31	41.36	40.95
4,000	67.63	59.45	56.41	55.15	54.60
5,000	84.54	74.31	70.51	68.93	68.25
6,000	101.45	89.18	84.61	82.72	81.90
7,000	118.36	104.04	98.71	96.50	95.55
8,000	135.26	118.90	112.81	110.29	109.20
9,000	152.17	133.76	126.91	124.07	122.85
10,000	169.08	148.62	141.01	137.86	136.50
20,000	338.15	297.24	282.01	275.71	272.99
30,000	507.23	445.86	423.02	413.57	409.49
40,000	676.30	594.47	564.02	551.42	545.98
50,000	845.38	743.09	705.03	689.28	682.47
60,000	1014.45	891.71	846.03	827.13	818.97
70,000	1183.53	1040.32	987.04	964.98	955.46
80,000	1352.60	1188.94	1128.04	1102.84	1091.95
90,000	1521.67	1337.56	1269.05	1240.69	1228.45
100,000	1690.75	1486.17	1410.05	1378.55	1364.94
110,000	1859.82	1634.79	1551.05	1516.40	1501.43
120,000	2028.90	1783.41	1692.06	1654.25	1637.93
130,000	2197.97	1932.02	1833.06	1792.11	1774.42
140,000	2367.05	2080.64	1974.07	1929.96	1910.91
150,000	2536.12	2229.26	2115.07	2067.82	2047.41
160,000	2705.19	2377.87	2256.08	2205.67	2183.90
170,000	2874.27	2526.49	2397.08	2343.52	2320.39
180,000	3043.34	2675.11	2538.09	2481.38	2456.89
190,000	3212.42	2823.72	2679.09	2619.23	2593.38
200,000	3381.49	2972.34	2820.10	2757.09	2729.87
250,000	4226.86	3715.42	3525.12	3446.36	3412.34
300,000	5072.23	4458.51	4230.14	4135.63	4094.81

MONTHLY PAYMENTS
ANNUAL INTEREST RATE: 16.5%

LOAN AMOUNT	LOAN MATURITY (YEARS)				
	10	15	20	25	30
50	0.86	0.76	0.72	0.70	0.70
100	1.71	1.51	1.43	1.40	1.39
200	3.42	3.01	2.86	2.80	2.78
300	5.12	4.52	4.29	4.20	4.16
400	6.83	6.02	5.72	5.60	5.55
500	8.54	7.52	7.15	7.00	6.93
600	10.24	9.03	8.58	8.39	8.32
700	11.95	10.53	10.01	9.79	9.70
800	13.66	12.03	11.44	11.19	11.09
900	15.36	13.54	12.87	12.59	12.47
1,000	17.07	15.04	14.29	13.99	13.86
2,000	34.13	30.08	28.58	27.97	27.71
3,000	51.20	45.12	42.87	41.95	41.56
4,000	68.26	60.15	57.16	55.93	55.41
5,000	85.33	75.19	71.45	69.92	69.26
6,000	102.39	90.23	85.74	83.90	83.11
7,000	119.45	105.26	100.03	97.88	96.97
8,000	136.52	120.30	114.32	111.86	110.82
9,000	153.58	135.34	128.61	125.85	124.67
10,000	170.65	150.38	142.90	139.83	138.52
20,000	341.29	300.75	285.79	279.65	277.03
30,000	511.93	451.12	428.68	419.48	415.55
40,000	682.58	601.49	571.57	559.30	554.06
50,000	853.22	751.86	714.46	699.13	692.58
60,000	1023.86	902.23	857.35	838.95	831.09
70,000	1194.50	1052.60	1000.24	978.78	969.61
80,000	1365.15	1202.97	1143.13	1118.60	1108.12
90,000	1535.79	1353.34	1286.02	1258.43	1246.64
100,000	1706.43	1503.71	1428.91	1398.25	1385.15
110,000	1877.07	1654.09	1571.80	1538.07	1523.67
120,000	2047.72	1804.46	1714.69	1677.90	1662.18
130,000	2218.36	1954.83	1857.58	1817.72	1800.70
140,000	2389.00	2105.20	2000.47	1957.55	1939.21
150,000	2559.64	2255.57	2143.36	2097.37	2077.73
160,000	2730.29	2405.94	2286.25	2237.20	2216.24
170,000	2900.93	2556.31	2429.14	2377.02	2354.76
180,000	3071.57	2706.68	2572.03	2516.85	2493.27
190,000	3242.21	2857.05	2714.92	2656.67	2631.79
200,000	3412.86	3007.42	2857.81	2796.49	2770.30
250,000	4266.07	3759.28	3572.26	3495.62	3462.88
300,000	5119.28	4511.13	4286.71	4194.74	4155.45

451

MONTHLY PAYMENTS
ANNUAL INTEREST RATE: 16.75%

LOAN AMOUNT	LOAN MATURITY (YEARS)				
	10	15	20	25	30
50	0.87	0.77	0.73	0.71	0.71
100	1.73	1.53	1.45	1.42	1.41
200	3.45	3.05	2.90	2.84	2.82
300	5.17	4.57	4.35	4.26	4.22
400	6.89	6.09	5.80	5.68	5.63
500	8.62	7.61	7.24	7.09	7.03
600	10.34	9.13	8.69	8.51	8.44
700	12.06	10.65	10.14	9.93	9.84
800	13.78	12.18	11.59	11.35	11.25
900	15.50	13.70	13.04	12.77	12.65
1,000	17.23	15.22	14.48	14.18	14.06
2,000	34.45	30.43	28.96	28.36	28.11
3,000	51.67	45.64	43.44	42.54	42.17
4,000	68.89	60.86	57.92	56.72	56.22
5,000	86.11	76.07	72.40	70.90	70.27
6,000	103.34	91.28	86.87	85.08	84.33
7,000	120.56	106.50	101.35	99.26	98.38
8,000	137.78	121.71	115.83	113.44	112.44
9,000	155.00	136.92	130.31	127.62	126.49
10,000	172.22	152.14	144.79	141.80	140.54
20,000	344.44	304.27	289.57	283.60	281.08
30,000	516.66	456.40	434.35	425.40	421.62
40,000	688.87	608.53	579.13	567.20	562.16
50,000	861.09	760.67	723.91	709.00	702.70
60,000	1033.31	912.80	868.70	850.80	843.24
70,000	1205.52	1064.93	1013.48	992.60	983.78
80,000	1377.74	1217.06	1158.26	1134.40	1124.32
90,000	1549.96	1369.19	1303.04	1276.20	1264.86
100,000	1722.17	1521.33	1447.82	1418.00	1405.40
110,000	1894.39	1673.46	1592.61	1559.80	1545.94
120,000	2066.61	1825.59	1737.39	1701.60	1686.48
130,000	2238.82	1977.72	1882.17	1843.40	1827.02
140,000	2411.04	2129.86	2026.95	1985.20	1967.56
150,000	2583.26	2281.99	2171.73	2127.00	2108.10
160,000	2755.47	2434.12	2316.52	2268.80	2248.64
170,000	2927.69	2586.25	2461.30	2410.60	2389.18
180,000	3099.91	2738.38	2606.08	2552.40	2529.72
190,000	3272.13	2890.52	2750.86	2694.20	2670.26
200,000	3444.34	3042.65	2895.64	2836.00	2810.80
250,000	4305.43	3803.31	3619.55	3545.00	3513.49
300,000	5166.51	4563.97	4343.46	4254.00	4216.19

MONTHLY PAYMENTS
ANNUAL INTEREST RATE: 17%

LOAN AMOUNT	\multicolumn LOAN MATURITY (YEARS)				
	10	15	20	25	30
50	0.87	0.77	0.74	0.72	0.72
100	1.74	1.54	1.47	1.44	1.43
200	3.48	3.08	2.94	2.88	2.86
300	5.22	4.62	4.41	4.32	4.28
400	6.96	6.16	5.87	5.76	5.71
500	8.69	7.70	7.34	7.19	7.13
600	10.43	9.24	8.81	8.63	8.56
700	12.17	10.78	10.27	10.07	9.98
800	13.91	12.32	11.74	11.51	11.41
900	15.65	13.86	13.21	12.95	12.84
1,000	17.38	15.40	14.67	14.38	14.26
2,000	34.76	30.79	29.34	28.76	28.52
3,000	52.14	46.18	44.01	43.14	42.78
4,000	69.52	61.57	58.68	57.52	57.03
5,000	86.90	76.96	73.34	71.89	71.29
6,000	104.28	92.35	88.01	86.27	85.55
7,000	121.66	107.74	102.68	100.65	99.80
8,000	139.04	123.13	117.35	115.03	114.06
9,000	156.42	138.52	132.02	129.41	128.32
10,000	173.80	153.91	146.68	143.78	142.57
20,000	347.60	307.81	293.36	287.56	285.14
30,000	521.40	461.71	440.04	431.34	427.71
40,000	695.19	615.61	586.72	575.12	570.28
50,000	868.99	769.51	733.40	718.90	712.84
60,000	1042.79	923.41	880.08	862.68	855.41
70,000	1216.59	1077.31	1026.76	1006.46	997.98
80,000	1390.38	1231.21	1173.44	1150.24	1140.55
90,000	1564.18	1385.11	1320.12	1294.02	1283.11
100,000	1737.98	1539.01	1466.80	1437.80	1425.68
110,000	1911.78	1692.91	1613.48	1581.58	1568.25
120,000	2085.57	1846.81	1760.16	1725.36	1710.82
130,000	2259.37	2000.71	1906.84	1869.14	1853.38
140,000	2433.17	2154.61	2053.52	2012.92	1995.95
150,000	2606.96	2308.51	2200.20	2156.70	2138.52
160,000	2780.76	2462.41	2346.88	2300.48	2281.09
170,000	2954.56	2616.31	2493.56	2444.26	2423.65
180,000	3128.36	2770.21	2640.24	2588.04	2566.22
190,000	3302.15	2924.11	2786.92	2731.82	2708.79
200,000	3475.95	3078.01	2933.60	2875.60	2851.36
250,000	4344.94	3847.51	3667.00	3594.50	3564.19
300,000	5213.92	4617.01	4400.40	4313.39	4277.03

453

MONTHLY PAYMENTS
ANNUAL INTEREST RATE: 17.25%

LOAN AMOUNT	LOAN MATURITY (YEARS)				
	10	15	20	25	30
50	0.88	0.78	0.75	0.73	0.73
100	1.76	1.56	1.49	1.46	1.45
200	3.51	3.12	2.98	2.92	2.90
300	5.27	4.68	4.46	4.38	4.34
400	7.02	6.23	5.95	5.84	5.79
500	8.77	7.79	7.43	7.29	7.23
600	10.53	9.35	8.92	8.75	8.68
700	12.28	10.90	10.41	10.21	10.13
800	14.04	12.46	11.89	11.67	11.57
900	15.79	14.02	13.38	13.12	13.02
1,000	17.54	15.57	14.86	14.58	14.46
2,000	35.08	31.14	29.72	29.16	28.92
3,000	52.62	46.71	44.58	43.73	43.38
4,000	70.16	62.28	59.44	58.31	57.84
5,000	87.70	77.84	74.30	72.89	72.30
6,000	105.24	93.41	89.16	87.46	86.76
7,000	122.77	108.98	104.01	102.04	101.22
8,000	140.31	124.55	118.87	116.62	115.68
9,000	157.85	140.11	133.73	131.19	130.14
10,000	175.39	155.68	148.59	145.77	144.60
20,000	350.78	311.36	297.17	291.53	289.20
30,000	526.16	467.03	445.76	437.30	433.80
40,000	701.55	622.71	594.34	583.06	578.40
50,000	876.93	778.38	742.93	728.83	723.00
60,000	1052.32	934.06	891.51	874.59	867.60
70,000	1227.70	1089.74	1040.09	1020.35	1012.20
80,000	1403.09	1245.41	1188.68	1166.12	1156.79
90,000	1578.47	1401.09	1337.26	1311.88	1301.39
100,000	1753.86	1556.76	1485.85	1457.65	1445.99
110,000	1929.24	1712.44	1634.43	1603.41	1590.59
120,000	2104.63	1868.11	1783.02	1749.18	1735.19
130,000	2280.01	2023.79	1931.60	1894.94	1879.79
140,000	2455.40	2179.47	2080.18	2040.70	2024.39
150,000	2630.78	2335.14	2228.77	2186.47	2168.98
160,000	2806.17	2490.82	2377.35	2332.23	2313.58
170,000	2981.55	2646.49	2525.94	2478.00	2458.18
180,000	3156.94	2802.17	2674.52	2623.76	2602.78
190,000	3332.32	2957.85	2823.11	2769.52	2747.38
200,000	3507.71	3113.52	2971.69	2915.29	2891.98
250,000	4384.64	3891.90	3714.61	3644.11	3614.97
300,000	5261.56	4670.28	4457.53	4372.93	4337.96

MONTHLY PAYMENTS
ANNUAL INTEREST RATE: 17.5%

LOAN AMOUNT	LOAN MATURITY (YEARS)				
	10	15	20	25	30
50	0.89	0.79	0.76	0.74	0.74
100	1.77	1.58	1.51	1.48	1.47
200	3.54	3.15	3.01	2.96	2.94
300	5.31	4.73	4.52	4.44	4.40
400	7.08	6.30	6.02	5.92	5.87
500	8.85	7.88	7.53	7.39	7.34
600	10.62	9.45	9.03	8.87	8.80
700	12.39	11.03	10.54	10.35	10.27
800	14.16	12.60	12.04	11.83	11.74
900	15.93	14.18	13.55	13.30	13.20
1,000	17.70	15.75	15.05	14.78	14.67
2,000	35.40	31.50	30.10	29.56	29.33
3,000	53.10	47.24	45.15	44.33	43.99
4,000	70.80	62.99	60.20	59.11	58.66
5,000	88.49	78.73	75.25	73.88	73.32
6,000	106.19	94.48	90.30	88.66	87.98
7,000	123.89	110.23	105.35	103.43	102.65
8,000	141.59	125.97	120.40	118.21	117.31
9,000	159.29	141.72	135.45	132.98	131.97
10,000	176.98	157.46	150.50	147.76	146.64
20,000	353.96	314.92	300.99	295.51	293.27
30,000	530.94	472.38	451.49	443.26	439.90
40,000	707.92	629.84	601.98	591.02	586.54
50,000	884.90	787.29	752.48	738.77	733.17
60,000	1061.88	944.75	902.97	886.52	879.80
70,000	1238.86	1102.21	1053.46	1034.28	1026.43
80,000	1415.84	1259.67	1203.96	1182.03	1173.07
90,000	1592.81	1417.13	1354.45	1329.78	1319.70
100,000	1769.79	1574.58	1504.95	1477.53	1466.33
110,000	1946.77	1732.04	1655.44	1625.29	1612.96
120,000	2123.75	1889.50	1805.94	1773.04	1759.60
130,000	2300.73	2046.96	1956.43	1920.79	1906.23
140,000	2477.71	2204.41	2106.92	2068.55	2052.86
150,000	2654.69	2361.87	2257.42	2216.30	2199.49
160,000	2831.67	2519.33	2407.91	2364.05	2346.13
170,000	3008.65	2676.79	2558.41	2511.81	2492.76
180,000	3185.62	2834.25	2708.90	2659.56	2639.39
190,000	3362.60	2991.70	2859.39	2807.31	2786.02
200,000	3539.58	3149.16	3009.89	2955.06	2932.66
250,000	4424.48	3936.45	3762.36	3693.83	3665.82
300,000	5309.37	4723.74	4514.83	4432.59	4398.98

MONTHLY PAYMENTS
ANNUAL INTEREST RATE: 17.75%

LOAN AMOUNT	LOAN MATURITY (YEARS)				
	10	15	20	25	30
50	0.90	0.80	0.77	0.75	0.75
100	1.79	1.60	1.53	1.50	1.49
200	3.58	3.19	3.05	3.00	2.98
300	5.36	4.78	4.58	4.50	4.47
400	7.15	6.37	6.10	5.99	5.95
500	8.93	7.97	7.63	7.49	
600	10.72	9.56	9.15	8.99	8.93
700	12.51	11.15	10.67	10.49	10.41
800	14.29	12.74	12.20	11.98	11.90
900	16.08	14.34	13.72	13.48	13.39
1,000	17.86	15.93	15.25	14.98	14.87
2,000	35.72	31.85	30.49	29.95	29.74
3,000	53.58	47.78	45.73	44.93	44.61
4,000	71.44	63.70	60.97	59.90	59.47
5,000	89.29	79.63	76.21	74.88	74.34
6,000	107.15	95.55	91.45	89.85	89.21
7,000	125.01	111.48	106.69	104.83	104.07
8,000	142.87	127.40	121.93	119.80	118.94
9,000	160.73	143.33	137.17	134.78	133.81
10,000	178.58	159.25	152.41	149.75	148.67
20,000	357.16	318.50	304.82	299.50	297.34
30,000	535.74	477.75	457.24	449.24	446.01
40,000	714.32	636.99	609.64	598.99	594.68
50,000	892.90	796.24	762.06	748.74	743.35
60,000	1071.48	955.49	914.47	898.48	892.02
70,000	1250.06	1114.73	1066.88	1048.23	1040.69
80,000	1428.64	1273.98	1219.28	1197.97	1189.36
90,000	1607.22	1433.23	1371.70	1347.72	1338.03
100,000	1785.80	1592.47	1524.11	1497.47	1486.70
110,000	1964.38	1751.72	1676.51	1647.21	1635.37
120,000	2142.96	1910.97	1828.93	1796.96	1784.04
130,000	2321.54	2070.21	1981.34	1946.70	1932.71
140,000	2500.11	2229.46	2133.74	2096.45	2081.37
150,000	2678.69	2388.71	2286.15	2246.20	2230.04
160,000	2857.27	2547.95	2438.56	2395.94	2378.71
170,000	3035.85	2707.20	2590.97	2545.69	2527.38
180,000	3214.43	2866.45	2743.38	2695.43	2676.05
190,000	3393.01	3025.70	2895.79	2845.18	2824.72
200,000	3571.59	3184.94	3048.20	2994.93	2973.39
250,000	4464.49	3981.18	3810.25	3743.66	3716.74
300,000	5357.38	4777.41	4572.30	4492.39	4460.08

456

MONTHLY PAYMENTS
ANNUAL INTEREST RATE: 18%

LOAN AMOUNT	LOAN MATURITY (YEARS)				
	10	15	20	25	30
50	0.91	0.81	0.78	0.76	0.76
100	1.81	1.62	1.55	1.52	1.51
200	3.61	3.23	3.09	3.04	3.02
300	5.41	4.84	4.63	4.56	4.53
400	7.21	6.45	6.18	6.07	6.03
500	9.01	8.06	7.72	7.59	7.54
600	10.82	9.67	9.26	9.11	9.05
700	12.62	11.28	10.81	10.63	10.55
800	14.42	12.89	12.35	12.14	12.06
900	16.22	14.50	13.89	13.66	13.57
1,000	18.02	16.11	15.44	15.18	15.08
2,000	36.04	32.21	30.87	30.35	30.15
3,000	54.06	48.32	46.30	45.53	45.22
4,000	72.08	64.42	61.74	60.70	60.29
5,000	90.10	80.53	77.17	75.88	75.36
6,000	108.12	96.63	92.60	91.05	90.43
7,000	126.13	112.73	108.04	106.23	105.50
8,000	144.15	128.84	123.47	121.40	120.57
9,000	162.17	144.94	138.90	136.57	135.64
10,000	180.19	161.05	154.34	151.75	150.71
20,000	360.38	322.09	308.67	303.49	301.42
30,000	540.56	483.13	463.00	455.23	452.13
40,000	720.75	644.17	617.33	606.98	602.84
50,000	900.93	805.22	771.66	758.72	753.55
60,000	1081.12	966.26	925.99	910.46	904.26
70,000	1261.30	1127.30	1080.32	1062.21	1054.96
80,000	1441.49	1288.34	1234.65	1213.95	1205.67
90,000	1621.67	1449.38	1388.99	1365.69	1356.38
100,000	1801.86	1610.43	1543.32	1517.44	1507.09
110,000	1982.04	1771.47	1697.65	1669.18	1657.80
120,000	2162.23	1932.51	1851.98	1820.92	1808.51
130,000	2342.42	2093.55	2006.31	1972.66	1959.22
140,000	2522.60	2254.60	2160.64	2124.41	2109.92
150,000	2702.79	2415.64	2314.97	2276.15	2260.63
160,000	2882.97	2576.68	2469.30	2427.89	2411.34
170,000	3063.16	2737.72	2623.64	2579.64	2562.05
180,000	3243.34	2898.76	2777.97	2731.38	2712.76
190,000	3423.53	3059.81	2932.30	2883.12	2863.47
200,000	3603.71	3220.85	3086.63	3034.87	3014.18
250,000	4504.64	4026.06	3858.29	3793.58	3767.72
300,000	5405.57	4831.27	4629.94	4552.30	4521.26

MONTHLY PAYMENTS
ANNUAL INTEREST RATE: 18.25%

LOAN AMOUNT	LOAN MATURITY (YEARS)				
	10	15	20	25	30
50	0.91	0.82	0.79	0.77	0.77
100	1.82	1.63	1.57	1.54	1.53
200	3.64	3.26	3.13	3.08	3.06
300	5.46	4.89	4.69	4.62	4.59
400	7.28	6.52	6.26	6.15	6.12
500	9.09	8.15	7.82	7.69	7.64
600	10.91	9.78	9.38	9.23	9.17
700	12.73	11.40	10.94	10.77	10.70
800	14.55	13.03	12.51	12.30	12.23
900	16.37	14.66	14.07	13.84	13.75
1,000	18.18	16.29	15.63	15.38	15.28
2,000	36.36	32.57	31.26	30.75	30.56
3,000	54.54	48.86	46.88	46.13	45.83
4,000	72.72	65.14	62.51	61.50	61.11
5,000	90.90	81.43	78.13	76.88	76.38
6,000	109.08	97.71	93.76	92.25	91.66
7,000	127.26	114.00	109.39	107.63	106.93
8,000	145.44	130.28	125.01	123.00	122.21
9,000	163.62	146.56	140.64	138.37	137.48
10,000	181.80	162.85	156.26	153.75	152.76
20,000	363.60	325.69	312.52	307.49	305.51
30,000	545.40	488.54	468.78	461.24	458.26
40,000	727.20	651.38	625.04	614.98	611.01
50,000	908.99	814.23	781.29	768.72	763.76
60,000	1090.79	977.07	937.55	922.47	916.51
70,000	1272.59	1139.91	1093.81	1076.21	1069.26
80,000	1454.39	1302.76	1250.07	1229.96	1222.01
90,000	1636.18	1465.60	1406.33	1383.70	1374.76
100,000	1817.98	1628.45	1562.58	1537.44	1527.51
110,000	1999.78	1791.29	1718.84	1691.19	1680.26
120,000	2181.58	1954.13	1875.10	1844.93	1833.01
130,000	2363.38	2116.98	2031.36	1998.68	1985.76
140,000	2545.17	2279.82	2187.61	2152.42	2138.51
150,000	2726.97	2442.67	2343.87	2306.16	2291.26
160,000	2908.77	2605.51	2500.13	2459.91	2444.01
170,000	3090.57	2768.35	2656.39	2613.65	2596.76
180,000	3272.36	2931.20	2812.65	2767.39	2749.51
190,000	3454.16	3094.04	2968.90	2921.14	2902.26
200,000	3635.96	3256.89	3125.16	3074.88	3055.01
250,000	4544.95	4071.11	3906.45	3843.60	3818.76
300,000	5453.94	4885.33	4687.74	4612.32	4582.51

458

MONTHLY PAYMENTS
ANNUAL INTEREST RATE: 18.5%

LOAN AMOUNT	LOAN MATURITY (YEARS)				
	10	15	20	25	30
50	0.92	0.83	0.80	0.78	0.78
100	1.84	1.65	1.59	1.56	1.55
200	3.67	3.30	3.17	3.12	3.10
300	5.51	4.94	4.75	4.68	4.65
400	7.34	6.59	6.33	6.23	6.20
500	9.18	8.24	7.91	7.79	7.74
600	11.01	9.88	9.50	9.35	9.29
700	12.84	11.53	11.08	10.91	10.84
800	14.68	13.18	12.66	12.46	12.39
900	16.51	14.82	14.24	14.02	13.94
1,000	18.35	16.47	15.82	15.58	15.48
2,000	36.69	32.94	31.64	31.15	30.96
3,000	55.03	49.40	47.46	46.73	46.44
4,000	73.37	65.87	63.28	62.30	61.92
5,000	91.71	82.33	79.10	77.88	77.40
6,000	110.06	98.80	94.92	93.45	92.88
7,000	128.40	115.26	110.74	109.03	108.36
8,000	146.74	131.73	126.56	124.60	123.84
9,000	165.08	148.19	142.38	140.18	139.32
10,000	183.42	164.66	158.19	155.75	154.80
20,000	366.84	329.31	316.38	311.50	309.59
30,000	550.26	493.96	474.57	467.25	464.39
40,000	733.67	658.61	632.76	623.00	619.18
50,000	917.09	823.27	790.95	778.75	773.98
60,000	1100.51	987.92	949.14	934.50	928.77
70,000	1283.92	1152.57	1107.33	1090.24	1083.57
80,000	1467.34	1317.22	1265.52	1245.99	1238.36
90,000	1650.76	1481.88	1423.71	1401.74	1393.16
100,000	1834.17	1646.53	1581.90	1557.49	1547.95
110,000	2017.59	1811.18	1740.09	1713.24	1702.74
120,000	2201.01	1975.83	1898.28	1868.99	1857.54
130,000	2384.42	2140.49	2056.47	2024.73	2012.33
140,000	2567.84	2305.14	2214.66	2180.48	2167.13
150,000	2751.26	2469.79	2372.85	2336.23	2321.92
160,000	2934.67	2634.44	2531.04	2491.98	2476.72
170,000	3118.09	2799.10	2689.23	2647.73	2631.51
180,000	3301.51	2963.75	2847.42	2803.48	2786.31
190,000	3484.92	3128.40	3005.61	2959.23	2941.10
200,000	3668.34	3293.05	3163.80	3114.97	3095.89
250,000	4585.42	4116.32	3954.75	3893.72	3869.87
300,000	5502.51	4939.58	4745.70	4672.46	4643.84

MONTHLY PAYMENTS
ANNUAL INTEREST RATE: 18.75%

LOAN AMOUNT	LOAN MATURITY (YEARS)				
	10	15	20	25	30
50	0.93	0.84	0.81	0.79	0.79
100	1.86	1.67	1.61	1.58	1.57
200	3.71	3.33	3.21	3.16	3.14
300	5.56	5.00	4.81	4.74	4.71
400	7.41	6.66	6.41	6.32	6.28
500	9.26	8.33	8.01	7.89	7.85
600	11.11	9.99	9.61	9.47	9.42
700	12.96	11.66	11.21	11.05	10.98
800	14.81	13.32	12.82	12.63	12.55
900	16.66	14.99	14.42	14.20	14.12
1,000	18.51	16.65	16.02	15.78	15.69
2,000	37.01	33.30	32.03	31.56	31.37
3,000	55.52	49.95	48.04	47.33	47.06
4,000	74.02	66.59	64.06	63.11	62.74
5,000	92.53	83.24	80.07	78.88	78.43
6,000	111.03	99.89	96.08	94.66	94.11
7,000	129.53	116.53	112.09	110.43	109.79
8,000	148.04	133.18	128.11	126.21	125.48
9,000	166.54	149.83	144.12	141.99	141.16
10,000	185.05	166.47	160.13	157.76	156.85
20,000	370.09	332.94	320.26	315.52	313.69
30,000	555.13	499.41	480.38	473.27	470.53
40,000	740.17	665.87	640.51	631.03	627.37
50,000	925.21	832.34	800.64	788.79	784.21
60,000	1110.25	998.81	960.76	946.54	941.05
70,000	1295.30	1165.27	1120.89	1104.30	1097.89
80,000	1480.34	1331.74	1281.02	1262.06	1254.73
90,000	1665.38	1498.21	1441.14	1419.81	1411.57
100,000	1850.42	1664.67	1601.27	1577.57	1568.41
110,000	2035.46	1831.14	1761.40	1735.33	1725.25
120,000	2220.50	1997.61	1921.52	1893.08	1882.09
130,000	2405.54	2164.08	2081.65	2050.84	2038.94
140,000	2590.59	2330.54	2241.78	2208.60	2195.78
150,000	2775.63	2497.01	2401.90	2366.35	2352.62
160,000	2960.67	2663.48	2562.03	2524.11	2509.46
170,000	3145.71	2829.94	2722.16	2681.87	2666.30
180,000	3330.75	2996.41	2882.28	2839.62	2823.14
190,000	3515.79	3162.88	3042.41	2997.38	2979.98
200,000	3700.84	3329.34	3202.54	3155.14	3136.82
250,000	4626.04	4161.68	4003.17	3943.92	3921.03
300,000	5551.25	4994.01	4803.80	4732.70	4705.23

MONTHLY PAYMENTS
ANNUAL INTEREST RATE: 19%

LOAN AMOUNT	LOAN MATURITY (YEARS)				
	10	15	20	25	30
50	0.94	0.85	0.82	0.80	0.80
100	1.87	1.69	1.63	1.60	1.59
200	3.74	3.37	3.25	3.20	3.18
300	5.61	5.05	4.87	4.80	4.77
400	7.47	6.74	6.49	6.40	6.36
500	9.34	8.42	8.11	7.99	7.95
600	11.21	10.10	9.73	9.59	9.54
700	13.07	11.79	11.35	11.19	11.13
800	14.94	13.47	12.97	12.79	12.72
900	16.81	15.15	14.59	14.38	14.31
1,000	18.67	16.83	16.21	15.98	15.89
2,000	37.34	33.66	32.42	31.96	31.78
3,000	56.01	50.49	48.63	47.94	47.67
4,000	74.67	67.32	64.83	63.91	63.56
5,000	93.34	84.15	81.04	79.89	79.45
6,000	112.01	100.98	97.25	95.87	95.34
7,000	130.68	117.81	113.45	111.84	111.23
8,000	149.34	134.64	129.66	127.82	127.12
9,000	168.01	151.46	145.87	143.80	143.01
10,000	186.68	168.29	162.07	159.77	158.89
20,000	373.35	336.58	324.14	319.54	317.78
30,000	560.02	504.87	486.21	479.31	476.67
40,000	746.69	673.16	648.28	639.08	635.56
50,000	933.37	841.44	810.35	798.84	794.45
60,000	1120.04	1009.73	972.42	958.61	953.34
70,000	1306.71	1178.02	1134.48	1118.38	1112.23
80,000	1493.38	1346.31	1296.55	1278.15	1271.12
90,000	1680.05	1514.59	1458.62	1437.92	1430.01
100,000	1866.73	1682.88	1620.69	1597.68	1588.90
110,000	2053.40	1851.17	1782.76	1757.45	1747.79
120,000	2240.07	2019.46	1944.83	1917.22	1906.68
130,000	2426.74	2187.74	2106.89	2076.99	2065.57
140,000	2613.42	2356.03	2268.96	2236.76	2224.45
150,000	2800.09	2524.32	2431.03	2396.52	2383.34
160,000	2986.76	2692.61	2593.10	2556.29	2542.23
170,000	3173.43	2860.89	2755.17	2716.06	2701.12
180,000	3360.10	3029.18	2917.24	2875.83	2860.01
190,000	3546.78	3197.47	3079.31	3035.60	3018.90
200,000	3733.45	3365.76	3241.37	3195.36	3177.79
250,000	4666.81	4207.19	4051.72	3994.20	3972.24
300,000	5600.17	5048.63	4862.06	4793.04	4766.68

MONTHLY PAYMENTS
ANNUAL INTEREST RATE: 19.25%

LOAN AMOUNT	LOAN MATURITY (YEARS)				
	10	15	20	25	30
50	0.95	0.86	0.83	0.81	0.81
100	1.89	1.71	1.65	1.62	1.61
200	3.77	3.41	3.29	3.24	3.22
300	5.65	5.11	4.93	4.86	4.83
400	7.54	6.81	6.57	6.48	6.44
500	9.42	8.51	8.21	8.09	8.05
600	11.30	10.21	9.85	9.71	9.66
700	13.19	11.91	11.49	11.33	11.27
800	15.07	13.61	13.13	12.95	12.88
900	16.95	15.32	14.77	14.57	14.49
1,000	18.84	17.02	16.41	16.18	16.10
2,000	37.67	34.03	32.81	32.36	32.19
3,000	56.50	51.04	49.21	48.54	48.29
4,000	75.33	68.05	65.61	64.72	64.38
5,000	94.16	85.06	82.01	80.90	80.47
6,000	112.99	102.07	98.41	97.07	96.57
7,000	131.82	119.09	114.82	113.25	112.66
8,000	150.65	136.10	131.22	129.43	128.76
9,000	169.48	153.11	147.62	145.61	144.85
10,000	188.31	170.12	164.02	161.79	160.94
20,000	376.62	340.23	328.04	323.57	321.88
30,000	564.93	510.35	492.05	485.35	482.82
40,000	753.24	680.46	656.07	647.14	643.76
50,000	941.55	850.58	820.08	808.92	804.70
60,000	1129.86	1020.69	984.10	970.70	965.64
70,000	1318.17	1190.81	1148.11	1132.48	1126.58
80,000	1506.48	1360.92	1312.13	1294.27	1287.52
90,000	1694.79	1531.03	1476.14	1456.05	1448.46
100,000	1883.10	1701.15	1640.16	1617.83	1609.40
110,000	2071.41	1871.26	1804.17	1779.62	1770.34
120,000	2259.72	2041.38	1968.19	1941.40	1931.28
130,000	2448.03	2211.49	2132.20	2103.18	2092.22
140,000	2636.34	2381.61	2296.22	2264.96	2253.16
150,000	2824.65	2551.72	2460.23	2426.75	2414.10
160,000	3012.95	2721.83	2624.25	2588.53	2575.04
170,000	3201.26	2891.95	2788.26	2750.31	2735.98
180,000	3389.57	3062.06	2952.28	2912.09	2896.92
190,000	3577.88	3232.18	3116.29	3073.88	3057.86
200,000	3766.19	3402.29	3280.31	3235.66	3218.80
250,000	4707.74	4252.86	4100.38	4044.57	4023.50
300,000	5649.29	5103.44	4920.46	4853.49	4828.20

MONTHLY PAYMENTS
ANNUAL INTEREST RATE: 19.5%

LOAN AMOUNT	LOAN MATURITY (YEARS)				
	10	15	20	25	30
50	0.95	0.86	0.83	0.82	0.82
100	1.90	1.72	1.66	1.64	1.63
200	3.80	3.44	3.32	3.28	3.26
300	5.70	5.16	4.98	4.92	4.89
400	7.60	6.88	6.64	6.56	6.52
500	9.50	8.60	8.30	8.20	8.15
600	11.40	10.32	9.96	9.83	9.78
700	13.30	12.04	11.62	11.47	11.41
800	15.20	13.76	13.28	13.11	13.04
900	17.10	15.48	14.94	14.75	14.67
1,000	19.00	17.20	16.60	16.39	16.30
2,000	38.00	34.39	33.20	32.77	32.60
3,000	56.99	51.59	49.79	49.15	48.90
4,000	75.99	68.78	66.39	65.53	65.20
5,000	94.98	85.98	82.99	81.91	81.50
6,000	113.98	103.17	99.58	98.29	97.80
7,000	132.97	120.37	116.18	114.67	114.10
8,000	151.97	137.56	132.78	131.05	130.40
9,000	170.96	154.76	149.37	147.43	146.70
10,000	189.96	171.95	165.97	163.81	163.00
20,000	379.91	343.90	331.94	327.61	325.99
30,000	569.86	515.85	497.90	491.41	488.98
40,000	759.81	687.79	663.87	655.21	651.97
50,000	949.77	859.74	829.84	819.01	814.97
60,000	1139.72	1031.69	995.80	982.81	977.96
70,000	1329.67	1203.63	1161.77	1146.61	1140.95
80,000	1519.62	1375.58	1327.74	1310.41	1303.94
90,000	1709.57	1547.53	1493.70	1474.21	1466.93
100,000	1899.53	1719.47	1659.67	1638.01	1629.93
110,000	2089.48	1891.42	1825.64	1801.81	1792.92
120,000	2279.43	2063.37	1991.60	1965.61	1955.91
130,000	2469.38	2235.32	2157.57	2129.41	2118.90
140,000	2659.34	2407.26	2323.54	2293.21	2281.89
150,000	2849.29	2579.21	2489.50	2457.01	2444.88
160,000	3039.24	2751.16	2655.47	2620.81	2607.88
170,000	3229.19	2923.10	2821.43	2784.62	2770.87
180,000	3419.14	3095.05	2987.40	2948.42	2933.86
190,000	3609.10	3267.00	3153.37	3112.22	3096.85
200,000	3799.05	3438.94	3319.33	3276.02	3259.85
250,000	4748.81	4298.68	4149.17	4095.02	4074.80
300,000	5698.57	5158.41	4979.00	4914.02	4889.76

463

MONTHLY PAYMENTS
ANNUAL INTEREST RATE: 19.75%

LOAN AMOUNT	LOAN MATURITY (YEARS)				
	10	15	20	25	30
50	0.96	0.87	0.84	0.83	0.83
100	1.92	1.74	1.68	1.66	1.66
200	3.84	3.48	3.36	3.32	3.31
300	5.75	5.22	5.04	4.98	4.96
400	7.67	6.96	6.72	6.64	6.61
500	9.59	8.69	8.40	8.30	8.26
600	11.50	10.43	10.08	9.95	9.91
700	13.42	12.17	11.76	11.61	11.56
800	15.33	13.91	13.44	13.27	13.21
900	17.25	15.65	15.12	14.93	14.86
1,000	19.17	17.38	16.80	16.59	16.51
2,000	38.33	34.76	33.59	33.17	33.01
3,000	57.49	52.14	50.38	49.75	49.52
4,000	76.65	69.52	67.17	66.33	66.02
5,000	95.81	86.90	83.97	82.92	82.53
6,000	114.97	104.28	100.76	99.50	99.03
7,000	134.13	121.65	117.55	116.08	115.54
8,000	153.29	139.03	134.34	132.66	132.04
9,000	172.45	156.41	151.14	149.24	148.55
10,000	191.61	173.79	167.93	165.83	165.05
20,000	383.21	347.58	335.85	331.65	330.10
30,000	574.81	521.36	503.77	497.47	495.14
40,000	766.41	695.15	671.69	663.29	660.19
50,000	958.01	868.93	839.62	829.11	825.24
60,000	1149.61	1042.72	1007.54	994.93	990.28
70,000	1341.21	1216.50	1175.46	1160.76	1155.33
80,000	1532.82	1390.29	1343.38	1326.58	1320.37
90,000	1724.42	1564.08	1511.31	1492.40	1485.42
100,000	1916.02	1737.86	1679.23	1658.22	1650.47
110,000	2107.62	1911.65	1847.15	1824.04	1815.51
120,000	2299.22	2085.43	2015.07	1989.86	1980.56
130,000	2490.82	2259.22	2183.00	2155.68	2145.60
140,000	2682.42	2433.00	2350.92	2321.51	2310.65
150,000	2874.02	2606.79	2518.84	2487.33	2475.70
160,000	3065.63	2780.57	2686.76	2653.15	2640.74
170,000	3257.23	2954.36	2854.68	2818.97	2805.79
180,000	3448.83	3128.15	3022.61	2984.79	2970.83
190,000	3640.43	3301.93	3190.53	3150.61	3135.88
200,000	3832.03	3475.72	3358.45	3316.43	3300.93
250,000	4790.04	4344.65	4198.06	4145.54	4126.16
300,000	5748.04	5213.57	5037.68	4974.65	4951.39

MONTHLY PAYMENTS
ANNUAL INTEREST RATE: 20%

LOAN AMOUNT	LOAN MATURITY (YEARS)				
	10	15	20	25	30
50	0.97	0.88	0.85	0.84	0.84
100	1.94	1.76	1.70	1.68	1.68
200	3.87	3.52	3.40	3.36	3.35
300	5.80	5.27	5.10	5.04	5.02
400	7.74	7.03	6.80	6.72	6.69
500	9.67	8.79	8.50	8.40	8.36
600	11.60	10.54	10.20	10.08	10.03
700	13.53	12.30	11.90	11.75	11.70
800	15.47	14.06	13.60	13.43	13.37
900	17.40	15.81	15.29	15.11	15.04
1,000	19.33	17.57	16.99	16.79	16.72
2,000	38.66	35.13	33.98	33.57	33.43
3,000	57.98	52.69	50.97	50.36	50.14
4,000	77.31	70.26	67.96	67.14	66.85
5,000	96.63	87.82	84.95	83.93	83.56
6,000	115.96	105.38	101.93	100.71	100.27
7,000	135.28	122.95	118.92	117.50	116.98
8,000	154.61	140.51	135.91	134.28	133.69
9,000	173.94	158.07	152.90	151.07	150.40
10,000	193.26	175.63	169.89	167.85	167.11
20,000	386.52	351.26	339.77	335.70	334.21
30,000	579.77	526.89	509.65	503.54	501.31
40,000	773.03	702.52	679.53	671.39	668.41
50,000	966.28	878.15	849.42	839.23	835.51
60,000	1159.54	1053.78	1019.30	1007.08	1002.62
70,000	1352.80	1229.41	1189.18	1174.92	1169.72
80,000	1546.05	1405.04	1359.06	1342.77	1336.82
90,000	1739.31	1580.67	1528.95	1510.61	1503.92
100,000	1932.56	1756.30	1698.83	1678.46	1671.02
110,000	2125.82	1931.93	1868.71	1846.30	1838.13
120,000	2319.07	2107.56	2038.59	2014.15	2005.23
130,000	2512.33	2283.19	2208.48	2181.99	2172.33
140,000	2705.59	2458.82	2378.36	2349.84	2339.43
150,000	2898.84	2634.45	2548.24	2517.68	2506.53
160,000	3092.10	2810.08	2718.12	2685.53	2673.63
170,000	3285.35	2985.71	2888.01	2853.37	2840.74
180,000	3478.61	3161.34	3057.89	3021.22	3007.84
190,000	3671.86	3336.97	3227.77	3189.06	3174.94
200,000	3865.12	3512.60	3397.65	3356.91	3342.04
250,000	4831.40	4390.75	4247.07	4196.13	4177.55
300,000	5797.68	5268.90	5096.48	5035.36	5013.06

MONTHLY PAYMENTS
ANNUAL INTEREST RATE: 20.25%

LOAN AMOUNT	LOAN MATURITY (YEARS)				
	10	15	20	25	30
50	0.98	0.89	0.86	0.85	0.85
100	1.95	1.78	1.72	1.70	1.70
200	3.90	3.55	3.44	3.40	3.39
300	5.85	5.33	5.16	5.10	5.08
400	7.80	7.10	6.88	6.80	6.77
500	9.75	8.88	8.60	8.50	8.46
600	11.70	10.65	10.32	10.20	10.15
700	13.65	12.43	12.03	11.90	11.85
800	15.60	14.20	13.75	13.59	13.54
900	17.55	15.98	15.47	15.29	15.23
1,000	19.50	17.75	17.19	16.99	16.92
2,000	38.99	35.50	34.37	33.98	33.84
3,000	58.48	53.25	51.56	50.97	50.75
4,000	77.97	71.00	68.74	67.95	67.67
5,000	97.46	88.74	85.93	84.94	84.58
6,000	116.95	106.49	103.11	101.93	101.50
7,000	136.45	124.24	120.30	118.92	118.42
8,000	155.94	141.99	137.48	135.90	135.33
9,000	175.43	159.74	154.67	152.89	152.25
10,000	194.92	177.48	171.85	169.88	169.16
20,000	389.84	354.96	343.70	339.75	338.32
30,000	584.75	532.44	515.55	509.62	507.48
40,000	779.67	709.92	687.39	679.49	676.64
50,000	974.59	887.40	859.24	849.36	845.80
60,000	1169.50	1064.88	1031.09	1019.23	1014.96
70,000	1364.42	1242.36	1202.93	1189.11	1184.12
80,000	1559.33	1419.84	1374.78	1358.98	1353.28
90,000	1754.25	1597.32	1546.63	1528.85	1522.44
100,000	1949.17	1774.80	1718.47	1698.72	1691.60
110,000	2144.08	1952.28	1890.32	1868.59	1860.76
120,000	2339.00	2129.76	2062.17	2038.46	2029.92
130,000	2533.91	2307.24	2234.01	2208.34	2199.08
140,000	2728.83	2484.72	2405.86	2378.21	2368.23
150,000	2923.75	2662.20	2577.71	2548.08	2537.39
160,000	3118.66	2839.67	2749.55	2717.95	2706.55
170,000	3313.58	3017.15	2921.40	2887.82	2875.71
180,000	3508.49	3194.63	3093.25	3057.69	3044.87
190,000	3703.41	3372.11	3265.10	3227.57	3214.03
200,000	3898.33	3549.59	3436.94	3397.44	3383.19
250,000	4872.91	4436.99	4296.18	4246.80	4228.99
300,000	5847.49	5324.39	5155.41	5096.15	5074.78

MONTHLY PAYMENTS
ANNUAL INTEREST RATE: 20.5%

LOAN AMOUNT	LOAN MATURITY (YEARS)				
	10	15	20	25	30
50	0.99	0.90	0.87	0.86	0.86
100	1.97	1.80	1.74	1.72	1.72
200	3.94	3.59	3.48	3.44	3.43
300	5.90	5.39	5.22	5.16	5.14
400	7.87	7.18	6.96	6.88	6.85
500	9.83	8.97	8.70	8.60	8.57
600	11.80	10.77	10.43	10.32	10.28
700	13.77	12.56	12.17	12.04	11.99
800	15.73	14.35	13.91	13.76	13.70
900	17.70	16.15	15.65	15.48	15.41
1,000	19.66	17.94	17.39	17.20	17.13
2,000	39.32	35.87	34.77	34.39	34.25
3,000	58.98	53.81	52.15	51.58	51.37
4,000	78.64	71.74	69.53	68.77	68.49
5,000	98.30	89.67	86.91	85.96	85.61
6,000	117.95	107.61	104.29	103.15	102.74
7,000	137.61	125.54	121.68	120.34	119.86
8,000	157.27	143.47	139.06	137.53	136.98
9,000	176.93	161.41	156.44	154.72	154.10
10,000	196.59	179.34	173.82	171.91	171.22
20,000	393.17	358.67	347.64	343.81	342.44
30,000	589.75	538.01	521.45	515.71	513.66
40,000	786.34	717.34	695.27	687.61	684.88
50,000	982.92	896.68	869.08	859.51	856.10
60,000	1179.50	1076.01	1042.90	1031.41	1027.31
70,000	1376.08	1255.35	1216.71	1203.31	1198.53
80,000	1572.67	1434.68	1390.53	1375.21	1369.75
90,000	1769.25	1614.02	1564.34	1547.11	1540.97
100,000	1965.83	1793.35	1738.16	1719.01	1712.19
110,000	2162.41	1972.69	1911.98	1890.91	1883.40
120,000	2359.00	2152.02	2085.79	2062.81	2054.62
130,000	2555.58	2331.36	2259.61	2234.71	2225.84
140,000	2752.16	2510.69	2433.42	2406.62	2397.06
150,000	2948.74	2690.03	2607.24	2578.52	2568.28
160,000	3145.33	2869.36	2781.05	2750.42	2739.49
170,000	3341.91	3048.70	2954.87	2922.32	2910.71
180,000	3538.49	3228.03	3128.68	3094.22	3081.93
190,000	3735.07	3407.37	3302.50	3266.12	3253.15
200,000	3931.66	3586.70	3476.31	3438.02	3424.37
250,000	4914.57	4483.38	4345.39	4297.52	4280.46
300,000	5897.48	5380.05	5214.47	5157.03	5136.55

467

MONTHLY PAYMENTS
ANNUAL INTEREST RATE: 20.75%

LOAN AMOUNT	LOAN MATURITY (YEARS)				
	10	15	20	25	30
50	1.00	0.91	0.88	0.87	0.87
100	1.99	1.82	1.76	1.74	1.74
200	3.97	3.63	3.52	3.48	3.47
300	5.95	5.44	5.28	5.22	5.20
400	7.94	7.25	7.04	6.96	6.94
500	9.92	9.06	8.79	8.70	8.67
600	11.90	10.88	10.55	10.44	10.40
700	13.88	12.69	12.31	12.18	12.13
800	15.87	14.50	14.07	13.92	13.87
900	17.85	16.31	15.83	15.66	15.60
1,000	19.83	18.12	17.58	17.40	17.33
2,000	39.66	36.24	35.16	34.79	34.66
3,000	59.48	54.36	52.74	52.18	51.99
4,000	79.31	72.48	70.32	69.58	69.32
5,000	99.13	90.60	87.90	86.97	86.64
6,000	118.96	108.72	105.48	104.36	103.97
7,000	138.78	126.84	123.06	121.76	121.30
8,000	158.61	144.96	140.64	139.15	138.63
9,000	178.43	163.08	158.21	156.54	155.96
10,000	198.26	181.20	175.79	173.94	173.28
20,000	396.51	362.40	351.58	347.87	346.56
30,000	594.77	543.59	527.37	521.80	519.84
40,000	793.02	724.79	703.16	695.73	693.12
50,000	991.28	905.98	878.94	869.67	866.40
60,000	1189.53	1087.18	1054.73	1043.60	1039.68
70,000	1387.78	1268.37	1230.52	1217.53	1212.95
80,000	1586.04	1449.57	1406.31	1391.46	1386.23
90,000	1784.29	1630.76	1582.10	1565.40	1559.51
100,000	1982.55	1811.96	1757.88	1739.33	1732.79
110,000	2180.80	1993.15	1933.67	1913.26	1906.07
120,000	2379.06	2174.35	2109.46	2087.19	2079.35
130,000	2577.31	2355.54	2285.25	2261.12	2252.62
140,000	2775.56	2536.74	2461.04	2435.06	2425.90
150,000	2973.82	2717.93	2636.82	2608.99	2599.18
160,000	3172.07	2899.13	2812.61	2782.92	2772.46
170,000	3370.33	3080.33	2988.40	2956.85	2945.74
180,000	3568.58	3261.52	3164.19	3130.79	3119.02
190,000	3766.84	3442.72	3339.98	3304.72	3292.29
200,000	3965.09	3623.91	3515.76	3478.65	3465.57
250,000	4956.36	4529.89	4394.70	4348.31	4331.96
300,000	5947.63	5435.86	5273.64	5217.97	5198.36

MONTHLY PAYMENTS
ANNUAL INTEREST RATE: 21%

LOAN AMOUNT	LOAN MATURITY (YEARS)				
	10	15	20	25	30
50	1.00	0.92	0.89	0.88	0.88
100	2.00	1.84	1.78	1.76	1.76
200	4.00	3.67	3.56	3.52	3.51
300	6.00	5.50	5.34	5.28	5.27
400	8.00	7.33	7.12	7.04	7.02
500	10.00	9.16	8.89	8.80	8.77
600	12.00	10.99	10.67	10.56	10.53
700	14.00	12.82	12.45	12.32	12.28
800	16.00	14.65	14.23	14.08	14.03
900	18.00	16.48	16.00	15.84	15.79
1,000	20.00	18.31	17.78	17.60	17.54
2,000	39.99	36.62	35.56	35.20	35.07
3,000	59.98	54.92	53.33	52.79	52.61
4,000	79.98	73.23	71.11	70.39	70.14
5,000	99.97	91.54	88.89	87.99	87.67
6,000	119.96	109.84	106.66	105.58	105.21
7,000	139.96	128.15	124.44	123.18	122.74
8,000	159.95	146.45	142.22	140.78	140.28
9,000	179.94	164.76	159.99	158.37	157.81
10,000	199.94	183.07	177.77	175.97	175.35
20,000	399.87	366.13	355.53	351.94	350.69
30,000	599.80	549.19	533.30	527.90	526.03
40,000	799.73	732.25	711.06	703.87	701.37
50,000	999.66	915.31	888.83	879.84	876.71
60,000	1199.59	1098.37	1066.59	1055.80	1052.05
70,000	1399.53	1281.43	1244.35	1231.77	1227.39
80,000	1599.46	1464.49	1422.12	1407.74	1402.73
90,000	1799.39	1647.56	1599.88	1583.70	1578.07
100,000	1999.32	1830.62	1777.65	1759.67	1753.41
110,000	2199.25	2013.68	1955.41	1935.63	1928.75
120,000	2399.18	2196.74	2133.18	2111.60	2104.09
130,000	2599.11	2379.80	2310.94	2287.57	2279.42
140,000	2799.05	2562.86	2488.70	2463.53	2454.77
150,000	2998.98	2745.92	2666.47	2639.50	2630.11
160,000	3198.91	2928.98	2844.23	2815.47	2805.44
170,000	3398.84	3112.04	3022.00	2991.43	2980.79
180,000	3598.77	3295.11	3199.76	3167.40	3156.13
190,000	3798.70	3478.17	3377.53	3343.36	3331.46
200,000	3998.63	3661.23	3555.29	3519.33	3506.81
250,000	4998.29	4576.53	4444.11	4399.16	4383.51
300,000	5997.95	5491.84	5332.93	5278.99	5260.21

MONTHLY PAYMENTS
ANNUAL INTEREST RATE: 21.25%

LOAN AMOUNT	LOAN MATURITY (YEARS)				
	10	15	20	25	30
50	1.01	0.93	0.90	0.90	0.89
100	2.02	1.85	1.80	1.79	1.78
200	4.04	3.70	3.60	3.57	3.55
300	6.05	5.55	5.40	5.35	5.33
400	8.07	7.40	7.19	7.13	7.10
500	10.09	9.25	8.99	8.91	8.88
600	12.10	11.10	10.79	10.69	10.65
700	14.12	12.95	12.59	12.47	12.42
800	16.13	14.80	14.38	14.25	14.20
900	18.15	16.65	16.18	16.03	15.97
1,000	20.17	18.50	17.98	17.81	17.75
2,000	40.33	36.99	35.95	35.61	35.49
3,000	60.49	55.48	53.93	53.41	53.23
4,000	80.65	73.98	71.90	71.21	70.97
5,000	100.81	92.47	89.88	89.01	88.71
6,000	120.97	110.96	107.85	106.81	106.45
7,000	141.14	129.46	125.83	124.61	124.19
8,000	161.30	147.95	143.80	142.41	141.93
9,000	181.46	166.44	161.78	160.21	159.67
10,000	201.62	184.94	179.75	178.01	177.41
20,000	403.23	369.87	359.49	356.01	354.81
30,000	604.85	554.80	539.24	534.01	532.21
40,000	806.46	739.73	718.98	712.02	709.62
50,000	1008.08	924.67	898.73	890.02	887.02
60,000	1209.70	1109.60	1078.47	1068.02	1064.42
70,000	1411.31	1294.53	1258.22	1246.02	1241.83
80,000	1612.92	1479.46	1437.96	1424.03	1419.23
90,000	1814.54	1664.40	1617.71	1602.03	1596.63
100,000	2016.15	1849.33	1797.45	1780.03	1774.03
110,000	2217.77	2034.26	1977.19	1958.03	1951.44
120,000	2419.38	2219.19	2156.94	2136.04	2128.84
130,000	2621.00	2404.13	2336.68	2314.04	2306.24
140,000	2822.61	2589.06	2516.43	2492.04	2483.65
150,000	3024.23	2773.99	2696.17	2670.04	2661.05
160,000	3225.84	2958.92	2875.92	2848.05	2838.45
170,000	3427.46	3143.86	3055.66	3026.05	3015.85
180,000	3629.07	3328.79	3235.41	3204.05	3193.26
190,000	3830.69	3513.72	3415.15	3382.05	3370.66
200,000	4032.30	3698.65	3594.89	3560.06	3548.06
250,000	5040.38	4623.32	4493.62	4450.07	4435.08
300,000	6048.45	5547.98	5392.34	5340.08	5322.09

MONTHLY PAYMENTS
ANNUAL INTEREST RATE: 21.5%

LOAN AMOUNT	LOAN MATURITY (YEARS)				
	10	15	20	25	30
50	1.02	0.94	0.91	0.91	0.90
100	2.04	1.87	1.82	1.81	1.80
200	4.07	3.74	3.64	3.61	3.59
300	6.10	5.61	5.46	5.41	5.39
400	8.14	7.48	7.27	7.21	7.18
500	10.17	9.35	9.09	9.01	8.98
600	12.20	11.21	10.91	10.81	0.77
700	14.24	13.08	12.73	12.61	12.57
800	16.27	14.95	14.54	14.41	14.36
900	18.30	16.82	16.36	16.21	16.16
1,000	20.34	18.69	18.18	18.01	17.95
2,000	40.67	37.37	36.35	36.01	35.90
3,000	61.00	56.05	54.52	54.02	53.85
4,000	81.33	74.73	72.70	72.02	71.79
5,000	101.66	93.41	90.87	90.03	89.74
6,000	121.99	112.09	109.04	108.03	107.69
7,000	142.32	130.77	127.21	126.03	125.63
8,000	162.65	149.45	145.39	144.04	143.58
9,000	182.98	168.13	163.56	162.04	161.53
10,000	203.31	186.81	181.73	180.05	179.47
20,000	406.61	373.62	363.46	360.09	358.94
30,000	609.91	560.43	545.19	540.13	538.41
40,000	813.22	747.24	726.92	720.17	717.87
50,000	1016.52	934.05	908.65	900.21	897.34
60,000	1219.82	1120.86	1090.37	1080.25	1076.81
70,000	1423.13	1307.66	1272.10	1260.29	1256.27
80,000	1626.43	1494.47	1453.83	1440.33	1435.74
90,000	1829.73	1681.28	1635.56	1620.37	1615.21
100,000	2033.04	1868.09	1817.29	1800.42	1794.67
110,000	2236.34	2054.90	1999.01	1980.46	1974.14
120,000	2439.64	2241.71	2180.74	2160.50	2153.61
130,000	2642.95	2428.51	2362.47	2340.54	2333.08
140,000	2846.25	2615.32	2544.20	2520.58	2512.54
150,000	3049.55	2802.13	2725.93	2700.62	2692.01
160,000	3252.86	2988.94	2907.65	2880.66	2871.48
170,000	3456.16	3175.75	3089.38	3060.70	3050.94
180,000	3659.46	3362.56	3271.11	3240.74	3230.41
190,000	3862.77	3549.37	3452.84	3420.78	3409.88
200,000	4066.07	3736.17	3634.57	3600.83	3589.34
250,000	5082.59	4670.22	4543.21	4501.03	4486.68
300,000	6099.10	5604.26	5451.85	5401.24	5384.01

MONTHLY PAYMENTS
ANNUAL INTEREST RATE: 21.75%

LOAN AMOUNT	\multicolumn{5}{c}{LOAN MATURITY (YEARS)}				
	10	15	20	25	30
50	1.03	0.95	0.92	0.92	0.91
100	2.05	1.89	1.84	1.83	1.82
200	4.10	3.78	3.68	3.65	3.64
300	6.15	5.67	5.52	5.47	5.45
400	8.20	7.55	7.35	7.29	7.27
500	10.25	9.44	9.19	9.11	9.08
600	12.30	11.33	11.03	10.93	10.90
700	14.35	13.21	12.87	12.75	12.71
800	16.40	15.10	14.70	14.57	14.53
900	18.45	16.99	16.54	16.39	16.34
1,000	20.50	18.87	18.38	18.21	18.16
2,000	41.00	37.74	36.75	36.42	36.31
3,000	61.50	56.61	55.12	54.63	54.46
4,000	82.00	75.48	73.49	72.84	72.62
5,000	102.50	94.35	91.86	91.05	90.77
6,000	123.00	113.22	110.23	109.25	108.92
7,000	143.50	132.09	128.61	127.46	127.08
8,000	164.00	150.96	146.98	145.67	145.23
9,000	184.50	169.83	165.35	163.88	163.38
10,000	205.00	188.69	183.72	182.09	181.54
20,000	410.00	377.38	367.44	364.17	363.07
30,000	615.00	566.07	551.15	546.25	544.60
40,000	819.99	754.76	734.87	728.33	726.13
50,000	1024.99	943.45	918.58	910.41	907.67
60,000	1229.99	1132.14	1102.30	1092.49	1089.20
70,000	1434.99	1320.83	1286.01	1274.58	1270.73
80,000	1639.98	1509.52	1469.73	1456.66	1452.26
90,000	1844.98	1698.21	1653.44	1638.74	1633.79
100,000	2049.98	1886.90	1837.16	1820.82	1815.33
110,000	2254.97	2075.59	2020.87	2002.90	1996.86
120,000	2459.97	2264.28	2204.59	2184.98	2178.39
130,000	2664.97	2452.97	2388.30	2367.07	2359.92
140,000	2869.97	2641.66	2572.02	2549.15	2541.46
150,000	3074.96	2830.35	2755.73	2731.23	2722.99
160,000	3279.96	3019.04	2939.45	2913.31	2904.52
170,000	3484.96	3207.73	3123.17	3095.39	3086.05
180,000	3689.95	3396.42	3306.88	3277.47	3267.58
190,000	3894.95	3585.11	3490.60	3459.56	3449.12
200,000	4099.95	3773.80	3674.31	3641.64	3630.65
250,000	5124.93	4717.24	4592.89	4552.05	4538.31
300,000	6149.92	5660.69	5511.47	5462.45	5445.97

LOAN PROGRESS TABLES
(Remaining Balance per $1,000 Original Loan)

Loan progress tables allow you to determine how much is still owed on a mortgage loan during the loan term. To use the tables you must know the following:

1. *The annual interest rate on the loan.* The rate is shown at the top of each table, and each table is for a different rate. Rates range from 7% to 21.75% by .25% intervals.

2. *The original amount borrowed.* The amounts in the table are per $1,000 of original loan. If the original principal was $30,000 then multiply the amount in the table by 30.

3. *The maturity of the loan.* The table shows amounts for 10, 15, 20, 25 and 30 year maturities.

4. *The age of the loan.* This is the number of years since the loan was originated and is shown in the left-most column.

The amounts shown in the table are the remaining balance of the loan at the end of the period shown.

Example: Suppose you obtained a mortgage loan 3½ years ago for $48,500. The interest rate is 7% and the maturity is 20 years. How much do you still owe on the loan?

Find the 7% table. Look at the row for "3.5" age of loan. At the intersection of this row with the "20" column is the amount of 908.94. Multiply this amount by the number of thousands originally borrowed (48.5) to get $44,083.59, the existing balance of the loan.

Example: Suppose you want to know how much interest you paid last year on your mortgage loan so you can deduct the amount from your taxable income. The amount of interest is the difference between your total payments over the year and the amount the loan amortized principal. You can find this latter amount with aid of the table.

Suppose the loan had been originated 5 years ago for $50,000. The interest rate is 7% and maturity is 30 years. At the beginning of last year the loan was 4 years old. At that time the amount owed was $954.75 ("4.0" row, "30" column) per thousand, or $47,737.50 total (50 times 954.75). At the end of the year, the 5-year old loan had a balance of $941.32 per thousand, or $47,066.00. The balance amortized by $47,737.50 minus $47,066.00, or $671.50, during the year. The total monthly payments were $332.66 times 12, or $3,991.92. Total interest paid was $3,991.92 minus $671.50, or $3,320.42.

Example: Suppose you take out a loan today at 7% for 25 years. How long will it take to pay off half of the principal?

Look down the column for 25 year loans. At the 17 year row the amount is 518.41. This is slightly more than half the original $1,000 of principal. The 18 year row shows 468.29, which is less than half. Therefore, you will pay off half the principal some time during the 17th year of the loan.

REMAINING BALANCE PER $1000 OF ORIGINAL LOAN
ANNUAL INTEREST RATE: 7%

AGE OF LOAN	LOAN MATURITY (YEARS)				
	10	15	20	25	30
0.5	964.83	980.79	988.31	992.48	995.01
1.0	928.40	960.90	976.21	984.70	989.84
1.5	890.68	940.31	963.68	976.64	984.49
2.0	851.63	918.98	950.70	968.30	978.95
2.5	811.18	896.89	937.26	959.66	973.21
3.0	769.30	874.02	923.35	950.71	967.27
3.5	725.94	850.34	908.94	941.44	961.12
4.0	681.03	825.82	894.02	931.85	954.75
4.5	634.53	800.42	878.57	921.91	948.15
5.0	586.37	774.13	862.57	911.62	941.32
5.5	536.51	746.90	846.00	900.97	934.24
6.0	484.87	718.70	828.84	889.93	926.92
6.5	431.40	689.50	811.08	878.51	919.33
7.0	376.03	659.27	792.68	866.68	911.47
7.5	318.70	627.96	773.63	854.43	903.34
8.0	259.33	595.54	753.90	841.74	894.92
8.5	197.85	561.97	733.48	828.61	886.19
9.0	134.19	527.20	712.32	815.01	877.16
9.5	68.26	491.20	690.42	800.92	867.81
10.0	0.00	453.93	667.74	786.33	858.12
11.0		375.35	619.93	755.59	837.71
12.0		291.10	568.66	722.62	815.82
13.0		200.75	513.69	687.27	792.35
14.0		103.88	454.75	649.37	767.18
15.0		0.00	391.54	608.72	740.19
16.0			323.77	565.14	711.25
17.0			251.09	518.41	680.22
18.0			173.16	468.29	646.94
19.0			89.60	414.56	611.26
20.0			0.00	356.94	573.00
21.0				295.15	531.98
22.0				226.90	487.98
23.0				157.86	440.81
24.0				81.68	390.23
25.0				0.00	335.99
26.0					277.83
27.0					215.47
28.0					148.60
29.0					76.89
30.0					0.00

REMAINING BALANCE PER $1000 OF ORIGINAL LOAN
ANNUAL INTEREST RATE: 7.25%

AGE OF LOAN	LOAN MATURITY (YEARS)				
	10	15	20	25	30
0.5	965.29	981.20	988.66	992.77	995.25
1.0	929.30	961.70	976.90	985.28	990.32
1.5	891.99	941.49	964.70	977.51	985.21
2.0	853.30	920.53	952.06	969.46	979.92
2.5	813.19	898.80	938.96	961.11	974.43
3.0	771.60	876.27	925.37	952.45	968.73
3.5	728.49	852.92	911.28	943.47	962.83
4.0	683.78	828.70	896.67	934.16	956.71
4.5	637.44	803.59	881.52	924.51	950.37
5.0	589.38	777.56	865.82	914.51	943.79
5.5	539.56	750.57	849.54	904.14	936.97
6.0	487.90	722.59	832.66	893.38	929.90
6.5	434.34	693.57	815.16	882.23	922.56
7.0	378.82	663.49	797.01	870.67	914.96
7.5	321.24	632.30	778.20	858.68	907.08
8.0	261.55	599.97	758.70	846.26	898.91
8.5	199.67	566.44	738.47	833.37	890.44
9.0	135.50	531.68	717.50	820.01	881.65
9.5	68.97	495.64	695.77	806.16	872.55
10.0	0.00	458.28	673.23	791.80	863.10
11.0		379.37	625.63	761.48	843.16
12.0		294.55	574.46	728.88	821.73
13.0		203.37	519.46	693.83	798.69
14.0		105.36	460.34	656.16	773.92
15.0		0.00	396.79	615.67	747.29
16.0			328.47	572.14	718.67
17.0			255.03	525.35	687.90
18.0			176.08	475.06	654.83
19.0			91.22	420.99	619.28
20.0			0.00	362.87	581.06
21.0				300.39	539.98
22.0				233.23	495.82
23.0				161.03	448.35
24.0				83.42	397.32
25.0				0.00	342.47
26.0					283.50
27.0					220.12
28.0					151.98
29.0					78.73
30.0					0.00

475

REMAINING BALANCE PER $1000 OF ORIGINAL LOAN
ANNUAL INTEREST RATE: 7.5 %

AGE OF LOAN	LOAN MATURITY (YEARS)				
	10	15	20	25	30
0.5	965.75	981.59	988.99	993.05	995.48
1.0	930.19	962.49	977.57	985.84	990.78
1.5	893.28	942.65	965.71	978.35	985.91
2.0	854.96	922.06	953.40	970.58	980.85
2.5	815.19	900.69	940.61	962.52	975.60
3.0	773.89	878.50	927.35	954.14	970.14
3.5	731.03	855.46	913.57	945.45	964.48
4.0	686.53	831.55	899.27	936.42	958.61
4.5	640.34	806.73	884.43	927.05	952.51
5.0	592.39	780.96	869.02	917.33	946.17
5.5	542.61	754.21	853.03	907.23	939.60
6.0	490.93	726.44	836.42	896.75	932.78
6.5	437.29	697.62	819.18	885.87	925.69
7.0	381.60	667.69	801.29	874.57	918.34
7.5	323.79	636.63	782.72	862.85	910.71
8.0	263.78	604.38	763.43	850.68	902.78
8.5	201.49	570.90	743.42	838.04	894.56
9.0	136.82	536.15	722.64	824.93	886.02
9.5	69.69	500.08	701.06	811.31	877.15
10.0	0.00	462.63	678.67	797.18	867.95
11.0		383.40	631.29	767.27	848.48
12.0		298.02	580.24	735.04	827.50
13.0		206.01	525.22	700.32	804.89
14.0		106.85	465.93	662.89	780.52
15.0		0.00	402.03	622.56	754.27
16.0			333.18	579.10	725.97
17.0			258.98	532.27	695.48
18.0			179.02	481.80	662.62
19.0			92.86	427.41	627.21
20.0			0.00	368.80	589.05
21.0				305.64	547.93
22.0				237.57	503.62
23.0				164.22	455.86
24.0				85.18	404.40
25.0				0.00	348.95
26.0					289.18
27.0					224.78
28.0					155.38
29.0					80.59
30.0					0.00

REMAINING BALANCE PER $1000 OF ORIGINAL LOAN
ANNUAL INTEREST RATE: 7.75%

AGE OF LOAN	10	15	20	25	30
			LOAN MATURITY (YEARS)		
0.5	966.20	981.98	989.32	993.32	995.70
1.0	931.07	963.26	978.22	986.38	991.22
1.5	894.56	943.80	966.69	979.17	986.57
2.0	856.61	923.57	954.70	971.67	981.74
2.5	817.17	902.54	942.24	963.88	976.72
3.0	776.17	880.69	929.28	955.78	971.50
3.5	733.55	857.98	915.82	947.36	966.07
4.0	689.26	834.37	901.83	938.61	960.43
4.5	643.23	809.83	887.28	929.52	954.57
5.0	595.38	784.33	872.17	920.07	948.48
5.5	545.65	757.82	856.45	910.24	942.14
6.0	493.96	730.26	840.12	900.03	935.56
6.5	440.23	701.63	823.15	889.42	928.72
7.0	384.39	671.86	805.50	878.39	921.61
7.5	326.35	640.92	787.17	866.92	914.22
8.0	266.02	608.77	768.11	855.00	906.54
8.5	203.32	575.35	748.30	842.62	898.55
9.0	138.14	540.61	727.71	829.74	890.25
9.5	70.41	504.50	706.31	816.36	881.63
10.0	0.00	466.97	684.06	802.45	872.66
11.0		387.42	636.91	772.97	853.66
12.0		301.49	585.97	741.12	833.13
13.0		208.65	530.95	706.71	810.95
14.0		108.35	471.50	669.54	786.99
15.0		0.00	407.28	629.38	761.11
16.0			337.90	586.00	733.14
17.0			262.95	539.14	702.93
18.0			181.97	488.51	670.30
19.0			94.50	433.81	635.04
20.0			0.00	374.72	596.96
21.0				310.89	555.81
22.0				241.93	511.36
23.0				167.43	463.34
24.0				86.95	411.46
25.0				0.00	355.42
26.0					294.87
27.0					229.46
28.0					158.80
29.0					82.47
30.0					0.00

REMAINING BALANCE PER $1000 OF ORIGINAL LOAN
ANNUAL INTEREST RATE: 8%

AGE OF LOAN	LOAN MATURITY (YEARS)				
	10	15	20	25	30
0.5	966.65	982.37	989.64	993.58	995.91
1.0	931.95	964.02	978.86	986.91	991.65
1.5	895.83	944.93	967.65	979.96	987.21
2.0	858.25	925.06	955.97	972.73	982.60
2.5	819.13	904.38	943.82	965.21	977.80
3.0	778.43	882.86	931.18	957.38	972.80
3.5	736.07	860.46	918.02	949.23	967.60
4.0	691.99	837.16	904.33	940.75	962.19
4.5	646.11	812.90	890.08	931.92	956.56
5.0	598.37	787.66	875.26	922.74	950.70
5.5	548.69	761.40	859.82	913.18	944.60
6.0	496.98	734.06	843.77	903.24	938.25
6.5	443.17	705.61	827.05	892.89	931.65
7.0	387.18	676.01	809.66	882.11	924.77
7.5	328.91	645.20	791.56	870.90	917.62
8.0	268.26	613.14	772.73	859.24	910.18
8.5	205.15	579.77	753.13	847.10	902.43
9.0	139.48	545.05	732.73	834.46	894.37
9.5	71.13	508.92	711.50	821.32	885.98
10.0	0.00	471.31	689.41	807.63	877.25
11.0		391.45	642.49	778.58	858.71
12.0		304.97	591.68	747.11	838.62
13.0		211.30	536.65	713.03	816.88
14.0		109.86	477.06	676.12	793.32
15.0		0.00	412.52	636.14	767.82
16.0			342.62	592.85	740.19
17.0			266.92	545.97	710.27
18.0			184.94	495.19	677.87
19.0			96.16	440.20	642.78
20.0			0.00	380.65	604.78
21.0				316.15	563.62
22.0				246.30	519.05
23.0				170.65	470.78
24.0				88.73	418.50
25.0				0.00	361.88
26.0					300.56
27.0					234.16
28.0					162.24
29.0					84.35
30.0					0.00

REMAINING BALANCE PER $1000 OF ORIGINAL LOAN
ANNUAL INTEREST RATE: 8.25%

AGE OF
LOAN

LOAN MATURITY (YEARS)

AGE OF LOAN	10	15	20	25	30
0.5	967.10	982.75	989.95	993.84	996.11
1.0	932.81	964.77	979.49	987.42	992.05
1.5	897.09	946.04	968.58	980.73	987.83
2.0	859.87	926.52	957.22	973.76	983.42
2.5	821.09	906.19	945.38	966.49	978.83
3.0	780.68	885.00	933.04	958.92	974.05
3.5	738.57	862.92	920.19	951.04	969.07
4.0	694.70	839.91	906.79	942.82	963.88
4.5	648.98	815.94	892.83	934.26	958.47
5.0	601.35	790.97	878.29	925.34	952.84
5.5	551.72	764.94	863.14	916.04	946.97
6.0	500.00	737.82	847.35	906.36	940.85
6.5	446.12	709.57	830.90	896.27	934.48
7.0	389.97	680.13	813.76	885.75	927.83
7.5	331.47	649.45	795.90	874.80	920.91
8.0	270.51	617.49	777.29	863.38	913.70
8.5	206.99	584.18	757.89	851.48	906.19
9.0	140.81	549.48	737.69	839.09	898.36
9.5	71.85	513.32	716.64	826.17	890.20
10.0	0.00	475.65	694.70	812.72	881.70
11.0		395.48	648.02	784.09	863.62
12.0		308.45	597.35	753.00	843.98
13.0		213.96	542.34	719.25	822.66
14.0		111.38	482.60	682.61	799.52
15.0		0.00	417.76	642.83	774.39
16.0			347.35	599.64	747.11
17.0			270.91	552.75	717.49
18.0			187.92	501.84	685.33
19.0			97.82	446.57	650.42
20.0			0.00	386.57	612.52
21.0				321.42	571.36
22.0				250.69	526.68
23.0				173.89	478.18
24.0				90.52	425.51
25.0				0.00	368.34
26.0					306.26
27.0					238.86
28.0					165.69
29.0					86.25
30.0					0.00

REMAINING BALANCE PER $1000 OF ORIGINAL LOAN
ANNUAL INTEREST RATE: 8.5%

AGE OF LOAN	LOAN MATURITY (YEARS)				
	10	15	20	25	30
0.5	967.54	983.12	990.26	994.08	996.30
1.0	933.67	965.51	980.10	987.91	992.44
1.5	898.34	947.13	969.50	981.47	988.41
2.0	861.48	927.97	958.44	974.75	984.21
2.5	823.03	907.97	946.90	967.74	979.83
3.0	782.91	887.11	934.86	960.43	975.26
3.5	741.06	865.34	922.30	952.80	970.49
4.0	697.40	842.64	909.20	944.84	965.51
4.5	651.84	818.95	895.53	936.53	960.32
5.0	604.32	794.24	881.27	927.87	954.90
5.5	554.74	768.45	866.39	918.83	949.25
6.0	503.02	741.56	850.87	909.40	943.36
6.5	449.06	713.50	834.68	899.57	937.21
7.0	392.76	684.22	817.79	889.30	930.79
7.5	334.03	653.68	800.17	878.60	924.10
8.0	272.76	621.82	781.78	867.43	917.11
8.5	208.84	588.58	762.60	855.78	909.83
9.0	142.15	553.90	742.59	843.62	902.23
9.5	72.58	517.72	721.72	830.94	894.30
10.0	0.00	479.97	699.94	817.70	886.02
11.0		399.52	653.51	789.50	868.39
12.0		311.95	602.98	758.80	849.20
13.0		216.64	547.99	725.39	828.31
14.0		112.90	488.13	689.03	805.57
15.0		0.00	422.99	649.45	780.83
16.0			352.08	606.37	753.90
17.0			274.91	559.49	724.58
18.0			190.92	508.46	692.68
19.0			99.50	452.92	657.95
20.0			0.00	392.48	620.16
21.0				326.69	579.03
22.0				255.08	534.26
23.0				177.15	485.53
24.0				92.32	432.50
25.0				0.00	374.78
26.0					311.95
27.0					243.58
28.0					169.16
29.0					88.16
30.0					0.00

REMAINING BALANCE PER $1000 OF ORIGINAL LOAN
ANNUAL INTEREST RATE: 8.75%

AGE OF LOAN	LOAN MATURITY (YEARS)				
	10	15	20	25	30
0.5	967.98	983.48	990.56	994.32	996.48
1.0	934.52	966.23	980.69	988.38	992.81
1.5	899.58	948.21	970.39	982.19	988.98
2.0	863.08	929.39	959.63	975.71	984.97
2.5	824.96	909.73	948.38	968.95	980.78
3.0	785.13	889.19	936.64	961.88	976.41
3.5	743.53	867.74	924.37	954.50	971.85
4.0	700.08	845.33	911.56	946.79	967.08
4.5	654.69	821.92	898.18	938.74	962.09
5.0	607.28	797.47	884.20	930.33	956.89
5.5	557.76	771.94	869.60	921.55	951.45
6.0	506.03	745.26	854.34	912.37	945.77
6.5	452.00	717.39	838.41	902.78	939.84
7.0	395.56	688.29	821.77	892.77	933.65
7.5	336.60	657.88	804.38	882.31	927.17
8.0	275.02	626.12	786.22	871.39	920.41
8.5	210.69	592.95	767.25	859.97	913.35
9.0	143.50	558.30	747.44	848.05	905.98
9.5	73.31	522.10	726.74	835.60	898.27
10.0	0.00	484.29	705.13	822.60	890.22
11.0		403.55	658.96	794.82	873.04
12.0		315.45	608.58	764.51	854.28
13.0		219.32	553.62	731.45	833.82
14.0		114.44	493.65	695.37	811.49
15.0		0.00	428.21	656.00	787.13
16.0			356.82	613.05	760.56
17.0			278.92	566.18	731.56
18.0			193.92	515.05	699.91
19.0			101.19	459.25	665.39
20.0			0.00	398.38	627.72
21.0				331.96	586.62
22.0				259.49	541.77
23.0				180.41	492.84
24.0				94.14	439.46
25.0				0.00	381.20
26.0					317.65
27.0					248.30
28.0					172.64
29.0					90.08
30.0					0.00

REMAINING BALANCE PER $1000 OF ORIGINAL LOAN
ANNUAL INTEREST RATE: 9%

AGE OF LOAN	LOAN MATURITY (YEARS)				
	10	15	20	25	30
0.5	968.41	983.84	990.85	994.55	996.66
1.0	935.37	966.95	981.27	988.84	993.17
1.5	900.81	949.28	971.26	982.88	989.52
2.0	864.67	930.79	960.79	976.64	985.70
2.5	826.87	911.46	949.84	970.12	981.70
3.0	787.34	891.25	938.38	963.29	977.52
3.5	746.00	870.11	926.41	956.16	973.15
4.0	702.76	847.99	913.88	948.69	968.58
4.5	657.54	824.87	900.77	940.89	963.80
5.0	610.24	800.68	887.07	932.73	958.80
5.5	560.78	775.38	872.74	924.19	953.57
6.0	509.04	748.93	857.75	915.26	948.11
6.5	454.94	721.26	842.07	905.92	942.39
7.0	398.36	692.32	825.68	896.15	936.41
7.5	339.18	662.06	808.53	885.94	930.15
8.0	277.28	630.41	790.60	875.25	923.61
8.5	212.55	597.31	771.85	864.08	916.77
9.0	144.85	562.68	752.23	852.40	909.61
9.5	74.05	526.48	731.72	840.18	902.13
10.0	0.00	488.61	710.26	827.39	894.30
11.0		407.58	664.35	800.05	877.55
12.0		318.96	614.14	770.13	859.23
13.0		222.02	559.22	737.41	839.20
14.0		115.98	499.14	701.62	817.28
15.0		0.00	433.43	662.48	793.31
16.0			361.55	619.66	767.09
17.0			282.94	572.82	738.40
18.0			196.94	521.60	707.03
19.0			102.88	465.56	672.72
20.0			0.00	404.27	635.19
21.0				337.23	594.13
22.0				263.90	549.23
23.0				183.69	500.11
24.0				95.96	446.38
25.0				0.00	387.62
26.0					323.34
27.0					253.03
28.0					176.13
29.0					92.01
30.0					0.00

REMAINING BALANCE PER $1000 OF ORIGINAL LOAN
ANNUAL INTEREST RATE: 9.25%

AGE OF LOAN	LOAN MATURITY (YEARS)				
	10	15	20	25	30
0.5	968.84	984.20	991.13	994.77	996.83
1.0	936.20	967.65	981.84	989.29	993.51
1.5	902.03	950.32	972.11	983.55	990.03
2.0	866.24	932.17	961.92	977.54	986.39
2.5	828.77	913.17	951.26	971.25	982.58
3.0	789.53	893.27	940.09	964.66	978.58
3.5	748.44	872.44	928.39	957.76	974.40
4.0	705.42	850.62	916.14	950.54	970.03
4.5	660.36	827.77	903.32	942.97	965.44
5.0	613.19	803.85	889.89	935.05	960.64
5.5	563.78	778.80	875.82	926.75	955.61
6.0	512.05	752.57	861.10	918.07	950.35
6.5	457.88	725.10	845.68	908.97	944.84
7.0	401.15	696.33	829.53	899.45	939.07
7.5	341.75	666.21	812.62	889.47	933.02
8.0	279.55	634.67	794.91	879.03	926.69
8.5	214.42	601.64	776.37	868.09	920.06
9.0	146.21	567.05	756.96	856.64	913.12
9.5	74.79	530.83	736.63	844.65	905.86
10.0	0.00	492.91	715.34	832.09	898.25
11.0		411.61	669.70	805.17	881.93
12.0		322.47	619.66	775.65	864.05
13.0		224.72	564.78	743.28	844.43
14.0		117.53	504.61	707.79	822.92
15.0		0.00	438.63	668.88	799.34
16.0			366.29	626.20	773.48
17.0			286.96	579.41	745.12
18.0			199.97	528.10	714.03
19.0			104.59	471.84	679.93
20.0			0.00	410.15	642.55
21.0				342.50	601.55
22.0				268.32	556.60
23.0				186.98	507.31
24.0				97.80	453.27
25.0				0.00	394.00
26.0					329.02
27.0					257.76
28.0					179.62
29.0					93.95
30.0					0.00

REMAINING BALANCE PER $1000 OF ORIGINAL LOAN
ANNUAL INTEREST RATE: 9.5%

AGE OF LOAN	LOAN MATURITY (YEARS)				
	10	15	20	25	30
0.5	969.26	984.54	991.40	994.98	996.99
1.0	937.03	968.34	982.39	989.72	993.83
1.5	903.24	951.35	972.94	984.20	990.52
2.0	867.81	933.53	963.03	978.41	987.06
2.5	830.66	914.86	952.65	972.35	983.42
3.0	791.71	895.28	941.76	965.99	979.60
3.5	750.88	874.74	930.34	959.32	975.61
4.0	708.07	853.22	918.37	952.33	971.41
4.5	663.18	830.65	905.81	945.00	967.02
5.0	616.12	806.99	892.65	937.31	962.41
5.5	566.78	782.18	878.86	929.25	957.58
6.0	515.05	756.17	864.39	920.81	952.51
6.5	460.82	728.90	849.22	911.95	947.20
7.0	403.95	700.31	833.32	902.66	941.63
7.5	344.33	670.33	816.65	892.93	935.80
8.0	281.82	638.91	799.17	882.72	929.67
8.5	216.29	605.95	780.84	872.02	923.26
9.0	147.57	571.41	761.63	860.79	916.53
9.5	75.53	535.18	741.48	849.03	909.47
10.0	0.00	497.21	720.36	836.70	902.08
11.0		415.64	675.00	810.20	886.19
12.0		325.99	625.14	781.08	868.73
13.0		227.43	570.32	749.07	849.54
14.0		119.09	510.07	713.88	828.44
15.0		0.00	443.83	675.20	805.24
16.0			371.03	632.69	779.75
17.0			290.99	585.95	751.72
18.0			203.02	534.57	720.91
19.0			106.31	478.09	687.05
20.0			0.00	416.01	649.82
21.0				347.77	608.90
22.0				272.75	563.92
23.0				190.29	514.47
24.0				99.64	460.12
25.0				0.00	400.37
26.0					334.69
27.0					262.50
28.0					183.14
29.0					95.90
30.0					0.00

REMAINING BALANCE PER $1000 OF ORIGINAL LOAN
ANNUAL INTEREST RATE: 9.75%

AGE OF LOAN	LOAN MATURITY (YEARS)				
	10	15	20	25	30
0.5	969.68	984.88	991.67	995.18	997.14
1.0	937.85	969.02	982.93	990.13	994.14
1.5	904.43	952.36	973.75	984.82	991.00
2.0	869.36	934.87	964.12	979.25	987.69
2.5	832.53	916.52	954.00	973.41	984.22
3.0	793.88	897.25	943.38	967.27	980.58
3.5	753.30	877.02	932.24	960.82	976.76
4.0	710.71	855.78	920.54	954.06	972.74
4.5	665.99	833.49	908.26	946.96	968.53
5.0	619.05	810.09	895.37	939.51	964.11
5.5	569.78	785.53	881.83	931.68	959.47
6.0	518.05	759.74	867.62	923.47	954.59
6.5	463.75	732.68	852.71	914.84	949.48
7.0	406.75	704.26	837.05	905.79	944.11
7.5	346.91	674.43	820.62	896.29	938.47
8.0	284.10	643.12	803.36	886.32	932.55
8.5	218.16	610.25	785.25	875.84	926.34
9.0	148.94	575.74	766.24	864.85	919.82
9.5	76.28	539.52	746.28	853.31	912.97
10.0	0.00	501.49	725.33	841.20	905.79
11.0		419.67	680.25	815.14	890.32
12.0		329.51	630.57	786.42	873.28
13.0		230.15	575.82	754.76	854.51
14.0		120.66	515.50	719.89	833.81
15.0		0.00	449.02	681.45	811.01
16.0			375.76	639.10	785.88
17.0			295.03	592.42	758.19
18.0			206.07	540.99	727.68
19.0			108.03	484.31	694.05
20.0			0.00	421.85	656.99
21.0				353.03	616.16
22.0				277.18	571.16
23.0				193.60	521.57
24.0				101.50	466.93
25.0				0.00	406.71
26.0					340.36
27.0					267.23
28.0					186.65
29.0					97.85
30.0					0.00

485

REMAINING BALANCE PER $1000 OF ORIGINAL LOAN
ANNUAL INTEREST RATE: 10%

AGE OF
LOAN

LOAN MATURITY (YEARS)

	10	15	20	25	30
0.5	970.09	985.22	991.93	995.38	997.29
1.0	938.66	969.68	983.45	990.53	994.44
1.5	905.62	953.35	974.54	985.43	991.45
2.0	870.89	936.19	965.17	980.07	988.30
2.5	834.39	918.15	955.33	974.43	984.99
3.0	796.03	899.19	944.98	968.51	981.52
3.5	755.71	879.26	934.10	962.28	977.86
4.0	713.33	858.32	922.67	955.74	974.02
4.5	668.79	836.30	910.65	948.87	969.99
5.0	621.97	813.17	898.02	941.64	965.74
5.5	572.76	788.85	884.75	934.04	961.28
6.0	521.05	763.28	870.80	926.06	956.60
6.5	466.69	736.42	856.13	917.66	951.67
7.0	409.55	708.18	840.72	908.84	946.49
7.5	349.50	678.50	824.52	899.57	941.05
8.0	286.38	647.31	807.50	889.83	935.33
8.5	220.04	614.52	789.60	879.58	929.32
9.0	150.31	580.06	770.79	868.82	923.00
9.5	77.03	543.84	751.02	857.51	916.36
10.0	0.00	505.77	730.24	845.61	909.38
11.0		423.70	685.45	819.98	894.33
12.0		333.03	635.96	791.65	877.71
13.0		232.88	581.30	760.37	859.34
14.0		122.23	520.90	725.81	839.06
15.0		0.00	454.19	687.62	816.64
16.0			380.49	645.44	791.89
17.0			299.07	598.85	764.54
18.0			209.13	547.37	734.32
19.0			109.77	490.50	700.94
20.0			0.00	427.68	664.07
21.0				358.28	623.33
22.0				281.62	578.33
23.0				196.92	528.62
24.0				103.36	473.70
25.0				0.00	413.03
26.0					346.01
27.0					271.97
28.0					190.18
29.0					99.82
30.0					0.00

REMAINING BALANCE PER $1000 OF ORIGINAL LOAN
ANNUAL INTEREST RATE: 10.25%

AGE OF LOAN	LOAN MATURITY (YEARS)				
	10	15	20	25	30
0.5	970.50	985.55	992.19	995.57	997.43
1.0	939.46	970.34	983.96	990.92	994.72
1.5	906.80	954.33	975.31	986.01	991.88
2.0	872.42	937.49	966.20	980.85	988.88
2.5	836.24	919.76	956.62	975.42	985.73
3.0	798.17	901.11	946.54	969.71	982.41
3.5	758.11	881.48	935.92	963.70	978.92
4.0	715.94	860.82	924.75	957.37	975.25
4.5	671.58	839.08	913.00	950.71	971.38
5.0	624.88	816.20	900.63	943.71	967.31
5.5	575.75	792.13	887.61	936.33	963.03
6.0	524.04	766.79	873.92	928.57	958.52
6.5	469.62	740.13	859.50	920.41	953.78
7.0	412.35	712.07	844.33	911.81	948.79
7.5	352.09	682.54	828.37	902.77	943.54
8.0	288.67	651.47	811.57	893.25	938.01
8.5	221.93	618.77	793.89	883.24	932.20
9.0	151.69	584.36	775.28	872.70	926.08
9.5	77.78	548.14	755.70	861.60	919.64
10.0	0.00	510.03	735.10	849.93	912.86
11.0		427.72	690.60	824.72	898.22
12.0		336.56	641.31	796.80	882.01
13.0		235.61	586.73	765.88	864.05
14.0		123.81	526.29	731.64	844.17
15.0		0.00	459.35	693.72	822.15
16.0			385.22	651.72	797.76
17.0			303.12	605.21	770.76
18.0			212.20	553.71	740.85
19.0			111.51	496.66	707.72
20.0			0.00	433.49	671.04
21.0				363.53	630.42
22.0				286.06	585.43
23.0				200.25	535.61
24.0				105.23	480.43
25.0				0.00	419.32
26.0					351.65
27.0					276.71
28.0					193.71
29.0					101.79
30.0					0.00

REMAINING BALANCE PER $1000 OF ORIGINAL LOAN
ANNUAL INTEREST RATE: 10.5%

AGE OF LOAN	LOAN MATURITY (YEARS)				
	10	15	20	25	30
0.5	970.91	985.87	992.43	995.76	997.56
1.0	940.26	970.98	984.46	991.29	994.99
1.5	907.96	955.29	976.06	986.58	992.29
2.0	873.93	938.77	967.21	981.61	989.44
2.5	838.07	921.35	957.88	976.38	986.43
3.0	800.29	903.00	948.06	970.87	983.27
3.5	760.49	883.66	937.70	965.07	979.93
4.0	718.54	863.29	926.79	958.95	976.42
4.5	674.35	841.83	915.30	952.50	972.72
5.0	627.78	819.21	903.18	945.71	968.82
5.5	578.72	795.38	890.42	938.56	964.71
6.0	527.02	770.27	876.98	931.02	960.38
6.5	472.55	743.81	862.81	923.07	955.81
7.0	415.15	715.93	847.88	914.70	951.00
7.5	354.68	686.56	832.15	905.88	945.94
8.0	290.96	655.61	815.58	896.59	940.60
8.5	223.82	623.00	798.11	886.80	934.97
9.0	153.08	588.64	779.71	876.48	929.05
9.5	78.54	552.43	760.32	865.61	922.80
10.0	0.00	514.28	739.90	854.15	916.22
11.0		431.74	695.69	829.37	901.99
12.0		340.10	646.62	801.85	886.18
13.0		238.36	592.13	771.30	868.63
14.0		125.40	531.65	737.38	849.15
15.0		0.00	464.49	699.73	827.52
16.0			389.94	657.93	803.51
17.0			307.17	611.51	776.85
18.0			215.28	559.99	747.25
19.0			113.26	502.79	714.39
20.0			0.00	439.28	677.91
21.0				368.77	637.41
22.0				290.49	592.45
23.0				203.59	542.53
24.0				107.11	487.11
25.0				0.00	425.58
26.0					357.27
27.0					281.44
28.0					197.24
29.0					103.77
30.0					0.00

REMAINING BALANCE PER $1000 OF ORIGINAL LOAN
ANNUAL INTEREST RATE: 10.75%

AGE OF LOAN	LOAN MATURITY (YEARS)				
	10	15	20	25	30
0.5	971.31	986.19	992.67	995.93	997.69
1.0	941.04	971.61	984.95	991.65	995.25
1.5	909.12	956.24	976.79	987.12	992.68
2.0	875.43	940.02	968.19	982.35	989.97
2.5	839.89	922.91	959.11	977.31	987.11
3.0	802.40	904.86	949.54	972.00	984.09
3.5	762.85	885.82	939.44	966.39	980.90
4.0	721.13	865.73	928.79	960.48	977.54
4.5	677.11	844.54	917.55	954.24	974.00
5.0	630.67	822.18	905.69	947.66	970.26
5.5	581.68	798.59	893.18	940.72	966.32
6.0	530.00	773.71	879.98	933.39	962.15
6.5	475.48	747.46	866.06	925.67	957.76
7.0	417.95	719.76	851.37	917.52	953.13
7.5	357.27	690.54	835.87	908.92	948.25
8.0	293.25	659.72	819.52	899.84	943.09
8.5	225.71	627.20	802.28	890.27	937.65
9.0	154.47	592.90	784.08	880.17	931.92
9.5	79.30	556.71	764.89	869.52	925.86
10.0	0.00	518.53	744.64	858.28	919.48
11.0		435.75	700.74	833.92	905.64
12.0		343.63	651.88	806.81	890.23
13.0		241.11	597.50	776.63	873.08
14.0		127.00	536.98	743.04	854.00
15.0		0.00	469.62	705.66	832.76
16.0			394.66	664.06	809.12
17.0			311.22	617.76	782.81
18.0			218.37	566.23	753.53
19.0			115.02	508.87	720.95
20.0			0.00	445.04	684.68
21.0				374.00	644.31
22.0				294.94	599.39
23.0				206.94	549.39
24.0				109.00	493.74
25.0				0.00	431.81
26.0					362.88
27.0					286.16
28.0					200.78
29.0					105.76
30.0					0.00

REMAINING BALANCE PER $1000 OF ORIGINAL LOAN
ANNUAL INTEREST RATE: 11%

AGE OF LOAN	LOAN MATURITY (YEARS)				
	10	15	20	25	30
0.5	971.71	986.50	992.91	996.10	997.81
1.0	941.83	972.24	985.42	991.99	995.50
1.5	910.26	957.17	977.50	987.64	993.06
2.0	876.92	941.26	969.15	983.05	990.48
2.5	841.70	924.45	960.32	978.21	987.75
3.0	804.50	906.70	950.99	973.08	984.87
3.5	765.21	887.95	941.14	967.67	981.83
4.0	723.70	868.14	930.74	961.96	978.62
4.5	679.86	847.22	919.75	955.92	975.23
5.0	633.55	825.12	908.14	949.55	971.65
5.5	584.64	801.77	895.88	942.81	967.86
6.0	532.97	777.12	882.93	935.70	963.86
6.5	478.40	751.07	869.25	928.19	959.64
7.0	420.76	723.56	854.80	920.25	955.18
7.5	359.87	694.50	839.53	911.87	950.47
8.0	295.55	663.81	823.41	903.01	945.49
8.5	227.62	631.38	806.38	893.66	940.24
9.0	155.86	597.14	788.39	883.78	934.69
9.5	80.06	560.97	769.39	873.35	928.82
10.0	0.00	522.76	749.32	862.32	922.63
11.0		439.77	705.73	838.38	909.17
12.0		347.17	657.09	811.67	894.16
13.0		243.86	602.83	781.87	877.41
14.0		128.60	542.29	748.62	858.72
15.0		0.00	474.74	711.52	837.87
16.0			399.37	670.12	814.61
17.0			315.28	623.94	788.66
18.0			221.46	572.42	759.70
19.0			116.79	514.93	727.39
20.0			0.00	450.78	691.34
21.0				379.22	651.12
22.0				299.38	606.25
23.0				210.29	556.19
24.0				110.90	500.33
25.0				0.00	438.00
26.0					368.47
27.0					290.89
28.0					204.33
29.0					107.75
30.0					0.00

REMAINING BALANCE PER $1000 OF ORIGINAL LOAN
ANNUAL INTEREST RATE: 11.25%

AGE OF LOAN	LOAN MATURITY (YEARS)				
	10	15	20	25	30
0.5	972.10	986.80	993.14	996.27	997.93
1.0	942.60	972.85	985.88	992.32	995.73
1.5	911.39	958.09	978.20	988.15	993.41
2.0	878.39	942.48	970.08	983.74	990.96
2.5	843.49	925.97	961.49	979.07	988.37
3.0	806.58	908.51	952.41	974.13	985.62
3.5	767.55	890.04	942.80	968.91	982.72
4.0	726.26	870.51	932.64	963.39	979.65
4.5	682.60	849.86	921.90	957.55	976.41
5.0	636.42	828.02	910.54	951.38	972.97
5.5	587.59	804.92	898.52	944.85	969.34
6.0	535.94	780.49	885.82	937.94	965.50
6.5	481.32	754.65	872.38	930.64	961.44
7.0	423.56	727.32	858.16	922.91	957.15
7.5	362.46	698.43	843.13	914.74	952.61
8.0	297.85	667.86	827.23	906.10	947.81
8.5	229.52	635.54	810.42	896.96	942.73
9.0	157.26	601.36	792.64	887.30	937.36
9.5	80.83	565.20	773.83	877.08	931.67
10.0	0.00	526.97	753.94	866.27	925.67
11.0		443.77	710.66	842.75	912.59
12.0		350.71	662.26	816.44	897.97
13.0		246.63	608.12	787.01	881.61
14.0		130.21	547.56	754.10	863.32
15.0		0.00	479.83	717.28	842.86
16.0			404.07	676.11	819.97
17.0			319.34	630.06	794.37
18.0			224.56	578.55	765.74
19.0			118.56	520.94	733.72
20.0			0.00	456.50	697.90
21.0				384.42	657.84
22.0				303.81	613.03
23.0				213.65	562.91
24.0				112.80	506.86
25.0				0.00	444.16
26.0					374.03
27.0					295.60
28.0					207.87
29.0					109.75
30.0					0.00

REMAINING BALANCE PER $1000 OF ORIGINAL LOAN
ANNUAL INTEREST RATE: 11.5%

AGE OF LOAN	10	15	20	25	30
		LOAN MATURITY (YEARS)			

AGE OF LOAN	10	15	20	25	30
0.5	972.49	987.10	993.36	996.43	998.04
1.0	943.36	973.45	986.32	992.64	995.96
1.5	912.52	958.99	978.87	988.64	993.75
2.0	879.86	943.67	970.99	984.40	991.42
2.5	845.27	927.46	962.63	979.90	988.95
3.0	808.65	910.29	953.79	975.15	986.34
3.5	769.87	892.11	944.43	970.11	983.57
4.0	728.81	872.86	934.51	964.78	980.64
4.5	685.33	852.47	924.01	959.13	977.53
5.0	639.28	830.89	912.89	953.15	974.25
5.5	590.53	808.03	901.12	946.82	970.77
6.0	538.91	783.83	888.65	940.11	967.08
6.5	484.24	758.20	875.45	933.01	963.18
7.0	426.36	731.06	861.47	925.50	959.04
7.5	365.06	702.32	846.67	917.54	954.67
8.0	300.16	671.90	830.99	909.11	950.03
8.5	231.43	639.68	814.40	900.18	945.13
9.0	158.66	605.56	796.82	890.73	939.93
9.5	81.60	569.43	778.21	880.72	934.43
10.0	0.00	531.17	758.51	870.12	928.60
11.0		447.77	715.55	847.02	915.90
12.0		354.25	667.38	821.11	901.66
13.0		249.40	613.37	792.06	885.69
14.0		131.83	552.81	759.49	867.79
15.0		0.00	484.90	722.97	847.71
16.0			408.77	682.03	825.20
17.0			323.40	636.11	799.97
18.0			227.67	584.63	771.67
19.0			120.34	526.91	739.93
20.0			0.00	462.19	704.36
21.0				389.62	664.46
22.0				308.24	619.73
23.0				217.01	569.58
24.0				114.71	513.34
25.0				0.00	450.28
26.0					379.58
27.0					300.31
28.0					211.42
29.0					111.75
30.0					0.00

REMAINING BALANCE PER $1000 OF ORIGINAL LOAN
ANNUAL INTEREST RATE: 11.75%

AGE OF LOAN	LOAN MATURITY (YEARS)				
	10	15	20	25	30
0.5	972.88	987.40	993.57	996.58	998.14
1.0	944.12	974.04	986.76	992.95	996.17
1.5	913.63	959.87	979.53	989.11	994.08
2.0	881.31	944.85	971.87	985.03	991.86
2.5	847.03	928.93	963.75	980.71	989.51
3.0	810.70	912.04	955.14	976.13	987.02
3.5	772.18	894.15	946.01	971.27	984.38
4.0	731.34	875.17	936.33	966.12	981.58
4.5	688.04	855.05	926.07	960.66	978.61
5.0	642.13	833.72	915.19	954.87	975.46
5.5	593.46	811.11	903.66	948.73	972.13
6.0	541.86	787.13	891.43	942.22	968.59
6.5	487.16	761.71	878.46	935.32	964.84
7.0	429.16	734.76	864.72	928.01	960.86
7.5	367.66	706.19	850.14	920.25	956.65
8.0	302.47	675.90	834.69	912.03	952.18
8.5	233.35	643.78	818.31	903.31	947.44
9.0	160.07	609.73	800.95	894.07	942.41
9.5	82.37	573.63	782.53	884.27	937.09
10.0	0.00	535.36	763.01	873.89	931.44
11.0		451.76	720.38	851.20	919.11
12.0		357.80	672.45	825.69	905.24
13.0		252.17	618.58	797.02	889.65
14.0		133.45	558.02	764.80	872.14
15.0		0.00	489.96	728.58	852.45
16.0			413.45	687.86	830.31
17.0			327.45	642.10	805.43
18.0			230.79	590.66	777.47
19.0			122.13	532.84	746.03
20.0			0.00	467.84	710.70
21.0				394.79	670.99
22.0				312.67	626.35
23.0				220.37	576.17
24.0				116.62	519.76
25.0				0.00	456.37
26.0					385.10
27.0					305.00
28.0					214.96
29.0					113.76
30.0					0.00

REMAINING BALANCE PER $1000 OF ORIGINAL LOAN
ANNUAL INTEREST RATE: 12%

AGE OF LOAN	LOAN MATURITY (YEARS)				
	10	15	20	25	30
0.5	973.26	987.69	993.78	996.73	998.24
1.0	944.87	974.61	987.18	993.25	996.37
1.5	914.73	960.74	980.17	989.56	994.39
2.0	882.74	946.01	972.73	985.64	992.28
2.5	848.79	930.37	964.84	981.49	990.05
3.0	812.74	913.77	956.46	977.07	987.67
3.5	774.48	896.15	947.56	972.39	985.16
4.0	733.86	877.45	938.11	967.41	982.48
4.5	690.74	857.60	928.09	962.14	979.64
5.0	644.97	836.52	917.44	956.53	976.63
5.5	596.39	814.15	906.15	950.58	973.43
6.0	544.82	790.40	894.15	944.27	970.04
6.5	490.07	765.20	881.42	937.57	966.44
7.0	431.96	738.44	867.91	930.45	962.61
7.5	370.27	710.03	853.56	922.90	958.55
8.0	304.78	679.88	838.34	914.88	954.24
8.5	235.27	647.87	822.17	906.37	949.67
9.0	161.48	613.89	805.01	897.33	944.81
9.5	83.15	577.82	786.80	887.74	939.65
10.0	0.00	539.54	767.46	877.56	934.18
11.0		455.75	725.15	855.29	922.20
12.0		361.34	677.47	830.18	908.71
13.0		254.96	623.75	801.89	893.50
14.0		135.08	563.21	770.02	876.37
15.0		0.00	494.99	734.10	857.06
16.0			418.13	693.63	835.30
17.0			331.51	648.02	810.78
18.0			233.91	596.64	783.16
19.0			123.93	538.73	752.03
20.0			0.00	473.48	716.95
21.0				399.95	677.42
22.0				317.10	632.88
23.0				223.74	582.69
24.0				118.54	526.14
25.0				0.00	462.41
26.0					390.60
27.0					309.69
28.0					218.51
29.0					115.77
30.0					0.00

REMAINING BALANCE PER $1000 OF ORIGINAL LOAN
ANNUAL INTEREST RATE: 12.25%

AGE OF LOAN	LOAN MATURITY (YEARS)				
	10	15	20	25	30
0.5	973.63	987.97	993.98	996.87	998.33
1.0	945.61	975.18	987.59	993.54	996.56
1.5	915.83	961.59	980.80	990.00	994.68
2.0	884.17	947.15	973.57	986.23	992.68
2.5	850.52	931.79	965.90	982.24	990.56
3.0	814.77	915.48	957.74	977.99	988.30
3.5	776.76	898.13	949.07	973.47	985.90
4.0	736.36	879.70	939.85	968.67	983.34
4.5	693.43	860.11	930.06	963.57	980.63
5.0	647.80	839.29	919.65	958.14	977.75
5.5	599.31	817.16	908.58	952.38	974.69
6.0	547.76	793.64	896.82	946.25	971.43
6.5	492.98	768.64	884.32	939.74	967.97
7.0	434.75	742.07	871.04	932.82	964.29
7.5	372.87	713.84	856.92	925.47	960.38
8.0	307.10	683.82	841.91	917.65	956.22
8.5	237.19	651.93	825.97	909.34	951.81
9.0	162.89	618.02	809.01	900.51	947.11
9.5	83.93	581.99	791.00	891.13	942.12
10.0	0.00	543.69	771.85	881.15	936.82
11.0		459.73	729.87	859.28	925.20
12.0		364.88	682.45	834.58	912.07
13.0		257.74	628.88	806.67	897.23
14.0		136.72	568.36	775.15	880.47
15.0		0.00	500.01	739.54	861.55
16.0			422.79	699.32	840.16
17.0			335.56	653.88	816.01
18.0			237.03	602.55	788.72
19.0			125.73	544.57	757.90
20.0			0.00	479.08	723.09
21.0				405.09	683.76
22.0				321.52	639.33
23.0				227.11	589.15
24.0				120.47	532.46
25.0				0.00	468.42
26.0					396.08
27.0					314.36
28.0					222.06
29.0					117.79
30.0					0.00

REMAINING BALANCE PER $1000 OF ORIGINAL LOAN
ANNUAL INTEREST RATE: 12.5%

AGE OF LOAN	LOAN MATURITY (YEARS)				
	10	15	20	25	30
0.5	974.01	988.25	994.18	997.00	998.42
1.0	946.34	975.74	987.99	993.81	996.75
1.5	916.91	962.43	981.40	990.42	994.96
2.0	885.58	948.26	974.39	986.80	993.06
2.5	852.25	933.19	966.93	982.96	991.04
3.0	816.77	917.15	958.99	978.87	988.89
3.5	779.03	900.08	950.54	974.51	986.60
4.0	738.86	881.92	941.55	969.88	984.17
4.5	696.11	862.59	931.98	964.95	981.58
5.0	650.62	842.02	921.80	959.70	978.82
5.5	602.21	820.14	910.97	954.12	975.88
6.0	550.70	796.84	899.44	948.17	972.76
6.5	495.88	772.06	887.17	941.85	969.44
7.0	437.55	745.68	874.11	935.12	965.90
7.5	375.47	717.61	860.22	927.96	962.14
8.0	309.41	687.74	845.43	920.34	958.13
8.5	239.12	655.96	829.70	912.23	953.87
9.0	164.31	622.13	812.95	903.61	949.33
9.5	84.71	586.14	795.14	894.42	944.51
10.0	0.00	547.84	776.18	884.65	939.37
11.0		463.70	734.53	863.19	928.09
12.0		368.43	687.37	838.88	915.31
13.0		260.53	633.96	811.36	900.85
14.0		138.36	573.48	780.19	884.46
15.0		0.00	505.00	744.90	865.91
16.0			427.44	704.93	844.90
17.0			339.62	659.67	821.11
18.0			240.16	608.41	794.17
19.0			127.54	550.37	763.67
20.0			0.00	484.64	729.12
21.0				410.21	690.00
22.0				325.93	645.69
23.0				230.48	595.53
24.0				122.40	538.71
25.0				0.00	474.38
26.0					401.53
27.0					319.02
28.0					225.60
29.0					119.80
30.0					0.00

REMAINING BALANCE PER $1000 OF ORIGINAL LOAN
ANNUAL INTEREST RATE: 12.75%

AGE OF	LOAN MATURITY (YEARS)				
LOAN	10	15	20	25	30
0.5	974.37	988.52	994.37	997.13	998.51
1.0	947.07	976.29	988.38	994.08	996.92
1.5	917.98	963.25	981.99	990.82	995.23
2.0	886.98	949.36	975.19	987.35	993.43
2.5	853.96	934.57	967.94	983.65	991.50
3.0	818.77	918.80	960.21	979.71	989.46
3.5	781.28	902.01	951.98	975.52	987.28
4.0	741.33	884.11	943.21	971.05	984.95
4.5	698.77	865.04	933.86	966.28	982.48
5.0	653.43	844.72	923.91	961.21	979.84
5.5	605.11	823.08	913.30	955.80	977.03
6.0	553.63	800.01	902.00	950.04	974.03
6.5	498.78	775.44	889.96	943.90	970.84
7.0	440.34	749.25	877.13	937.36	967.44
7.5	378.08	721.36	863.46	930.39	963.82
8.0	311.74	691.63	848.89	922.96	959.96
8.5	241.05	659.96	833.37	915.05	955.85
9.0	165.74	626.22	816.84	906.62	951.47
9.5	85.50	590.27	799.22	897.64	946.80
10.0	0.00	551.96	780.45	888.07	941.83
11.0		467.67	739.14	867.01	930.88
12.0		371.97	692.24	843.10	918.46
13.0		263.33	639.01	815.96	904.35
14.0		140.00	578.57	785.15	888.34
15.0		0.00	509.97	750.17	870.16
16.0			432.08	710.46	849.53
17.0			343.67	665.39	826.10
18.0			243.29	614.22	799.51
19.0			129.35	556.13	769.32
20.0			0.00	490.18	735.05
21.0				415.32	696.14
22.0				330.33	651.97
23.0				233.86	601.83
24.0				124.33	544.92
25.0				0.00	480.30
26.0					406.95
27.0					323.67
28.0					229.14
29.0					121.83
30.0					0.00

REMAINING BALANCE PER $1000 OF ORIGINAL LOAN
ANNUAL INTEREST RATE: 13%

AGE OF LOAN	LOAN MATURITY (YEARS)				
	10	15	20	25	30
0.5	974.74	988.79	994.56	997.26	998.59
1.0	947.79	976.82	988.76	994.33	997.09
1.5	919.04	964.06	982.57	991.21	995.48
2.0	888.37	950.45	975.96	987.88	993.77
2.5	855.65	935.92	968.92	984.32	991.95
3.0	820.75	920.43	961.40	980.53	990.00
3.5	783.52	903.90	953.38	976.49	987.92
4.0	743.80	886.27	944.83	972.18	985.70
4.5	701.43	867.46	935.70	967.57	983.34
5.0	656.22	847.39	925.97	962.67	980.82
5.5	608.00	825.98	915.59	957.43	978.13
6.0	556.56	803.15	904.51	951.84	975.26
6.5	501.68	778.78	892.69	945.88	972.19
7.0	443.14	752.80	880.08	939.52	968.93
7.5	380.69	725.07	866.63	932.74	965.44
8.0	314.06	695.50	852.29	925.51	961.72
8.5	242.99	663.94	836.98	917.79	957.76
9.0	167.17	630.29	820.66	909.55	953.53
9.5	86.29	594.38	803.24	900.77	949.01
10.0	0.00	556.08	784.66	891.40	944.20
11.0		471.62	743.69	870.74	933.58
12.0		375.51	697.07	847.23	921.50
13.0		266.13	644.01	820.47	907.75
14.0		141.66	583.63	790.02	892.11
15.0		0.00	514.91	755.36	874.30
16.0			436.71	715.92	854.04
17.0			347.71	671.04	830.97
18.0			246.43	619.96	804.73
19.0			131.17	561.84	774.86
20.0			0.00	495.69	740.87
21.0				420.40	702.19
22.0				334.73	658.17
23.0				237.23	608.07
24.0				126.27	551.06
25.0				0.00	486.18
26.0					412.34
27.0					328.31
28.0					232.68
29.0					123.85
30.0					0.00

REMAINING BALANCE PER $1000 OF ORIGINAL LOAN
ANNUAL INTEREST RATE: 13.25%

AGE OF LOAN	LOAN MATURITY (YEARS)				
	10	15	20	25	30
0.5	975.10	989.05	994.74	997.38	998.67
1.0	948.50	977.35	989.12	994.57	997.24
1.5	920.09	964.85	983.12	991.58	995.72
2.0	889.75	951.51	976.71	988.38	994.10
2.5	857.34	937.25	969.87	984.97	992.36
3.0	822.72	922.03	962.56	981.32	990.51
3.5	785.74	905.76	954.75	977.43	988.53
4.0	746.25	888.39	946.41	973.27	986.42
4.5	704.06	869.84	937.50	968.82	984.16
5.0	659.01	850.02	927.98	964.07	981.75
5.5	610.88	828.85	917.82	959.00	979.17
6.0	559.48	806.24	906.96	953.59	976.42
6.5	504.57	782.10	895.37	947.80	973.49
7.0	445.93	756.30	882.98	941.63	970.35
7.5	383.29	728.75	869.75	935.03	966.99
8.0	316.39	699.33	855.62	927.98	963.41
8.5	244.93	667.90	840.53	920.45	959.59
9.0	168.60	634.33	824.41	912.41	955.50
9.5	87.08	598.47	807.20	903.82	951.14
10.0	0.00	560.17	788.80	894.65	946.48
11.0		475.57	748.18	874.38	936.19
12.0		379.05	701.84	851.26	924.44
13.0		268.94	648.96	824.89	911.04
14.0		143.32	588.64	794.80	895.76
15.0		0.00	519.83	760.47	878.32
16.0			441.32	721.30	858.42
17.0			351.75	676.62	835.73
18.0			249.57	625.65	809.83
19.0			132.99	567.50	780.29
20.0			0.00	501.15	746.59
21.0				425.46	708.14
22.0				339.11	664.27
23.0				240.60	614.23
24.0				128.22	557.14
25.0				0.00	492.01
26.0					417.70
27.0					332.93
28.0					236.21
29.0					125.88
30.0					0.00

REMAINING BALANCE PER $1000 OF ORIGINAL LOAN
ANNUAL INTEREST RATE: 13.5%

AGE OF LOAN	LOAN MATURITY (YEARS)				
	10	15	20	25	30
0.5	975.45	989.30	994.92	997.49	998.74
1.0	949.20	977.87	989.48	994.81	997.39
1.5	921.13	965.63	983.67	991.94	995.95
2.0	891.11	952.55	977.45	988.87	994.41
2.5	859.00	938.56	970.80	985.59	992.76
3.0	824.67	923.60	963.69	982.08	991.00
3.5	787.95	907.60	956.08	978.33	989.12
4.0	748.68	890.49	947.95	974.32	987.10
4.5	706.69	872.19	939.25	970.03	984.95
5.0	661.78	852.62	929.95	965.44	982.64
5.5	613.75	831.69	920.01	960.53	980.18
6.0	562.39	809.31	909.37	955.28	977.54
6.5	507.46	785.37	897.99	949.67	974.72
7.0	448.72	759.78	885.83	943.67	971.71
7.5	385.90	732.40	872.82	937.25	968.48
8.0	318.72	703.13	858.90	930.38	965.04
8.5	246.87	671.82	844.02	923.04	961.35
9.0	170.04	638.34	828.11	915.19	957.41
9.5	87.87	602.54	811.09	906.79	953.19
10.0	0.00	564.25	792.90	897.81	948.68
11.0		479.50	752.62	877.94	938.70
12.0		382.59	706.56	855.21	927.29
13.0		271.75	653.88	829.22	914.23
14.0		144.98	593.63	799.49	899.30
15.0		0.00	524.72	765.49	882.23
16.0			445.92	726.61	862.70
17.0			355.79	682.14	840.37
18.0			252.71	631.28	814.83
19.0			134.82	573.11	785.61
20.0			0.00	506.59	752.20
21.0				430.50	714.00
22.0				343.49	670.30
23.0				243.98	620.32
24.0				130.16	563.16
25.0				0.00	497.79
26.0					423.03
27.0					337.53
28.0					239.74
29.0					127.91
30.0					0.00

REMAINING BALANCE PER $1000 OF ORIGINAL LOAN
ANNUAL INTEREST RATE: 13.75%

AGE OF LOAN	LOAN MATURITY (YEARS)				
	10	15	20	25	30
0.5	975.81	989.56	995.09	997.60	998.81
1.0	949.90	978.37	989.83	995.03	997.53
1.5	922.16	966.40	984.19	992.29	996.17
2.0	892.46	953.58	978.16	989.34	994.71
2.5	860.66	939.85	971.70	986.19	993.14
3.0	826.61	925.15	964.79	982.82	991.47
3.5	790.14	909.41	957.38	979.20	989.67
4.0	751.10	892.55	949.45	975.33	987.75
4.5	709.30	874.51	940.97	971.19	985.70
5.0	664.54	855.18	931.88	966.75	983.49
5.5	616.61	834.49	922.14	962.00	981.14
6.0	565.29	812.34	911.72	956.92	978.61
6.5	510.34	788.62	900.56	951.47	975.91
7.0	451.51	763.22	888.61	945.64	973.01
7.5	388.51	736.02	875.82	939.40	969.91
8.0	321.05	706.90	862.12	932.71	966.59
8.5	248.82	675.72	847.45	925.55	963.04
9.0	171.48	642.33	831.75	917.89	959.23
9.5	88.67	606.58	814.93	909.68	955.16
10.0	0.00	568.30	796.92	900.89	950.80
11.0		483.43	757.00	881.41	941.12
12.0		386.12	711.22	859.07	930.03
13.0		274.56	658.74	833.46	917.32
14.0		146.65	598.57	804.09	902.74
15.0		0.00	529.59	770.43	886.02
16.0			450.49	731.83	866.86
17.0			359.82	687.58	844.89
18.0			255.85	636.84	819.70
19.0			136.66	578.67	790.82
20.0			0.00	511.98	757.71
21.0				435.52	719.75
22.0				347.85	676.23
23.0				247.35	626.33
24.0				132.11	569.12
25.0				0.00	503.53
26.0					428.33
27.0					342.11
28.0					243.26
29.0					129.93
30.0					0.00

501

REMAINING BALANCE PER $1000 OF ORIGINAL LOAN
ANNUAL INTEREST RATE: 14%

AGE OF	LOAN MATURITY (YEARS)				
LOAN	10	15	20	25	30
0.5	976.15	989.80	995.25	997.71	998.88
1.0	950.59	978.87	990.16	995.25	997.67
1.5	923.18	967.15	984.71	992.62	996.38
2.0	893.80	954.58	978.85	989.79	994.99
2.5	862.30	941.11	972.58	986.77	993.51
3.0	828.53	926.67	965.86	983.52	991.91
3.5	792.32	911.19	958.65	980.04	990.21
4.0	753.51	894.59	950.92	976.31	988.37
4.5	711.90	876.79	942.64	972.31	986.41
5.0	667.29	857.71	933.76	968.03	984.31
5.5	619.46	837.26	924.23	963.43	982.05
6.0	568.19	815.33	914.02	958.50	979.63
6.5	513.22	791.83	903.08	953.22	977.04
7.0	454.29	766.62	891.35	947.56	974.26
7.5	391.12	739.61	878.77	941.49	971.28
8.0	323.38	710.64	865.28	934.98	968.09
8.5	250.77	679.59	850.82	928.00	964.66
9.0	172.93	646.30	835.33	920.52	960.99
9.5	89.47	610.61	818.71	912.50	957.06
10.0	0.00	572.34	800.89	903.90	952.84
11.0		487.34	761.32	884.80	943.46
12.0		389.65	715.84	862.85	932.69
13.0		277.37	663.56	837.62	920.31
14.0		148.32	603.48	808.62	906.07
15.0		0.00	534.43	775.29	889.72
16.0			455.06	736.98	870.92
17.0			363.84	692.95	849.31
18.0			259.00	642.35	824.47
19.0			138.50	584.19	795.93
20.0			0.00	517.34	763.12
21.0				440.51	725.41
22.0				352.21	682.08
23.0				250.72	632.27
24.0				134.07	575.02
25.0				0.00	509.22
26.0					433.60
27.0					346.68
28.0					246.78
29.0					131.96
30.0					0.00

REMAINING BALANCE PER $1000 OF ORIGINAL LOAN
ANNUAL INTEREST RATE: 14.25%

AGE OF LOAN	LOAN MATURITY (YEARS)				
	10	15	20	25	30
0.5	976.50	990.04	995.41	997.81	998.94
1.0	951.27	979.36	990.49	995.46	997.80
1.5	924.19	967.89	985.20	992.94	996.57
2.0	895.13	955.57	979.53	990.23	995.26
2.5	863.93	942.35	973.44	987.32	993.85
3.0	830.44	928.17	966.90	984.20	992.34
3.5	794.49	912.94	959.89	980.85	990.71
4.0	755.90	896.59	952.35	977.26	988.97
4.5	714.49	879.05	944.27	973.40	987.09
5.0	670.03	860.21	935.59	969.26	985.08
5.5	622.30	839.99	926.28	964.81	982.93
6.0	571.08	818.29	916.28	960.04	980.61
6.5	516.10	795.00	905.55	954.91	978.13
7.0	457.08	770.00	894.02	949.41	975.46
7.5	393.72	743.16	881.66	943.51	972.60
8.0	325.72	714.35	868.39	937.18	969.52
8.5	252.73	683.43	854.14	930.37	966.22
9.0	174.38	650.24	838.84	923.07	962.68
9.5	90.28	614.61	822.43	915.24	958.88
10.0	0.00	576.36	804.81	906.83	954.80
11.0		491.25	765.59	888.11	945.72
12.0		393.18	720.40	866.54	935.25
13.0		280.19	668.34	841.69	923.20
14.0		150.00	608.36	813.05	909.31
15.0		0.00	539.24	780.06	893.30
16.0			459.61	742.05	874.86
17.0			367.86	698.26	853.61
18.0			262.14	647.79	829.13
19.0			140.34	589.65	800.93
20.0			0.00	522.66	768.43
21.0				445.48	730.98
22.0				356.55	687.84
23.0				254.08	638.13
24.0				136.03	580.86
25.0				0.00	514.87
26.0					438.83
27.0					351.23
28.0					250.29
29.0					134.00
30.0					0.00

REMAINING BALANCE PER $1000 OF ORIGINAL LOAN
ANNUAL INTEREST RATE: 14.5%

AGE OF LOAN	LOAN MATURITY (YEARS)				
	10	15	20	25	30
0.5	976.84	990.28	995.57	997.91	999.00
1.0	951.95	979.83	990.80	995.66	997.92
1.5	925.19	968.61	985.69	993.24	996.76
2.0	896.44	956.54	980.18	990.65	995.51
2.5	865.54	943.58	974.27	987.85	994.18
3.0	832.33	929.64	967.92	984.86	992.74
3.5	796.64	914.66	961.09	981.63	991.19
4.0	758.28	898.57	953.75	978.17	989.53
4.5	717.06	881.27	945.86	974.44	987.74
5.0	672.75	862.67	937.38	970.44	985.83
5.5	625.13	842.69	928.27	966.14	983.76
6.0	573.96	821.22	918.48	961.52	981.55
6.5	518.96	798.14	907.96	956.55	979.16
7.0	459.85	773.34	896.65	951.21	976.60
7.5	396.33	746.68	884.49	945.47	973.85
8.0	328.06	718.03	871.43	939.31	970.90
8.5	254.69	687.24	857.39	932.68	967.72
9.0	175.83	654.15	842.30	925.56	964.30
9.5	91.08	618.59	826.08	917.90	960.63
10.0	0.00	580.36	808.66	909.67	956.69
11.0		495.14	769.80	891.33	947.89
12.0		396.71	724.91	870.14	937.73
13.0		283.01	673.07	845.67	925.99
14.0		151.68	613.19	817.40	912.44
15.0		0.00	544.02	784.75	896.78
16.0			464.14	747.04	878.70
17.0			371.86	703.48	857.81
18.0			265.29	653.17	833.68
19.0			142.19	595.06	805.82
20.0			0.00	527.94	773.63
21.0				450.42	736.45
22.0				360.87	693.51
23.0				257.45	643.92
24.0				137.98	586.63
25.0				0.00	520.46
26.0					444.03
27.0					355.76
28.0					253.80
29.0					136.03
30.0					0.00

REMAINING BALANCE PER $1000 OF ORIGINAL LOAN
ANNUAL INTEREST RATE: 14.75%

AGE OF LOAN	LOAN MATURITY (YEARS)				
	10	15	20	25	30
0.5	977.17	990.51	995.72	998.00	999.05
1.0	952.61	980.30	991.11	995.85	998.03
1.5	926.18	969.32	986.16	993.54	996.94
2.0	897.74	957.50	980.82	991.05	995.76
2.5	867.14	944.78	975.08	988.37	994.49
3.0	834.21	931.09	968.91	985.48	993.12
3.5	798.77	916.36	962.26	982.38	991.65
4.0	760.64	900.51	955.11	979.04	990.07
4.5	719.61	883.46	947.41	975.45	988.36
5.0	675.46	865.11	939.13	971.59	986.53
5.5	627.96	845.36	930.22	967.43	984.56
6.0	576.83	824.11	920.64	962.95	982.44
6.5	521.83	801.25	910.32	958.14	980.16
7.0	462.63	776.64	899.22	952.95	977.70
7.5	398.94	750.17	887.27	947.38	975.06
8.0	330.40	721.68	874.42	941.38	972.21
8.5	256.65	691.02	860.58	934.92	969.15
9.0	177.29	658.04	845.70	927.97	965.86
9.5	91.89	622.54	829.68	920.49	962.31
10.0	0.00	584.35	812.45	912.45	958.50
11.0		499.02	773.95	894.48	949.98
12.0		400.23	729.37	873.67	940.12
13.0		285.83	677.75	849.57	928.70
14.0		153.37	617.98	821.67	915.47
15.0		0.00	548.78	789.37	900.16
16.0			468.65	751.96	882.43
17.0			375.87	708.65	861.90
18.0			268.43	658.50	838.13
19.0			144.04	600.43	810.60
20.0			0.00	533.19	778.73
21.0				455.33	741.83
22.0				365.19	699.10
23.0				260.81	649.63
24.0				139.94	592.34
25.0				0.00	526.01
26.0					449.20
27.0					360.27
28.0					257.29
29.0					138.06
30.0					0.00

REMAINING BALANCE PER $1000 OF ORIGINAL LOAN
ANNUAL INTEREST RATE: 15%

AGE OF LOAN	LOAN MATURITY (YEARS)				
	10	15	20	25	30
0.5	977.51	990.74	995.87	998.09	999.11
1.0	953.27	980.76	991.41	996.04	998.14
1.5	927.16	970.01	986.61	993.82	997.10
2.0	899.03	958.43	981.44	991.43	995.99
2.5	868.73	945.96	975.87	988.86	994.78
3.0	836.07	932.51	969.87	986.09	993.48
3.5	800.89	918.03	963.40	983.11	992.09
4.0	762.99	902.43	956.43	979.89	990.58
4.5	722.16	885.62	948.93	976.43	988.96
5.0	678.17	867.50	940.84	972.69	987.21
5.5	630.77	847.99	932.13	968.67	985.32
6.0	579.70	826.97	922.74	964.34	983.29
6.5	524.68	804.32	912.63	959.67	981.11
7.0	465.41	779.91	901.73	954.64	978.75
7.5	401.55	753.62	890.00	949.22	976.21
8.0	332.74	725.30	877.35	943.38	973.48
8.5	258.61	694.78	863.72	937.09	970.53
9.0	178.75	661.90	849.04	930.32	967.35
9.5	92.70	626.48	833.23	923.02	963.93
10.0	0.00	588.31	816.18	915.15	960.25
11.0		502.89	778.05	897.54	952.00
12.0		403.74	733.78	877.11	942.43
13.0		288.66	682.39	853.39	931.31
14.0		155.07	622.74	825.86	918.41
15.0		0.00	553.51	793.90	903.44
16.0			473.14	756.80	886.06
17.0			379.86	713.74	865.89
18.0			271.58	663.76	842.47
19.0			145.89	605.74	815.29
20.0			0.00	538.39	783.74
21.0				460.22	747.12
22.0				369.49	704.61
23.0				264.16	655.26
24.0				141.91	597.99
25.0				0.00	531.51
26.0					454.34
27.0					364.76
28.0					260.78
29.0					140.09
30.0					0.00

REMAINING BALANCE PER $1000 OF ORIGINAL LOAN
ANNUAL INTEREST RATE: 15.25%

AGE OF LOAN	LOAN MATURITY (YEARS)				
	10	15	20	25	30
0.5	977.83	990.96	996.01	998.18	999.16
1.0	953.92	981.21	991.70	996.21	998.25
1.5	928.13	970.70	987.05	994.09	997.26
2.0	900.31	959.35	982.04	991.80	996.20
2.5	870.30	947.11	976.64	989.34	995.06
3.0	837.92	933.91	970.80	986.67	993.83
3.5	803.00	919.67	964.51	983.80	992.50
4.0	765.33	904.31	957.73	980.70	991.06
4.5	724.69	887.74	950.41	977.36	989.52
5.0	680.85	869.87	942.51	973.76	987.85
5.5	633.57	850.59	933.99	969.87	986.05
6.0	582.56	829.79	924.80	965.68	984.11
6.5	527.53	807.35	914.89	961.15	982.01
7.0	468.18	783.15	904.20	956.27	979.75
7.5	404.15	757.04	892.66	951.01	977.31
8.0	335.08	728.88	880.22	945.33	974.68
8.5	260.58	698.50	866.80	939.20	971.85
9.0	180.21	665.73	852.32	932.59	968.79
9.5	93.52	630.38	836.71	925.46	965.49
10.0	0.00	592.25	819.86	917.78	961.93
11.0		506.75	782.08	900.53	953.94
12.0		407.25	738.13	880.47	944.65
13.0		291.48	686.98	857.12	933.84
14.0		156.76	627.46	829.96	921.26
15.0		0.00	558.20	798.34	906.62
16.0			477.61	761.56	889.59
17.0			383.84	718.76	869.77
18.0			274.72	668.95	846.71
19.0			147.75	610.99	819.87
20.0			0.00	543.55	788.64
21.0				465.08	752.31
22.0				373.77	710.02
23.0				267.51	660.82
24.0				143.87	603.57
25.0				0.00	536.95
26.0					459.43
27.0					369.23
28.0					264.26
29.0					142.12
30.0					0.00

REMAINING BALANCE PER $1000 OF ORIGINAL LOAN
ANNUAL INTEREST RATE: 15.5%

AGE OF LOAN	LOAN MATURITY (YEARS)				
	10	15	20	25	30
0.5	978.16	991.18	996.14	998.26	999.20
1.0	954.57	981.65	991.98	996.38	998.34
1.5	929.09	971.37	987.48	994.35	997.41
2.0	901.58	960.25	982.63	992.16	996.41
2.5	871.86	948.25	977.38	989.79	995.33
3.0	839.76	935.29	971.71	987.23	994.16
3.5	805.09	921.29	965.59	984.47	992.89
4.0	767.65	906.17	958.98	981.49	991.53
4.5	727.21	889.84	951.85	978.27	990.05
5.0	683.53	872.20	944.14	974.79	988.46
5.5	636.36	853.15	935.81	971.03	986.74
6.0	585.41	832.58	926.81	966.97	984.88
6.5	530.38	810.36	917.10	962.59	982.88
7.0	470.95	786.36	906.61	957.85	980.71
7.5	406.76	760.43	895.28	952.74	978.37
8.0	337.43	732.44	883.04	947.21	975.84
8.5	262.55	702.20	869.82	941.25	973.11
9.0	181.68	669.54	855.55	934.81	970.16
9.5	94.34	634.27	840.13	927.85	966.98
10.0	0.00	596.18	823.48	920.33	963.54
11.0		510.59	786.07	903.45	955.81
12.0		410.76	742.43	883.75	946.80
13.0		294.31	691.52	860.78	936.28
14.0		158.46	632.14	833.98	924.02
15.0		0.00	562.87	802.71	909.71
16.0			482.07	766.25	893.02
17.0			387.81	723.71	873.55
18.0			277.86	674.09	850.84
19.0			149.61	616.20	824.35
20.0			0.00	548.68	793.45
21.0				469.91	757.41
22.0				378.04	715.36
23.0				270.86	666.31
24.0				145.84	609.09
25.0				0.00	542.35
26.0					464.49
27.0					373.67
28.0					267.73
29.0					144.15
30.0					0.00

508

REMAINING BALANCE PER $1000 OF ORIGINAL LOAN
ANNUAL INTEREST RATE: 15.75%

AGE OF LOAN	LOAN MATURITY (YEARS)				
	10	15	20	25	30
0.5	978.48	991.39	996.28	998.34	999.25
1.0	955.21	982.09	992.25	996.54	998.44
1.5	930.04	972.02	987.90	994.60	997.56
2.0	902.83	961.14	983.19	992.50	996.61
2.5	873.40	949.37	978.10	990.23	995.58
3.0	841.58	936.64	972.60	987.77	994.47
3.5	807.16	922.88	966.65	985.12	993.27
4.0	769.95	908.00	960.21	982.24	991.97
4.5	729.71	891.90	953.25	979.14	990.56
5.0	686.19	874.50	945.72	975.78	989.04
5.5	639.13	855.68	937.58	972.15	987.40
6.0	588.25	835.33	928.78	968.22	985.63
6.5	533.22	813.32	919.26	963.97	983.70
7.0	473.71	789.52	908.97	959.38	981.63
7.5	409.36	763.79	897.84	954.41	979.38
8.0	339.77	735.96	885.80	949.04	976.95
8.5	264.52	705.86	872.79	943.23	974.32
9.0	183.15	673.32	858.71	936.95	971.48
9.5	95.16	638.13	843.49	930.16	968.41
10.0	0.00	600.07	827.03	922.81	965.09
11.0		514.42	789.99	906.28	957.61
12.0		414.26	746.67	886.95	948.87
13.0		297.13	696.01	864.35	938.64
14.0		160.17	636.77	837.91	926.69
15.0		0.00	567.50	807.00	912.70
16.0			486.50	770.85	896.35
17.0			391.77	728.58	877.24
18.0			281.00	679.15	854.88
19.0			151.47	621.35	828.73
20.0			0.00	553.76	798.16
21.0				474.71	762.41
22.0				382.28	720.60
23.0				274.20	671.71
24.0				147.80	614.54
25.0				0.00	547.69
26.0					469.51
27.0					378.10
28.0					271.19
29.0					146.18
30.0					0.00

REMAINING BALANCE PER $1000 OF ORIGINAL LOAN
ANNUAL INTEREST RATE: 16%

AGE OF LOAN	LOAN MATURITY (YEARS)				
	10	15	20	25	30
0.5	978.80	991.60	996.41	998.41	999.29
1.0	955.84	982.51	992.52	996.70	998.52
1.5	930.98	972.67	988.30	994.84	997.69
2.0	904.07	962.01	983.74	992.83	996.79
2.5	874.93	950.47	978.81	990.65	995.82
3.0	843.38	937.97	973.46	988.29	994.77
3.5	809.22	924.44	967.67	985.74	993.62
4.0	772.24	909.80	961.40	982.97	992.39
4.5	732.20	893.94	954.62	979.98	991.05
5.0	688.84	876.77	947.27	976.74	989.60
5.5	641.90	858.18	939.31	973.23	988.03
6.0	591.08	838.05	930.70	969.43	986.33
6.5	536.05	816.25	921.38	965.31	984.49
7.0	476.47	792.66	911.28	960.86	982.50
7.5	411.96	767.11	900.35	956.03	980.35
8.0	342.12	739.45	888.51	950.81	978.01
8.5	266.50	709.50	875.70	945.16	975.48
9.0	184.63	677.07	861.82	939.04	972.75
9.5	95.98	641.97	846.80	932.41	969.79
10.0	0.00	603.95	830.54	925.23	966.58
11.0		518.24	793.86	909.05	959.34
12.0		417.75	750.86	890.08	950.86
13.0		299.96	700.46	867.84	940.92
14.0		161.87	641.37	841.77	929.27
15.0		0.00	572.11	811.21	915.61
16.0			490.91	775.39	899.60
17.0			395.73	733.39	880.82
18.0			284.14	684.16	858.82
19.0			153.34	626.45	833.02
20.0			0.00	558.80	802.78
21.0				479.49	767.32
22.0				386.52	725.77
23.0				277.53	677.05
24.0				149.77	619.94
25.0				0.00	552.99
26.0					474.50
27.0					382.50
28.0					274.65
29.0					148.21
30.0					0.00

REMAINING BALANCE PER $1000 OF ORIGINAL LOAN
ANNUAL INTEREST RATE: 16.25%

AGE OF	LOAN MATURITY (YEARS)				
LOAN	10	15	20	25	30
0.5	979.11	991.81	996.53	998.49	999.33
1.0	956.46	982.93	992.77	996.85	998.61
1.5	931.91	973.30	988.70	995.07	997.82
2.0	905.30	962.86	984.28	993.14	996.97
2.5	876.45	951.54	979.49	991.05	996.05
3.0	845.17	939.28	974.30	988.79	995.05
3.5	811.27	925.98	968.67	986.33	993.96
4.0	774.52	911.57	962.56	983.67	992.79
4.5	734.67	895.94	955.95	980.79	991.51
5.0	691.48	879.00	948.78	977.66	990.13
5.5	644.66	860.64	941.01	974.27	988.63
6.0	593.90	840.73	932.58	970.59	987.01
6.5	538.88	819.15	923.44	966.61	985.25
7.0	479.23	795.76	913.54	962.29	983.34
7.5	414.57	770.40	902.81	957.60	981.27
8.0	344.47	742.91	891.17	952.53	979.03
8.5	268.48	713.11	878.55	947.02	976.60
9.0	186.10	680.80	864.88	941.06	973.96
9.5	96.81	645.78	850.05	934.59	971.10
10.0	0.00	607.81	833.98	927.58	968.01
11.0		522.04	797.67	911.74	961.01
12.0		421.24	755.00	893.13	952.79
13.0		302.79	704.86	871.26	943.13
14.0		163.59	645.93	845.55	931.77
15.0		0.00	576.68	815.35	918.43
16.0			495.30	779.85	902.74
17.0			399.67	738.13	884.31
18.0			287.28	689.11	862.66
19.0			155.21	631.50	837.21
20.0			0.00	563.80	807.30
21.0				484.23	772.15
22.0				390.74	730.85
23.0				280.86	682.31
24.0				151.74	625.27
25.0				0.00	558.23
26.0					479.46
27.0					386.88
28.0					278.09
29.0					150.24
30.0					0.00

REMAINING BALANCE PER $1000 OF ORIGINAL LOAN
ANNUAL INTEREST RATE: REMAINING BALANCE PER $1000 OF
ORIGINAL LOAN ANNUAL INTEREST RATE:16.5%

AGE OF LOAN	LOAN MATURITY (YEARS)				
	10	15	20	25	30
0.5	979.42	992.01	996.65	998.56	999.37
1.0	957.08	983.33	993.02	996.99	998.69
1.5	932.83	973.92	989.08	995.29	997.94
2.0	906.52	963.70	984.80	993.44	997.14
2.5	877.95	952.60	980.15	991.44	996.26
3.0	846.95	940.56	975.11	989.27	995.31
3.5	813.30	927.49	969.64	986.91	994.28
4.0	776.77	913.31	963.70	984.34	993.16
4.5	737.13	897.91	957.25	981.56	991.95
5.0	694.10	881.20	950.25	978.55	990.63
5.5	647.40	863.07	942.66	975.27	989.20
6.0	596.71	843.38	934.41	971.71	987.65
6.5	541.70	822.02	925.46	967.86	985.97
7.0	481.98	798.83	915.75	963.67	984.14
7.5	417.17	773.65	905.21	959.12	982.15
8.0	346.82	746.33	893.77	954.19	980.00
8.5	270.46	716.68	881.35	948.83	977.66
9.0	187.59	684.50	867.87	943.02	975.12
9.5	97.63	649.56	853.24	936.71	972.37
10.0	0.00	611.65	837.37	929.86	969.38
11.0		525.83	801.43	914.36	962.61
12.0		424.72	759.08	896.11	954.64
13.0		305.62	709.21	874.59	945.25
14.0		165.30	650.44	849.25	934.19
15.0		0.00	581.22	819.40	921.15
16.0			499.67	784.23	905.80
17.0			403.59	742.80	887.71
18.0			290.41	693.99	866.40
19.0			157.08	636.49	841.30
20.0			0.00	568.75	811.73
21.0				488.95	776.89
22.0				394.93	735.84
23.0				284.18	687.49
24.0				153.71	630.53
25.0				0.00	563.42
26.0					484.37
27.0					391.24
28.0					281.52
29.0					152.27
30.0					0.00

512

REMAINING BALANCE PER $1000 OF ORIGINAL LOAN
ANNUAL INTEREST RATE: 16.75%

AGE OF LOAN	LOAN MATURITY (YEARS)				
	10	15	20	25	30
0.5	979.72	992.20	996.77	998.62	999.41
1.0	957.69	983.73	993.26	997.13	998.76
1.5	933.74	974.52	989.45	995.50	998.06
2.0	907.72	964.52	985.30	993.73	997.30
2.5	879.44	953.64	980.79	991.81	996.47
3.0	848.71	941.82	975.90	989.72	995.57
3.5	815.31	928.98	970.58	987.46	994.59
4.0	779.02	915.02	964.80	984.99	993.52
4.5	739.58	899.86	958.51	982.31	992.37
5.0	696.72	883.38	951.69	979.40	991.11
5.5	650.14	865.46	944.27	976.24	989.75
6.0	599.52	846.00	936.20	972.80	988.26
6.5	544.51	824.85	927.44	969.06	986.65
7.0	484.73	801.86	917.92	965.00	984.90
7.5	419.76	776.88	907.57	960.59	983.00
8.0	349.17	749.73	896.32	955.80	980.93
8.5	272.45	720.23	884.10	950.59	978.68
9.0	189.07	688.17	870.82	944.92	976.24
9.5	98.46	653.32	856.38	938.77	973.58
10.0	0.00	615.46	840.70	932.08	970.70
11.0		529.60	805.13	916.92	964.16
12.0		428.20	763.12	899.01	956.43
13.0		308.45	713.51	877.86	947.30
14.0		167.02	654.92	852.88	936.53
15.0		0.00	585.73	823.38	923.80
16.0			504.01	788.54	908.77
17.0			407.51	747.40	891.02
18.0			293.54	698.81	870.06
19.0			158.95	641.43	845.30
20.0			0.00	573.66	816.06
21.0				493.63	781.53
22.0				399.12	740.76
23.0				287.50	692.60
24.0				155.68	635.73
25.0				0.00	568.56
26.0					489.24
27.0					395.57
28.0					284.94
29.0					154.29
30.0					0.00

513

REMAINING BALANCE PER $1000 OF ORIGINAL LOAN
ANNUAL INTEREST RATE: 17%

AGE OF LOAN	LOAN MATURITY (YEARS)				
	10	15	20	25	30
0.5	980.03	992.39	996.88	998.69	999.44
1.0	958.29	984.12	993.49	997.26	998.83
1.5	934.64	975.12	989.80	995.70	998.17
2.0	908.91	965.32	985.79	994.01	997.45
2.5	880.92	954.66	981.42	992.17	996.66
3.0	850.46	943.06	976.67	990.17	995.81
3.5	817.31	930.44	971.50	987.99	994.88
4.0	781.25	916.71	965.87	985.61	993.87
4.5	742.01	901.77	959.75	983.03	992.77
5.0	699.32	885.52	953.08	980.23	991.57
5.5	652.86	867.83	945.84	977.17	990.27
6.0	602.31	848.58	937.95	973.85	988.85
6.5	547.32	827.64	929.37	970.23	987.31
7.0	487.47	804.86	920.03	966.30	985.63
7.5	422.36	780.07	909.87	962.01	983.80
8.0	351.52	753.09	898.82	957.36	981.82
8.5	274.43	723.74	886.79	952.29	979.66
9.0	190.56	691.81	873.70	946.77	977.31
9.5	99.30	657.06	859.46	940.77	974.75
10.0	0.00	619.25	843.97	934.24	971.96
11.0		533.36	808.77	919.40	965.64
12.0		431.67	767.10	901.84	958.15
13.0		311.27	717.76	881.05	949.28
14.0		168.74	659.35	856.43	938.79
15.0		0.00	590.20	827.28	926.36
16.0			508.34	792.78	911.65
17.0			411.41	751.93	894.24
18.0			296.67	703.57	873.62
19.0			160.83	646.31	849.21
20.0			0.00	578.53	820.31
21.0				498.28	786.10
22.0				403.28	745.59
23.0				290.80	697.64
24.0				157.65	640.87
25.0				0.00	573.65
26.0					494.08
27.0					399.88
28.0					288.35
29.0					156.32
30.0					0.00

REMAINING BALANCE PER $1000 OF ORIGINAL LOAN
ANNUAL INTEREST RATE: 17.25%

AGE OF LOAN	LOAN MATURITY (YEARS)				
	10	15	20	25	30
0.5	980.32	992.58	996.99	998.75	999.47
1.0	958.89	984.50	993.72	997.38	998.90
1.5	935.54	975.70	990.15	995.90	998.27
2.0	910.10	966.11	986.26	994.28	997.59
2.5	882.38	955.66	982.03	992.51	996.84
3.0	852.19	944.28	977.41	990.59	996.04
3.5	819.30	931.88	972.39	988.49	995.15
4.0	783.46	918.37	966.91	986.21	994.19
4.5	744.43	903.65	960.95	983.73	993.14
5.0	701.90	887.62	954.45	981.02	992.00
5.5	655.57	870.16	947.37	978.07	990.76
6.0	605.10	851.13	939.65	974.86	989.41
6.5	550.11	830.40	931.25	971.36	987.93
7.0	490.21	807.82	922.10	967.54	986.33
7.5	424.96	783.22	912.13	963.39	984.57
8.0	353.87	756.42	901.26	958.86	982.67
8.5	276.42	727.23	889.43	953.93	980.59
9.0	192.05	695.42	876.54	948.56	978.33
9.5	100.13	660.77	862.49	942.71	975.86
10.0	0.00	623.02	847.19	936.33	973.18
11.0		537.10	812.36	921.82	967.06
12.0		435.12	771.02	904.60	959.81
13.0		314.10	721.96	884.16	951.19
14.0		170.47	663.74	859.90	940.97
15.0		0.00	594.64	831.11	928.84
16.0			512.63	796.94	914.45
17.0			415.30	756.39	897.36
18.0			299.79	708.26	877.09
19.0			162.70	651.14	853.02
20.0			0.00	583.35	824.46
21.0				502.90	790.57
22.0				407.42	750.34
23.0				294.10	702.60
24.0				159.61	645.94
25.0				0.00	578.69
26.0					498.88
27.0					404.16
28.0					291.75
29.0					158.34
30.0					0.00

REMAINING BALANCE PER $1000 OF ORIGINAL LOAN
ANNUAL INTEREST RATE: 17.5%

AGE OF LOAN	LOAN MATURITY (YEARS)				
	10	15	20	25	30
0.5	980.62	992.77	997.10	998.81	999.50
1.0	959.48	984.88	993.94	997.50	998.96
1.5	936.42	976.27	990.48	996.08	998.37
2.0	911.27	966.88	986.72	994.53	997.72
2.5	883.83	956.64	982.62	992.84	997.02
3.0	853.91	945.47	978.14	991.00	996.25
3.5	821.27	933.29	973.25	988.98	995.41
4.0	785.66	920.00	967.92	986.79	994.50
4.5	746.83	905.51	962.11	984.40	993.50
5.0	704.47	889.70	955.77	981.79	992.42
5.5	658.27	872.45	948.86	978.94	991.23
6.0	607.87	853.65	941.32	975.83	989.94
6.5	552.91	833.13	933.09	972.44	988.53
7.0	492.95	810.75	924.12	968.75	986.99
7.5	427.55	786.34	914.33	964.72	985.31
8.0	356.22	759.72	903.66	960.32	983.48
8.5	278.41	730.68	892.02	955.52	981.48
9.0	193.54	699.00	879.31	950.29	979.31
9.5	100.97	664.45	865.46	944.59	976.93
10.0	0.00	626.77	850.35	938.37	974.34
11.0		540.82	815.89	924.17	968.43
12.0		438.58	774.90	907.29	961.40
13.0		316.93	726.12	887.20	953.04
14.0		172.19	668.09	863.30	943.09
15.0		0.00	599.05	834.86	931.25
16.0			516.91	801.03	917.16
17.0			419.18	760.78	900.41
18.0			302.91	712.89	880.47
19.0			164.58	655.92	856.75
20.0			0.00	588.14	828.53
21.0				507.49	794.96
22.0				411.54	755.01
23.0				297.39	707.49
24.0				161.58	650.95
25.0				0.00	583.68
26.0					503.64
27.0					408.42
28.0					295.14
29.0					160.36
30.0					0.00

REMAINING BALANCE PER $1000 OF ORIGINAL LOAN
ANNUAL INTEREST RATE: REMAINING BALANCE PER $1000 OF ORIGINAL LOAN ANNUAL INTEREST RATE:17.75%

AGE OF LOAN	LOAN MATURITY (YEARS)				
	10	15	20	25	30
0.5	980.91	992.95	997.20	998.86	999.53
1.0	960.06	985.24	994.15	997.62	999.02
1.5	937.29	976.83	990.81	996.26	998.46
2.0	912.42	967.64	987.17	994.78	997.85
2.5	885.27	957.60	983.19	993.15	997.18
3.0	855.61	946.65	978.84	991.39	996.46
3.5	823.22	934.68	974.09	989.45	995.66
4.0	787.85	921.61	968.91	987.34	994.79
4.5	749.22	907.33	963.25	985.04	993.84
5.0	707.03	891.74	957.07	982.52	992.81
5.5	660.96	874.72	950.32	979.77	991.68
6.0	610.64	856.13	942.94	976.77	990.44
6.5	555.69	835.82	934.89	973.49	989.09
7.0	495.68	813.65	926.10	969.91	987.62
7.5	430.14	789.43	916.49	966.00	986.01
8.0	358.57	762.98	906.00	961.73	984.26
8.5	280.40	734.10	894.55	957.07	982.34
9.0	195.04	702.56	882.04	951.98	980.24
9.5	101.81	668.11	868.38	946.41	977.95
10.0	0.00	630.49	853.46	940.34	975.46
11.0		544.53	819.37	926.46	969.75
12.0		442.02	778.71	909.91	962.94
13.0		319.75	730.23	890.17	954.82
14.0		173.92	672.39	866.62	945.13
15.0		0.00	603.42	838.54	933.58
16.0			521.16	805.05	919.80
17.0			423.04	765.10	903.37
18.0			306.02	717.46	883.77
19.0			166.46	660.64	860.39
20.0			0.00	592.87	832.51
21.0				512.05	799.26
22.0				415.65	759.60
23.0				300.67	712.30
24.0				163.55	655.89
25.0				0.00	588.61
26.0					508.36
27.0					412.66
28.0					298.51
29.0					162.37
30.0					0.00

517

REMAINING BALANCE PER $1000 OF ORIGINAL LOAN
ANNUAL INTEREST RATE: 18%

AGE OF	LOAN MATURITY (YEARS)				
LOAN	10	15	20	25	30
0.5	981.20	993.12	997.30	998.91	999.56
1.0	960.63	985.60	994.35	997.73	999.08
1.5	938.15	977.38	991.13	996.43	998.55
2.0	913.57	968.38	987.60	995.01	997.97
2.5	886.69	958.55	983.74	993.46	997.34
3.0	857.30	947.80	979.52	991.76	996.65
3.5	825.16	936.04	974.91	989.90	995.90
4.0	790.02	923.19	969.87	987.87	995.07
4.5	751.59	909.13	964.36	985.66	994.17
5.0	709.57	893.76	958.33	983.23	993.18
5.5	663.63	876.95	951.74	980.58	992.10
6.0	613.40	858.58	944.53	977.68	990.93
6.5	558.47	838.48	936.65	974.50	989.64
7.0	498.40	816.51	928.03	971.04	988.23
7.5	432.73	792.49	918.60	967.24	986.68
8.0	360.92	766.22	908.30	963.10	985.00
8.5	282.40	737.49	897.03	958.56	983.16
9.0	196.54	706.08	884.71	953.61	981.14
9.5	102.65	671.74	871.24	948.18	978.94
10.0	0.00	634.19	856.51	942.26	976.53
11.0		548.23	822.80	928.69	971.01
12.0		445.45	782.48	912.46	964.42
13.0		322.57	734.29	893.07	956.53
14.0		175.66	676.66	869.88	947.10
15.0		0.00	607.76	842.15	935.83
16.0			525.38	809.00	922.36
17.0			426.89	769.36	906.24
18.0			309.13	721.97	886.98
19.0			168.34	665.31	863.95
20.0			0.00	597.57	836.41
21.0				516.57	803.48
22.0				419.73	764.12
23.0				303.95	717.05
24.0				165.51	660.78
25.0				0.00	593.49
26.0					513.05
27.0					416.87
28.0					301.87
29.0					164.38
30.0					0.00

REMAINING BALANCE PER $1000 OF ORIGINAL LOAN
ANNUAL INTEREST RATE: 18.25%

AGE OF LOAN	LOAN MATURITY (YEARS)				
	10	15	20	25	30
0.5	981.48	993.29	997.40	998.97	999.58
1.0	961.20	985.95	994.55	997.83	999.13
1.5	939.01	977.91	991.43	996.59	998.63
2.0	914.70	969.11	988.02	995.23	998.09
2.5	888.10	959.48	984.28	993.75	997.49
3.0	858.97	948.93	980.19	992.12	996.83
3.5	827.08	937.38	975.71	990.34	996.12
4.0	792.17	924.74	970.80	988.39	995.33
4.5	753.95	910.90	965.43	986.25	994.48
5.0	712.11	895.74	959.55	983.91	993.54
5.5	666.30	879.15	953.12	981.35	992.51
6.0	616.14	860.99	946.07	978.55	991.38
6.5	561.24	841.11	938.36	975.48	990.15
7.0	501.13	819.34	929.92	972.12	988.80
7.5	435.32	795.51	920.67	968.44	987.32
8.0	363.27	769.42	910.55	964.42	985.71
8.5	284.39	740.85	899.47	960.01	983.94
9.0	198.04	709.58	887.34	955.18	982.00
9.5	103.50	675.34	874.05	949.90	979.88
10.0	0.00	637.86	859.51	944.12	977.55
11.0		551.91	826.17	930.85	972.23
12.0		448.88	786.20	914.95	965.84
13.0		325.40	738.30	895.90	958.19
14.0		177.39	680.88	873.06	949.01
15.0		0.00	612.06	845.69	938.02
16.0			529.58	812.88	924.84
17.0			430.72	773.55	909.04
18.0			312.23	726.42	890.11
19.0			170.22	669.93	867.42
20.0			0.00	602.22	840.22
21.0				521.06	807.62
22.0				423.79	768.55
23.0				307.21	721.72
24.0				167.48	665.60
25.0				0.00	598.33
26.0					517.70
27.0					421.06
28.0					305.23
29.0					166.40
30.0					0.00

REMAINING BALANCE PER $1000 OF ORIGINAL LOAN
ANNUAL INTEREST RATE: 18.5%

AGE OF LOAN	LOAN MATURITY (YEARS)				
	10	15	20	25	30
0.5	981.76	993.46	997.49	999.01	999.61
1.0	961.77	986.29	994.74	997.93	999.18
1.5	939.85	978.44	991.73	996.75	998.71
2.0	915.83	969.82	988.42	995.45	998.19
2.5	889.49	960.38	984.80	994.02	997.63
3.0	860.63	950.04	980.83	992.46	997.01
3.5	828.99	938.69	976.48	990.75	996.33
4.0	794.31	926.26	971.71	988.88	995.59
4.5	756.29	912.63	966.48	986.82	994.77
5.0	714.62	897.70	960.75	984.57	993.87
5.5	668.95	881.32	954.47	982.10	992.89
6.0	618.88	863.37	947.58	979.39	991.82
6.5	564.00	843.70	940.03	976.42	990.64
7.0	503.84	822.13	931.76	973.17	989.35
7.5	437.90	798.49	922.69	969.60	987.94
8.0	365.62	772.58	912.75	965.69	986.38
8.5	286.39	744.18	901.85	961.41	984.68
9.0	199.54	713.05	889.91	956.71	982.82
9.5	104.35	678.92	876.81	951.57	980.78
10.0	0.00	641.51	862.46	945.92	978.54
11.0		555.56	829.48	932.96	973.39
12.0		452.29	789.86	917.38	967.21
13.0		328.21	742.26	898.66	959.78
14.0		179.13	685.06	876.17	950.85
15.0		0.00	616.33	849.15	940.13
16.0			533.76	816.68	927.24
17.0			434.54	777.67	911.76
18.0			315.33	730.80	893.16
19.0			172.10	674.49	870.81
20.0			0.00	606.82	843.95
21.0				525.52	811.68
22.0				427.84	772.91
23.0				310.47	726.33
24.0				169.44	670.36
25.0				0.00	603.11
26.0					522.30
27.0					425.22
28.0					308.56
29.0					168.40
30.0					0.00

REMAINING BALANCE PER $1000 OF ORIGINAL LOAN
ANNUAL INTEREST RATE: 18.75%

AGE OF LOAN	LOAN MATURITY (YEARS)				
	10	15	20	25	30
0.5	982.04	993.63	997.58	999.06	999.63
1.0	962.32	986.63	994.93	998.03	999.23
1.5	940.68	978.95	992.01	996.90	998.78
2.0	916.94	970.52	988.82	995.65	998.30
2.5	890.88	961.28	985.31	994.29	997.76
3.0	862.27	951.13	981.46	992.79	997.17
3.5	830.88	939.99	977.23	991.15	996.53
4.0	796.43	927.76	972.59	989.35	995.82
4.5	758.62	914.34	967.50	987.37	995.05
5.0	717.13	899.62	961.91	985.20	994.20
5.5	671.58	883.46	955.78	982.82	993.26
6.0	621.60	865.72	949.05	980.20	992.24
6.5	566.75	846.26	941.67	977.33	991.11
7.0	506.55	824.89	933.56	974.18	989.87
7.5	440.48	801.45	924.66	970.72	988.52
8.0	367.97	775.72	914.90	966.93	987.03
8.5	288.39	747.48	904.19	962.76	985.40
9.0	201.05	716.49	892.43	958.19	983.61
9.5	105.20	682.47	879.52	953.18	981.64
10.0	0.00	645.14	865.36	947.67	979.48
11.0		559.21	832.75	935.00	974.51
12.0		455.70	793.48	919.74	968.53
13.0		331.03	746.17	901.36	961.32
14.0		180.87	689.20	879.22	952.63
15.0		0.00	620.57	852.55	942.17
16.0			537.91	820.42	929.58
17.0			438.35	781.73	914.40
18.0			318.42	735.13	896.13
19.0			173.98	678.99	874.11
20.0			0.00	611.38	847.60
21.0				529.95	815.66
22.0				431.86	777.19
23.0				313.71	730.86
24.0				171.40	675.05
25.0				0.00	607.83
26.0					526.87
27.0					429.35
28.0					311.89
29.0					170.41
30.0					0.00

521

REMAINING BALANCE PER $1000 OF ORIGINAL LOAN
ANNUAL INTEREST RATE: 19%

AGE OF LOAN	LOAN MATURITY (YEARS)				
	10	15	20	25	30
0.5	982.31	993.79	997.67	999.10	999.65
1.0	962.87	986.96	995.11	998.12	999.27
1.5	941.51	979.45	992.29	997.04	998.85
2.0	918.04	971.21	989.20	995.85	998.39
2.5	892.24	962.15	985.80	994.54	997.89
3.0	863.90	952.20	982.06	993.11	997.33
3.5	832.76	941.26	977.96	991.53	996.72
4.0	798.54	929.24	973.45	989.80	996.05
4.5	760.94	916.03	968.49	987.90	995.31
5.0	719.62	901.51	963.05	985.81	994.50
5.5	674.21	885.57	957.06	983.51	993.61
6.0	624.32	868.04	950.48	980.98	992.63
6.5	569.50	848.78	943.26	978.21	991.56
7.0	509.25	827.62	935.32	975.16	990.37
7.5	443.06	804.37	926.59	971.80	989.07
8.0	370.32	778.82	917.01	968.12	987.65
8.5	290.39	750.75	906.47	964.08	986.08
9.0	202.56	719.89	894.90	959.63	984.36
9.5	106.05	685.99	882.18	954.74	982.46
10.0	0.00	648.74	868.20	949.38	980.38
11.0		562.83	835.96	936.99	975.59
12.0		459.10	797.04	922.04	969.79
13.0		333.85	750.04	903.99	962.80
14.0		182.61	693.29	882.19	954.35
15.0		0.00	624.77	855.87	944.15
16.0			542.03	824.10	931.84
17.0			442.13	785.72	916.97
18.0			321.51	739.39	899.02
19.0			175.86	683.45	877.34
20.0			0.00	615.90	851.17
21.0				534.34	819.56
22.0				435.86	781.40
23.0				316.95	735.33
24.0				173.37	679.69
25.0				0.00	612.51
26.0					531.40
27.0					433.46
28.0					315.20
29.0					172.41
30.0					0.00

REMAINING BALANCE PER $1000 OF ORIGINAL LOAN
ANNUAL INTEREST RATE: 19.25%

AGE OF LOAN	LOAN MATURITY (YEARS)				
	10	15	20	25	30
0.5	982.58	993.94	997.75	999.15	999.67
1.0	963.41	987.28	995.28	998.21	999.31
1.5	942.32	979.95	992.56	997.18	998.92
2.0	919.12	971.88	989.57	996.04	998.48
2.5	893.60	963.01	986.27	994.79	998.00
3.0	865.52	953.24	982.65	993.41	997.48
3.5	834.62	942.50	978.66	991.90	996.90
4.0	800.63	930.68	974.28	990.24	996.26
4.5	763.24	917.68	969.45	988.40	995.56
5.0	722.09	903.38	964.15	986.39	994.79
5.5	676.83	887.64	958.31	984.17	993.94
6.0	627.02	870.32	951.88	981.73	993.01
6.5	572.23	851.27	944.81	979.05	991.98
7.0	511.95	830.32	937.04	976.10	990.85
7.5	445.63	807.26	928.48	972.85	989.60
8.0	372.67	781.89	919.07	969.28	988.24
8.5	292.39	753.98	908.71	965.34	986.73
9.0	204.07	723.27	897.32	961.02	985.08
9.5	106.90	689.49	884.78	956.26	983.25
10.0	0.00	652.32	870.99	951.02	981.25
11.0		566.44	839.12	938.93	976.62
12.0		462.49	800.55	924.28	971.01
13.0		336.66	753.86	906.56	964.22
14.0		184.35	697.34	885.10	956.01
15.0		0.00	628.93	859.13	946.07
16.0			546.13	827.70	934.03
17.0			445.90	789.65	919.47
18.0			324.59	743.60	901.83
19.0			177.74	687.85	880.49
20.0			0.00	620.37	854.66
21.0				538.70	823.39
22.0				439.84	785.54
23.0				320.17	739.72
24.0				175.32	684.26
25.0				0.00	617.14
26.0					535.89
27.0					437.54
28.0					318.50
29.0					174.41
30.0					0.00

REMAINING BALANCE PER $1000 OF ORIGINAL LOAN
ANNUAL INTEREST RATE: 19.5%

AGE OF LOAN	LOAN MATURITY (YEARS)				
	10	15	20	25	30
0.5	982.84	994.10	997.83	999.19	999.69
1.0	963.95	987.59	995.45	998.29	999.35
1.5	943.13	980.43	992.82	997.31	998.98
2.0	920.20	972.54	989.92	996.22	998.57
2.5	894.94	963.85	986.73	995.02	998.12
3.0	867.12	954.27	983.22	993.70	997.62
3.5	836.47	943.73	979.35	992.25	997.07
4.0	802.71	932.11	975.09	990.65	996.46
4.5	765.52	919.31	970.39	988.89	995.80
5.0	724.55	905.21	965.22	986.95	995.06
5.5	679.43	889.68	959.52	984.81	994.25
6.0	629.72	872.58	953.24	982.46	993.36
6.5	574.96	853.73	946.33	979.86	992.38
7.0	514.65	832.98	938.71	977.01	991.30
7.5	448.20	810.11	930.32	973.86	990.11
8.0	375.02	784.93	921.08	970.39	988.80
8.5	294.39	757.18	910.90	966.57	987.35
9.0	205.59	726.62	899.69	962.36	985.76
9.5	107.76	692.96	887.33	957.73	984.01
10.0	0.00	655.87	873.73	952.62	982.08
11.0		570.03	842.23	940.80	977.61
12.0		465.86	804.01	926.46	972.18
13.0		339.47	757.63	909.06	965.60
14.0		186.10	701.35	887.95	957.61
15.0		0.00	633.06	862.33	947.92
16.0			550.20	831.24	936.16
17.0			449.66	793.51	921.89
18.0			327.66	747.74	904.57
19.0			179.63	692.20	883.56
20.0			0.00	624.80	858.07
21.0				543.02	827.13
22.0				443.79	789.60
23.0				323.39	744.05
24.0				177.28	688.78
25.0				0.00	621.72
26.0					540.34
27.0					441.60
28.0					321.79
29.0					176.41
30.0					0.00

REMAINING BALANCE PER $1000 OF ORIGINAL LOAN
ANNUAL INTEREST RATE: 19.75%

AGE OF LOAN	LOAN MATURITY (YEARS)				
	10	15	20	25	30
0.5	983.11	994.25	997.91	999.23	999.71
1.0	964.48	987.90	995.61	998.37	999.39
1.5	943.93	980.90	993.07	997.43	999.04
2.0	921.27	973.18	990.27	996.39	998.65
2.5	896.27	964.67	987.18	995.25	998.22
3.0	868.71	955.28	983.77	993.98	997.75
3.5	838.30	944.93	980.02	992.59	997.23
4.0	804.77	933.51	975.87	991.05	996.66
4.5	767.79	920.91	971.30	989.36	996.02
5.0	727.00	907.02	966.26	987.49	995.32
5.5	682.02	891.70	960.70	985.43	994.55
6.0	632.40	874.80	954.57	983.15	993.70
6.5	577.68	856.16	947.81	980.65	992.77
7.0	517.33	835.60	940.35	977.88	991.73
7.5	450.77	812.93	932.12	974.83	990.59
8.0	377.36	787.93	923.05	971.47	989.34
8.5	296.40	760.35	913.05	967.76	987.95
9.0	207.10	729.94	902.01	963.66	986.42
9.5	108.62	696.40	889.84	959.15	984.73
10.0	0.00	659.40	876.42	954.17	982.87
11.0		573.60	845.28	942.63	978.56
12.0		469.23	807.41	928.59	973.31
13.0		342.27	761.35	911.50	966.92
14.0		187.85	705.31	890.73	959.16
15.0		0.00	637.15	865.45	949.71
16.0			554.25	834.71	938.22
17.0			453.40	797.31	924.24
18.0			330.73	751.82	907.24
19.0			181.51	696.49	886.56
20.0			0.00	629.18	861.40
21.0				547.31	830.80
22.0				447.73	793.58
23.0				326.59	748.31
24.0				179.24	693.23
25.0				0.00	626.24
26.0					544.75
27.0					445.63
28.0					325.06
29.0					178.40
30.0					0.00

REMAINING BALANCE PER $1000 OF ORIGINAL LOAN
ANNUAL INTEREST RATE: 20%

AGE OF LOAN	LOAN MATURITY (YEARS)				
	10	15	20	25	30
0.5	983.37	994.39	997.99	999.26	999.73
1.0	965.00	988.20	995.77	998.45	999.43
1.5	944.72	981.36	993.31	997.55	999.10
2.0	922.32	973.81	990.61	996.56	998.73
2.5	897.59	965.48	987.61	995.46	998.32
3.0	870.28	956.27	984.31	994.25	997.88
3.5	840.12	946.11	980.66	992.91	997.38
4.0	806.82	934.88	976.64	991.44	996.84
4.5	770.04	922.48	972.19	989.81	996.24
5.0	729.43	908.79	967.28	988.01	995.57
5.5	684.59	893.68	961.85	986.02	994.84
6.0	635.07	876.99	955.86	983.83	994.03
6.5	580.39	858.55	949.25	981.40	993.13
7.0	520.01	838.20	941.95	978.73	992.14
7.5	453.34	815.72	933.88	975.77	991.05
8.0	379.71	790.90	924.98	972.51	989.85
8.5	298.40	763.50	915.15	968.90	988.52
9.0	208.62	733.23	904.29	964.92	987.05
9.5	109.48	699.81	892.30	960.53	985.42
10.0	0.00	662.91	879.06	955.68	983.63
11.0		577.15	848.29	944.40	979.47
12.0		472.59	810.77	930.65	974.39
13.0		345.08	765.02	913.89	968.20
14.0		189.59	709.24	893.44	960.65
15.0		0.00	641.21	868.51	951.44
16.0			558.27	838.12	940.22
17.0			457.12	801.05	926.53
18.0			333.78	755.85	909.84
19.0			183.39	700.73	889.49
20.0			0.00	633.52	864.67
21.0				551.57	834.40
22.0				451.64	797.50
23.0				329.78	752.50
24.0				181.19	697.63
25.0				0.00	630.72
26.0					549.13
27.0					449.64
28.0					328.32
29.0					180.39
30.0					0.00

REMAINING BALANCE PER $1000 OF ORIGINAL LOAN
ANNUAL INTEREST RATE: 20.25%

AGE OF LOAN	LOAN MATURITY (YEARS)				
	10	15	20	25	30
0.5	983.62	994.54	998.06	999.30	999.74
1.0	965.52	988.50	995.92	998.52	999.46
1.5	945.50	981.82	993.55	997.66	999.15
2.0	923.36	974.43	990.93	996.71	998.80
2.5	898.89	966.27	988.03	995.67	998.42
3.0	871.84	957.24	984.83	994.51	998.00
3.5	841.92	947.26	981.29	993.22	997.53
4.0	808.85	936.23	977.38	991.81	997.01
4.5	772.28	924.03	973.05	990.24	996.44
5.0	731.85	910.54	968.26	988.51	995.81
5.5	687.16	895.63	962.97	986.59	995.11
6.0	637.74	879.14	957.12	984.47	994.33
6.5	583.10	860.92	950.66	982.13	993.48
7.0	522.69	840.76	943.51	979.54	992.54
7.5	455.90	818.48	935.60	976.68	991.49
8.0	382.05	793.84	926.86	973.51	990.34
8.5	300.41	766.61	917.20	970.01	989.06
9.0	210.14	736.49	906.52	966.14	987.65
9.5	110.34	703.20	894.71	961.86	986.09
10.0	0.00	666.38	881.65	957.13	984.36
11.0		580.69	851.24	946.12	980.34
12.0		475.93	814.08	932.66	975.43
13.0		347.88	768.65	916.21	969.43
14.0		191.34	713.12	896.10	962.09
15.0		0.00	645.24	871.51	953.12
16.0			562.26	841.46	942.16
17.0			460.83	804.72	928.75
18.0			336.84	759.82	912.37
19.0			185.27	704.92	892.34
20.0			0.00	637.82	867.86
21.0				555.80	837.93
22.0				455.53	801.35
23.0				332.96	756.63
24.0				183.14	701.97
25.0				0.00	635.15
26.0					553.46
27.0					453.62
28.0					331.57
29.0					182.37
30.0					0.00

REMAINING BALANCE PER $1000 OF ORIGINAL LOAN
ANNUAL INTEREST RATE: 20.5%

AGE OF LOAN	LOAN MATURITY (YEARS)				
	10	15	20	25	30
0.5	983.88	994.68	998.13	999.33	999.76
1.0	966.03	988.78	996.07	998.59	999.49
1.5	946.27	982.26	993.78	997.77	999.20
2.0	924.39	975.04	991.24	996.87	998.87
2.5	900.18	967.04	988.44	995.86	998.51
3.0	873.38	958.19	985.34	994.75	998.11
3.5	843.71	948.40	981.90	993.52	997.66
4.0	810.86	937.55	978.10	992.16	997.17
4.5	774.51	925.55	973.88	990.65	996.63
5.0	734.26	912.26	969.22	988.98	996.03
5.5	689.71	897.55	964.06	987.14	995.36
6.0	640.39	881.27	958.35	985.09	994.63
6.5	585.79	863.24	952.03	982.83	993.81
7.0	525.36	843.29	945.03	980.32	992.91
7.5	458.45	821.20	937.28	977.55	991.91
8.0	384.40	796.75	928.70	974.48	990.80
8.5	302.42	769.68	919.21	971.08	989.58
9.0	211.67	739.72	908.70	967.32	988.22
9.5	111.21	706.55	897.06	963.16	986.72
10.0	0.00	669.84	884.19	958.55	985.06
11.0		584.20	854.15	947.79	981.18
12.0		479.26	817.34	934.62	976.43
13.0		350.67	772.23	918.47	970.61
14.0		193.09	716.95	898.69	963.48
15.0		0.00	649.22	874.45	954.74
16.0			566.22	844.74	944.03
17.0			464.51	808.33	930.91
18.0			339.88	763.72	914.83
19.0			187.15	709.06	895.12
20.0			0.00	642.07	870.97
21.0				559.98	841.38
22.0				459.39	805.12
23.0				336.13	760.69
24.0				185.09	706.24
25.0				0.00	639.52
26.0					557.76
27.0					457.57
28.0					334.80
29.0					184.35
30.0					0.00

REMAINING BALANCE PER $1000 OF ORIGINAL LOAN
ANNUAL INTEREST RATE: 20.75%

AGE OF LOAN	LOAN MATURITY (YEARS)				
	10	15	20	25	30
0.5	984.12	994.81	998.20	999.36	999.77
1.0	966.53	989.06	996.21	998.66	999.52
1.5	947.03	982.69	994.00	997.88	999.24
2.0	925.41	975.63	991.55	997.01	998.94
2.5	901.46	967.80	988.83	996.05	998.59
3.0	874.91	959.13	985.82	994.99	998.21
3.5	845.48	949.51	982.49	993.81	997.79
4.0	812.87	938.86	978.79	992.50	997.33
4.5	776.72	927.05	974.70	991.05	996.81
5.0	736.65	913.95	970.16	989.44	996.24
5.5	692.24	899.45	965.12	987.66	995.61
6.0	643.03	883.36	959.55	985.69	994.90
6.5	588.48	865.54	953.37	983.50	994.12
7.0	528.02	845.79	946.51	981.08	993.26
7.5	461.01	823.89	938.92	978.39	992.31
8.0	386.74	799.63	930.50	975.42	991.25
8.5	304.42	772.73	921.18	972.12	990.07
9.0	213.19	742.92	910.84	968.46	988.77
9.5	112.07	709.88	899.38	964.41	987.32
10.0	0.00	673.26	886.68	959.92	985.72
11.0		587.70	857.00	949.42	981.99
12.0		482.58	820.55	936.52	977.39
13.0		353.46	775.76	920.68	971.75
14.0		194.85	720.75	901.22	964.82
15.0		0.00	653.17	877.32	956.31
16.0			570.16	847.96	945.85
17.0			468.18	811.88	933.00
18.0			342.91	767.57	917.22
19.0			189.03	713.14	897.84
20.0			0.00	646.28	874.02
21.0				564.14	844.77
22.0				463.24	808.83
23.0				339.29	764.69
24.0				187.04	710.46
25.0				0.00	643.85
26.0					562.02
27.0					461.50
28.0					338.02
29.0					186.33
30.0					0.00

REMAINING BALANCE PER $1000 OF ORIGINAL LOAN
ANNUAL INTEREST RATE: 21%

AGE OF LOAN	LOAN MATURITY (YEARS)				
	10	15	20	25	30
0.5	984.37	994.95	998.27	999.39	999.79
1.0	967.03	989.34	996.34	998.72	999.55
1.5	947.78	983.12	994.21	997.98	999.29
2.0	926.42	976.21	991.84	997.15	999.00
2.5	902.72	968.55	989.21	996.23	998.67
3.0	876.42	960.04	986.30	995.21	998.31
3.5	847.24	950.61	983.06	994.08	997.92
4.0	814.85	940.14	979.47	992.82	997.48
4.5	778.91	928.51	975.49	991.43	996.98
5.0	739.03	915.62	971.06	989.89	996.44
5.5	694.77	901.31	966.16	988.17	995.84
6.0	645.66	885.43	960.71	986.27	995.17
6.5	591.15	867.81	954.67	984.15	994.42
7.0	530.67	848.25	947.96	981.81	993.60
7.5	463.56	826.55	940.52	979.21	992.68
8.0	389.08	802.47	932.26	976.32	991.67
8.5	306.43	775.75	923.10	973.12	990.54
9.0	214.72	746.09	912.93	969.57	989.29
9.5	112.94	713.19	901.65	965.62	987.90
10.0	0.00	676.67	889.13	961.24	986.36
11.0		591.18	859.81	951.00	982.76
12.0		485.90	823.71	938.38	978.32
13.0		356.25	779.25	922.84	972.85
14.0		196.60	724.51	903.70	966.11
15.0		0.00	657.09	880.13	957.82
16.0			574.07	851.11	947.61
17.0			471.84	815.38	935.04
18.0			345.94	771.37	919.55
19.0			190.91	717.18	900.48
20.0			0.00	650.44	877.00
21.0				568.26	848.08
22.0				467.06	812.47
23.0				342.44	768.62
24.0				188.98	714.62
25.0				0.00	648.13
26.0					566.24
27.0					465.40
28.0					341.22
29.0					188.31
30.0					0.00

REMAINING BALANCE PER $1000 OF ORIGINAL LOAN
ANNUAL INTEREST RATE: 21.25%

AGE OF LOAN	LOAN MATURITY (YEARS)				
	10	15	20	25	30
0.5	984.61	995.08	998.33	999.42	999.80
1.0	967.52	989.61	996.48	998.78	999.58
1.5	948.53	983.53	994.42	998.07	999.33
2.0	927.42	976.78	992.13	997.28	999.05
2.5	903.97	969.28	989.58	996.40	998.75
3.0	877.92	960.94	986.76	995.43	998.41
3.5	848.98	951.68	983.62	994.34	998.03
4.0	816.82	941.39	980.13	993.14	997.61
4.5	781.09	929.96	976.25	991.80	997.15
5.0	741.39	917.26	971.95	990.31	996.63
5.5	697.28	903.14	967.16	988.66	996.06
6.0	648.27	887.46	961.85	986.82	995.42
6.5	593.82	870.04	955.94	984.78	994.71
7.0	533.32	850.68	949.38	982.51	993.92
7.5	466.10	829.18	942.08	979.99	993.04
8.0	391.42	805.28	933.98	977.20	992.07
8.5	308.44	778.73	924.98	974.09	990.99
9.0	216.25	749.23	914.98	970.63	989.79
9.5	113.81	716.46	903.87	966.79	988.46
10.0	0.00	680.04	891.52	962.53	986.97
11.0		594.63	862.57	952.52	983.50
12.0		489.19	826.82	940.18	979.20
13.0		359.03	782.69	924.93	973.90
14.0		198.35	728.21	906.11	967.36
15.0		0.00	660.96	882.88	959.28
16.0			577.95	854.21	949.32
17.0			475.47	818.81	937.01
18.0			348.96	775.10	921.82
19.0			192.79	721.16	903.06
20.0			0.00	654.56	879.91
21.0				572.35	851.33
22.0				470.86	816.05
23.0				345.58	772.49
24.0				190.92	718.73
25.0				0.00	652.35
26.0					570.42
27.0					469.27
28.0					344.41
29.0					190.28
30.0					0.00

REMAINING BALANCE PER $1000 OF ORIGINAL LOAN
ANNUAL INTEREST RATE: 21.5%

AGE OF LOAN	10	15	20	25	30
			LOAN MATURITY (YEARS)		
0.5	984.85	995.20	998.39	999.45	999.81
1.0	968.00	989.87	996.60	998.84	999.60
1.5	949.26	983.94	994.62	998.16	999.37
2.0	928.41	977.33	992.40	997.41	999.11
2.5	905.21	969.99	989.94	996.57	998.82
3.0	879.41	961.82	987.20	995.63	998.50
3.5	850.71	952.73	984.16	994.59	998.14
4.0	818.77	942.62	980.77	993.43	997.75
4.5	783.25	931.38	977.00	992.15	997.30
5.0	743.74	918.87	972.80	990.72	996.81
5.5	699.78	904.95	968.14	989.12	996.26
6.0	650.88	889.47	962.95	987.35	995.66
6.5	596.48	872.24	957.18	985.38	994.98
7.0	535.96	853.08	950.76	983.19	994.23
7.5	468.65	831.77	943.61	980.75	993.39
8.0	393.76	808.06	935.66	978.04	992.46
8.5	310.45	781.69	926.82	975.02	991.42
9.0	217.78	752.34	916.99	971.66	990.27
9.5	114.68	719.70	906.05	967.93	988.98
10.0	0.00	683.39	893.88	963.77	987.56
11.0		598.07	865.28	954.01	984.20
12.0		492.48	829.88	941.93	980.05
13.0		361.81	786.08	926.98	974.92
14.0		200.11	731.88	908.48	968.56
15.0		0.00	664.81	885.58	960.70
16.0			581.80	857.24	950.97
17.0			479.09	822.18	938.93
18.0			351.97	778.79	924.02
19.0			194.67	725.09	905.58
20.0			0.00	658.64	882.75
21.0				576.40	854.51
22.0				474.64	819.56
23.0				348.70	776.30
24.0				192.86	722.78
25.0				0.00	656.54
26.0					574.57
27.0					473.13
28.0					347.59
29.0					192.24
30.0					0.00

REMAINING BALANCE PER $1000 OF ORIGINAL LOAN
ANNUAL INTEREST RATE: 21.75%

AGE OF LOAN	LOAN MATURITY (YEARS)				
	10	15	20	25	30
0.5	985.09	995.33	998.45	999.48	999.82
1.0	968.48	990.13	996.73	998.90	999.63
1.5	949.99	984.33	994.81	998.25	999.41
2.0	929.39	977.88	992.67	997.53	999.16
2.5	906.44	970.69	990.29	996.72	998.89
3.0	880.88	962.68	987.63	995.83	998.58
3.5	852.42	953.77	984.68	994.83	998.25
4.0	820.71	943.83	981.39	993.72	997.87
4.5	785.40	932.77	977.72	992.48	997.45
5.0	746.07	920.45	973.64	991.11	996.98
5.5	702.26	906.73	969.09	989.57	996.46
6.0	653.47	891.44	964.03	987.86	995.88
6.5	599.13	874.42	958.38	985.96	995.24
7.0	538.60	855.45	952.10	983.84	994.52
7.5	471.18	834.33	945.10	981.48	993.72
8.0	396.09	810.81	937.31	978.85	992.82
8.5	312.46	784.61	928.62	975.92	991.83
9.0	219.31	755.43	918.95	972.66	990.72
9.5	115.56	722.92	908.18	969.03	989.49
10.0	0.00	686.72	896.18	964.98	988.12
11.0		601.49	867.94	955.45	984.88
12.0		495.75	832.90	943.63	980.87
13.0		364.58	789.43	928.97	975.90
14.0		201.86	735.51	910.78	969.73
15.0		0.00	668.62	888.22	962.07
16.0			585.63	860.22	952.57
17.0			482.68	825.49	940.79
18.0			354.97	782.41	926.17
19.0			196.54	728.97	908.03
20.0			0.00	662.67	885.54
21.0				580.42	857.63
22.0				478.39	823.00
23.0				351.82	780.05
24.0				194.79	726.77
25.0				0.00	660.67
26.0					578.67
27.0					476.95
28.0					350.76
29.0					194.21
30.0					0.00

MORTGAGE VALUE TABLES
(Value of Amortizing Mortgage Loans as Percentage of Face Value)

Mortgage loans can be an investment medium as well as a method for financing a home purchase. When viewed as an investment, a loan has a market value just as a share of stock or a bond. The value of the loan depends in part on the face interest rate of the loan compared with current interest rates. The following tables provide the relative value of mortgage loans for various combinations of face rates and market rates.

To use the tables, you need the following information:

1. *The interest rate on the loan* (face interest rate). Each page covers a different rate ranging from 6% to 17.75% in intervals of .25%.

2. *The yield demanded by secondary investors* (yield to maturity). Even though the loan is contracted at a certain interest rate, the yield may be raised or lowered by adjusting the price paid for the loan. The yield to maturity is the rate desired by the investor. Each page covers yields from 10 to 19.00% in .25% intervals.

3. *The remaining term of the loan.* How many years will the loan run after being purchased by the investor? The tables cover terms of 10, 15, 20, 25, and 30 years. Use the column which is closest to the actual remaining term.

4. *The remaining balance of the loan* (face value). What is the balance of the loan when the investor makes the purchase?

Example. A home seller provides a loan as part of the sales arrangement. After holding the loan for two years, the seller decides to sell the loan to secondary investors. The loan still has 23 years until maturity and a remaining principal balance of $45,000. The interest rate on the loan is 6%. If investors require a yield to maturity of 15% on 25-year amortizing home mortgage loans, what is the loan worth in the market?

Look at the first table. At the top is listed the "FACE INTEREST RATE" of 6%. Under the column for "YIELD TO MATURITY" find the yield of 15.0%. Follow this row over to the column under "TERM OF LOAN 25" (this is the closest to the actual term of 23 years). The value factor is 50.303. That is, the loan is worth 50.303 cents per dollar of face value. Multiply this percentage by the balance of the loan, or $45,000. The result is $22,636, which is the market value of the loan.

Example. A home seller is willing to provide financing to assist in making a sale. The seller makes an offer to provide a loan at 6% interest over a term of 20 years. The seller intends to sell the loan to investors who desire a yield to maturity of 12%. What should be the amount of the loan if the seller wants to get $50,000 cash from its sale?

Look at the table for "FACE INTEREST RATE" of 6%. Under the column "YIELD TO MATURITY" find the rate 12.0%. Follow the row to the column under "TERM OF LOAN 20." The value factor is 65.066. Divide the value desired, $50,000, by the percentage value factor, .65066, to obtain the result of $76,845. This is the face value of the loan which serves the seller's purpose.

VALUE OF AMORTIZING MORTGAGE LOANS
AS PERCENTAGE OF FACE VALUE
FACE INTEREST RATE: 6%

YIELD TO MATURITY	TERM OF LOAN (YEARS)				
	10	15	20	25	30
10.00	84.010	78.527	74.240	70.903	68.319
10.25	83.137	77.422	72.983	69.550	66.907
10.50	82.277	76.339	71.759	68.239	65.543
10.75	81.430	75.281	70.568	66.969	64.227
11.00	80.596	74.244	69.409	65.737	62.957
11.25	79.774	73.229	68.280	64.544	61.729
11.50	78.964	72.236	67.180	63.386	60.543
11.75	78.167	71.263	66.109	62.263	59.396
12.00	77.382	70.312	65.066	61.174	58.287
12.25	76.608	69.379	64.049	60.117	57.215
12.50	75.846	68.466	63.058	59.091	56.177
12.75	75.095	67.571	62.093	58.095	55.172
13.00	74.355	66.695	61.151	57.127	54.199
13.25	73.626	65.837	60.233	56.187	53.257
13.50	72.908	64.996	59.338	55.274	52.344
13.75	72.200	64.172	58.465	54.387	51.459
14.00	71.503	63.365	57.613	53.524	50.600
14.25	70.816	62.574	56.782	52.685	49.768
14.50	70.139	61.798	55.971	51.869	48.961
14.75	69.471	61.038	55.180	51.076	48.177
15.00	68.814	60.293	54.407	50.303	47.416
15.25	68.165	59.563	53.653	49.552	46.677
15.50	67.526	58.847	52.917	48.820	45.960
15.75	66.896	58.144	52.198	48.108	45.262
16.00	66.276	57.456	51.495	47.414	44.584
16.25	65.664	56.781	50.809	46.738	43.925
16.50	65.060	56.118	50.139	46.079	43.284
16.75	64.466	55.469	49.483	45.437	42.661
17.00	63.879	54.831	48.843	44.812	42.054
17.25	63.301	54.206	48.217	44.202	41.463
17.50	62.731	53.593	47.605	43.607	40.888
17.75	62.169	52.990	47.007	43.026	40.328
18.00	61.615	52.400	46.422	42.460	39.782
18.25	61.068	51.820	45.849	41.907	39.250
18.50	60.529	51.251	45.289	41.368	38.732
18.75	59.998	50.692	44.742	40.841	38.227
19.00	59.473	50.144	44.205	40.327	37.734

536

VALUE OF AMORTIZING MORTGAGE LOANS
AS PERCENTAGE OF FACE VALUE
FACE INTEREST RATE: 6.25%

YIELD TO MATURITY	TERM OF LOAN (YEARS)				
	10	15	20	25	30
10.00	84.963	79.789	75.742	72.594	70.161
10.25	84.080	78.666	74.459	71.209	68.710
10.50	83.210	77.566	73.211	69.866	67.310
10.75	82.353	76.490	71.996	68.566	65.959
11.00	81.510	75.437	70.813	67.305	64.654
11.25	80.678	74.406	69.661	66.083	63.393
11.50	79.860	73.397	68.539	64.898	62.175
11.75	79.053	72.409	67.446	63.748	60.997
12.00	78.259	71.441	66.382	62.633	59.859
12.25	77.477	70.494	65.345	61.551	58.757
12.50	76.706	69.566	64.334	60.500	57.691
12.75	75.946	68.657	63.349	59.480	56.659
13.00	75.198	67.767	62.388	58.490	55.660
13.25	74.461	66.895	61.452	57.527	54.693
13.50	73.735	66.041	60.538	56.592	53.755
13.75	73.019	65.203	59.647	55.684	52.846
14.00	72.314	64.383	58.779	54.800	51.965
14.25	71.619	63.579	57.931	53.942	51.110
14.50	70.934	62.791	57.104	53.106	50.281
14.75	70.259	62.019	56.296	52.294	49.476
15.00	69.594	61.262	55.508	51.503	48.695
15.25	68.938	60.520	54.739	50.733	47.936
15.50	68.292	59.792	53.987	49.984	47.199
15.75	67.655	59.079	53.254	49.255	46.482
16.00	67.027	58.379	52.537	48.545	45.786
16.25	66.408	57.693	51.837	47.852	45.109
16.50	65.798	57.020	51.153	47.178	44.451
16.75	65.196	56.360	50.484	46.521	43.811
17.00	64.604	55.713	49.831	45.880	43.188
17.25	64.019	55.077	49.193	45.256	42.581
17.50	63.442	54.454	48.568	44.647	41.990
17.75	62.874	53.842	47.958	44.052	41.415
18.00	62.313	53.242	47.361	43.473	40.855
18.25	61.760	52.653	46.777	42.907	40.309
18.50	61.215	52.074	46.206	42.355	39.776
18.75	60.678	51.507	45.647	41.815	39.257
19.00	60.148	50.950	45.100	41.289	38.751

VALUE OF AMORTIZING MORTGAGE LOANS
AS PERCENTAGE OF FACE VALUE
FACE INTEREST RATE: 6.5%

YIELD TO MATURITY	TERM OF LOAN (YEARS)				
	10	15	20	25	30
10.00	85.923	81.063	77.260	74.305	72.025
10.25	85.030	79.922	75.952	72.887	70.536
10.50	84.150	78.805	74.679	71.513	69.098
10.75	83.284	77.712	73.439	70.181	67.711
11.00	82.431	76.642	72.233	68.891	66.371
11.25	81.590	75.595	71.058	67.640	65.077
11.50	80.763	74.569	69.913	66.427	63.827
11.75	79.947	73.565	68.799	65.250	62.618
12.00	79.144	72.582	67.713	64.109	61.449
12.25	78.353	71.620	66.655	63.001	60.318
12.50	77.573	70.677	65.624	61.926	59.224
12.75	76.805	69.754	64.619	60.882	58.164
13.00	76.049	68.849	63.639	59.868	57.139
13.25	75.303	67.963	62.683	58.883	56.145
13.50	74.569	67.095	61.752	57.926	55.183
13.75	73.844	66.245	60.843	56.996	54.250
14.00	73.131	65.411	59.957	56.092	53.345
14.25	72.429	64.595	59.092	55.213	52.468
14.50	71.736	63.794	58.248	54.358	51.616
14.75	71.053	63.010	57.425	53.526	50.790
15.00	70.381	62.241	56.621	52.717	49.988
15.25	69.718	61.487	55.836	51.929	49.209
15.50	69.064	60.747	55.070	51.162	48.452
15.75	68.420	60.022	54.321	50.415	47.717
16.00	67.785	59.312	53.590	49.688	47.003
16.25	67.159	58.615	52.876	48.980	46.308
16.50	66.542	57.931	52.178	48.290	45.632
16.75	65.934	57.260	51.496	47.617	44.975
17.00	65.334	56.602	50.830	46.961	44.335
17.25	64.742	55.957	50.179	46.322	43.712
17.50	64.159	55.323	49.542	45.699	43.106
17.75	63.584	54.702	48.919	45.090	42.515
18.00	63.018	54.092	48.310	44.497	41.940
18.25	62.459	53.494	47.714	43.918	41.379
18.50	61.907	52.906	47.132	43.353	40.833
18.75	61.364	52.329	46.562	42.801	40.300
19.00	60.828	51.763	46.004	42.262	39.781

VALUE OF AMORTIZING MORTGAGE LOANS
AS PERCENTAGE OF FACE VALUE
FACE INTEREST RATE: 6.75%

YIELD TO MATURITY	TERM OF LOAN (YEARS)				
	10	15	20	25	30
10.00	86.889	82.347	78.792	76.033	73.908
10.25	85.986	81.188	77.458	74.582	72.380
10.50	85.096	80.053	76.160	73.176	70.905
10.75	84.220	78.943	74.896	71.813	69.482
11.00	83.357	77.856	73.665	70.493	68.107
11.25	82.507	76.792	72.467	69.213	66.779
11.50	81.670	75.751	71.300	67.972	65.496
11.75	80.845	74.730	70.163	66.768	64.255
12.00	80.033	73.732	69.056	65.600	63.056
12.25	79.233	72.754	67.977	64.466	61.895
12.50	78.444	71.797	66.925	63.366	60.772
12.75	77.668	70.859	65.900	62.298	59.686
13.00	76.903	69.940	64.901	61.260	58.633
13.25	76.149	69.040	63.927	60.252	57.614
13.50	75.406	68.158	62.977	59.273	56.626
13.75	74.674	67.294	62.050	58.321	55.668
14.00	73.953	66.448	61.146	57.396	54.740
14.25	73.242	65.618	60.264	56.497	53.840
14.50	72.542	64.805	59.404	55.622	52.966
14.75	71.852	64.008	58.564	54.771	52.118
15.00	71.171	63.227	57.744	53.943	51.295
15.25	70.501	62.461	56.943	53.137	50.496
15.50	69.840	61.710	56.162	52.352	49.719
15.75	69.188	60.973	55.399	51.588	48.965
16.00	68.546	60.251	54.653	50.844	48.232
16.25	67.913	59.543	53.925	50.119	47.519
16.50	67.289	58.848	53.213	49.413	46.825
16.75	66.674	58.167	52.518	48.724	46.151
17.00	66.068	57.499	51.838	48.054	45.494
17.25	65.470	56.843	51.174	47.399	44.855
17.50	64.880	56.200	50.525	46.761	44.233
17.75	64.299	55.568	49.889	46.139	43.627
18.00	63.726	54.949	49.268	45.532	43.037
18.25	63.160	54.341	48.661	44.939	42.461
18.50	62.603	53.744	48.067	44.361	41.901
18.75	62.053	53.158	47.485	43.796	41.354
19.00	61.511	52.583	46.916	43.245	40.821

VALUE OF AMORTIZING MORTGAGE LOANS
AS PERCENTAGE OF FACE VALUE
FACE INTEREST RATE: 7%

YIELD TO MATURITY	TERM OF LOAN (YEARS)				
	10	15	20	25	30
10.00	87.860	83.642	80.340	77.779	75.812
10.25	86.947	82.465	78.980	76.294	74.244
10.50	86.047	81.312	77.656	74.856	72.731
10.75	85.162	80.184	76.367	73.463	71.271
11.00	84.289	79.081	75.112	72.112	69.861
11.25	83.430	78.000	73.890	70.802	68.499
11.50	82.583	76.942	72.700	69.533	67.182
11.75	81.749	75.906	71.541	68.301	65.910
12.00	80.928	74.892	70.412	67.106	64.680
12.25	80.119	73.899	69.312	65.947	63.489
12.50	79.322	72.926	68.240	64.821	62.337
12.75	78.536	71.973	67.194	63.728	61.223
13.00	77.763	71.040	66.176	62.667	60.143
13.25	77.000	70.126	65.182	61.636	59.097
13.50	76.250	69.230	64.214	60.634	58.084
13.75	75.509	68.352	63.269	59.661	57.102
14.00	74.780	67.493	62.347	58.714	56.150
14.25	74.061	66.650	61.448	57.794	55.226
14.50	73.353	65.824	60.570	56.899	54.330
14.75	72.655	65.014	59.714	56.028	53.460
15.00	71.967	64.221	58.878	55.181	52.616
15.25	71.289	63.443	58.062	54.357	51.796
15.50	70.621	62.680	57.265	53.554	51.000
15.75	69.962	61.932	56.487	52.773	50.226
16.00	69.313	61.199	55.726	52.011	49.474
16.25	68.673	60.480	54.984	51.270	48.742
16.50	68.042	59.774	54.258	50.548	48.031
16.75	67.420	59.082	53.549	49.843	47.339
17.00	66.807	58.403	52.856	49.157	46.666
17.25	66.202	57.737	52.179	48.488	46.010
17.50	65.606	57.084	51.517	47.835	45.372
17.75	65.018	56.442	50.869	47.198	44.750
18.00	64.438	55.813	50.236	46.577	44.145
18.25	63.867	55.196	49.617	45.971	43.555
18.50	63.303	54.589	49.011	45.379	42.980
18.75	62.747	53.994	48.418	44.802	42.419
19.00	62.199	53.410	47.838	44.238	41.872

VALUE OF AMORTIZING MORTGAGE LOANS
AS PERCENTAGE OF FACE VALUE
FACE INTEREST RATE: 7.25%

YIELD TO MATURITY	TERM OF LOAN (YEARS)				
	10	15	20	25	30
10.00	88.839	84.949	81.903	79.543	77.735
10.25	87.916	83.753	80.516	78.025	76.127
10.50	87.006	82.582	79.166	76.554	74.576
10.75	86.110	81.437	77.852	75.129	73.079
11.00	85.228	80.316	76.573	73.748	71.633
11.25	84.359	79.218	75.327	72.408	70.236
11.50	83.503	78.144	74.114	71.110	68.887
11.75	82.660	77.091	72.933	69.850	67.582
12.00	81.829	76.062	71.782	68.628	66.320
12.25	81.011	75.053	70.660	67.442	65.100
12.50	80.205	74.065	69.567	66.291	63.919
12.75	79.411	73.097	68.501	65.174	62.776
13.00	78.629	72.150	67.463	64.088	61.669
13.25	77.858	71.221	66.450	63.034	60.596
13.50	77.099	70.312	65.463	62.009	59.557
13.75	76.350	69.420	64.499	61.014	58.550
14.00	75.613	68.547	63.560	60.046	57.574
14.25	74.886	67.691	62.643	59.105	56.627
14.50	74.170	66.852	61.748	58.189	55.708
14.75	73.464	66.030	60.875	57.299	54.816
15.00	72.769	65.224	60.023	56.433	53.951
15.25	72.083	64.434	59.191	55.590	53.110
15.50	71.408	63.659	58.379	54.769	52.294
15.75	70.741	62.899	57.585	53.970	51.500
16.00	70.085	62.155	56.810	53.191	50.729
16.25	69.438	61.424	56.053	52.433	49.979
16.50	68.800	60.708	55.314	51.694	49.249
16.75	68.171	60.005	54.591	50.974	48.540
17.00	67.551	59.315	53.885	50.272	47.849
17.25	66.939	58.639	53.194	49.588	47.177
17.50	66.336	57.975	52.519	48.920	46.523
17.75	65.742	57.324	51.859	48.269	45.886
18.00	65.156	56.685	51.213	47.634	45.265
18.25	64.578	56.058	50.582	47.014	44.660
18.50	64.008	55.442	49.964	46.409	44.070
18.75	63.446	54.838	49.360	45.818	43.495
19.00	62.892	54.244	48.768	45.241	42.934

VALUE OF AMORTIZING MORTGAGE LOANS
AS PERCENTAGE OF FACE VALUE
FACE INTEREST RATE: 7.5%

YIELD TO MATURITY	TERM OF LOAN (YEARS)				
	10	15	20	25	30
10.00	89.822	86.265	83.479	81.324	79.676
10.25	88.889	85.051	82.066	79.772	78.028
10.50	87.969	83.862	80.690	78.268	76.438
10.75	87.063	82.699	79.351	76.811	74.904
11.00	86.172	81.560	78.047	75.398	73.422
11.25	85.293	80.445	76.777	74.029	71.990
11.50	84.428	79.354	75.541	72.702	70.607
11.75	83.575	78.286	74.336	71.414	69.269
12.00	82.735	77.240	73.163	70.165	67.976
12.25	81.908	76.216	72.020	68.952	66.725
12.50	81.093	75.212	70.906	67.775	65.515
12.75	80.290	74.230	69.820	66.633	64.343
13.00	79.500	73.267	68.761	65.523	63.209
13.25	78.720	72.324	67.729	64.445	62.110
13.50	77.952	71.401	66.723	63.398	61.045
13.75	77.195	70.496	65.741	62.380	60.012
14.00	76.450	69.609	64.783	61.390	59.012
14.25	75.715	68.740	63.849	60.428	58.041
14.50	74.991	67.888	62.937	59.492	57.099
14.75	74.278	67.053	62.047	58.582	56.185
15.00	73.575	66.235	61.178	57.696	55.298
15.25	72.881	65.432	60.330	56.834	54.436
15.50	72.198	64.645	59.502	55.995	53.599
15.75	71.525	63.874	58.694	55.178	52.786
16.00	70.861	63.118	57.904	54.382	51.996
16.25	70.207	62.376	57.132	53.607	51.227
16.50	69.561	61.648	56.378	52.851	50.479
16.75	68.925	60.934	55.642	52.115	49.752
17.00	68.299	60.234	54.922	51.397	49.044
17.25	67.680	59.547	54.218	50.698	48.355
17.50	67.071	58.873	53.530	50.015	47.685
17.75	66.470	58.212	52.857	49.350	47.031
18.00	65.877	57.563	52.199	48.700	46.395
18.25	65.293	56.926	51.555	48.066	45.775
18.50	64.717	56.301	50.926	47.448	45.170
18.75	64.148	55.687	50.310	46.844	44.581
19.00	63.588	55.085	49.707	46.254	44.006

VALUE OF AMORTIZING MORTGAGE LOANS
AS PERCENTAGE OF FACE VALUE
FACE INTEREST RATE: 7.75%

YIELD TO MATURITY	TERM OF LOAN (YEARS)				
	10	15	20	25	30
10.00	90.814	87.593	85.071	83.122	81.636
10.25	89.870	86.360	83.630	81.535	79.948
10.50	88.940	85.153	82.228	79.998	78.319
10.75	88.024	83.972	80.864	78.509	76.746
11.00	87.123	82.816	79.535	77.066	75.228
11.25	86.234	81.684	78.241	75.666	73.761
11.50	85.359	80.576	76.981	74.309	72.344
11.75	84.497	79.491	75.754	72.993	70.973
12.00	83.648	78.429	74.558	71.716	69.649
12.25	82.812	77.389	73.393	70.477	68.367
12.50	81.988	76.370	72.258	69.274	67.127
12.75	81.177	75.372	71.151	68.106	65.926
13.00	80.377	74.395	70.072	66.972	64.764
13.25	79.589	73.438	69.021	65.870	63.637
13.50	78.813	72.500	67.995	64.799	62.546
13.75	78.047	71.581	66.994	63.759	61.489
14.00	77.294	70.680	66.018	62.748	60.463
14.25	76.551	69.798	65.066	61.764	59.469
14.50	75.819	68.933	64.137	60.808	58.504
14.75	75.097	68.085	63.230	59.877	57.568
15.00	74.387	67.254	62.345	58.972	56.658
15.25	73.686	66.439	61.481	58.091	55.776
15.50	72.995	65.641	60.637	57.233	54.918
15.75	72.314	64.857	59.813	56.398	54.085
16.00	71.643	64.089	59.008	55.584	53.275
16.25	70.981	63.336	58.222	54.792	52.487
16.50	70.329	62.597	57.453	54.020	51.721
16.75	69.686	61.873	56.703	53.267	50.976
17.00	69.052	61.162	55.969	52.534	50.251
17.25	68.427	60.464	55.252	51.819	49.545
17.50	67.811	59.780	54.550	51.121	48.858
17.75	67.203	59.108	53.865	50.441	48.188
18.00	66.604	58.449	53.194	49.777	47.536
18.25	66.014	57.803	52.538	49.129	46.901
18.50	65.431	57.168	51.897	48.497	46.282
18.75	64.856	56.545	51.269	47.880	45.678
19.00	64.290	55.933	50.655	47.277	45.089

VALUE OF AMORTIZING MORTGAGE LOANS
AS PERCENTAGE OF FACE VALUE
FACE INTEREST RATE: 8%

YIELD TO MATURITY	TERM OF LOAN (YEARS)				
	10	15	20	25	30
10.00	91.810	88.930	86.676	84.936	83.613
10.25	90.856	87.679	85.208	83.315	81.884
10.50	89.915	86.453	83.780	81.744	80.216
10.75	88.990	85.254	82.389	80.223	78.605
11.00	88.078	84.080	81.036	78.748	77.050
11.25	87.180	82.931	79.717	77.318	75.548
11.50	86.295	81.806	78.434	75.931	74.096
11.75	85.424	80.705	77.183	74.586	72.692
12.00	84.566	79.626	75.965	73.281	71.335
12.25	83.720	78.570	74.778	72.015	70.023
12.50	82.887	77.536	73.621	70.786	68.752
12.75	82.067	76.523	72.494	69.592	67.523
13.00	81.259	75.531	71.394	68.433	66.332
13.25	80.462	74.559	70.323	67.308	65.179
13.50	79.677	73.607	69.278	66.214	64.061
13.75	78.903	72.674	68.258	65.150	62.978
14.00	78.141	71.760	67.264	64.117	61.928
14.25	77.391	70.864	66.294	63.112	60.909
14.50	76.650	69.985	65.347	62.135	59.921
14.75	75.921	69.125	64.423	61.184	58.962
15.00	75.202	68.281	63.521	60.259	58.031
15.25	74.494	67.454	62.641	59.359	57.126
15.50	73.796	66.643	61.781	58.482	56.248
15.75	73.107	65.848	60.941	57.629	55.394
16.00	72.429	65.068	60.121	56.798	54.565
16.25	71.760	64.303	59.320	55.988	53.758
16.50	71.100	63.553	58.537	55.199	52.974
16.75	70.450	62.817	57.772	54.430	52.211
17.00	69.810	62.096	57.025	53.681	51.468
17.25	69.178	61.387	56.294	52.950	50.745
17.50	68.555	60.693	55.580	52.237	50.041
17.75	67.940	60.011	54.881	51.542	49.356
18.00	67.335	59.342	54.198	50.863	48.688
18.25	66.738	58.685	53.529	50.201	48.037
18.50	66.149	58.041	52.876	49.555	47.402
18.75	65.568	57.408	52.236	48.925	46.784
19.00	64.995	56.787	51.610	48.309	46.181

VALUE OF AMORTIZING MORTGAGE LOANS
AS PERCENTAGE OF FACE VALUE
FACE INTEREST RATE: 8.25%

YIELD TO MATURITY	TERM OF LOAN (YEARS)				
	10	15	20	25	30
10.00	92.812	90.279	88.295	86.767	85.607
10.25	91.848	89.008	86.800	85.111	83.837
10.50	90.897	87.764	85.345	83.506	82.129
10.75	89.962	86.546	83.928	81.952	80.480
11.00	89.040	85.355	82.549	80.445	78.888
11.25	88.132	84.188	81.207	78.984	77.350
11.50	87.238	83.046	79.899	77.568	75.863
11.75	86.357	81.928	78.625	76.193	74.426
12.00	85.489	80.834	77.384	74.861	73.037
12.25	84.635	79.762	76.175	73.567	71.693
12.50	83.792	78.712	74.996	72.311	70.392
12.75	82.963	77.683	73.848	71.092	69.133
13.00	82.146	76.676	72.728	69.908	67.914
13.25	81.340	75.689	71.636	68.758	66.733
13.50	80.547	74.723	70.572	67.641	65.589
13.75	79.765	73.775	69.533	66.555	64.480
14.00	78.995	72.847	68.520	65.499	63.405
14.25	78.236	71.938	67.532	64.472	62.362
14.50	77.487	71.046	66.568	63.474	61.350
14.75	76.750	70.173	65.626	62.503	60.368
15.00	76.024	69.316	64.708	61.558	59.415
15.25	75.307	68.476	63.811	60.638	58.489
15.50	74.601	67.653	62.935	59.743	57.590
15.75	73.905	66.846	62.080	58.871	56.716
16.00	73.220	66.054	61.244	58.022	55.866
16.25	72.544	65.278	60.428	57.194	55.040
16.50	71.877	64.516	59.631	56.389	54.237
16.75	71.220	63.770	58.852	55.603	53.456
17.00	70.572	63.037	58.090	54.837	52.695
17.25	69.933	62.318	57.346	54.091	51.955
17.50	69.303	61.613	56.618	53.363	51.235
17.75	68.682	60.920	55.906	52.652	50.533
18.00	68.070	60.241	55.210	51.960	49.849
18.25	67.466	59.575	54.529	51.283	49.183
18.50	66.871	58.920	53.864	50.623	48.533
18.75	66.284	58.278	53.212	49.979	47.900
19.00	65.705	57.648	52.574	49.350	47.282

VALUE OF AMORTIZING MORTGAGE LOANS
AS PERCENTAGE OF FACE VALUE
FACE INTEREST RATE: 8.5%

YIELD TO MATURITY	TERM OF LOAN (YEARS)				
	10	15	20	25	30
10.00	93.822	91.637	89.928	88.613	87.618
10.25	92.847	90.348	88.405	86.922	85.807
10.50	91.886	89.085	86.923	85.283	84.058
10.75	90.940	87.849	85.481	83.695	82.371
11.00	90.008	86.640	84.076	82.157	80.741
11.25	89.090	85.455	82.709	80.665	79.167
11.50	88.186	84.296	81.377	79.218	77.645
11.75	87.296	83.161	80.079	77.815	76.175
12.00	86.419	82.050	78.815	76.454	74.753
12.25	85.555	80.962	77.584	75.133	73.377
12.50	84.704	79.896	76.384	73.850	72.046
12.75	83.865	78.853	75.214	72.605	70.757
13.00	83.039	77.830	74.073	71.396	69.510
13.25	82.225	76.829	72.961	70.221	68.301
13.50	81.423	75.848	71.877	69.080	67.130
13.75	80.632	74.886	70.819	67.971	65.995
14.00	79.854	73.944	69.788	66.893	64.894
14.25	79.086	73.021	68.781	65.844	63.827
14.50	78.330	72.116	67.799	64.825	62.791
14.75	77.585	71.229	66.840	63.833	61.786
15.00	76.850	70.360	65.905	62.868	60.810
15.25	76.126	69.507	64.991	61.928	59.863
15.50	75.413	68.672	64.099	61.014	58.942
15.75	74.709	67.852	63.228	60.124	58.048
16.00	74.016	67.048	62.377	59.256	57.179
16.25	73.332	66.261	61.546	58.412	56.333
16.50	72.658	65.488	60.734	57.589	55.511
16.75	71.994	64.729	59.940	56.786	54.712
17.00	71.340	63.986	59.165	56.004	53.933
17.25	70.694	63.256	58.406	55.242	53.176
17.50	70.057	62.540	57.665	54.498	52.438
17.75	69.429	61.837	56.940	53.773	51.720
18.00	68.810	61.148	56.231	53.065	51.020
18.25	68.200	60.472	55.538	52.375	50.338
18.50	67.598	59.807	54.860	51.701	49.673
18.75	67.004	59.155	54.196	51.042	49.025
19.00	66.419	58.515	53.547	50.400	48.393

VALUE OF AMORTIZING MORTGAGE LOANS
AS PERCENTAGE OF FACE VALUE
FACE INTEREST RATE: 8.75%

YIELD TO MATURITY	TERM OF LOAN (YEARS)				
	10	15	20	25	30
10.00	94.836	93.006	91.574	90.475	89.645
10.25	93.850	91.697	90.024	88.748	87.791
10.50	92.879	90.415	88.514	87.075	86.003
10.75	91.923	89.161	87.045	85.454	84.276
11.00	90.981	87.934	85.615	83.883	82.609
11.25	90.053	86.732	84.222	82.359	80.998
11.50	89.140	85.555	82.866	80.882	79.441
11.75	88.239	84.403	81.545	79.450	77.937
12.00	87.353	83.276	80.258	78.060	76.482
12.25	86.480	82.171	79.004	76.711	75.074
12.50	85.619	81.090	77.782	75.401	73.712
12.75	84.772	80.030	76.591	74.130	72.394
13.00	83.937	78.993	75.429	72.896	71.117
13.25	83.114	77.976	74.297	71.696	69.881
13.50	82.303	76.980	73.193	70.531	68.683
13.75	81.504	76.004	72.116	69.399	67.521
14.00	80.717	75.048	71.065	68.298	66.395
14.25	79.942	74.111	70.040	67.228	65.303
14.50	79.177	73.193	69.040	66.186	64.244
14.75	78.424	72.293	68.064	65.174	63.215
15.00	77.681	71.410	67.111	64.188	62.217
15.25	76.949	70.545	66.181	63.229	61.248
15.50	76.228	69.697	65.272	62.296	60.306
15.75	75.517	68.865	64.385	61.387	59.391
16.00	74.816	68.050	63.519	60.501	58.501
16.25	74.125	67.250	62.672	59.639	57.636
16.50	73.444	66.466	61.845	58.798	56.795
16.75	72.773	65.696	61.037	57.979	55.977
17.00	72.111	64.941	60.248	57.181	55.181
17.25	71.458	64.201	59.475	56.402	54.406
17.50	70.815	63.474	58.721	55.643	53.651
17.75	70.180	62.761	57.982	54.903	52.916
18.00	69.554	62.061	57.261	54.180	52.200
18.25	68.937	61.375	56.555	53.475	51.502
18.50	68.329	60.700	55.864	52.787	50.822
18.75	67.729	60.039	55.188	52.115	50.159
19.00	67.137	59.389	54.527	51.459	49.512

VALUE OF AMORTIZING MORTGAGE LOANS
AS PERCENTAGE OF FACE VALUE
FACE INTEREST RATE: 9%

YIELD TO MATURITY	TERM OF LOAN (YEARS)				
	10	15	20	25	30
10.00	95.856	94.384	93.233	92.351	91.687
10.25	94.860	93.056	91.655	90.588	89.791
10.50	93.878	91.755	90.118	88.880	87.962
10.75	92.912	90.482	88.623	87.226	86.196
11.00	91.960	89.237	87.167	85.622	84.490
11.25	91.022	88.017	85.749	84.067	82.843
11.50	90.099	86.823	84.368	82.560	81.251
11.75	89.189	85.654	83.023	81.097	79.712
12.00	88.293	84.510	81.712	79.679	78.224
12.25	87.410	83.389	80.435	78.302	76.784
12.50	86.541	82.291	79.191	76.965	75.391
12.75	85.684	81.217	77.978	75.668	74.043
13.00	84.840	80.164	76.796	74.408	72.737
13.25	84.008	79.132	75.643	73.183	71.473
13.50	83.189	78.121	74.519	71.994	70.247
13.75	82.381	77.131	73.422	70.838	69.059
14.00	81.585	76.161	72.353	69.714	67.908
14.25	80.802	75.210	71.309	68.622	66.791
14.50	80.029	74.278	70.291	67.559	65.707
14.75	79.267	73.364	69.297	66.525	64.655
15.00	78.517	72.469	68.327	65.520	63.634
15.25	77.777	71.591	67.380	64.541	62.643
15.50	77.048	70.730	66.455	63.588	61.680
15.75	76.329	69.886	65.552	62.660	60.744
16.00	75.621	69.058	64.670	61.756	59.834
16.25	74.923	68.247	63.808	60.876	58.949
16.50	74.234	67.451	62.966	60.018	58.089
16.75	73.556	66.670	62.143	59.182	57.252
17.00	72.887	65.904	61.339	58.367	56.438
17.25	72.227	65.152	60.553	57.572	55.645
17.50	71.576	64.415	59.785	56.797	54.873
17.75	70.935	63.691	59.033	56.041	54.122
18.00	70.303	62.981	58.298	55.304	53.389
18.25	69.679	62.284	57.579	54.584	52.676
18.50	69.064	61.600	56.876	53.881	51.980
18.75	68.458	60.929	56.188	53.196	51.302
19.00	67.860	60.270	55.515	52.526	50.640

VALUE OF AMORTIZING MORTGAGE LOANS
AS PERCENTAGE OF FACE VALUE
FACE INTEREST RATE: 9.25%

YIELD TO MATURITY	TERM OF LOAN (YEARS)				
	10	15	20	25	30
10.00	96.884	95.774	94.906	94.243	93.745
10.25	95.877	94.426	93.300	92.444	91.806
10.50	94.885	93.106	91.735	90.701	89.936
10.75	93.908	91.815	90.213	89.013	88.130
11.00	92.946	90.551	88.731	87.376	86.386
11.25	91.998	89.313	87.287	85.789	84.702
11.50	91.065	88.102	85.882	84.251	83.074
11.75	90.145	86.915	84.512	82.758	81.501
12.00	89.240	85.754	83.179	81.311	79.979
12.25	88.348	84.617	81.879	79.906	78.507
12.50	87.468	83.503	80.612	78.542	77.083
12.75	86.603	82.412	79.378	77.218	75.705
13.00	85.750	81.344	78.174	75.932	74.370
13.25	84.909	80.297	77.001	74.682	73.077
13.50	84.081	79.272	75.856	73.469	71.824
13.75	83.264	78.266	74.740	72.289	70.609
14.00	82.460	77.282	73.651	71.142	69.432
14.25	81.668	76.317	72.589	70.027	68.290
14.50	80.887	75.371	71.552	68.943	67.182
14.75	80.117	74.444	70.541	67.888	66.106
15.00	79.359	73.536	69.553	66.862	65.062
15.25	78.611	72.645	68.589	65.863	64.049
15.50	77.874	71.772	67.648	64.890	63.064
15.75	77.148	70.915	66.728	63.943	62.107
16.00	76.432	70.075	65.830	63.021	61.177
16.25	75.726	69.252	64.953	62.122	60.272
16.50	75.030	68.444	64.096	61.247	59.393
16.75	74.344	67.651	63.259	60.394	58.537
17.00	73.668	66.874	62.440	59.562	57.704
17.25	73.001	66.111	61.640	58.751	56.894
17.50	72.344	65.363	60.857	57.960	56.105
17.75	71.695	64.629	60.092	57.189	55.336
18.00	71.056	63.908	59.344	56.436	54.587
18.25	70.426	63.201	58.613	55.702	53.858
18.50	69.805	62.507	57.897	54.985	53.146
18.75	69.192	61.826	57.197	54.285	52.453
19.00	68.587	61.157	56.511	53.602	51.777

VALUE OF AMORTIZING MORTGAGE LOANS
AS PERCENTAGE OF FACE VALUE
FACE INTEREST RATE: 9.5%

YIELD TO MATURITY	TERM OF LOAN (YEARS)				
	10	15	20	25	30
10.00	97.916	97.172	96.591	96.148	95.816
10.25	96.899	95.805	94.956	94.313	93.835
10.50	95.896	94.465	93.364	92.535	91.923
10.75	94.909	93.155	91.815	90.812	90.077
11.00	93.936	91.873	90.306	89.142	88.295
11.25	92.978	90.617	88.837	87.524	86.573
11.50	92.035	89.388	87.407	85.954	84.910
11.75	91.105	88.184	86.013	84.431	83.301
12.00	90.190	87.006	84.655	82.954	81.746
12.25	89.289	85.852	83.333	81.521	80.242
12.50	88.400	84.722	82.043	80.129	78.786
12.75	87.525	83.616	80.787	78.779	77.377
13.00	86.663	82.531	79.562	77.467	76.013
13.25	85.813	81.469	78.368	76.192	74.691
13.50	84.977	80.429	77.203	74.954	73.411
13.75	84.151	79.409	76.067	73.750	72.169
14.00	83.339	78.410	74.959	72.580	70.966
14.25	82.538	77.431	73.878	71.443	69.799
14.50	81.748	76.472	72.823	70.337	68.666
14.75	80.971	75.531	71.793	69.260	67.567
15.00	80.204	74.609	70.788	68.213	66.500
15.25	79.448	73.705	69.807	67.194	65.464
15.50	78.704	72.819	68.849	66.202	64.457
15.75	77.969	71.950	67.913	65.236	63.479
16.00	77.246	71.098	66.999	64.295	62.528
16.25	76.533	70.263	66.106	63.378	61.604
16.50	75.829	69.443	65.234	62.485	60.705
16.75	75.136	68.639	64.382	61.615	59.830
17.00	74.453	67.851	63.549	60.766	58.979
17.25	73.779	67.077	62.734	59.939	58.151
17.50	73.114	66.318	61.938	59.132	57.344
17.75	72.459	65.573	61.159	58.345	56.559
18.00	71.813	64.842	60.398	57.577	55.793
18.25	71.176	64.124	59.653	56.828	55.048
18.50	70.548	63.420	58.925	56.097	54.321
18.75	69.929	62.728	58.212	55.383	53.612
19.00	69.318	62.050	57.515	54.685	52.921

VALUE OF AMORTIZING MORTGAGE LOANS
AS PERCENTAGE OF FACE VALUE
FACE INTEREST RATE: 9.75%

YIELD TO MATURITY	TERM OF LOAN (YEARS)				
	10	15	20	25	30
10.00	98.955	98.582	98.290	98.067	97.901
10.25	97.927	97.194	96.626	96.195	95.877
10.50	96.914	95.835	95.006	94.382	93.923
10.75	95.916	94.506	93.429	92.625	92.038
11.00	94.934	93.205	91.894	90.922	90.217
11.25	93.965	91.931	90.399	89.271	88.458
11.50	93.012	90.684	88.943	87.670	86.758
11.75	92.072	89.463	87.525	86.117	85.115
12.00	91.148	88.268	86.144	84.611	83.526
12.25	90.237	87.097	84.798	83.148	81.989
12.50	89.339	85.951	83.486	81.729	80.501
12.75	88.454	84.828	82.207	80.351	79.061
13.00	87.583	83.728	80.961	79.013	77.667
13.25	86.724	82.651	79.746	77.713	76.317
13.50	85.879	81.595	78.560	76.450	75.008
13.75	85.044	80.561	77.404	75.223	73.740
14.00	84.223	79.547	76.277	74.029	72.510
14.25	83.414	78.554	75.177	72.869	71.318
14.50	82.616	77.581	74.103	71.741	70.161
14.75	81.830	76.627	73.055	70.643	69.038
15.00	81.056	75.691	72.033	69.575	67.947
15.25	80.292	74.774	71.034	68.535	66.889
15.50	79.539	73.875	70.059	67.524	65.860
15.75	78.797	72.994	69.107	66.538	64.861
16.00	78.066	72.129	68.177	65.578	63.889
16.25	77.345	71.282	67.269	64.644	62.945
16.50	76.634	70.450	66.381	63.733	62.026
16.75	75.934	69.635	65.514	62.845	61.133
17.00	75.243	68.835	64.666	61.979	60.263
17.25	74.562	68.049	63.837	61.136	59.417
17.50	73.891	67.279	63.027	60.313	58.592
17.75	73.228	66.523	62.235	59.510	57.790
18.00	72.576	65.782	61.460	58.727	57.008
18.25	71.932	65.054	60.702	57.963	56.246
18.50	71.297	64.339	59.961	57.217	55.503
18.75	70.671	63.638	59.236	56.488	54.779
19.00	70.054	62.950	58.526	55.777	54.073

VALUE OF AMORTIZING MORTGAGE LOANS
AS PERCENTAGE OF FACE VALUE
FACE INTEREST RATE: 10%

YIELD TO MATURITY	TERM OF LOAN (YEARS)				
	10	15	20	25	30
10.00	100.000	100.000	100.000	100.000	100.000
10.25	98.961	98.592	98.307	98.091	97.932
10.50	97.937	97.214	96.659	96.242	95.937
10.75	96.928	95.866	95.055	94.451	94.011
11.00	95.936	94.546	93.493	92.714	92.151
11.25	94.957	93.254	91.972	91.030	90.354
11.50	93.994	91.989	90.491	89.398	88.618
11.75	93.044	90.750	89.048	87.814	86.939
12.00	92.110	89.538	87.643	86.278	85.316
12.25	91.189	88.351	86.273	84.787	83.746
12.50	90.282	87.188	84.939	83.340	82.227
12.75	89.388	86.049	83.638	81.935	80.756
13.00	88.508	84.933	82.370	80.570	79.332
13.25	87.640	83.840	81.133	79.245	77.953
13.50	86.785	82.769	79.927	77.957	76.616
13.75	85.942	81.720	78.751	76.705	75.321
14.00	85.112	80.692	77.604	75.489	74.065
14.25	84.295	79.684	76.485	74.305	72.846
14.50	83.488	78.697	75.392	73.155	71.665
14.75	82.694	77.729	74.327	72.035	70.517
15.00	81.911	76.780	73.286	70.946	69.404
15.25	81.139	75.850	72.270	69.886	68.322
15.50	80.379	74.938	71.278	68.854	67.272
15.75	79.629	74.044	70.310	67.849	66.251
16.00	78.890	73.167	69.363	66.871	65.259
16.25	78.162	72.307	68.439	65.918	64.294
16.50	77.443	71.464	67.536	64.989	63.356
16.75	76.735	70.636	66.654	64.083	62.443
17.00	76.037	69.825	65.791	63.201	61.555
17.25	75.349	69.029	64.948	62.341	60.690
17.50	74.671	68.247	64.124	61.501	59.848
17.75	74.001	67.481	63.318	60.683	59.028
18.00	73.342	66.728	62.529	59.884	58.230
18.25	72.691	65.990	61.758	59.105	57.451
18.50	72.050	65.265	61.004	58.344	56.693
18.75	71.417	64.554	60.266	57.602	55.953
19.00	70.793	63.855	59.544	56.876	55.232

VALUE OF AMORTIZING MORTGAGE LOANS
AS PERCENTAGE OF FACE VALUE
FACE INTEREST RATE: 10.25%

YIELD TO MATURITY	TERM OF LOAN (YEARS)				
	10	15	20	25	30
10.00	101.050	101.428	101.722	101.946	102.111
10.25	100.000	100.000	100.000	100.000	100.000
10.50	98.965	98.602	98.323	98.115	97.962
10.75	97.946	97.235	96.692	96.288	95.996
11.00	96.943	95.896	95.103	94.518	94.096
11.25	95.954	94.585	93.556	92.802	92.262
11.50	94.981	93.302	92.049	91.137	90.489
11.75	94.021	92.046	90.582	89.523	88.775
12.00	93.077	90.816	89.152	87.957	87.117
12.25	92.147	89.612	87.759	86.437	85.514
12.50	91.230	88.432	86.401	84.962	83.963
12.75	90.327	87.277	85.078	83.529	82.461
13.00	89.437	86.146	83.788	82.138	81.007
13.25	88.560	85.037	82.530	80.787	79.599
13.50	87.696	83.951	81.304	79.474	78.234
13.75	86.845	82.887	80.107	78.198	76.911
14.00	86.006	81.844	78.941	76.957	75.629
14.25	85.180	80.822	77.802	75.751	74.385
14.50	84.365	79.820	76.691	74.578	73.178
14.75	83.562	78.839	75.607	73.437	72.006
15.00	82.771	77.877	74.548	72.327	70.869
15.25	81.991	76.933	73.515	71.246	69.765
15.50	81.223	76.008	72.506	70.194	68.692
15.75	80.465	75.101	71.520	69.170	67.650
16.00	79.718	74.212	70.558	68.172	66.637
16.25	78.982	73.340	69.618	67.200	65.652
16.50	78.256	72.484	68.699	66.253	64.694
16.75	77.541	71.645	67.801	65.330	63.761
17.00	76.836	70.822	66.924	64.431	62.855
17.25	76.140	70.014	66.066	63.554	61.972
17.50	75.455	69.222	65.228	62.698	61.112
17.75	74.778	68.444	64.408	61.864	60.275
18.00	74.112	67.681	63.606	61.049	59.459
18.25	73.455	66.932	62.822	60.255	58.664
18.50	72.806	66.197	62.055	59.479	57.890
18.75	72.167	65.475	61.304	58.722	57.134
19.00	71.537	64.767	60.570	57.983	56.398

VALUE OF AMORTIZING MORTGAGE LOANS
AS PERCENTAGE OF FACE VALUE
FACE INTEREST RATE: 10.5%

YIELD TO MATURITY	TERM OF LOAN (YEARS)				
	10	15	20	25	30
10.00	102.107	102.866	103.457	103.905	104.235
10.25	101.046	101.418	101.705	101.921	102.080
10.50	100.000	100.000	100.000	100.000	100.000
10.75	98.971	98.613	98.340	98.138	97.992
11.00	97.957	97.255	96.725	96.334	96.054
11.25	96.958	95.926	95.151	94.585	94.181
11.50	95.974	94.625	93.619	92.888	92.371
11.75	95.005	93.351	92.126	91.243	90.621
12.00	94.051	92.104	90.672	89.647	88.929
12.25	93.110	90.882	89.256	88.098	87.293
12.50	92.184	89.686	87.875	86.594	85.709
12.75	91.271	88.514	86.529	85.134	84.176
13.00	90.372	87.367	85.217	83.716	82.692
13.25	89.486	86.242	83.938	82.339	81.254
13.50	88.614	85.141	82.690	81.001	79.861
13.75	87.753	84.062	81.473	79.700	78.511
14.00	86.906	83.004	80.287	78.436	77.202
14.25	86.071	81.968	79.129	77.207	75.932
14.50	85.247	80.952	77.999	76.011	74.700
14.75	84.436	79.956	76.896	74.848	73.504
15.00	83.637	78.981	75.819	73.716	72.343
15.25	82.849	78.024	74.768	72.615	71.216
15.50	82.072	77.086	73.742	71.543	70.121
15.75	81.307	76.166	72.740	70.499	69.057
16.00	80.552	75.264	71.761	69.482	68.023
16.25	79.808	74.379	70.805	68.491	67.017
16.50	79.075	73.512	69.871	67.526	66.039
16.75	78.352	72.661	68.958	66.586	65.088
17.00	77.639	71.826	68.065	65.669	64.162
17.25	76.937	71.007	67.193	64.775	63.261
17.50	76.244	70.203	66.340	63.903	62.383
17.75	75.560	69.414	65.506	63.052	61.529
18.00	74.887	68.640	64.691	62.222	60.696
18.25	74.223	67.881	63.893	61.413	59.885
18.50	73.568	67.135	63.113	60.622	59.094
18.75	72.922	66.404	62.349	59.851	58.323
19.00	72.285	65.685	61.602	59.097	57.571

VALUE OF AMORTIZING MORTGAGE LOANS
AS PERCENTAGE OF FACE VALUE
FACE INTEREST RATE: 10.75%

YIELD TO MATURITY	TERM OF LOAN (YEARS)				
	10	15	20	25	30
10.00	103.169	104.312	105.203	105.876	106.371
10.25	102.097	102.844	103.421	103.855	104.171
10.50	101.040	101.407	101.688	101.897	102.049
10.75	100.000	100.000	100.000	100.000	100.000
11.00	98.976	98.623	98.357	98.162	98.022
11.25	97.966	97.275	96.757	96.379	96.110
11.50	96.972	95.956	95.199	94.650	94.263
11.75	95.993	94.664	93.681	92.974	92.478
12.00	95.029	93.399	92.203	91.347	90.752
12.25	94.079	92.161	90.762	89.769	89.081
12.50	93.143	90.947	89.358	88.237	87.465
12.75	92.221	89.759	87.989	86.749	85.901
13.00	91.312	88.596	86.655	85.304	84.386
13.25	90.417	87.455	85.354	83.901	82.919
13.50	89.535	86.339	84.086	82.537	81.497
13.75	88.666	85.244	82.848	81.212	80.119
14.00	87.809	84.172	81.641	79.924	78.783
14.25	86.966	83.121	80.464	78.671	77.487
14.50	86.134	82.091	79.315	77.453	76.230
14.75	85.314	81.081	78.193	76.268	75.010
15.00	84.507	80.091	77.099	75.115	73.825
15.25	83.710	79.121	76.030	73.992	72.675
15.50	82.926	78.170	74.987	72.900	71.558
15.75	82.152	77.237	73.967	71.836	70.472
16.00	81.390	76.322	72.972	70.800	69.416
16.25	80.638	75.425	72.000	69.791	68.390
16.50	79.897	74.546	71.050	68.807	67.392
16.75	79.167	73.683	70.121	67.849	66.421
17.00	78.447	72.836	69.214	66.914	65.476
17.25	77.737	72.005	68.327	66.003	64.557
17.50	77.037	71.190	67.460	65.115	63.661
17.75	76.346	70.391	66.612	64.248	62.789
18.00	75.666	69.606	65.783	63.403	61.940
18.25	74.995	68.836	64.971	62.578	61.112
18.50	74.333	68.080	64.178	61.772	60.305
18.75	73.680	67.338	63.402	60.986	59.518
19.00	73.036	66.609	62.642	60.218	58.750

VALUE OF AMORTIZING MORTGAGE LOANS
AS PERCENTAGE OF FACE VALUE
FACE INTEREST RATE: 11%

YIELD TO MATURITY	TERM OF LOAN (YEARS)				
	10	15	20	25	30
10.00	104.237	105.768	106.960	107.859	108.518
10.25	103.153	104.280	105.149	105.800	106.274
10.50	102.086	102.822	103.386	103.805	104.109
10.75	101.035	101.396	101.670	101.873	102.018
11.00	100.000	100.000	100.000	100.000	100.000
11.25	98.980	98.633	98.373	98.184	98.050
11.50	97.976	97.295	96.789	96.423	96.166
11.75	96.986	95.985	95.246	94.715	94.344
12.00	96.012	94.703	93.743	93.058	92.583
12.25	95.052	93.447	92.278	91.450	90.879
12.50	94.106	92.217	90.850	89.889	89.231
12.75	93.175	91.012	89.459	88.374	87.635
13.00	92.257	89.832	88.103	86.902	86.090
13.25	91.353	88.676	86.780	85.472	84.593
13.50	90.462	87.544	85.490	84.083	83.142
13.75	89.583	86.434	84.232	82.733	81.737
14.00	88.718	85.346	83.005	81.421	80.373
14.25	87.866	84.281	81.808	80.145	79.051
14.50	87.025	83.236	80.640	78.904	77.769
14.75	86.197	82.213	79.500	77.696	76.524
15.00	85.381	81.209	78.387	76.522	75.316
15.25	84.577	80.226	77.300	75.378	74.142
15.50	83.784	79.261	76.239	74.265	73.002
15.75	83.002	78.315	75.203	73.181	71.894
16.00	82.232	77.388	74.191	72.126	70.817
16.25	81.473	76.478	73.202	71.098	69.771
16.50	80.724	75.586	72.236	70.096	68.752
16.75	79.986	74.711	71.293	69.119	67.762
17.00	79.259	73.853	70.370	68.168	66.798
17.25	78.541	73.010	69.468	67.240	65.860
17.50	77.834	72.184	68.587	66.335	64.946
17.75	77.136	71.373	67.724	65.452	64.056
18.00	76.449	70.577	66.881	64.590	63.190
18.25	75.771	69.797	66.057	63.750	62.345
18.50	75.102	69.030	65.250	62.929	61.522
18.75	74.443	68.278	64.461	62.128	60.719
19.00	73.792	67.539	63.688	61.346	59.936

VALUE OF AMORTIZING MORTGAGE LOANS
AS PERCENTAGE OF FACE VALUE
FACE INTEREST RATE: 11.25%

YIELD TO MATURITY	TERM OF LOAN (YEARS)				
	10	15	20	25	30
10.00	105.311	107.234	108.729	109.853	110.676
10.25	104.216	105.725	106.888	107.757	108.388
10.50	103.138	104.247	105.096	105.725	106.179
10.75	102.076	102.801	103.352	103.757	104.047
11.00	101.031	101.386	101.654	101.850	101.989
11.25	100.000	100.000	100.000	100.000	100.000
11.50	98.986	98.644	98.390	98.207	98.078
11.75	97.986	97.315	96.821	96.467	96.221
12.00	97.002	96.015	95.293	94.779	94.424
12.25	96.032	94.742	93.804	93.142	92.687
12.50	95.076	93.495	92.353	91.552	91.005
12.75	94.135	92.274	90.938	90.008	89.378
13.00	93.208	91.077	89.560	88.509	87.802
13.25	92.294	89.905	88.215	87.053	86.275
13.50	91.394	88.757	86.904	85.639	84.796
13.75	90.506	87.632	85.625	84.263	83.362
14.00	89.632	86.529	84.378	82.927	81.972
14.25	88.771	85.449	83.161	81.627	80.624
14.50	87.922	84.390	81.973	80.363	79.315
14.75	87.086	83.352	80.814	79.133	78.046
15.00	86.261	82.335	79.683	77.937	76.813
15.25	85.448	81.337	78.578	76.772	75.616
15.50	84.648	80.360	77.500	75.639	74.454
15.75	83.858	79.400	76.447	74.535	73.324
16.00	83.080	78.460	75.418	73.460	72.226
16.25	82.313	77.538	74.413	72.413	71.158
16.50	81.556	76.634	73.431	71.392	70.120
16.75	80.810	75.746	72.472	70.398	69.110
17.00	80.076	74.876	71.534	69.429	68.126
17.25	79.351	74.022	70.617	68.483	67.170
17.50	78.636	73.184	69.721	67.561	66.238
17.75	77.931	72.362	68.844	66.662	65.330
18.00	77.237	71.556	67.987	65.785	64.446
18.25	76.552	70.764	67.149	64.929	63.585
18.50	75.876	69.987	66.329	64.093	62.745
18.75	75.210	69.224	65.527	63.277	61.927
19.00	74.553	68.475	64.742	62.481	61.128

VALUE OF AMORTIZING MORTGAGE LOANS
AS PERCENTAGE OF FACE VALUE
FACE INTEREST RATE: 11.5%

YIELD TO	TERM OF LOAN (YEARS)				
MATURITY	10	15	20	25	30
10.00	106.390	108.709	110.508	111.860	112.844
10.25	105.284	107.178	108.637	109.725	110.511
10.50	104.195	105.680	106.816	107.656	108.259
10.75	103.122	104.214	105.043	105.652	106.086
11.00	102.066	102.780	103.317	103.709	103.987
11.25	101.025	101.375	101.637	101.826	101.959
11.50	100.000	100.000	100.000	100.000	100.000
11.75	98.990	98.653	98.405	98.229	98.106
12.00	97.996	97.336	96.853	96.510	96.275
12.25	97.016	96.045	95.339	94.843	94.503
12.50	96.051	94.780	93.864	93.224	92.788
12.75	95.100	93.542	92.427	91.652	91.129
13.00	94.163	92.329	91.025	90.126	89.522
13.25	93.240	91.141	89.659	88.643	87.965
13.50	92.331	89.977	88.326	87.202	86.457
13.75	91.434	88.836	87.027	85.802	84.995
14.00	90.551	87.719	85.759	84.441	83.578
14.25	89.681	86.624	84.522	83.118	82.203
14.50	88.823	85.550	83.315	81.831	80.869
14.75	87.978	84.498	82.137	80.578	79.575
15.00	87.145	83.467	80.987	79.360	78.318
15.25	86.324	82.456	79.865	78.174	77.098
15.50	85.515	81.464	78.768	77.020	75.913
15.75	84.717	80.492	77.698	75.896	74.761
16.00	83.931	79.539	76.652	74.801	73.641
16.25	83.156	78.604	75.631	73.735	72.552
16.50	82.392	77.687	74.633	72.696	71.494
16.75	81.639	76.788	73.658	71.683	70.464
17.00	80.896	75.906	72.705	70.696	69.461
17.25	80.164	75.040	71.773	69.734	68.486
17.50	79.442	74.191	70.862	68.795	67.536
17.75	78.730	73.357	69.971	67.880	66.610
18.00	78.028	72.539	69.100	66.986	65.709
18.25	77.336	71.737	68.248	66.114	64.831
18.50	76.654	70.949	67.415	65.264	63.975
18.75	75.981	70.176	66.599	64.433	63.140
19.00	75.317	69.416	65.801	63.622	62.326

VALUE OF AMORTIZING MORTGAGE LOANS
AS PERCENTAGE OF FACE VALUE
FACE INTEREST RATE: 11.75%

YIELD TO MATURITY	TERM OF LOAN (YEARS)				
	10	15	20	25	30
10.00	107.476	110.192	112.299	113.877	115.023
10.25	106.359	108.641	110.398	111.703	112.645
10.50	105.258	107.123	108.547	109.597	110.350
10.75	104.174	105.637	106.745	107.557	108.134
11.00	103.107	104.183	104.992	105.580	105.995
11.25	102.056	102.759	103.284	103.662	103.928
11.50	101.020	101.365	101.620	101.803	101.931
11.75	100.000	100.000	100.000	100.000	100.000
12.00	98.996	98.664	98.422	98.251	98.133
12.25	98.006	97.356	96.884	96.553	96.327
12.50	97.031	96.074	95.385	94.905	94.580
12.75	96.070	94.819	93.924	93.305	92.888
13.00	95.124	93.590	92.500	91.751	91.250
13.25	94.191	92.385	91.112	90.242	89.664
13.50	93.273	91.205	89.758	88.775	88.126
13.75	92.367	90.049	88.437	87.349	86.636
14.00	91.475	88.916	87.148	85.964	85.192
14.25	90.596	87.806	85.892	84.617	83.790
14.50	89.729	86.718	84.665	83.306	82.431
14.75	88.876	85.651	83.468	82.032	81.111
15.00	88.035	84.606	82.299	80.791	79.830
15.25	87.205	83.581	81.159	79.584	78.586
15.50	86.388	82.576	80.045	78.409	77.378
15.75	85.582	81.591	78.957	77.265	76.204
16.00	84.787	80.625	77.894	76.150	75.063
16.25	84.005	79.677	76.856	75.065	73.953
16.50	83.233	78.748	75.842	74.007	72.874
16.75	82.472	77.836	74.851	72.976	71.824
17.00	81.722	76.942	73.883	71.971	70.802
17.25	80.982	76.064	72.936	70.991	69.808
17.50	80.253	75.203	72.010	70.036	68.839
17.75	79.533	74.358	71.105	69.104	67.896
18.00	78.824	73.530	70.220	68.194	66.978
18.25	78.125	72.716	69.354	67.307	66.082
18.50	77.436	71.917	68.507	66.440	65.210
18.75	76.756	71.133	67.678	65.595	64.359
19.00	76.085	70.364	66.867	64.769	63.529

VALUE OF AMORTIZING MORTGAGE LOANS
AS PERCENTAGE OF FACE VALUE
FACE INTEREST RATE: 12%

YIELD TO MATURITY	TERM OF LOAN (YEARS)				
	10	15	20	25	30
10.00	108.566	111.684	114.100	115.904	117.211
10.25	107.438	110.112	112.168	113.692	114.788
10.50	106.326	108.573	110.287	111.549	112.449
10.75	105.231	107.067	108.457	109.472	110.191
11.00	104.153	105.593	106.675	107.460	108.011
11.25	103.091	104.150	104.940	105.508	105.905
11.50	102.045	102.737	103.250	103.616	103.870
11.75	101.014	101.354	101.603	101.780	101.902
12.00	100.000	100.000	100.000	100.000	100.000
12.25	99.000	98.674	98.437	98.272	98.160
12.50	98.015	97.375	96.915	96.595	96.379
12.75	97.045	96.103	95.430	94.966	94.655
13.00	96.089	94.857	93.983	93.385	92.986
13.25	95.147	93.636	92.573	91.848	91.369
13.50	94.219	92.440	91.197	90.356	89.803
13.75	93.304	91.268	89.855	88.905	88.284
14.00	92.403	90.120	88.546	87.494	86.812
14.25	91.515	88.995	87.269	86.123	85.384
14.50	90.640	87.892	86.022	84.790	83.999
14.75	89.777	86.811	84.806	83.492	82.654
15.00	88.928	85.752	83.619	82.230	81.349
15.25	88.090	84.713	82.460	81.001	80.081
15.50	87.264	83.694	81.328	79.805	78.850
15.75	86.450	82.696	80.223	78.640	77.654
16.00	85.648	81.716	79.143	77.506	76.491
16.25	84.857	80.756	78.089	76.401	75.360
16.50	84.077	79.814	77.058	75.325	74.260
16.75	83.308	78.890	76.051	74.275	73.190
17.00	82.551	77.984	75.067	73.253	72.149
17.25	81.803	77.094	74.105	72.255	71.136
17.50	81.067	76.222	73.165	71.283	70.149
17.75	80.340	75.365	72.245	70.334	69.188
18.00	79.624	74.525	71.346	69.408	68.252
18.25	78.918	73.700	70.466	68.505	67.339
18.50	78.221	72.891	69.605	67.623	66.450
18.75	77.534	72.096	68.763	66.763	65.583
19.00	76.857	71.317	67.940	65.922	64.738

VALUE OF AMORTIZING MORTGAGE LOANS
AS PERCENTAGE OF FACE VALUE
FACE INTEREST RATE: 12.25%

YIELD TO MATURITY	TERM OF LOAN (YEARS)				
	10	15	20	25	30
10.00	109.662	113.185	115.911	117.942	119.409
10.25	108.523	111.592	113.948	115.691	116.940
10.50	107.399	110.032	112.038	113.510	114.557
10.75	106.294	108.506	110.179	111.397	112.257
11.00	105.205	107.012	108.368	109.349	110.036
11.25	104.132	105.550	106.605	107.363	107.890
11.50	103.076	104.118	104.889	105.438	105.817
11.75	102.035	102.716	103.216	103.570	103.813
12.00	101.010	101.344	101.587	101.758	101.875
12.25	100.000	100.000	100.000	100.000	100.000
12.50	99.005	98.684	98.453	98.293	98.186
12.75	98.025	97.394	96.945	96.636	96.430
13.00	97.059	96.132	95.475	95.027	94.729
13.25	96.108	94.895	94.042	93.463	93.082
13.50	95.171	93.683	92.644	91.944	91.486
13.75	94.246	92.495	91.281	90.468	89.939
14.00	93.336	91.331	89.951	89.033	88.440
14.25	92.439	90.191	88.654	87.638	86.985
14.50	91.555	89.073	87.388	86.280	85.574
14.75	90.684	87.978	86.152	84.960	84.204
15.00	89.826	86.904	84.946	83.676	82.874
15.25	88.979	85.851	83.769	82.425	81.583
15.50	88.145	84.819	82.619	81.208	80.328
15.75	87.323	83.807	81.496	80.023	79.109
16.00	86.512	82.815	80.400	78.869	77.925
16.25	85.714	81.841	79.328	77.745	76.773
16.50	84.926	80.887	78.281	76.649	75.652
16.75	84.150	79.950	77.259	75.582	74.562
17.00	83.384	79.032	76.259	74.541	73.502
17.25	82.629	78.130	75.282	73.526	72.469
17.50	81.885	77.246	74.326	72.536	71.464
17.75	81.152	76.378	73.392	.71.571	70.485
18.00	80.428	75.527	72.478	70.629	69.531
18.25	79.715	74.691	71.585	69.710	68.602
18.50	79.011	73.871	70.710	68.812	67.696
18.75	78.318	73.065	69.855	67.937	66.813
19.00	77.633	72.275	69.018	67.081	65.951

VALUE OF AMORTIZING MORTGAGE LOANS
AS PERCENTAGE OF FACE VALUE
FACE INTEREST RATE: 12.5%

YIELD TO MATURITY	TERM OF LOAN (YEARS)				
	10	15	20	25	30
10.00	110.765	114.695	117.732	119.990	121.615
10.25	109.614	113.081	115.739	117.700	119.100
10.50	108.479	111.500	113.798	115.481	116.673
10.75	107.362	109.954	111.910	113.332	114.331
11.00	106.263	108.440	110.071	111.248	112.069
11.25	105.179	106.958	108.281	109.228	109.884
11.50	104.112	105.507	106.537	107.269	107.772
11.75	103.060	104.086	104.838	105.369	105.731
12.00	102.025	102.696	103.184	103.525	103.757
12.25	101.005	101.334	101.571	101.737	101.848
12.50	100.000	100.000	100.000	100.000	100.000
12.75	99.010	98.694	98.469	98.314	98.212
13.00	98.035	97.414	96.976	96.677	96.480
13.25	97.074	96.160	95.520	95.086	94.802
13.50	96.127	94.932	94.100	93.541	93.177
13.75	95.194	93.729	92.715	92.039	91.601
14.00	94.274	92.550	91.365	90.579	90.074
14.25	93.369	91.394	90.047	89.159	88.592
14.50	92.475	90.262	88.761	87.779	87.155
14.75	91.596	89.152	87.506	86.436	85.760
15.00	90.729	88.064	86.281	85.129	84.405
15.25	89.874	86.997	85.085	83.857	83.090
15.50	89.031	85.951	83.917	82.619	81.813
15.75	88.201	84.925	82.777	81.413	80.571
16.00	87.382	83.919	81.663	80.239	79.364
16.25	86.575	82.933	80.575	79.095	78.191
16.50	85.780	81.966	79.512	77.980	77.050
16.75	84.995	81.017	78.473	76.894	75.940
17.00	84.223	80.086	77.457	75.835	74.860
17.25	83.460	79.172	76.464	74.803	73.808
17.50	82.709	78.276	75.494	73.796	72.785
17.75	81.967	77.397	74.545	72.814	71.787
18.00	81.237	76.534	73.617	71.855	70.816
18.25	80.516	75.687	72.709	70.920	69.869
18.50	79.805	74.856	71.821	70.007	68.947
18.75	79.105	74.040	70.953	69.116	68.047
19.00	78.414	73.239	70.103	68.246	67.170

VALUE OF AMORTIZING MORTGAGE LOANS
AS PERCENTAGE OF FACE VALUE
FACE INTEREST RATE: 12.75%

YIELD TO MATURITY	TERM OF LOAN (YEARS)				
	10	15	20	25	30
10.00	111.872	116.213	119.563	122.048	123.830
10.25	110.709	114.578	117.539	119.719	121.269
10.50	109.563	112.976	115.568	117.462	118.798
10.75	108.436	111.409	113.650	115.275	116.413
11.00	107.325	109.875	111.783	113.156	114.110
11.25	106.230	108.373	109.965	111.101	111.885
11.50	105.153	106.904	108.194	109.108	109.735
11.75	104.090	105.464	106.469	107.176	107.656
12.00	103.045	104.055	104.789	105.301	105.647
12.25	102.015	102.675	103.151	103.481	103.702
12.50	101.000	101.324	101.555	101.715	101.821
12.75	100.000	100.000	100.000	100.000	100.000
13.00	99.015	98.704	98.484	98.335	98.237
13.25	98.044	97.433	97.005	96.717	96.529
13.50	97.088	96.189	95.564	95.145	94.874
13.75	96.145	94.969	94.157	93.617	93.269
14.00	95.217	93.775	92.786	92.132	91.714
14.25	94.302	92.604	91.448	90.688	90.205
14.50	93.400	91.456	90.142	89.284	88.742
14.75	92.511	90.332	88.867	87.918	87.321
15.00	91.636	89.229	87.623	86.589	85.942
15.25	90.772	88.148	86.408	85.295	84.603
15.50	89.921	87.088	85.223	84.035	83.302
15.75	89.082	86.049	84.064	82.809	82.038
16.00	88.256	85.030	82.933	81.615	80.810
16.25	87.441	84.031	81.828	80.451	79.615
16.50	86.637	83.050	80.748	79.317	78.453
16.75	85.845	82.089	79.693	78.213	77.323
17.00	85.065	81.146	78.662	77.136	76.223
17.25	84.294	80.220	77.654	76.085	75.152
17.50	83.535	79.312	76.668	75.061	74.110
17.75	82.787	78.421	75.704	74.062	73.095
18.00	82.049	77.547	74.762	73.088	72.106
18.25	81.321	76.689	73.840	72.136	71.142
18.50	80.603	75.847	72.938	71.208	70.202
18.75	79.896	75.020	72.056	70.302	69.286
19.00	79.198	74.209	71.193	69.416	68.393

VALUE OF AMORTIZING MORTGAGE LOANS
AS PERCENTAGE OF FACE VALUE
FACE INTEREST RATE: 13%

YIELD TO MATURITY	TERM OF LOAN (YEARS)				
	10	15	20	25	30
10.00	112.985	117.740	121.404	124.115	126.052
10.25	111.811	116.083	119.348	121.746	123.446
10.50	110.653	114.460	117.347	119.451	120.930
10.75	109.514	112.872	115.400	117.227	118.503
11.00	108.393	111.319	113.504	115.072	116.158
11.25	107.287	109.797	111.658	112.982	113.893
11.50	106.199	108.308	109.860	110.956	111.704
11.75	105.126	106.849	108.108	108.991	109.589
12.00	104.070	105.422	106.402	107.084	107.543
12.25	103.030	104.024	104.739	105.234	105.564
12.50	102.004	102.654	103.119	103.437	103.649
12.75	100.995	101.314	101.540	101.694	101.795
13.00	100.000	100.000	100.000	100.000	100.000
13.25	99.020	98.713	98.499	98.355	98.261
13.50	98.054	97.452	97.035	96.756	96.577
13.75	97.102	96.217	95.607	95.203	94.943
14.00	96.164	95.006	94.214	93.693	93.360
14.25	95.240	93.820	92.856	92.224	91.825
14.50	94.329	92.658	91.529	90.796	90.335
14.75	93.431	91.518	90.235	89.407	88.889
15.00	92.547	90.401	88.972	88.055	87.485
15.25	91.675	89.306	87.739	86.739	86.122
15.50	90.816	88.232	86.535	85.459	84.798
15.75	89.968	87.179	85.358	84.211	83.511
16.00	89.134	86.147	84.210	82.997	82.260
16.25	88.311	85.134	83.088	81.814	81.044
16.50	87.499	84.141	81.991	80.661	79.861
16.75	86.699	83.167	80.920	79.537	78.711
17.00	85.911	82.212	79.873	78.442	77.591
17.25	85.133	81.274	78.849	77.374	76.501
17.50	84.366	80.354	77.849	76.332	75.440
17.75	83.610	79.452	76.870	75.317	74.407
18.00	82.865	78.566	75.913	74.325	73.400
18.25	82.130	77.696	74.977	73.358	72.419
18.50	81.405	76.843	74.061	72.414	71.462
18.75	80.690	76.006	73.166	71.492	70.530
19.00	79.985	75.183	72.289	70.592	69.621

VALUE OF AMORTIZING MORTGAGE LOANS
AS PERCENTAGE OF FACE VALUE
FACE INTEREST RATE: 13.25%

YIELD TO MATURITY	TERM OF LOAN (YEARS)				
	10	15	20	25	30
10.00	114.104	119.275	123.254	126.191	128.283
10.25	112.918	117.596	121.167	123.783	125.630
10.50	111.749	115.952	119.136	121.449	123.070
10.75	110.599	114.344	117.159	119.188	120.599
11.00	109.466	112.770	115.234	116.997	118.213
11.25	108.349	111.228	113.359	114.872	115.908
11.50	107.250	109.720	111.534	112.812	113.681
11.75	106.167	108.242	109.756	110.814	111.528
12.00	105.101	106.796	108.023	108.875	109.446
12.25	104.050	105.380	106.335	106.994	107.432
12.50	103.014	103.993	104.690	105.168	105.483
12.75	101.995	102.634	103.087	103.395	103.596
13.00	100.990	101.304	101.524	101.673	101.770
13.25	100.000	100.000	100.000	100.000	100.000
13.50	99.025	98.723	98.514	98.375	98.285
13.75	98.063	97.471	97.064	96.795	96.624
14.00	97.116	96.245	95.650	95.260	95.012
14.25	96.183	95.044	94.271	93.767	93.449
14.50	95.263	93.866	92.924	92.315	91.933
14.75	94.357	92.711	91.611	90.902	90.462
15.00	93.464	91.580	90.328	89.528	89.033
15.25	92.583	90.470	89.076	88.190	87.646
15.50	91.715	89.383	87.854	86.888	86.298
15.75	90.859	88.316	86.659	85.620	84.989
16.00	90.016	87.270	85.493	84.385	83.716
16.25	89.185	86.244	84.354	83.182	82.478
16.50	88.365	85.238	83.241	82.010	81.275
16.75	87.558	84.252	82.153	80.868	80.104
17.00	86.761	83.284	81.090	79.754	78.964
17.25	85.976	82.334	80.051	78.668	77.855
17.50	85.202	81.402	79.035	77.609	76.775
17.75	84.438	80.487	78.042	76.576	75.723
18.00	83.685	79.590	77.070	75.569	74.699
18.25	82.943	78.709	76.120	74.585	73.700
18.50	82.211	77.845	75.190	73.625	72.727
18.75	81.489	76.996	74.281	72.688	71.778
19.00	80.777	76.164	73.391	71.773	70.853

VALUE OF AMORTIZING MORTGAGE LOANS
AS PERCENTAGE OF FACE VALUE
FACE INTEREST RATE: 13.5%

YIELD TO MATURITY	TERM OF LOAN (YEARS)				
	10	15	20	25	30
10.00	115.227	120.818	125.113	128.276	130.521
10.25	114.030	119.117	122.995	125.827	127.822
10.50	112.850	117.452	120.933	123.455	125.217
10.75	111.688	115.823	118.926	121.157	122.703
11.00	110.544	114.229	116.972	118.930	120.276
11.25	109.416	112.667	115.069	116.770	117.930
11.50	108.306	111.139	113.216	114.676	115.664
11.75	107.212	109.643	111.411	112.644	113.473
12.00	106.136	108.178	109.653	110.674	111.355
12.25	105.075	106.743	107.940	108.761	109.306
12.50	104.029	105.338	106.270	106.905	107.323
12.75	102.999	103.962	104.642	105.103	105.403
13.00	101.985	102.614	103.056	103.352	103.545
13.25	100.985	101.294	101.508	101.652	101.744
13.50	100.000	100.000	100.000	100.000	100.000
13.75	99.029	98.732	98.528	98.394	98.309
14.00	98.073	97.490	97.093	96.833	96.670
14.25	97.130	96.273	95.693	95.316	95.080
14.50	96.201	95.080	94.326	93.840	93.537
14.75	95.286	93.910	92.993	92.404	92.040
15.00	94.384	92.764	91.691	91.007	90.586
15.25	93.494	91.640	90.420	89.647	89.175
15.50	92.618	90.539	89.179	88.323	87.804
15.75	91.754	89.458	87.967	87.034	86.471
16.00	90.903	88.399	86.783	85.779	85.176
16.25	90.063	87.360	85.627	84.556	83.917
16.50	89.236	86.341	84.497	83.365	82.692
16.75	88.420	85.341	83.393	82.204	81.501
17.00	87.616	84.361	82.313	81.072	80.342
17.25	86.823	83.399	81.259	79.968	79.213
17.50	86.041	82.455	80.227	78.891	78.114
17.75	85.270	81.529	79.219	77.841	77.044
18.00	84.510	80.620	78.233	76.817	76.002
18.25	83.760	79.728	77.268	75.817	74.986
18.50	83.021	78.852	76.324	74.841	73.996
18.75	82.292	77.992	75.401	73.889	73.030
19.00	81.573	77.149	74.498	72.959	72.089

VALUE OF AMORTIZING MORTGAGE LOANS
AS PERCENTAGE OF FACE VALUE
FACE INTEREST RATE: 13.75%

YIELD TO MATURITY	TERM OF LOAN (YEARS)				
	10	15	20	25	30
10.00	116.357	122.369	126.982	130.369	132.766
10.25	115.148	120.647	124.832	127.881	130.020
10.50	113.956	118.960	122.739	125.470	127.371
10.75	112.783	117.310	120.702	123.134	124.814
11.00	111.628	115.696	118.719	120.871	122.344
11.25	110.489	114.114	116.788	118.676	119.959
11.50	109.369	112.566	114.907	116.547	117.654
11.75	108.264	111.051	113.075	114.483	115.425
12.00	107.177	109.567	111.291	112.480	113.270
12.25	106.105	108.114	109.552	110.536	111.186
12.50	105.049	106.691	107.857	108.650	109.169
12.75	104.009	105.297	106.205	106.818	107.216
13.00	102.985	103.932	104.595	105.039	105.326
13.25	101.975	102.594	103.025	103.311	103.494
13.50	100.981	101.284	101.494	101.632	101.720
13.75	100.000	100.000	100.000	100.000	100.000
14.00	99.034	98.742	98.543	98.414	98.332
14.25	98.083	97.509	97.122	96.871	96.715
14.50	97.145	96.301	95.735	95.371	95.146
14.75	96.220	95.117	94.381	93.912	93.623
15.00	95.310	93.956	93.060	92.492	92.144
15.25	94.411	92.817	91.770	91.110	90.709
15.50	93.527	91.702	90.511	89.765	89.314
15.75	92.654	90.607	89.281	88.455	87.958
16.00	91.794	89.534	88.079	87.179	86.641
16.25	90.947	88.482	86.906	85.936	85.360
16.50	90.111	87.450	85.759	84.725	84.115
16.75	89.287	86.437	84.638	83.545	82.903
17.00	88.475	85.444	83.543	82.395	81.724
17.25	87.674	84.470	82.472	81.273	80.576
17.50	86.885	83.514	81.426	80.179	79.458
17.75	86.106	82.576	80.402	79.112	78.369
18.00	85.338	81.655	79.401	78.071	77.309
18.25	84.582	80.752	78.422	77.055	76.276
18.50	83.835	79.865	77.464	76.063	75.268
18.75	83.099	78.994	76.527	75.095	74.286
19.00	82.373	78.139	75.610	74.149	73.329

VALUE OF AMORTIZING MORTGAGE LOANS
AS PERCENTAGE OF FACE VALUE
FACE INTEREST RATE: 14%

YIELD TO MATURITY	TERM OF LOAN (YEARS)				
	10	15	20	25	30
10.00	117.492	123.928	128.859	132.470	135.017
10.25	116.271	122.184	126.678	129.942	132.225
10.50	115.067	120.476	124.554	127.492	129.531
10.75	113.883	118.805	122.487	125.119	126.930
11.00	112.716	117.169	120.474	122.819	124.419
11.25	111.567	115.568	118.514	120.588	121.993
11.50	110.435	114.000	116.606	118.426	119.649
11.75	109.319	112.465	114.747	116.328	117.383
12.00	108.222	110.963	112.936	114.293	115.191
12.25	107.140	109.491	111.171	112.318	113.071
12.50	106.073	108.050	109.451	110.401	111.020
12.75	105.024	106.639	107.775	108.540	109.035
13.00	103.989	105.256	106.141	106.732	107.112
13.25	102.969	103.901	104.548	104.976	105.250
13.50	101.965	102.575	102.994	103.270	103.445
13.75	100.975	101.274	101.478	101.612	101.696
14.00	100.000	100.000	100.000	100.000	100.000
14.25	99.039	98.752	98.558	98.433	98.355
14.50	98.092	97.528	97.150	96.908	96.759
14.75	97.158	96.328	95.777	95.426	95.211
15.00	96.239	95.153	94.436	93.983	93.707
15.25	95.332	94.000	93.127	92.579	92.247
15.50	94.439	92.870	91.849	91.212	90.828
15.75	93.557	91.761	90.600	89.881	89.450
16.00	92.689	90.675	89.381	88.584	88.110
16.25	91.833	89.609	88.190	87.321	86.808
16.50	90.989	88.564	87.026	86.091	85.541
16.75	90.158	87.539	85.889	84.892	84.309
17.00	89.338	86.533	84.778	83.723	83.110
17.25	88.529	85.546	83.691	82.583	81.942
17.50	87.732	84.578	82.629	81.471	80.806
17.75	86.945	83.628	81.591	80.387	79.699
18.00	86.170	82.695	80.575	79.329	78.620
18.25	85.406	81.780	79.581	78.297	77.569
18.50	84.652	80.882	78.610	77.289	76.545
18.75	83.909	80.000	77.659	76.305	75.546
19.00	83.176	79.135	76.728	75.344	74.572

VALUE OF AMORTIZING MORTGAGE LOANS
AS PERCENTAGE OF FACE VALUE
FACE INTEREST RATE: 14.25%

YIELD TO MATURITY	TERM OF LOAN (YEARS)				
	10	15	20	25	30
10.00	118.632	125.495	130.745	134.580	137.275
10.25	117.399	123.728	128.531	132.011	134.436
10.50	116.184	121.999	126.376	129.522	131.697
10.75	114.988	120.307	124.279	127.111	129.053
11.00	113.810	118.651	122.237	124.774	126.500
11.25	112.649	117.029	120.249	122.508	124.033
11.50	111.506	115.442	118.312	120.311	121.650
11.75	110.380	113.887	116.426	118.180	119.346
12.00	109.271	112.366	114.589	116.113	117.118
12.25	108.179	110.876	112.798	114.106	114.962
12.50	107.102	109.416	111.053	112.159	112.877
12.75	106.042	107.987	109.352	110.268	110.858
13.00	104.998	106.587	107.694	108.431	108.903
13.25	103.968	105.215	106.077	106.647	107.010
13.50	102.954	103.871	104.501	104.914	105.175
13.75	101.955	102.554	102.963	103.230	103.397
14.00	100.970	101.264	101.463	101.592	101.672
14.25	100.000	100.000	100.000	100.000	100.000
14.50	99.043	98.761	98.572	98.451	98.377
14.75	98.101	97.546	97.178	96.945	96.803
15.00	97.173	96.356	95.818	95.479	95.274
15.25	96.257	95.188	94.490	94.053	93.789
15.50	95.355	94.044	93.193	92.664	92.347
15.75	94.465	92.921	91.926	91.312	90.946
16.00	93.588	91.821	90.689	89.995	89.584
16.25	92.724	90.742	89.481	88.712	88.260
16.50	91.872	89.683	88.300	87.462	86.972
16.75	91.032	88.645	87.146	86.243	85.719
17.00	90.204	87.627	86.018	85.056	84.499
17.25	89.388	86.627	84.916	83.898	83.312
17.50	88.583	85.647	83.838	82.768	82.157
17.75	87.789	84.685	82.784	81.667	81.031
18.00	87.006	83.741	81.754	80.592	79.935
18.25	86.235	82.814	80.746	79.543	78.866
18.50	85.474	81.905	79.760	78.519	77.825
18.75	84.723	81.012	78.795	77.520	76.810
19.00	83.983	80.135	77.851	76.544	75.819

VALUE OF AMORTIZING MORTGAGE LOANS
AS PERCENTAGE OF FACE VALUE
FACE INTEREST RATE: 14.5%

YIELD TO MATURITY	TERM OF LOAN (YEARS)				
	10	15	20	25	30
10.00	119.777	127.070	132.639	136.696	139.539
10.25	118.533	125.281	130.394	134.087	136.654
10.50	117.306	123.530	128.207	131.560	133.869
10.75	116.098	121.817	126.080	129.111	131.182
11.00	114.909	120.140	124.008	126.737	128.586
11.25	113.737	118.498	121.991	124.435	126.079
11.50	112.583	116.890	120.027	122.204	123.656
11.75	111.446	115.316	118.113	120.039	121.314
12.00	110.327	113.776	116.249	117.939	119.049
12.25	109.224	112.267	114.432	115.901	116.859
12.50	108.137	110.789	112.662	113.923	114.739
12.75	107.067	109.342	110.937	112.002	112.686
13.00	106.012	107.924	109.255	110.137	110.699
13.25	104.973	106.535	107.614	108.325	108.775
13.50	103.949	105.175	106.015	106.565	106.910
13.75	102.939	103.841	104.455	104.853	105.102
14.00	101.945	102.535	102.933	103.190	103.349
14.25	100.966	101.255	101.449	101.573	101.649
14.50	100.000	100.000	100.000	100.000	100.000
14.75	99.049	98.770	98.586	98.470	98.399
15.00	98.111	97.565	97.206	96.981	96.845
15.25	97.186	96.383	95.859	95.532	95.336
15.50	96.276	95.224	94.543	94.121	93.870
15.75	95.377	94.088	93.258	92.748	92.446
16.00	94.492	92.973	92.003	91.410	91.062
16.25	93.620	91.881	90.777	90.107	89.715
16.50	92.759	90.809	89.579	88.837	88.406
16.75	91.911	89.758	88.409	87.600	87.132
17.00	91.076	88.726	87.265	86.394	85.893
17.25	90.251	87.714	86.146	85.217	84.687
17.50	89.438	86.722	85.053	84.070	83.512
17.75	88.637	85.748	83.984	82.951	82.368
18.00	87.847	84.792	82.938	81.860	81.253
18.25	87.068	83.853	81.916	80.794	80.167
18.50	86.299	82.932	80.915	79.754	79.109
18.75	85.541	82.028	79.937	78.739	78.076
19.00	84.794	81.141	78.979	77.748	77.070

VALUE OF AMORTIZING MORTGAGE LOANS
AS PERCENTAGE OF FACE VALUE
FACE INTEREST RATE: 14.75%

YIELD TO MATURITY	TERM OF LOAN (YEARS)				
	10	15	20	25	30
10.00	120.928	128.652	134.541	138.821	141.809
10.25	119.671	126.841	132.264	136.171	138.877
10.50	118.433	125.068	130.046	133.604	136.047
10.75	117.214	123.333	127.888	131.117	133.316
11.00	116.013	121.636	125.787	128.706	130.678
11.25	114.830	119.973	123.740	126.369	128.130
11.50	113.665	118.346	121.748	124.103	125.668
11.75	112.517	116.752	119.807	121.904	123.287
12.00	111.387	115.193	117.916	119.772	120.986
12.25	110.273	113.665	116.073	117.702	118.759
12.50	109.176	112.169	114.278	115.693	116.605
12.75	108.095	110.703	112.528	113.743	114.520
13.00	107.030	109.268	110.821	111.848	112.500
13.25	105.981	107.862	109.158	110.008	110.544
13.50	104.947	106.484	107.536	108.220	108.649
13.75	103.928	105.134	105.953	106.483	106.812
14.00	102.925	103.812	104.410	104.794	105.030
14.25	101.936	102.516	102.904	103.151	103.303
14.50	100.961	101.245	101.434	101.554	101.627
14.75	100.000	100.000	100.000	100.000	100.000
15.00	99.054	98.780	98.600	98.488	98.421
15.25	98.120	97.583	97.233	97.016	96.887
15.50	97.200	96.410	95.899	95.584	95.397
15.75	96.293	95.259	94.595	94.189	93.950
16.00	95.400	94.131	93.323	92.831	92.543
16.25	94.519	93.025	92.079	91.507	91.175
16.50	93.651	91.940	90.864	90.218	89.844
16.75	92.794	90.875	89.677	88.961	88.550
17.00	91.951	89.831	88.516	87.736	87.290
17.25	91.118	88.807	87.382	86.541	86.064
17.50	90.298	87.802	86.273	85.377	84.870
17.75	89.488	86.815	85.188	84.240	83.708
18.00	88.691	85.847	84.128	83.132	82.575
18.25	87.904	84.897	83.091	82.050	81.471
18.50	87.128	83.965	82.076	80.994	80.395
18.75	86.363	83.050	81.083	79.963	79.346
19.00	85.609	82.151	80.112	78.956	78.323

VALUE OF AMORTIZING MORTGAGE LOANS
AS PERCENTAGE OF FACE VALUE
FACE INTEREST RATE: 15%

YIELD TO MATURITY	TERM OF LOAN (YEARS)				
	10	15	20	25	30
10.00	122.083	130.242	136.452	140.952	144.084
10.25	120.815	128.408	134.141	138.261	141.105
10.50	119.564	126.613	131.892	135.655	138.230
10.75	118.334	124.857	129.704	133.130	135.455
11.00	117.122	123.138	127.573	130.682	132.775
11.25	115.927	121.455	125.497	128.309	130.186
11.50	114.751	119.808	123.476	126.008	127.684
11.75	113.592	118.195	121.507	123.776	125.266
12.00	112.451	116.616	119.590	121.610	122.927
12.25	111.327	115.069	117.721	119.509	120.665
12.50	110.219	113.554	115.900	117.469	118.476
12.75	109.128	112.071	114.125	115.489	116.357
13.00	108.053	110.618	112.395	113.565	114.305
13.25	106.994	109.194	110.707	111.697	112.318
13.50	105.950	107.800	109.062	109.882	110.392
13.75	104.921	106.433	107.457	108.117	108.525
14.00	103.908	105.094	105.892	106.402	106.716
14.25	102.910	103.782	104.365	104.735	104.960
14.50	101.925	102.496	102.874	103.113	103.257
14.75	100.956	101.235	101.420	101.535	101.605
15.00	100.000	100.000	100.000	100.000	100.000
15.25	99.058	98.788	98.614	98.506	98.442
15.50	98.129	97.601	97.260	97.051	96.928
15.75	97.214	96.436	95.938	95.635	95.457
16.00	96.312	95.294	94.647	94.256	94.028
16.25	95.422	94.174	93.386	92.912	92.638
16.50	94.545	93.075	92.154	91.603	91.286
16.75	93.681	91.998	90.950	90.327	89.971
17.00	92.829	90.941	89.773	89.083	88.691
17.25	91.989	89.904	88.622	87.870	87.445
17.50	91.160	88.886	87.498	86.687	86.232
17.75	90.343	87.888	86.398	85.533	85.051
18.00	89.538	86.908	85.322	84.408	83.900
18.25	88.744	85.946	84.270	83.309	82.778
18.50	87.961	85.002	83.241	82.237	81.685
18.75	87.188	84.076	82.234	81.190	80.620
19.00	86.427	83.166	81.249	80.168	79.580

VALUE OF AMORTIZING MORTGAGE LOANS
AS PERCENTAGE OF FACE VALUE
FACE INTEREST RATE: 15.25%

YIELD TO MATURITY	TERM OF LOAN (YEARS)				
	10	15	20	25	30
10.00	123.245	131.839	138.370	143.090	146.365
10.25	121.964	129.983	136.027	140.359	143.339
10.50	120.702	128.166	133.746	137.713	140.418
10.75	119.459	126.389	131.527	135.149	137.599
11.00	118.236	124.649	129.366	132.664	134.876
11.25	117.030	122.945	127.261	130.255	132.246
11.50	115.843	121.277	125.212	127.919	129.705
11.75	114.672	119.644	123.216	125.653	127.248
12.00	113.521	118.046	121.271	123.455	124.873
12.25	112.386	116.480	119.376	121.322	122.575
12.50	111.267	114.947	117.529	119.251	120.351
12.75	110.166	113.446	115.729	117.240	118.199
13.00	109.081	111.975	113.975	115.288	116.115
13.25	108.011	110.534	112.264	113.391	114.096
13.50	106.958	109.122	110.595	111.548	112.139
13.75	105.919	107.738	108.968	109.757	110.243
14.00	104.897	106.383	107.380	108.016	108.405
14.25	103.889	105.055	105.832	106.323	106.622
14.50	102.895	103.753	104.320	104.677	104.892
14.75	101.916	102.477	102.845	103.075	103.213
15.00	100.951	101.226	101.406	101.517	101.583
15.25	100.000	100.000	100.000	100.000	100.000
15.50	99.063	98.798	98.628	98.523	98.462
15.75	98.138	97.619	97.287	97.086	96.968
16.00	97.228	96.463	95.978	95.685	95.516
16.25	96.330	95.329	94.699	94.321	94.104
16.50	95.445	94.217	93.449	92.992	92.731
16.75	94.572	93.126	92.228	91.697	91.395
17.00	93.712	92.056	91.035	90.434	90.095
17.25	92.864	91.006	89.868	89.203	88.829
17.50	92.028	89.976	88.728	88.002	87.597
17.75	91.203	88.966	87.612	86.831	86.397
18.00	90.390	87.974	86.522	85.688	85.228
18.25	89.588	87.000	85.455	84.573	84.089
18.50	88.798	86.045	84.411	83.485	82.978
18.75	88.018	85.107	83.390	82.422	81.896
19.00	87.249	84.186	82.391	81.384	80.840

VALUE OF AMORTIZING MORTGAGE LOANS
AS PERCENTAGE OF FACE VALUE
FACE INTEREST RATE: 15.5%

YIELD TO MATURITY	TERM OF LOAN (YEARS)				
	10	15	20	25	30
10.00	124.411	133.443	140.295	145.234	148.651
10.25	123.118	131.565	137.920	142.462	145.577
10.50	121.844	129.726	135.608	139.776	142.611
10.75	120.590	127.926	133.357	137.174	139.747
11.00	119.354	126.165	131.166	134.652	136.983
11.25	118.137	124.441	129.032	132.207	134.312
11.50	116.939	122.753	126.954	129.836	131.731
11.75	115.757	121.100	124.930	127.536	129.235
12.00	114.595	119.482	122.959	125.305	126.823
12.25	113.449	117.898	121.037	123.140	124.489
12.50	112.320	116.346	119.165	121.038	122.231
12.75	111.208	114.826	117.340	118.998	120.045
13.00	110.113	113.337	115.561	117.016	117.928
13.25	109.033	111.879	113.826	115.091	115.877
13.50	107.970	110.450	112.134	113.220	113.891
13.75	106.921	109.049	110.484	111.402	111.965
14.00	105.889	107.678	108.875	109.635	110.098
14.25	104.872	106.333	107.304	107.917	108.287
14.50	103.868	105.015	105.772	106.246	106.530
14.75	102.880	103.724	104.276	104.620	104.825
15.00	101.906	102.458	102.817	103.038	103.169
15.25	100.946	101.217	101.392	101.499	101.562
15.50	100.000	100.000	100.000	100.000	100.000
15.75	99.067	98.807	98.641	98.541	98.483
16.00	98.148	97.636	97.313	97.119	97.008
16.25	97.241	96.489	96.017	95.735	95.574
16.50	96.348	95.363	94.750	94.386	94.179
16.75	95.467	94.259	93.512	93.071	92.822
17.00	94.599	93.177	92.302	91.789	91.502
17.25	93.742	92.114	91.119	90.540	90.216
17.50	92.898	91.071	89.962	89.321	88.965
17.75	92.066	90.048	88.831	88.132	87.746
18.00	91.245	89.044	87.726	86.972	86.559
18.25	90.436	88.059	86.644	85.840	85.402
18.50	89.638	87.092	85.586	84.736	84.274
18.75	88.850	86.143	84.551	83.657	83.175
19.00	88.074	85.211	83.538	82.604	82.102

VALUE OF AMORTIZING MORTGAGE LOANS
AS PERCENTAGE OF FACE VALUE
FACE INTEREST RATE: 15.75%

YIELD TO MATURITY	TERM OF LOAN (YEARS)				
	10	15	20	25	30
10.00	125.583	135.055	142.228	147.385	150.941
10.25	124.278	133.154	139.820	144.572	147.820
10.50	122.991	131.293	137.476	141.847	144.808
10.75	121.725	129.472	135.195	139.206	141.901
11.00	120.479	127.689	132.973	136.647	139.093
11.25	119.250	125.944	130.810	134.165	136.381
11.50	118.040	124.236	128.704	131.759	133.760
11.75	116.848	122.563	126.652	129.425	131.227
12.00	115.674	120.926	124.653	127.161	128.777
12.25	114.518	119.322	122.705	124.964	126.407
12.50	113.378	117.751	120.807	122.831	124.114
12.75	112.256	116.213	118.957	120.760	121.894
13.00	111.150	114.706	117.153	118.749	119.745
13.25	110.060	113.230	115.394	116.795	117.663
13.50	108.987	111.784	113.679	114.897	115.646
13.75	107.929	110.367	112.006	113.052	113.690
14.00	106.886	108.978	110.375	111.259	111.794
14.25	105.859	107.618	108.783	109.515	109.955
14.50	104.847	106.284	107.229	107.819	108.171
14.75	103.849	104.977	105.713	106.169	106.440
15.00	102.866	103.696	104.234	104.564	104.759
15.25	101.897	102.439	102.789	103.002	103.127
15.50	100.942	101.208	101.378	101.481	101.541
15.75	100.000	100.000	100.000	100.000	100.000
16.00	99.072	98.816	98.654	98.558	98.502
16.25	98.157	97.655	97.340	97.153	97.046
16.50	97.255	96.515	96.055	95.784	95.630
16.75	96.366	95.398	94.800	94.449	94.252
17.00	95.490	94.302	93.573	93.149	92.912
17.25	94.625	93.226	92.374	91.881	91.607
17.50	93.773	92.171	91.202	90.644	90.336
17.75	92.933	91.136	90.055	89.437	89.098
18.00	92.104	90.120	88.934	88.260	87.893
18.25	91.288	89.123	87.838	87.112	86.718
18.50	90.482	88.144	86.765	85.991	85.573
18.75	89.687	87.183	85.716	84.896	84.456
19.00	88.904	86.240	84.689	83.827	83.367

VALUE OF AMORTIZING MORTGAGE LOANS
AS PERCENTAGE OF FACE VALUE
FACE INTEREST RATE: 16%

YIELD TO MATURITY	TERM OF LOAN (YEARS)				
	10	15	20	25	30
10.00	126.759	136.673	144.168	149.542	153.236
10.25	125.442	134.749	141.727	146.688	150.068
10.50	124.143	132.866	139.351	143.922	147.010
10.75	122.865	131.023	137.039	141.243	144.058
11.00	121.607	129.219	134.787	138.646	141.208
11.25	120.367	127.453	132.594	136.128	138.455
11.50	119.146	125.725	130.459	133.687	135.794
11.75	117.942	124.032	128.379	131.319	133.222
12.00	116.758	122.375	126.353	129.022	130.735
12.25	115.590	120.752	124.379	126.792	128.329
12.50	114.440	119.162	122.454	124.628	126.001
12.75	113.307	117.606	120.579	122.527	123.748
13.00	112.191	116.081	118.751	120.487	121.566
13.25	111.091	114.587	116.968	118.504	119.452
13.50	110.008	113.124	115.230	116.578	117.404
13.75	108.939	111.689	113.534	114.706	115.419
14.00	107.888	110.284	111.880	112.887	113.494
14.25	106.851	108.907	110.267	111.118	111.627
14.50	105.829	107.558	108.692	109.397	109.816
14.75	104.822	106.235	107.155	107.723	108.058
15.00	103.830	104.938	105.655	106.094	106.352
15.25	102.851	103.667	104.191	104.509	104.694
15.50	101.887	102.421	102.761	102.966	103.085
15.75	100.937	101.198	101.364	101.463	101.520
16.00	100.000	100.000	100.000	100.000	100.000
16.25	99.077	98.825	98.668	98.574	98.522
16.50	98.166	97.672	97.365	97.185	97.084
16.75	97.269	96.541	96.093	95.832	95.685
17.00	96.384	95.432	94.850	94.512	94.324
17.25	95.512	94.344	93.634	93.225	92.999
17.50	94.652	93.276	92.446	91.970	91.709
17.75	93.803	92.228	91.284	90.746	90.453
18.00	92.967	91.200	90.147	89.552	89.229
18.25	92.143	90.191	89.036	88.387	88.036
18.50	91.329	89.200	87.949	87.249	86.874
18.75	90.527	88.228	86.885	86.138	85.740
19.00	89.737	87.273	85.844	85.054	84.635

576

VALUE OF AMORTIZING MORTGAGE LOANS
AS PERCENTAGE OF FACE VALUE
FACE INTEREST RATE: 16.25%

YIELD TO MATURITY	TERM OF LOAN (YEARS)				
	10	15	20	25	30
10.00	127.940	138.299	146.115	151.704	155.535
10.25	126.611	136.352	143.641	148.809	152.319
10.50	125.300	134.446	141.233	146.004	149.216
10.75	124.010	132.581	138.889	143.286	146.220
11.00	122.740	130.756	136.608	140.651	143.327
11.25	121.488	128.969	134.385	138.097	140.532
11.50	120.256	127.220	132.221	135.621	137.832
11.75	119.041	125.507	130.113	133.218	135.221
12.00	117.846	123.830	128.059	130.888	132.697
12.25	116.667	122.188	126.058	128.626	130.255
12.50	115.506	120.579	124.108	126.430	127.892
12.75	114.363	119.004	122.208	124.299	125.604
13.00	113.237	117.461	120.355	122.229	123.390
13.25	112.126	115.949	118.548	120.218	121.244
13.50	111.033	114.469	116.786	118.264	119.165
13.75	109.955	113.017	115.067	116.365	117.150
14.00	108.893	111.596	113.391	114.519	115.197
14.25	107.847	110.203	111.756	112.725	113.302
14.50	106.815	108.837	110.160	110.979	111.464
14.75	105.799	107.498	108.602	109.281	109.679
15.00	104.797	106.186	107.082	107.629	107.947
15.25	103.810	104.900	105.598	106.021	106.265
15.50	102.837	103.639	104.148	104.455	104.631
15.75	101.877	102.402	102.733	102.931	103.044
16.00	100.932	101.189	101.350	101.446	101.500
16.25	100.000	100.000	100.000	100.000	100.000
16.50	99.081	98.833	98.680	98.591	98.541
16.75	98.175	97.689	97.391	97.217	97.121
17.00	97.282	96.567	96.131	95.879	95.740
17.25	96.402	95.466	94.899	94.573	94.395
17.50	95.534	94.385	93.694	93.300	93.085
17.75	94.677	93.325	92.517	92.059	91.810
18.00	93.833	92.284	91.365	90.847	90.568
18.25	93.001	91.263	90.238	89.665	89.357
18.50	92.180	90.261	89.136	88.511	88.177
18.75	91.371	89.277	88.058	87.384	87.027
19.00	90.573	88.311	87.003	86.284	85.905

VALUE OF AMORTIZING MORTGAGE LOANS
AS PERCENTAGE OF FACE VALUE
FACE INTEREST RATE: 16.5%

YIELD TO MATURITY	TERM OF LOAN (YEARS)				
	10	15	20	25	30
10.00	129.127	139.931	148.069	153.873	157.839
10.25	127.785	137.961	145.562	150.936	154.575
10.50	126.462	136.033	143.122	148.091	151.425
10.75	125.161	134.146	140.747	145.334	148.385
11.00	123.879	132.300	138.434	142.662	145.449
11.25	122.615	130.491	136.182	140.071	142.613
11.50	121.371	128.721	133.989	137.559	139.873
11.75	120.145	126.988	131.853	135.122	137.223
12.00	118.939	125.292	129.772	132.759	134.662
12.25	117.750	123.630	127.744	130.464	132.184
12.50	116.578	122.002	125.768	128.238	129.786
12.75	115.424	120.409	123.842	126.076	127.465
13.00	114.287	118.848	121.964	123.976	125.217
13.25	113.166	117.318	120.133	121.936	123.040
13.50	112.063	115.820	118.348	119.955	120.930
13.75	110.974	114.351	116.606	118.029	118.885
14.00	109.903	112.913	114.908	116.156	116.903
14.25	108.847	111.503	113.250	114.336	114.980
14.50	107.806	110.121	111.633	112.565	113.114
14.75	106.780	108.767	110.055	110.843	111.304
15.00	105.769	107.440	108.514	109.167	109.546
15.25	104.773	106.138	107.010	107.536	107.839
15.50	103.791	104.862	105.541	105.948	106.181
15.75	102.822	103.611	104.107	104.402	104.570
16.00	101.868	102.384	102.706	102.896	103.004
16.25	100.928	101.180	101.337	101.429	101.481
16.50	100.000	100.000	100.000	100.000	100.000
16.75	99.086	98.842	98.693	98.607	98.559
17.00	98.185	97.707	97.416	97.249	97.157
17.25	97.296	96.592	96.168	95.925	95.793
17.50	96.420	95.499	94.947	94.634	94.464
17.75	95.556	94.426	93.754	93.374	93.170
18.00	94.704	93.374	92.587	92.146	91.909
18.25	93.864	92.340	91.445	90.946	90.681
18.50	93.035	91.326	90.328	89.776	89.483
18.75	92.219	90.331	89.236	88.633	88.316
19.00	91.413	89.354	88.167	87.517	87.177

VALUE OF AMORTIZING MORTGAGE LOANS
AS PERCENTAGE OF FACE VALUE
FACE INTEREST RATE: 16.75%

YIELD TO MATURITY	TERM OF LOAN (YEARS)				
	10	15	20	25	30
10.00	130.318	141.570	150.030	156.046	160.146
10.25	128.964	139.577	147.490	153.068	156.835
10.50	127.629	137.626	145.017	150.183	153.639
10.75	126.315	135.717	142.610	147.387	150.554
11.00	125.022	133.849	140.267	144.677	147.576
11.25	123.746	132.019	137.985	142.050	144.698
11.50	122.491	130.229	135.763	139.502	141.917
11.75	121.254	128.475	133.599	137.031	139.229
12.00	120.036	126.759	131.490	134.634	136.630
12.25	118.836	125.078	129.436	132.307	134.116
12.50	117.653	123.431	127.433	130.049	131.683
12.75	116.489	121.819	125.481	127.857	129.328
13.00	115.341	120.240	123.579	125.727	127.047
13.25	114.210	118.692	121.724	123.659	124.838
13.50	113.097	117.176	119.915	121.649	122.698
13.75	111.998	115.691	118.150	119.696	120.623
14.00	110.917	114.235	116.429	117.797	118.612
14.25	109.851	112.809	114.750	115.951	116.661
14.50	108.800	111.411	113.111	114.155	114.768
14.75	107.765	110.041	111.512	112.409	112.931
15.00	106.745	108.698	109.951	110.709	111.147
15.25	105.739	107.381	108.427	109.055	109.415
15.50	104.748	106.090	106.939	107.445	107.733
15.75	103.771	104.824	105.485	105.877	106.098
16.00	102.808	103.583	104.066	104.350	104.509
16.25	101.859	102.365	102.679	102.862	102.964
16.50	100.923	101.171	101.324	101.413	101.462
16.75	100.000	100.000	100.000	100.000	100.000
17.00	99.091	98.851	98.706	98.623	98.578
17.25	98.193	97.724	97.441	97.280	97.193
17.50	97.309	96.618	96.204	95.971	95.845
17.75	96.437	95.532	94.995	94.693	94.532
18.00	95.578	94.467	93.813	93.447	93.253
18.25	94.730	93.422	92.656	92.231	92.006
18.50	93.894	92.396	91.524	91.044	90.791
18.75	93.069	91.389	90.417	89.885	89.607
19.00	92.256	90.400	89.334	88.754	88.451

VALUE OF AMORTIZING MORTGAGE LOANS
AS PERCENTAGE OF FACE VALUE
FACE INTEREST RATE: 17%

YIELD TO MATURITY	TERM OF LOAN (YEARS)				
	10	15	20	25	30
10.00	131.514	143.215	151.996	158.225	162.457
10.25	130.147	141.199	149.423	155.205	159.098
10.50	128.800	139.226	146.918	152.279	155.856
10.75	127.475	137.295	144.480	149.445	152.727
11.00	126.169	135.405	142.106	146.697	149.705
11.25	124.882	133.554	139.794	144.033	146.786
11.50	123.615	131.742	137.543	141.450	143.965
11.75	122.366	129.968	135.350	138.944	141.238
12.00	121.138	128.232	133.214	136.514	138.602
12.25	119.926	126.532	131.132	134.155	136.051
12.50	118.733	124.866	129.104	131.865	133.583
12.75	117.558	123.235	127.126	129.642	131.194
13.00	116.400	121.637	125.199	127.483	128.880
13.25	115.259	120.072	123.319	125.385	126.640
13.50	114.135	118.538	121.487	123.348	124.468
13.75	113.026	117.035	119.699	121.367	122.364
14.00	111.935	115.563	117.955	119.442	120.323
14.25	110.859	114.120	116.254	117.570	118.344
14.50	109.799	112.706	114.594	115.749	116.424
14.75	108.754	111.320	112.974	113.978	114.560
15.00	107.725	109.961	111.392	112.255	112.751
15.25	106.710	108.629	109.848	110.578	110.994
15.50	105.710	107.323	108.340	108.945	109.288
15.75	104.723	106.042	106.868	107.355	107.629
16.00	103.751	104.787	105.430	105.807	106.017
16.25	102.793	103.555	104.025	104.298	104.450
16.50	101.849	102.347	102.652	102.829	102.926
16.75	100.918	101.162	101.311	101.396	101.443
17.00	100.000	100.000	100.000	100.000	100.000
17.25	99.095	98.859	98.718	98.639	98.595
17.50	98.202	97.741	97.466	97.311	97.228
17.75	97.322	96.643	96.240	96.016	95.896
18.00	96.455	95.565	95.042	94.752	94.598
18.25	95.599	94.508	93.871	93.519	93.334
18.50	94.755	93.470	92.724	92.315	92.101
18.75	93.923	92.451	91.602	91.140	90.900
19.00	93.103	91.451	90.505	89.993	89.728

VALUE OF AMORTIZING MORTGAGE LOANS
AS PERCENTAGE OF FACE VALUE
FACE INTEREST RATE: 17.25%

YIELD TO MATURITY	TERM OF LOAN (YEARS)				
	10	15	20	25	30
10.00	132.716	144.868	153.970	160.409	164.771
10.25	131.337	142.828	151.363	157.348	161.364
10.50	129.977	140.832	148.825	154.381	158.076
10.75	128.639	138.879	146.355	151.507	154.902
11.00	127.322	136.967	143.951	148.722	151.838
11.25	126.023	135.095	141.609	146.021	148.877
11.50	124.745	133.262	139.329	143.402	146.016
11.75	123.484	131.468	137.107	140.862	143.250
12.00	122.244	129.712	134.943	138.398	140.576
12.25	121.022	127.991	132.835	136.007	137.989
12.50	119.818	126.307	130.780	133.685	135.486
12.75	118.632	124.657	128.777	131.431	133.063
13.00	117.463	123.040	126.824	129.242	130.717
13.25	116.312	121.457	124.920	127.116	128.444
13.50	115.177	119.906	123.064	125.050	126.242
13.75	114.059	118.386	121.253	123.042	124.107
14.00	112.957	116.896	119.487	121.091	122.037
14.25	111.872	115.437	117.763	119.193	120.030
14.50	110.802	114.006	116.082	117.347	118.082
14.75	109.748	112.604	114.440	115.552	116.192
15.00	108.709	111.230	112.838	113.804	114.357
15.25	107.685	109.882	111.274	112.104	112.576
15.50	106.675	108.561	109.747	110.449	110.845
15.75	105.680	107.266	108.255	108.837	109.163
16.00	104.699	105.996	106.799	107.267	107.528
16.25	103.733	104.750	105.376	105.738	105.938
16.50	102.779	103.528	103.985	104.248	104.392
16.75	101.840	102.329	102.626	102.796	102.888
17.00	100.914	101.154	101.298	101.380	101.425
17.25	100.000	100.000	100.000	100.000	100.000
17.50	99.100	98.868	98.731	98.654	98.613
17.75	98.211	97.758	97.490	97.341	97.262
18.00	97.336	96.668	96.276	96.060	95.946
18.25	96.473	95.598	95.089	94.810	94.663
18.50	95.621	94.548	93.928	93.589	93.413
18.75	94.782	93.518	92.792	92.398	92.194
19.00	93.954	92.506	91.680	91.235	91.006

VALUE OF AMORTIZING MORTGAGE LOANS
AS PERCENTAGE OF FACE VALUE
FACE INTEREST RATE: 17.5%

YIELD TO MATURITY	TERM OF LOAN (YEARS)				
	10	15	20	25	30
10.00	133.922	146.526	155.949	162.598	167.089
10.25	132.530	144.463	153.309	159.495	163.634
10.50	131.158	142.444	150.738	156.488	160.300
10.75	129.808	140.468	148.237	153.575	157.081
11.00	128.479	138.535	145.801	150.751	153.974
11.25	127.168	136.641	143.429	148.013	150.971
11.50	125.878	134.788	141.120	145.359	148.070
11.75	124.607	132.973	138.869	142.784	145.265
12.00	123.355	131.197	136.678	140.286	142.554
12.25	122.122	129.457	134.542	137.862	139.930
12.50	120.907	127.752	132.461	135.509	137.392
12.75	119.710	126.084	130.432	133.225	134.935
13.00	118.531	124.449	128.455	131.006	132.555
13.25	117.369	122.847	126.526	128.851	130.250
13.50	116.224	121.278	124.646	126.756	128.017
13.75	115.095	119.741	122.812	124.721	125.853
14.00	113.984	118.234	121.023	122.743	123.754
14.25	112.889	116.758	119.277	120.819	121.718
14.50	111.809	115.311	117.574	118.948	119.743
14.75	110.745	113.893	115.911	117.128	117.827
15.00	109.697	112.503	114.289	115.357	115.966
15.25	108.663	111.140	112.704	113.634	114.159
15.50	107.645	109.804	111.158	111.956	112.404
15.75	106.640	108.494	109.647	110.322	110.698
16.00	105.651	107.209	108.171	108.731	109.040
16.25	104.675	105.949	106.730	107.181	107.428
16.50	103.713	104.713	105.322	105.670	105.861
16.75	102.765	103.501	103.945	104.198	104.335
17.00	101.831	102.312	102.600	102.764	102.851
17.25	100.909	101.145	101.285	101.364	101.407
17.50	100.000	100.000	100.000	100.000	100.000
17.75	99.104	98.877	98.743	98.669	98.630
18.00	98.220	97.774	97.514	97.371	97.295
18.25	97.349	96.692	96.311	96.103	95.995
18.50	96.490	95.630	95.135	94.866	94.727
18.75	95.643	94.588	93.985	93.659	93.491
19.00	94.807	93.565	92.858	92.480	92.286

VALUE OF AMORTIZING MORTGAGE LOANS
AS PERCENTAGE OF FACE VALUE
FACE INTEREST RATE: 17.75%

YIELD TO MATURITY	TERM OF LOAN (YEARS)				
	10	15	20	25	30
10.00	135.133	148.191	157.934	164.791	169.410
10.25	133.728	146.105	155.260	161.646	165.907
10.50	132.344	144.063	152.657	158.599	162.526
10.75	130.982	142.064	150.124	155.646	159.263
11.00	129.640	140.109	147.657	152.785	156.112
11.25	128.318	138.194	145.255	150.010	153.068
11.50	127.016	136.319	142.916	147.320	150.127
11.75	125.733	134.484	140.637	144.710	147.283
12.00	124.471	132.687	138.418	142.179	144.534
12.25	123.226	130.927	136.255	139.722	141.874
12.50	122.000	129.204	134.147	137.337	139.300
12.75	120.792	127.516	132.093	135.022	136.809
13.00	119.603	125.863	130.090	132.773	134.396
13.25	118.430	124.243	128.137	130.589	132.060
13.50	117.275	122.656	126.233	128.466	129.795
13.75	116.136	121.101	124.375	126.403	127.601
14.00	115.015	119.578	122.563	124.398	125.473
14.25	113.910	118.085	120.796	122.449	123.409
14.50	112.820	116.621	119.070	120.553	121.407
14.75	111.746	115.187	117.387	118.708	119.463
15.00	110.689	113.781	115.744	116.913	117.577
15.25	109.646	112.403	114.139	115.166	115.745
15.50	108.618	111.052	112.573	113.466	113.965
15.75	107.605	109.726	111.043	111.810	112.236
16.00	106.606	108.427	109.548	110.197	110.555
16.25	105.622	107.153	108.089	108.626	108.920
16.50	104.651	105.903	106.662	107.096	107.331
16.75	103.694	104.677	105.269	105.604	105.785
17.00	102.751	103.474	103.906	104.150	104.280
17.25	101.821	102.294	102.575	102.732	102.815
17.50	100.904	101.136	101.273	101.349	101.389
17.75	100.000	100.000	100.000	100.000	100.000
18.00	99.109	98.885	98.755	98.684	98.647
18.25	98.230	97.791	97.538	97.400	97.328
18.50	97.363	96.717	96.346	96.146	96.043
18.75	96.508	95.663	95.181	94.922	94.790
19.00	95.665	94.628	94.041	93.727	93.568

PREMIUMS FOR ASSUMABLE LOANS
(Maximum Premiums for Assumable Loans as Percentage of Loan Balance)

Homes are often sold with a provision for the buyer to assume the existing mortgage, rather than arrange new financing. Some older loans carry interest rates below the rates charged on new loans. When the buyer assumes such a loan (and the lender does not have the authority to escalate the rate), monthly loan payments will be lower than for a comparable loan at the higher market rate of interest. Consequently, buyers are often willing to pay a higher price for the home because of the assumable mortgage.

The tables which follow provide indications of the highest additional price sellers should expect to receive for specific assumable loans. At the premium shown in the table, a buyer would be indifferent between assuming the loan and arranging new financing, assuming the buyer has enough additional cash to pay the premium. In the actual market, the price will be set through negotiation between buyer and seller, so the actual premium paid for the favorable assumption tends to be lower than the maximum indicated in the table.

To use the tables, you need the following information:

1. *The market value of the home with new financing.* How much would the home be worth if the assumable loan did not exist? A knowledgeable real estate appraiser should be able to provide an indication.

2. *The interest rate on new financing* (current rate). What is the current interest rate on new mortgage loans with a maturity similar to the remaining term on the assumable loan? The tables cover current rates ranging from 9% to 18% in .25% intervals.

3. *The interest rate on the assumable loan* (face interest rate). This is the rate you are paying on the existing loan and that the buyer will be paying on the assumed loan. In some cases, lenders may raise the rate above what the seller has paid but keep it below that of new financing. The rate charged to the buyer is the rate to use. The tables cover face rates from 6% to 17.75% in intervals of .25%.

4. *The remaining term of the existing loan.* How many more years are left on the loan that will be assumed? The tables cover terms of 15, 20, 25, 27, and 30 years. Select the term which is closest to the actual remaining term on the loan.

5. *The remaining balance of the assumable loan.* How much is still owed on the existing loan? This represents the amount of the purchase price that will be covered by the assumed loan.

Example. A home is valued at $60,000. The owner has an assumable loan with a remaining principal balance of $30,000 and a 21-year remaining term. The loan may be assumed at the existing interest rate of 6%. What is the maximum price the seller can expect to receive if the current market interest rate for 20-year loans is 14%?

Look at the first table covering face interest rates of 6%. Look down the "CURRENT RATE" column to find 14.00%. Follow this row over to the column under 20-year remaining term. (The table has no 21-year re-

maining term column, so use the column which most closely matches the actual remaining term in the problem.) The premium listed in the table is 42.387%. Multiply this percentage by the remaining balance of the assumed loan, or $30,000. The result is $12,716 which is added to the home's market value of $60,000. The home could sell for as much as $72,716 owing to the assumable loan.

Example. A home is for sale. The seller wants $70,000 cash which is in line with prices of similar homes on the market. Alternatively, the seller is willing to provide financing for $50,000 of the price with an amortizing loan at 10% interest over 25 years. If the financing is included, the seller will demand a higher price. If current mortgage interest rates for 25-year loans is 15%, what is the highest price a buyer should pay under the favorable financing arrangement?

Look for the table with a "FACE INTEREST RATE" of 10%. Follow down the "CURRENT RATE" column to find 15.00%. Follow this row to the "25" column and read the premium of 29.054%. Multiply this percentage by the balance of $50,000 to obtain the amount of $14,527. The buyer could pay up to $70,000 plus $14,527, or $84,527, for the home with the seller financing.

MAXIMUM PREMIUM FOR ASSUMABLE LOANS
AS PERCENTAGE OF LOAN BALANCE
FACE INTEREST RATE: 6%

CURRENT RATE	REMAINING TERM OF LOAN (YEARS)				
	15	20	25	27	30
9.00	16.801	20.372	23.224	24.193	25.487
9.25	18.008	21.776	24.765	25.776	27.122
9.50	19.188	23.140	26.256	27.305	28.697
9.75	20.343	24.468	27.699	28.783	30.216
10.00	21.473	25.760	29.097	30.211	31.681
10.25	22.578	27.017	30.450	31.591	33.093
10.50	23.661	28.241	31.761	32.927	34.457
10.75	24.719	29.432	33.031	34.219	35.773
11.00	25.756	30.591	34.263	35.469	37.043
11.25	26.771	31.720	35.456	36.679	38.271
11.50	27.764	32.820	36.614	37.851	39.457
11.75	28.737	33.891	37.737	38.986	40.604
12.00	29.688	34.934	38.826	40.085	41.713
12.25	30.621	35.951	39.883	41.150	42.785
12.50	31.534	36.942	40.909	42.183	43.823
12.75	32.429	37.907	41.905	43.185	44.828
13.00	33.305	38.849	42.873	44.156	45.801
13.25	34.163	39.767	43.813	45.099	46.743
13.50	35.004	40.662	44.726	46.013	47.656
13.75	35.828	41.535	45.613	46.901	48.541
14.00	36.635	42.387	46.476	47.763	49.400
14.25	37.426	43.218	47.315	48.601	50.232
14.50	38.202	44.029	48.131	49.414	51.039
14.75	38.962	44.820	48.924	50.205	51.823
15.00	39.707	45.593	49.697	50.973	52.584
15.25	40.437	46.347	50.448	51.720	53.323
15.50	41.153	47.083	51.180	52.447	54.040
15.75	41.856	47.802	51.892	53.154	54.738
16.00	42.544	48.505	52.586	53.842	55.416
16.25	43.219	49.191	53.262	54.511	56.075
16.50	43.882	49.861	53.921	55.163	56.716
16.75	44.531	50.517	54.563	55.798	57.339
17.00	45.169	51.157	55.188	56.416	57.946
17.25	45.794	51.783	55.798	57.018	58.537
17.50	46.407	52.395	56.393	57.605	59.112
17.75	47.010	52.993	56.974	58.177	59.672
18.00	47.600	53.578	57.540	58.735	60.218

MAXIMUM PREMIUM FOR ASSUMABLE LOANS
AS PERCENTAGE OF LOAN BALANCE
FACE INTEREST RATE: 6.25%

CURRENT RATE	REMAINING TERM OF LOAN (YEARS)				
	15	20	25	27	30
9.00	15.464	18.761	21.393	22.286	23.478
9.25	16.691	20.193	22.971	23.909	25.157
9.50	17.889	21.586	24.497	25.477	26.775
9.75	19.063	22.940	25.975	26.991	28.335
10.00	20.211	24.258	27.406	28.455	29.839
10.25	21.334	25.541	28.791	29.871	31.290
10.50	22.434	26.789	30.134	31.240	32.690
10.75	23.510	28.004	31.434	32.564	34.041
11.00	24.563	29.187	32.695	33.846	35.346
11.25	25.594	30.339	33.917	35.086	36.607
11.50	26.603	31.461	35.102	36.287	37.825
11.75	27.591	32.554	36.252	37.451	39.003
12.00	28.559	33.618	37.367	38.578	40.141
12.25	29.506	34.655	38.449	39.670	41.243
12.50	30.434	35.666	39.500	40.729	42.309
12.75	31.343	36.651	40.520	41.756	43.341
13.00	32.233	37.612	41.510	42.752	44.340
13.25	33.105	38.548	42.473	43.718	45.307
13.50	33.959	39.462	43.408	44.655	46.245
13.75	34.797	40.353	44.316	45.566	47.154
14.00	35.617	41.221	45.200	46.449	48.035
14.25	36.421	42.069	46.058	47.308	48.890
14.50	37.209	42.896	46.894	48.142	49.719
14.75	37.981	43.704	47.706	48.952	50.524
15.00	38.738	44.492	48.497	49.740	51.305
15.25	39.480	45.261	49.267	50.506	52.064
15.50	40.208	46.013	50.016	51.251	52.801
15.75	40.921	46.746	50.745	51.975	53.518
16.00	41.621	47.463	51.455	52.681	54.214
16.25	42.307	48.163	52.148	53.367	54.891
16.50	42.980	48.847	52.822	54.035	55.549
16.75	43.640	49.516	53.479	54.686	56.189
17.00	44.287	50.169	54.120	55.320	56.812
17.25	44.923	50.807	54.744	55.937	57.419
17.50	45.546	51.432	55.353	56.539	58.010
17.75	46.158	52.042	55.948	57.125	58.585
18.00	46.758	52.639	56.527	57.697	59.145

MAXIMUM PREMIUM FOR ASSUMABLE LOANS
AS PERCENTAGE OF LOAN BALANCE
FACE INTEREST RATE: 6.5%

CURRENT RATE	REMAINING TERM OF LOAN (YEARS)				
	15	20	25	27	30
9.00	14.114	17.133	19.541	20.357	21.445
9.25	15.360	18.594	21.156	22.021	23.169
9.50	16.578	20.014	22.718	23.627	24.830
9.75	17.770	21.396	24.231	25.179	26.431
10.00	18.937	22.740	25.695	26.680	27.975
10.25	20.078	24.048	27.113	28.130	29.464
10.50	21.195	25.321	28.487	29.533	30.902
10.75	22.288	26.561	29.819	30.890	32.289
11.00	23.358	27.767	31.109	32.204	33.629
11.25	24.405	28.942	32.360	33.475	34.923
11.50	25.431	30.087	33.573	34.706	36.173
11.75	26.435	31.201	34.750	35.898	37.382
12.00	27.418	32.287	35.891	37.053	38.551
12.25	28.380	33.345	36.999	38.173	39.682
12.50	29.323	34.376	38.074	39.258	40.776
12.75	30.246	35.381	39.118	40.310	41.836
13.00	31.151	36.361	40.132	41.331	42.861
13.25	32.037	37.317	41.117	42.321	43.855
13.50	32.905	38.248	42.074	43.282	44.817
13.75	33.755	39.157	43.004	44.215	45.750
14.00	34.589	40.043	43.908	45.120	46.655
14.25	35.405	40.908	44.787	46.000	47.532
14.50	36.206	41.752	45.642	46.855	48.384
14.75	36.990	42.575	46.474	47.685	49.210
15.00	37.759	43.379	47.283	48.492	50.012
15.25	38.513	44.164	48.071	49.277	50.791
15.50	39.253	44.930	48.838	50.041	51.548
15.75	39.978	45.679	49.585	50.783	52.283
16.00	40.688	46.410	50.312	51.506	52.997
16.25	41.385	47.124	51.020	52.209	53.692
16.50	42.069	47.822	51.710	52.894	54.368
16.75	42.740	48.504	52.383	53.561	55.025
17.00	43.398	49.170	53.039	54.211	55.665
17.25	44.043	49.821	53.678	54.843	56.288
17.50	44.677	50.458	54.301	55.460	56.894
17.75	45.298	51.081	54.910	56.061	57.485
18.00	45.908	51.690	55.503	56.647	58.060

MAXIMUM PREMIUM FOR ASSUMABLE LOANS
AS PERCENTAGE OF LOAN BALANCE
FACE INTEREST RATE: 6.75%

CURRENT RATE	REMAINING TERM OF LOAN (YEARS)				
	15	20	25	27	30
9.00	12.753	15.489	17.670	18.408	19.391
9.25	14.019	16.979	19.322	20.112	21.160
9.50	15.257	18.427	20.921	21.758	22.864
9.75	16.468	19.837	22.469	23.348	24.507
10.00	17.653	21.208	23.967	24.885	26.092
10.25	18.812	22.542	25.418	26.371	27.620
10.50	19.947	23.840	26.824	27.808	29.095
10.75	21.057	25.104	28.187	29.199	30.518
11.00	22.144	26.335	29.507	30.544	31.893
11.25	23.208	27.533	30.787	31.847	33.221
11.50	24.249	28.700	32.028	33.108	34.504
11.75	25.270	29.837	33.232	34.330	35.745
12.00	26.268	30.944	34.400	35.513	36.944
12.25	27.246	32.023	35.534	36.660	38.105
12.50	28.203	33.075	36.634	37.771	39.228
12.75	29.141	34.100	37.703	38.849	40.314
13.00	30.060	35.099	38.740	39.895	41.367
13.25	30.960	36.073	39.748	40.909	42.386
13.50	31.842	37.023	40.727	41.894	43.374
13.75	32.706	37.950	41.679	42.849	44.332
14.00	33.552	38.854	42.604	43.777	45.260
14.25	34.382	39.736	43.503	44.678	46.160
14.50	35.195	40.596	44.378	45.554	47.034
14.75	35.992	41.436	45.229	46.405	47.882
15.00	36.773	42.256	46.057	47.232	48.705
15.25	37.539	43.057	46.863	48.036	49.504
15.50	38.290	43.838	47.648	48.818	50.281
15.75	39.027	44.601	48.412	49.579	51.035
16.00	39.749	45.347	49.156	50.319	51.768
16.25	40.457	46.075	49.881	51.040	52.481
16.50	41.152	46.787	50.587	51.741	53.175
16.75	41.833	47.482	51.276	52.425	53.849
17.00	42.501	48.162	51.946	53.090	54.506
17.25	43.157	48.826	52.601	53.738	55.145
17.50	43.800	49.476	53.239	54.370	55.767
17.75	44.432	50.111	53.861	54.986	56.373
18.00	45.051	50.732	54.468	55.586	56.963

MAXIMUM PREMIUM FOR ASSUMABLE LOANS
AS PERCENTAGE OF LOAN BALANCE
FACE INTEREST RATE: 7%

CURRENT RATE	REMAINING TERM OF LOAN (YEARS) 15	20	25	27	30
9.00	11.381	13.829	15.779	16.439	17.315
9.25	12.667	15.348	17.469	18.184	19.130
9.50	13.924	16.825	19.105	19.869	20.878
9.75	15.154	18.262	20.688	21.498	22.563
10.00	16.358	19.660	22.221	23.072	24.188
10.25	17.535	21.020	23.706	24.594	25.756
10.50	18.688	22.344	25.144	26.066	27.269
10.75	19.816	23.633	26.537	27.490	28.729
11.00	20.919	24.888	27.888	28.868	30.139
11.25	22.000	26.110	29.198	30.202	31.501
11.50	23.058	27.300	30.467	31.493	32.818
11.75	24.094	28.459	31.699	32.744	34.090
12.00	25.108	29.588	32.894	33.956	35.320
12.25	26.101	30.688	34.053	35.131	36.511
12.50	27.074	31.760	35.179	36.269	37.663
12.75	28.027	32.806	36.272	37.373	38.777
13.00	28.960	33.824	37.333	38.444	39.857
13.25	29.874	34.818	38.364	39.483	40.903
13.50	30.770	35.786	39.366	40.491	41.916
13.75	31.648	36.731	40.339	41.470	42.898
14.00	32.507	37.653	41.286	42.420	43.850
14.25	33.350	38.552	42.206	43.343	44.774
14.50	34.176	39.430	43.101	44.239	45.670
14.75	34.986	40.286	43.972	45.111	46.540
15.00	35.779	41.122	44.819	45.958	47.384
15.25	36.557	41.938	45.643	46.781	48.204
15.50	37.320	42.735	46.446	47.582	49.000
15.75	38.068	43.513	47.227	48.362	49.774
16.00	38.801	44.274	47.989	49.120	50.526
16.25	39.520	45.016	48.730	49.858	51.258
16.50	40.226	45.742	49.452	50.576	51.969
16.75	40.918	46.451	50.157	51.276	52.661
17.00	41.597	47.144	50.843	51.957	53.334
17.25	42.263	47.821	51.512	52.621	53.990
17.50	42.916	48.483	52.165	53.268	54.628
17.75	43.558	49.131	52.802	53.899	55.250
18.00	44.187	49.764	53.423	54.514	55.855

MAXIMUM PREMIUM FOR ASSUMABLE LOANS
AS PERCENTAGE OF LOAN BALANCE
FACE INTEREST RATE: 7.25%

CURRENT RATE	REMAINING TERM OF LOAN (YEARS)				
	15	20	25	27	30
9.00	9.997	12.153	13.869	14.448	15.218
9.25	11.303	13.702	15.598	16.235	17.078
9.50	12.579	15.207	17.270	17.960	18.871
9.75	13.829	16.672	18.889	19.628	20.599
10.00	15.051	18.097	20.457	21.240	22.265
10.25	16.247	19.484	21.975	22.798	23.873
10.50	17.418	20.834	23.446	24.305	25.424
10.75	18.563	22.148	24.871	25.763	26.921
11.00	19.684	23.427	26.252	27.173	28.367
11.25	20.782	24.673	27.592	28.539	29.764
11.50	21.856	25.886	28.890	29.862	31.113
11.75	22.909	27.067	30.150	31.142	32.418
12.00	23.939	28.218	31.372	32.383	33.680
12.25	24.947	29.340	32.558	33.586	34.900
12.50	25.935	30.433	33.709	34.751	36.081
12.75	26.903	31.499	34.826	35.881	37.224
13.00	27.850	32.537	35.912	36.978	38.331
13.25	28.779	33.550	36.966	38.041	39.404
13.50	29.688	34.537	37.991	39.074	40.443
13.75	30.580	35.501	38.986	40.076	41.450
14.00	31.453	36.440	39.954	41.048	42.426
14.25	32.309	37.357	40.895	41.993	43.373
14.50	33.148	38.252	41.811	42.911	44.292
14.75	33.970	39.125	42.701	43.804	45.184
15.00	34.776	39.977	43.567	44.671	46.049
15.25	35.566	40.809	44.410	45.514	46.890
15.50	36.341	41.621	45.231	46.334	47.706
15.75	37.101	42.415	46.030	47.132	48.500
16.00	37.845	43.190	46.809	47.908	49.271
16.25	38.576	43.947	47.567	48.664	50.021
16.50	39.292	44.686	48.306	49.399	50.751
16.75	39.995	45.409	49.026	50.116	51.460
17.00	40.685	46.115	49.728	50.813	52.151
17.25	41.361	46.806	50.412	51.493	52.823
17.50	42.025	47.481	51.080	52.156	53.477
17.75	42.676	48.141	51.731	52.801	54.114
18.00	43.315	48.787	52.366	53.431	54.735

MAXIMUM PREMIUM FOR ASSUMABLE LOANS
AS PERCENTAGE OF LOAN BALANCE
FACE INTEREST RATE: 7.5%

CURRENT RATE	REMAINING TERM OF LOAN (YEARS)				
	15	20	25	27	30
9.00	8.603	10.462	11.941	12.439	13.100
9.25	9.929	12.041	13.708	14.268	15.007
9.50	11.225	13.575	15.418	16.034	16.845
9.75	12.494	15.068	17.074	17.741	18.616
10.00	13.735	16.521	18.676	19.390	20.324
10.25	14.949	17.934	20.228	20.985	21.972
10.50	16.138	19.310	21.732	22.527	23.562
10.75	17.301	20.649	23.189	24.019	25.096
11.00	18.440	21.953	24.602	25.463	26.578
11.25	19.555	23.223	25.971	26.861	28.010
11.50	20.646	24.459	27.298	28.214	29.393
11.75	21.714	25.664	28.586	29.525	30.731
12.00	22.760	26.837	29.835	30.795	32.024
12.25	23.784	27.980	31.048	32.026	33.275
12.50	24.788	29.094	32.225	33.219	34.485
12.75	25.770	30.180	33.367	34.376	35.657
13.00	26.733	31.239	34.477	35.498	36.791
13.25	27.676	32.271	35.555	36.586	37.890
13.50	28.599	33.277	36.602	37.643	38.955
13.75	29.504	34.259	37.620	38.668	39.988
14.00	30.391	35.217	38.610	39.664	40.988
14.25	31.260	36.151	39.572	40.631	41.959
14.50	32.112	37.063	40.508	41.571	42.901
14.75	32.947	37.953	41.418	42.484	43.815
15.00	33.765	38.822	42.304	43.371	44.702
15.25	34.568	39.670	43.166	44.234	45.564
15.50	35.355	40.498	44.005	45.074	46.401
15.75	36.126	41.306	44.822	45.890	47.214
16.00	36.882	42.096	45.618	46.685	48.005
16.25	37.624	42.868	46.393	47.458	48.773
16.50	38.352	43.622	47.149	48.211	49.521
16.75	39.066	44.358	47.885	48.944	50.248
17.00	39.766	45.078	48.603	49.658	50.956
17.25	40.453	45.782	49.302	50.354	51.645
17.50	41.127	46.470	49.985	51.032	52.315
17.75	41.788	47.143	50.650	51.693	52.969
18.00	42.437	47.801	51.300	52.337	53.605

MAXIMUM PREMIUM FOR ASSUMABLE LOANS
AS PERCENTAGE OF LOAN BALANCE
FACE INTEREST RATE: 7.75%

CURRENT RATE	REMAINING TERM OF LOAN (YEARS)				
	15	20	25	27	30
9.00	7.196	8.755	9.993	10.411	10.963
9.25	8.542	10.364	11.800	12.281	12.917
9.50	9.858	11.927	13.548	14.088	14.799
9.75	11.147	13.449	15.240	15.835	16.614
10.00	12.407	14.929	16.878	17.522	18.364
10.25	13.640	16.370	18.465	19.154	20.052
10.50	14.847	17.772	20.002	20.732	21.681
10.75	16.028	19.136	21.491	22.259	23.254
11.00	17.184	20.465	22.934	23.736	24.772
11.25	18.316	21.759	24.334	25.166	26.239
11.50	19.424	23.019	25.691	26.551	27.656
11.75	20.509	24.246	27.007	27.892	29.027
12.00	21.571	25.442	28.284	29.192	30.351
12.25	22.611	26.607	29.523	30.451	31.633
12.50	23.630	27.742	30.726	31.672	32.873
12.75	24.628	28.849	31.894	32.855	34.074
13.00	25.605	29.928	33.028	34.003	35.236
13.25	26.562	30.979	34.130	35.117	36.363
13.50	27.500	32.005	35.201	36.198	37.454
13.75	28.419	33.006	36.241	37.247	38.511
14.00	29.320	33.982	37.252	38.266	39.537
14.25	30.202	34.934	38.236	39.256	40.531
14.50	31.067	35.863	39.192	40.217	41.496
14.75	31.915	36.770	40.123	41.151	42.432
15.00	32.746	37.655	41.028	42.059	43.342
15.25	33.561	38.519	41.909	42.942	44.224
15.50	34.359	39.363	42.767	43.801	45.082
15.75	35.143	40.187	43.602	44.637	45.915
16.00	35.911	40.992	44.416	45.449	46.725
16.25	36.664	41.778	45.208	46.241	47.513
16.50	37.403	42.547	45.980	47.011	48.279
16.75	38.128	43.297	46.733	47.761	49.024
17.00	38.838	44.031	47.466	48.492	49.749
17.25	39.536	44.748	48.181	49.204	50.455
17.50	40.220	45.450	48.879	49.897	51.142
17.75	40.892	46.135	49.559	50.574	51.812
18.00	41.551	46.806	50.223	51.233	52.464

594

MAXIMUM PREMIUM FOR ASSUMABLE LOANS
AS PERCENTAGE OF LOAN BALANCE
FACE INTEREST RATE: 8%

CURRENT RATE	REMAINING TERM OF LOAN (YEARS)				
	15	20	25	27	30
9.00	5.779	7.034	8.029	8.364	8.806
9.25	7.146	8.673	9.875	10.277	10.808
9.50	8.482	10.266	11.661	12.126	12.736
9.75	9.790	11.816	13.390	13.912	14.595
10.00	11.070	13.324	15.064	15.638	16.387
10.25	12.321	14.792	16.685	17.307	18.116
10.50	13.547	16.220	18.256	18.921	19.784
10.75	14.746	17.611	19.777	20.483	21.395
11.00	15.920	18.964	21.252	21.994	22.950
11.25	17.069	20.283	22.682	23.457	24.452
11.50	18.194	21.566	24.069	24.873	25.904
11.75	19.295	22.817	25.414	26.245	27.308
12.00	20.374	24.035	26.719	27.574	28.665
12.25	21.430	25.222	27.985	28.862	29.977
12.50	22.464	26.379	29.214	30.111	31.248
12.75	23.477	27.506	30.408	31.321	32.477
13.00	24.469	28.606	31.567	32.495	33.668
13.25	25.441	29.677	32.692	33.635	34.821
13.50	26.393	30.722	33.786	34.740	35.939
13.75	27.326	31.742	34.850	35.814	37.022
14.00	28.240	32.736	35.883	36.856	38.072
14.25	29.136	33.706	36.888	37.868	39.091
14.50	30.015	34.653	37.865	38.851	40.079
14.75	30.875	35.577	38.816	39.807	41.038
15.00	31.719	36.479	39.741	40.736	41.969
15.25	32.546	37.359	40.641	41.639	42.874
15.50	33.357	38.219	41.518	42.517	43.752
15.75	34.152	39.059	42.371	43.372	44.606
16.00	34.932	39.879	43.202	44.203	45.435
16.25	35.697	40.680	44.012	45.012	46.242
16.50	36.447	41.463	44.801	45.800	47.026
16.75	37.183	42.228	45.570	46.568	47.789
17.00	37.904	42.975	46.320	47.315	48.532
17.25	38.613	43.706	47.050	48.043	49.255
17.50	39.307	44.420	47.763	48.753	49.959
17.75	39.989	45.119	48.458	49.444	50.644
18.00	40.658	45.802	49.137	50.119	51.312

MAXIMUM PREMIUM FOR ASSUMABLE LOANS
AS PERCENTAGE OF LOAN BALANCE
FACE INTEREST RATE: 8.25%

CURRENT RATE	REMAINING TERM OF LOAN (YEARS)				
	15	20	25	27	30
9.00	4.350	5.297	6.047	6.299	6.631
9.25	5.738	6.966	7.933	8.256	8.680
9.50	7.095	8.589	9.757	10.145	10.654
9.75	8.423	10.169	11.523	11.972	12.558
10.00	9.721	11.705	13.233	13.737	14.393
10.25	10.992	13.200	14.889	15.443	16.163
10.50	12.236	14.655	16.494	17.094	17.871
10.75	13.454	16.072	18.048	18.691	19.520
11.00	14.645	17.451	19.555	20.236	21.112
11.25	15.812	18.794	21.016	21.732	22.650
11.50	16.954	20.101	22.433	23.180	24.137
11.75	18.072	21.375	23.807	24.583	25.574
12.00	19.166	22.616	25.139	25.942	26.963
12.25	20.238	23.825	26.433	27.259	28.307
12.50	21.288	25.004	27.689	28.536	29.608
12.75	22.317	26.152	28.908	29.774	30.867
13.00	23.324	27.272	30.092	30.974	32.086
13.25	24.311	28.364	31.242	32.139	33.267
13.50	25.277	29.428	32.359	33.270	34.411
13.75	26.225	30.467	33.445	34.367	35.520
14.00	27.153	31.480	34.501	35.433	36.595
14.25	28.062	32.468	35.528	36.468	37.638
14.50	28.954	33.432	36.526	37.473	38.650
14.75	29.827	34.374	37.497	38.450	39.632
15.00	30.684	35.292	38.442	39.400	40.585
15.25	31.524	36.189	39.362	40.324	41.511
15.50	32.347	37.065	40.257	41.222	42.410
15.75	33.154	37.920	41.129	42.096	43.284
16.00	33.946	38.756	41.978	42.946	44.134
16.25	34.722	39.572	42.806	43.773	44.960
16.50	35.484	40.369	43.611	44.579	45.763
16.75	36.230	41.148	44.397	45.364	46.544
17.00	36.963	41.910	45.163	46.128	47.305
17.25	37.682	42.654	45.909	46.872	48.045
17.50	38.387	43.382	46.637	47.598	48.765
17.75	39.080	44.094	47.348	48.305	49.467
18.00	39.759	44.790	48.040	48.995	50.151

MAXIMUM PREMIUM FOR ASSUMABLE LOANS
AS PERCENTAGE OF LOAN BALANCE
FACE INTEREST RATE: 8.5%

CURRENT RATE	REMAINING TERM OF LOAN (YEARS)				
	15	20	25	27	30
9.00	2.910	3.545	4.047	4.216	4.438
9.25	4.319	5.246	5.973	6.216	6.535
9.50	5.696	6.899	7.836	8.148	8.555
9.75	7.044	8.507	9.640	10.015	10.503
10.00	8.363	10.072	11.387	11.819	12.382
10.25	9.652	11.595	13.078	13.564	14.193
10.50	10.915	13.077	14.717	15.251	15.942
10.75	12.151	14.519	16.305	16.883	17.629
11.00	13.360	15.924	17.843	18.463	19.259
11.25	14.545	17.291	19.335	19.992	20.833
11.50	15.704	18.623	20.782	21.473	22.355
11.75	16.839	19.921	22.185	22.907	23.825
12.00	17.950	21.185	23.546	24.296	25.247
12.25	19.038	22.416	24.867	25.642	26.623
12.50	20.104	23.616	26.150	26.947	27.954
12.75	21.147	24.786	27.395	28.212	29.243
13.00	22.170	25.927	28.604	29.440	30.490
13.25	23.171	27.039	29.779	30.631	31.699
13.50	24.152	28.123	30.920	31.786	32.870
13.75	25.114	29.181	32.029	32.908	34.005
14.00	26.056	30.212	33.107	33.997	35.106
14.25	26.979	31.219	34.156	35.055	36.173
14.50	27.884	32.201	35.175	36.083	37.209
14.75	28.771	33.160	36.167	37.082	38.214
15.00	29.640	34.095	37.132	38.053	39.190
15.25	30.493	35.009	38.072	38.997	40.137
15.50	31.328	35.901	38.986	39.915	41.058
15.75	32.148	36.772	39.876	40.808	41.952
16.00	32.952	37.623	40.744	41.678	42.821
16.25	33.739	38.454	41.588	42.523	43.667
16.50	34.512	39.266	42.411	43.347	44.489
16.75	35.271	40.060	43.214	44.149	45.288
17.00	36.014	40.835	43.996	44.930	46.067
17.25	36.744	41.594	44.758	45.691	46.824
17.50	37.460	42.335	45.502	46.433	47.562
17.75	38.163	43.060	46.227	47.156	48.280
18.00	38.852	43.769	46.935	47.861	48.980

MAXIMUM PREMIUM FOR ASSUMABLE LOANS
AS PERCENTAGE OF LOAN BALANCE
FACE INTEREST RATE: 8.75%

CURRENT RATE	REMAINING TERM OF LOAN (YEARS)				
	15	20	25	27	30
9.00	1.461	1.780	2.032	2.116	2.227
9.25	2.890	3.511	3.998	4.160	4.373
9.50	4.288	5.194	5.900	6.134	6.440
9.75	5.656	6.833	7.742	8.042	8.433
10.00	6.994	8.426	9.525	9.886	10.355
10.25	8.303	9.976	11.252	11.669	12.209
10.50	9.585	11.486	12.925	13.393	13.997
10.75	10.839	12.955	14.546	15.061	15.724
11.00	12.066	14.385	16.117	16.676	17.391
11.25	13.268	15.778	17.641	18.238	19.002
11.50	14.445	17.134	19.118	19.751	20.559
11.75	15.597	18.455	20.550	21.217	22.063
12.00	16.724	19.742	21.940	22.636	23.518
12.25	17.829	20.996	23.289	24.012	24.926
12.50	18.910	22.218	24.599	25.346	26.288
12.75	19.970	23.409	25.870	26.639	27.606
13.00	21.007	24.571	27.104	27.893	28.883
13.25	22.024	25.703	28.304	29.110	30.119
13.50	23.020	26.807	29.469	30.291	31.317
13.75	23.996	27.884	30.601	31.438	32.479
14.00	24.952	28.935	31.702	32.551	33.605
14.25	25.889	29.960	32.773	33.632	34.697
14.50	26.807	30.960	33.814	34.682	35.756
14.75	27.707	31.936	34.826	35.703	36.785
15.00	28.590	32.889	35.812	36.695	37.783
15.25	29.455	33.819	36.771	37.660	38.752
15.50	30.303	34.728	37.704	38.598	39.694
15.75	31.135	35.615	38.613	39.511	40.609
16.00	31.950	36.481	39.499	40.399	41.499
16.25	32.750	37.328	40.361	41.264	42.364
16.50	33.534	38.155	41.202	42.105	43.205
16.75	34.304	38.963	42.021	42.925	44.023
17.00	35.059	39.752	42.819	43.723	44.819
17.25	35.799	40.525	43.598	44.501	45.594
17.50	36.526	41.279	44.357	45.259	46.349
17.75	37.239	42.018	45.097	45.998	47.084
18.00	37.939	42.739	45.820	46.718	47.800

MAXIMUM PREMIUM FOR ASSUMABLE LOANS
AS PERCENTAGE OF LOAN BALANCE
FACE INTEREST RATE: 9%

CURRENT RATE	\multicolumn REMAINING TERM OF LOAN (YEARS)				
	15	20	25	27	30
9.00	0.000	0.000	0.000	0.000	0.000
9.25	1.451	1.763	2.007	2.088	2.195
9.50	2.869	3.477	3.949	4.105	4.309
9.75	4.258	5.144	5.829	6.054	6.347
10.00	5.616	6.767	7.649	7.938	8.313
10.25	6.944	8.345	9.412	9.759	10.209
10.50	8.245	9.882	11.120	11.521	12.038
10.75	9.518	11.377	12.774	13.225	13.804
11.00	10.763	12.833	14.378	14.874	15.510
11.25	11.983	14.251	15.933	16.471	17.157
11.50	13.177	15.632	17.440	18.016	18.749
11.75	14.346	16.978	18.903	19.513	20.288
12.00	15.490	18.288	20.321	20.964	21.776
12.25	16.611	19.565	21.698	22.369	23.216
12.50	17.709	20.809	23.035	23.732	24.609
12.75	18.783	22.022	24.332	25.053	25.957
13.00	19.836	23.204	25.592	26.334	27.263
13.25	20.868	24.357	26.817	27.577	28.527
13.50	21.879	25.481	28.006	28.784	29.753
13.75	22.869	26.578	29.162	29.955	30.941
14.00	23.839	27.647	30.286	31.092	32.092
14.25	24.790	28.691	31.378	32.197	33.209
14.50	25.722	29.709	32.441	33.270	34.293
14.75	26.636	30.703	33.475	34.313	35.345
15.00	27.531	31.673	34.480	35.327	36.366
15.25	28.409	32.620	35.459	36.312	37.357
15.50	29.270	33.545	36.412	37.271	38.320
15.75	30.114	34.448	37.340	38.203	39.256
16.00	30.942	35.330	38.244	39.111	40.166
16.25	31.753	36.192	39.124	39.994	41.051
16.50	32.549	37.034	39.982	40.854	41.911
16.75	33.330	37.857	40.818	41.691	42.748
17.00	34.096	38.661	41.633	42.506	43.562
17.25	34.848	39.447	42.428	43.301	44.355
17.50	35.585	40.215	43.203	44.075	45.127
17.75	36.309	40.967	43.959	44.830	45.878
18.00	37.019	41.702	44.696	45.566	46.611

MAXIMUM PREMIUM FOR ASSUMABLE LOANS
AS PERCENTAGE OF LOAN BALANCE
FACE INTEREST RATE: 9.25%

CURRENT RATE	REMAINING TERM OF LOAN (YEARS)				
	15	20	25	27	30
9.00	-1.472	-1.795	-2.048	-2.133	-2.244
9.25	0.000	0.000	0.000	0.000	0.000
9.50	1.439	1.744	1.981	2.060	2.162
9.75	2.848	3.442	3.900	4.051	4.246
10.00	4.226	5.094	5.757	5.975	6.255
10.25	5.574	6.700	7.556	7.835	8.194
10.50	6.894	8.265	9.299	9.634	10.064
10.75	8.185	9.787	10.987	11.374	11.870
11.00	9.449	11.269	12.624	13.059	13.614
11.25	10.687	12.713	14.211	14.689	15.298
11.50	11.898	14.118	15.749	16.268	16.926
11.75	13.085	15.488	17.242	17.797	18.499
12.00	14.246	16.821	18.689	19.278	20.021
12.25	15.383	18.121	20.094	20.713	21.493
12.50	16.497	19.388	21.458	22.105	22.917
12.75	17.588	20.622	22.782	23.454	24.295
13.00	18.656	21.826	24.068	24.763	25.630
13.25	19.703	22.999	25.318	26.033	26.923
13.50	20.728	24.144	26.531	27.265	28.176
13.75	21.734	25.260	27.711	28.461	29.391
14.00	22.718	26.349	28.858	29.623	30.568
14.25	23.683	27.411	29.973	30.751	31.710
14.50	24.629	28.448	31.057	31.847	32.818
14.75	25.556	29.459	32.112	32.912	33.894
15.00	26.464	30.447	33.138	33.947	34.938
15.25	27.355	31.411	34.137	34.954	35.951
15.50	28.228	32.352	35.110	35.933	36.936
15.75	29.085	33.272	36.057	36.885	37.893
16.00	29.925	34.170	36.979	37.812	38.823
16.25	30.748	35.047	37.878	38.714	39.728
16.50	31.556	35.904	38.753	39.592	40.607
16.75	32.349	36.742	39.606	40.447	41.463
17.00	33.126	37.560	40.438	41.280	42.296
17.25	33.889	38.360	41.249	42.092	43.106
17.50	34.637	39.143	42.040	42.882	43.895
17.75	35.371	39.908	42.811	43.653	44.664
18.00	36.092	40.656	43.564	44.405	45.413

MAXIMUM PREMIUM FOR ASSUMABLE LOANS
AS PERCENTAGE OF LOAN BALANCE
FACE INTEREST RATE: 9.5%

CURRENT RATE	REMAINING TERM OF LOAN (YEARS)				
	15	20	25	27	30
9.00	−2.954	−3.602	−4.111	−4.281	−4.503
9.25	−1.460	−1.775	−2.022	−2.103	−2.209
9.50	0.000	0.000	0.000	0.000	0.000
9.75	1.429	1.728	1.957	2.033	2.130
10.00	2.828	3.409	3.852	3.997	4.184
10.25	4.195	5.044	5.687	5.896	6.165
10.50	5.535	6.636	7.465	7.733	8.077
10.75	6.845	8.185	9.188	9.510	9.923
11.00	8.127	9.694	10.858	11.230	11.705
11.25	9.383	11.163	12.476	12.895	13.427
11.50	10.612	12.593	14.046	14.507	15.090
11.75	11.816	13.987	15.569	16.068	16.699
12.00	12.994	15.345	17.046	17.580	18.254
12.25	14.148	16.667	18.479	19.046	19.758
12.50	15.278	17.957	19.871	20.467	21.214
12.75	16.384	19.213	21.221	21.844	22.623
13.00	17.469	20.438	22.533	23.181	23.987
13.25	18.531	21.632	23.808	24.477	25.309
13.50	19.571	22.797	25.046	25.735	26.589
13.75	20.591	23.933	26.250	26.957	27.831
14.00	21.590	25.041	27.420	28.143	29.034
14.25	22.569	26.122	28.557	29.294	30.202
14.50	23.528	27.177	29.663	30.413	31.334
14.75	24.469	28.207	30.740	31.501	32.433
15.00	25.391	29.212	31.787	32.558	33.500
15.25	26.295	30.193	32.806	33.586	34.536
15.50	27.181	31.151	33.798	34.585	35.543
15.75	28.050	32.087	34.764	35.558	36.521
16.00	28.902	33.001	35.705	36.504	37.472
16.25	29.737	33.894	36.622	37.425	38.396
16.50	30.557	34.766	37.515	38.322	39.295
16.75	31.361	35.618	38.385	39.195	40.170
17.00	32.149	36.451	39.234	40.045	41.021
17.25	32.923	37.266	40.061	40.874	41.849
17.50	33.682	38.062	40.868	41.681	42.656
17.75	34.427	38.841	41.655	42.468	43.441
18.00	35.158	39.602	42.423	43.236	44.207

MAXIMUM PREMIUM FOR ASSUMABLE LOANS
AS PERCENTAGE OF LOAN BALANCE
FACE INTEREST RATE: 9.75%

CURRENT RATE	REMAINING TERM OF LOAN (YEARS)				
	15	20	25	27	30
9.00	− 4.447	− 5.423	− 6.190	− 6.445	− 6.778
9.25	− 2.931	− 3.565	− 4.058	− 4.222	− 4.434
9.50	− 1.450	− 1.758	− 1.996	− 2.075	− 2.177
9.75	0.000	0.000	0.000	0.000	0.000
10.00	1.418	1.710	1.933	2.005	2.099
10.25	2.806	3.374	3.805	3.944	4.123
10.50	4.165	4.994	5.618	5.819	6.077
10.75	5.494	6.571	7.375	7.633	7.962
11.00	6.795	8.106	9.078	9.388	9.783
11.25	8.069	9.601	10.729	11.088	11.542
11.50	9.316	11.057	12.330	12.733	13.242
11.75	10.537	12.475	13.883	14.326	14.885
12.00	11.732	13.856	15.389	15.870	16.474
12.25	12.903	15.202	16.852	17.366	18.011
12.50	14.049	16.514	18.271	18.817	19.499
12.75	15.172	17.793	19.649	20.223	20.939
13.00	16.272	19.039	20.987	21.587	22.333
13.25	17.349	20.254	22.287	22.910	23.683
13.50	18.405	21.440	23.550	24.194	24.992
13.75	19.439	22.596	24.777	25.441	26.260
14.00	20.453	23.723	25.971	26.652	27.490
14.25	21.446	24.823	27.131	27.827	28.682
14.50	22.419	25.897	28.259	28.970	29.839
14.75	23.373	26.945	29.357	30.080	30.962
15.00	24.309	27.967	30.425	31.159	32.053
15.25	25.226	28.966	31.465	32.208	33.111
15.50	26.125	29.941	32.476	33.228	34.140
15.75	27.006	30.893	33.462	34.221	35.139
16.00	27.871	31.823	34.422	35.187	36.111
16.25	28.718	32.731	35.356	36.127	37.055
16.50	29.550	33.619	36.267	37.042	37.974
16.75	30.365	34.486	37.155	37.933	38.867
17.00	31.165	35.334	38.021	38.801	39.737
17.25	31.951	36.163	38.864	39.647	40.583
17.50	32.721	36.973	39.687	40.471	41.408
17.75	33.477	37.765	40.490	41.275	42.210
18.00	34.218	38.540	41.273	42.058	42.992

MAXIMUM PREMIUM FOR ASSUMABLE LOANS
AS PERCENTAGE OF LOAN BALANCE
FACE INTEREST RATE: 10%

CURRENT RATE	REMAINING TERM OF LOAN (YEARS)				
	15	20	25	27	30
9.00	−5.950	−7.258	−8.283	−8.623	−9.067
9.25	−4.412	−5.367	−6.109	−6.354	−6.673
9.50	−2.910	−3.529	−4.007	−4.164	−4.367
9.75	−1.439	−1.740	−1.971	−2.046	−2.144
10.00	0.000	0.000	0.000	0.000	0.000
10.25	1.408	1.693	1.909	1.978	2.068
10.50	2.786	3.341	3.758	3.892	4.063
10.75	4.134	4.945	5.550	5.743	5.989
11.00	5.454	6.507	7.286	7.534	7.849
11.25	6.746	8.028	8.970	9.268	9.646
11.50	8.011	9.509	10.602	10.947	11.382
11.75	9.250	10.952	12.186	12.573	13.061
12.00	10.462	12.357	13.722	14.149	14.684
12.25	11.649	13.727	15.213	15.675	16.254
12.50	12.812	15.061	16.660	17.155	17.773
12.75	13.951	16.362	18.065	18.590	19.244
13.00	15.067	17.630	19.430	19.982	20.668
13.25	16.160	18.867	20.755	21.333	22.047
13.50	17.231	20.073	22.043	22.643	23.384
13.75	18.280	21.249	23.295	23.916	24.679
14.00	19.308	22.396	24.511	25.151	25.935
14.25	20.316	23.515	25.695	26.351	27.154
14.50	21.303	24.607	26.845	27.516	28.335
14.75	22.271	25.673	27.965	28.649	29.483
15.00	23.220	26.714	29.054	29.750	30.596
15.25	24.150	27.730	30.114	30.821	31.678
15.50	25.062	28.722	31.146	31.862	32.728
15.75	25.956	29.690	32.150	32.875	33.749
16.00	26.833	30.637	33.129	33.860	34.741
16.25	27.693	31.561	34.082	34.820	35.706
16.50	28.536	32.464	35.011	35.754	36.644
16.75	29.364	33.346	35.917	36.663	37.557
17.00	30.175	34.209	36.799	37.549	38.445
17.25	30.971	35.052	37.659	38.412	39.310
17.50	31.753	35.876	38.499	39.253	40.152
17.75	32.519	36.682	39.317	40.073	40.972
18.00	33.272	37.471	40.116	40.872	41.770

MAXIMUM PREMIUM FOR ASSUMABLE LOANS
AS PERCENTAGE OF LOAN BALANCE
FACE INTEREST RATE: 10.25%

CURRENT RATE	REMAINING TERM OF LOAN (YEARS)				
	15	20	25	27	30
9.00	−7.462	−9.105	−10.390	−10.815	−11.369
9.25	−5.903	−7.182	−8.174	−8.501	−8.925
9.50	−4.379	−5.312	−6.030	−6.266	−6.570
9.75	−2.887	−3.492	−3.955	−4.106	−4.300
10.00	−1.428	−1.722	−1.946	−2.018	−2.111
10.25	0.000	0.000	0.000	0.000	0.000
10.50	1.398	1.677	1.885	1.952	2.038
10.75	2.765	3.308	3.712	3.841	4.004
11.00	4.104	4.897	5.482	5.668	5.904
11.25	5.415	6.444	7.198	7.437	7.738
11.50	6.698	7.951	8.863	9.150	9.511
11.75	7.954	9.418	10.477	10.809	11.225
12.00	9.184	10.848	12.043	12.416	12.883
12.25	10.388	12.241	13.563	13.973	14.486
12.50	11.568	13.599	15.038	15.483	16.037
12.75	12.723	14.922	16.471	16.947	17.539
13.00	13.854	16.212	17.862	18.367	18.993
13.25	14.963	17.470	19.213	19.745	20.401
13.50	16.049	18.696	20.526	21.082	21.766
13.75	17.113	19.893	21.802	22.380	23.089
14.00	18.156	21.059	23.043	23.640	24.371
14.25	19.178	22.198	24.249	24.864	25.615
14.50	20.180	23.309	25.422	26.053	26.822
14.75	21.161	24.393	26.563	27.209	27.994
15.00	22.123	25.452	27.673	28.332	29.131
15.25	23.067	26.485	28.754	29.424	30.235
15.50	23.992	27.494	29.806	30.487	31.308
15.75	24.899	28.480	30.830	31.520	32.350
16.00	25.788	29.442	31.828	32.525	33.363
16.25	26.660	30.382	32.800	33.504	34.348
16.50	27.516	31.301	33.747	34.457	35.306
16.75	28.355	32.199	34.670	35.385	36.239
17.00	29.178	33.076	35.569	36.288	37.145
17.25	29.986	33.934	36.446	37.169	38.028
17.50	30.778	34.772	37.302	38.027	38.888
17.75	31.556	35.592	38.136	38.864	39.725
18.00	32.319	36.394	38.951	39.679	40.541

MAXIMUM PREMIUM FOR ASSUMABLE LOANS
AS PERCENTAGE OF LOAN BALANCE
FACE INTEREST RATE: 10.5%

CURRENT RATE	REMAINING TERM OF LOAN (YEARS) 15	20	25	27	30
9.00	− 8.986	− 10.965	− 12.511	− 13.021	− 13.686
9.25	− 7.404	− 9.009	− 10.252	− 10.661	− 11.191
9.50	− 5.859	− 7.108	− 8.068	− 8.382	− 8.787
9.75	− 4.346	− 5.257	− 5.952	− 6.179	− 6.470
10.00	− 2.866	− 3.457	− 3.905	− 4.049	− 4.235
10.25	− 1.418	− 1.705	− 1.921	− 1.991	− 2.080
10.50	0.000	0.000	0.000	0.000	0.000
10.75	1.387	1.660	1.862	1.926	2.008
11.00	2.745	3.275	3.666	3.790	3.946
11.25	4.074	4.849	5.415	5.594	5.819
11.50	5.375	6.381	7.112	7.341	7.629
11.75	6.649	7.874	8.757	9.033	9.379
12.00	7.896	9.328	10.353	10.672	11.071
12.25	9.118	10.744	11.902	12.261	12.707
12.50	10.314	12.125	13.406	13.801	14.291
12.75	11.486	13.471	14.866	15.294	15.824
13.00	12.633	14.783	16.284	16.742	17.308
13.25	13.758	16.062	17.661	18.147	18.746
13.50	14.859	17.310	18.999	19.511	20.139
13.75	15.938	18.527	20.300	20.835	21.489
14.00	16.996	19.713	21.564	22.120	22.798
14.25	18.032	20.871	22.793	23.368	24.068
14.50	19.048	22.001	23.989	24.581	25.300
14.75	20.044	23.104	25.152	25.760	26.496
15.00	21.019	24.181	26.284	26.905	27.657
15.25	21.976	25.232	27.385	28.019	28.784
15.50	22.914	26.258	28.457	29.103	29.879
15.75	23.834	27.260	29.501	30.156	30.943
16.00	24.736	28.239	30.518	31.182	31.977
16.25	25.621	29.195	31.509	32.180	32.983
16.50	26.488	30.129	32.474	33.152	33.961
16.75	27.339	31.042	33.414	34.098	34.912
17.00	28.174	31.935	34.331	35.020	35.838
17.25	28.993	32.807	35.225	35.918	36.739
17.50	29.797	33.660	36.097	36.793	37.617
17.75	30.586	34.494	36.948	37.646	38.471
18.00	31.360	35.309	37.778	38.478	39.304

MAXIMUM PREMIUM FOR ASSUMABLE LOANS
AS PERCENTAGE OF LOAN BALANCE
FACE INTEREST RATE: 10.75%

CURRENT RATE	REMAINING TERM OF LOAN (YEARS)				
	15	20	25	27	30
9.00	−10.519	−12.838	−14.645	−15.241	−16.015
9.25	−8.915	−10.849	−12.344	−12.834	−13.469
9.50	−7.348	−8.915	−10.118	−10.510	−11.016
9.75	−5.813	−7.033	−7.962	−8.264	−8.651
10.00	−4.312	−5.203	−5.876	−6.093	−6.371
10.25	−2.844	−3.421	−3.855	−3.994	−4.171
10.50	−1.407	−1.688	−1.897	−1.964	−2.049
10.75	0.000	0.000	0.000	0.000	0.000
11.00	1.377	1.643	1.838	1.900	1.978
11.25	2.725	3.243	3.621	3.740	3.890
11.50	4.044	4.801	5.350	5.521	5.737
11.75	5.336	6.319	7.026	7.247	7.522
12.00	6.601	7.797	8.653	8.918	9.248
12.25	7.839	9.238	10.231	10.538	10.919
12.50	9.053	10.642	11.763	12.108	12.535
12.75	10.241	12.011	13.251	13.630	14.099
13.00	11.404	13.345	14.696	15.107	15.614
13.25	12.545	14.646	16.099	16.540	17.081
13.50	13.661	15.914	17.463	17.930	18.503
13.75	14.756	17.152	18.788	19.280	19.881
14.00	15.828	18.359	20.076	20.590	21.217
14.25	16.879	19.536	21.329	21.863	22.513
14.50	17.909	20.685	22.547	23.100	23.770
14.75	18.919	21.807	23.732	24.302	24.990
15.00	19.909	22.901	24.885	25.470	26.175
15.25	20.879	23.970	26.008	26.606	27.325
15.50	21.830	25.013	27.100	27.710	28.442
15.75	22.763	26.033	28.164	28.785	29.528
16.00	23.678	27.028	29.200	29.831	30.584
16.25	24.575	28.000	30.209	30.848	31.610
16.50	25.454	28.950	31.193	31.839	32.608
16.75	26.317	29.879	32.151	32.804	33.579
17.00	27.164	30.786	33.086	33.744	34.524
17.25	27.995	31.673	33.997	34.660	35.443
17.50	28.810	32.540	34.885	35.552	36.339
17.75	29.609	33.388	35.752	36.422	37.211
18.00	30.394	34.218	36.597	37.270	38.060

MAXIMUM PREMIUM FOR ASSUMABLE LOANS
AS PERCENTAGE OF LOAN BALANCE
FACE INTEREST RATE: 11%

CURRENT RATE	REMAINING TERM OF LOAN (YEARS)				
	15	20	25	27	30
9.00	− 12.061	− 14.723	− 16.792	− 17.473	− 18.357
9.25	− 10.435	− 12.700	− 14.448	− 15.020	− 15.759
9.50	− 8.846	− 10.734	− 12.180	− 12.651	− 13.257
9.75	− 7.290	− 8.821	− 9.984	− 10.361	− 10.844
10.00	− 5.768	− 6.960	− 7.859	− 8.148	− 8.518
10.25	− 4.280	− 5.149	− 5.800	− 6.008	− 6.274
10.50	− 2.822	− 3.386	− 3.805	− 3.939	− 4.109
10.75	− 1.396	− 1.670	− 1.873	− 1.937	− 2.018
11.00	0.000	0.000	0.000	0.000	0.000
11.25	1.367	1.627	1.816	1.875	1.950
11.50	2.705	3.211	3.577	3.691	3.834
11.75	4.015	4.754	5.285	5.450	5.656
12.00	5.297	6.257	6.942	7.153	7.417
12.25	6.553	7.722	8.550	8.805	9.121
12.50	7.783	9.150	10.111	10.405	10.769
12.75	8.988	10.541	11.626	11.957	12.365
13.00	10.168	11.897	13.098	13.462	13.910
13.25	11.324	13.220	14.528	14.923	15.407
13.50	12.456	14.510	15.917	16.340	16.858
13.75	13.566	15.768	17.267	17.716	18.263
14.00	14.654	16.995	18.579	19.052	19.627
14.25	15.719	18.192	19.855	20.350	20.949
14.50	16.764	19.360	21.096	21.610	22.231
14.75	17.787	20.500	22.304	22.835	23.476
15.00	18.791	21.613	23.478	24.026	24.684
15.25	19.774	22.700	24.622	25.184	25.858
15.50	20.739	23.761	25.735	26.310	26.998
15.75	21.685	24.797	26.819	27.405	28.106
16.00	22.612	25.809	27.874	28.471	29.183
16.25	23.522	26.798	28.902	29.509	30.229
16.50	24.414	27.764	29.904	30.519	31.248
16.75	25.289	28.707	30.881	31.502	32.238
17.00	26.147	29.630	31.832	32.460	33.202
17.25	26.990	30.532	32.760	33.394	34.140
17.50	27.816	31.413	33.665	34.303	35.054
17.75	28.627	32.276	34.548	35.190	35.944
18.00	29.423	33.119	35.410	36.055	36.810

MAXIMUM PREMIUM FOR ASSUMABLE LOANS
AS PERCENTAGE OF LOAN BALANCE
FACE INTEREST RATE: 11.25%

CURRENT RATE	REMAINING TERM OF LOAN (YEARS)				
	15	20	25	27	30
9.00	− 13.614	− 16.620	− 18.952	− 19.718	− 20.710
9.25	− 11.966	− 14.564	− 16.565	− 17.218	− 18.061
9.50	− 10.355	− 12.566	− 14.255	− 14.804	− 15.509
9.75	− 8.777	− 10.621	− 12.019	− 12.470	− 13.048
10.00	− 7.234	− 8.729	− 9.853	− 10.215	− 10.676
10.25	− 5.725	− 6.888	− 7.757	− 8.035	− 8.388
10.50	− 4.247	− 5.096	− 5.725	− 5.926	− 6.179
10.75	− 2.801	− 3.352	− 3.757	− 3.885	− 4.047
11.00	− 1.386	− 1.654	− 1.850	− 1.911	− 1.989
11.25	0.000	0.000	0.000	0.000	0.000
11.50	1.356	1.610	1.793	1.850	1.922
11.75	2.685	3.179	3.533	3.643	3.779
12.00	3.985	4.707	5.221	5.379	5.576
12.25	5.258	6.196	6.858	7.062	7.313
12.50	6.505	7.647	8.448	8.693	8.995
12.75	7.726	9.062	9.992	10.274	10.622
13.00	8.923	10.440	11.491	11.809	12.198
13.25	10.095	11.785	12.947	13.297	13.725
13.50	11.243	13.096	14.361	14.741	15.204
13.75	12.368	14.375	15.737	16.144	16.638
14.00	13.471	15.622	17.073	17.505	18.028
14.25	14.551	16.839	18.373	18.827	19.376
14.50	15.610	18.027	19.637	20.112	20.685
14.75	16.648	19.186	20.867	21.360	21.954
15.00	17.665	20.317	22.063	22.574	23.187
15.25	18.663	21.422	23.228	23.754	24.384
15.50	19.640	22.500	24.361	24.901	25.546
15.75	20.600	23.553	25.465	26.018	26.676
16.00	21.540	24.582	26.540	27.104	27.774
16.25	22.462	25.587	27.587	28.161	28.842
16.50	23.366	26.569	28.608	29.191	29.880
16.75	24.254	27.528	29.602	30.193	30.890
17.00	25.124	28.466	30.572	31.170	31.874
17.25	25.978	29.383	31.517	32.121	32.830
17.50	26.816	30.279	32.439	33.048	33.762
17.75	27.638	31.156	33.338	33.952	34.670
18.00	28.444	32.013	34.215	34.833	35.554

MAXIMUM PREMIUM FOR ASSUMABLE LOANS
AS PERCENTAGE OF LOAN BALANCE
FACE INTEREST RATE: 11.5%

CURRENT RATE	REMAINING TERM OF LOAN (YEARS)				
	15	20	25	27	30
9.00	− 15.176	− 18.529	− 21.124	− 21.975	− 23.076
9.25	− 13.505	− 16.439	− 18.693	− 19.428	− 20.374
9.50	− 11.872	− 14.408	− 16.341	− 16.968	− 17.772
9.75	− 10.273	− 12.431	− 14.064	− 14.591	− 15.263
10.00	− 8.709	− 10.508	− 11.860	− 12.293	− 12.844
10.25	− 7.178	− 8.637	− 9.725	− 10.071	− 10.511
10.50	− 5.680	− 6.816	− 7.656	− 7.922	− 8.259
10.75	− 4.214	− 5.043	− 5.652	− 5.844	− 6.086
11.00	− 2.780	− 3.317	− 3.709	− 3.833	− 3.987
11.25	− 1.375	− 1.637	− 1.826	− 1.885	− 1.959
11.50	0.000	0.000	0.000	0.000	0.000
11.75	1.347	1.595	1.771	1.826	1.894
12.00	2.664	3.147	3.490	3.595	3.726
12.25	3.955	4.661	5.157	5.310	5.497
12.50	5.220	6.136	6.776	6.971	7.212
12.75	6.458	7.573	8.348	8.583	8.871
13.00	7.671	8.975	9.874	10.146	10.478
13.25	8.859	10.341	11.357	11.662	12.035
13.50	10.023	11.674	12.798	13.134	13.543
13.75	11.164	12.973	14.198	14.563	15.005
14.00	12.281	14.241	15.559	15.950	16.422
14.25	13.376	15.478	16.882	17.297	17.797
14.50	14.450	16.685	18.169	18.606	19.131
14.75	15.502	17.863	19.422	19.878	20.425
15.00	16.533	19.013	20.640	21.114	21.682
15.25	17.544	20.135	21.826	22.317	22.902
15.50	18.536	21.232	22.980	23.486	24.087
15.75	19.508	22.302	24.104	24.623	25.239
16.00	20.461	23.348	25.199	25.730	26.359
16.25	21.396	24.369	26.265	26.807	27.448
16.50	22.313	25.367	27.304	27.856	28.506
16.75	23.212	26.342	28.317	28.877	29.536
17.00	24.094	27.295	29.304	29.872	30.539
17.25	24.960	28.227	30.266	30.841	31.514
17.50	25.809	29.138	31.205	31.786	32.464
17.75	26.643	30.029	32.120	32.706	33.390
18.00	27.461	30.900	33.014	33.604	34.291

MAXIMUM PREMIUM FOR ASSUMABLE LOANS
AS PERCENTAGE OF LOAN BALANCE
FACE INTEREST RATE: 11.75%

CURRENT RATE	REMAINING TERM OF LOAN (YEARS)				
	15	20	25	27	30
9.00	− 16.749	− 20.449	− 23.309	− 24.244	− 25.452
9.25	− 15.054	− 18.326	− 20.834	− 21.650	− 22.698
9.50	− 13.399	− 16.262	− 18.439	− 19.144	− 20.046
9.75	− 11.778	− 14.253	− 16.121	− 16.722	− 17.489
10.00	− 10.192	− 12.299	− 13.877	− 14.382	− 15.023
10.25	− 8.641	− 10.398	− 11.703	− 12.119	− 12.645
10.50	− 7.123	− 8.547	− 9.597	− 9.930	− 10.349
10.75	− 5.637	− 6.745	− 7.557	− 7.813	− 8.134
11.00	− 4.183	− 4.992	− 5.580	− 5.764	− 5.995
11.25	− 2.759	− 3.284	− 3.662	− 3.780	− 3.928
11.50	− 1.365	− 1.620	− 1.803	− 1.860	− 1.931
11.75	0.000	0.000	0.000	0.000	0.000
12.00	1.336	1.578	1.749	1.802	1.867
12.25	2.644	3.116	3.447	3.548	3.673
12.50	3.926	4.615	5.095	5.241	5.420
12.75	5.181	6.076	6.695	6.882	7.112
13.00	6.410	7.500	8.249	8.475	8.750
13.25	7.615	8.888	9.758	10.019	10.336
13.50	8.795	10.242	11.225	11.518	11.874
13.75	9.951	11.563	12.651	12.973	13.364
14.00	11.084	12.852	14.036	14.386	14.808
14.25	12.194	14.108	15.383	15.759	16.210
14.50	13.282	15.335	16.694	17.092	17.569
14.75	14.349	16.532	17.968	18.388	18.889
15.00	15.394	17.701	19.209	19.647	20.170
15.25	16.419	18.841	20.416	20.872	21.414
15.50	17.424	19.955	21.591	22.062	22.622
15.75	18.409	21.043	22.735	23.221	23.796
16.00	19.375	22.106	23.850	24.348	24.937
16.25	20.323	23.144	24.935	25.446	26.047
16.50	21.252	24.158	25.993	26.514	27.126
16.75	22.164	25.149	27.024	27.554	28.176
17.00	23.058	26.117	28.029	28.567	29.198
17.25	23.936	27.064	29.009	29.555	30.192
17.50	24.797	27.990	29.964	30.517	31.161
17.75	25.642	28.895	30.896	31.455	32.104
18.00	26.470	29.780	31.806	32.369	33.022

MAXIMUM PREMIUM FOR ASSUMABLE LOANS
AS PERCENTAGE OF LOAN BALANCE
FACE INTEREST RATE: 12%

CURRENT RATE	REMAINING TERM OF LOAN (YEARS)				
	15	20	25	27	30
9.00	− 18.329	− 22.381	− 25.504	− 26.524	− 27.838
9.25	− 16.612	− 20.223	− 22.985	− 23.882	− 25.032
9.50	− 14.934	− 18.126	− 20.548	− 21.330	− 22.330
9.75	− 13.291	− 16.085	− 18.189	− 18.864	− 19.724
10.00	− 11.684	− 14.099	− 15.904	− 16.480	− 17.211
10.25	− 10.112	− 12.168	− 13.692	− 14.176	− 14.788
10.50	− 8.573	− 10.287	− 11.549	− 11.947	− 12.449
10.75	− 7.067	− 8.457	− 9.472	− 9.791	− 10.191
11.00	− 5.593	− 6.675	− 7.460	− 7.705	− 8.011
11.25	− 4.150	− 4.940	− 5.508	− 5.685	− 5.905
11.50	− 2.737	− 3.250	− 3.616	− 3.729	− 3.870
11.75	− 1.354	− 1.603	− 1.780	− 1.835	− 1.902
12.00	0.000	0.000	0.000	0.000	0.000
12.25	1.326	1.563	1.728	1.778	1.840
12.50	2.625	3.085	3.405	3.502	3.621
12.75	3.897	4.570	5.034	5.174	5.345
13.00	5.143	6.017	6.615	6.795	7.014
13.25	6.364	7.427	8.152	8.368	8.631
13.50	7.560	8.803	9.644	9.895	10.197
13.75	8.732	10.145	11.095	11.377	11.716
14.00	9.880	11.454	12.506	12.815	13.188
14.25	11.005	12.731	13.877	14.213	14.616
14.50	12.108	13.978	15.210	15.571	16.001
14.75	13.189	15.194	16.508	16.890	17.346
15.00	14.248	16.381	17.770	18.173	18.651
15.25	15.287	17.540	18.999	19.420	19.919
15.50	16.306	18.672	20.195	20.632	21.150
15.75	17.304	19.777	21.360	21.812	22.346
16.00	18.284	20.857	22.494	22.960	23.509
16.25	19.244	21.911	23.599	24.078	24.640
16.50	20.186	22.942	24.675	25.166	25.740
16.75	21.110	23.949	25.725	26.225	26.810
17.00	22.016	24.933	26.747	27.257	27.851
17.25	22.906	25.895	27.745	28.262	28.864
17.50	23.778	26.835	28.717	29.242	29.851
17.75	24.635	27.755	29.666	30.197	30.812
18.00	25.475	28.654	30.592	31.128	31.748

MAXIMUM PREMIUM FOR ASSUMABLE LOANS
AS PERCENTAGE OF LOAN BALANCE
FACE INTEREST RATE: 12.25%

CURRENT RATE	REMAINING TERM OF LOAN (YEARS)				
	15	20	25	27	30
9.00	− 19.920	− 24.323	− 27.711	− 28.815	− 30.235
9.25	− 18.180	− 22.132	− 25.148	− 26.125	− 27.376
9.50	− 16.479	− 20.001	− 22.668	− 23.527	− 24.623
9.75	− 14.814	− 17.928	− 20.267	− 21.016	− 21.968
10.00	− 13.185	− 15.911	− 17.942	− 18.589	− 19.409
10.25	− 11.592	− 13.948	− 15.691	− 16.243	− 16.940
10.50	− 10.032	− 12.038	− 13.510	− 13.974	− 14.557
10.75	− 8.506	− 10.179	− 11.397	− 11.779	− 12.257
11.00	− 7.012	− 8.368	− 9.349	− 9.655	− 10.036
11.25	− 5.550	− 6.605	− 7.363	− 7.598	− 7.890
11.50	− 4.118	− 4.889	− 5.438	− 5.607	− 5.817
11.75	− 2.716	− 3.216	− 3.570	− 3.679	− 3.813
12.00	− 1.344	− 1.587	− 1.758	− 1.811	− 1.875
12.25	0.000	0.000	0.000	0.000	0.000
12.50	1.316	1.547	1.707	1.755	1.814
12.75	2.606	3.055	3.364	3.457	3.570
13.00	3.868	4.525	4.973	5.108	5.271
13.25	5.105	5.958	6.537	6.709	6.918
13.50	6.317	7.356	8.056	8.263	8.514
13.75	7.505	8.719	9.532	9.772	10.061
14.00	8.669	10.049	10.967	11.237	11.560
14.25	9.809	11.346	12.362	12.660	13.015
14.50	10.927	12.612	13.720	14.042	14.426
14.75	12.022	13.848	15.040	15.385	15.796
15.00	13.096	15.054	16.324	16.691	17.126
15.25	14.149	16.231	17.575	17.961	18.417
15.50	15.181	17.381	18.792	19.195	19.672
15.75	16.193	18.504	19.977	20.397	20.891
16.00	17.185	19.600	21.131	21.565	22.075
16.25	18.159	20.672	22.255	22.703	23.227
16.50	19.113	21.719	23.351	23.811	24.348
16.75	20.050	22.741	24.418	24.889	25.438
17.00	20.968	23.741	25.459	25.940	26.498
17.25	21.870	24.718	26.474	26.963	27.531
17.50	22.754	25.674	27.464	27.961	28.536
17.75	23.622	26.608	28.429	28.933	29.515
18.00	24.473	27.522	29.371	29.881	30.469

MAXIMUM PREMIUM FOR ASSUMABLE LOANS
AS PERCENTAGE OF LOAN BALANCE
FACE INTEREST RATE: 12.5%

CURRENT RATE	REMAINING TERM OF LOAN (YEARS)				
	15	20	25	27	30
9.00	− 21.519	− 26.277	− 29.929	− 31.116	− 32.641
9.25	− 19.756	− 24.051	− 27.321	− 28.378	− 29.730
9.50	− 18.033	− 21.887	− 24.798	− 25.734	− 26.926
9.75	− 16.346	− 19.781	− 22.355	− 23.178	− 24.222
10.00	− 14.695	− 17.732	− 19.990	− 20.708	− 21.615
10.25	− 13.081	− 15.739	− 17.700	− 18.320	− 19.100
10.50	− 11.500	− 13.798	− 15.481	− 16.010	− 16.673
10.75	− 9.954	− 11.910	− 13.332	− 13.776	− 14.331
11.00	− 8.440	− 10.071	− 11.248	− 11.614	− 12.069
11.25	− 6.958	− 8.281	− 9.228	− 9.520	− 9.884
11.50	− 5.507	− 6.537	− 7.269	− 7.494	− 7.772
11.75	− 4.086	− 4.838	− 5.369	− 5.531	− 5.731
12.00	− 2.696	− 3.184	− 3.525	− 3.629	− 3.757
12.25	− 1.334	− 1.571	− 1.737	− 1.787	− 1.848
12.50	0.000	0.000	0.000	0.000	0.000
12.75	1.306	1.531	1.686	1.732	1.788
13.00	2.586	3.024	3.323	3.412	3.520
13.25	3.840	4.480	4.914	5.042	5.198
13.50	5.068	5.900	6.459	6.624	6.823
13.75	6.271	7.285	7.961	8.160	8.399
14.00	7.450	8.635	9.421	9.651	9.926
14.25	8.606	9.953	10.841	11.099	11.408
14.50	9.738	11.239	12.221	12.506	12.845
14.75	10.848	12.494	13.564	13.874	14.240
15.00	11.936	13.719	14.871	15.203	15.595
15.25	13.003	14.915	16.143	16.495	16.910
15.50	14.049	16.083	17.381	17.752	18.187
15.75	15.075	17.223	18.587	18.974	19.429
16.00	16.081	18.337	19.761	20.164	20.636
16.25	17.067	19.425	20.905	21.322	21.809
16.50	18.034	20.488	22.020	22.449	22.950
16.75	18.983	21.527	23.106	23.547	24.060
17.00	19.914	22.543	24.165	24.617	25.140
17.25	20.828	23.536	25.197	25.658	26.192
17.50	21.724	24.506	26.204	26.674	27.215
17.75	22.603	25.455	27.186	27.663	28.213
18.00	23.466	26.383	28.145	28.628	29.184

MAXIMUM PREMIUM FOR ASSUMABLE LOANS
AS PERCENTAGE OF LOAN BALANCE
FACE INTEREST RATE: 12.75%

CURRENT RATE	REMAINING TERM OF LOAN (YEARS) 15	20	25	27	30
9.00	− 23.128	− 28.241	− 32.157	− 33.427	− 35.057
9.25	− 21.341	− 25.980	− 29.504	− 30.641	− 32.092
9.50	− 19.595	− 23.782	− 26.938	− 27.950	− 29.237
9.75	− 17.885	− 21.644	− 24.453	− 25.349	− 26.484
10.00	− 16.213	− 19.563	− 22.048	− 22.836	− 23.830
10.25	− 14.578	− 17.539	− 19.719	− 20.406	− 21.269
10.50	− 12.976	− 15.568	− 17.462	− 18.055	− 18.798
10.75	− 11.409	− 13.650	− 15.275	− 15.781	− 16.413
11.00	− 9.875	− 11.783	− 13.156	− 13.581	− 14.110
11.25	− 8.373	− 9.965	− 11.101	− 11.451	− 11.885
11.50	− 6.904	− 8.194	− 9.108	− 9.389	− 9.735
11.75	− 5.464	− 6.469	− 7.176	− 7.391	− 7.656
12.00	− 4.055	− 4.788	− 5.301	− 5.456	− 5.647
12.25	− 2.675	− 3.151	− 3.481	− 3.581	− 3.702
12.50	− 1.324	− 1.555	− 1.715	− 1.763	− 1.821
12.75	0.000	0.000	0.000	0.000	0.000
13.00	1.297	1.516	1.665	1.710	1.763
13.25	2.567	2.995	3.283	3.369	3.471
13.50	3.811	4.436	4.855	4.978	5.126
13.75	5.031	5.843	6.383	6.541	6.731
14.00	6.225	7.214	7.868	8.058	8.286
14.25	7.396	8.552	9.312	9.532	9.795
14.50	8.544	9.858	10.716	10.964	11.258
14.75	9.668	11.133	12.082	12.355	12.679
15.00	10.771	12.377	13.411	13.708	14.058
15.25	11.852	13.592	14.705	15.023	15.397
15.50	12.912	14.777	15.965	16.302	16.698
15.75	13.951	15.936	17.191	17.546	17.962
16.00	14.970	17.067	18.385	18.757	19.190
16.25	15.969	18.172	19.549	19.935	20.385
16.50	16.950	19.252	20.683	21.082	21.547
16.75	17.911	20.307	21.787	22.200	22.677
17.00	18.854	21.338	22.864	23.288	23.777
17.25	19.780	22.346	23.915	24.348	24.848
17.50	20.688	23.332	24.939	25.381	25.890
17.75	21.579	24.296	25.938	26.388	26.905
18.00	22.453	25.238	26.912	27.370	27.894

MAXIMUM PREMIUM FOR ASSUMABLE LOANS
AS PERCENTAGE OF LOAN BALANCE
FACE INTEREST RATE: 13%

CURRENT RATE	REMAINING TERM OF LOAN (YEARS)				
	15	20	25	27	30
9.00	−24.745	−30.215	−34.395	−35.748	−37.481
9.25	−22.935	−27.919	−31.697	−32.913	−34.463
9.50	−21.166	−25.688	−29.088	−30.176	−31.557
9.75	−19.434	−23.516	−26.561	−27.530	−28.754
10.00	−17.740	−21.404	−24.115	−24.972	−26.052
10.25	−16.083	−19.348	−21.746	−22.500	−23.446
10.50	−14.460	−17.347	−19.451	−20.109	−20.930
10.75	−12.872	−15.400	−17.227	−17.795	−18.503
11.00	−11.319	−13.504	−15.072	−15.557	−16.158
11.25	−9.797	−11.658	−12.982	−13.390	−13.893
11.50	−8.308	−9.860	−10.956	−11.292	−11.704
11.75	−6.849	−8.108	−8.991	−9.259	−9.589
12.00	−5.422	−6.402	−7.084	−7.290	−7.543
12.25	−4.024	−4.739	−5.234	−5.382	−5.564
12.50	−2.654	−3.119	−3.437	−3.533	−3.649
12.75	−1.314	−1.540	−1.694	−1.739	−1.795
13.00	0.000	0.000	0.000	0.000	0.000
13.25	1.287	1.501	1.645	1.688	1.739
13.50	2.548	2.965	3.244	3.325	3.423
13.75	3.783	4.393	4.797	4.915	5.056
14.00	4.994	5.786	6.307	6.459	6.640
14.25	6.180	7.144	7.776	7.959	8.175
14.50	7.342	8.471	9.204	9.415	9.665
14.75	8.482	9.765	10.593	10.831	11.111
15.00	9.599	11.028	11.945	12.207	12.515
15.25	10.694	12.261	13.261	13.545	13.878
15.50	11.768	13.465	14.541	14.846	15.202
15.75	12.821	14.642	15.789	16.112	16.489
16.00	13.853	15.790	17.003	17.344	17.740
16.25	14.866	16.912	18.186	18.543	18.956
16.50	15.859	18.009	19.339	19.710	20.139
16.75	16.833	19.080	20.463	20.846	21.289
17.00	17.788	20.127	21.558	21.953	22.409
17.25	18.726	21.151	22.626	23.032	23.499
17.50	19.646	22.151	23.668	24.083	24.560
17.75	20.548	23.130	24.683	25.108	25.593
18.00	21.434	24.087	25.675	26.107	26.600

MAXIMUM PREMIUM FOR ASSUMABLE LOANS
AS PERCENTAGE OF LOAN BALANCE
FACE INTEREST RATE: 13.25%

CURRENT RATE	REMAINING TERM OF LOAN (YEARS)				
	15	20	25	27	30
9.00	− 26.371	− 32.200	− 36.643	− 38.079	− 39.914
9.25	− 24.538	− 29.869	− 33.900	− 35.195	− 36.843
9.50	− 22.746	− 27.604	− 31.247	− 32.410	− 33.885
9.75	− 20.991	− 25.399	− 28.678	− 29.719	− 31.033
10.00	− 19.275	− 23.254	− 26.191	− 27.118	− 28.283
10.25	− 17.596	− 21.167	− 23.783	− 24.603	− 25.630
10.50	− 15.952	− 19.136	− 21.449	− 22.170	− 23.070
10.75	− 14.344	− 17.159	− 19.188	− 19.817	− 20.599
11.00	− 12.770	− 15.234	− 16.997	− 17.541	− 18.213
11.25	− 11.228	− 13.359	− 14.872	− 15.336	− 15.908
11.50	− 9.720	− 11.534	− 12.812	− 13.202	− 13.681
11.75	− 8.242	− 9.755	− 10.814	− 11.135	− 11.528
12.00	− 6.796	− 8.023	− 8.875	− 9.132	− 9.446
12.25	− 5.380	− 6.335	− 6.994	− 7.192	− 7.432
12.50	− 3.993	− 4.690	− 5.168	− 5.310	− 5.483
12.75	− 2.634	− 3.087	− 3.395	− 3.486	− 3.596
13.00	− 1.304	− 1.524	− 1.673	− 1.717	− 1.770
13.25	0.000	0.000	0.000	0.000	0.000
13.50	1.277	1.486	1.625	1.666	1.715
13.75	2.529	2.936	3.205	3.283	3.376
14.00	3.755	4.350	4.740	4.853	4.988
14.25	4.956	5.729	6.233	6.378	6.551
14.50	6.134	7.076	7.685	7.860	8.067
14.75	7.289	8.389	9.098	9.300	9.538
15.00	8.420	9.672	10.472	10.700	10.967
15.25	9.530	10.924	11.810	12.061	12.354
15.50	10.617	12.146	13.112	13.384	13.702
15.75	11.684	13.341	14.380	14.672	15.011
16.00	12.730	14.507	15.615	15.925	16.284
16.25	13.756	15.646	16.818	17.144	17.522
16.50	14.762	16.759	17.990	18.331	18.725
16.75	15.748	17.847	19.132	19.488	19.896
17.00	16.716	18.910	20.246	20.614	21.036
17.25	17.666	19.949	21.332	21.711	22.145
17.50	18.598	20.965	22.391	22.780	23.225
17.75	19.513	21.958	23.424	23.822	24.277
18.00	20.410	22.930	24.431	24.838	25.301

MAXIMUM PREMIUM FOR ASSUMABLE LOANS
AS PERCENTAGE OF LOAN BALANCE
FACE INTEREST RATE: 13.5%

CURRENT RATE	REMAINING TERM OF LOAN (YEARS)				
	15	20	25	27	30
9.00	− 28.006	− 34.194	− 38.900	− 40.418	− 42.354
9.25	− 26.149	− 31.828	− 36.112	− 37.485	− 39.230
9.50	− 24.333	− 29.529	− 33.415	− 34.653	− 36.220
9.75	− 22.556	− 27.290	− 30.804	− 31.916	− 33.318
10.00	− 20.818	− 25.113	− 28.276	− 29.271	− 30.521
10.25	− 19.117	− 22.995	− 25.827	− 26.714	− 27.822
10.50	− 17.452	− 20.933	− 23.455	− 24.240	− 25.217
10.75	− 15.823	− 18.926	− 21.157	− 21.847	− 22.703
11.00	− 14.229	− 16.972	− 18.930	− 19.532	− 20.276
11.25	− 12.667	− 15.069	− 16.770	− 17.290	− 17.930
11.50	− 11.139	− 13.216	− 14.676	− 15.120	− 15.664
11.75	− 9.643	− 11.411	− 12.644	− 13.018	− 13.473
12.00	− 8.178	− 9.653	− 10.674	− 10.981	− 11.355
12.25	− 6.743	− 7.940	− 8.761	− 9.007	− 9.306
12.50	− 5.338	− 6.270	− 6.905	− 7.094	− 7.323
12.75	− 3.962	− 4.642	− 5.103	− 5.239	− 5.403
13.00	− 2.614	− 3.056	− 3.352	− 3.440	− 3.545
13.25	− 1.294	− 1.508	− 1.652	− 1.694	− 1.744
13.50	0.000	0.000	0.000	0.000	0.000
13.75	1.268	1.472	1.606	1.645	1.691
14.00	2.510	2.907	3.167	3.242	3.330
14.25	3.727	4.307	4.684	4.792	4.920
14.50	4.920	5.674	6.160	6.299	6.463
14.75	6.090	7.007	7.596	7.764	7.960
15.00	7.236	8.309	8.993	9.187	9.414
15.25	8.360	9.580	10.353	10.571	10.825
15.50	9.461	10.821	11.677	11.917	12.196
15.75	10.542	12.033	12.966	13.226	13.529
16.00	11.601	13.217	14.221	14.500	14.824
16.25	12.640	14.373	15.444	15.741	16.083
16.50	13.659	15.503	16.635	16.948	17.308
16.75	14.659	16.607	17.796	18.124	18.499
17.00	15.639	17.687	18.928	19.269	19.658
17.25	16.601	18.741	20.032	20.385	20.787
17.50	17.545	19.773	21.109	21.472	21.886
17.75	18.471	20.781	22.159	22.532	22.956
18.00	19.380	21.767	23.183	23.565	23.998

MAXIMUM PREMIUM FOR ASSUMABLE LOANS
AS PERCENTAGE OF LOAN BALANCE
FACE INTEREST RATE: 13.75%

CURRENT RATE	\multicolumn REMAINING TERM OF LOAN (YEARS)				
	15	20	25	27	30
9.00	− 29.650	− 36.198	− 41.167	− 42.766	− 44.803
9.25	− 27.769	− 33.797	− 38.334	− 39.784	− 41.625
9.50	− 25.930	− 31.463	− 35.593	− 36.905	− 38.563
9.75	− 24.130	− 29.192	− 32.939	− 34.122	− 35.612
10.00	− 22.369	− 26.982	− 30.369	− 31.433	− 32.766
10.25	− 20.647	− 24.832	− 27.881	− 28.833	− 30.020
10.50	− 18.960	− 22.739	− 25.470	− 26.318	− 27.371
10.75	− 17.310	− 20.702	− 23.134	− 23.885	− 24.814
11.00	− 15.696	− 18.719	− 20.871	− 21.531	− 22.344
11.25	− 14.114	− 16.788	− 18.676	− 19.251	− 19.959
11.50	− 12.566	− 14.907	− 16.547	− 17.045	− 17.654
11.75	− 11.051	− 13.075	− 14.483	− 14.907	− 15.425
12.00	− 9.567	− 11.291	− 12.480	− 12.837	− 13.270
12.25	− 8.114	− 9.552	− 10.536	− 10.830	− 11.186
12.50	− 6.691	− 7.857	− 8.650	− 8.885	− 9.169
12.75	− 5.297	− 6.205	− 6.818	− 6.999	− 7.216
13.00	− 3.932	− 4.595	− 5.039	− 5.170	− 5.326
13.25	− 2.594	− 3.025	− 3.311	− 3.395	− 3.494
13.50	− 1.284	− 1.494	− 1.632	− 1.672	− 1.720
13.75	0.000	0.000	0.000	0.000	0.000
14.00	1.258	1.457	1.586	1.624	1.668
14.25	2.491	2.878	3.129	3.200	3.285
14.50	3.699	4.265	4.629	4.732	4.854
14.75	4.883	5.619	6.088	6.221	6.377
15.00	6.044	6.940	7.508	7.668	7.856
15.25	7.183	8.230	8.890	9.076	9.291
15.50	8.298	9.489	10.235	10.444	10.686
15.75	9.393	10.719	11.545	11.775	12.042
16.00	10.466	11.921	12.821	13.071	13.359
16.25	11.518	13.094	14.064	14.332	14.640
16.50	12.550	14.241	15.275	15.559	15.885
16.75	13.563	15.362	16.455	16.754	17.097
17.00	14.556	16.457	17.605	17.919	18.276
17.25	15.530	17.528	18.727	19.053	19.424
17.50	16.486	18.574	19.821	20.159	20.542
17.75	17.424	19.598	20.888	21.236	21.631
18.00	18.345	20.599	21.929	22.287	22.691

MAXIMUM PREMIUM FOR ASSUMABLE LOANS
AS PERCENTAGE OF LOAN BALANCE
FACE INTEREST RATE: 14%

CURRENT RATE	REMAINING TERM OF LOAN (YEARS)				
	15	20	25	27	30
9.00	− 31.302	− 38.212	− 43.443	− 45.122	− 47.258
9.25	− 29.396	− 35.775	− 40.563	− 42.091	− 44.026
9.50	− 27.534	− 33.407	− 37.778	− 39.164	− 40.913
9.75	− 25.711	− 31.101	− 35.081	− 36.336	− 37.911
10.00	− 23.928	− 28.859	− 32.470	− 33.602	− 35.017
10.25	− 22.184	− 26.678	− 29.942	− 30.959	− 32.225
10.50	− 20.476	− 24.554	− 27.492	− 28.402	− 29.531
10.75	− 18.805	− 22.487	− 25.119	− 25.929	− 26.930
11.00	− 17.169	− 20.474	− 22.819	− 23.536	− 24.419
11.25	− 15.568	− 18.514	− 20.588	− 21.219	− 21.993
11.50	− 14.000	− 16.606	− 18.426	− 18.976	− 19.649
11.75	− 12.465	− 14.747	− 16.328	− 16.804	− 17.383
12.00	− 10.963	− 12.936	− 14.293	− 14.699	− 15.191
12.25	− 9.491	− 11.171	− 12.318	− 12.659	− 13.071
12.50	− 8.050	− 9.451	− 10.401	− 10.682	− 11.020
12.75	− 6.639	− 7.775	− 8.540	− 8.765	− 9.035
13.00	− 5.256	− 6.141	− 6.732	− 6.905	− 7.112
13.25	− 3.901	− 4.548	− 4.976	− 5.101	− 5.250
13.50	− 2.575	− 2.994	− 3.270	− 3.350	− 3.445
13.75	− 1.274	− 1.478	− 1.612	− 1.650	− 1.696
14.00	0.000	0.000	0.000	0.000	0.000
14.25	1.248	1.442	1.567	1.603	1.645
14.50	2.472	2.850	3.092	3.160	3.241
14.75	3.672	4.223	4.574	4.674	4.789
15.00	4.847	5.564	6.017	6.145	6.293
15.25	6.000	6.873	7.421	7.575	7.753
15.50	7.130	8.151	8.788	8.966	9.172
15.75	8.239	9.400	10.119	10.319	10.550
16.00	9.325	10.619	11.416	11.636	11.890
16.25	10.391	11.810	12.679	12.918	13.192
16.50	11.436	12.974	13.909	14.166	14.459
16.75	12.461	14.111	15.108	15.381	15.691
17.00	13.467	15.222	16.277	16.564	16.890
17.25	14.454	16.309	17.417	17.717	18.058
17.50	15.422	17.371	18.529	18.841	19.194
17.75	16.372	18.409	19.613	19.936	20.301
18.00	17.305	19.425	20.671	21.004	21.380

MAXIMUM PREMIUM FOR ASSUMABLE LOANS
AS PERCENTAGE OF LOAN BALANCE
FACE INTEREST RATE: 14.25%

CURRENT RATE	REMAINING TERM OF LOAN (YEARS)				
	15	20	25	27	30
9.00	− 32.962	− 40.234	− 45.726	− 47.486	− 49.721
9.25	− 31.032	− 37.762	− 42.801	− 44.406	− 46.435
9.50	− 29.147	− 35.359	− 39.972	− 41.431	− 43.270
9.75	− 27.301	− 33.020	− 37.232	− 38.557	− 40.218
10.00	− 25.495	− 30.745	− 34.580	− 35.778	− 37.275
10.25	− 23.728	− 28.531	− 32.011	− 33.092	− 34.437
10.50	− 21.999	− 26.376	− 29.522	− 30.494	− 31.697
10.75	− 20.307	− 24.279	− 27.111	− 27.981	− 29.053
11.00	− 18.651	− 22.237	− 24.774	− 25.549	− 26.500
11.25	− 17.029	− 20.249	− 22.508	− 23.194	− 24.033
11.50	− 15.442	− 18.312	− 20.311	− 20.915	− 21.650
11.75	− 13.887	− 16.426	− 18.180	− 18.706	− 19.346
12.00	− 12.366	− 14.588	− 16.113	− 16.568	− 17.118
12.25	− 10.876	− 12.798	− 14.106	− 14.495	− 14.962
12.50	− 9.416	− 11.053	− 12.159	− 12.485	− 12.877
12.75	− 7.987	− 9.352	− 10.268	− 10.537	− 10.858
13.00	− 6.587	− 7.694	− 8.431	− 8.647	− 8.903
13.25	− 5.215	− 6.077	− 6.647	− 6.813	− 7.010
13.50	− 3.871	− 4.501	− 4.914	− 5.034	− 5.175
13.75	− 2.554	− 2.963	− 3.230	− 3.306	− 3.397
14.00	− 1.264	− 1.463	− 1.592	− 1.629	− 1.672
14.25	0.000	0.000	0.000	0.000	0.000
14.50	1.239	1.428	1.549	1.583	1.623
14.75	2.454	2.822	3.055	3.121	3.197
15.00	3.644	4.182	4.521	4.616	4.726
15.25	4.812	5.510	5.947	6.069	6.211
15.50	5.956	6.807	7.336	7.483	7.653
15.75	7.079	8.074	8.688	8.858	9.054
16.00	8.179	9.311	10.005	10.197	10.416
16.25	9.258	10.519	11.288	11.499	11.740
16.50	10.317	11.700	12.538	12.767	13.028
16.75	11.355	12.854	13.757	14.002	14.281
17.00	12.373	13.982	14.944	15.205	15.501
17.25	13.373	15.084	16.102	16.377	16.688
17.50	14.353	16.162	17.232	17.519	17.843
17.75	15.315	17.216	18.333	18.632	18.969
18.00	16.259	18.246	19.408	19.718	20.065

MAXIMUM PREMIUM FOR ASSUMABLE LOANS
AS PERCENTAGE OF LOAN BALANCE
FACE INTEREST RATE: 14.5%

CURRENT RATE	\ 15	REMAINING TERM OF LOAN (YEARS)\ 20	\ 25	\ 27	\ 30
9.00	− 34.630	− 42.266	− 48.019	− 49.858	− 52.190
9.25	− 32.677	− 39.758	− 45.048	− 46.728	− 48.850
9.50	− 30.767	− 37.320	− 42.174	− 43.706	− 45.633
9.75	− 28.898	− 34.947	− 39.391	− 40.785	− 42.530
10.00	− 27.070	− 32.639	− 36.697	− 37.962	− 39.539
10.25	− 25.281	− 30.394	− 34.087	− 35.233	− 36.654
10.50	− 23.530	− 28.207	− 31.560	− 32.593	− 33.869
10.75	− 21.817	− 26.080	− 29.111	− 30.039	− 31.182
11.00	− 20.140	− 24.008	− 26.737	− 27.568	− 28.586
11.25	− 18.498	− 21.991	− 24.435	− 25.175	− 26.079
11.50	− 16.890	− 20.027	− 22.204	− 22.859	− 23.656
11.75	− 15.316	− 18.113	− 20.039	− 20.615	− 21.314
12.00	− 13.776	− 16.249	− 17.939	− 18.442	− 19.049
12.25	− 12.267	− 14.432	− 15.901	− 16.336	− 16.859
12.50	− 10.789	− 12.662	− 13.923	− 14.294	− 14.739
12.75	− 9.342	− 10.937	− 12.002	− 12.314	− 12.686
13.00	− 7.924	− 9.255	− 10.137	− 10.394	− 10.699
13.25	− 6.535	− 7.614	− 8.325	− 8.531	− 8.775
13.50	− 5.175	− 6.015	− 6.565	− 6.723	− 6.910
13.75	− 3.841	− 4.455	− 4.853	− 4.968	− 5.102
14.00	− 2.535	− 2.933	− 3.190	− 3.263	− 3.349
14.25	− 1.255	− 1.449	− 1.573	− 1.608	− 1.649
14.50	0.000	0.000	0.000	0.000	0.000
14.75	1.230	1.414	1.530	1.563	1.601
15.00	2.435	2.794	3.019	3.082	3.155
15.25	3.617	4.141	4.468	4.559	4.664
15.50	4.776	5.457	5.879	5.995	6.130
15.75	5.912	6.742	7.252	7.393	7.554
16.00	7.027	7.997	8.590	8.752	8.938
16.25	8.119	9.223	9.893	10.076	10.285
16.50	9.191	10.421	11.163	11.364	11.594
16.75	10.242	11.591	12.400	12.619	12.868
17.00	11.274	12.735	13.606	13.841	14.107
17.25	12.286	13.854	14.783	15.032	15.313
17.50	13.278	14.947	15.930	16.193	16.488
17.75	14.252	16.016	17.049	17.324	17.632
18.00	15.208	17.062	18.140	18.426	18.747

MAXIMUM PREMIUM FOR ASSUMABLE LOANS
AS PERCENTAGE OF LOAN BALANCE
FACE INTEREST RATE: 14.75%

CURRENT RATE	REMAINING TERM OF LOAN (YEARS)				
	15	20	25	27	30
9.00	− 36.306	− 44.306	− 50.319	− 52.237	− 54.666
9.25	− 34.329	− 41.762	− 47.301	− 49.058	− 51.272
9.50	− 32.396	− 39.289	− 44.383	− 45.987	− 48.002
9.75	− 30.503	− 36.883	− 41.557	− 43.020	− 44.849
10.00	− 28.652	− 34.541	− 38.821	− 40.152	− 41.809
10.25	− 26.841	− 32.264	− 36.171	− 37.379	− 38.877
10.50	− 25.068	− 30.046	− 33.604	− 34.698	− 36.047
10.75	− 23.333	− 27.888	− 31.117	− 32.103	− 33.316
11.00	− 21.636	− 25.787	− 28.706	− 29.593	− 30.678
11.25	− 19.973	− 23.740	− 26.369	− 27.162	− 28.130
11.50	− 18.346	− 21.748	− 24.103	− 24.810	− 25.668
11.75	− 16.752	− 19.807	− 21.904	− 22.530	− 23.287
12.00	− 15.193	− 17.916	− 19.772	− 20.322	− 20.986
12.25	− 13.665	− 16.073	− 17.702	− 18.183	− 18.759
12.50	− 12.169	− 14.278	− 15.693	− 16.108	− 16.605
12.75	− 10.703	− 12.528	− 13.743	− 14.097	− 14.520
13.00	− 9.268	− 10.821	− 11.848	− 12.146	− 12.500
13.25	− 7.862	− 9.158	− 10.008	− 10.254	− 10.544
13.50	− 6.484	− 7.536	− 8.220	− 8.417	− 8.649
13.75	− 5.134	− 5.953	− 6.483	− 6.634	− 6.812
14.00	− 3.812	− 4.410	− 4.794	− 4.903	− 5.030
14.25	− 2.516	− 2.904	− 3.151	− 3.221	− 3.303
14.50	− 1.245	− 1.434	− 1.554	− 1.588	− 1.627
14.75	0.000	0.000	0.000	0.000	0.000
15.00	1.220	1.400	1.512	1.543	1.579
15.25	2.417	2.767	2.984	3.044	3.113
15.50	3.590	4.101	4.416	4.503	4.603
15.75	4.741	5.405	5.811	5.923	6.050
16.00	5.869	6.677	7.169	7.304	7.457
16.25	6.975	7.921	8.493	8.648	8.825
16.50	8.060	9.136	9.782	9.957	10.156
16.75	9.125	10.323	11.039	11.232	11.450
17.00	10.169	11.484	12.264	12.474	12.710
17.25	11.193	12.618	13.459	13.683	13.936
17.50	12.198	13.727	14.623	14.862	15.130
17.75	13.185	14.812	15.760	16.011	16.292
18.00	14.153	15.872	16.868	17.131	17.425

MAXIMUM PREMIUM FOR ASSUMABLE LOANS
AS PERCENTAGE OF LOAN BALANCE
FACE INTEREST RATE: 15%

CURRENT RATE	REMAINING TERM OF LOAN (YEARS)				
	15	20	25	27	30
9.00	− 37.990	− 46.355	− 52.626	− 54.623	− 57.148
9.25	− 35.988	− 43.775	− 49.563	− 51.394	− 53.699
9.50	− 34.031	− 41.267	− 46.599	− 48.275	− 50.376
9.75	− 32.115	− 38.826	− 43.730	− 45.262	− 47.173
10.00	− 30.242	− 36.452	− 40.952	− 42.349	− 44.084
10.25	− 28.408	− 34.141	− 38.261	− 39.533	− 41.105
10.50	− 26.613	− 31.892	− 35.655	− 36.809	− 38.230
10.75	− 24.857	− 29.704	− 33.130	− 34.174	− 35.455
11.00	− 23.138	− 27.573	− 30.682	− 31.624	− 32.775
11.25	− 21.455	− 25.497	− 28.309	− 29.156	− 30.186
11.50	− 19.808	− 23.476	− 26.008	− 26.766	− 27.684
11.75	− 18.195	− 21.507	− 23.776	− 24.451	− 25.266
12.00	− 16.616	− 19.590	− 21.610	− 22.208	− 22.927
12.25	− 15.069	− 17.721	− 19.509	− 20.035	− 20.665
12.50	− 13.554	− 15.900	− 17.469	− 17.928	− 18.476
12.75	− 12.071	− 14.125	− 15.489	− 15.885	− 16.357
13.00	− 10.618	− 12.395	− 13.565	− 13.904	− 14.305
13.25	− 9.194	− 10.707	− 11.697	− 11.982	− 12.318
13.50	− 7.800	− 9.062	− 9.882	− 10.116	− 10.392
13.75	− 6.433	− 7.457	− 8.117	− 8.305	− 8.525
14.00	− 5.094	− 5.892	− 6.402	− 6.547	− 6.716
14.25	− 3.782	− 4.365	− 4.735	− 4.839	− 4.960
14.50	− 2.496	− 2.874	− 3.113	− 3.180	− 3.257
14.75	− 1.235	− 1.420	− 1.535	− 1.567	− 1.605
15.00	0.000	0.000	0.000	0.000	0.000
15.25	1.212	1.386	1.494	1.524	1.558
15.50	2.399	2.740	2.949	3.006	3.072
15.75	3.564	4.062	4.365	4.448	4.543
16.00	4.706	5.353	5.744	5.851	5.972
16.25	5.826	6.614	7.088	7.217	7.362
16.50	6.925	7.846	8.397	8.546	8.714
16.75	8.002	9.050	9.673	9.841	10.029
17.00	9.059	10.227	10.917	11.102	11.309
17.25	10.096	11.378	12.130	12.330	12.555
17.50	11.114	12.502	13.313	13.528	13.768
17.75	12.112	13.602	14.467	14.695	14.949
18.00	13.092	14.678	15.592	15.833	16.100

MAXIMUM PREMIUM FOR ASSUMABLE LOANS
AS PERCENTAGE OF LOAN BALANCE
FACE INTEREST RATE: 15.25%

CURRENT RATE	REMAINING TERM OF LOAN (YEARS)				
	15	20	25	27	30
9.00	− 39.683	− 48.412	− 54.941	− 57.016	− 59.635
9.25	− 37.656	− 45.796	− 51.831	− 53.737	− 56.132
9.50	− 35.675	− 43.253	− 48.823	− 50.570	− 52.757
9.75	− 33.736	− 40.777	− 45.910	− 47.510	− 49.503
10.00	− 31.839	− 38.370	− 43.090	− 44.552	− 46.365
10.25	− 29.983	− 36.027	− 40.359	− 41.692	− 43.339
10.50	− 28.166	− 33.746	− 37.713	− 38.926	− 40.418
10.75	− 26.389	− 31.527	− 35.149	− 36.250	− 37.599
11.00	− 24.649	− 29.366	− 32.664	− 33.661	− 34.876
11.25	− 22.945	− 27.261	− 30.255	− 31.154	− 32.246
11.50	− 21.277	− 25.212	− 27.919	− 28.727	− 29.705
11.75	− 19.644	− 23.216	− 25.653	− 26.377	− 27.248
12.00	− 18.046	− 21.271	− 23.455	− 24.100	− 24.873
12.25	− 16.480	− 19.376	− 21.322	− 21.893	− 22.575
12.50	− 14.947	− 17.529	− 19.251	− 19.753	− 20.351
12.75	− 13.446	− 15.729	− 17.240	− 17.679	− 18.199
13.00	− 11.975	− 13.975	− 15.288	− 15.667	− 16.115
13.25	− 10.534	− 12.264	− 13.391	− 13.715	− 14.096
13.50	− 9.122	− 10.595	− 11.548	− 11.820	− 12.139
13.75	− 7.738	− 8.968	− 9.757	− 9.981	− 10.243
14.00	− 6.383	− 7.380	− 8.016	− 8.196	− 8.405
14.25	− 5.055	− 5.832	− 6.323	− 6.462	− 6.622
14.50	− 3.753	− 4.320	− 4.677	− 4.777	− 4.892
14.75	− 2.477	− 2.845	− 3.075	− 3.139	− 3.213
15.00	− 1.226	− 1.406	− 1.517	− 1.548	− 1.583
15.25	0.000	0.000	0.000	0.000	0.000
15.50	1.202	1.372	1.477	1.505	1.538
15.75	2.381	2.713	2.914	2.969	3.032
16.00	3.537	4.022	4.315	4.394	4.484
16.25	4.671	5.301	5.679	5.781	5.896
16.50	5.783	6.551	7.008	7.131	7.269
16.75	6.874	7.772	8.303	8.445	8.605
17.00	7.944	8.965	9.566	9.726	9.905
17.25	8.994	10.132	10.797	10.974	11.171
17.50	10.024	11.272	11.998	12.189	12.403
17.75	11.034	12.388	13.169	13.375	13.603
18.00	12.026	13.478	14.312	14.530	14.772

MAXIMUM PREMIUM FOR ASSUMABLE LOANS
AS PERCENTAGE OF LOAN BALANCE
FACE INTEREST RATE: 15.5%

CURRENT RATE	REMAINING TERM OF LOAN (YEARS)				
	15	20	25	27	30
9.00	− 41.383	− 50.477	− 57.263	− 59.415	− 62.128
9.25	− 39.331	− 47.825	− 54.107	− 56.086	− 58.570
9.50	− 37.326	− 45.246	− 51.053	− 52.871	− 55.142
9.75	− 35.363	− 42.736	− 48.096	− 49.764	− 51.837
10.00	− 33.443	− 40.295	− 45.234	− 46.760	− 48.651
10.25	− 31.565	− 37.920	− 42.462	− 43.857	− 45.577
10.50	− 29.726	− 35.608	− 39.776	− 41.049	− 42.611
10.75	− 27.926	− 33.357	− 37.174	− 38.332	− 39.747
11.00	− 26.165	− 31.166	− 34.652	− 35.703	− 36.983
11.25	− 24.441	− 29.032	− 32.207	− 33.158	− 34.312
11.50	− 22.753	− 26.954	− 29.836	− 30.694	− 31.731
11.75	− 21.100	− 24.930	− 27.536	− 28.308	− 29.235
12.00	− 19.482	− 22.959	− 25.305	− 25.996	− 26.823
12.25	− 17.898	− 21.037	− 23.140	− 23.755	− 24.489
12.50	− 16.346	− 19.165	− 21.038	− 21.583	− 22.231
12.75	− 14.826	− 17.340	− 18.998	− 19.477	− 20.045
13.00	− 13.337	− 15.561	− 17.016	− 17.434	− 17.928
13.25	− 11.879	− 13.826	− 15.091	− 15.452	− 15.877
13.50	− 10.450	− 12.134	− 13.220	− 13.529	− 13.891
13.75	− 9.049	− 10.484	− 11.402	− 11.662	− 11.965
14.00	− 7.678	− 8.875	− 9.635	− 9.849	− 10.098
14.25	− 6.333	− 7.304	− 7.917	− 8.088	− 8.287
14.50	− 5.015	− 5.772	− 6.246	− 6.378	− 6.530
14.75	− 3.724	− 4.276	− 4.620	− 4.715	− 4.825
15.00	− 2.458	− 2.817	− 3.038	− 3.099	− 3.169
15.25	− 1.217	− 1.392	− 1.499	− 1.528	− 1.562
15.50	0.000	0.000	0.000	0.000	0.000
15.75	1.193	1.359	1.459	1.487	1.517
16.00	2.364	2.687	2.881	2.933	2.992
16.25	3.511	3.983	4.265	4.341	4.426
16.50	4.637	5.250	5.614	5.712	5.821
16.75	5.741	6.488	6.929	7.046	7.178
17.00	6.823	7.698	8.211	8.346	8.498
17.25	7.886	8.881	9.460	9.613	9.784
17.50	8.929	10.038	10.679	10.848	11.035
17.75	9.952	11.169	11.868	12.051	12.254
18.00	10.956	12.274	13.028	13.224	13.441

MAXIMUM PREMIUM FOR ASSUMABLE LOANS
AS PERCENTAGE OF LOAN BALANCE
FACE INTEREST RATE: 15.75%

CURRENT RATE	REMAINING TERM OF LOAN (YEARS)				
	15	20	25	27	30
9.00	− 43.090	− 52.551	− 59.592	− 61.821	− 64.626
9.25	− 41.014	− 49.861	− 56.389	− 58.441	− 61.013
9.50	− 38.985	− 47.247	− 53.290	− 55.178	− 57.533
9.75	− 36.998	− 44.703	− 50.290	− 52.024	− 54.177
10.00	− 35.055	− 42.228	− 47.385	− 48.975	− 50.941
10.25	− 33.154	− 39.820	− 44.572	− 46.028	− 47.820
10.50	− 31.293	− 37.476	− 41.847	− 43.177	− 44.808
10.75	− 29.472	− 35.195	− 39.206	− 40.420	− 41.901
11.00	− 27.689	− 32.973	− 36.647	− 37.751	− 39.093
11.25	− 25.944	− 30.810	− 34.165	− 35.168	− 36.381
11.50	− 24.236	− 28.704	− 31.759	− 32.667	− 33.760
11.75	− 22.563	− 26.652	− 29.425	− 30.244	− 31.227
12.00	− 20.926	− 24.653	− 27.161	− 27.897	− 28.777
12.25	− 19.322	− 22.705	− 24.964	− 25.623	− 26.407
12.50	− 17.751	− 20.807	− 22.831	− 23.418	− 24.114
12.75	− 16.213	− 18.957	− 20.760	− 21.280	− 21.894
13.00	− 14.706	− 17.153	− 18.749	− 19.207	− 19.745
13.25	− 13.230	− 15.394	− 16.795	− 17.195	− 17.663
13.50	− 11.784	− 13.679	− 14.897	− 15.242	− 15.646
13.75	− 10.367	− 12.006	− 13.052	− 13.347	− 13.690
14.00	− 8.978	− 10.375	− 11.259	− 11.507	− 11.794
14.25	− 7.618	− 8.783	− 9.515	− 9.719	− 9.955
14.50	− 6.284	− 7.229	− 7.819	− 7.983	− 8.171
14.75	− 4.977	− 5.713	− 6.169	− 6.295	− 6.440
15.00	− 3.696	− 4.234	− 4.564	− 4.655	− 4.759
15.25	− 2.439	− 2.789	− 3.002	− 3.060	− 3.127
15.50	− 1.208	− 1.378	− 1.481	− 1.509	− 1.541
15.75	0.000	0.000	0.000	0.000	0.000
16.00	1.184	1.346	1.442	1.468	1.498
16.25	2.345	2.660	2.847	2.897	2.954
16.50	3.485	3.945	4.216	4.289	4.370
16.75	4.602	5.200	5.551	5.644	5.748
17.00	5.698	6.427	6.851	6.963	7.088
17.25	6.774	7.626	8.119	8.249	8.393
17.50	7.829	8.798	9.356	9.502	9.664
17.75	8.864	9.945	10.563	10.724	10.902
18.00	9.880	11.066	11.740	11.915	12.107

MAXIMUM PREMIUM FOR ASSUMABLE LOANS
AS PERCENTAGE OF LOAN BALANCE
FACE INTEREST RATE: 16%

CURRENT RATE	REMAINING TERM OF LOAN (YEARS)				
	15	20	25	27	30
9.00	− 44.805	− 54.632	− 61.928	− 64.232	− 67.129
9.25	− 42.704	− 51.906	− 58.678	− 60.802	− 63.461
9.50	− 40.650	− 49.256	− 55.534	− 57.490	− 59.928
9.75	− 38.640	− 46.677	− 52.489	− 54.289	− 56.521
10.00	− 36.673	− 44.168	− 49.542	− 51.195	− 53.236
10.25	− 34.750	− 41.727	− 46.688	− 48.204	− 50.068
10.50	− 32.866	− 39.351	− 43.922	− 45.311	− 47.010
10.75	− 31.023	− 37.039	− 41.243	− 42.512	− 44.058
11.00	− 29.219	− 34.787	− 38.646	− 39.804	− 41.208
11.25	− 27.453	− 32.594	− 36.128	− 37.182	− 38.455
11.50	− 25.725	− 30.459	− 33.687	− 34.644	− 35.794
11.75	− 24.032	− 28.379	− 31.319	− 32.185	− 33.222
12.00	− 22.375	− 26.353	− 29.022	− 29.803	− 30.735
12.25	− 20.752	− 24.379	− 26.792	− 27.495	− 28.329
12.50	− 19.162	− 22.454	− 24.628	− 25.257	− 26.001
12.75	− 17.606	− 20.579	− 22.527	− 23.087	− 23.748
13.00	− 16.081	− 18.751	− 20.487	− 20.983	− 21.566
13.25	− 14.587	− 16.968	− 18.504	− 18.941	− 19.452
13.50	− 13.124	− 15.230	− 16.578	− 16.960	− 17.404
13.75	− 11.689	− 13.534	− 14.706	− 15.036	− 15.419
14.00	− 10.284	− 11.880	− 12.887	− 13.168	− 13.494
14.25	− 8.907	− 10.267	− 11.118	− 11.354	− 11.627
14.50	− 7.558	− 8.692	− 9.397	− 9.592	− 9.816
14.75	− 6.235	− 7.155	− 7.723	− 7.879	− 8.058
15.00	− 4.938	− 5.655	− 6.094	− 6.215	− 6.352
15.25	− 3.667	− 4.191	− 4.509	− 4.596	− 4.694
15.50	− 2.421	− 2.761	− 2.966	− 3.022	− 3.085
15.75	− 1.198	− 1.364	− 1.463	− 1.490	− 1.520
16.00	0.000	0.000	0.000	0.000	0.000
16.25	1.175	1.332	1.426	1.450	1.478
16.50	2.328	2.635	2.815	2.863	2.916
16.75	3.459	3.907	4.168	4.238	4.315
17.00	4.568	5.150	5.488	5.577	5.676
17.25	5.656	6.366	6.775	6.882	7.001
17.50	6.724	7.554	8.030	8.154	8.291
17.75	7.772	8.716	9.254	9.393	9.547
18.00	8.800	9.853	10.448	10.602	10.771

MAXIMUM PREMIUM FOR ASSUMABLE LOANS
AS PERCENTAGE OF LOAN BALANCE
FACE INTEREST RATE: 16.25%

CURRENT RATE	REMAINING TERM OF LOAN (YEARS)				
	15	20	25	27	30
9.00	− 46.527	− 56.720	− 64.270	− 66.649	− 69.637
9.25	− 44.401	− 53.957	− 60.972	− 63.169	− 65.914
9.50	− 42.323	− 51.271	− 57.783	− 59.808	− 62.327
9.75	− 40.289	− 48.658	− 54.694	− 56.560	− 58.869
10.00	− 38.299	− 46.115	− 51.704	− 53.420	− 55.535
10.25	− 36.352	− 43.641	− 48.809	− 50.385	− 52.319
10.50	− 34.446	− 41.233	− 46.004	− 47.449	− 49.216
10.75	− 32.581	− 38.889	− 43.286	− 44.610	− 46.220
11.00	− 30.756	− 36.608	− 40.651	− 41.862	− 43.327
11.25	− 28.969	− 34.385	− 38.097	− 39.201	− 40.532
11.50	− 27.220	− 32.221	− 35.621	− 36.625	− 37.832
11.75	− 25.507	− 30.113	− 33.218	− 34.130	− 35.221
12.00	− 23.830	− 28.059	− 30.888	− 31.714	− 32.697
12.25	− 22.188	− 26.058	− 28.626	− 29.371	− 30.255
12.50	− 20.579	− 24.108	− 26.431	− 27.101	− 27.892
12.75	− 19.004	− 22.208	− 24.299	− 24.899	− 25.604
13.00	− 17.461	− 20.355	− 22.229	− 22.763	− 23.390
13.25	− 15.949	− 18.548	− 20.218	− 20.692	− 21.244
13.50	− 14.469	− 16.786	− 18.264	− 18.681	− 19.165
13.75	− 13.017	− 15.067	− 16.365	− 16.729	− 17.150
14.00	− 11.596	− 13.391	− 14.519	− 14.834	− 15.197
14.25	− 10.203	− 11.756	− 12.725	− 12.993	− 13.302
14.50	− 8.837	− 10.160	− 10.979	− 11.205	− 11.464
14.75	− 7.498	− 8.602	− 9.281	− 9.467	− 9.679
15.00	− 6.186	− 7.082	− 7.629	− 7.778	− 7.947
15.25	− 4.900	− 5.598	− 6.021	− 6.135	− 6.265
15.50	− 3.639	− 4.148	− 4.455	− 4.538	− 4.631
15.75	− 2.402	− 2.733	− 2.931	− 2.984	− 3.044
16.00	− 1.189	− 1.350	− 1.446	− 1.472	− 1.500
16.25	0.000	0.000	0.000	0.000	0.000
16.50	1.167	1.320	1.409	1.433	1.459
16.75	2.311	2.609	2.783	2.828	2.879
17.00	3.433	3.869	4.121	4.187	4.260
17.25	4.534	5.101	5.427	5.512	5.605
17.50	5.615	6.306	6.700	6.802	6.915
17.75	6.675	7.483	7.941	8.060	8.190
18.00	7.716	8.635	9.153	9.286	9.432

MAXIMUM PREMIUM FOR ASSUMABLE LOANS
AS PERCENTAGE OF LOAN BALANCE
FACE INTEREST RATE: 16.5%

CURRENT RATE	REMAINING TERM OF LOAN (YEARS)				
	15	20	25	27	30
9.00	− 48.257	− 58.816	− 66.618	− 69.072	− 72.149
9.25	− 46.105	− 56.016	− 63.273	− 65.541	− 68.371
9.50	− 44.003	− 53.294	− 60.038	− 62.131	− 64.731
9.75	− 41.944	− 50.646	− 56.905	− 58.836	− 61.222
10.00	− 39.931	− 48.069	− 53.873	− 55.651	− 57.839
10.25	− 37.961	− 45.562	− 50.936	− 52.571	− 54.575
10.50	− 36.033	− 43.122	− 48.091	− 49.593	− 51.425
10.75	− 34.146	− 40.747	− 45.334	− 46.712	− 48.385
11.00	− 32.300	− 38.434	− 42.662	− 43.924	− 45.449
11.25	− 30.491	− 36.182	− 40.071	− 41.225	− 42.613
11.50	− 28.721	− 33.989	− 37.559	− 38.611	− 39.873
11.75	− 26.988	− 31.853	− 35.122	− 36.080	− 37.223
12.00	− 25.292	− 29.772	− 32.759	− 33.628	− 34.662
12.25	− 23.630	− 27.744	− 30.464	− 31.252	− 32.184
12.50	− 22.002	− 25.768	− 28.238	− 28.948	− 29.786
12.75	− 20.409	− 23.842	− 26.076	− 26.715	− 27.465
13.00	− 18.848	− 21.964	− 23.976	− 24.548	− 25.217
13.25	− 17.318	− 20.133	− 21.936	− 22.446	− 23.040
13.50	− 15.820	− 18.348	− 19.955	− 20.406	− 20.930
13.75	− 14.351	− 16.606	− 18.029	− 18.426	− 18.885
14.00	− 12.913	− 14.908	− 16.156	− 16.503	− 16.903
14.25	− 11.503	− 13.250	− 14.336	− 14.636	− 14.980
14.50	− 10.121	− 11.633	− 12.565	− 12.822	− 13.114
14.75	− 8.767	− 10.055	− 10.843	− 11.058	− 11.304
15.00	− 7.440	− 8.514	− 9.167	− 9.345	− 9.546
15.25	− 6.138	− 7.010	− 7.536	− 7.678	− 7.839
15.50	− 4.862	− 5.541	− 5.948	− 6.058	− 6.181
15.75	− 3.611	− 4.107	− 4.402	− 4.481	− 4.570
16.00	− 2.384	− 2.706	− 2.896	− 2.947	− 3.004
16.25	− 1.180	− 1.337	− 1.429	− 1.454	− 1.481
16.50	0.000	0.000	0.000	0.000	0.000
16.75	1.158	1.307	1.393	1.416	1.441
17.00	2.293	2.584	2.751	2.794	2.843
17.25	3.408	3.832	4.075	4.138	4.207
17.50	4.501	5.053	5.366	5.447	5.536
17.75	5.574	6.246	6.626	6.723	6.830
18.00	6.626	7.413	7.854	7.967	8.091

MAXIMUM PREMIUM FOR ASSUMABLE LOANS
AS PERCENTAGE OF LOAN BALANCE
FACE INTEREST RATE: 16.75%

CURRENT RATE	REMAINING TERM OF LOAN (YEARS)				
	15	20	25	27	30
9.00	− 49.993	− 60.918	− 68.971	− 71.500	− 74.666
9.25	− 47.817	− 58.082	− 65.580	− 67.918	− 70.832
9.50	− 45.689	− 55.324	− 62.299	− 64.459	− 67.139
9.75	− 43.607	− 52.640	− 59.122	− 61.116	− 63.579
10.00	− 41.570	− 50.030	− 56.047	− 57.886	− 60.146
10.25	− 39.577	− 47.490	− 53.068	− 54.762	− 56.835
10.50	− 37.626	− 45.017	− 50.183	− 51.741	− 53.639
10.75	− 35.717	− 42.610	− 47.387	− 48.819	− 50.554
11.00	− 33.849	− 40.267	− 44.677	− 45.990	− 47.576
11.25	− 32.019	− 37.985	− 42.050	− 43.253	− 44.698
11.50	− 30.229	− 35.763	− 39.502	− 40.602	− 41.917
11.75	− 28.475	− 33.599	− 37.031	− 38.034	− 39.229
12.00	− 26.759	− 31.490	− 34.634	− 35.547	− 36.630
12.25	− 25.078	− 29.436	− 32.307	− 33.137	− 34.116
12.50	− 23.431	− 27.433	− 30.049	− 30.800	− 31.683
12.75	− 21.819	− 25.481	− 27.857	− 28.534	− 29.328
13.00	− 20.240	− 23.579	− 25.727	− 26.337	− 27.047
13.25	− 18.692	− 21.724	− 23.659	− 24.204	− 24.838
13.50	− 17.176	− 19.915	− 21.649	− 22.135	− 22.698
13.75	− 15.691	− 18.150	− 19.696	− 20.127	− 20.623
14.00	− 14.235	− 16.429	− 17.797	− 18.176	− 18.612
14.25	− 12.809	− 14.750	− 15.951	− 16.282	− 16.661
14.50	− 11.411	− 13.111	− 14.155	− 14.442	− 14.768
14.75	− 10.041	− 11.512	− 12.409	− 12.653	− 12.931
15.00	− 8.698	− 9.951	− 10.709	− 10.915	− 11.147
15.25	− 7.381	− 8.427	− 9.055	− 9.224	− 9.415
15.50	− 6.090	− 6.939	− 7.445	− 7.581	− 7.733
15.75	− 4.824	− 5.485	− 5.877	− 5.981	− 6.098
16.00	− 3.583	− 4.066	− 4.350	− 4.425	− 4.509
16.25	− 2.365	− 2.679	− 2.862	− 2.911	− 2.964
16.50	− 1.171	− 1.324	− 1.413	− 1.436	− 1.462
16.75	0.000	0.000	0.000	0.000	0.000
17.00	1.149	1.294	1.377	1.399	1.422
17.25	2.276	2.559	2.720	2.761	2.807
17.50	3.382	3.796	4.029	4.089	4.155
17.75	4.468	5.005	5.307	5.384	5.468
18.00	5.533	6.187	6.553	6.646	6.747

MAXIMUM PREMIUM FOR ASSUMABLE LOANS
AS PERCENTAGE OF LOAN BALANCE
FACE INTEREST RATE: 17%

CURRENT RATE	REMAINING TERM OF LOAN (YEARS)				
	15	20	25	27	30
9.00	− 51.736	− 63.028	− 71.331	− 73.932	− 77.186
9.25	− 49.534	− 60.154	− 67.892	− 70.300	− 73.297
9.50	− 47.383	− 57.360	− 64.565	− 66.792	− 69.551
9.75	− 45.276	− 54.641	− 61.344	− 63.402	− 65.939
10.00	− 43.215	− 51.996	− 58.225	− 60.125	− 62.457
10.25	− 41.199	− 49.423	− 55.205	− 56.958	− 59.098
10.50	− 39.226	− 46.918	− 52.279	− 53.893	− 55.856
10.75	− 37.295	− 44.480	− 49.445	− 50.929	− 52.727
11.00	− 35.405	− 42.106	− 46.697	− 48.061	− 49.705
11.25	− 33.554	− 39.794	− 44.033	− 45.285	− 46.786
11.50	− 31.742	− 37.543	− 41.450	− 42.596	− 43.965
11.75	− 29.968	− 35.350	− 38.944	− 39.992	− 41.238
12.00	− 28.232	− 33.214	− 36.514	− 37.470	− 38.602
12.25	− 26.532	− 31.132	− 34.155	− 35.025	− 36.051
12.50	− 24.866	− 29.104	− 31.865	− 32.655	− 33.583
12.75	− 23.235	− 27.126	− 29.642	− 30.357	− 31.194
13.00	− 21.637	− 25.199	− 27.483	− 28.129	− 28.880
13.25	− 20.072	− 23.319	− 25.385	− 25.966	− 26.640
13.50	− 18.538	− 21.487	− 23.348	− 23.868	− 24.468
13.75	− 17.035	− 19.699	− 21.367	− 21.830	− 22.364
14.00	− 15.563	− 17.955	− 19.442	− 19.853	− 20.323
14.25	− 14.120	− 16.254	− 17.570	− 17.931	− 18.344
14.50	− 12.706	− 14.594	− 15.749	− 16.065	− 16.424
14.75	− 11.320	− 12.974	− 13.978	− 14.251	− 14.560
15.00	− 9.961	− 11.392	− 12.255	− 12.488	− 12.751
15.25	− 8.629	− 9.848	− 10.578	− 10.774	− 10.994
15.50	− 7.323	− 8.340	− 8.945	− 9.107	− 9.288
15.75	− 6.042	− 6.868	− 7.355	− 7.485	− 7.629
16.00	− 4.787	− 5.430	− 5.807	− 5.906	− 6.017
16.25	− 3.555	− 4.025	− 4.298	− 4.370	− 4.450
16.50	− 2.347	− 2.652	− 2.829	− 2.875	− 2.926
16.75	− 1.162	− 1.311	− 1.396	− 1.418	− 1.443
17.00	0.000	0.000	0.000	0.000	0.000
17.25	1.141	1.282	1.361	1.382	1.405
17.50	2.259	2.534	2.689	2.729	2.772
17.75	3.357	3.760	3.984	4.042	4.104
18.00	4.435	4.958	5.248	5.322	5.402

MAXIMUM PREMIUM FOR ASSUMABLE LOANS
AS PERCENTAGE OF LOAN BALANCE
FACE INTEREST RATE: 17.25%

CURRENT RATE	REMAINING TERM OF LOAN (YEARS) 15	20	25	27	30
9.00	− 53.487	− 65.144	− 73.695	− 76.370	− 79.710
9.25	− 51.260	− 62.233	− 70.209	− 72.687	− 75.766
9.50	− 49.083	− 59.403	− 66.836	− 69.130	− 71.966
9.75	− 46.952	− 56.649	− 63.571	− 65.692	− 68.303
10.00	− 44.868	− 53.970	− 60.409	− 62.369	− 64.771
10.25	− 42.828	− 51.363	− 57.348	− 59.157	− 61.364
10.50	− 40.832	− 48.825	− 54.381	− 56.050	− 58.076
10.75	− 38.879	− 46.355	− 51.507	− 53.045	− 54.902
11.00	− 36.967	− 43.951	− 48.722	− 50.136	− 51.838
11.25	− 35.095	− 41.609	− 46.021	− 47.321	− 48.877
11.50	− 33.262	− 39.329	− 43.402	− 44.595	− 46.016
11.75	− 31.468	− 37.107	− 40.862	− 41.954	− 43.250
12.00	− 29.712	− 34.943	− 38.398	− 39.396	− 40.576
12.25	− 27.991	− 32.835	− 36.007	− 36.917	− 37.989
12.50	− 26.307	− 30.780	− 33.685	− 34.514	− 35.486
12.75	− 24.657	− 28.777	− 31.431	− 32.184	− 33.063
13.00	− 23.040	− 26.824	− 29.242	− 29.924	− 30.717
13.25	− 21.457	− 24.920	− 27.116	− 27.732	− 28.444
13.50	− 19.906	− 23.064	− 25.050	− 25.604	− 26.242
13.75	− 18.386	− 21.253	− 23.042	− 23.538	− 24.107
14.00	− 16.896	− 19.487	− 21.091	− 21.532	− 22.037
14.25	− 15.437	− 17.763	− 19.193	− 19.584	− 20.030
14.50	− 14.006	− 16.082	− 17.347	− 17.692	− 18.082
14.75	− 12.604	− 14.440	− 15.552	− 15.852	− 16.192
15.00	− 11.230	− 12.838	− 13.804	− 14.065	− 14.357
15.25	− 9.882	− 11.274	− 12.104	− 12.326	− 12.576
15.50	− 8.561	− 9.747	− 10.449	− 10.636	− 10.845
15.75	− 7.266	− 8.255	− 8.837	− 8.991	− 9.163
16.00	− 5.996	− 6.799	− 7.267	− 7.391	− 7.528
16.25	− 4.750	− 5.376	− 5.738	− 5.833	− 5.938
16.50	− 3.528	− 3.985	− 4.248	− 4.317	− 4.392
16.75	− 2.329	− 2.626	− 2.796	− 2.840	− 2.888
17.00	− 1.154	− 1.298	− 1.380	− 1.401	− 1.425
17.25	0.000	0.000	0.000	0.000	0.000
17.50	1.132	1.269	1.346	1.366	1.387
17.75	2.242	2.510	2.659	2.697	2.738
18.00	3.332	3.724	3.940	3.995	4.054

MAXIMUM PREMIUM FOR ASSUMABLE LOANS
AS PERCENTAGE OF LOAN BALANCE
FACE INTEREST RATE: 17.5%

CURRENT RATE	REMAINING TERM OF LOAN (YEARS)				
	15	20	25	27	30
9.00	− 55.244	− 67.267	− 76.065	− 78.812	− 82.238
9.25	− 52.991	− 64.318	− 72.531	− 75.078	− 78.238
9.50	− 50.790	− 61.452	− 69.113	− 71.471	− 74.385
9.75	− 48.634	− 58.662	− 65.802	− 67.986	− 70.671
10.00	− 46.526	− 55.949	− 62.598	− 64.618	− 67.089
10.25	− 44.463	− 53.309	− 59.495	− 61.361	− 63.634
10.50	− 42.444	− 50.738	− 56.488	− 58.211	− 60.300
10.75	− 40.468	− 48.237	− 53.575	− 55.164	− 57.081
11.00	− 38.535	− 45.801	− 50.751	− 52.215	− 53.974
11.25	− 36.641	− 43.429	− 48.013	− 49.360	− 50.971
11.50	− 34.788	− 41.120	− 45.359	− 46.597	− 48.070
11.75	− 32.973	− 38.869	− 42.784	− 43.920	− 45.265
12.00	− 31.196	− 36.678	− 40.286	− 41.326	− 42.554
12.25	− 29.457	− 34.542	− 37.862	− 38.813	− 39.930
12.50	− 27.752	− 32.461	− 35.509	− 36.377	− 37.392
12.75	− 26.084	− 30.432	− 33.225	− 34.014	− 34.935
13.00	− 24.449	− 28.455	− 31.006	− 31.723	− 32.555
13.25	− 22.847	− 26.526	− 28.851	− 29.500	− 30.250
13.50	− 21.278	− 24.646	− 26.756	− 27.343	− 28.017
13.75	− 19.741	− 22.812	− 24.721	− 25.248	− 25.853
14.00	− 18.234	− 21.023	− 22.743	− 23.215	− 23.754
14.25	− 16.758	− 19.277	− 20.819	− 21.240	− 21.718
14.50	− 15.311	− 17.574	− 18.948	− 19.321	− 19.743
14.75	− 13.893	− 15.911	− 17.128	− 17.456	− 17.827
15.00	− 12.503	− 14.289	− 15.357	− 15.644	− 15.966
15.25	− 11.140	− 12.704	− 13.634	− 13.881	− 14.159
15.50	− 9.804	− 11.158	− 11.956	− 12.167	− 12.404
15.75	− 8.494	− 9.647	− 10.322	− 10.500	− 10.698
16.00	− 7.209	− 8.171	− 8.731	− 8.878	− 9.040
16.25	− 5.949	− 6.730	− 7.181	− 7.298	− 7.428
16.50	− 4.713	− 5.322	− 5.670	− 5.761	− 5.861
16.75	− 3.501	− 3.945	− 4.198	− 4.264	− 4.335
17.00	− 2.312	− 2.600	− 2.764	− 2.805	− 2.851
17.25	− 1.145	− 1.285	− 1.364	− 1.385	− 1.407
17.50	0.000	0.000	0.000	0.000	0.000
17.75	1.123	1.257	1.331	1.350	1.370
18.00	2.226	2.486	2.629	2.666	2.705

MAXIMUM PREMIUM FOR ASSUMABLE LOANS
AS PERCENTAGE OF LOAN BALANCE
FACE INTEREST RATE: 17.75%

CURRENT RATE	REMAINING TERM OF LOAN (YEARS)				
	15	20	25	27	30
9.00	-57.008	-69.397	-78.440	-81.258	-84.769
9.25	-54.729	-66.410	-74.859	-77.473	-80.714
9.50	-52.503	-63.507	-71.394	-73.817	-76.808
9.75	-50.323	-60.682	-68.039	-70.284	-73.041
10.00	-48.191	-57.934	-64.791	-66.870	-69.410
10.25	-46.105	-55.260	-61.646	-63.569	-65.907
10.50	-44.063	-52.657	-58.599	-60.375	-62.526
10.75	-42.064	-50.124	-55.646	-57.287	-59.263
11.00	-40.109	-47.657	-52.785	-54.298	-56.112
11.25	-38.194	-45.255	-50.010	-51.404	-53.068
11.50	-36.319	-42.916	-47.320	-48.602	-50.127
11.75	-34.484	-40.637	-44.710	-45.889	-47.283
12.00	-32.687	-38.418	-42.179	-43.260	-44.534
12.25	-30.927	-36.255	-39.722	-40.712	-41.874
12.50	-29.204	-34.147	-37.337	-38.243	-39.300
12.75	-27.516	-32.093	-35.022	-35.848	-36.809
13.00	-25.863	-30.090	-32.773	-33.525	-34.396
13.25	-24.243	-28.137	-30.589	-31.272	-32.060
13.50	-22.656	-26.233	-28.466	-29.085	-29.795
13.75	-21.101	-24.375	-26.403	-26.962	-27.601
14.00	-19.578	-22.563	-24.398	-24.901	-25.473
14.25	-18.085	-20.796	-22.449	-22.899	-23.409
14.50	-16.621	-19.070	-20.553	-20.954	-21.407
14.75	-15.187	-17.387	-18.708	-19.063	-19.463
15.00	-13.781	-15.744	-16.913	-17.226	-17.577
15.25	-12.403	-14.139	-15.166	-15.440	-15.745
15.50	-11.052	-12.573	-13.466	-13.702	-13.965
15.75	-9.726	-11.043	-11.810	-12.012	-12.236
16.00	-8.427	-9.548	-10.197	-10.367	-10.555
16.25	-7.153	-8.089	-8.626	-8.766	-8.920
16.50	-5.903	-6.662	-7.096	-7.208	-7.331
16.75	-4.677	-5.269	-5.604	-5.690	-5.785
17.00	-3.474	-3.906	-4.150	-4.212	-4.280
17.25	-2.294	-2.575	-2.732	-2.772	-2.815
17.50	-1.136	-1.273	-1.349	-1.368	-1.389
17.75	0.000	0.000	0.000	0.000	0.000
18.00	1.115	1.245	1.316	1.334	1.353

634

DISCOUNT POINT TABLE
(Effective Annual Interest Rates on Loan Held to Maturity)

The following tables indicate the effective interest rate paid over the term of a mortgage loan when discount points are charged at origination. Discount points are commonly charged to either or both the seller and buyer when a home mortgage loan is made. Each point is equal to 1% of the amount borrowed on the loan. Points are generally considered interest. Their effect is to raise the interest rate above the rate stated in the mortgage contract. The tables assume that loans run to their full amortization term. If the loan is paid off before maturity, the effective rate is higher than that shown in the table. The difference is not substantial, however, unless the loan is paid off in the early part of the term.

To use the table, you must know the following items:

1. *The loan maturity.* There are two tables each for loans with maturities of 15, 20, 25, and 30 years.

2. *The contract or face rate of interest.* This is the rate of interest stated in the mortgage contract. Contract rates are shown in the left-most column of each table. One table covers rates from 7% to 13.75% and the other from 14% to 20.75% in .25% increments.

3. *The number of discount points charged.* These are listed in the heading of each table and vary from 1 to 5 points.

Example: A loan with a maturity of 15 years is originated at a contract rate of 10%. If three points are charged and the loan is held to maturity, what is the effective annual rate of interest?

Look at the first table for 15-year loans. Find "10.00" in the column under "CONTRACT RATE." Follow this row across to the column under "3 DISCOUNT POINTS." This is the effective interest rate of 10.54%

Example. A loan is originated for 15 years at a contract interest rate of 14. 5%. If the lender wants to earn an effective rate of 15.5% on the loan, how many discount points should be charged?

Look at the second table for 15-year loans. Find the row under "CONTRACT RATE" for 14.50%. Follow this row across until a rate of at least 15.5% is found. The column under "5 DISCOUNT POINTS" shows an effective rate of 15.55%, so the lender should charge 5 points.

EFFECTIVE INTEREST RATE
ON LOAN HELD TO MATURITY
LOAN TERM: 15 YEARS

CONTRACT RATE	DISCOUNT POINTS				
	1	2	3	4	5
7.00	7.16	7.33	7.49	7.66	7.83
7.25	7.41	7.58	7.75	7.92	8.09
7.50	7.66	7.83	8.00	8.17	8.35
7.75	7.92	8.08	8.25	8.43	8.60
8.00	8.17	8.34	8.51	8.68	8.86
8.25	8.42	8.59	8.76	8.94	9.12
8.50	8.67	8.84	9.02	9.19	9.37
8.75	8.92	9.09	9.27	9.45	9.63
9.00	9.17	9.35	9.52	9.70	9.89
9.25	9.42	9.60	9.78	9.96	10.14
9.50	9.67	9.85	10.03	10.21	10.40
9.75	9.93	10.10	10.29	10.47	10.66
10.00	10.18	10.36	10.54	10.72	10.91
10.25	10.43	10.61	10.79	10.98	11.17
10.50	10.68	10.86	11.05	11.24	11.43
10.75	10.93	11.11	11.30	11.49	11.68
11.00	11.18	11.37	11.56	11.75	11.94
11.25	11.43	11.62	11.81	12.00	12.20
11.50	11.69	11.87	12.06	12.26	12.46
11.75	11.94	12.13	12.32	12.51	12.71
12.00	12.19	12.38	12.57	12.77	12.97
12.25	12.44	12.63	12.83	13.03	13.23
12.50	12.69	12.88	13.08	13.28	13.49
12.75	12.94	13.14	13.34	13.54	13.74
13.00	13.19	13.39	13.59	13.79	14.00
13.25	13.45	13.64	13.85	14.05	14.26
13.50	13.70	13.90	14.10	14.31	14.52
13.75	13.95	14.15	14.35	14.56	14.77

EFFECTIVE INTEREST RATE
ON LOAN HELD TO MATURITY
LOAN TERM: 15 YEARS

CONTRACT RATE	DISCOUNT POINTS				
	1	2	3	4	5
14.00	14.20	14.40	14.61	14.82	15.03
14.25	14.45	14.66	14.86	15.08	15.29
14.50	14.70	14.91	15.12	15.33	15.55
14.75	14.95	15.16	15.37	15.59	15.81
15.00	15.21	15.42	15.63	15.84	16.07
15.25	15.46	15.67	15.88	16.10	16.32
15.50	15.71	15.92	16.14	16.36	16.58
15.75	15.96	16.18	16.39	16.61	16.84
16.00	16.21	16.43	16.65	16.87	17.10
16.25	16.46	16.68	16.90	17.13	17.36
16.50	16.72	16.94	17.16	17.38	17.62
16.75	16.97	17.19	17.41	17.64	17.87
17.00	17.22	17.44	17.67	17.90	18.13
17.25	17.47	17.69	17.92	18.16	18.39
17.50	17.72	17.95	18.18	18.41	18.65
17.75	17.97	18.20	18.43	18.67	18.91
18.00	18.23	18.46	18.69	18.93	19.17
18.25	18.48	18.71	18.94	19.18	19.43
18.50	18.73	18.96	19.20	19.44	19.69
18.75	18.98	19.22	19.45	19.70	19.95
19.00	19.23	19.47	19.71	19.96	20.20
19.25	19.48	19.72	19.97	20.21	20.46
19.50	19.74	19.98	20.22	20.47	20.72
19.75	19.99	20.23	20.48	20.73	20.98
20.00	20.24	20.48	20.73	20.98	21.24
20.25	20.49	20.74	20.99	21.24	21.50
20.50	20.74	20.99	21.24	21.50	21.76
20.75	21.00	21.24	21.50	21.76	22.02

EFFECTIVE INTEREST RATE
ON LOAN HELD TO MATURITY
LOAN TERM: 20 YEARS

CONTRACT RATE	DISCOUNT POINTS				
	1	2	3	4	5
7.00	7.13	7.26	7.40	7.53	7.67
7.25	7.38	7.51	7.65	7.79	7.93
7.50	7.63	7.77	7.90	8.04	8.18
7.75	7.88	8.02	8.16	8.30	8.44
8.00	8.14	8.27	8.41	8.55	8.70
8.25	8.39	8.53	8.67	8.81	8.96
8.50	8.64	8.78	8.92	9.07	9.21
8.75	8.89	9.03	9.18	9.32	9.47
9.00	9.14	9.28	9.43	9.58	9.73
9.25	9.39	9.54	9.68	9.83	9.99
9.50	9.64	9.79	9.94	10.09	10.24
9.75	9.90	10.04	10.19	10.35	10.50
10.00	10.15	10.30	10.45	10.60	10.76
10.25	10.40	10.55	10.70	10.86	11.02
10.50	10.65	10.80	10.96	11.11	11.27
10.75	10.90	11.06	11.21	11.37	11.53
11.00	11.15	11.31	11.47	11.63	11.79
11.25	11.40	11.56	11.72	11.88	12.05
11.50	11.66	11.81	11.98	12.14	12.31
11.75	11.91	12.07	12.23	12.40	12.57
12.00	12.16	12.32	12.49	12.65	12.82
12.25	12.41	12.57	12.74	12.91	13.08
12.50	12.66	12.83	13.00	13.17	13.34
12.75	12.91	13.08	13.25	13.42	13.60
13.00	13.17	13.33	13.51	13.68	13.86
13.25	13.42	13.59	13.76	13.94	14.12
13.50	13.67	13.84	14.02	14.19	14.38
13.75	13.92	14.09	14.27	14.45	14.63

EFFECTIVE INTEREST RATE
ON LOAN HELD TO MATURITY
LOAN TERM: 20 YEARS

CONTRACT RATE	DISCOUNT POINTS				
	1	2	3	4	5
14.00	14.17	14.35	14.53	14.71	14.89
14.25	14.42	14.60	14.78	14.97	15.15
14.50	14.68	14.86	15.04	15.22	15.41
14.75	14.93	15.11	15.29	15.48	15.67
15.00	15.18	15.36	15.55	15.74	15.93
15.25	15.43	15.62	15.80	16.00	16.19
15.50	15.68	15.87	16.06	16.25	16.45
15.75	15.94	16.12	16.32	16.51	16.71
16.00	16.19	16.38	16.57	16.77	16.97
16.25	16.44	16.63	16.83	17.03	17.23
16.50	16.69	16.89	17.08	17.28	17.49
16.75	16.94	17.14	17.34	17.54	17.75
17.00	17.19	17.39	17.59	17.80	18.01
17.25	17.45	17.65	17.85	18.06	18.27
17.50	17.70	17.90	18.11	18.32	18.53
17.75	17.95	18.15	18.36	18.57	18.79
18.00	18.20	18.41	18.62	18.83	19.05
18.25	18.45	18.66	18.87	19.09	19.31
18.50	18.71	18.92	19.13	19.35	19.57
18.75	18.96	19.17	19.39	19.61	19.83
19.00	19.21	19.42	19.64	19.86	20.09
19.25	19.46	19.68	19.90	20.12	20.35
19.50	19.71	19.93	20.15	20.38	20.61
19.75	19.97	20.19	20.41	20.64	20.87
20.00	20.22	20.44	20.67	20.90	21.13
20.25	20.47	20.70	20.92	21.16	21.39
20.50	20.72	20.95	21.18	21.42	21.66
20.75	20.97	21.20	21.44	21.67	21.92

EFFECTIVE INTEREST RATE
ON LOAN HELD TO MATURITY
LOAN TERM: 25 YEARS

CONTRACT RATE	DISCOUNT POINTS				
	1	2	3	4	5
7.00	7.11	7.23	7.34	7.46	7.58
7.25	7.36	7.48	7.59	7.71	7.83
7.50	7.61	7.73	7.85	7.97	8.09
7.75	7.87	7.98	8.10	8.23	8.35
8.00	8.12	8.24	8.36	8.48	8.61
8.25	8.37	8.49	8.61	8.74	8.86
8.50	8.62	8.74	8.87	8.99	9.12
8.75	8.87	9.00	9.12	9.25	9.38
9.00	9.12	9.25	9.38	9.51	9.64
9.25	9.38	9.50	9.63	9.76	9.90
9.50	9.63	9.76	9.89	10.02	10.16
9.75	9.88	10.01	10.14	10.28	10.41
10.00	10.13	10.26	10.40	10.53	10.67
10.25	10.38	10.52	10.65	10.79	10.93
10.50	10.63	10.77	10.91	11.05	11.19
10.75	10.88	11.02	11.16	11.30	11.45
11.00	11.14	11.28	11.42	11.56	11.71
11.25	11.39	11.53	11.67	11.82	11.97
11.50	11.64	11.78	11.93	12.08	12.23
11.75	11.89	12.04	12.18	12.33	12.49
12.00	12.14	12.29	12.44	12.59	12.74
12.25	12.40	12.54	12.69	12.85	13.00
12.50	12.65	12.80	12.95	13.11	13.26
12.75	12.90	13.05	13.21	13.36	13.52
13.00	13.15	13.30	13.46	13.62	13.78
13.25	13.40	13.56	13.72	13.88	14.04
13.50	13.65	13.81	13.97	14.14	14.30
13.75	13.91	14.07	14.23	14.39	14.56

EFFECTIVE INTEREST RATE
ON LOAN HELD TO MATURITY
LOAN TERM: 25 YEARS

CONTACT RATE	DISCOUNT POINTS				
	1	2	3	4	5
14.00	14.16	14.32	14.48	14.65	14.82
14.25	14.41	14.57	14.74	14.91	15.08
14.50	14.66	14.83	15.00	15.17	15.34
14.75	14.91	15.08	15.25	15.43	15.60
15.00	15.17	15.34	15.51	15.68	15.86
15.25	15.42	15.59	15.77	15.94	16.12
15.50	15.67	15.84	16.02	16.20	16.39
15.75	15.92	16.10	16.28	16.46	16.65
16.00	16.17	16.35	16.53	16.72	16.91
16.25	16.43	16.61	16.79	16.98	17.17
16.50	16.68	16.86	17.05	17.24	17.43
16.75	16.93	17.12	17.30	17.49	17.69
17.00	17.18	17.37	17.56	17.75	17.95
17.25	17.44	17.62	17.82	18.01	18.21
17.50	17.69	17.88	18.07	18.27	18.47
17.75	17.94	18.13	18.33	18.53	18.73
18.00	18.19	18.39	18.59	18.79	19.00
18.25	18.44	18.64	18.84	19.05	19.26
18.50	18.70	18.90	19.10	19.31	19.52
18.75	18.95	19.15	19.36	19.57	19.78
19.00	19.20	19.40	19.61	19.82	20.04
19.25	19.45	19.66	19.87	20.08	20.30
19.50	19.70	19.91	20.13	20.34	20.56
19.75	19.96	20.17	20.38	20.60	20.83
20.00	20.21	20.42	20.64	20.86	21.09
20.25	20.46	20.68	20.90	21.12	21.35
20.50	20.71	20.93	21.15	21.38	21.61
20.75	20.97	21.19	21.41	21.64	21.87

EFFECTIVE INTEREST RATE
ON LOAN HELD TO MATURITY
LOAN TERM: 30 YEARS

CONTRACT RATE	DISCOUNT POINTS				
	1	2	3	4	5
7.00	7.10	7.20	7.30	7.41	7.52
7.25	7.35	7.45	7.56	7.67	7.77
7.50	7.60	7.71	7.81	7.92	8.03
7.75	7.85	7.96	8.07	8.18	8.29
8.00	8.11	8.21	8.32	8.44	8.55
8.25	8.36	8.47	8.58	8.69	8.81
8.50	8.61	8.72	8.83	8.95	9.07
8.75	8.86	8.97	9.09	9.21	9.32
9.00	9.11	9.23	9.34	9.46	9.58
9.25	9.36	9.48	9.60	9.72	9.84
9.50	9.62	9.73	9.85	9.98	10.10
9.75	9.87	9.99	10.11	10.23	10.36
10.00	10.12	10.24	10.37	10.49	10.62
10.25	10.37	10.50	10.62	10.75	10.88
10.50	10.62	10.75	10.88	11.01	11.14
10.75	10.88	11.00	11.13	11.26	11.40
11.00	11.13	11.26	11.39	11.52	11.66
11.25	11.38	11.51	11.64	11.78	11.92
11.50	11.63	11.76	11.90	12.04	12.18
11.75	11.88	12.02	12.16	12.30	12.44
12.00	12.13	12.27	12.41	12.55	12.70
12.25	12.39	12.53	12.67	12.81	12.96
12.50	12.64	12.78	12.92	13.07	13.22
12.75	12.89	13.03	13.18	13.33	13.48
13.00	13.14	13.29	13.44	13.59	13.74
13.25	13.39	13.54	13.69	13.85	14.00
13.50	13.65	13.80	13.95	14.10	14.26
13.75	13.90	14.05	14.21	14.36	14.52

EFFECTIVE INTEREST RATE
ON LOAN HELD TO MATURITY
LOAN TERM: 30 YEARS

CONTRACT RATE	DISCOUNT POINTS				
	1	2	3	4	5
14.00	14.15	14.31	14.46	14.62	14.78
14.25	14.40	14.56	14.72	14.88	15.05
14.50	14.66	14.81	14.97	15.14	15.31
14.75	14.91	15.07	15.23	15.40	15.57
15.00	15.16	15.32	15.49	15.66	15.83
15.25	15.41	15.58	15.74	15.92	16.09
15.50	15.66	15.83	16.00	16.17	16.35
15.75	15.92	16.09	16.26	16.43	16.61
16.00	16.17	16.34	16.51	16.69	16.87
16.25	16.42	16.59	16.77	16.95	17.14
16.50	16.67	16.85	17.03	17.21	17.40
16.75	16.92	17.10	17.29	17.47	17.66
17.00	17.18	17.36	17.54	17.73	17.92
17.25	17.43	17.61	17.80	17.99	18.18
17.50	17.68	17.87	18.06	18.25	18.45
17.75	17.93	18.12	18.31	18.51	18.71
18.00	18.19	18.38	18.57	18.77	18.97
18.25	18.44	18.63	18.83	19.03	19.23
18.50	18.69	18.89	19.08	19.29	19.49
18.75	18.94	19.14	19.34	19.55	19.76
19.00	19.20	19.40	19.60	19.81	20.02
19.25	19.45	19.65	19.86	20.07	20.28
19.50	19.70	19.90	20.11	20.33	20.54
19.75	19.95	20.16	20.37	20.59	20.81
20.00	20.21	20.41	20.63	20.85	21.07
20.25	20.46	20.67	20.88	21.11	21.33
20.50	20.71	20.92	21.14	21.37	21.59
20.75	20.96	21.18	21.40	21.62	21.85

GRADUATED PAYMENT MORTGAGES
(Monthly Payment per $1,000 of Principal)

The following tables allow you to compute a payment schedule for a common form of graduated payment mortgage loan. This type of loan features a 5-year period in the beginning of the loan term in which monthly payments are lower than with a conventional fixed-payment loan. For each year of this period, monthly payments are increased by 7.5% compared with the previous year. The payment reaches its highest level in the sixth year and is constant over the remaining term of the loan.

The table allows you to calculate what the payments will be for each year of the initial term and the constant payment for the remaining term. You will need the following information:

1. *The interest rate on the loan.* Interest rates ranging from 8% to 21.75% in .25% intervals are listed in the left-most column of the tables.

2. *The amount of the loan.* The factors in the tables represent the monthly payment in dollars for each thousand dollars of original loan principal. To calculate the payments for your loan, you must multiply the factor by the number of thousands in the loan amount.

Example. A graduated payment mortgage, following the form of FHA 245 plan III, is originated at 12% interest. The amount of the loan is $55,500. What is the monthly payment in the first year? In the sixth year?

Find the column under "INTEREST RATE" and look for the rate of 12.00%. Follow this row to the column under "YEAR 1st." The factor is 7.91. Multiply this factor by 55.5 to obtain the first-year payment of $439.01.

Now follow the row for the 12% interest rate to the column under "YEAR 6-30." The factor shown is 11.36. Multiplying this factor by 55.5 gives $630.48, the payment in the sixth year and every year thereafter.

Example. You can afford to pay up to $400 in monthly payments in the first year. If the interest rate on graduated payment mortgages is 15%, how much can you afford to borrow?

Look under "INTEREST RATE" to find 15.00 (second page of tables). The factor under the 1st year is 9.90. Divide $400 by the factor to obtain 40.4. Multiply this figure by $1,000 to obtain the maximum loan you can afford, $40,400.

GRADUATED PAYMENT MORTGAGE
MONTHLY PAYMENT PER $1000 OF PRINCIPAL
FHA 245 PLAN III
LOAN TERM = 30 YEARS

INTEREST RATE	YEAR					
	1	2	3	4	5	6–30
7.00	4.97	5.34	5.74	6.17	6.63	7.13
7.25	5.10	5.48	5.89	6.34	6.81	7.32
7.50	5.23	5.63	6.05	6.50	6.99	7.52
7.75	5.37	5.77	6.21	6.67	7.17	7.71
8.00	5.51	5.92	6.37	6.85	7.36	7.91
8.25	5.65	6.07	6.53	7.02	7.55	8.11
8.50	5.79	6.23	6.69	7.19	7.73	8.31
8.75	5.93	6.38	6.86	7.37	7.93	8.52
9.00	6.08	6.53	7.02	7.55	8.12	8.73
9.25	6.22	6.69	7.19	7.73	8.31	8.94
9.50	6.37	6.85	7.36	7.92	8.51	9.15
9.75	6.52	7.01	7.54	8.10	8.71	9.36
10.00	6.67	7.17	7.71	8.29	8.91	9.58
10.25	6.82	7.33	7.88	8.47	9.11	9.79
10.50	6.97	7.50	8.06	8.66	9.31	10.01
10.75	7.13	7.66	8.24	8.85	9.52	10.23
11.00	7.28	7.83	8.42	9.05	9.73	10.46
11.25	7.44	8.00	8.60	9.24	9.93	10.68
11.50	7.60	8.17	8.78	·9.44	10.14	10.90
11.75	7.75	8.34	8.96	9.63	10.36	11.13
12.00	7.91	8.51	9.15	9.83	10.57	11.36
12.25	8.07	8.68	9.33	10.03	10.78	11.59
12.50	8.24	8.85	9.52	10.23	11.00	11.82
12.75	8.40	9.03	9.71	10.43	11.22	12.06
13.00	8.56	9.20	9.89	10.64	11.43	12.29
13.25	8.73	9.38	10.08	10.84	11.65	12.53
13.50	8.89	9.56	10.28	11.05	11.87	12.77
13.75	9.06	9.74	10.47	11.25	12.10	13.00
14.00	9.23	9.92	10.66	11.46	12.32	13.24
14.25	9.39	10.10	10.86	11.67	12.54	13.49
14.50	9.56	10.28	11.05	11.88	12.77	13.73
14.75	9.73	10.46	11.25	12.09	13.00	13.97

GRADUATED PAYMENT MORTGAGE
MONTHLY PAYMENT PER $1000 OF PRINCIPAL
FHA 245 PLAN III
LOAN TERM = 30 YEARS

INTEREST RATE	YEAR 1	2	3	4	5	6–30
15.00	9.90	10.65	11.44	12.30	13.22	14.22
15.25	10.07	10.83	11.64	12.51	13.45	14.46
15.50	10.25	11.01	11.84	12.73	13.68	14.71
15.75	10.42	11.20	12.04	12.94	13.91	14.96
16.00	10.59	11.39	12.24	13.16	14.15	15.21
16.25	10.77	11.57	12.44	13.37	14.38	15.46
16.50	10.94	11.76	12.64	13.59	14.61	15.71
16.75	11.12	11.95	12.85	13.81	14.85	15.96
17.00	11.29	12.14	13.05	14.03	15.08	16.21
17.25	11.47	12.33	13.25	14.25	15.32	16.47
17.50	11.65	12.52	13.46	14.47	15.55	16.72
17.75	11.82	12.71	13.66	14.69	15.79	16.98
18.00	12.00	12.90	13.87	14.91	16.03	17.23
18.25	12.18	13.10	14.08	15.13	16.27	17.49
18.50	12.36	13.29	14.29	15.36	16.51	17.75
18.75	12.54	13.48	14.49	15.58	16.75	18.01
19.00	12.72	13.68	14.70	15.81	16.99	18.27
19.25	12.90	13.87	14.91	16.03	17.23	18.53
19.50	13.09	14.07	15.12	16.26	17.48	18.79
19.75	13.27	14.26	15.33	16.48	17.72	19.05
20.00	13.45	14.46	15.54	16.71	17.96	19.31
20.25	13.63	14.66	15.76	16.94	18.21	19.57
20.50	13.82	14.85	15.97	17.17	18.45	19.84
20.75	14.00	15.05	16.18	17.39	18.70	20.10
21.00	14.19	15.25	16.39	17.62	18.95	20.37
21.25	14.37	15.45	16.61	17.85	19.19	20.63
21.50	14.56	15.65	16.82	18.08	19.44	20.90
21.75	14.74	15.85	17.04	18.31	19.69	21.16
22.00	14.93	16.05	17.25	18.55	19.94	21.43
22.25	15.12	16.25	17.47	18.78	20.19	21.70
22.50	15.30	16.45	17.68	19.01	20.44	21.97
22.75	15.49	16.65	17.90	19.24	20.69	22.24

Depreciation Rates

The Tax Reform Act of 1986

The body of these tables shows the rate of depreciation that may be claimed each year for assets eligible for depreciation. The tables shown here include those offered by the Tax Reform Act of 1986 and those used for standard accounting purposes.

Depreciation deductions may be claimed for tax purposes on most structural assets or equipment used in a trade or business. These deductions may be thought of as providing a tax incentive for the use of productive assets, allowing for the cost of assets to be recovered over time, or as an allowance for exhaustion, wear and tear, and normal obsolescence.

To be eligible for depreciation deductions, an asset must be used in a trade or business or held for the production of income. This excludes personal cars or residences since they are not used in a trade or business. It also excludes land since land does not wear out. For example, a single family home that is rented to a tenant can be depreciated, but not the land under it.

Depreciation under the Tax Reform Act of 1986. The Tax Reform Act of 1986 (TRA) prescribed the rate at which asset cost may be depreciated each year. This is based on the class of property. Classes include 3-, 5-, 7-, 10-, 15-, 20-, 27½-, 31½-year life property. Apartment buildings and other residential rental properties are generally in the 27½-year category; most other buildings such as offices and retail stores are depreciable over a 31½-year life. The depreciation to be claimed is shown in the following tables as a fraction of original cost.

For personal property, such as refrigerators and furniture, the annual depreciation allowance under TRA will vary depending on the year it is placed in service. For real estate, the allowance for the first and last year depends upon the month placed in service.

To use the tables you need to know the year the property was placed in service (for buildings the month is needed), the recovery class, and the asset cost. Select the appropriate table considering the year and class of property. For most personal property (short-lived) find the intersection of the class life (year) with the year of use. Apply the rate in the table to the asset cost. For a building, find the column for the month it was placed in service. Multiply the rate by the building cost to derive the annual depreciation allowance.

Example. A warehouse was acquired in July 1988 for $1,000,000, exclusive of land. How much depreciation may be deducted under TRA in 1988 and 1989? Turn to the table which offers recovery amounts for nonresidential real property other than low-income housing. The intersection of July with year 1 provides the number .015. Thus, 1.5% of the asset cost, or $15,000 for the warehouse, is deductible in 1988. The intersection of July with recovery year 2 provides .032. Therefore 3.2% of the asset cost, or $32,000 may be deducted in the second year (1989).

Example. What are the first and second year deductions for furniture that cost $500 and is placed in service in 1990? Most furniture is in the 7-year property class, so you may find the column for 7-year property. The appropriate first year rate is .143. Then 14.3 percent of its cost may be deducted in 1990 regardless of the month of acquisition. This is a $71.50 deduction. The second year rate is .245. The second year deduction is 24.5% of $500 or $122.50.

647

Example. A duplex was purchased for rental use in January 1990 at a cost of $125,000. Of the purchase price $25,000 was for land, leaving $100,000 to be depreciated. How much depreciation may be claimed in 1990 and each year thereafter?

Locate the table with the heading: Annual Straight-Line Depreciation Rates For Real Estate, 27^1/$_2$ Year Residential Real Property. At the intersection of Jan with Recovery Year 1 you will find .035. In the first year of ownership 3.5% of the cost is allowed for tax purposes as depreciation, which is $3,500 for a $100,000 asset. From years 2 through 27 3.6% may be claimed, providing a $3,600 annual tax deduction.

ANNUAL STRAIGHT-LINE DEPRECIATION RATES FOR REAL ESTATE

27½-YEAR RESIDENTIAL REAL PROPERTY

Recovery Year(s)	Jan	Feb	Mar	Apr	May	Jun	Jul	Aug	Sep	Oct	Nov	Dec
1	.035	.032	.029	.026	.023	.020	.017	.014	.011	.008	.005	.002
2-27	.036	.036	.036	.036	.036	.036	.036	.036	.036	.036	.036	.036
28	.029	.032	.035	.036	.036	.036	.036	.036	.036	.036	.036	.036
29	0	0	0	.002	.005	.008	.011	.014	.017	.020	.023	.026
Total	1.000	1.000	1.000	1.000	1.000	1.000	1.000	1.000	1.000	1.000	1.000	1.000

31½-YEAR NONRESIDENTIAL REAL PROPERTY

Recovery Years(s)	Jan	Feb	Mar	Apr	May	Jun	Jul	Aug	Sep	Oct	Nov	Dec
1	.030	.028	.025	.022	.020	.017	.015	.012	.009	.007	.004	.001
-27	.032	.032	.032	.032	.032	.032	.032	.032	.032	.032	.032	.032
28	.010	.012	.015	.018	.020	.023	.025	.028	.031	.032	.032	.032
29	0	0	0	0	0	0	0	0	0	.001	.004	.007
Total	1.000	1.000	1.000	1.000	1.000	1.000	1.000	1.000	1.000	1.000	1.000	1.000

UNOFFICIAL ALTERNATIVE DEPRECIATION SYSTEM FOR REAL ESTATE

DEPRECIATION RATES FOR 27 OR 31 YEAR REAL PROPERTY (40 YEARS)*

Recovery Year(s)	Jan	Feb	Mar	Apr	May	Jun	Jul	Aug	Sep	Oct	Nov	Dec
1	.024	.022	.020	.018	.016	.014	.011	.009	.007	.005	.003	.001
2-40	.025	.025	.025	.025	.025	.025	.025	.025	.025	.025	.025	.025
41	.001	.003	.005	.007	.009	.011	.014	.016	.018	.020	.022	.024
Total	1.000	1.000	1.000	1.000	1.000	1.000	1.000	1.000	1.000	1.000	1.000	1.000

STRAIGHT-LINE DEPRECIATION FOR PROPERTY OTHER THAN REAL ESTATE

ACRS Class	First Recovery Year %	Other Recovery Years Years	%	Last Recovery Year Year	%	Depreciation Total
3-Year	.167	2-3	.333	4	.167	1.000
5-Year	.100	2-5	.200	6	.100	1.000
7-Year	.071	2-7	.143	8	.071	1.000
10-Year	.050	2-10	.100	11	.050	1.000
15-Year	.033	2-15	.067	16	.029	1.000
20-Year	.025	2-20	.050	21	.025	1.000

ESTIMATED DEPRECIATION RATES**
ACCELERATED DEPRECIATION FOR PROPERTY OTHER THAN REAL ESTATE

Recovery Year	ACRS Class					
	3-Year (200% DB)	5-Year (200% DB)	7-Year (200% DB)	10-Year (200% DB)	15-Year (150% DB)	20-Year (150% DB)
1	.33	.200	.143	.100	.050	.038
2	.45	.320	.245	.180	.095	.072
3	.15	.192	.175	.144	.086	.067
4	.07	.115†	.125	.115	.077	.062
5		.115	.089†	.092	.069	.057
6		.058	.089	.074	.062	.053
7			.089	.066†	.059†	.049
8			.045	.066	.059	.045
9				.065	.059	.045†
10				.065	.059	.045
11				.030	.059	.045
12					.059	.045
13					.059	.045
14					.059	.045
15					.059	.045
16					.030	.045
17						.045
18						.045
19						.045
20						.045
21						.017
Total	1.00	1.000	1.000	1.000	1.000	1.000

* Multiply depreciation rates by the property's original depreciation base.
** Assumes half-year convention applies.
† Switchover to S-L depreciation over remaining useful life.

PRORATION PERCENTAGES

The following tables allow you to prorate expenses for closing dates within the 365-day calendar year. Using the percentages in the tables, you may calculate how much of prepaid or postpaid property expenses should be allocated to the buying and selling party. To use the tables, you need the following information:

1. *The closing date.* The day of the month on which the property is to be closed. According to convention the day of closing is allocated to the seller. This is reflected in the tables.

2. *When the expense was paid or is due to be paid.* Has the seller paid the expense covering the entire year or will the bill fall due after the closing and be paid by the buyer?

3. *The amount of the expense.* The expense should cover the calendar year in which the closing takes place. If the expense covers multiple years, use only that portion which covers the year of closing.

Example. Brown sells a home to Jones. The closing is scheduled for May 22. In January, Brown paid an insurance premium covering the entire calendar year in the amount of $200. Property taxes for the year are due on November 1 and will be paid by the buyer. The tax bill is expect to be $500. How should these expenses be prorated at the closing?

The insurance premium was paid by Brown, the seller. Brown should get a credit for the premium less the proportion covering the time the home was owned by Brown. Look at the tables and find the column marked "MAY." Follow this column down to the 22 under the column "DAY OF MO." This is the percentage of the year from January 1 through May 22, the day of closing. The percentage is 38.90%. Brown has used 38.9% of the insurance, the premium for which is .389 times $200, or $77.80. Brown gets a credit for the remaining $122.20 of the prepaid premium.

The same percentage is used to prorate the tax expense. Brown is debited for 38.9% of the $500 bill which covers the time Brown owned the home. Accordingly, Brown's closing statement is reduced by .389 times $500, or $194.50.

PRORATION PERCENTAGES DAYS
FROM JANUARY 1

DAY OF MO.	JAN	FEB	MARCH	APRIL	MAY	JUNE
1	0.27	8.77	16.44	24.93	33.15	41.64
2	0.55	9.04	16.71	25.21	33.42	41.92
3	0.82	9.32	16.99	25.48	33.70	42.19
4	1.10	9.59	17.26	25.75	33.97	42.47
5	1.37	9.86	17.53	26.03	34.25	42.74
6	1.64	10.14	17.81	26.30	34.52	43.01
7	1.92	10.41	18.08	26.58	34.79	43.29
8	2.19	10.68	18.36	26.85	35.07	43.56
9	2.47	10.96	18.63	27.12	35.34	43.84
10	2.74	11.23	18.90	27.40	35.62	44.11
11	3.01	11.51	19.18	27.67	35.89	44.38
12	3.29	11.78	19.45	27.95	36.16	44.66
13	3.56	12.05	19.73	28.22	36.44	44.93
14	3.84	12.33	20.00	28.49	36.71	45.21
15	4.11	12.60	20.27	28.77	36.99	45.48
16	4.38	12.88	20.55	29.04	37.26	45.75
17	4.66	13.15	20.82	29.32	37.53	46.03
18	4.93	13.42	21.10	29.59	37.81	46.30
19	5.21	13.70	21.37	29.86	38.08	46.58
20	5.48	13.97	21.64	30.14	38.36	46.85
21	5.75	14.25	21.92	30.41	38.63	47.12
22	6.03	14.52	22.19	30.68	38.90	47.40
23	6.30	14.79	22.47	30.96	39.18	47.67
24	6.58	15.07	22.74	31.23	39.45	47.95
25	6.85	15.34	23.01	31.51	39.73	48.22
26	7.12	15.62	23.29	31.78	40.00	48.49
27	7.40	15.89	23.56	32.05	40.27	48.77
28	7.67	16.16	23.84	32.33	40.55	49.04
29	7.95		24.11	32.60	40.82	49.32
30	8.22		24.38	32.88	41.10	49.59
31	8.49		24.66		41.37	

PRORATION PERCENTAGES DAYS
FROM JANUARY 1

DAY OF MO.	JULY	AUG	SEPT	OCT	NOV	DEC
			MONTH			
1	49.86	58.36	66.85	75.07	83.56	91.78
2	50.14	58.63	67.12	75.34	83.84	92.05
3	50.41	58.90	67.40	75.62	84.11	92.33
4	50.68	59.18	67.67	75.89	84.38	92.60
5	50.96	59.45	67.95	76.16	84.66	92.88
6	51.23	59.73	68.22	76.44	84.93	93.15
7	51.51	60.00	68.49	76.71	85.21	93.42
8	51.78	60.27	68.77	76.99	85.48	93.70
9	52.05	60.55	69.04	77.26	85.75	93.97
10	52.33	60.82	69.32	77.53	86.03	94.25
11	52.60	61.10	69.59	77.81	86.30	94.52
12	52.88	61.37	69.86	78.08	86.58	94.79
13	53.15	61.64	70.14	78.36	86.85	95.07
14	53.42	61.92	70.41	78.63	87.12	95.34
15	53.70	62.19	70.68	78.90	87.40	95.62
16	53.97	62.47	70.96	79.18	87.67	95.89
17	54.25	62.74	71.23	79.45	87.95	96.16
18	54.52	63.01	71.51	79.73	88.22	96.44
19	54.79	63.29	71.78	80.00	88.49	96.71
20	55.07	63.56	72.05	80.27	88.77	96.99
21	55.34	63.84	72.33	80.55	89.04	97.26
22	55.62	64.11	72.60	80.82	89.32	97.53
23	55.89	64.38	72.88	81.10	89.59	97.81
24	56.16	64.66	73.15	81.37	89.86	98.08
25	56.44	64.93	73.42	81.64	90.14	98.36
26	56.71	65.21	73.70	81.92	90.41	98.63
27	56.99	65.48	73.97	82.19	90.68	98.90
28	57.26	65.75	74.25	82.47	90.96	99.18
29	57.53	66.03	74.52	82.74	91.23	99.45
30	57.81	66.30	74.79	83.01	91.51	99.73
31	58.08	66.58		83.29		100.00

APPENDIX

House Cross Section

Description of Number Parts in House

1—Collar beam	18—Girder
2—Ceiling joist	19—Footing for foundation wall
3—Chimney cap	20—Foundation drain tile
4—Chimney pots	21—Diagonal subflooring
5—Chimney flashing	22—Foundation wall
6—Rafters	23—Termite shield
7—Roof boards	24—Wall studs
8—Stud	25—Pilaster
9—Eave trough or gutter	26—Window casing
10—Downspout or leader gooseneck	27—Wainscoting
11—Frieze	28—Baseboard
12—Door jamb	29—Floor joists
13—Basement stair riser	30—Fire brick
14—Stair stringer	31—Newel cap
15—Girder post	32—Window sash
16—Chair rail	33—Mantel
17—Furring strips	34—Newel

FIGURE 188

From Boyce's *Real Estate Appraisal Terminology*, Copyright 1975, The American Institute of Real Estate Appraisers and The Society of Real Estate Appraisers. Reprinted with permission from Ballinger Publishing Company.

APPENDIX

ABBREVIATIONS

A/C air conditioning

ACRS accelerated cost recovery system

ADR asset depreciation range

AIREA American Institute of Real Estate Appraisers

ALTA American Land Title Association

AMI alternative mortgage instrument

AML adjustable mortgage loan

APA American Planning Association

app appreciation (in appraisal terminology)

APR annual percentage rate

AREUEA American Real Estate and Urban Economics Association

ARM adjustable rate mortgage

ASA American Society of Appraisers

ASREC American Society of Real Estate Counselors

BOMA Building Owners and Managers Association

CAI Community Associations Institute

CBD central business district

CCIM Certified Commercial-Investment Member (RNMI)

CD certificate of deposit

CPI consumer price index (see cost of living index)

CPM Certified Property Manager (IREM)

CRB Certified Real Estate Brokerage Manager (RNMI)

CRE Counselor in Real Estate (ASREC)

CRS Certified Residential Specialist (RNMI)

DCR debt coverage ratio

dep depreciation (in appraisal terminology)

EIS environmental impact statement

EPA Environmental Protection Agency

FAR floor-area ratio

FDIC Federal Deposit Insurance Corporation

FHA Federal Housing Administration

FHLB Federal Home Loan Bank

FHLMC Federal Home Loan Mortgage Corporation (Freddie Mac)

FmHA Farmers Home Administration

FMRR financial management rate of return

FMV fair market value

FNMA Federal National Mortgage Association (Fannie Mae)

FPM flexible payment mortgage

FSLIC Federal Savings and Loan Insurance Corporation

FTC Federal Trade Commission

FY fiscal year

GEM growing equity mortgage

GIM gross income multiplier

GNMA Government National Mortgage Association (Ginnie Mae)

GPM graduated payment mortgage

GRI Graduate, Realtors® Institute

GRM gross rent multiplier

HOW homeowners warranty

HUD Department of Housing and Urban Development

HVAC heating, ventilation, and air conditioning

IAAO International Association of Assessing Officers

IRA individual retirement account

IREM Institute of Real Estate Management

IRR internal rate of return

IRS Internal Revenue Service

IRWA International Right-of-Way Association

L/V loan-to-value ratio

MAI Member, Appraisal Institute (AIREA)

MBA Mortgage Bankers Association of America

MGIC Mortgage Guaranty Insurance Corporation

MLS multiple listing service

MMC money market certificate of deposit

NAA National Apartment Association

NACORE National Association of Corporate Real Estate Executives

NAHB National Association of Home Builders

NAR National Association of Realtors®

NAREB National Association of Real Estate Brokers

NARELLO National Association of Real Estate Licensing Law Officials

NOI net operating income

NOW negotiable order of withdrawal (account)

NPV net present value

OAR overall rate of capitalization

OILSR Office of Interstate Land Sales Registration

PAM pledged account mortgage

P & I principal and interest (payment)

PITI principal, interest, taxes and insurance (payment)

PMI private mortgage insurance

PUD planned unit development

RAM reverse annuity mortgage

REIT real estate investment trust

RESPA Real Estate Settlement Procedures Act

RESSI Real Estate Securities and Syndication Institute

RM Residential Member (AIREA)

RNMI Realtors® National Marketing Institute

RRM renegotiated rate mortgage

R/W right-of-way

SAM shared appreciation mortgage

SBA Small Business Administration

SEC Securities and Exchange Commission

SIR Society of Industrial Realtors®

S&L savings and loan association

SMSA standard metropolitan statistical area

SRA Senior Residential Appraiser (SREA)

SREA Senior Real Estate Analyst (SREA)

SREA Society of Real Estate Appraisers

SRPA Senior Real Property Appraiser (SREA)

SYD sum-of-the-years-digits (method of depreciation)

TDR transferable development rights

TIL truth-in-lending law

UCC Uniform Commercial Code

ULI Urban Land Institute

VA Veterans Administration

VRM variable rate mortgage

WCR Women's Council of Realtors

YTM yield to maturity

MEASUREMENT TABLES

ENGLISH SYSTEM

Linear Measure

12 inches (in or ″)	= 1 foot (ft or ′)
3 feet	= 1 yard (yd)
5½ yards	= 1 rod (rd), pole, or perch (16½ feet)
40 rods	= 1 furlong (fur)
	= 220 yards
	= 660 feet
6076.11549 feet	= 1 international nautical mile

Gunter's or Surveyor's Chain Measure

7.92 inches (in)	= 1 link
100 links	= 1 chain (ch)
	= 4 rods
	= 66 feet
80 chains	= 1 statute mile (mi)
	= 320 rods
	= 5,280 feet

Area Measure

Squares and cubes of units are sometimes abbreviated by using "superior" figures. For example, ft^2 means square foot, and ft^3 means cubic foot.

144 square inches	= 1 square foot (ft^2)
9 square feet	= 1 square yard (yd^2)
	= 1,296 square inches
30¼ square yards	= 1 square rod (rd^2)
	= 272¼ square feet
160 square rods	= 1 acre
	= 4,840 square yards
	= 43,560 square feet
640 acres	= 1 square mile (mi^2)
1 mile square	= 1 section (of land)
6 miles square	= 1 township
	= 36 sections
	= 36 square miles

APPENDIX

METRIC SYSTEM

Linear Measure

10 millimeters (mm)	= 1 centimeter (cm)
10 centimeters	= 1 decimeter (dm)
	= 100 millimeters
10 decimeters	= 1 meter (m)
	= 1,000 millimeters
10 meters	= 1 dekameter (dam)
10 dekameters	= 1 hectometer (hm)
	= 100 meters
10 hectometers	= 1 kilometer (km)
	= 1,000 meters

Area Measure

100 square millimeters (mm^2)	= 1 square centimeter (cm^2)
10,000 square centimeters	= 1 square meter (m^2)
	= 1,000,000 square millimeters
100 square meters	= 1 are (a)
100 ares	= 1 hectare (ha)
	= 10,000 square meters
100 hectares	= 1 square kilometer (km^2)
	= 1,000,000 square meters

EQUIVALENTS BETWEEN ENGLISH AND METRIC SYSTEMS

Lengths

angstrom	= 0.1 nanometer (exactly)
	= 0.000 1 micron (exactly)
	= 0.000 000 1 millimeter (exactly)
	= 0.000 000 004 inch
1 cable's length	= 120 fathoms
	= 720 feet
	= 219.456 meters (exactly)
1 centimeter (cm)	= 0.3937 inch
1 chain (ch), (Gunter's or surveyor's)	= 66 feet
	= 20.1168 meters (exactly)
1 chain (engineer's)	= 100 feet
	= 30.48 meters (exactly)
1 decimeter (dm)	= 3.937 inches
1 dekameter (dam)	= 32.808 feet
1 fathom	= 6 feet
	= 1.8288 meters (exactly)

1 foot (ft)	= 0.3048 meters (exactly)
1 inch (in)	= 2.54 centimeters (exactly)
1 kilometer (km)	= 0.621 mile
	= 3,280.8 feet
1 league (land)	= 3 statute miles
	= 4.828 kilometers
1 link (Gunter's or surveyor's)	= 7.92 inches
	= 0.201 meter
1 link (engineer's)	= 1 foot
	= 0.305 meter
1 meter (m)	= 39.37 inches
	= 1.094 yards
1 mile (mi) (statute or land)	= 5,280 feet
	= 1.609 kilometers
1 international nautical mile (INM)	= 1,852 kilometers (exactly)
	= 1.150779 statute miles
	= 6,076.11549 feet
1 rod (rd), pole, or perch	= 16½ feet
	= 5½ yards
	= 5.029 meters
1 yard (yd)	= 0.9144 meter (exactly)

Areas or Surfaces

1 acre	= 43,560 square feet
	= 4,840 square yards
	= 0.405 hectare
1 are (a) (100 square meters)	= 119.599 square yards
	= 0.025 acre
1 hectare (ha) (10,000 square meters)	= 2.471 acres
[1 square (building)]	= 100 square feet
1 square centimeter (cm^2)	= 0.155 square inch
1 square decimeter (dm^2)	= 15.500 square inches
1 square foot (ft^2)	= 929.030 square centimeters
1 square inch (in^2)	= 6.452 square centimeters
1 square kilometer (km^2)	= 247.105 acres
	= 0.386 square mile
	= 1,196 square yards
1 square meter (m^2)	= 10.764 square feet
1 square mile (mi^2)	= 640 acres 258.999 hectares
1 square millimeter (mm^2)	= 0.002 square inch
1 square rod (rd^2), sq. pole, or sq. perch	= 25.293 square meters
1 square yard (yd^2)	= 0.836 square meter

APPENDIX

MATHEMATICAL FORMULAS

To find the **CIRCUMFERENCE** of a:

Circle—Multiply the diameter by 3.14159265 (usually 3.1416).

To find the **AREA** of a:

Circle—Multiply the square of the diameter by .785398 (usually .7854).

Rectangle—Multiply the length of the base by the height.

Sphere (surface)—Multiply the square of the radius by 3.1416 and multiply by 4.

Square—Square the length of one side.

Trapezoid—Add the length of the 2 parallel sides, multiply by the height and divide by 2.

Triangle—Multiply the length of the base by the height and divide by 2.

REAL ESTATE FORMS AND WORKSHEETS

Standard real estate forms that are mentioned in the text are reproduced in this section for the convenience of the reader. Although they have been reduced to fit on the page, these forms are more than adequate for anyone who wishes to become familiar with their contents.

In addition several worksheets are provided to facilitate analyses that must be prepared by the prospective home buyer or home seller.

The following forms and worksheets are included:
Qualifying Income Worksheet
Debt Obligation Worksheet
Residential Purchase Agreement and Deposit Receipt
Residential Loan Application
Request for Verification of Employment
Request for Verification of Deposit
Seller's Estimated Receipts Worksheet
Settlement Statement
Form 2119 Sale or Exchange of Principal Residence
Form 3903 Moving Expenses

Debt Obligations Worksheet

For all entries, use average monthly payment.

Loans from lending institutions and credit companies (if term of loan is at least ten months):

Creditor	Payment
_____	_____
_____	_____
_____	_____

Credit cards and lines of credit (if balance maintained):

Source	Payment
_____	_____
_____	_____
_____	_____

Mortgage debt on rental property or second home:

Property	Payment
_____	_____

Child support: _____
Alimony: _____

Total obligations: _____

Qualifying Income Worksheet

Source of Income	Borrower	Spouse
Annual Salary:	_____	_____

Variable income (list annual average for last two years):

	Borrower	Spouse
Overtime pay:	_____	_____
Bonus pay:	_____	_____
Commissions:	_____	_____
Second job:	_____	_____
Self-employment:	_____	_____

Investment income (list average if at least $1,200 per year):

	Borrower	Spouse
Interest:	_____	_____
Dividends:	_____	_____
Royalties:	_____	_____
Rental property net operating income:	_____	_____
Business profits:	_____	_____

Other income (optional):

	Borrower	Spouse
Alimony:	_____	_____
Child support:	_____	_____
Welfare:	_____	_____
Social security:	_____	_____
Pension:	_____	_____

Total income:	_____	_____

Add two totals: _____
Monthly income (divide by 12): _____

Note: All income listed must be consistent and expected to continue in the future. The lender may ask you to verify past income.

RESIDENTIAL PURCHASE AGREEMENT AND DEPOSIT RECEIPT

RECEIVED from _____

_____, hereinafter designated as PURCHASER, the amount set forth below as **DEPOSIT** on account of the

PURCHASE PRICE of $_____ (_____**DOLLARS**),

for the real property in the City of_____, County of_____, State of_____,

described as_____, upon the following **TERMS AND CONDITIONS:**

1. FINANCING TERMS. *(Also refer to Items 8,9, and 10 on the reverse side)*

A. $_____ **DEPOSIT** evidenced by ☐ Cash, ☐ Cashiers Check, ☐ Note, ☐ Personal Check, ☐ Other:_____,

held uncashed until acceptance and one day thereafter deposited with:_____.

B. $_____ **ADDITIONAL CASH DEPOSIT In escrow** ☐ within____days from acceptance, ☐ upon removal of all contingen-

cies.

C. $_____ **BALANCE OF CASH PAYMENT at close of escrow.**

FIRST LOAN

D. $_____ **PROCEEDS FROM NEW FIRST LOAN:** ☐ FHA, ☐ VA, ☐ CONVENTIONAL ☐ FIXED RATE,

☐ OTHER:_____

for _____ years, with Interest not to exceed _____%, payable at approximately $_____ p/mo,

☐ including Taxes and Insurance, with the balance due not less than _____ years. ☐ Other terms:_____

_____. Loan fee not to exceed _____% plus $_____

Seller agrees to pay discount points not to exceed_____%. Purchaser agrees to pay discount points not to exceed

_____%. FHA — MIP to be ☐ Financed, ☐ Paid in Cash.

E. $_____ **EXISTING FIRST LOAN:** ☐ ASSUMPTION OF, ☐ SUBJECT TO existing first loan of record:

☐ FHA, ☐ VA, ☐ CONVENTIONAL, ☐ PRIVATE _____ ☐ FIXED RATE, ☐ OTHER: _____

payable at $_____ per month, with interest currently at _____%, ☐ including Taxes and Insurance,

with Interest Rate to be adjusted not to exceed _____%. Other terms: _____

Held by: _____. Assumption Fee, if any, not to exceed_____%.

All charges related to assumption shall be paid by Purchaser.

☐ ASSUMPTION OF VA LOAN WITH RELEASE OF LIABILITY: Purchaser shall assume Seller's Potential Indemnity

Liability to the U.S. Government for the repayment of the loan.

F. $_____ **SELLER FINANCING:** First Loan secured by the property, payable at $_____ per month, or more, including

_____% interest, with the balance due _____ years from date of conveyance, ☐ due on sale.

A late charge of $_____ shall be due on monthly payments tendered more than _____ days late.

JUNIOR LOANS

G. $_____ **PROCEEDS FROM NEW SECOND LOAN:** ☐ FIXED RATE ☐ OTHER:_____

amortization _____ years, with Interest not to exceed _____%, payable at approximately $_____ p/mo,

with the balance due not less than _____ years. ☐ Other terms:_____

_____. Loan fee not to exceed _____%.

H. $_____ **EXISTING SECOND LOAN** ☐ ASSUMPTION OF, ☐ SUBJECT TO existing second loan of record:

☐ FIXED RATE, ☐ Other:_____

payable at $_____ per month, with interest currently at _____%. Interest Rate to be adjusted

to: _____%. Other terms: _____

Held by: _____. Assumption Fee, if any, not to exceed_____%.

All charges related to assumption shall be paid by purchaser.

I. $_____ **SELLER FINANCING:** ☐ SECOND, ☐ THIRD LOAN secured by the property, payable at $_____ per

month, or more, including _____% interest, with the balance due _____ years from date of conveyance, ☐ due on sale.

A late charge of $_____ shall be due on monthly payments tendered more than _____ days late.

J. $_____ **OTHER FINANCIAL TERMS:** ☐ BELOW, ☐ IN ATTACHED ADDENDUM

K. $_____ **BONDS AND ASSESSMENTS** of record assumed by Purchaser. (See Item 22 on page 101-R.2)

L. $_____ **TOTAL PURCHASE PRICE** (not including closing costs). Any net differences between the approximate balances

of encumbrances shown above, which are to be assumed or taken subject to, and the actual balances of said encumbrances

at close of escrow shall be adjusted in ☐ Cash, ☐ Other:_____

M. LOAN APPROVAL: Conditioned upon Lender's ☐ written, ☐ verbal LOAN APPROVAL within _____ days of acceptance, per Item 8

on reverse side.

2. ADDITIONAL TERMS AND CONDITIONS:

3. ADDENDUM. Addendum(s), identified as _____, signed by the parties, is attached.

4. SELLER'S PROPERTY DISCLOSURE STATEMENT [Professional Publishing Form 109.1 & 109.2 or 109.5 CAL] ☐ is, ☐ is not to be provided to Purchaser.

(continued on reverse side)

PROVISIONS ON REVERSE SIDE ARE PART OF THIS AGREEMENT Purchaser's Initials: [_____] [_____] Seller's Initials: [_____] [_____]

FORM 101-R.1 (12-87) COPYRIGHT © 1985, BY PROFESSIONAL PUBLISHING CORP., 122 PAUL DR., SAN RAFAEL, CA 94903, (415) 472-1964 **PROFESSIONAL PUBLISHING**

APPENDIX

. . . PROPERTY DISCLOSURE STATEMENT *(continued).* On or before delivery of the accepted offer or counter offer, Purchaser shall receive, in addition to any Transfer Statements required by law, a Property Disclosure Statement prepared and signed by Seller. If Purchaser is not satisfied with any condition of the property disclosed in the statement, and which was not previously known to Purchaser, he may terminate the transaction by written notice delivered to Seller's broker or agent *within 72 hours of receipt* of Seller's Property Disclosure Statement, or notify Seller's broker or agent in writing *within said 72 hours* of Purchaser's election to order additional inspections of the property by appropriate professionals.

If Purchaser is not satisfied with the result of any such inspections, he may terminate the transaction by written notice delivered to Seller's broker or agent, together with copies of all inspection reports, *within fifteen (15) days of receipt* of Seller's Property Disclosure Statement.

Purchaser understands that Seller's Property Disclosure Statement is not a substitute for property inspections by professionals, including but not limited to engineers, architects, general contractors, and structural pest control operators, and Purchaser has the opportunity to retain and pay for such professionals as he believes are appropriate. Purchaser understands and acknowledges that the brokers and agents in the transaction cannot warrant the condition of the property or guarantee that all defects have been disclosed by Seller.

Seller agrees to hold all brokers and agents in the transaction harmless and to defend and indemnify them from any claim, demand, action or proceedings resulting from any omission or alleged omission by Seller in his Property Disclosure Statement. Unless otherwise required by this agreement, *(i.e., Clause #26, MAINTENANCE)* Seller shall not be obligated to make any repair or remedy any defect set forth in his Property Disclosure Statement.

5. TIME. Time is of the essence of this agreement. All modifications and extensions shall be in writing and signed by all parties.

6. DEFINITIONS. The term "Broker" includes cooperating brokers and all sales persons, and the term "days" means calendar days unless otherwise specified.

7. CONDITIONS SATISFIED IN WRITING. Each condition contained herein shall be satisfied according to its terms or waived in writing by the party responsible within the time specified (or any extension thereof agreed to by the parties in writing), or this agreement shall be null and void and all deposits returned to Purchaser less expenses incurred by Purchaser to the date of cancellation of this transaction. This paragraph contemplates that each party shall diligently pursue the completion of this transaction.

8. LOAN APPROVAL. Within the number of days and in the manner specified under **Item 1-M**, Purchaser shall provide Seller with evidence of loan commitment for the New Financing, from a lender of Purchaser's choice, and/or consent to assumption of Existing Financing provided for in this agreement. Purchaser shall use his best efforts to qualify for and obtain said financing and shall complete and submit a loan application **within five (5) days of acceptance.**

8A. LOAN CLOSING. In the event a loan commitment and/or consent is obtained but not honored without fault of Purchaser, this agreement shall be null and void and all deposits returned to Purchaser less expenses incurred by Purchaser to the date of cancellation of this transaction.

9. EXISTING LOANS.

LOAN DOCUMENTS. Seller shall within **three (3) days of acceptance,** provide Purchaser with copies of all Notes and Deeds of Trust or Mortgages to be assumed or taken subject to, and **within five (5) days of receipt** thereof Purchaser shall in writing notify Seller of his approval or disapproval of such terms, which shall not be unreasonably withheld. **Within three (3) days of acceptance,** Seller shall submit written request for a current Beneficiary Statement on the above loan or loans.

10. SELLER FINANCING. In the event of Seller Financing, Purchaser shall furnish Seller **within three (3) days of acceptance,** a customary financial statement for the sole purpose of credit approval, which approval shall not be unreasonably withheld. Purchaser authorizes Seller to engage the services of a reputable credit reporting agency for this purpose at Purchaser's expense and Seller shall notify Purchaser **within ten (10) days of receipt** of financial statement, of approval or disapproval of Purchaser's credit.

11. EXAMINATION OF TITLE. Fifteen (15) days from date of acceptance hereof are allowed the Purchaser to examine the title to the property and to report in writing any valid objections thereto. Any exceptions to the title, which would be disclosed by examination of the records, shall be deemed to have been accepted unless reported in writing **within said fifteen (15) days.** If Purchaser objects to any exceptions to the title, Seller shall use due diligence to remove such exceptions at his own expense **before close of escrow.** But if such exceptions cannot be removed **before close of escrow,** all rights and obligations hereunder may, at the election of the Purchaser, terminate and the deposit shall be returned to Purchaser, unless he elects to purchase the property subject to such exceptions.

12. ENCUMBRANCES. In addition to any encumbrances referred to herein, Purchaser shall take title to the property subject to: [1] Real Estate Taxes not yet due, and [2] Covenants, Conditions, Restrictions, Rights of Way, and Easements of record, if any, which do not materially affect the value or intended use of the property. Such encumbrances shall be deemed approved unless written notice to the contrary is delivered to Seller or his agent **within fifteen (15) days of acceptance.**

13. PRORATIONS. Rents, taxes, interest, and other expenses of the property to be prorated as of the date of recordation of the deed. Security deposits, advance rentals, or considerations involving future lease credits shall be credited to Purchaser.

13A. REASSESSMENT. Purchaser is advised that the property may be reassessed as of the date of conveyance which may result in a tax increase.

14. INSURANCE. Purchaser to obtain hazard insurance prepaid for one year in an amount satisfactory to the loan holders and covering one hundred percent replacement cost of improvements, and to name holders of the secured loans as additional loss payees. Purchaser agrees further to annually increase said insurance if necessary, to equal the current replacement cost of the property during the term of the loan holders' mortgages. In the event of Seller Financing, Purchaser shall instruct the insurance carrier to deliver to Seller before close of escrow a certificate providing for 30 days written notice in the event of cancellation.

14A. DESTRUCTION OF IMPROVEMENTS. If the improvements of the property are destroyed, materially damaged, or found to be materially defective prior to close of escrow, Purchaser may terminate the transaction by written notice delivered to Seller's broker or agent, and all deposits shall be returned to Purchaser. In the event Purchaser does not elect to terminate the agreement, Purchaser shall be entitled to receive in addition to the property any insurance proceeds payable on account of the damage or destruction.

15. NOTICES. By acceptance hereof Seller warrants that he has no notice of violations relating to the property from City, County, or State agencies.

15A. ACCESS TO PROPERTY. Seller agrees to provide reasonable access to the property to Purchaser and inspectors representing Purchaser as provided in this agreement and to representatives of lending institutions for appraisal purposes.

16. DUE ON SALE CLAUSE. IF the note and deed of trust or mortgage for any existing loan contains an acceleration or DUE ON SALE clause, the lender may demand full payment of the entire loan balance as a result of this transaction. Both parties acknowledge that they are not relying on any representation by the other party or the broker with respect to the enforceability of such a provision in existing notes and deeds of trust or mortgages, or deeds of trust or mortgages to be executed in accordance with this agreement. Both parties have been advised by the broker to seek independent legal advice with respect to these matters.

17. BALLOON PAYMENT. Both parties acknowledge they have not received or relied upon any statements or representations made to them by Broker regarding availability of funds, or rate of interest at which funds might be available, when Purchaser becomes obligated to refinance or pay off the remaining balance of any loan pursuant to the terms of this agreement.

18. DEFAULT. In the event that Purchaser shall default in the performance of this agreement, unless the parties have agreed to a provision for liquidated damages, Seller may, subject to any rights of the Broker herein, retain Purchaser's deposit on account of damages sustained and may take such actions as he deems appropriate to collect such additional damages as may have been actually sustained, and Purchaser shall have the right to take such action as he deems appropriate to recover such portion of the deposit as may be allowed by law. **In the event that Purchaser shall so default, unless Purchaser and Seller have agreed to liquidated damages, Purchaser agrees to pay the Broker(s) entitled thereto such commissions as would be payable by Seller in the absence of such default.** Purchaser's obligation to said Broker(s) shall be in addition to any rights which said Broker(s) may have against Seller in the event of default. In the event legal action is instituted by the Broker(s), or any party to this agreement, or arising out of the execution of this agreement or the sale, or to collect commissions, the prevailing party shall be entitled to receive from the other party a reasonable attorney fee to be determined by the court in which such action is brought.

19. FOREIGN INVESTMENT AND REAL PROPERTY TAX ACT. The Foreign Investment and Real Property Tax Act requires a buyer purchasing real property from a foreign person to withhold tax from the sale proceeds unless an exemption applies. Seller agrees to provide Purchaser with a certification establishing that no federal income tax is required to be withheld under the act, or to consent to withholding of tax from the proceeds of sale as required, unless it is established that the transaction is exempt because the purchase price is $300,000 or less and the Purchaser intends to use the property as his residence.

NCR (No Carbon Required)　　Property Address _____ PAGE 3 of 4 PAGES

20.　CLOSING on or before _____, or within _____ days of acceptance, whichever is later, both parties shall deposit with an authorized Escrow Holder, to be selected by ☐ Purchaser, ☐ Seller, all funds and instruments necessary to complete the sale in accordance with the terms hereof. ☐ Signed Escrow Instructions to be delivered to Escrow Holder **within** _____ **days of acceptance.** The representations and warranties shall not be terminated by conveyance of the property. Escrow Fee to be paid by _____. Transfer Tax(es), if any, to be paid by _____

21.　EVIDENCE OF TITLE in the form of ☐ a policy of _____ Title Insurance, ☐ Other: _____ paid by _____, who shall order a Preliminary Title Report **within** _____ **days of acceptance.**

22.　BONDS. The amount of any bond or assessment which is a lien shall be ☐ paid by Seller, ☐ assumed by Purchaser.

23.　PHYSICAL POSSESSION. Physical possession, with all keys and garage door openers, shall be delivered to Purchaser (check either item [1] or item [2]): ☐ 1. UPON recordation of the deed. ☐ 2. AFTER recordation, **but not later than midnight of**_____. Unless Seller has vacated the premises prior to recordation of the deed, Seller agrees to pay Purchaser $_____ per day from recordation to date possession is delivered and to leave in escrow a sum equal to the above per diem amount multiplied by the number of days from date of closing to date allowed above for delivery of possession. Said sum to be disbursed to the persons entitled thereto on the date possession is delivered.

24.　FIXTURES. All items permanently attached to the property, including attached floor coverings, draperies with hardware, shades, blinds, window and door screens, storm sash, combination doors, awnings, light fixtures, television antennas, electric garage door openers with controls, outdoor plants and trees, are included in the purchase price free of liens, EXCLUDING:_____

25.　PERSONAL PROPERTY. The following personal property, on the premises when inspected by Purchaser, is included in the purchase price and shall be transferred to Purchaser by a Bill of Sale at close of escrow. No warranty is implied as to the condition of said property:_____

26.　MAINTENANCE. Seller covenants that the heating, air-conditioning (if any), electrical, sewer, septic system, drainage, sprinkler (if any), and plumbing systems including the water heater, as well as built-in appliances and other mechanical apparatus shall be in **normal working order** on the date occupancy is delivered. Seller shall replace any cracked or broken glass including windows, mirrors, shower and tub enclosures. Until occupancy is delivered Seller shall maintain landscaping, grounds and pool (if any). Seller agrees to deliver the property in a neat and clean condition with all debris removed. The following items are specifically excluded from the above: _____
Purchaser and Seller understand and acknowledge that Broker shall not in any circumstances be liable for any breach in this clause.

27.　PROVISIONS ON THE REVERSE SIDE. The provisions marked ☒ below, printed in full on the reverse side, are included in this agreement.

☐　A. Pest Control Inspection, paid by ☐ Purchaser, ☐ Seller
☐　B. Existing Pest Control Report Dated:_____ By _____
☐　C. "As Is," but Subject to Purchaser's Approval
☐　D. Waiver of Pest Control Inspection
☐　E. Roof Inspection Report within _____ days of acceptance
☐　F. City and County Inspections within _____ days of acceptance
☐　G. Condominium Disclosure
☐　H. Home Protect. Ctr. ☐ paid by _____ waived by _____
☐　I. Arbitration Clause

☐　J. Contingent upon the sale of_____
☐　K. Inspection of Property Condition, Pool, and Septic Tank, approved within _____ days of receipt of report(s)
☐　L. VA Appraisal Clause
☐　M. FHA Appraisal Clause
☐　N. Smoke Detectors provided by _____
☐　O. Flood Hazard Zone

28.　EXPIRATION. This offer shall expire unless a copy with Seller's written acceptance is delivered to Purchaser or the Purchaser's agent on or before _____ o'clock ☐ AM ☐ PM, on _____, 19_____.

29.　OWNER OCCUPANCY. Purchaser ☐ does, ☐ does not intend to occupy the property as Purchaser's residence.

30.　TITLE shall vest as _____, unless otherwise designated in Escrow Instructions.
(The manner of taking title may have significant legal and tax consequences. If in doubt, Purchasers should obtain advice from legal or tax counsel.)

31.　AGENCY DECLARATION. The following agency relationship(s) are hereby confirmed.
_____ is the agent of (check one):　　_____ is the agent of (check one):
(Name of Listing Agent)　　(Name of Selling Agent if not the same as the Listing Agent)

☐ the seller exclusively; or　　☐ the buyer exclusively; or　☐ the seller exclusively; or
☐ both the buyer and seller.　　☐ both the buyer and seller.

The undersigned Purchaser *has read all 4 pages of this agreement* and hereby acknowledges receipt of a copy of pages 1, 2, 3 and 4. Purchaser acknowledges further that he has not received or relied upon statements or representations by the undersigned Broker which are not herein expressed.

_____ Purchaser's Broker　　DATED: _____ TIME: _____
By _____　　_____ Purchaser
Broker's Initials: _____ Dated: _____　　_____ Purchaser

ACCEPTANCE

Seller accepts the foregoing offer and agrees to sell the herein described property for the price and on the terms and conditions herein specified. Subject to:

COMMISSION. Seller hereby irrevocably assigns and agrees to pay to _____, the Broker in this transaction, in Cash from proceeds at close of escrow, for services rendered:_____

In the event that Purchaser defaults and fails to complete the sale, the Broker shall be entitled to receive one-half of Purchaser's deposit, but not more than the commission earned, without prejudice to Broker's rights to recover the balance of the commission from Purchaser. The mutual rescission of this agreement by Purchaser and Seller shall not relieve said parties of their obligations to Broker hereunder. This agreement shall not limit the rights of Broker provided for in any listing or other agreement which may be in effect between Seller and Broker, except that the amount of the commission shall be as specified herein.

The undersigned Seller *has read all 4 pages of this agreement* and hereby acknowledges receipt of a copy of pages 1, 2, 3 and 4. Broker is hereby authorized to deliver a signed copy to Purchaser and to disclose the terms of sale to Multiple Listing Service or Real Estate Board members.

_____ Seller's Broker　　DATED: _____ TIME: _____
By _____　　_____ Seller
Broker's Initials: _____ Dated: _____　　_____ Seller
Purchaser acknowledges receipt of a copy of the accepted agreement. DATE: _____ TIME: _____　_____ Purchaser

FORM 101-R.2 (12-87)　COPYRIGHT © 1985, BY PROFESSIONAL PUBLISHING CORP., 122 PAUL DR., SAN RAFAEL, CA 94903, (415) 472-1964　**PROFESSIONAL PUBLISHING**

APPENDIX

_____ **27-A. PEST CONTROL INSPECTION.** The main building and all attached structures to be inspected by a licensed structural pest control operator. Seller to pay for: (1) Elimination of infestation and/or infection of wood-destroying pests or organisms, (2) For repair of damage caused by such infestation and/or infection, (3) For correction of conditions which caused said damage and (4) For repair of plumbing and other leaks affecting wood members, including repair of leaking stall showers, in accordance with said pest control operator's report. Seller shall not be responsible for preventive work where no damage is found, except where required for FHA or VA financing.

If the inspecting structural pest control operator shall recommend further inspection of inaccessible areas, Purchaser may require that said areas be inspected. If any infestation or infection is discovered by such inspection, the additional cost of such inspection and additional required work shall be paid by Seller. If no such infestation or infection is discovered, the additional cost of inspecting such inaccessible areas and the work required to return the property to its original condition shall be paid by Purchaser.

Funds for work specified in said report to be done at Seller's expense shall be held in escrow and disbursed by escrow holder upon receipt of Notice of Work Completed by a licensed structural pest control operator selected by Seller certifying that the property is free of evidence of active infestation or infection.

As soon as the same are available, copies of the report, and any certification or other proof of completion of the work shall be delivered to the agents of Purchaser and Seller who are authorized to receive the same on behalf of their principals.

_____ **27-B. EXISTING PEST CONTROL REPORT ACCEPTED BY PURCHASER.** Purchaser accepts existing pest control report on the property by the licensed structural pest control operator listed under **Item 27-B.** Seller's obligations shall be as set forth in **Item 27-A** above.

_____ **27-C. AS IS, BUT SUBJECT TO PURCHASER'S APPROVAL OF INSPECTION REPORT.** Property to be purchased in its present condition with no charge to Seller for any pest control work. However, Purchaser shall have the right to have the property inspected and to obtain a report from a licensed structural pest control operator. Purchaser shall be deemed to have approved said report unless written notice to the contrary is delivered to Seller or his agent **within fifteen (15) days of acceptance.** In the event Purchaser does not approve the report, he may have his deposit returned and both parties shall be relieved of all obligations hereunder. Purchaser acknowledges that he has not received or relied upon any representations by either the Broker or the Seller, with respect to the condition of the property.

_____ **27-D. WAIVER OF PEST CONTROL INSPECTION.** Purchaser has satisfied himself about the condition of the property and agrees to purchase the property in its present condition without the benefit of a structural pest control inspection.

Purchaser acknowledges that he has not received or relied upon any representations by either the Broker or the Seller, with respect to the condition of the property.

_____ **27-E. ROOF INSPECTION.** Purchaser, at his expense, may order a roof inspection report from a licensed general or roofing contractor. **Within the number of days specified under Item 27-E,** copies of the report shall be delivered to the agents of Purchaser and Seller who are authorized to receive the same on behalf of their principals.

Within three (3) days following receipt of the report, Seller may [a]: elect to pay the cost of all work recommended by such report; or [b]: elect to pay none or only a portion of the cost of such work. Written notice of such election shall be delivered to Purchaser or his agent.

In the event Seller does not agree to pay for all such work, Purchaser may elect to pay the balance of the cost of such work or terminate all rights and obligations to the parties under this agreement. Written notice of such election shall be delivered to Seller or his agent **within seven (7) days following receipt** of Seller's notice. In the event of such termination, Purchaser shall be entitled to a full refund of all deposits excluding the cost of the above roof inspection report. If no written election is made **within seven (7) days,** Purchaser shall have no right to terminate this agreement, and Seller shall be responsible for the cost of that portion of the work which he elected to pay.

In the event Seller shall have elected to pay the cost of all such work, he shall have the right to have such work performed by a licensed general or roofing contractor of his choice.

_____ **27-F. CITY AND COUNTY INSPECTION REPORT.** Local ordinance requires that the property be inspected **or a report issued** for compliance with local building and permit regulations, standards and ordinances as a condition to sale or transfer. **Within the number of days specified under Item 27-F** Seller shall notify the appropriate local agency to cause the property to be inspected, **or to issue the required report** at the earliest practicable date. If Seller is unable or unwilling to pay for correction of any violations shown in the report, this agreement shall terminate and all deposits be returned to Purchaser, unless Purchaser agrees to pay the cost of corrections required.

_____ **27-G. CONDOMINIUM DISCLOSURE.** Purchaser shall take title subject to Condominium Declaration, Covenants, Conditions and Restrictions, Articles of Incorporation, By-Laws, Rules and Regulations currently in force, and Financial Statements of the condominium owners association, to be delivered to Purchaser for his approval **within five (5) days of acceptance.** Purchaser shall be deemed to have approved said documents unless written notice to the contrary is delivered to Seller or his agent **within five (5) days of receipt** by Purchaser, in which case Purchaser may have his deposit returned and both parties shall be relieved of all obligations hereunder.

In addition, Seller shall deliver to Purchaser before close of escrow a written statement from the condominium owners association documenting the amount of any delinquent assessments including penalties, attorney's fees, and other charges provided for in the management documents. Such charges shall be credited to Purchaser at close of escrow.

_____ **27-H. HOME PROTECTION CONTRACT,** paid for by the party specified under **Item 27-H,** shall become effective upon close of escrow for not less than one year, unless both parties have waived such Home Protection Contract, as specified under **Item 27-H.** The brokers herein have informed both parties that such protection programs are available, but do not approve or endorse any particular program.

_____ **27-I. ARBITRATION.** Purchaser, Seller and Broker(s) agree that in the event any party defaults in the performance of the obligations of such party under the agreement, or in the event there is a dispute between any of them with respect to their obligations under the agreement, or their obligations arising out of the purchase and sale, exchange or lease of the property, that the matter shall be submitted to arbitration in accordance with the Commercial Rules of Arbitration of the American Arbitration Association.

The parties do further agree that the party or parties prevailing in such arbitration shall be entitled to receive from the other party or parties a reasonable attorney's fee and all costs incurred in connection with the arbitration in an amount to be determined by the arbitrator or arbitrators, and in the event that any party shall fail to pay the amount due under the award of the arbitrator or arbitrators, and legal action is commenced for the enforcement of the award, the prevailing party or parties shall be entitled to receive a reasonable attorney's fee incurred in such action to be determined by the court in which such action is brought.

The parties further agree that they shall each have the rights of discovery set forth in provisions of local law, which is by this reference incorporated herein.

_____ **27-J. CONTINGENCY RELEASE CLAUSE.** Subject to the sale and conveyance of "Purchaser's Property," described in **Item 27-J,** within the time specified for closing of Seller's property. Seller shall have the right to continue to offer the herein property for sale and to accept offers subject to the rights of Purchaser. Should Seller accept such an offer, then Purchaser shall be given written notice of such acceptance. In the event Purchaser will not waive this condition in writing **within three (3) days** of receipt of such notice, then this agreement shall be terminated and all deposits be returned to Purchaser and escrow cancelled. Said notice may be personally delivered or mailed by certified mail and addressed to Purchaser, in care of his agent identified herein. In the event of mailing, such notice shall be deemed to have been given on the day following the date of mailing evidenced by the postmark on the envelope containing such notice.

_____ **27-K. INSPECTION OF PHYSICAL CONDITION OF PROPERTY, POOL, SEPTIC TANK.** Inspection report(s) of physical condition of the property including swimming pool, wells, if any, by a representative of Purchaser's choice and at Purchaser's expense to be ordered **within two (2) days of acceptance.** Seller to provide a septic tank inspection report at his expense. Approval of the report(s), at the discretion of the Purchaser, to be given in writing **within the number of days of receipt of said report(s) specified under Item 27-K,** which approval shall not be unreasonably withheld. In the event Purchaser does not approve of the report, he may have his deposit returned and both parties shall be relieved of all obligations hereunder. Seller, or seller's agent, to be provided with copies of the report(s).

_____ **27-L. VA APPRAISED VALUE CLAUSE.** It is expressly agreed that, notwithstanding any other provisions of this contract, the Purchaser shall not incur any penalty by forfeiture of earnest money or otherwise be obligated to complete the purchase of the property described herein, if the contract purchase price or cost exceeds the Reasonable Value of the property established by the Veterans Administration. The Purchaser shall, however, have the privilege and option of proceeding with the consummation of this contract without regard to the amount of the Reasonable Value established by the Veterans Administration. Escrow Fee to be paid by Seller.

_____ **27-M. FHA APPRAISED VALUE CLAUSE.** It is expressly agreed that, notwithstanding any other provisions of this contract, the Purchaser shall not be obligated to complete the purchase of the property described herein or to incur any penalty by forfeiture of earnest money deposits or otherwise unless the Seller has delivered to the Purchaser a written statement, issued by the Federal Housing Commissioner, setting forth the appraised value of the property for mortgage insurance purposes of not less than $_____, which statement the Seller hereby agrees to deliver to the Purchaser promptly after such appraised value statement is made available to the Seller. The Purchaser shall, however, have the privilege and option of proceeding with the consummation of this contract without regard to the amount of the appraised valuation made by the Federal Housing Commissioner.

The appraised valuation is arrived at to determine the maximum mortgage the Department of Housing and Urban Development will insure. HUD does not warrant the value or the condition of the property. The Purchaser should satisfy himself/herself that the price and condition of the property are acceptable.

_____ **27-N. SMOKE DETECTORS.** In accordance with local ordinance smoke detectors shall be installed at the expense of the party indicated under **Item 27-N.** If required, said smoke detectors shall be inspected by the appropriate City or County agency prior to close of escrow and a compliance report obtained.

_____ **27-O. FLOOD HAZARD ZONE.** Purchaser has been advised that the property is located in an area which the Secretary of HUD has found to have special flood hazards and that it will be necessary to purchase flood insurance in order to obtain any loan secured by the property from any federally regulated financial institution or a loan insured or guaranteed by an agency of the U.S. Government.

Residential Loan Application

MORTGAGE APPLIED FOR	☐ Conventional ☐ FHA ☐ VA	Amount $	Interest Rate %	No. of Months	Monthly Payment Principal & Interest $	Escrow/Impounds (to be collected monthly) ☐ Taxes ☐ Hazard Ins. ☐ Mtg. Ins. ☐

Prepayment Option

Subject Property

Property Street Address	City	County	State	Zip	No. Units

Legal Description (Attach description if necessary)	Year Built

Purpose of Loan: ☐ Purchase ☐ Construction-Permanent ☐ Construction ☐ Refinance ☐ Other (Explain)

Complete this line if Construction-Permanent or Construction Loan	Lot Value Data	Original Cost	Present Value (a)	Cost of Imps. (b)	Total (a + b)	ENTER TOTAL AS PURCHASE PRICE IN DETAILS OF PURCHASE.
Year Acquired $	$	$	$	$	$	

Complete this line if a Refinance Loan	Purpose of Refinance	Describe Improvements [] made [] to be made
Year Acquired Original Cost Amt. Existing Liens $ $		Cost: $

Title Will Be Held In What Name(s)	Manner In Which Title Will Be Held

Source of Down Payment and Settlement Charges

This application is designed to be completed by the borrower(s) with the lender's assistance. The Co-Borrower Section and all other Co-Borrower questions must be completed and the appropriate box(es) checked if ☐ another person will be jointly obligated with the Borrower on the loan, or ☐ the Borrower is relying on income from alimony, child support or separate maintenance or on the income or assets of another person as a basis for repayment of the loan, or ☐ the Borrower is married and resides, or the property is located, in a community property state.

Borrower				Co-Borrower			
Name		Age	School Yrs	Name		Age	School Yrs
Present Address No. Years ☐ Own ☐ Rent				Present Address No. Years ☐ Own ☐ Rent			
Street				Street			
City/State/Zip				City/State/Zip			
Former address if less than 2 years at present address				Former address if less than 2 years at present address			
Street				Street			
City/State/Zip				City/State/Zip			
Years at former address ☐ Own ☐ Rent				Years at former address ☐ Own ☐ Rent			
Marital Status ☐ Married ☐ Separated ☐ Unmarried (incl. single, divorced, widowed)	DEPENDENTS OTHER THAN LISTED BY CO BORROWER NO. AGES			Marital Status ☐ Married ☐ Separated ☐ Unmarried (incl. single, divorced, widowed)	DEPENDENTS OTHER THAN LISTED BY BORROWER NO. AGES		
Name and Address of Employer		Years employed in this line of work or profession? years Years on this job ____ ☐ Self Employed*		Name and Address of Employer		Years employed in this line of work or profession? years Years on this job ____ ☐ Self Employed*	
Position/Title	Type of Business			Position/Title	Type of Business		
Social Security Number ***	Home Phone	Business Phone		Social Security Number ***	Home Phone	Business Phone	

Gross Monthly Income				Monthly Housing Expense**			Details of Purchase	
Item	Borrower	Co-Borrower	Total		PRESENT	PROPOSED	Do Not Complete If Refinance	
Base Empl. Income	$	$	$	Rent	$		a. Purchase Price	$
Overtime				First Mortgage (P&I)		$	b. Total Closing Costs (Est.)	
Bonuses				Other Financing (P&I)			c. Prepaid Escrows (Est.)	
Commissions				Hazard Insurance			d. Total (a + b + c)	$
Dividends/Interest				Real Estate Taxes			e. Amount This Mortgage	()
Net Rental Income				Mortgage Insurance			f. Other Financing	()
Other† (Before completing, see notice under Describe Other Income below.)				Homeowner Assn. Dues			g. Other Equity	()
				Other:			h. Amount of Cash Deposit	()
				Total Monthly Pmt.	$	$	i. Closing Costs Paid by Seller	()
				Utilities			j. Cash Reqd. For Closing (Est.)	$
Total	$	$	$	Total	$	$		

Describe Other Income		
▷ B—Borrower C—Co-Borrower	NOTICE:† Alimony, child support, or separate maintenance income need not be revealed if the Borrower or Co-Borrower does not choose to have it considered as a basis for repaying this loan.	Monthly Amount
		$

If Employed In Current Position For Less Than Two Years, Complete the Following						
B/C	Previous Employer/School	City/State	Type of Business	Position/Title	Dates From/To	Monthly Income
						$

These Questions Apply To Both Borrower and Co-Borrower		

If a "yes" answer is given to a question in this column, please explain on an attached sheet.

	Borrower Yes or No	Co-Borrower Yes or No
Are there any outstanding judgments against you?		
Have you been declared bankrupt within the past 7 years?		
Have you had property foreclosed upon or given title or deed in lieu thereof in the last 7 years?		
Are you a party to a law suit?		
Are you obligated to pay alimony, child support, or separate maintenance?		
Is any part of the down payment borrowed?		
Are you a co-maker or endorser on a note?		

	Borrower Yes or No	Co-Borrower Yes or No
Are you a U.S. citizen?		
If "no," are you a resident alien?		
If "no," are you a non-resident alien?		
Explain Other Financing or Other Equity (if any).		

*FHLMC/FNMA require business credit report, signed Federal Income Tax returns for last two years; and, if available, audited Profit and Loss Statement plus balance sheet for same period.
**All Present Monthly Housing Expenses of Borrower and Co-Borrower should be listed on a combined basis.
***Optional for FHLMC

FHLMC 65 Rev. 10/86

669

Fannie Mae Form 1003 Rev. 10/86

Federal National Mortgage Association

REQUEST FOR VERIFICATION OF EMPLOYMENT

INSTRUCTIONS: LENDER- Complete items 1 thru 7. Have applicant complete item 8. Forward directly to employer named in item 1.

EMPLOYER-Please complete either Part II or Part III as applicable. Sign and return directly to lender named in item 2.

PART I - REQUEST

1. TO *(Name and address of employer)*	2. FROM*(Name and address of lender)*		
3. SIGNATURE OF LENDER	4. TITLE	5. DATE	6. LENDER'S NUMBER *(optional)*

I have applied for a mortgage loan and stated that I am now or was formerly employed by you. My signature below authorizes verification of this information.

7. NAME AND ADDRESS OF APPLICANT *(Include employee or badge number)*	8. SIGNATURE OF APPLICANT

PART II - VERIFICATION OF PRESENT EMPLOYMENT

EMPLOYMENT DATA	PAY DATA				
9. APPLICANT'S DATE OF EMPLOYMENT	12A. CURRENT BASE PAY (Enter Amount and Check Period) ☐ ANNUAL ☐ HOURLY ☐ MONTHLY ☐ OTHER ☐ WEEKLY *(Specify)* $ _____		12C.FOR MILITARY PERSONNEL ONLY		
			PAY GRADE		
10. PRESENT POSITION			TYPE	MONTHLY AMOUNT	
	12B. EARNINGS		BASE PAY	$	
11. PROBABILITY OF CONTINUED EMPLOYMENT	TYPE	YEAR TO DATE	PAST YEAR	RATIONS	$
13.IF OVERTIME OR BONUS IS APPLICABLE, IS ITS CONTINUANCE LIKELY?	BASE PAY	$	$	FLIGHT OR HAZARD	$
	OVERTIME	$	$	CLOTHING	$
				QUARTERS	$
	COMMISSIONS	$	$	PRO PAY	$
OVERTIME ☐ YES ☐ NO BONUS ☐ YES ☐ NO	BONUS	$	$	OVER SEAS OR COMBAT	$

14. REMARKS *(if paid hourly, please indicate average hours worked each week during current and past year)*

PART III - VERIFICATION OF PREVIOUS EMPLOYMENT

15. DATES OF EMPLOYMENT	16. SALARY/WAGE AT TERMINATION PER (Year) (Month)(Week)
	BASE _____ OVERTIME _____ COMMISSIONS _____ BONUS _____
17. REASON FOR LEAVING	18. POSITION HELD

19. SIGNATURE OF EMPLOYER	20. TITLE	21. DATE

The confidentiality of the information you have furnished will be preserved except where disclosure of this information is required by applicable law. The form is to be transmitted directly to the lender and is not to be transmitted through the applicant or any other party.

PREVIOUS EDITION WILL BE USED UNTIL STOCK IS EXHAUSTED

FNMA Form 1005
Rev. June 78

This Statement and any applicable supporting schedules may be completed jointly by both married and unmarried co-borrowers if their assets and liabilities are sufficiently joined so that the Statement can be meaningfully and fairly presented on a combined basis; otherwise separate Statements and Schedules are required (FHLMC 65A/FNMA 1003A). If the co-borrower section was completed about a spouse, this statement and supporting schedules must be completed about that spouse also. ☐ Completed Jointly ☐ Not Completed Jointly

Assets Liabilities and Pledged Assets

Indicate by (*) those liabilities or pledged assets which will be satisfied upon sale of real estate owned or upon refinancing of subject property

Description	Cash or Market Value	Creditors' Name, Address and Account Number		Acct. Name if Not Borrower's	Mo. Pmt. and Mos. Left to Pay	Unpaid Balance
Cash Deposit Toward Purchase Held By	$	Installment Debts (Include "revolving" charge accounts)			$ Pmt/Mos.	$
		Co.	Acct. No.			
Checking and Savings Accounts (Show Names of Institutions (Account Numbers) Bank, S & L or Credit Union		Addr.				
		City			/	
		Co.	Acct. No.			
Addr.		Addr.				
City		City			/	
Acct. No.		Co.	Acct. No.			
Bank, S & L or Credit Union		Addr.				
		City				
Addr.		Co.	Acct. No.			
City		Addr.				
Acct. No.		City				
Bank, S & L or Credit Union		Co.	Acct. No.			
		Addr.				
Addr.		City			/	
City		Other Debts including Stock Pledges				
Acct. No.						
Stocks and Bonds (No./Description)					/	
		Real Estate Loans Co.	Acct. No.			
		Addr.				
		City				
Life Insurance Net Cash Value Face Amount $		Co.	Acct. No.			
		Addr.				
Subtotal Liquid Assets		City				
Real Estate Owned (Enter Market Value from Schedule of Real Estate Owned)		Automobile Loans Co.	Acct. No.			
Vested Interest in Retirement Fund		Addr.			/	
Net worth of Business Owned (ATTACH FINANCIAL STATEMENT)		City				
		Co.	Acct. No.			
Automobiles Owned (Make and Year)						
		City				
Furniture and Personal Property		Alimony/Child Support/Separate Maintenance Payments Owed to			/	
Other Assets (Itemize)						
		Total Monthly Payments			$	
Total Assets	A $	Net Worth (A minus B) $			Total Liabilities	B $

SCHEDULE OF REAL ESTATE OWNED (If Additional Properties Owned Attach Separate Schedule)

Address of Property (Indicate S if Sold, PS if Pending Sale or R if Rental being held for income)		Type of Property	Present Market Value	Amount of Mortgages & Liens	Gross Rental Income	Mortgage Payments	Taxes, Ins. Maintenance and Misc.	Net Rental Income
			$	$	$	$	$	$
		TOTALS →	$	$	$	$	$	$

List Previous Credit References

B–Borrower C–Co-Borrower	Creditor's Name and Address	Account Number	Purpose	Highest Balance	Date Paid
				$	

List any additional names under which credit has previously been received _____

AGREEMENT: The undersigned applies for the loan indicated in this application to be secured by a first mortgage or deed of trust on the property described herein, and represents that the property will not be used for any illegal or restricted purpose, and that all statements made in this application are true and are made for the purpose of obtaining the loan. Verification may be obtained from any source named in this application. The original or a copy of this application will be retained by the lender, even if the loan is not granted. The undersigned ☐ intend or ☐ do not intend to occupy the property as their primary residence.

I/we fully understand that it is a federal crime punishable by fine or imprisonment, or both, to knowingly make any false statements concerning any of the above facts as applicable under the provisions of Title 18, United States Code, Section 1014.

_____ Date _____ _____ Date _____
Borrower's Signature Co-Borrower's Signature

Information for Government Monitoring Purposes

The following information is requested by the Federal Government for certain types of loans related to a dwelling, in order to monitor the lender's compliance with equal credit opportunity and fair housing laws. You are not required to furnish this information, but are encouraged to do so. The law provides that a lender may neither discriminate on the basis of this information, nor on whether you choose to furnish it. However, if you choose not to furnish it, under Federal regulations this lender is required to note race and sex on the basis of visual observation or surname. If you do not wish to furnish the above information, please check the box below. (Lender must review the above material to assure that the disclosures satisfy all requirements to which the Lender is subject under applicable state law for the particular type of loan applied for.)

Borrower: ☐ I do not wish to furnish this information
Race/National Origin:
☐ American Indian, Alaskan Native ☐ Asian, Pacific Islander
☐ Black ☐ Hispanic ☐ White
☐ Other (specify): _____
Sex: ☐ Female ☐ Male

Co-Borrower: ☐ I do not wish to furnish this information
Race/National Origin:
☐ American Indian, Alaskan Native ☐ Asian, Pacific Islander
☐ Black ☐ Hispanic ☐ White
☐ Other (specify): _____
Sex: ☐ Female ☐ Male

To Be Completed by Interviewer

This application was taken by:
☐ face to face interview
☐ by mail
☐ by telephone

_____ _____
Interviewer Name of Interviewer's Employer

_____ _____
Interviewer's Phone Number Address of Interviewer's Employer

APPENDIX

Federal National Mortgage Association

REQUEST FOR VERIFICATION OF DEPOSIT

INSTRUCTIONS: LENDER - Complete Items 1 thru 8. Have applicant(s) complete Item 9. Forward directly to depository named in Item 1.

DEPOSITORY - Please complete Items 10 thru 15 and return DIRECTLY to lender named in Item 2.

PART I - REQUEST

1. TO (Name and address of depository)	2. FROM (Name and address of lender)		

3. SIGNATURE OF LENDER	4. TITLE	5. DATE	6. LENDER'S NUMBER (Optional)

7. INFORMATION TO BE VERIFIED

TYPE OF ACCOUNT	ACCOUNT IN NAME OF	ACCOUNT NUMBER	BALANCE
			$
			$
			$
			$

TO DEPOSITORY: I have applied for a mortgage loan and stated in my financial statement that the balance on deposit with you is as shown above. You are authorized to verify this information and to supply the lender identified above with the information requested in Items 10 thru 12. Your response is solely a matter of courtesy for which no responsibility is attached to your institution or any of your officers.

8. NAME AND ADDRESS OF APPLICANT(s)	9. SIGNATURE OF APPLICANT(s)

TO BE COMPLETED BY DEPOSITORY

PART II - VERIFICATION OF DEPOSITORY

10. DEPOSIT ACCOUNTS OF APPLICANT(s)

TYPE OF ACCOUNT	ACCOUNT NUMBER	CURRENT BALANCE	AVERAGE BALANCE FOR PREVIOUS TWO MONTHS	DATE OPENED
		$	$	
		$	$	
		$	$	
		$	$	

11. LOANS OUTSTANDING TO APPLICANT(s)

LOAN NUMBER	DATE OF LOAN	ORIGINAL AMOUNT	CURRENT BALANCE	INSTALLMENTS (Monthly/Quarterly)	SECURED BY	NUMBER OF LATE PAYMENTS
		$	$	$ per		
		$	$	$ per		
		$	$	$ per		

12. ADDITIONAL INFORMATION WHICH MAY BE OF ASSISTANCE IN DETERMINATION OF CREDIT WORTHINESS:
(Please include information on loans paid-in-full as in Item 11 above)

13. SIGNATURE OF DEPOSITORY	14. TITLE	15. DATE

The confidentiality of the information you have furnished will be preserved except where disclosure of this information is required by applicable law. The form is to be transmitted directly to the lender and is not to be transmitted through the applicant or any other party.

PREVIOUS EDITION WILL BE USED UNTIL STOCK IS EXHAUSTED

FNMA Form 1006
Rev. June 78

SELLER'S ESTIMATED RECEIPTS
ALL FIGURES ARE APPROXIMATE Date_____

PROPERTY DESCRIPTION	SELLER'S NAME

	Seller Receives
SELLING PRICE ..	$

OUTSTANDING MORTGAGES

1st Mortgage ...	$
2nd Mortgage ..	
Other Encumbrances	
Subtract Total Mortgages→	$
Gross Equity ..→	$

LESS SELLER'S ESTIMATED EXPENSES Seller Pays

Title Insurance Policy	$
Attorneys Fees ...	
Release of Lien ..	
Survey of Property ..	
Escrow Fees ...	
Termite Inspection ..	
Recording Fees ..	
Brokers Professional Service Fee	
Prepayment Penalty On Loan	
Photographs ...	
Loan Discount Fee ...	
Home Warranty ..	
..	
..	
..	
Total Estimated Expenses→	$
ESTIMATED RECEIPTS ..→	$

Note: 1. These figures are only estimated and are subject to verification by the Seller.
2. Prorations of taxes, interest and insurance are not included on this statement.
3. Our insurance estimates are based on minimum coverage since types and amounts of coverage varies so much from individual to individual.

Notes: _____

APPENDIX

A	

B. TYPE OF LOAN

1. ☐ FHA 2. ☐ FMHA 3. ☐ CONV. UNINS.

4. ☐ VA 5. ☐ CONV. INS.

6. File Number:

7. Loan Number:

8. Mortgage Insurance Case Number:

SETTLEMENT STATEMENT
U.S. DEPARTMENT OF HOUSING AND URBAN DEVELOPMENT

C. NOTE: This form is furnished to give you a statement of actual settlement costs. Amounts paid to and by the settlement agent are shown. Items marked "(p.o.c.)" were paid outside the closing; they are shown here for informational purposes and are not included in the totals. **WARNING:** It is a crime to knowingly make false statements to the United States on this or any other similar form. Penalties upon conviction can include a fine and imprisonment. For details see: Title 18U, S. Code Section 1001 and Section 1010 PREVIOUS EDITION IS OBSOLETE

D. NAME OF BORROWER:
 ADDRESS:

E. NAME OF SELLER:
 ADDRESS:

F. NAME OF LENDER:
 ADDRESS:

SELLER'S IDENTIFICATION NUMBER:

G. PROPERTY LOCATION: STREET:
 LEGAL:

☐ PRINCIPAL RESIDENCE ☐ OTHER REAL ESTATE

H. SETTLEMENT AGENT: UNIVERSITY TITLE COMPANY
 ADDRESS: 1021 UNIVERSITY DRIVE EAST, COLLEGE STATION, TX 77841

SETTLEMENT AGENT'S IDENTIFICATION NUMBER: 74-1753734

PLACE OF SETTLEMENT:
 ADDRESS:

I. SETTLEMENT DATE:

J. SUMMARY OF BORROWER'S TRANSACTION		K. SUMMARY OF SELLER'S TRANSACTION	
100. GROSS AMOUNT DUE FROM BORROWER		**400. GROSS AMOUNT DUE TO SELLER:**	
101. Contract sales price		401. Contract sales price	
102. Personal property		402. Personal property	
103. Settlement charges to borrower (line 1400)		403.	
104.		404.	
105.		405.	
Adjustments for items paid by seller in advance		*Adjustments for items paid by seller in advance*	
106. City/town taxes to		406. City/town taxes to	
107. County taxes to		407. County taxes to	
108. Assessments to		408. Assessments to	
109.		409.	
110.		410.	
111.		411.	
112.		412.	
120. GROSS AMOUNT DUE FROM BORROWER		**420. GROSS AMOUNT DUE TO SELLER**	
200. AMOUNTS PAID BY OR IN BEHALF OF BORROWER:		**500. REDUCTIONS IN AMOUNT DUE TO SELLER:**	
201. Deposit or earnest money		501. Excess deposit (see instructions)	
202. Principal amount of new loan(s)		502. Settlement charges to seller (line 1400)	
203. Existing loan(s) taken subject to		503. Existing loan(s) taken subject to	
204.		504. Payoff of first mortgage loan	
205.		505. Payoff of second mortgage loan	
206.		506.	
207.		507.	
208.		508.	
209.		509.	
Adjustments for items unpaid by seller		*Adjustments for items unpaid by seller*	
210. City/town taxes to		510. City/town taxes to	
211. County taxes to		511. County taxes to	
212. Assessments to		512. Assessments to	
213.		513.	
214.		514.	
215.		515.	
216.		516.	
217.		517.	
218.		518.	
219.		519.	
220. TOTAL PAID BY/FOR BORROWER		**520. TOTAL REDUCTIONS AMOUNT DUE SELLER**	
300. CASH AT SETTLEMENT FROM/TO BORROWER		**600. CASH AT SETTLEMENT TO/FROM SELLER**	
301. Gross amount due from borrower (line 120)		601. Gross amount due to seller (line 420)	
302. Less amounts paid by/for borrower (line 220)	()	602. Less reductions in amount due seller (line 520)	()
303. CASH (☐ FROM) (☐ TO) BORROWER		**603. CASH (☐ FROM) (☐ TO) SELLER**	

SOLICITATION: You are required by law to provide **UNIVERSITY TITLE COMPANY** with your correct taxpayer identification number. If you do not provide **UNIVERSITY TITLE COMPANY** with your correct taxpayer identification number, you may be subject to civil or criminal penalties imposed by law.

Under penalties of perjury, I certify that the number shown on this statement is my correct taxpayer identification number.

Seller's Signature _____ Seller's Signature _____ Seller's Signature _____

The information contained in Blocks E, G, H, I, and on line 401 (or if line 401 has an asterick, line 403 and 404) is important tax information and is being furnished to the Internal Revenue Service. If you are required to file a return, a negligence penalty or other sanction will be imposed on you if this item is required to be reported and the IRS determines that it has not been reported

L. SETTLEMENT CHARGES

		PAID FROM BORROWER'S FUNDS AT SETTLEMENT	PAID FROM SELLER'S FUNDS AT SETTLEMENT
700.	**TOTAL SALES/BROKER'S COMMISSION** based on price $ @ % =		
	Division of commission (line 700) as follows:		
701.	$ to		
702.	$ to		
703.	Commission paid at Settlement (Money retained by broker applied to commission $_____)		
704.			
800.	**ITEMS PAYABLE IN CONNECTION WITH LOAN**		
801.	Loan Origination Fee %		
802.	Loan Discount %		
803.	Appraisal Fee to		
804.	Credit Report to		
805.	Lender's Inspection Fee		
806.	Mortgage Insurance Application Fee to		
807.	Assumption Fee		
808.			
809.			
900.	**ITEMS REQUIRED BY LENDER TO BE PAID IN ADVANCE**		
901.	Interest from to @ $ /day		
902.	Mortgage Insurance Premium for months to		
903.	Hazard Insurance Premium for years to		
904.	years to		
905.			
1000.	**RESERVES DEPOSITED WITH LENDER**		
1001.	Hazard insurance month @ $ per month		
1002.	Mortgage insurance month @ $ per month		
1003.	City property taxes month @ $ per month		
1004.	County property taxes month @ $ per month		
1005.	Annual assessments month @ $ per month		
1006.	month @ $ per month		
1007.	month @ $ per month		
1008.	month @ $ per month		
1100.	**TITLE CHARGES**		
1101.	Settlement or closing fee to		
1102.	Abstract or title search to		
1103.	Title examination to		
1104.	Title insurance binder to		
1105.	Document preparation to		
1106.	Notary fees to		
1107.	Attorney's fees to		
	(includes above items numbers;		
1108.	Title insurance to		
	(includes above items numbers;		
1109.	Lender's coverage $		
1110.	Owner's coverage $		
1111.			
1112.			
1113.			
1200.	**GOVERNMENT RECORDING AND TRANSFER CHARGES**		
1201.	Recording fees: Deed $; Mortgage $; Release $		
1202.	City/county tax/stamps: Deed $; Mortgage $		
1203.	State tax/stamps: Deed $; Mortgage $		
1204.			
1205.			
1300.	**ADDITIONAL SETTLEMENT CHARGES**		
1301.	Survey to		
1302.	Pest inspection to		
1303.			
1304.			
1305.			
1306.			
1307.			
1400.	**TOTAL SETTLEMENT CHARGES (enter on lines 103, Section J and 502, Section K)**		

I have carefully reviewed the HUD-1 Settlement Statement and to the best of my knowledge and belief, it is a true and accurate statement of all receipts and disbursements made on my account in this transaction. I further certify that I have received a copy of the HUD-1 Settlement Statement.

Borrower_____ Seller_____

The HUD-1 Settlement Statement which I have prepared is a true and accurate account of this transmission. I have caused or will cause funds to be disbursed in accordance with this statement.

_____ _____
 Settlement Agent Date

WARNING: It is a crime to knowingly make false statements to the United States on this or any other similar form. Penalties upon conviction can include a fine and imprisonment. For details see: Title 18 U. S. Code Section 1001 and Section 1010.

HUD-1
RESPA HB 4305.2

APPENDIX

Form **2119**	**Sale or Exchange of Principal Residence**	OMB No. 1545–0072
	▶ See instructions on back.	**19 87**
Department of the Treasury Internal Revenue Service (X)	▶ Attach to Form 1040 for year of sale (see instruction B).	Attachment Sequence No. **22**
Name(s) as shown on Form 1040.		Your social security number

Do not include expenses that you deduct as moving expenses.

			Yes	No
1 a	Date former residence sold ▶			
b	Enter the face amount of any mortgage, note (for example, second trust), or other financial instrument on which you will receive periodic payments of principal or interest from this sale ▶			
2 a	If you bought or built a new residence, enter date you occupied it; otherwise enter ''None'' ▶			
b	Are any rooms in either residence rented out or used for business for which a deduction is allowed? (If ''Yes,'' see instructions.)			
3 a	Were you 55 or over on date of sale? .			
b	Was your spouse 55 or over on date of sale? . If you answered ''No'' to 3a and 3b, do not complete 3c through 3f and Part II.			
c	Did the person who answered ''Yes'' to 3a or 3b own and use the property sold as his or her principal residence for a total of at least 3 years (except for short absences) of the 5-year period before the sale?			
d	If you answered ''Yes'' to 3c, do you elect to take the once in a lifetime exclusion of the gain on the sale?			
e	At time of sale, was the residence owned by: ☐ you, ☐ your spouse, ☐ both of you?			
f	Social security number of spouse, at time of sale, if different from number on Form 1040 ▶ (Enter ''None'' if you were not married at time of sale.)			

Part I Computation of Gain

4	Selling price of residence (Do not include personal property items.)	**4**	
5	Expense of sale (Include sales commissions, advertising, legal, etc.)	**5**	
6	Subtract line 5 from line 4. This is the amount realized	**6**	
7	Basis of residence sold .	**7**	
8	Gain on sale (subtract line 7 from line 6). If zero or less, enter zero and do not complete the rest of form. Enter the gain from this line on Schedule D, line 3 or 10,* unless you bought another principal residence or checked ''Yes'' to 3d. Then continue with this form	**8**	

If you haven't replaced your residence, do you plan to do so within the replacement period? ☐ Yes ☐ No
(If ''Yes'' see instruction B.)

Part II Age 55 or Over One-Time Exclusion

Complete this part only if you checked "yes" to 3(d) to elect the once in a lifetime exclusion; otherwise, skip to Part III.

9	Enter the smaller of line 8 or $125,000 ($62,500, if married filing separate return)	**9**	
10	Gain (subtract line 9 from line 8). If zero, do not complete rest of form. Enter the gain from this line on Schedule D, line 10,* unless you bought another principal residence. Then continue with this form . .	**10**	

Part III Gain To Be Postponed and Adjusted Basis of New Residence

Complete this part if you bought another principal residence.

11	Fixing-up expenses (see instructions for time limits)	**11**	
12	Adjusted sales price (subtract line 11 from line 6)	**12**	
13	Cost of new residence .	**13**	
14	Gain taxable this year (subtract line 13 plus line 9 (if applicable) from line 12). If result is zero or less, enter zero. Do not enter more than line 8 or line 10 (if applicable). Enter the gain from this line on Schedule D, line 3 or 10* .	**14**	
15	Gain to be postponed (Subtract line 14 from line 8. However, if Part II applies, subtract line 14 from line 10.) .	**15**	
16	Adjusted basis of new residence (subtract line 15 from line 13)	**16**	

*****Caution:** If you completed Form 6252 for the residence in 1a, do not enter your taxable gain from Form 2119 on Schedule D.

For Paperwork Reduction Act Notice, see back of form. Form **2119** (1987)

Form **3903**

Department of the Treasury
Internal Revenue Service (X)

Moving Expenses

▶ Attach to Form 1040.

▶ See separate Instructions.

OMB No. 1545-0062

1987

Attachment
Sequence No. **62**

Name(s) as shown on Form 1040 | Your social security number

1	Enter the number of miles from your **old** residence to your **new** workplace	1
2	Enter the number of miles from your **old** residence to your **old** workplace	2
3	Subtract line 2 from line 1. Enter the result (but not less than zero) ▶	3

If line **3** is 35 or more miles, complete the rest of this form. If line 3 is less than 35 miles, you may not take a deduction for moving expenses. This rule does not apply to members of the armed forces.

Part I Moving Expenses

Section A.—Transportation of Household Goods

4 Transportation and storage for household goods and personal effects	4

Section B.—Expenses of Moving From Old to New Residence

5 Travel and lodging **not** including meals	5	
6 Total meals .	6	
7 Reimbursements for meals on line 6 on which no income tax was withheld (see **Meal Expenses** in the Instructions). Do not enter more than the amount shown on line 6 . .	7	
8 Subtract line 7 from line 6	8	
9 Multiply line 8 by 80% (.80)	9	
10 Add lines 5, 7, and 9 .	10	

Section C.—Pre-move Househunting Expenses

11 Travel and lodging **not** including meals	11	
12 Total meals .	12	
13 Reimbursements for meals on line 12 on which no income tax was withheld (see **Meal Expenses** in the Instructions). Do not enter more than the amount shown on line 12 .	13	
14 Subtract line 13 from line 12	14	
15 Multiply line 14 by 80% (.80)	15	
16 Add lines 11, 13, and 15	16	

Section D.—Temporary Quarters (for any 30 days in a row after getting your job)

17 Lodging expenses **not** including meals	17	
18 Total meals .	18	
19 Reimbursements for meals on line 18 on which no income tax was withheld (see **Meal Expenses** in the Instructions). Do not enter more than the amount shown on line 18 . .	19	
20 Subtract line 19 from line 18	20	
21 Multiply line 20 by 80% (.80)	21	
22 Add lines 17, 19, and 21	22	

Section E.—Qualified Real Estate Expenses

23 Expenses of (check one): **a** ☐ selling or exchanging your old residence; or **b** ☐ if renting, settling an unexpired lease	23	
24 Expenses of (check one): **a** ☐ buying your new residence; or **b** ☐ if renting, getting a new lease	24	

Part II Dollar Limitations

25 Add lines 16 and 22	25	
26 Enter the smaller of line 25 or $1,500 ($750 if married, filing a separate return, and at the end of the tax year you lived with your spouse who also started work during the tax year) .	26	
27 Add lines 23, 24, and 26	27	
28 Enter the smaller of line 27 or $3,000 ($1,500 if married, filing a separate return, and at the end of the tax year you lived with your spouse who also started work during the tax year)	28	
29 Add lines 4, 10, and 28. This is your moving expense deduction. **Enter here and on Schedule A (Form 1040), line 19. (Note:** Any payments your employer made for any part of your move (including the value of any services furnished in kind) should be included on Form W-2. Report that amount on **Form 1040, line 7.** See **Reimbursements** in the Instructions.) ▶	29	

For Paperwork Reduction Act Notice, see separate Instructions.

Form **3903** (1987)

BIBLIOGRAPHY

This section lists selected publications on a wide variety of real estate topics. It is intended as a reference for use by those who want information about a special aspect of real estate or land development. It contains references to recent and relevant articles, books, and monographs on selected topics; it is not an exhaustive list of publications.

Persons helpful in compiling this list include (alphabetically): Don Albrecht, Waldo Born, Wayne Etter. Judon Fambrough, Jack Friedman, Charles Gilliland, Terry Grissom, Jack Harris. Ted Jones, Robert Lyon, Gary Maler, Ivan Schmedemann, and Arthur Wright, all with the Real Estate Center at Texas A&M University. Appreciation to the Real Estate Center, Richard L. Floyd, Director.

TOPIC

Agriculture
Appraisal (General)
Appraisal (Rural)
Appraisal Terminology
 and Definitions
Assessment
Associations (Directories)
Bibliographies
Brokerage
Capitalization
Careers
Commercial Real Estate
Computers and Calculators
Condominium
Condemnation Appraisal
Construction
Corporate Real Estate
Cost Indexes
Counseling
Demographics
Depreciation
Development
Easements
Economics, Land
Eminent Domain
Employee Transfer
Energy
Feasibility Study
Finance
Financial Tables
Floodplain
Foreign Ownership
Forms
Glossaries
Highest and Best Use
Historic Properties
Home Selling
Hotel/Motel
Housing, Multi-Family
Housing, Single-Family
Housing, Urban

Income Property
Industrial Parks
Industrial Property
Insurance
Investment
Land and Land Use
Land Planning
Law
Leases and Leasehold
 Interests
Licensing Exam Preparation
Limited Partnerships
Management (Brokerage)
Management (Property)
Market Analysis
Marketing
Mathematics
Medical Facilities
Mineral Leasing
Mortgage, Alternative Instruments
Mortgage Market
Multiple Regression
Office Buildings
Parking Facilities
Principles (of Real Estate)
Regulations
Rent and Rent Control
Right of Way
Rural Properties
Savings and Loan Associations
Shopping Centers
Site Selection
Syndication
Tax (Income)
Tax (Property)
Timber and Timberland
Timesharing
Transfer of Development Rights
Waterfront Property
Water Rights
Zoning

Entire page

AGRICULTURE (SEE RURAL PROPERTIES)

Periodicals

Agricultural Economics Research. Superintendent of Documents, Government Printing Office, Washington, DC 20402. Quarterly.

Agricultural Outlook. Superintendent of Documents, Government Printing Office, Washington, DC 20402. Monthly.

Farmline. Superintendent of Documents, Government Printing Office, Washington, DC 20402. 11 issues a year.

Journal of the American Society of Farm Managers and Rural Appraisers. Box 6857, Denver, CO 80206. Semiannual.

APPRAISAL (GENERAL)

MARSHALL VALUATION SERVICE (Cost estimation information). Marshall and Swift Publication Co., 1617 Beverly Boulevard, Los Angeles, CA 90026.

Periodicals

Appraisal Journal, The, American Institute of Real Estate Appraisers, 430 North Michigan Avenue, Chicago, IL 60611. Quarterly.

Appraisal Review Journal. National Association of Review Appraisers, Suite 410 Midwest Federal Bldg., St. Paul, MN 55101.

Journal of the American Society of Farm Managers and Rural Appraisers. Box 6857, Denver, CO 80206.

Real Estate Appraiser & Analyst. Society of Real Estate Appraisers, 225 North Michigan Avenue, Chicago, IL 60611. Bimonthly.

Valuation. American Society of Appraisers, P.O. Box 17265, Washington, DC 20041.

Books

Appraisal of Real Estate, The. 8th ed. Chicago: American Institute of Real Estate Appraisers, 1983.

Bloom, George F., and Harrison, Henry S. *Appraising The Single Family Residence.* Chicago: American Institute of Real Estate Appraisers, 1978.

Friedman, Jack P., and Ordway, Nicholas. *Income Property Appraisal and Analysis.* 2nd ed. Englewood Cliffs, NJ: Prentice-Hall, 1987.

MacBride, Dexter D., ed. *The Bibliography of Appraisal Literature.* Washington, DC: American Society of Appraisers, 1974.

Ring, Alfred, and Boykin, Jack. *The Valuation of Real Estate.* 3rd ed. Englewood Cliffs, NJ: Prentice-Hall, 1986.

Smith, Halbert, and Belloit, Jerry. *Real Estate Appraisal.* 2nd ed. Dayton, OH: Century VII Publishing Co., 1987.

APPRAISAL (RURAL)

Articles

Schott, Reid, and White, Fred C. "Multiple Regression Analysis of Farmland Values by Land Classes." *Appraisal Journal* XLV (July 1977): 427–34.

Books

Appraisal of Rural Property, The. Chicago: American Institute of Real Estate Appraisers, 1983.

Murray, William. *Farm Appraisal and Valuation.* 5th ed. Ames, IA: Iowa State University Press, 1969.

Rural Appraisal Manual. 5th ed. Denver: American Society of Farm Managers and Rural Appraisers, 1979.

Suter, Robert. *The Appraisal of Farm Real Estate.* Denver: The Interstate Printers and Publishers, 1974.

BIBLIOGRAPHY

APPRAISAL TERMINOLOGY AND DEFINITIONS

Books

Boyce, Byrl N. *Real Estate Appraisal Terminology.* Cambridge, MA: Ballinger Publishing Co., 1984.

Dictionary of Real Estate Appraisal, The. Chicago: American Institute of Real Estate Appraisers, 1984.

Friedman, Edith. *Encyclopedia of Real Estate Appraising.* Englewood Cliffs, NJ: Prentice-Hall, 1978.

ASSESSMENT

Periodicals

Assessment and Valuation Legal Reporter. International Association of Assessing Officers, 1313 East 60th Street, Chicago, IL 60637-9990. Monthly.

Articles

Rienmuth, James E. "Measurement of Valuation Accuracy." *Assessors Journal* 9 (1976): 3–14.

Books

Improving Real Property Assessment: A Reference Manual. Chicago: International Association of Assessing Officers, 1978.

Property Assessment Valuation. Chicago: International Association of Assessing Officers, 1977.

ASSOCIATIONS (DIRECTORIES)

Periodicals

CAI News. Community Associations Institute, 300 South Eads Street, Arlington, VA 22202. Monthly.

Community Association Law Reporter. Community Associations Institute, 3000 South Eads Street, Arlington, VA 22202. Monthly.

Housing and Development Reporter. Warren, Gorham, and Lamont, 210 South Street, Boston, MA 02111.

National Real Estate Investor. Communication Channels, Inc., 6285 Barfield Road, Atlanta, GA 30328. Monthly.

BIBLIOGRAPHIES

Books

Johnsich, John Robert. *Real Estate Books and Periodicals in Print.* Sacramento, CA: Real Estate Publishing Company, 1982–83 edition.

BROKERAGE

Periodicals

Real Estate Today. National Association of Realtors, 430 North Michigan Avenue, Chicago, IL 60611. Monthly.

Books

Lindeman, Bruce. *Real Estate Brokerage Management.* Englewood Cliffs, NJ: Prentice-Hall, 1987.

National Association of Realtors. *Inside the Real Estate Business.* Washington, DC: Acropolis Books, 1982.

CAPITALIZATION

Articles

Gettel, Ronald E. "Good Grief, Another Method of Selecting Capitalization Rates!" *Appraisal Journal* XLVI (January 1978): 90–100.

Hanford, Lloyd. "The Capitalization Process Revisited." *Appraisal Journal XLIV (July 1976): 393–404.*

Books

Akerson, Charles B. *Capitalization Theory and Technique*. Chicago: AIREA, 1984.

Mortgage-Equity Capitalization: An Introduction. Chicago: American Institute of Real Estate Appraisers, 1975.

Johnson, Irvin E. *Instant Mortgage-Equity Technique*. Lexington, MA: Lexington Books, 1971.

CAREERS

Books

Edwards, Kenneth. *Your Successful Real Estate Career*. New York: American Management Assn., 1982.

Shenkel, William M. *The Real Estate Professional*. New York: Dow Jones-Irwin Books, 1976.

COMMERCIAL REAL ESTATE

Periodicals

Commercial Investment Journal. Realtors National Marketing Institute, Chicago, IL 60611.

Journal of Real Estate Development. Federal Research Press, 210 Lincoln Street, Boston, MA 02111-9903.

Real Estate Review. Warren, Gorham & Lamont, Inc., 210 South Street, Boston, MA 02111. Quarterly.

Articles

Kelley, Hugh F. "Forecasting Office Space Demand in Urban Areas," *Real Estate Review* 13 (Fall 1983): 87–95.

Martin, William B., and English, Wilke D. "Forecasting Demand for Multi-Tenant Office Space." *Commercial Investment Journal* IV (Winter 1985): 7–9 and 27.

Rosen, Kenneth T. "Toward a Model of the Office Building Sector." *AREUEA Journal* 12 (Fall 1984): 261–69.

COMPUTERS & CALCULATORS

Books

Dilmore, Gene. *Quantitative Techniques in Real Estate Counseling*. Lexington, MA: Lexington Books, 1981.

CONDOMINIUM

Books

Dombal, Robert W. *Residential Condominiums: A Guide to Analysis & Appraisal*. Chicago: The American Institute of Real Estate Appraisers, 1976.

Romney, Keith B. *Condominium Development Guide*. Boston: Warren, Gorham & Lamont, 1976.

BIBLIOGRAPHY

CONDEMNATION APPRAISAL

Articles

Davis, William D., Sr. "The Impact of Public Announcement on Value." *The Appraisal Journal* XLIV (October 1976): 533–46.

Lewis, Harold J. "The Appraisal of Highway Noise Damages." *The Appraisal Journal* XLV (October 1977): 499–504.

Books

Bonbright, James C. *The Valuation of Property*. Vols I and II. Charlottesville, VA: The Wichie Co., 1965.

Condemnation Appraisal Practice. Vol. II. Chicago: American Institute of Real Estate Appraisers, 1973.

Real Estate Valuation in Litigation. Chicago: AIREA, 1983.

CONSTRUCTION

Periodicals

Builder. National Association of Home Builders, 15th & M Streets NW, Washington, DC 20005. Monthly.

Construction Review. U.S. Department of Commerce, Washington, DC. Bimonthly.

Multi-Housing News. Gralla Publications, 1515 Broadway, New York, NY 10036. Monthly.

Professional Builder/Apartment Business. Cahners Publishing Co. Inc., 270 St.Paul Street, Denver, CO 80206. Monthly.

Books

Boeckh Building Cost Manual. 525 E. Michigan, Milwaukee, WI

Construction Cost Control Manual. Washington, DC: National Association of Homebuilders, 1982.

Construction Dictionary. Washington, DC: National Association of Homebuilders, 1985.

Dodge Building Cost Calculator. New York: McGraw-Hill Information Systems. Updated regularly.

Marshall Valuation Service. Los Angeles, CA: Marshall & Swift Publication Co. Updated regularly.

CORPORATE REAL ESTATE

Periodicals

Corporate Real Estate Executive. National Association of Corporate Real Estate Executives, 471 Spencer Drive, West Palm Beach, FL 33409.

Articles

Friedman, Jack P., and Moores, John H. "A Mixed Bag of Blessings: Corporate Real Estate." *Financial Executive* XLVI (October 1978): 56–67.

Books

Collins, Webster A., Spaulding, Charles H., et al. *Real Estate: A Hidden Corporate Asset*. Chicago: American Society of Real Estate Counselors, 1986.

COST INDEXES

Boeckh Building Cost Manual. 525 E. Michigan, Milwaukee, WI.

Dodge Services, F. W. Dodge, 1221 Avenue of the Americas, New York, NY.

Marshall Valuation Service, 1617 Beverly Blvd., Los Angeles, CA 90026.

COUNSELING

Periodicals

Real Estate Issues. American Society of Real Estate Counselors, 430 N. Michigan Avenue, Chicago, IL 60611. Quarterly.

Books

Boykin, James H., ed. *Real Estate Counseling*. Chicago: American Society of Real Estate Counselors, 1984.

DEMOGRAPHICS

Periodicals

Annual Survey of Buying Power. Sales and Marketing Management Magazine, Bill Publication Co., New York, NY. Annual.

Current Population Reports. Bureau of the Census, Government Printing Office, Washington, DC.

New One-Family Houses Sold and for Sale. Bureau of the Census, U.S. Department of Commence, Washington, DC.

DEPRECIATION

Books

Young, James C., and Dilley, Steven C., eds. *The Tax Reform Act of 1986: The New ACRS Rules*. Paramus, NJ: Prentice-Hall Information Services, 1987.

DEVELOPMENT

Periodicals

Journal of Real Estate Development. Federal Research Press, 210 Lincoln Street, Boston, MA 02111. Quarterly.

National Real Estate Investor. Communication Channels, Inc., 6285 Barfield Road, Atlanta, GA 30328. Monthly.

Books

Halpin, Michael C. *Profit Planning for Real Estate Development*, New York: Dow Jones-Irwin, 1977.

Roulac, Stephen. *Case Studies in Property Development*. San Francisco: Property Press, 1973.

EASEMENTS

Periodicals

Right Of Way. International Right of Way Assn., 6133 Bristol Parkway, Suite 270, Culver City, CA 90230. Bimonthly.

Books

Clark, Louis, Jr., and Treadway, F. H. *Impact of Electric Power Transmission Line Easements on Real Estate*. Chicago: American Institute of Real Estate Appraisers, 1972.

ECONOMICS, LAND

Periodicals

Land Economics. University of Wisconsin Press, Journals Dept., 114 North Murray Street, Madison, WI 53715. Quarterly.

Books

Barlowe, Raleigh. *Land Resource Economics*. 3rd ed. Englewood Cliffs, NJ: Prentice-Hall, 1978.

EMINENT DOMAIN

Books

Federal Law of Eminent Domain, The. Charlottesville, VA: Federal Law Library, Wichie Co., 1982.

EMPLOYEE TRANSFER

Periodicals

Mobility. Jerry Holloman, ed., Employee Relocation Council, 1627 K Street NW, Washington, DC 20006.

ENERGY

Articles

Webb, James. "The Influence of Solar Energy Systems on the Value of Dwellings," *Real Estate Appraiser & Analyst* 46 (January–February 1980): 4–7.

Books

Energy Conservation Opportunities and Strategies. Chicago: Institute of Real Estate Management, 1981.

FEASIBILITY STUDY

Periodicals

Site Selection Handbook. Conway Data Inc., 1954 Airport Road NE, Atlanta, GA 30341-4996.

Books

Barrett, G. V., and Blair, John P. *How to Conduct and Analyze Real Estate Market and Feasibility Studies.* New York: Van Nostrand Reinhold Company, 1982.

Cannestaso, James C. *Real Estate Financial Feasibility Analysis Handbook & Workbook.* Chicago: American Institute of Real Estate Appraisers, 1982.

Graaskamp, James A. *A Guide to Feasibility Analysis.* Chicago: Society of Real Estate Appraisers, 1970.

Lukens, Reaves C., Jr. *The Appraiser & Real Estate Feasibility Studies.* Chicago: American Institute of Real Estate Appraisers, 1972.

Messner, S.D., Boyce, B.N., Trimble, M.G., and Ward, R.L. *Analyzing Real Estate Opportunities — Market and Feasibility Studies.* Chicago: Realtors National Marketing Institutions, 1977.

FINANCE

Periodicals

Crittenden Report. Crittenden Publishing Inc., Box 1150, Novato, CA 94948. Weekly.

Federal Home Loan Bank Board Journal. Superintendent of Documents, Government Printing Office, Washington, DC 20402. Monthly.

Mortgage Banking. Mortgage Bankers Association of America, 1125 15th Street NW, Washington, DC 20005. Monthly.

Novick's Income Property Finance Report. IPFR Publishing Corp., 111 John Street, Penthouse, New York, NY 10038. 22 issues a year.

Real Estate Finance. Federal Research Press, 210 Lincoln St., Suite 700, Boston, MA 02111. Quarterly.

Real Estate Finance Journal. Warren, Gorham & Lamont, 210 South Street, Boston, MA 02111-9902.

Books

Brueggeman, William B., and Stone, Leo D. *Real Estate Finance*. 7th ed. Homewood, IL: Richard D. Irwin, 1981. Maisel, Sherman J., and Roulac, Stephen E.

Real Estate Investment & Finance. New York: McGraw-Hill, 1976.

Mason, James J. *AIREA Financial Tables*. Chicago: American Institute of Real Estate Appraisers, 1981.

Weidemer, John. *Real Estate Finance*. Englewood Cliffs, NJ: Prentice-Hall, 1986.

FINANCIAL TABLES

Capitalization Rate Tables. Boston, MA: Financial Publishing Company, 1974.

Ellwood, L. W. *Ellwood Tables*. Cambridge, MA: Ballinger Publishing Co., 1977.

Friedman, Jack P., and Harris, Jack C. *Adjustable Rate Tables*. Hauppauge, NY: Barron's Educational Series, 1987.

Friedman, Jack P., and Pearson, Peggy. *Real Estate Finance and Investment Tables*. Englewood Cliffs, NJ: Prentice-Hall, 1983.

FLOOD PLAIN

H.V.D. flood hazard maps available from: National Flood Insurance Program, Box 34294, Bethesda, MD 20034. Phone: 1-800-638-6620.

Maps of flood plains from: U.S. Corps of Engineers, SWFPLF, Box 17300, Fort Worth, TX 76102. Phone: 1-817-334-3207.

FOREIGN OWNERSHIP

Books

Hinds, Dudley S., and Ordway, Nicholas. *International Real Estate Investment*. Chicago: Real Estate Education Co., 1982.

Meyers, Myron. *Foreign Investment in United States Real Estate*. New York: Dow Jones-Irwin Books, 1982.

U.S. Department of Agriculture. *Monitoring Foreign Ownership of U.S. Real Estate*. (A Report to Congress). Vol. 1, Chap. 2.

Periodicals

International Real Estate Federation, FIABCI, American Chapter, 430 N. Michigan Avenue, Chicago, IL 60611.

FORMS

Books

Arnold, Alvin L. *Modern Real Estate & Mortgage Forms*. New York: Warren, Gorham & Lamont, 1979.

, and Smith, Owen T. *Modern Ownership & Investment Forms*. New York: Warren, Gorham & Lamont, 1976.

Kushet, Jack, and Lopatin, Robert. *Modern Real Estate Forms*. New York: Warren, Gorham & Lamont, 1981.

Kushet, Robert, and Lopatin, Robert. *Modern Real Estate Leasing Forms*. New York: Warren, Gorham & Lamont, 1980.

Kushet, Jack, and Smith, Owen T. *Modern Construction & Development Forms*. New York: Warren, Gorham & Lamont, 1976.

GLOSSARIES

Books

Arnold, Alvin. *Encyclopedia of Real Estate*. Boston: Warren Gorham & Lamont. Boston. Updated annually.

Boyce, Byrl N. *Real Estate Appraisal Terminology*. Chicago: American Institute of Real Estate Appraisers and Society of Real Estate Appraisers, 1984.

Dictionary of Real Estate Appraisal, The. Chicago: American Institute of Real Estate Appraisers, 1984.

Friedman, Jack P., Harris, Jack C., and Lindeman, Bruce. *Dictionary of Real Estate Terms*. Hauppauge, NY: Barron's Educational Series, 1987.

Reilly, John W. *The Language of Real Estate*. Chicago: Real Estate Education Company, 1982.

HIGHEST AND BEST USE

Books

Readings in Highest & Best Use. Chicago: American Institute of Real Estate Appraisers, 1981.

HISTORIC PROPERTIES

Periodicals

Old House Journal, The. Old House Journal Corp., 69A Seventh Ave, Brooklyn, NY 11217. 10 issues per year.

Articles

Ragas, Wade R., and Meitchovich, Ivan J. Jr., "Historic Preservation and the 1976 Tax Reform Act." *Appraisal Journal* XLVI (January 1978): 44–52.

Oldham, Sally G. "Historic Properties: Variable Valuations." *Appraisal Journal L (July 1982): 364–377.*

Books

Reynolds, Judith. *Historic Properties: Preservation and the Valuation Process*. Chicago: American Institute of Real Estate Appraisers, 1982.

HOME SELLING

Books

Real Estate Advertising Handbook. Chicago: Realtors National Marketing Institute, 1984.

Rosenauer, Johnie L. *Effective Real Estate Sales & Marketing*. Chicago: Real Estate Education Co., 1982.

HOTEL/MOTEL

Periodicals

Cornell Hotel and Restaurant Administration Quarterly. School of Hotel Administration, Cornell University, Statler Hall, Ithaca, NY 14853. Quarterly.

Lodging Hospitality. Penton/IPC, Inc., 1111 Chester Avenue, Cleveland, OH 44114. Monthly.

Books

Rushmore, Stephen. *How to Perform an Economic Feasibility Study of a Proposed Hotel/Motel*. Chicago: American Society of Real Estate Counselors, 1986.

HOUSING, MULTI-FAMILY

Periodicals

Apartment Management Newsletter. Mattco Equities, Inc., 48 West 21st Street, New York, NY 10010-6976. Monthly.

Income/Expense Analysis: Apartments. Institute of Real Estate Management. Annual.

Multi-Housing News. Gralla Publications, 1515 Broadway, New York, NY 10036. Monthly.

Books

Downs, James C., Jr. *Principles of Real Estate Management*. Chicago: Institute of Real Estate Management, National Association of Realtors, 1980.

Freeman, Roland. *The Encyclopedia of Apartment Management*. Washington, DC: National Apartment Association, 1976.

Kelley, Edward N. *Practical Apartment Management*. Chicago: Institute of Real Estate Management, National Association of Realtors, 1981.

HOUSING, SINGLE-FAMILY

Periodicals

Existing Home Sales. National Association of Realtors, Economics & Research Division, 777 14th Street NW, Washington, DC 20005. Monthly and annual reports.

Books:

Harrison, Henry S. *Houses*. Chicago: National Association of Realtors, 1976.

HOUSING, URBAN

Articles

Weicher, John. "The Affordability of New Homes." *AREUEA Journal* 5 (Summer 1977): 209–26.

Books:

Smith, Wallace. *Housing*. Berkeley, CA: University of California Press, 1970.

Starr, Roger. *Housing & The Money Market*. New York: Basic Books, 1975.

Sumichrast, Michael, et al. *Housing Fact Book*. Washington, DC: National Association of Home Builders, 1979.

INCOME PROPERTY

Books

Epley, Donald R., and Boykin, James H. *Basic Income Property Appraisal*. Reading, MA: Addison-Wesley, 1983.

Friedman, Jack P., and Ordway, Nicholas. *Income Property Appraisal and Analysis*. Englewood Cliffs, NJ: Prentice-Hall, 1987.

687

Readings in the Income Approach to Real Property Valuation. Vol. I. Chicago: American Institute of Real Estate Appraisers, 1977.

Readings in the Income Capitalization Approach to Real Property Valuation. Vol. II. Chicago: American Institute of Real Estate Appraisers, 1985.

INDUSTRIAL PARKS

Periodicals

The SIR Professionals. Department of Finance, University of Akron, Akron, OH 44325. Semiannual.

Books

Kinnard, William N., Jr., and Messner, Stephen D. *Industrial Real Estate*. 2nd ed. Washington, DC: Society of Industrial Realtors, 1984. Chapters 15, 16, and 17.

INDUSTRIAL PROPERTY

Periodicals

Industrial Development. Conway Research, Inc., 1954 Airport Road, Atlanta, GA 30341. Bimonthly.

Industrial Market Survey. Society of Industrial Realtors, 777 14th Street NW, Washington, DC 20005. Semiannual.

SIR Reports. Society of Industrial Realtors, 777 14th Street NW, Washington, DC 20005. 10 issues a year.

Articles

Atkins, Robert J., and Shrives, Richard, H. "New Approach to Facilities Location." *Harvard Business Review* 46 (May–June 1968).

Fulton, Maurice. "New Factors in Plant Location." *Harvard Business Review* 49 (May–June 1971).

Schmeiner, Roger W. "Look Beyond the Obvious in Plant Location." *Harvard Business Review* 57 (January–February 1979).

Books

Kinnard, William N., Jr., and Messner, Stephen D. *Industrial Real Estate*. 2nd ed. Washington, DC: Society of Industrial Realtors, 1984.

Lochmoeller, Donald C., Muncy, Dorothy, Thorne, Oakleigh, and Viets, Mark. *Industrial Development Handbook*. Washington, DC: Urban Land Institute, 1975.

INSURANCE

Book

Rubin, Harvey W. *Dictionary of Insurance Terms*. Hauppauge, New York: Barron's Educational Series, 1987.

INVESTMENT

Periodicals

Commercial Investment Journal. Realtors National Marketing Institute, 430 North Michigan Avenue, Chicago, IL 60611. Quarterly.

Books

Friedman, Jack, and Ordway, Nicholas. *Income Property Appraisal and Analysis*. Englewood Cliffs, NJ: Prentice-Hall, 1987.

Messner, Stephen D., et al. *Marketing Investment Real Estate*. Chicago: Realtors National Marketing Institute, National Association of Realtors, 1982.

Pyhrr, Stephen A., and Cooper, James R. *Real Estate Investment: Strategy, Analysis & Decision*. Boston: Warren, Gorham & Lamont, 1982.

LAND AND LAND USE

Books

Netter, Edith. *Land Use Law: Issues for the Eighties*. Chicago: American Planning Association, 1981.

Robinson, Shepard D. *Land Use Guide for Builders, Developers and Planners*. New York: McGraw-Hill, 1981.

LAND PLANNING

Periodicals

Journal of the American Planning Association. 1313 East 60th Street, Chicago, IL 60637. Quarterly.

Planning. American Planning Association, 1313 East 60th Street, Chicago, IL 60637. Monthly.

Books

Mandelker, Daniel R., and Cunningham, Roger A. *Planning & Control of Land Development*. Charlottesville, VA: Wichie Co., 1979.

LAW

Periodicals

Real Estate Law Journal. Warren, Gorham & Lamont, Inc. Quarterly.

Real Estate Law Report. Warren, Gorham & Lamont, Inc. Monthly.

Books

Cribbet, John E. *Principles of the Law of Property*. 2nd ed. Mineola, NY: University Text Book Series, 1975.

Eaton, James D. *Real Estate Valuation in Litigation*. Chicago: American Institute of Real Estate Appraisers, 1982.

Jacobus, Charles J., and Levi, Donald R. *Real Estate Law*. Englewood Cliffs, NJ: Prentice-Hall, 1980.

Kratovil, Robert, and Werner, Raymond J. *Real Estate Law*. 8th ed. Englewood Cliffs, NJ: Prentice-Hall, 1983.

Kusnet, Jack, Arnold, Alvin L., and Steckler, David. *Real Estate Law Digest.* Boston: Warren, Gorham & Lamont, 1976.

Madison, Michael T., and Dwyer, Jeffrey R. *The Law of Real Estate Financing*. Boston: Warren, Gorham & Lamont, 1981.

LEASES & LEASEHOLD INTERESTS

Periodicals

Real Estate Leasing Report. Federal Research Press, 210 Lincoln St., Suite 700, Boston, MA 02111.

Books

Britton, James A., ed. *Financing Income-Producing Real Estate*. New York: McGraw Hill, 1979.

Friedman, Jack P., and Ordway, Nicholas. *Income Property Appraisal and Analysis*. Englewood Cliffs, NJ: Prentice-Hall, 1987. Chap. 19.

Kusnet, Jack. *Modern Real Estate Leasing Forms*. New York: Warren, Gorham & Lamont, 1980.

Roulac, Stephen E. *Tax Shelter Sale-Leaseback Financing*. Cambridge, MA: Ballinger Publishing Co., 1976.

Seldin, Maury, ed. *The Real Estate Handbook*, New York: Dow Jones-Irwin, 1980.

LICENSING EXAM PREPARATION

Books

Friedman, Jack P., and Lindeman, Bruce. *Barron's How to Prepare for Real Estate Licensing Examinations*, 3rd ed. Hauppauge, NY: Barron's Educational Series, 1987.

LIMITED PARTNERSHIPS

Books

Lynn, Theodore S., and Goldberg, Harry F. *Real Estate Limited Partnerships*. Somerset, NY: Ronald Press, 1983.

MANAGEMENT (BROKERAGE)

Books

Lindeman, Bruce. *Real Estate Brokerage Management*. Englewood Cliffs, NJ: Prentice-Hall, 1987.

Marcus, Bruce. *Marketing Professional Services in Real Estate: Advertising, Promotion, Public Relations*. Chicago: Realtors National Marketing Institute, 1981.

MANAGEMENT (PROPERTY)

Periodicals

Journal of Property Management. Institute of Real Estate Management, 430 North Michigan Avenue, Chicago, IL 60611. Bimonthly.

Books

Downs, James C., Jr. *Principles of Real Estate Management*. 12th ed. Chicago: Institute of Real Estate Management, 1980.

MARKET ANALYSIS

Articles

Seldin, Maury. "A Reclassification of Real Estate and Market Analyses: Toward Improving the Line of Reasoning." *Real Estate Issues* 9 (Spring/Summer 1984): 44–49.

Books

Barrett, Vincent G., and Blair, John O. *How to Conduct and Analyze Real Estate Market and Feasibility Studies*. New York: Van Nostrand and Reinhold Company, 1982.

Boyd, Harper W., and Westfall, Ralph. *Marketing Research*. Homewood, IL: Richard D. Irwin, 1972.

Boykin, James H. *Real Estate Counseling*. Englewood Cliffs, NJ: Prentice-Hall, 1984.

Graaskamp, James A. *A Guide to Feasibility Analysis*. Chicago: Society of Real Estate Appraisers, 1970.

Lukens, Reaves. *The Appraisers & Real Estate Feasibility Studies*. Chicago: American Institute of Real Estate Appraisers, 1972.

Vernor, James D, ed. *Readings in Market Research for Real Estate*. Chicago: American Institute of Real Estate Appraisers, 1985.

MARKETING

Books

Real Estate Sales Handbook. Chicago: Realtors National Marketing Institute, 1984.

Realtors Institute Reference & Practice Book. Chicago: National Association of Realtors, 1977. Vols. 1, 2, & 3.

Shenkel, William. *Marketing Real Estate*. Englewood Cliffs, NJ: Prentice-Hall, 1980.

MATHEMATICS

Books

Ordway, Nicholas, Ordway, Kathy, and Tosh, Dennis S. *Real Estate Math Made Easy*. Englewood Cliffs, NJ: Prentice-Hall, 1985.

Ventolo, William L., Jr., Marks, Lynette K., and Allaway, Wellington J. *Mastering Real Estate Mathematics*. 2nd ed. Chicago: Real Estate Education Company, 1984.

MEDICAL FACILITIES

Articles

Gimmy, Arthur E. "The Doctor's Office — An Intimate Examination." *Appraisal Journal* XLIII (October 1975): 527–539.

Scott, John E., and Whitaker, David A., Jr. "The Economics of Nursing Home Development." *Appraisal Journal* XLIII (July 1975): 390–99.

MINERAL LEASING

Books

Oil and Gas Law. 8 vols. New York: Matthew Bender & Co.

MORTGAGE, ALTERNATIVE INSTRUMENTS

Periodicals

Mortgage & Real Estate Executives Report, The. Warren, Gorham & Lamont, Inc. Twice monthly.

Books

Friedman, Jack P., and Harris, Jack C. *Adjustable Mortgage Loans*. Hauppauge, NY: Barron's Educational Series, 1987.

MORTGAGE MARKET

Articles

Vartanian, Thomas. "The Garn-St. Germain Depository Institutions Act of 1982," *Housing Finance Review* 2 (April 1983): 167–76.

American Real Estate & Urban Economics Association Journal 8 (Spring 1980): Entire issue.

MULTIPLE REGRESSION

Articles

Clettenberg, Karel J. "Statistical Applications for the SREA Market Data Centers, Inc., Part 1." *Real Estate Appraiser* 39 (September–October 1973): 43–59.

Mullett, Gary M. "A Statistician Appraises Multiple Regression Analysis." *Real Estate Appraiser* 42 (1976): 39–43.

Shenkel, William M. "Developing and Using an Appraisal Data Base." *Real Estate Appraiser* 42 (January–February 1976): 17–32.

BIBLIOGRAPHY

OFFICE BUILDINGS

Periodicals

Income/Expense Analysis: Office Buildings. Institute of Real Estate Management, Chicago. Annually.

Office Building Experience Exchange Report. Building Owners and Managers Association International (BOMA), Washington, DC.

Books

Bearden, Thomas H., Farber, Joseph, and Trione, Gerard W. *Office Buildings: Development, Marketing and Leasing.* Chicago: American Society of Real Estate Counselors, 1981.

Britton, James A., ed. *Financing Income-Producing Real Estate.* New York: McGraw-Hill, 197. Pp. 574–619 and 665–86.

Managing the Office Building. Chicago: Institute of Real Estate Management, 1981.

Roberts, Duane F. *Marketing & Leasing of Office Space.* Chicago: Institute of Real Estate Management, 1979.

PARKING FACILITIES

Articles

Gottesman, Jerome. "Parking Feasibility Checklist." *Appraisal Digest* 27 (October–November–December 1976): 7–16.

Books

The Dimensions of Parking. 2nd ed. Washington, DC: The Urban Land Institute, 1983.

Parking Requirements for Shopping Centers: Summary Recommendation and Research Study Report. Washington, DC: The Urban Land Institute, 1982.

PRINCIPLES (OF REAL ESTATE)

Books

Dasso, Jerome, and Ring, Alfred. *Real Estate Principles.* Englewood Cliffs, NJ: Prentice-Hall, 1986.

Hines, M.A. *Principles and Practices of Real Estate.* Homewood, IL: Richard D. Irwin, 1976.

Unger, M., and Karvel, G. *Real Estate Principles and Practices.* Cincinnati: South-Western Publishing Co., 1987.

REGULATIONS

Periodicals

Housing & Development Reporter. Bureau of National Affairs, 1231 25th Street NW, Washington, DC 20037. Weekly.

Books

Barron, Paul E. *Federal Regulation of Real Estate.* Boston: Warren, Gorham & Lamont, 1975.

RENT AND RENT CONTROL

Books

Lett, Monica R. *Rent Control: Concepts, Realties and Mechanisms.* New Brunswick, NJ: The Center for Urban Policy Research, 1976.

RIGHT OF WAY (SEE EASEMENTS)

Periodicals

Right of Way. International Right of Way Assn., 6133 Bristol Parkway, Suite 270, Culver City, CA 90230. Bimonthly.

Articles

Beetle, George R. "Railroad Right-of-Way Use & Economic Value." *Appraisal Journal* XLV (October 1977): 511–18.

Reiger, Arthur J. "Appraising the Sun: Experience to Date." *Appraisal Journal* XLVIII (April 1980): 224–29.

Reynolds, Judith. "Preservation Easements." *Appraisal Journal* XLIV (July 1976): 355–60.

Smith, Walstein, Jr. "Some Enchanting Easements." *Appraisal Journal* XLVIII (October 1980): 527–39.

RURAL PROPERTIES

Periodicals

American Journal of Agricultural Economics. Dept. of Economics, Iowa State University, Ames, IA 50011.

Agricultural Economics Research. U.S. Department of Agriculture. Superintendent of Documents, Government Printing Office, Washington, DC 20402. Quarterly.

SAVINGS & LOAN ASSOCIATIONS

Periodicals

National Savings & Loan League Journal. National Savings & Loan League, Suite 400, 1101 15th Street, NW, Washington, DC 20005. Monthly.

Savings & Loan News. U.S. League of Savings Associations, 111 East Wacker Drive, Chicago IL 60601. Monthly.

SHOPPING CENTERS

Periodicals

Dollars & Cents of Shopping Centers. Urban Land Institute. Annually.

Articles

Lamm, Robert R. "Selling or Buying Shopping Centers in Today's Market." *Urban Land* 42 (May 1983): 8–11.

Books:

Berry, Brian J. *Geography of Market Centers and Detail Distribution*. Englewood Cliffs, NJ: Prentice-Hall, 1967.

Davies, R. L., and Rogers, D. S. *Store Location and Store Assessment Research*. New York: Wiley & Sons, 1984.

Garret, Robert L., Hunter, Hogan A., Jr., and Stanton, Robert M. *The Valuation of Shopping Centers*. Chicago: American Institute of Real Estate Appraisers, 1976.

Managing the Shopping Center. Chicago: Institute of Real Estate Management, 1983.

Seldin, Maury, ed. *The Real Estate Handbook*. Homewood, IL: Dow Jones-Irwin, 1981.

Shopping Center Development Handbook. Urban Land Institute, Washington, DC: 1985.

SITE SELECTION

Periodicals

Industrial Development Site Selection Handbook. Conway Data, Inc., 40 Technology Park, Norcross, GA 30092-9990.

Books

Applebaum, William. *Retail Site Selection. A Guide to the Location of Shopping Centers*. New York: International Council of Shopping Centers, 1970.

Richey, Clyde W. *Freestanding Retail Site Requirements*. Boulder, CO: Business Research Division, University of Colorado, 1978.

SYNDICATION

Periodicals

RESSI Review. Real Estate Securities & Syndication Institute, 430 North Michigan Avenue, Chicago, IL 60611. Monthly.

Securities Regulation Law Journal. Warren, Gorham & Lamont, Inc., Boston, MA 02111. Quarterly.

TAXATION (INCOME)

Periodicals

Journal of Real Estate Taxation. Warren, Gorham & Lamont, Inc., Boston, MA 02111. Quarterly.

Real Estate Newsletter. Coopers & Lybrand, 222 South Riverside Plaza, Chicago, IL 60606. Quarterly.

Real Estate Tax Ideas. Warren, Gorham & Lamont, Inc., Boston, MA 02111. Monthly.

Books

Kau, James B., and Sirmans, C. F. *Tax Planning for Real Estate Investors*. Englewood Cliffs, NJ: Prentice Hall, 1980.

Robinson, Gerald J. *Federal Income Taxation of Real Estate*. 3rd ed. New York: Warren, Gorham & Lamont, 1979.

Smith, David A. *Subsidized Housing as a Tax Shelter*. Fair Haven, NJ: Robert A. Stanger Co., 1982.

Young, James C., and Dilley, Steven C., eds. *The Tax Reform Act of 1986: Taxation of Real Estate Transactions*. Paramus, NJ: Prentice-Hall Information Services, 1987.

TAX (PROPERTY)

Articles

Blake, D. R. "Property Tax Incidence: an Alternative View." *Land Economics* 55 (1979): 521–31.

Miezskowski, P. M. "Tax Incidence Theory: The Effects of Taxes on the Distribution of Income." *Journal of Political Economics* 75 (1967): 250–62.

Books

Aaron, H.J. *Who Pays the Property Tax*. Washington, DC: The Brookings Institute, 1975.

Netzer, D. *Economics of the Property Tax*. Washington, DC: The Brookings Institute, 1966.

TIMBER AND TIMBERLAND

Periodicals

Forest Farmers. Forest Farmers Association, Box 95385, 4 Executive Park East NE, Atlanta, GA 30347.

Articles

Klemperer, David W. "Segregating Land & Timber Values From Sales of Uneven-aged Forests." *Appraisal Journal* XLVIII (January 1979): 16–25.

TIMESHARING

Periodicals

Resort Timesharing Today. CHB Co. Inc., Drawer 730, Los Altos, CA 94022. Monthly.

Timesharing Law Reporter. Land Development Institute, Ltd., 1401 16th Street NW, Washington, DC 20036. Monthly.

TRANSFER OF DEVELOPMENT RIGHTS

Books

Costonis, John. *Space Adrift*. University of Illinois for the National Trust for Historic Preservation, 1976.

Heffley, Dennis S. *Transferable Development Rights: A Spatial Equilibrium Analysis*. Storrs, CT: Center for Real Estate and Urban Economic Studies, 1980.

WATERFRONT PROPERTY

Books

Richardson, Don K. *The Cost of Environmental Protection: Regulating Housing Development in the Coastal Zone*. New Brunswick, NJ: The Center for Urban Policy Research, 1978.

Rick, William B. *Planning & Developing Waterfront Property*. Washington, DC: Urban Land Institute, 1984.

WATER RIGHTS

Books

Waters and Water Rights. 7 vols. Indianapolis: The Allen Smith Company, 1967.

ZONING

Books

Hinds, Dudley, Carn, Neil, and Ordway, Nicholas. *Winning at Zoning*. New York: McGraw-Hill, 1980.

Mandelker, Daniel R. *Managing our Urban Environment*. Indianapolis: Bobbs-Merrill, 1982.

PUBLISHERS' ADDRESSES

The American Institute of Real Estate Appraisers
430 N. Michigan Avenue
Chicago, IL 60611

American Society of Farm Managers
& Rural Appraisers
Box 295
DeKalb, IL 60115

American Society of Appraisers
Dulles International Airport
Box 17265
Washington, DC 20041

Addison-Wesley Publishing Co.
Reading, MA 01867

Ballinger Publishing Co.
Cambridge, MA

Barron's Educational Series, Inc.
250 Wireless Blvd.
Hauppauge, NY 11788

Bobbs-Merrill Co.
4300 W. 62nd Street
Indianapolis, IN 46268

Communication Channels, Inc.
6285 Barfield Road
Atlanta, GA 30328

Community Associations Institute
300 South Eads Street
Arlington, VA 22202

Cahners Publishing Company
270 St. Paul Street
Denver, CO 80206

Conway Data Inc.
1954 Airport Road NE
Atlanta, GA 30341

Crittenden Publishing Inc.
Box 1150
Novato, CA 94948

Dow Jones-Irwin
1818 Ridge Road
Homewood, IL 60430

Dorsey Press
1818 Ridge Road
Homewood, IL 60430

Environmental Protection Agency
U.S. Government Printing Office
Washington, DC 20402

Employee Relocation Council
1627 K Street NW
Washington, DC 20006

Farm & Land Institute
430 North Michigan Avenue
Chicago, IL 60611

FIABCI
America Chapter
430 N. Michigan Avenue
Chicago, IL 60611

Gralla Publications
1515 Broadway
New York, NY 10036

International Association of Assessing Officers
1313 East 60th Street
Chicago, IL 60637-9990

Institute of Real Estate Management
437 Investment Bldg.
1511 K Street NW
Washington, DC 20005

International Right of Way Association
6133 Bristol Parkway, Suite 270
Culver City, CA 90230

IPFR Publishing Corp.
111 John Street
Penthouse
New York, NY 10038

McGraw-Hill Book Company
Princeton Road
Heightstown, NJ 08520

Mortgage Bankers Association of America
1125 15th Street NW
Washington, DC 20005

Mattco Equities, Inc.
48 West 21st Street
New York, NY 10010-6976

National Association of Review Appraisers
Suite 410, Midwest Federal Bldg.
St. Paul, MN 55101

National Apartment Association
1111 14th Street NW, Suite 900
Washington, DC 20005

National Association of Homebuilders
The National Housing Center
15th and M Streets NW
Washington, DC 20005

National Association of Realtors
Economics & Research Division
777 14th Street NW
Washington, DC 20005

Prentice-Hall, Inc.
Englewood Cliffs, NJ 07632

Property Press
Menlo Park, CA

Penton/IPC Inc.
1111 Chester Avenue
Cleveland, OH 44114

Real Estate Publishing Company
Box 41177
Sacramento, CA 95841

Random House, Inc.
201 E. 50th Street
New York, NY 10022

Real Estate Education Company
500 N. Dearborn Street
Chicago, IL 60610

Real Estate Law Institute
Box 12528
San Antonio, TX 78212

Realtors National Marketing Institute
430 N. Michigan
Chicago, IL 60611

School of Hotel Administration
Cornell University
Statler Hall
Ithaca, NY 14853

Scott, Foresman & Co.
1900 E. Lake Ave.
Glenview, IL 60025

Society of Real Estate Appraisers
225 North Michigan Avenue
Chicago, IL 60611

South-Western Publishing Co.
Cincinnati, OH

Superintendent of Documents
U.S. Government Printing Office
Washington, DC 20402

Urban Land Institute
1200 18th Street NW
Washington, DC 20036

University of Wisconsin Press
Journals Dept.
114 North Murray Street
Madison, WI 53715

U.S. Department of Agriculture
Washington, DC 20250

Van Nostrand Reinhold Company
450 W. 33rd Street
New York, NY 10001

Warren, Gorham & Lamont
One Penn Plaza
New York, NY 10119

West Publishing Company
Box 3526
St. Paul, MN 55165

INDEX

Asterisks indicate entries that appear in the Glossary.

INDEX

Federal Water Pollution Control Act, 63
Financing, 3, *
 financial status, determination of, 8–9
 prequalifying, 9–11
 sources for, 11–12
 types of, 12–15
Fixed expenses, 51
Fixed rate mortgage, 13, *
Fixing up (house), 27–28
Flood Disaster Protection Act, 63–64
Foreign Investment in Real Property
 Tax Act, 64
Form 2119 (IRS), 32

G

Garn-St. Germain Depository
 Institutions Act, 64
Glossary, 91–409
Government agencies, 12
Government controls, 40
Graduated payment mortgage
 (GPM), 14, 644–646
Gross rent multiplier (GRM), 48, 53, *
Growing equity mortgage (GEM), 15, *

H

Hazard and liability insurance, 4
Home finance companies, 12
Home Mortgage Disclosure Act, 64
Home shopping, 2
Hurdle rate, 57

I

Illiquidity, 40
Improvement ratio, 54–55
Income stream, 50–52, *
Income taxes, 37–38, 52
Index of interest cost, 14
Individual (private) financing, 12
Inflation, 52
Interest expense, 46
Interest saving loans, 14–15
Interior appearance, 27–28
Internal rate of return (IRR) 48, 58, *
Interstate Land Sales Full
 Disclosure Act, 64
Investment analysis, *
 advantages of, 37–39
 benchmark example, 41–48
 disadvantages of, 40–41
 financial benefit conflicts, 49–50
 income stream, 50–52
 rate of return, 52–58
Investments, 8–9

L

Land, 52, *
Land and Water Conservation Act, 64
Lease options, 7–8
Leasing phase, 51
Leverage, 38–39, 52, *
Liabilities, 9
Listing, 21, *
 period of, 23
 types of, 22–23

Loan assumptions, 15
Loan disclosure, 17
Loan progress tables, 473–533
Loan-to-value ratio, 13, 55, *
Loans, 3
 sources of, 11–12
 types of, 12–15
Lock box, 28

M

Magnuson-Moss Warranty, 65
Management, burden of, 40
Manufactured homes, 7
Market rent, 50
Market value, 24, 25–27, *
Mathematical formulas, 662
Measurement tables, 659–661
 ☐ English System, 659
 ☐ Equivalents, 660
 ☐ Metric system, 660
Mechanical systems, 28
Miscellaneous income, 42, 51
Monthly mortgage payments (tables),
 411–471
Mortgage companies, 11–12
Mortgage interest payments, 18
Mortgage loan officer, 83–84
Mortgage note, 17
Mortgage reduction, 49
Mortgage value tables, 535–583
Moving expenses, 32–33
Multiple listing service (MLS), 23, *
Multiple listings, 2, 23, *
Multiplier, 53

N

National Flood Insurance Act, 63
National Historic Preservation Act, 65
National Mobile Home and Construction
 Safety Standards Act, 65
Negative amortization, 14, *
Negotiation, 2–3, *
Neighborhood Self–Help Development
 Act, 65
Net listings, 22–23, *
Net operating income (NOI), 42, 50–51, *
Net present value (NPV), 57
Net spendable income technique, 55
New construction, 51

O

Occupational Safety and Health
 act (OSHA), 66
Open listings, 22, *
Operating expense ratio, 56–57
Operating expenses, 42, 51, *
Over age 55 home sale exemption, 31, *
Overall rate of return (OAR), 48, 53–54, *

P

Parts of a house, 655
Passive losses, 47, 48
Patio homes, 6
Planner, 85–86
Potential gross income, 42, 50–51, *